The Works of William James

Editors
Frederick H. Burkhardt, General Editor
Fredson Bowers, Textual Editor
Ignas K. Skrupskelis, Associate Editor

*This edition of the Works of William James
is sponsored by the American Council of
Learned Societies*

Introduction to this volume by
Michael M. Sokal

William James in 1892

photograph by Pach; courtesy Houghton Library, Harvard University

Psychology: Briefer Course

William James

HARVARD UNIVERSITY PRESS
Cambridge, Massachusetts
and London, England
1984

CENTER FOR
SCHOLARLY EDITIONS

AN APPROVED EDITION

MODERN LANGUAGE
ASSOCIATION OF AMERICA

This book is printed on acid-free paper, and its binding materials have been
chosen for strength and durability.

Library of Congress Cataloging in Publication Data

James, William, 1842–1910.
Psychology, briefer course.
(The Works of William James)
Abridged ed. of: Principles of psychology.
Includes bibliographical references and indexes.
1. Psychology. I. Title. II. Series: James, William, 1842–1910. Works. 1975.
BF131.J2 1984   150   84–528
ISBN 0–674–72102–0 (alk. paper)

Foreword

Psychology: Briefer Course is the undergraduate textbook version of James's monumental *Principles of Psychology*. To Harvard students it was known as "Jimmy," to distinguish it from the larger "James." Published in 1892, it was soon widely adopted in colleges and universities, and by the turn of the century it was the book by which thousands of students were instructed in psychology as an empirical natural science. As such it was a potent influence in the academic movement that culminated years later in the establishment of psychology as an independent discipline, separate from philosophy.

Although it was adapted from *Principles*, *Briefer Course* is more than simply a condensation. As the Introduction to this volume makes clear, James added important new material, made a number of revisions, and developed some concepts, like the famous "stream of consciousness," more fully, so that it represents James's latest thinking in the field. After more than ninety years it is still a useful and highly readable introduction to its subject.

Psychology: Briefer Course is the twelfth title and the fourteenth volume in THE WORKS OF WILLIAM JAMES. Like its predecessors it seeks to provide an authoritative text which, so far as the evidence will allow, represents James's final intentions.

The principles and techniques involved in the preparation of such a text are set forth in the Note on the Editorial Method by the Textual Editor of the WORKS, Fredson Bowers, Linden Kent Professor of English, Emeritus, at the University of Virginia. Professor Bowers also provides a discussion of the text and its relationship to *Principles* and textual apparatus with which the text of the documents used in the editing can be reconstructed.

Reference notes to the text and an index have been prepared by the Associate Editor, Ignas K. Skrupskelis.

Professor Michael M. Sokal of the Department of Humanities of Worcester Polytechnic Institute has written the Introduction. It gives a full account of the publishing history of the work as well as an analysis of its relationship to James's other works in psychology and philosophy.

The Advisory Board of scholars listed in the front matter was appointed by the American Council of Learned Societies, the sponsor of this edition of the WORKS. The Board has supplied general editorial policy guidance and has given help to the editors on many specific substantive questions.

The editors also wish to acknowledge their gratitude to the institutions and individuals that have in their several ways been important in making this volume possible.

The National Endowment for the Humanities has generously continued its support of this edition of THE WORKS OF WILLIAM JAMES by providing funds for the editorial work and for the preparation of camera-ready copy for the apparatus and other end matter. The staff members of the Division of Research Grants, and especially Kathy Fuller and George F. Farr, Jr., have been a steady source of advice and guidance for the entire project.

The editors are also grateful to the Barra Foundation and to its President, Robert L. McNeil, Jr., for generous and timely matching grants in support of the edition.

Alexander James and Dr. William Bond of the Houghton Library have granted permission to use and reproduce both printed and manuscript texts and illustrations in the James Collection at Harvard University. The Houghton Library staff members have given generous and patient help to the editors in their work with the James Papers.

The Reference Room staff of the Alderman Library of the University of Virginia have furnished expert assistance in locating references and source material pertinent to the editorial work.

The University of South Carolina has provided the Associate Editor with research assistance and working space.

The editors also wish to acknowledge their indebtedness to the following:

Richard Ludwig, Director of Special Collections, Princeton University Library, provided access to the Henry Holt Archives.

C. A. Ferrari di Valbona, Rome, made available a letter of January 30, 1906, to Giulio Cesare Ferrari.

Foreword

Professor Robert Hirst, University of California, Berkeley, has examined the volume for the seal of the Center for Scholarly Editions.

Audrone Skrupskelis assisted the Associate Editor in the preparation of the reference notes and index.

Charlotte Bowman contributed her services as Administrative Assistant to the General Editor.

Finally, Anne McCoy, Editorial Coordinator of the WORKS, and her staff, Elizabeth Berkeley, Mary Mikalson, Judith Nelson, Wilma Bradbeer, and Bernice Grohskopf, prepared the manuscript for publication with their usual skill and meticulous attention to detail.

Frederick H. Burkhardt

Contents

Introduction
by
Michael M. Sokal

Of all the books by William James, *Psychology: Briefer Course* is held in lowest regard. *The Principles of Psychology* was praised from its initial publication, and even twenty-five years later psychologists recognized it as "a declaration of independence [that] defin[ed] the boundary lines of a new science with unapproachable genius."[1] Today, of course, *Principles* is recognized as a classic text in both philosophy and psychology.[2] Similarly, *The Will to Believe, The Varieties of Religious Experience, Pragmatism*, and *A Pluralistic Universe* all called forth praise at their publication and are constantly used by philosophers today. But even the title *Briefer Course* (which James himself did not select) suggests a second-rate effort. The phrase calls to mind something undone, something incomplete, perhaps a textbook designed for those not completely serious about its subject. James himself disparaged the book and looked upon it almost as a literary stepchild. In an oft-cited letter to his publisher Henry Holt (quoted in this volume by Fredson Bowers; below, p. 467), James himself claimed that "by adding some twaddle about the senses, by leaving out all polemics and history, all bibliography and experimental details, all metaphysical subtleties and digressions, all quotations, all humor and pathos, all *interest* in short, and by blackening the tops of all the paragraphs, I think I have produced a tome of pedagogic classic which will enrich both you and me, if not the student's mind."[3]

[1] James McKeen Cattell, "Our Psychological Association and Research," *Science*, 45 (23 March 1917), 275–284.

[2] See Gerald E. Myers, "Introduction: The Intellectual Context," and Rand B. Evans, "Introduction: The Historical Context," *The Principles of Psychology*, Works, pp. xi–xl, xli–lxviii.

[3] James to Holt, 24 July 1891, James Papers, Houghton Library, Harvard.

Two of James's predictions were essentially accurate. *Briefer Course* is a pedagogic classic, and it did make a good deal of money for James and Holt even if it did not enrich them. The textual introduction to this volume details Holt's need to prepare four printings of the text within a year of its publication. A biography of Holt claims that 47,531 copies of *Briefer Course* were sold by 1902, while to that date only 8,115 sets of *Principles* had been sold.[4] As these figures indicate, James's comments were wrong in at least two respects: *Briefer Course* had (and has) much to interest the reader, and evidence exists to suggest that the minds of many students were enriched by the book. However, the most interesting and enriching aspect of this text was (and is) James's approach to psychology as a Darwinian natural science.

It is a historical and philosophical commonplace, of course, to stress the Darwinian roots of James's psychology, and this introduction will not review the evidence. Recent analyses by William R. Woodward and Robert J. Richards do so brilliantly.[5] Here it is sufficient to stress that, for James, the mind—or consciousness, or thought—was to be studied as part of nature, with a focus on how it helped the human organism live in the world. That is, if all living things were engaged in a struggle for existence, those organisms that were best adapted to their environment were more apt to survive than those less well adapted. This condition implies that all traits exhibited by a living organism must play (or must have played) a role in helping that organism (or its ancestors) in the struggle. James's psychology therefore ignored the faculty theories of the Scottish realists (and of those in American colleges) and the elemental ideas of the British associationists,[6] and focused on such psychological phenomena as habit, the self, and thought to explain just how they helped human beings live in the world. In *Briefer Course*, this position is spelled out clearly in James's Introductory chapter, in paragraphs that stress (in boldface) that

4 Charles A. Madison, *The Owl among Colophons: Henry Holt as Publisher and Editor* (New York: Holt, Rinehart and Winston, 1966), p. 51.
5 William R. Woodward, "Introduction," *Essays in Psychology*, WORKS, pp. xi–xxxix; Robert J. Richards, "The Personal Equation in Science: William James's Psychological and Moral Uses of the Darwinian Theory," *A William James Renaissance: Four Essays by Young Scholars*, ed. Mark R. Schwehn, *Harvard Library Bulletin*, 30 (October 1982), 387–425.
6 Evans, "The Historical Context," pp. xlvi–xlvii.

"mental facts cannot be properly studied apart from the physical environment of which they take cognizance" and that "mental life is primarily teleological." James explained this last statement by stating (p. 11) that "our various ways of feeling and thinking have grown to be what they are because of their utility in shaping our *reactions* on the outer world." (References to *Psychology: Briefer Course,* hereafter designated as *BC,* are to the present edition.) Here then is seen James's Darwinian approach to psychology.

However, this Darwinian naturalism played down the metaphysical concerns of many of those who studied psychology before James and put his psychology in opposition to theirs. Some have called his position positivistic, in that it slights metaphysical questions, whereas other analysts write of it as phenomenological, in that it approaches the mind as a given and concerns itself with describing the role played by the mind in everyday life.[7] Both characterizations are correct as far as they go and as long as they are not used to distort the essential evolutionary character of James's psychology. While evidence of the evolutionary character is found throughout *Briefer Course,* James's approach to psychology as a Darwinian natural science was reinforced by the context in which his book was published. Before the content of this text is analyzed, the context and the way in which James structured the volume should be reviewed.

Both *The Principles of Psychology* (1890) and *Psychology: Briefer Course* (1892) were published as part of Holt's American Science Series.[8] First projected in 1874, the series was designed as a money-making venture that would also do much to stimulate American science. Edward L. Youmans, the editor of the *Popular Science Monthly* (in which James published), had earlier begun an International Scientific Series, published in America by Appleton and in England by Kegan Paul. Despite its name, it was composed primarily of books by English scientists.[9] Holt wanted to give Ameri-

---

[7] See ibid., pp. xlvii–xlviii; Woodward, "Introduction," p. xiii.

[8] For a full history of this series, see Madison, *Owl among Colophons,* pp. 14–20, 44–66.

[9] Roy M. MacLeod, "Evolutionism, Internationalism and Commercial Enterprise in Science: The International Scientific Series, 1871–1910," *Development of Science Publishing in Europe,* ed. A. J. Meadows (Amsterdam, New York, Oxford: Elsevier Science Publishers, 1980), pp. 63–93.

can scientists a showcase in which they could display their own achievements and through which he could appeal to the chauvinism of American educational institutions, explicitly hoping that the series would become a set of "Science Text-Books for American High Schools and Colleges." For him, the principal objects of the series were "to supply the lack—in some subjects very great, of authoritative books whose principles are, so far as practicable, illustrated by familiar American facts, and . . . of text-books which at least do not contradict the latest generalizations."[10]

The most important of these "generalizations" for Holt was clearly "the doctrine of Evolution." Youmans had founded both his journal and his series as the "herald archangel" in the crusade to spread Herbert Spencer's ideas, and Holt was no less ardent a believer in the significance of evolution. No evidence has been found to suggest that Holt grasped the subtleties of Darwin's theory of natural selection, his mechanism for evolutionary change, or that he realized the differences between Darwin's and Spencer's ideas. Whether he did or not, Holt believed that "the doctrine of Evolution" was the foundation upon which late nineteenth-century science had to be built and that Americans had as much to contribute to such an edifice as did Europeans. To be sure, Holt projected volumes for his series in the classical physical sciences—astronomy, physics, and chemistry—but he believed that all other books, such as those on geology, zoology, and botany, should approach their subjects from an evolutionary perspective. He also projected volumes on less traditional topics—the human body, political economy, government, and ethics—believing strongly that evolutionary theory would allow their authors to approach their subjects as natural sciences, at least to some degree. Of course, in planning these books, Holt had in mind the markets that existed for them in American schools and colleges, but he also wanted to bring to these markets new ideas that he had faith in.

To prepare these volumes, Holt sought out leading scholars in all fields. For example, his *Astronomy* was written by Simon Newcomb and Edward S. Holden, both of the U.S. Naval Observatory, his *Zoology* by Alpheus S. Packard of the Salem Institute and Brown University, and his *Botany* by Charles E. Bessey of the University of

Nebraska. Other texts were written by professors at Johns Hopkins University, whose president, Daniel Coit Gilman, was an old friend of Holt's. Thus Ira Remsen, professor of chemistry at Johns Hopkins and author (in 1877) of a text in theoretical chemistry that had attracted international attention, wrote the volume *Inorganic Chemistry* for Holt's series. Similarly, H. Newell Martin, English physiologist and author (who had collaborated with his teacher Thomas Henry Huxley on *A Course of Practical Instruction in Elementary Biology* before coming to Johns Hopkins as professor of biology in 1876), wrote *The Human Body*.[11] In all, the contributors to the series formed a distinguished group, and James's contribution to it must be seen in this context.

From the beginning, Holt had thought that a volume on psychology would be an important part of his series. He had read at least some of Spencer's writings on psychology and knew that the subject could be approached from an evolutionary perspective. He also had in mind the many "mental philosophy" and "intellectual philosophy" courses then required of most seniors in American colleges. For both reasons, Holt first asked John Fiske to write the psychology volume for the series. Fiske was a popular author, a fervent disciple of Spencer's, librarian at Harvard, and a close friend of Holt's, who regarded him as a "universal genius." But Fiske could not accept Holt's commission and advised his friend to "go for James." Fiske and James had known each other since the early 1870s, and both had taken part in the activities of the Cambridge Metaphysical Club in the middle of the decade. During the 1876–1877 academic year, when James taught "physiological psychology" at Harvard, his perspective on the subject was compared by his students to Fiske's. Fiske thus knew that James was approaching psychology from the evolutionary position that Holt wanted. Holt quickly followed Fiske's advice, and by the middle of 1878 James had agreed to prepare the American Science Series contribution on psychology.[12] Twelve years later *The Principles of Psychology* appeared, followed in 1892 by *Psychology: Briefer Course.*

[11] Publication data for all contributions to the American Science Series can be found in the multivolume *National Union Catalog: Pre-1956 Imprints* (London: Mansell).

[12] See Evans, "The Historical Context"; Ralph Barton Perry, *The Thought and Character of William James* (Boston: Little, Brown, 1935), vol. 1, pp. 330, 465, 476, 535–536.

These two books took their subject further than it had ever gone before from its roots in philosophical concerns. To be sure, James did not divorce psychology entirely from philosophy, as will emerge here. But James in these books approached psychology as a branch of Darwinian natural science, thus fulfilling for Holt one of his major goals for the series.

Just as James's natural-science perspective on psychology reflected the intellectual focus of the American Science Series, its social history—that is, the way it was produced—shared much with the other volumes. For example, much has been made of the long time it took James to write *Principles*.[13] Holt, in 1878, was "a little staggered by the length of time which you think it would take you to write the Psychology" when James asked if he could submit his manuscript in 1880.[14] But Holt was to grow used to authors' delays with the American Science Series; he certainly encountered many. He first planned the series in 1872 and in 1874 announced his hope of publishing the first volumes in 1878. But the earliest books in the series, *Astronomy* and *Zoology*, did not appear until the following year and only a few other works trickled from the presses through the 1880s and 1890s. Still others—for example, two contributions by four scholars at the University of Chicago: *Geology* (3 vols.), by Thomas C. Chamberlin and Rollin D. Salisbury, and *Ethics*, by John Dewey and James H. Tufts—were not published until after the turn of the century. To be sure, the authors of these books were all recruited after James, but his delay was not unusual.

Similarly, many have commented on the length of James's *Principles*—almost 1,400 pages in two volumes—and even James himself was shocked at its size: "No one could be more disgusted than I at the sight of the book. *No* subject is worth being treated of in 1000 pages! Had I ten years more, I could rewrite it in 500; but as it stands it is this or nothing—a loathsome, distended, tumefied, bloated, dropsical mass."[15]

Holt himself had projected that the volumes in the series would each be about 500 pages long, or about 200,000 words. But of the first volumes published, only *Astronomy*—at 512 pages—came close

[13] See, e.g., Fredson Bowers, "The Text of *The Principles of Psychology*," *The Principles of Psychology*, pp. 1532–79.
[14] Holt to James, 8 June 1878, James Papers.
[15] James to Holt, 9 May 1890, James Papers.

to this length. *Botany*, for example, was 611 pages long, and *Zoology* was 719 pages; Martin's volume *The Human Body*, which was to be so important to James's books, had 655 pages, including a 34-page appendix on human reproduction. These excessive lengths led Holt to have his authors abridge their texts as volumes in an "American Science Series—Briefer Course." He also issued all "regular" volumes in the series published after 1882 (and later editions of all earlier full-scale volumes) as the "American Science Series—Advanced Course." The first "Briefer Course" abridgments appeared in 1883, when shorter versions of *The Human Body* (355 pages), *Astronomy* (338 pages), and *Zoology* (334 pages) were published. In 1884 Holt also began publishing an "American Science Series—Elementary Course," and at one point several of the contributions to the series were issued in four different versions. In 1892, for example, Holt advertised Remsen's *Inorganic Chemistry* (827 pages) as part of the Advanced Course, his *Introduction to the Study of Chemistry* (455 pages) as part of the Briefer Course, his *Elements of Chemistry: A Text-Book for Beginners* (272 pages) as part of the Elementary Course, and his *Laboratory Manual: Containing Directions for a Course of Experiments in General Chemistry* (196 pages) for use with either the Briefer Course or the Elementary Course. Martin's book *The Human Body* was also issued in Advanced, Briefer, and Elementary versions, and Holt also had available, "at the solicitation of the Women's Christian Temperance Union," an edition of the Briefer volume that stressed the harmful effects of alcohol and other narcotics. In addition, a special printing of the Advanced volume could be ordered without the appendix on sexual reproduction.[16] (No wonder, then, that Holt had James rewrite several sexually explicit passages in his *Briefer Course*; see below, pp. 473, 479.) Holt was not one to let a possible market go begging, and his editorial experience did much to help him fit his authors' books to readers' needs.

Consequently, Holt had good business reasons to urge James, soon after the publication of *The Principles of Psychology*, to prepare a condensation of it for his Briefer Course series. All of the volumes in this series of shorter books had done much to educate

---

[16] See advertisement for "The American Science Series" bound with the early printings of *Psychology: Briefer Course*.

American students, all were reprinted many times and apparently sold well, and several went through many editions. For example, the seventh edition of Bessey's *Essentials of Botany* was published in 1900, and the eighth edition of Remsen's *Introduction to the Study of Chemistry* appeared in 1909 and was reprinted as late as 1923. The volumes in the Advanced Course also did well. Holt reprinted a revised version of *Ethics* by Dewey and Tufts as late as 1942, and various versions of *The Human Body*, without significant revisions after Martin's death in 1896, appeared in 1909. If almost fifty thousand copies of *Psychology: Briefer Course* were sold in its first ten years, one wonders how many hundreds of thousands—or indeed millions—of copies of books in the entire series were sold during its lifetime.

More important, many of the books—in one or more of their versions—were classics in their fields. Reviews of the careers of Bessey, Martin, Packard, and Remsen stress the way in which their texts stimulated the development of their sciences in America.[17] In many cases, their influence depended on the evolutionary and natural-science perspective they took. Bessey's book, for example, "reoriented botanical instruction" in the United States by approaching plant anatomy physiologically and stressing how the different structures of plants helped them to develop, adapt, and survive. *Ethics* by Dewey and Tufts took a dynamic view of its subject, emphasizing morality as the making of correct choices in difficult situations, rather than as simple obedience to duty.[18] Two other books in the series helped their subjects emerge as social sciences: *The Science of Finance* (1898), by Henry Carter Adams, was "the first comprehensive treatise on public finance by an American" and helped determine much government financial policy in the early years of the twentieth century, while *Political Economy* (1883), by Holt's close friend Francis A. Walker, president of the Massachusetts Institute of Technology, was so influential in its various versions through the 1880s and 1890s that it was used extensively in Britain. The most explicitly evolutionary book in the

17 See *Dictionary of Scientific Biography*, vol. 2, pp. 102–104; vol. 9, pp. 142–143; vol. 10, pp. 272–274; vol. 11, pp. 370–371.

18 See *Dictionary of American Biography*, 3rd supplement, pp. 779–781; 5th supplement, pp. 169–173; George Dykhuizen, *The Life and Mind of John Dewey* (Carbondale: Southern Illinois University Press, 1973), pp. 136–137.

series was *General Biology* (1886), by William T. Sedgwick and Edmund B. Wilson, both of whom had been greatly influenced by Martin. In this text, living things were considered as adapting organisms within an environment, and its authors' viewpoint was "more analytic and integrated" than any previously available. As such, this book did even more than Bessey's to draw biology away from the "taxonomically and phylogenetically oriented introductory courses" of the period and to redefine it as a dynamic experimental science.[19] In all, no matter how distinguished and important James's two books were and continue to be, it would be difficult—though perhaps not impossible—to argue that they were much more influential than the other volumes of the American Science Series. In most cases, the volumes' approach to their subjects as evolutionary natural sciences did much to make them as important as they were.

This review of the publishing history of the American Science Series may do much to help put *Psychology: Briefer Course* into its context, but something should be noted here about its title. Although the title page of its first printing in 1892 merely carries the title *Psychology* below the heading "American Science Series, Briefer Course" (the spine is stamped "Psychology | Briefer Course | James"), the book was never, apparently, referred to simply as *Psychology*. James himself always referred to it as his *Briefer Course*, and students immediately labeled it "Jimmy," to distinguish it from the larger "James." In the same year as the American publication, Macmillan issued an edition of the volume in England as *Textbook in Psychology*, just as it had earlier published a briefer version of Walker's *Political Economy* as *A Brief Textbook of Political Economy*.[20] Holt continued to reprint James's book as *Psychology*, with the "American Science Series, Briefer Course" heading, until 1920. In that year, Holt began reprinting the volume as *Psychology: Briefer Course*—the title by which it had been known for almost thirty years and under which it is issued here—and noted that "earlier editions were published in the Ameri-

[19] See *Encyclopædia of the Social Sciences*, vol. 1, pp. 432–433; James Phinney Munroe, *A Life of Francis Amasa Walker* (New York: Henry Holt and Company, 1923), pp. 251–255, 297–298, 348; *Dictionary of Scientific Biography*, vol. 14, pp. 423–436.

[20] See *British Museum Catalogue of Printed Books to 1955: Compact Edition* (New York: Readex Microprint Corporation, 1967), vol. 13, pp. 281–282; vol. 26, p. 559.

can science series, briefer course." The year 1920 was also when James's widow renewed the copyright on the book after Holt's copyright on it expired, and this event may have led in some way to the title change. However, no evidence has been found to support this speculation.

William James wrote two descriptions of how he prepared *Psychology: Briefer Course*. The first, part of a letter to Henry Holt, has already been quoted here; the second appears in his own Preface to this volume. In both he stressed what the abridgment left out of *Principles*, and since *Briefer Course* is less than half the length of the two-volume set, such emphasis is appropriate. James's deletions, as well as what he retained, reveal a good deal about his hopes for *Briefer Course*, and, as this Introduction seeks to demonstrate, the book is more than "scissors and paste." But James did cut and rearrange material from *Principles* for this volume, and one can learn much by examining just what he did.

For example, Chapter 3 in *Principles*, "On Some General Conditions of Brain-Activity" (pp. 88–108; all references to *Principles* in this introduction are to the edition in WORKS), became Chapter 9, "Some General Conditions of Neural Activity," in *Briefer Course* (pp. 113–124). James changed "Brain" to "Neural" in the chapter title to stress and to reflect more accurately his view of what occurred in reaction-time experiments, the subject of much of the chapter. In both *Principles* (p. 93) and *Briefer Course* (p. 114), James stressed that "Just what happens during the actual time occupied by the reaction . . . is not made out at present, either from the neural or from the mental point of view." But in *Principles* (p. 95), James did try to lay out the "stages" that he believed were involved in reactions, and stressed that only one of them was "psycho-physical," while all the rest were "purely physiological," or neural, without involving the brain. James's new title is thus more accurate, though the second discussion does not appear in this volume. Here then, perhaps, is an example of the way in which James simplified his discussion in *Principles* for *Briefer Course*, omitting a detailed analysis that he apparently believed was not necessary for understanding the thrust of his discussion.

Other examples of omission abound. As he noted in his letter to Holt, he cut here "all bibliography" (compare *Principles*, pp.

89–92, with James's essentially unreferenced discussion in this volume), and, even if he did not leave out all "experimental details," his presentation in *Briefer Course* (pp. 114–115) oversimplified the longer discussion of *Principles* (pp. 93–94) to the point where it is misleading. By deleting mention of several instruments and an illustration of one of them in *Briefer Course,* James destroyed the rhetorical parallelism of his presentation. By removing his comparison of the Hipp Chronoscope with a stop-watch, he leads the reader to believe that this instrument produced the "time-line" on the "revolving drum," or kymograph (Figure 49)—an erroneous interpretation reinforced by the fact that the misleading passage appears immediately after the figure.[21] To be sure, James did add two sentences after this passage that describe the chronoscope and its operation more accurately. But the damage had already been done, and they are not really successful. Of course, James was never totally comfortable as an experimenter, and in 1892, as he was preparing *Briefer Course,* he was also making plans to yield the direction of the Harvard psychological laboratory to Hugo Münsterberg. No wonder, then, that his descriptions of the apparatus of this period are less than perfect.

The material remaining in the *Principles* chapter after these deletions was rearranged for *Briefer Course.* The *Principles* chapter, after a paragraph on neural anatomy that concludes that "too much anatomy has been found to order for theoretic purposes," opens with a long discussion of the effects of "The Summation of Stimuli," which includes two long quotations from German sources, and then passes on to the focus of the chapter, reaction-times (pp. 88–92). The chapter in *Briefer Course,* however, starts off with a short and clear explanatory paragraph on "The Nervous Discharge" that sets the stage for the discussion of reaction-times that follows immediately (*BC,* pp. 114–120); the paragraphs on "The Summation of Stimuli," without their long quotations, have been shifted to a position *after* the section on reaction-times (pp. 120–121). It is not totally clear why James made this change; both

21 For a discussion of how the Hipp Chronoscope actually operated, see Michael M. Sokal, ed., *An Education in Psychology: James McKeen Cattell's Journal and Letters from Germany and England, 1880–1888* (Cambridge, Mass.: MIT Press, 1981), pp. 98–99; and Michael M. Sokal, Audrey B. Davis, and Uta C. Merzbach, "Laboratory Instruments in the History of Psychology," *Journal of the History of the Behavioral Sciences,* 12 (January 1976), 59–64.

presentations are clear and neither is noticeably more suitable for classroom use than the other. But it serves as an example of how James felt compelled to rework his earlier book.

Other examples of reworking are easier to explain and shed much light not only on what James believed he could delete from *Principles,* but on what he believed he had to retain in *Briefer Course.* In both books, James stressed that simple reaction-time experiments were "in no sense measurements of the swiftness of *thought"* (*Principles,* p. 100; *BC,* p. 116). In *Principles* this statement follows James's detailed analysis of the "stages" involved in reactions and a long discussion of the work of Wilhelm Wundt and other Germans who had performed reaction-time experiments. The first part of this discussion criticizes Wundt's view, set forth in the second edition of his *Physiologische Psychologie* of 1880, that mental activity is involved in simple reactions. The second part, however, was clearly written sometime later, as it opens with James's statement that "I am happy to say that since the preceding paragraphs . . . were written, Wundt has himself become converted to the view which I defend" (*Principles,* p. 98) and cites the third edition of Wundt's book, published in 1887.[22] James then went on to trace Wundt's "conversion" to a series of experiments by Ludwig Lange, performed at Wundt's laboratory in Leipzig, that distinguished between "sensorial" and "muscular" reactions and supposedly showed that while the first did involve some mental activity, the second did not, and thus were identical to the simple reactions that James had stressed earlier. In *Briefer Course,* however, James merely led into the statement quoted at the head of this paragraph by mentioning how Lange's work supported his views. There was no need in the shorter book for the longer analysis, and thus James could readily omit most of it and condense what was left.

After stressing the limitations of simple reaction-time experiments, James went on to describe how they might be made useful for psychology. "Only when we complicate them is there a chance for anything like an intellectual operation to occur," he noted in both books (*Principles,* p. 100; *BC,* p. 116), and went on to explain

---

[22] Wilhelm Wundt, *Grundzüge der physiologischen Psychologie* (Leipzig: W. Engelmann). See the highly informative note on the different editions of this book and on how James used them; *Principles,* p. 1315.

briefly how such "complicated" experiments might be performed, so as to involve the mental processes of discrimination and choice. In *Principles* James noted that "we shall see, however, in the appropriate chapters, that the discrimination and choice involved in such a reaction are widely different from the intellectual operations of which we are ordinarily conscious under those names." And in his chapters "Discrimination and Comparison," "Association," and "The Perception of Things," James included discussions of what were called the discrimination-time, the association-time, and the perception-time (*Principles*, pp. 494–498, 525–529, 773–775). In each of these presentations, James was certain to stress the artificiality of the experimental situation and that what was being studied in the laboratory was not "the intellectual operations of which we are ordinarily conscious" (*Principles*, p. 100). As he explained the situation with respect to discrimination-time, James noted: "I trust I have said enough to convince the student that this minimum time by no means measures what we consciously know as discrimination. It only measures something which, under the experimental conditions, leads to a similar result. But it is the bane of psychology to suppose that where results are similar, processes must be the same" (*Principles*, p. 498).

In *Briefer Course*, however, James reworked these discussions of "complicated" reactions into his chapter on neural activity immediately after his section on simple reactions (*BC*, pp. 117–120). In introducing this analysis, James stated that "the rational place in which to report of them would be under the head of the various intellectual operations concerned"—just the procedure he followed in *Principles*. "But," James continued, "certain persons prefer to see all these measurements bunched together regardless of context," and so, he claimed, he chose to present the material at this point. Yet it would appear that James is being a little disingenuous here. He does not indicate who the "certain persons" were, and there are reasons to believe that he preferred this organizational scheme. It allowed him to condense his discussions of "complicated" reactions and thus delete the constant references to his analysis of simple reactions needed in each of the dispersed analyses. It also permitted him to consolidate and condense all of his discussions of the experiments involved in reaction-time study. After all, James was never at ease in the laboratory. More important, this organization made it possible for him to dispose of reaction-time experiments quickly and to proceed to what were for him more important topics; he constantly stressed how artificial the experiments were and how little they had to do with the way in which individuals actually thought.

Indeed, one of the most important points of his analyses of "complicated" reaction-times of *Principles* that James made sure to bring into *Briefer Course* was just this stress on their limitations. It was one conclusion that he could not delete or dilute with condensation. As he noted in this volume, "the only times we can measure are the *minimum* times of certain determinate and very simple intellectual operations" (*BC*, p. 117). These, he implied, were not the processes involved in actual everyday life. Instead they were limited and artificial, determined by the conditions of the laboratory. The results of reaction-time experiments thus may have contributed, according to James, to psychology as an experimental science, but they had little to say to psychology as a Darwinian natural science, concerned with the way in which individuals lived and functioned in the world. One can thus see clearly why James stressed their limitations in both *Principles* and *Briefer Course*— making sure to keep this analysis in both versions of his text— and why he brought his dispersed discussions of reaction-times together as he did. His approach to psychology as a Darwinian natural science thus determined how he used his "scissors-and-paste."

Within a few years, however, several American psychologists, using reaction-time experiments as part of a functional psychology, argued that the way in which individuals were raised and matured —how they adapted to the world—determined the way in which they would react.[23] This work was carried out by psychologists whom James knew well, primarily James McKeen Cattell of Columbia University and James Mark Baldwin of Princeton. Indeed, much of James's discussion on reaction-times is based on, and includes long quotations from, Cattell's work (*Principles*, pp. 98, 496–497; *BC*, pp. 117–120). By 1893, however, when Cattell had

---

[23] These studies are analyzed in David L. Krantz, "The Baldwin-Titchener Controversy: A Case Study in the Functioning and Malfunctioning of Schools," in *Schools of Psychology*, ed. David L. Krantz (New York: Appleton-Century-Crofts, 1969), pp. 1–19; Michael M. Sokal, *The Education and Psychological Career of James McKeen Cattell, 1860–1904* (diss., Case Western Reserve University, 1972; University Microfilms order no. 73–6341), pp. 505–514.

published the results of his first experiments on this question, James had withdrawn so much from the laboratory that he did not even note this work in his own copies of *Principles* or *Briefer Course* for use in any possible revision. Since he had never been especially interested in this work and had already concluded that reaction-time experiments had little to tell him about psychology as a Darwinian science, he ignored these studies, although they would have reinforced his evolutionary perspective. Thus by 1893, in at least this one case, James had lost touch with literature in experimental psychology relevant to his own concerns. Here, perhaps, is one reason why he resisted the temptation to revise either *Principles* or *Briefer Course*. (For a different conclusion see below, pp. 413–414.)

One can also learn much about James, his psychology, and *Briefer Course* by examining the material that he added to the volume, primarily on the different human senses in the early chapters. These discussions—this "twaddle about the senses" as James referred to them—traditionally have not been considered important, and indeed in one reprint edition of the volume, these chapters were omitted.[24] Nevertheless, these opinions are not fair to James or to *Briefer Course*.

In his Preface to this volume, James wrote that "knowing how ignorant the average student is of physiology, I have added brief chapters on the various senses." These are introduced, however, by a carefully written chapter on "Sensation in General" (drawn primarily from the chapter "Sensation" in *Principles*) that does much to set the stage for the material that follows. Here, for example, appears James's marvelous description of the baby's perceptual world as "one big blooming buzzing Confusion" (*BC*, p. 21, drawn from *Principles*, p. 462). More important, this chapter includes James's discussions of the cognitive nature of sensation and his distinction between "Knowledge of Acquaintance" and "Knowledge-about" (*BC*, p. 19). These metaphysical discussions are greatly condensed from longer analyses in *Principles* (pp. 653–661) and give the student for whom *Briefer Course* was designed just enough

[24] Gordon W. Allport, "Introduction to the Torchbook Edition," in William James, *Psychology: Briefer Course* (New York: Harper and Row, 1961), pp. xiii–xxiii.

philosophy to be able to proceed to James's chapters that approach psychology as a natural science. Even in deemphasizing metaphysical concerns, however, James was careful to distinguish his psychology from the narrowly focused experimental psychology of late nineteenth-century Germany. Consequently, this chapter also includes his discussion of the psychophysical work of Ernst Heinrich Weber and Gustav Theodor Fechner (*BC*, pp. 21–28). Despite his claim to "have left out all the polemical . . . matter" (*BC*, p. 1) of *Principles* in *Briefer Course*—a claim that is for the most part accurate—James could not resist some satirical comments about Fechner's work. For example, he briefly described some of Fechner's procedures "as an instance of . . . how patient German investigators can be," but only after he had concluded that "Fechner's psycho-physic formula . . . has been attacked on every hand; and [that] absolutely nothing practical has come of it" (*BC*, p. 26).[25] In fewer than ten pages James had shown that his psychology was not metaphysics and not psychophysics. Most of the rest of the volume was devoted to illustrating just what psychology was.

James's chapters on the specific senses were written primarily to make *Briefer Course* more useful as a textbook, and they probably did much to help Holt sell as many copies of it as he did. The attention that James paid to each sense varied. His chapter entitled "Sight" (*BC*, pp. 31–48), for example, is quite detailed because of the importance of this sense for the psychological questions in which James was interested. More specifically, sight does much to help people live in the world—for instance, by allowing them to perceive the world in three dimensions—and so is important for psychology as a Darwinian natural science. Consequently, some of the discussion and two of the illustrations (Figures 9 and 10, pp. 38, 39) in this chapter were taken from "The Perception of Space" (pp. 776–912). Although James did include a chapter on "The Perception of Space" in *Briefer Course* (*BC*, pp. 292–304), its thirteen pages could not include all that was discussed so extensively in *Principles*. As noted in The Text of *Psychology: Briefer Course*, much of the material in this "long and sprawling chapter" was considerably reworked for *Briefer Course*.

25 Compare this judgment with that of *Principles* (p. 517), in the chapter "Discrimination and Comparison": "The whole outcome of the discussion, so far as Fechner's theories are concerned, is indeed *nil*."

The chapter "Sight" also includes a long footnote (*BC*, p. 31) giving directions that students could readily follow for the dissection of the mammalian eye, thus providing elementary classes in psychology with one of their first laboratory exercises, and giving teachers trained in an older tradition a demonstration that they could use to link psychology with other sciences. By 1892, however, James was moving away from the laboratory and did not devote too much time to phenomena that he considered of lesser importance to psychology as a natural science. These topics included the perception of size, the duration of luminous sensations, and negative after-images; for these discussions James used another book in the American Science Series, Martin's *Human Body*, from which he drew extensive quotations (see *BC*, pp. 41–47). By including this material, James not only spared himself the effort of becoming expert on topics he considered less important, he also satisfied his publisher, who wanted to get the volume into classrooms as soon as possible. More important, however, he gave his readers the benefit of Martin's undisputed authority on material concerning human physiology. While it may not have been his intention, James's use of Martin's discussion also helped him merge his *Briefer Course* into the American Science Series, thus contributing to Holt's aim—first expressed almost twenty years earlier—of "an organic series."[26]

James also made extensive use of Martin's volume in his chapters "Hearing" (*BC*, pp. 49–60) and "Touch, the Temperature Sense, the Muscular Sense, and Pain" (pp. 61–69), quoting at length from *The Human Body*. Yet even in these chapters James prepared certain sections himself: for example, those entitled "Harmony and Discord," "Discriminative Sensibility of the Ear," and "Muscular Sensation" (pp. 59–60, 66–67). These areas treated topics of greater psychological than physiological importance, and in them James did not want merely to follow Martin.

After his chapters on the senses, James included one entitled "Sensations of Motion" (*BC*, pp. 70–75), drawn primarily from the section in *Principles* (pp. 810–814) called "The Sensation of Motion over Surfaces," itself part of the long chapter "The Perception of Space." Here James again took the opportunity to rework material of prime psychological importance. This is followed

[26] See Holt, "Preliminary and Confidential" Announcement.

by an entirely new chapter, "The Structure of the Brain" (*BC*, pp. 76–88), which opens with a relatively short "embryological sketch" of brain development and devotes most of its attention to a detailed set of instructions for the "dissection of sheep's brain." This section thus provided another important laboratory exercise for classes in psychology taught by James and others in the 1890s and after. James himself even had this chapter prepared as an eight-leaf pamphlet in 1891, before *Briefer Course* was formally published so it could be used by his students that fall. (See below, pp. 480–482.) As soon as the volume was published and adopted, several of James's students began using this exercise with considerable success. For example, at Wellesley College, Mary Whiton Calkins introduced her students to brain anatomy using James's instructions early in 1892.[27]

Brain anatomy was clearly not one of James's major concerns, however. In *Principles* (p. 24), at the very end of his introductory chapter "The Scope of Psychology," James included a note on the dissection of a sheep's brain that claimed that "nothing is easier than to familiarize one's self with the mammalian brain" and that directed his reader to several anatomical texts. He also mentioned these texts at the start of his dissection directions in *Briefer Course* (p. 79), but he closed this chapter with the admission that "when all is said and done, the fact remains that, for the beginner, the understanding of the brain's structure is not an easy thing" (p. 88). To be sure, as James himself always stressed, familiarity (or knowledge of acquaintance) is not the same thing as understanding (or knowledge-about), and *Briefer Course* was designed more for beginners than was *Principles*, which was issued as part of the Advanced Course of the American Science Series. But between 1890 and 1892, James had clearly changed his mind about the difficulty of dissection and the study of brain anatomy.

One final point should be made about *Briefer Course*'s chapters on the senses. In these, as noted, James based much of his text on the work of others, notably Martin's *Human Body*. In the same

27 Mary Whiton Calkins, "Experimental Psychology at Wellesley College," *American Journal of Psychology*, 5 (November 1892), 260–271. See also Laurel Furumoto, "The College Laboratory of Psychology as a Scientific Institution, 1885–1930," unpublished paper read before Cheiron, the International Society for the History of the Behavioral and Social Sciences, Carleton University, Ottawa, Ontario, Canada, 6 June 1975.

way, he took his illustrations for these chapters from other sources, sometimes without explicit credit. No attempt has been made to find the origins of all of James's figures, though the Notes include all the known sources. James took his figures from books and articles by authors he knew he could trust. For example, the illustrations in the *Briefer Course* chapter "Hearing" were derived from *The Human Body*, as was much of the text itself. In addition, Fredson Bowers (see below, p. 468n) has traced two figures to Thomas Henry Huxley's *Manual of the Anatomy of the Vertebrated Animals* (1871) and one to Hermann von Helmholtz's *Handbuch der physiologischen Optik* (1856–1860), and Ignas Skrupskelis has shown that James relied on both of these sources for *Principles* (pp. 1326–1327, 1329). Other figures are labeled "after Henle" or "Schematic, after Starr," or otherwise have their sources acknowledged. These borrowings show that James continued to make use of the work of men he cited in *Principles*, such as Johann Nepomuk Czermak (whose illustration—printed in *Briefer Course* as Figure 17—came to James by way of Martin's book), Jakob Henle (whose anatomy texts James studied while a medical student), Heinrich Obersteiner, and Moses Allen Starr. (See *Principles*, pp. 1312, 1320, 1355, 1359, 1389, 1390, 1409.) In his reliance on those sources that were familiar to him, James showed just how much he wanted to move from laboratory experimentation to areas he found of more interest.

Of all the changes that James made in converting *Principles* to *Briefer Course*, perhaps none is more striking than the one he made in defining psychology, and in the way that he explicated this change throughout the shorter book. The opening sentence of *Principles* (p. 15) reads: "Psychology is the Science of Mental Life, both of its phenomena and of their conditions"; *Briefer Course* (p. 9), however, begins with the statement that "the definition of Psychology may be best given in the words of Professor Ladd, as the *description and explanation of states of consciousness as such*." This change, in fact, has attracted much commentary and even criticism from some scholars. Before its implications can be reviewed and the validity of the criticism evaluated, the background of this change should be sketched.

In both *Principles* and *Briefer Course* James stressed that he approached psychology as a natural science, a perspective, as noted above, that derived from Darwinian ideas and that meshed well with that of the other volumes of the American Science Series. Soon after *Principles* appeared, however, this aspect of James's psychology was criticized severely by George Trumbull Ladd, Professor of Philosophy at Yale.[28] Ladd approached psychology as a branch of philosophy, although an interest in the experimental psychology of late nineteenth-century Germany had resulted in his *Elements of Physiological Psychology*.[29] Even in this book, however, he stressed the "nature of the mind." He thus found James's approach to psychology as a "So-called 'Natural Science' " less than satisfactory and argued that in *Principles* James distorted or ignored many important philosophical questions.[30]

Ladd was a major figure among American philosophers and psychologists in the 1890s, and James could not ignore these criticisms even had he wanted to. In "A Plea for Psychology as a 'Natural Science,' " James replied to Ladd,[31] admitting that, when he wrote *Principles*, psychology was not yet what he hoped it would become, and stressing that he "wished, by treating Psychology *like* a natural science, to help her to become one" (*Essays in Psychology*, WORKS, p. 270). He went on to ask the question, "What may one lawfully mean by saying that Psychology ought to be treated after the fashion of a 'natural science'?" (Ibid., p. 271), and answered it in part by referring explicitly to the Introductory and Epilogue chapters of the newly published *Briefer Course*. In this first chapter, James forcefully stressed the Darwinian concerns of his psychology; but because he knew that this book would be used by philosophers approaching psychology traditionally, he also emphasized the distinctions between psychology-as-natural-science, on the one hand, and the Theory of Knowledge and Rational Psychology on the other. He admitted the philosophical unity of all these subjects but argued

[28] On Ladd, see Ignas K. Skrupskelis' notes to *Principles*, pp. 1303–4; and Eugene S. Mills, *George Trumbull Ladd: Pioneer American Psychologist* (Cleveland: Press of Case Western Reserve University, 1969).

[29] George Trumbull Ladd, *Elements of Physiological Psychology: A Treatise of the Activities and Nature of the Mind from the Physical and Experimental Point of View* (New York: Scribner's, 1888).

[30] George Trumbull Ladd, "Psychology as So-called 'Natural Science,' " *Philosophical Review*, 1 (January 1892), 24–53.

[31] "A Plea for Psychology as a 'Natural Science,' " *Philosophical Review*, 1 (March 1892), 146–153; rpt. in *Essays in Psychology*, WORKS, pp. 270–277.

that he could not consider them all in this volume. "If critics find that this natural-science point of view cuts things too arbitrarily short," he wrote, "they must not blame the book which confines itself to that point of view; rather must they go on themselves to complete it by their deeper thought" (*BC*, p. 10). This sentence was written before Ladd's criticisms appeared, but the fact that James found it necessary to cite Ladd in the opening sentence of the book suggests that the two men had previously debated this point. One wonders if this sentence was meant as an implicit challenge to Ladd.

Whether or not James meant to challenge Ladd is speculation, but he knew that the majority of psychology teachers in America in the 1890s shared Ladd's perspective. James, with Holt's active encouragement, wanted to reach these teachers and their students. Despite their philosophical concerns, most of them—going back to John Locke and his followers in the British associationist tradition—accepted the importance of sensation and the idea that the physiology of the sense organs was worthy of study. It was in part to satisfy their needs that James introduced his chapters on the senses into *Briefer Course,* and their position at the beginning of the book reflects the traditional role of sensations as the building blocks from which all other mental events were constructed. James's adoption of this structure, however, does not imply that he accepted the view of psychology that usually accompanied it. The Darwinian naturalism of most of his book easily demonstrates this point. In the same way, the fact that James adopted an older definition of psychology—"the description and explanation of states of consciousness as such," rather than "the Science of Mental Life"—does not mean that he abandoned his naturalistic perspective. In fact, it can be argued that this new definition was adopted primarily as a ploy to help James's book gain entry into traditional courses and so to spread his new ideas. But it was probably much more.

In commenting on the way in which James made this change, one distinguished psychologist has claimed that through it James "capitulated" to Ladd and that it "blunted" James's revolution against traditional psychology.[32] Certainly the study of "states of consciousness" was more traditional than "the science of mental life." The

[32] Ernest R. Hilgard, "Consciousness in Contemporary Psychology," *Annual Review of Psychology,* 31 (1980), 1–26.

Thought," whereas in *Briefer Course* (p. 140) he submits only "Four Characters in Consciousness." These two schemata may be compared to each other as follows:

Principles	*Briefer Course*
1. "Every thought tends to be part of a personal consciousness."	1. "Every 'state' tends to be part of a personal consciousness."
2. "Within each personal consciousness thought is always changing."	2. "Within each personal consciousness states are always changing."
3. "Within each personal consciousness thought is sensibly continuous."	3. "Each personal consciousness is sensibly continuous."
4. "It always appears to deal with objects independent of itself."	
5. "It is interested in some parts of these objects to the exclusion of others, and welcomes or rejects—*chooses* from among them, in a word—all the while."	4. "It is interested in some parts of its object to the exclusion of others, and welcomes or rejects—*chooses* from among them, in a word—all the while."

The psychological equivalence of the two expositions is clear, and they illustrate Evans' point about how James regularly used "thought" and "consciousness" as effective synonyms. James's use of quotation marks around "state" in the *Briefer Course* formulation shows that he did not want the term, or indeed the concept of "state of consciousness," taken literally, despite the opening sentence of the book. Also evident is the rhetorical strength of the term "consciousness." For example, the force of the third "character"—the idea of the streamlike nature of mental activity—is much stronger in the later formulation than it is in the earlier one. To be sure, James felt so strongly about the rhetorical advantages of "consciousness" that he used the term in *Principles*, even in outlining the "characters of thought." But it is in *Briefer Course* that he made more effective use of the term.

Of course, the most notable point of distinction between the two outlines is the absence in *Briefer Course* of the fourth "character" spelled out in *Principles*, which sets forth James's dualistic belief in a world outside the mind, but of which the mind is cognizant. This is a metaphysical point, perhaps not expected in a book approaching psychology as a natural science. But James was a philosopher as well as a psychologist, and he knew, philosophically, that the existence of an external world had to be established before he could claim the cognitive power of consciousness—that is, the ability to know this world—for his psychology. He apparently had no qualms about raising this point and explicating it in *Principles* (pp. 262–267). James also raised other philosophical questions in *Principles*. For example, as Gerald E. Myers notes,[36] at the end of the chapter "Memory" (p. 647) James adds "a word, in closing, about the metaphysics involved in remembering." The sentences (not merely a word) that follow reveal much about the philosophical bases of James's psychology:

According to the assumptions of this book, thoughts accompany the brain's workings, and those thoughts are cognitive of realities. The whole relation is one which we can only write down empirically, confessing that no glimmer of explanation of it is yet in sight. That brains should give rise to a knowing consciousness at all, this is the one mystery which returns, no matter of what sort the consciousness and of what sort the knowledge may be.

In other words, from James's dualistic position, the relation between the mind and the brain was a "mystery" that psychology as a Darwinian natural science could not explain and about which, perhaps, it should not be concerned. Except for a short section on the "relation of consciousness to the brain" in his "Epilogue. Psychology and Philosophy" (*BC*, pp. 395–401), James did not raise this topic in his *Briefer Course*. For James, the book was almost purely an exposition of psychology as a Darwinian natural science, designed for first courses in the subject. It was not, to use Holt's term, an "advanced" treatment of the subject. Just as James knew "how ignorant the average student is of physiology" (above, p. xxv), he also knew the students' philosophical naïveté. Consequently, he saw that for most students "metaphysical discussions" (to quote his Preface) and "metaphysical subtleties and digressions" (to quote his letter to Holt; above, p. xi) would be at best distractions, and

[36] Myers, "The Intellectual Context," pp. xii–xiii.

might even lead his readers to abandon the book. No wonder he omitted such philosophical discussions in reworking *Principles* into *Briefer Course*.

James did not, however, banish all philosophy from *Briefer Course*. He knew that even if psychology is seen as a Darwinian natural science, and even if a dualism between the mind and an external world is assumed explicitly, he had to claim for the mind the cognitive power to know the world. This he did in the opening chapter, immediately after noting that his book would approach psychology as a science, but before his discussion on the distinction between psychology-as-a-natural-science on one hand and the Theory of Knowledge and Rational Psychology on the other—and even before he explicated the Darwinian nature of his approach. Here he simply claimed that the data of psychology, as distinct from philosophy, included "1. *Thoughts and feelings*, or whatever other names transitory *states of consciousness* may be known by" and "2. *Knowledge*, by these states of consciousness, of other facts."[37] In making this statement so baldly, James knew that he was on thin ice metaphysically, so he followed it with his discussion of the theory of knowledge and rational psychology. He then stressed that "incomplete statements are often practically necessary" in approaching psychology as a natural science, and concluded that, "to go beyond the usual 'scientific' assumptions in the present case, would require, not a volume, but a shelfful of volumes, and by the present author such a shelfful could not be written at all" (*BC*, pp. 10–11). Nevertheless James's later books do return to the question of cognition and go far beyond *Briefer Course* (and even *Principles*) in considering it. However, the relatively short and simple treatment of this topic was sufficient for *Briefer Course* and its uses.

Psychology: Briefer Course was well-received. The one review of it that appeared in an American psychological or philosophical journal called it "an admirable text-book" and concluded that "it commends itself by a wealth of facts, an orderliness of arrangement, a recentness and variety of interest, and a clear, forcible, and glow-

---

37 Here, within a page of adopting Ladd's phrase "states of consciousness," James used it again. But note that he carefully qualifies it with an adjective that denies any static implication.

ingly stimulating style."[38] Perhaps in part because of this review, it sold thousands of copies—more than five times as many as *Principles* by 1902—and by 1909 had been translated into French and German. The English edition, which appeared soon after the book was published in America, interestingly enough prompted the only detailed review the book received. James Ward was a Fellow at Trinity College, Cambridge, who had written the renowned article on psychology in the ninth edition (1886) of the *Encyclopædia Britannica*—an article that James had read carefully as soon as it appeared. Ward and James had met even earlier, in 1880, and James made extensive use of Ward's work in *Principles*, citing it many times.[39] Their friendship did not prevent Ward from writing a "Critical Notice" of *Briefer Course* that was truly critical.[40] Ward found the book to be unsystematic, took issue with James's theory of emotion, questioned the inclusion of physiological material in the early chapters, and generally doubted that it would be useful as a classroom text. His harshest comments, however, were reserved for "the licence the author allows himself in the use of fundamental terms," which Ward claimed "involves him [James] sometimes in what might fairly be called logical barbarisms." Here he was reacting against James's use of thought and mind and consciousness as equivalents, which had frustrated readers of *Principles*, and which, to Ward, was metaphysically unsound. Moreover, he took James to task for playing down the "fair amount of philosophical prolegomena to psychology" that "exists already," arguing that "no science can afford to be slovenly about its fundamental conceptions."[41] In doing so, of course, he criticized James for approaching psychology as a Darwinian science. Ward even disapproved of James's prose: "A severe critic, I am afraid, would say that Mr. James's facile pencil often runs away with him . . . [and that] there is not infrequently a needless but picturesque elaboration of

[38] Schurman, *Philosophical Review*, 1 (May 1892), 315.

[39] James Ward, "Psychology," *Encyclopædia Britannica*, 9th ed. (Edinburgh: Adam and Charles Black, 1886), vol. 20, pp. 37–85. James cited this article alone three times in *Principles* (pp. 164, 530, 595). On Ward and his relations with James see Perry, *Thought and Character*, vol. 1, p. 602, and vol. 2, pp. 57–59, 644–657; see also the notes to *Principles*, p. 1318.

[40] James Ward, "Critical Notices: *Text-book of Psychology*, by William James," *Mind*, n.s., 1 (October 1892), 531–539.

[41] Ibid., pp. 536–537.

stage scenery."[42] Certainly this response to James's style—especially in view of the praise it received from American reviewers—was idiosyncratic.

James took the review seriously and, while not allowing it to interfere with his friendly relations with Ward, tried to defend himself to his English friend: "Yes, I *am* too unsystematic & loose! But in this case I permitted myself to remain so deliberately, on account of the strong aversion with which I am filled for the humbugging pretense of exactitude in the way of definition of terms and description of states that has prevailed in psychological literature."[43] Ward replied to this letter, stressing his "craze" for "straining after exactitude that you say you cannot abide," and James responded, again defending his position.[44] At this point, the two friends dropped the topic from their correspondence but continued to exchange letters for many years.

Meanwhile, *Briefer Course* was being put to good use in the United States. As early as December 1891 Holt had received at least one request for an examination copy of the book, from Joseph Jastrow, professor of psychology at the University of Wisconsin. Once the book was published, James and Holt began distributing copies of it to others who were likely to want to use it in their classes. John Dewey, then at the University of Michigan, received one and reacted favorably to it: "I'm glad enough it is to be made accessible to a wider circle of students as it will be in this form. I've only had time to glance it through & read the preface—which I was glad to read."[45] Holt advertised the book in such journals as the *Psychological Review*, quoting the opinion of Harry N. Gardiner, a philosopher who taught psychology at Smith College and who thus represented those who traditionally had approached the subject from an older perspective. According to Gardiner, "a better

42 Ibid., p. 539.

43 James to Ward, 1 November 1892, James Papers.

44 Ward to James, 10 November 1892; James to Ward, 15 November 1892; James Papers. See also Perry, *Thought and Character*, vol. 2, pp. 95–101.

45 Dewey to James, 8 February 1892, James Papers. In this letter, Dewey also passed on to James a comment he had heard about James Sully's review of *Principles*, excerpted in the note to 1.22. As Dewey reported: "One of my friends summed up Sully's review in Mind for me as follows: 'A good book, but too lively to make a good corpse and every scientific book should be a corpse.' If we weren't indebted to you for many specific things, we should be indebted to you for what you did to break down this superstition."

text-book of psychology for college use, one clearer, simpler, more stimulating does not exist."[46] Although no evidence of the advertisement's influence exists, it is easy to speculate that other college teachers were introduced to *Briefer Course* by this notice. One who did not need the text brought to her attention was Mary Whiton Calkins, who used the volume for many years in her courses at Wellesley.

Despite its title, *Briefer Course* was adopted extensively for classroom use by philosophers and psychologists who taught at universities. James, as already noted, used the volume in his introductory classes at Harvard as early as the fall before its publication. Later, when James was on leave, Josiah Royce adopted it for the introductory classes he taught, and Herbert Nichols, a psychologist from Clark University, used *Principles* in the advanced course while substituting for James.[47] Psychologists who had studied with James also used *Briefer Course* extensively in their teaching. For example, Charles M. Bakewell, a philosopher who was the literary executor of James's friend, Thomas Davidson, based his introductory courses in psychology at the University of California, through the 1890s, on the book. Similarly, James Rowland Angell used *Briefer Course* in his classes at the University of Minnesota (in 1894) and at the University of Chicago (from 1895), until his own text was published in 1904. And as early as 1892, at Columbia University, James H. Hyslop—a younger contemporary of James— taught psychology from *Briefer Course*.[48] A systematic survey of college and university catalogs of the turn of the century would probably reveal many other adoptions.

Classroom use is one thing, however, and influence on students is another. Referring to both *Principles* and *Briefer Course*, James's

[46] Holt advertisement, *Psychological Review*, 1 (January 1894), third cover.

[47] "Letters and Notes," *American Journal of Psychology*, 4 (April 1892), 500; Harvard advertisement, *Psychological Review*, 4 (January 1897), advertising section, v–vi.

[48] See the following three memoirs in the History of Psychology in Autobiography series: Knight Dunlap, vol. 2, ed. Carl Murchison (Worcester: Clark University Press, 1932), pp. 35–61; Shepherd Ivory Franz, vol. 2, pp. 89–113; and James Rowland Angell, vol. 3, pp. 1–38. Angell's text—*Psychology: An Introductory Study of the Structure and Function of Human Consciousness*—was also published by Holt, and its author later claimed (in his autobiography; p. 23) that "for many years, it shared with the [*Briefer Course*] the larger part of the college market for psychological texts."

son once wrote that "during the thirty years that have passed since
[1890], the majority of the English-speaking students who have
entered the field of psychology have entered by the door which
James's pages threw wide to them."[49] This statement clearly refers
more to the two-volume set than to the shorter book, and direct and
indirect evidence for the influence of *Principles* is easy to find. But
how many of the students led to a career in psychology by James's
"door" were attracted to *Principles* by the use of *Briefer Course*
in their first psychology classes? Certainly thousands of students read
Briefer Course; Holt reprinted it at least ten times before 1920
and at least another seven times between 1920 and 1945.[50] At least
one eminent psychologist—Walter S. Hunter, an animal behaviorist
prominent in the 1920s and 1930s—read *Briefer Course* in prepara-
tory school and, under the influence of the book, "decided to become a psychologist."[51] Probably many others were equally struck
by the volume, but the influence of an introductory text, like that of
a high school teacher, is difficult to demonstrate directly.

James and Holt often discussed revising *Briefer Course* (see below, pp. 475–477), and James's friends and colleagues even offered
to revise the text for him. Nothing came of these discussions, however, and Henry Holt and Company issued its last printing of
Briefer Course in 1945. Three years later—when the book's copyright expired—the World Publishing Company issued a reprint
edition of the book, with an introduction by Ralph Barton Perry,
the Harvard philosopher, as part of its Living Library. Other reprints appeared during the paperback boom of the early 1960s:
a Torchbook edition, published by Harper and Row, came out in
1961 with an introduction by Gordon W. Allport, the Harvard
psychologist; a Premier Books edition, published by Fawcett, came
out in 1963 with an introduction by Ashley Montagu, the ubiqui-
tous compiler and introducer; and a Collier Books edition, published by Macmillan, came out in 1966 with an introduction
by Gardner Murphy, the distinguished student of James's psychical research. Chapters from the book were also reprinted
during this period—for example, in Gay Wilson Allen's *Wil-*

49 Henry James, ed., *The Letters of William James*, 2 vols. (Boston: Atlantic
Monthly Press, 1920), vol. 1, p. 301.
50 See *National Union Catalog: Pre-1956 Imprints*, vol. 276, pp. 668–688.
51 Walter S. Hunter, "Autobiography," *A History of Psychology in Autobiography*,
vol. 4, ed. Edwin G. Boring et al. (Worcester: Clark University Press, 1952), 163–187.

Introduction

liam James Reader (1971) and John J. McDermott's edition of *The Writings of William James* (1967).[52] This publishing activity attests to many things, including the relative wealth of the American academic community in the 1960s and the existence of what might be called a William James industry even before the volumes of the WORKS began appearing. But it especially demonstrates the continuing value of *Briefer Course*, evidence of which may be found in the dozens of times the book is still cited annually.[53] To be sure, many of those who cite James today do so only as a pro forma tip of the hat to one of the great men of psychology. Most scholars studying James's ideas work only from *Principles*, ignoring the significant way in which James's psychology developed after 1890, as most notably seen in *Briefer Course*. Nevertheless, there are scholars who are making substantive use of this book. For example, James's criticisms in this volume of Fechner's psychophysics have been used recently by several psychologists and philosophers studying the nature of sensation.[54] Similarly, James's concept of the Self as formulated in *Briefer Course* has proved important in the 1970s and 1980s to psychoanalysts and sociologists, as well as to psychologists.[55] The intellectual activity inspired by *Briefer Course* can be correlated to the many contemporary references to the book, both to the Holt printings and to later versions. This edition, however, with its definitive text and authoritative notes should be even more valuable in leading scholars to *Briefer Course*, while students of James are invited to explore further the book's significance and its relation to *Principles*. Then, perhaps, *Briefer Course* will be seen as more than James's literary stepchild.

[52] Allen reprinted the chapters "Habit" and "The Stream of Consciousness"; McDermott the chapter "Habit."

[53] For evidence of this point, see any of the volumes of the *Social Science Citation Index*, published annually since 1972 by the Institute for Scientific Information, Philadelphia, Pennsylvania.

[54] For example, see Uffe Juul Jensen, "Conceptual Epiphenomenalism," *The Monist*, 56 (April 1972), 250–275; and V. Siomopoulos, "On the Psychophysical Law: An Information Theory Interpretation," *Perceptual and Motor Skills*, 40 (1975), 8–10.

[55] For example, see Anthony J. Blasi, "Symbolic Interactionism as Theory," *Sociology and Social Research*, 56 (July 1972), 453–465; Joseph Barnett, "Interpersonal Processes, Cognition, and the Analysis of Character," *Contemporary Psychoanalysis*, 16 (1980), 397–416; and Robert L. Dipboye, "Alternative Approaches to Deindividuation," *Psychological Bulletin*, 84 (1977), 1057–75.

Psychology: Briefer Course

Preface

In preparing the following abridgment of my larger work, the *Principles of Psychology*, my chief aim has been to make it more directly available for class-room use. For this purpose I have omitted several whole chapters and rewritten others. I have left out all the polemical and historical matter, all the metaphysical discussions and purely speculative passages, most of the quotations, all the book-references, and (I trust) all the impertinences, of the larger work, leaving to the teacher the choice of orally restoring as much of this material as may seem to him good, along with his own remarks on the topics successively studied. Knowing how ignorant the average student is of physiology, I have added brief chapters on the various senses. In this shorter work the general point of view, which I have adopted as that of 'natural science,' has, I imagine, gained in clearness by its extrication from so much critical matter and its more simple and dogmatic statement. About two fifths of the volume is either new or rewritten, the rest is 'scissors and paste.' I regret to have been unable to supply chapters on pleasure and pain, æsthetics, and the moral sense. Possibly the defect may be made up in a later edition, if such a thing should ever be demanded.

I cannot forbear taking advantage of this preface to make a statement about the composition of the *Principles of Psychology*. My critics in the main have been so indulgent that I must cordially thank them; but they have been unanimous in one reproach, namely, that my order of chapters is planless and unnatural; and in one charitable excuse for this, namely, that the work, being largely a collection of review-articles, could not be expected to show as much system as a treatise cast in a single mould. Both the reproach and the excuse misapprehend the facts of the case. The order of composition is doubtless unshapely, or it would not be found so by so many. But planless it is not, for I deliberately followed what seemed to me a good pedagogic order, in proceeding from the more concrete mental aspects with which we are best acquainted to the so-called elements which we naturally come to know later by way of abstraction. The opposite order, of 'building-up' the mind out of its 'units of composition,' has the merit of expository elegance, and gives a neatly subdivided table of contents; but it often purchases these advantages at the cost of reality and truth. I admit that my 'analytic' order was stumblingly carried out; but this again was in consequence of what I thought were pedagogic necessities. On the whole, in spite of my critics, I venture still to think that the 'unsystematic' form charged upon the book is more apparent than profound, and that we really gain a more living understanding of the mind by keeping our attention as long as possible upon our entire conscious states as they are concretely given to us, than by the *post-mortem* study of their comminuted 'elements.' This last is the study of artificial abstractions, not of natural things.[1]

But whether the critics are right, or I am, on this first point, the critics are wrong about the relation of the magazine-articles to the book. With a single exception all the chapters were written for the book; and then by an afterthought some of them were sent to magazines, because the completion of the whole work seemed so distant. My lack of capacity has doubtless been great, but the charge of not having taken the utmost pains, according to my lights, in the composition of the volumes, cannot justly be laid at my door.

[1] In the present volume I have given so much extension to the details of 'Sensation' that I have obeyed custom and put that subject first, although by no means persuaded that such order intrinsically is the best. I feel now (when it is too late for the change to be made) that the chapters on the Production of Motion, on Instinct, and on Emotion ought, for purposes of teaching, to follow immediately upon that on Habit, and that the chapter on Reasoning ought to come in very early, perhaps immediately after that upon the Self. I advise teachers to adopt this modified order, in spite of the fact that with the change of place of 'Reasoning' there ought properly to go a slight amount of re-writing.

Contents

Contents

are not compounded of 'fused' sensations. The 'soul' as a combining medium. The sense of personal identity. Explained by identity of function in successive passing thoughts. Mutations of the self. Insane delusions. Alternating personalities. Mediumships or possessions. Who is the Thinker.

Contents

Chapter I

Introductory

The definition of Psychology may be best given in the words of Professor Ladd, as the *description and explanation of states of consciousness as such*. By states of consciousness are meant such things as sensations, desires, emotions, cognitions, reasonings, decisions, volitions, and the like. Their 'explanation' must of course include the study of their causes, conditions, and immediate consequences, so far as these can be ascertained.

Psychology is to be treated as a natural science in this book. This requires a word of commentary. Most thinkers have a faith that at bottom there is but one Science of all things, and that until all is known, no one thing can be completely known. Such a science, if realized, would be Philosophy. Meanwhile it is far from being realized; and instead of it, we have a lot of beginnings of knowledge made in different places, and kept separate from each other merely for practical convenience' sake, until with later growth they may run into one body of Truth. These provisional beginnings of learning we call 'the Sciences' in the plural. In order not to be unwieldy, every such science has to stick to its own arbitrarily-selected problems, and to ignore all others. Every science thus accepts certain data unquestioningly, leaving it to the other parts of Philosophy to scrutinize their significance and truth. All the natural sciences, for example, in spite of the fact that farther reflection leads to Idealism, assume that a world of matter exists altogether independently of the perceiving mind. Mechanical Science assumes this matter to have 'mass' and to exert 'force,' defining these terms merely phenomenally, and not troubling itself about certain unintelligibilities which they present on nearer reflection. Motion similarly is assumed by mechanical science to exist independently of the mind, in spite of the difficulties involved in the assumption. So Physics assumes atoms, action at a distance, etc., uncritically; Chemistry uncritically adopts all the data of Physics; and Physiology adopts those of Chemistry. Psychology as a natural science deals with things in the same partial and provisional way. In addition to the 'material world' with all its determinations, which the other sciences of nature assume, she assumes additional data peculiarly her own, and leaves it to more developed parts of Philosophy to test their ulterior significance and truth. These data are—

1. *Thoughts and feelings*, or whatever other names transitory *states of consciousness* may be known by.

2. *Knowledge*, by these states of consciousness, of other facts. These things may be material objects and events, or other states of mind. The material objects may be either near or distant in time and space, and the states of mind may be those of other people, or of the thinker himself at some other time.

How one thing *can* know another is the problem of what is called the Theory of Knowledge. How such a thing as a 'state of mind' can be at all is the problem of what has been called Rational, as distinguished from Empirical, Psychology. The *full* truth about states of mind cannot be known until both Theory of Knowledge and Rational Psychology have said their say. Meanwhile an immense amount of provisional truth about them can be got together, which will work in with the larger truth and be interpreted by it when the proper time arrives. Such a provisional body of propositions about states of mind, and about the cognitions which they enjoy, is what I mean by Psychology considered as a natural science. On any ulterior theory of matter, mind, and knowledge, the facts and laws of Psychology thus understood will have their value. If critics find that this natural-science point of view cuts things too arbitrarily short, they must not blame the book which confines itself to that point of view; rather must they go on themselves to complete it by their deeper thought. Incomplete statements are often practically necessary. To go beyond the usual 'scientific' assumptions in the present case, would require, not a volume, but a shelfful of volumes, and by the present author such a shelfful could not be written at all.

Let it also be added that **the human mind is all that can be touched upon** in this book. Although the mental life of lower creatures has been examined into of late years with some success, we have no space for its consideration here, and can only allude to its manifestations incidentally when they throw light upon our own.

Mental facts cannot be properly studied apart from the physical environment of which they take cognizance. The great fault of the older rational psychology was to set up the soul as an absolute spiritual being with certain faculties of its own by which the several activities of remembering, imagining, reasoning, willing, etc., were explained, almost without reference to the peculiarities of the world with which these activities deal. But the richer insight of modern days perceives that our inner faculties are *adapted* in advance to the features of the world in which we dwell, adapted, I mean, so as to secure our safety and prosperity in its midst. Not only are our capacities for forming new habits, for remembering sequences, and for abstracting general properties from things and associating their usual consequences with them, exactly the faculties needed for steering us in this world of mixed variety and uniformity, but our emotions and instincts are adapted to very special features of that world. In the main, if a phenomenon is important for our welfare, it interests and excites us the first time we come into its presence. Dangerous things fill us with involuntary fear; poisonous things with distaste; indispensable things with appetite. Mind and world in short have been evolved together, and in consequence are something of a mutual fit. The special interactions between the outer order and the order of consciousness, by which this harmony, such as it is, may in the course of time have come about, have been made the subject of many evolutionary speculations, which, though they cannot so far be said to be conclusive, have at least refreshed and enriched the whole subject, and brought all sorts of new questions to the light.

The chief result of all this more modern view is the gradually growing conviction that **mental life is primarily teleological**; that is to say, that our various ways of feeling and thinking have grown to be what they are because of their utility in shaping our *reactions* on the outer world. On the whole, few recent formulas have done more service in psychology than the Spencerian one that the essence of mental life and bodily life are one, namely, 'the adjustment of inner to outer relations.' The adjustment is to immediately present objects in lower animals and in infants. It is to objects more and more remote in time and space, and inferred by means of more and more complex and exact processes of reasoning, when the grade of mental development grows more advanced.

Primarily then, and fundamentally, the mental life is for the sake of action of a preservative sort. Secondarily and incidentally it does many other things, and may even, when ill 'adapted,' lead to its possessor's destruction. Psychology, taken in the widest way, ought to study every sort of mental activity, the useless and harmful sorts as well as that which is 'adapted.' But the study of the harmful in mental life has been made the subject of a special branch called 'Psychiatry'—the science of insanity—and the study of the useless is made over to 'Æsthetics.' Æsthetics and Psychiatry will receive no special notice in this book.

All mental states (no matter what their character as regards utility may be) **are followed by bodily activity of some sort.** They lead to inconspicuous changes in breathing, circulation, general muscular tension, and glandular or other visceral activity, even if they do not lead to conspicuous movements of the muscles of voluntary life. Not only certain particular states of mind, then (such as those called volitions, for example), but states of mind as such, *all* states of mind, even mere thoughts and feelings, are *motor* in their consequences. This will be made manifest in detail as our study advances. Meanwhile let it be set down as one of the fundamental facts of the science with which we are engaged.

It was said above that the 'conditions' of states of consciousness must be studied. **The immediate condition of a state of consciousness is an activity of some sort in the cerebral hemispheres.** This proposition is supported by so many pathological facts, and laid by physiologists at the base of so many of their reasonings, that to the medically educated mind it seems almost axiomatic. It would be hard, however, to give any short and peremptory proof of the unconditional dependence of mental action upon neural change. That a general and usual amount of dependence exists cannot possibly be ignored. One has only to consider how quickly consciousness may be (so far as we know) abolished by a blow on the head, by rapid loss of blood, by an epileptic discharge, by a full dose of alcohol, opium, ether, or nitrous oxide—or how easily it may be altered in quality by a smaller dose of any of these agents or of others, or by a fever,—to see how at the mercy of bodily happenings our spirit is. A little stoppage of the gall-duct, a swallow of cathartic medicine, a cup of strong coffee at the proper moment, will entirely overturn for the time a man's views of life. Our moods and resolutions are more determined by the condition of our circulation than by our logical grounds. Whether a man shall be a hero or a coward is a matter of his temporary 'nerves.' In many kinds of insanity, though by no means in all, distinct alterations of the brain-tissue have been found. Destruction of certain definite portions of the cerebral hemispheres involves losses of memory and of acquired motor faculty of quite determinate sorts, to which we shall revert again under the title of *aphasias*. Taking all such facts together, the simple and radical conception dawns upon the mind that mental action may be uniformly and absolutely a function of brain-action, varying as the latter varies, and being to the brain-action as effect to cause.

This conception is the 'working hypothesis' which underlies all the 'physiological psychology' of recent years, and it will be the working hypothesis of this book. Taken thus absolutely, it may possibly be too sweeping a statement of what in reality is only a partial truth. But the only way to make sure of its unsatisfactoriness is to apply it seriously to every possible case that can turn up. To work an hypothesis 'for all it is worth' is the real, and often the only, way to prove its insufficiency. I shall therefore assume without scruple at the outset that the uniform correlation of brain-states with mind-states is a law of nature. The interpretation of the law in detail will best show where its facilities and where its difficulties lie. To some readers such an assumption will seem like the most unjustifiable *a priori* materialism. In one sense it doubtless is materialism: it puts the Higher at the mercy of the Lower. But although we affirm that the *coming to pass* of thought is a consequence of mechanical laws,—for, according to another 'working hypothesis,' that namely of physiology, the laws of brain-action are at bottom mechanical laws,—we do not in the least explain the *nature* of thought by affirming this dependence, and in that latter sense our proposition is not materialism. The authors who most unconditionally affirm the dependence of our thoughts on our brain to be a fact are often the loudest to insist that the fact is inexplicable, and that the intimate essence of consciousness can never be rationally accounted for by any material cause. It will doubtless take several generations of psychologists to test the hypothesis of dependence with anything like minuteness. The books which postulate it will be to some extent on conjectural ground. But the student will remember that the Sciences constantly have to take these risks, and habitually advance by zig-zagging from one absolute formula to another which corrects it by going too far the other way. At present Psychology is on the materialistic tack, and ought in the interests of ultimate success to be allowed full headway even by those who are certain she will never fetch the port without putting down the helm once more. The only thing that is perfectly certain is that when taken up into the total body of Philosophy, the formulas of Psychology will appear with a very different meaning from that which they suggest so long as they are studied from the point of view of an abstract and truncated 'natural science,' however practically necessary and indispensable their study from such a provisional point of view may be.

The Divisions of Psychology.—So far as possible, then, we are to study states of consciousness in correlation with their probable neural conditions. Now the nervous system is well understood today to be nothing but a machine for receiving impressions and discharging reactions preservative to the individual and his kind—so much of physiology the reader will surely know. Anatomically, therefore, the nervous system falls into three main divisions, comprising—

1) The fibres which carry currents in;
2) The organs of central redirection of them; and
3) The fibres which carry them out.

Functionally, we have sensation, central reflection, and motion, to correspond to these anatomical divisions. In Psychology we may divide our work according to a similar scheme, and treat successively of three fundamental conscious processes and their conditions. The first will be Sensation; the second will be Cerebration or Intellection; the third will be the Tendency to Action. Much vagueness results from this division, but it has practical conveniences for such a book as this, and they may be allowed to prevail over whatever objections may be urged.

Chapter II

Sensation in General

Incoming nerve-currents are the only agents which normally affect the brain. The human nerve-centres are surrounded by many dense wrappings of which the effect is to protect them from the direct action of the forces of the outer world. The hair, the thick skin of the scalp, the skull, and two membranes at least, one of them a tough one, surround the brain; and this organ moreover, like the spinal cord, is bathed by a serous fluid in which it floats suspended. Under these circumstances the only things that can *happen* to the brain are:

1) The dullest and feeblest mechanical jars;

2) Changes in the quantity and quality of the blood-supply; and

3) Currents running in through the so-called afferent or centripetal nerves.

The mechanical jars are usually ineffective; the effects of the blood-changes are usually transient; the nerve-currents, on the contrary, produce consequences of the most vital sort, both at the moment of their arrival, and later, through the invisible paths of escape which they plough in the substance of the organ and which, as we believe, remain as more or less permanent features of its structure, modifying its action throughout all future time.

Each afferent nerve comes from a determinate part of the periphery and is played upon and excited to its inward activity by a particular force of the outer world. Usually it is insensible to other forces: thus the optic nerves are not impressible by air-waves, nor those of the skin by light-waves. The lingual nerve is not excited by aromatic effluvia, the auditory nerve is unaffected by heat. Each selects from the vibrations of the outer world some one rate to which it responds exclusively. The result is that our sensations form a discontinuous series, broken by enormous gaps. There is no reason to suppose that the order of vibrations in the outer world is anything like as interrupted as the order of our sensations. Between the quickest audible air-waves (40,000 vibrations a second at the outside) and the slowest sensible heat-waves (which number probably billions), Nature must somewhere have realized innumerable intermediary rates which we have no nerves for perceiving. The process in the nerve-fibres themselves is very likely the same, or much the same, in all the different nerves. It is the so-called 'current'; but the current is *started* by one order of outer vibrations in the retina, and in the ear, for example, by another. This is due to the different *terminal organs* with which the several afferent nerves are armed. Just as we arm ourselves with a spoon to pick up soup, and with a fork to pick up meat, so our nerve-fibres arm themselves with one sort of end-apparatus to pick up air-waves, with another to pick up ether-waves. The terminal apparatus always consists of modified epithelial cells with which the fibre is continuous. The fibre itself is not directly excitable by the outer agent which impresses the terminal organ. The optic fibres are unmoved by the direct rays of the sun; a cutaneous nerve-trunk may be touched with ice without feeling cold.[1] The fibres are mere transmitters; the terminal organs are so many imperfect telephones into which the material world speaks, and each of which takes up but a portion of what it says; the brain-cells at the fibres' central end are as many others at which the mind listens to the far-off call.

The 'Specific Energies' of the Various Parts of the Brain.—To a certain extent anatomists have traced definitely the paths which the sensory nerve-fibres follow after their entrance into the centres, as far as their termination in the gray matter of the cerebral convolutions.[2] It will be shown on a later page that the con-

[1] The subject may feel *pain*, however, in this experiment; and it must be admitted that nerve-fibres of every description, terminal organs as well, are to some degree excitable by mechanical violence and by the electric current.

[2] Thus the optic nerve-fibres are traced to the occipital lobes, the olfactory tracts go to the lower part of the temporal lobe (hippocampal convolution), the auditory nerve-fibres pass first to the cerebellum, and probably from thence to the upper part of the temporal lobe. These anatomical terms used in this chapter will be explained later. The *cortex* is the gray surface of the convolutions.

sciousness which accompanies the excitement of this gray matter varies from one portion of it to another. It is consciousness of things seen, when the occipital lobes, and of things heard, when the upper part of the temporal lobes, share in the excitement. Each region of the cerebral cortex responds to the stimulation which its afferent fibres bring to it, in a manner with which a peculiar quality of feeling seems invariably correlated. This is what has been called the law of 'specific energies' in the nervous system. Of course we are without even a conjectural explanation of the *ground* of such a law. Psychologists (as Lewes, Wundt, Rosenthal, Goldscheider, etc.) have debated a good deal as to whether the specific quality of the feeling depends solely on the *place* stimulated in the cortex, or on the *sort of current* which the nerve pours in. Doubtless the sort of outer force habitually impinging on the end-organ gradually modifies the end-organ, the sort of commotion received from the end-organ modifies the fibre, and the sort of current a so-modified fibre pours into the cortical centre modifies the centre. The modification of the centre in turn (though no man can guess how or why) seems to modify the resultant consciousness. But these adaptive modifications must be excessively slow; and as matters actually stand in any adult individual, it is safe to say that, more than anything else, the *place* excited in his cortex decides what kind of thing he shall feel. Whether we press the retina, or prick, cut, pinch, or galvanize the living optic nerve, the Subject always feels flashes of light, since the ultimate result of our operations is to stimulate the cortex of his occipital region. Our habitual ways of feeling outer things thus depend on which convolutions happen to be connected with the particular end-organs which those things impress. We *see* the sunshine and the fire, simply because the only peripheral end-organ susceptible of taking up the ether-waves which these objects radiate excites those particular fibres which run to the centres of sight. If we could interchange the inward connections, we should feel the world in altogether new ways. If, for instance, we could splice the outer extremity of our optic nerves to our ears, and that of our auditory nerves to our eyes, we should hear the lightning and see the thunder, see the symphony and hear the conductor's movements. Such hypotheses as these form a good training for neophytes in the idealistic philosophy!

Sensation distinguished from Perception.—It is impossible rigorously to *define* a sensation; and in the actual life of consciousness sensations, popularly so called, and perceptions merge into each other by insensible degrees. All we can say is that *what we mean by sensations are* FIRST *things in the way of consciousness.* They are the *immediate* results upon consciousness of nerve-currents as they enter the brain, and before they have awakened any suggestions or associations with past experience. But it is obvious that *such immediate sensations can only be realized in the earliest days of life.* They are all but impossible to adults with memories and stores of associations acquired. Prior to all impressions on sense-organs, the brain is plunged in deep sleep and consciousness is practically non-existent. Even the first weeks after birth are passed in almost unbroken sleep by human infants. It takes a strong message from the sense-organs to break this slumber. In a new-born brain this gives rise to an absolutely pure sensation. But the experience leaves its 'unimaginable touch' on the matter of the convolutions, and the next impression which a sense-organ transmits produces a cerebral reaction in which the awakened vestige of the last impression plays its part. Another sort of feeling and a higher grade of cognition are the consequence. 'Ideas' *about* the object mingle with the awareness of its mere sensible presence, we name it, class it, compare it, utter propositions concerning it, and the complication of the possible consciousness which an incoming current may arouse, goes on increasing to the end of life. In general, this higher consciousness about things is called Perception, the mere inarticulate feeling of their presence is Sensation, so far as we have it at all. To some degree we seem able to lapse into this inarticulate feeling at moments when our attention is entirely dispersed.

Sensations are cognitive. A sensation is thus an abstraction seldom realized by itself; and the object which a sensation knows is an abstract object which cannot exist alone. *'Sensible qualities' are the objects of sensation.* The sensations of the eye are aware of the *colors* of things, those of the ear are acquainted with their *sounds*; those of the skin feel their tangible *heaviness, sharpness, warmth* or *coldness*, etc., etc. From all the organs of the body currents may come which reveal to us the quality of *pain*, and to a certain extent that of *pleasure*.

Such qualities as *stickiness, roughness*, etc., are supposed to be felt through the coöperation of muscular sensations with those of the skin. The geometrical qualities of things, on the other hand, their *shapes, bignesses, distances*, etc. (so far as we discriminate and identify them), are by most psychologists supposed to be impossible without the evocation of memories from the past; and the cognition of these attributes is thus considered to exceed the power of sensation pure and simple.

'Knowledge of Acquaintance' and 'Knowledge-about.'—Sensation, thus considered, differs from perception only in the extreme simplicity of its object or content. Its object, being a simple quality, is sensibly *homogeneous*; and its function is that of mere *acquaintance* with this homogeneous seeming fact. Perception's function, on the other hand, is that of knowing something *about* the fact. But we must know *what* and *which* fact we mean, all the while, and the various *whats* and *whiches* are what sensations give. Our earliest thoughts are almost exclusively sensational. They give us a set of *whats*, or *thats*, or *its*; of subjects of discourse in other words, with their relations not yet brought out. The first time we see *light*, in Condillac's phrase we *are* it rather than see it. But all our later optical knowledge is about what this experience gives. And though we were struck blind from that first moment, our scholarship in the subject would lack no essential feature so long as our memory remained. In training-institutions for the blind they teach the pupils as much *about* light as in ordinary schools. Reflection, refraction, the spectrum, the ether-theory, etc., are all studied. But the best taught born-blind pupil of such an establishment yet lacks a knowledge which the least instructed seeing baby has. They can never show him *what* light is in its 'first intention'; and the loss of that sensible knowledge no book-learning can replace. All this is so obvious that we usually find sensation 'postulated' as an element of experience, even by those philosophers who are least inclined to make much of its importance, or to pay respect to the knowledge which it brings.

Sensations distinguished from Images.—Both sensation and perception, for all their difference, are yet alike in that their objects appear *vivid*, *lively*, and *present*. Objects merely *thought of, recollected*, or *imagined*, on the contrary, are relatively faint and devoid of this pungency, or tang, this quality of *real presence* which the objects of sensation possess. Now the cortical brain-processes to which sensations are attached are due to incoming currents from the periphery of the body—an external object must excite the eye, ear, etc., before the sensation comes. Those cortical processes, on the other hand, to which mere ideas or images are attached are

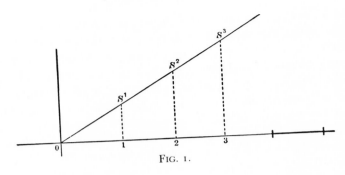

FIG. I.

Let the verticals dropped from the slanting line stand for the sensations aroused. At 0 there will be no sensation; at 1 there will be a sensation represented by the length of the vertical S^1—1, at 2 the sensation will be represented by S^2—2, and so on. The line of S's will rise evenly because by the hypothesis the verticals (or sensations) increase at the same rate as the horizontals (or stimuli) to which they severally correspond. But in Nature, as aforesaid, they increase at a slower rate. If each step forwards in the horizontal direction be equal to the last, then each step upwards in the vertical direction will have to be somewhat shorter than the last; the line of sensations will be convex on top instead of straight.

Fig. 2 represents this actual state of things, 0 being the zero-point of the stimulus, and conscious sensation, represented by the curved line, not beginning until the 'threshold' is reached, at which the stimulus has the value 3. From here onwards the sensation increases, but it increases less at each step, until at last, the 'acme' being reached, the sensation-line grows flat. The exact law of retardation is called *Weber's law*, from the fact that he first ob-

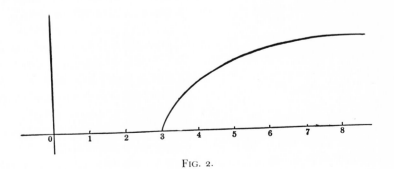

FIG. 2.

tify them), are by most psychologists supposed to be impossible without the evocation of memories from the past; and the cognition of these attributes is thus considered to exceed the power of sensation pure and simple.

'Knowledge of Acquaintance' and 'Knowledge-about.'—Sensation, thus considered, differs from perception only in the extreme simplicity of its object or content. Its object, being a simple quality, is sensibly *homogeneous*; and its function is that of mere *acquaintance* with this homogeneous seeming fact. Perception's function, on the other hand, is that of knowing something *about* the fact. But we must know *what* and *which* fact we mean, all the while, and the various *whats* and *whiches* are what sensations give. Our earliest thoughts are almost exclusively sensational. They give us a set of *whats*, or *thats*, or *its*; of subjects of discourse in other words, with their relations not yet brought out. The first time we see *light*, in Condillac's phrase we *are* it rather than see it. But all our later optical knowledge is about what this experience gives. And though we were struck blind from that first moment, our scholarship in the subject would lack no essential feature so long as our memory remained. In training-institutions for the blind they teach the pupils as much *about* light as in ordinary schools. Reflection, refraction, the spectrum, the ether-theory, etc., are all studied. But the best taught born-blind pupil of such an establishment yet lacks a knowledge which the least instructed seeing baby has. They can never show him *what* light is in its 'first intention'; and the loss of that sensible knowledge no book-learning can replace. All this is so obvious that we usually find sensation 'postulated' as an element of experience, even by those philosophers who are least inclined to make much of its importance, or to pay respect to the knowledge which it brings.

Sensations distinguished from Images.—Both sensation and perception, for all their difference, are yet alike in that their objects appear *vivid, lively,* and *present.* Objects merely *thought of, recollected,* or *imagined,* on the contrary, are relatively faint and devoid of this pungency, or tang, this quality of *real presence* which the objects of sensation possess. Now the cortical brain-processes to which sensations are attached are due to incoming currents from the periphery of the body—an external object must excite the eye, ear, etc., before the sensation comes. Those cortical processes, on the other hand, to which mere ideas or images are attached are due in all probability to currents from other convolutions. It would seem, then, that the currents from the periphery normally awaken a kind of brain-activity which the currents from other convolutions are inadequate to arouse. To this sort of activity—a profounder degree of disintegration, perhaps—the quality of vividness, presence, or reality in the object of the resultant consciousness seems correlated.

The Exteriority of Objects of Sensation.—Every thing or quality felt is felt in outer space. It is impossible to conceive a brightness or a color otherwise than as extended and outside of the mind. Sounds also appear in space. Contacts are against the body's surface; and pains always occupy some organ. An opinion which has had much currency in psychology is that sensible qualities are first apprehended as *in the mind itself*, and then 'projected' from it, or 'extradited,' by a secondary intellectual or super-sensational mental act. There is no ground whatever for this opinion. The only facts which even seem to make for it can be much better explained in another way, as we shall see later on. The very first sensation which an infant gets *is* for him the outer universe. And the universe which he comes to know in later life is nothing but an amplification of that first simple germ which, by accretion on the one hand and intussusception on the other, has grown so big and complex and articulate that its first estate is unrememberable. In his dumb awakening to the consciousness of *something there*, a mere *this* as yet (or something for which even the term *this* would perhaps be too discriminative, and the intellectual acknowledgment of which would be better expressed by the bare interjection 'lo!'), the infant encounters an object in which (though it be given in a pure sensation) all the 'categories of the understanding' are contained. *It has externality, objectivity, unity, substantiality, causality, in the full sense in which any later object or system of objects has these things.* Here the young knower meets and greets his world; and the miracle of knowledge bursts forth, as Voltaire says, as much in the infant's lowest sensation as in the highest achievement of a Newton's brain.

The physiological condition of this first sensible experience is probably many nerve-currents coming in from various peripheral organs at once; but this multitude of organic conditions does not prevent the consciousness from being one consciousness. We shall see as we go on that it can be one consciousness, even though it be due to the coöperation of numerous organs and be a consciousness of many things together. The Object which the numerous inpouring currents of the baby bring to his consciousness is one big blooming buzzing Confusion. That Confusion is the baby's universe; and the universe of all of us is still to a great extent such a Confusion, potentially resolvable, and demanding to be resolved, but not yet actually resolved, into parts. It appears from first to last as a space-occupying thing. So far as it is unanalyzed and unresolved we may be said to know it sensationally; but as fast as parts are distinguished in it and we become aware of their relations, our knowledge becomes perceptual or even conceptual, and as such need not concern us in the present chapter.

The Intensity of Sensations.—A light may be so weak as not sensibly to dispel the darkness, a sound so low as not to be heard, a contact so faint that we fail to notice it. In other words, a certain finite amount of the outward stimulus is required to produce any sensation of its presence at all. This is called by Fechner the law of the *threshold*—something must be stepped over before the object can gain entrance to the mind. An impression just above the threshold is called the *minimum visibile, audibile,* etc. From this point onwards, as the impressing force increases, the sensation increases also, though at a slower rate, until at last an *acme* of the sensation is reached which no increase in the stimulus can make sensibly more great. Usually, before the acme, *pain* begins to mix with the specific character of the sensation. This is definitely observable in the cases of great pressure, intense heat, cold, light, and sound; and in those of smell and taste less definitely so only from the fact that we can less easily increase the force of the stimuli here. On the other hand, all sensations, however unpleasant when more intense, are rather agreeable than otherwise in their very lowest degrees. A faintly bitter taste, or putrid smell, may at least be *interesting*.

Weber's Law.—I said that the intensity of the sensation increases by slower steps than those by which its exciting cause increases. If there were no threshold, and if every equal increment in the outer stimulus produced an equal increment in the sensation's intensity, a simple straight line would represent graphically the 'curve' of the relation between the two things. Let the horizontal line stand for the scale of intensities of the objective stimulus, so that at o it has no intensity, at 1 intensity 1, and so forth.

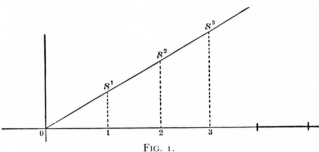

FIG. 1.

Let the verticals dropped from the slanting line stand for the sensations aroused. At o there will be no sensation; at 1 there will be a sensation represented by the length of the vertical S^1—1, at 2 the sensation will be represented by S^2—2, and so on. The line of S's will rise evenly because by the hypothesis the verticals (or sensations) increase at the same rate as the horizontals (or stimuli) to which they severally correspond. But in Nature, as aforesaid, they increase at a slower rate. If each step forwards in the horizontal direction be equal to the last, then each step upwards in the vertical direction will have to be somewhat shorter than the last; the line of sensations will be convex on top instead of straight.

Fig. 2 represents this actual state of things, o being the zero-point of the stimulus, and conscious sensation, represented by the curved line, not beginning until the 'threshold' is reached, at which the stimulus has the value 3. From here onwards the sensation increases, but it increases less at each step, until at last, the 'acme' being reached, the sensation-line grows flat. The exact law of retardation is called *Weber's law*, from the fact that he first ob-

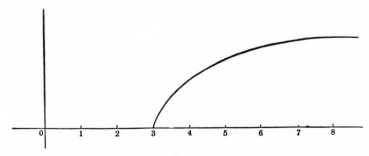

FIG. 2.

served it in the case of weights. I will quote Wundt's account of the law and of the facts on which it is based.

"Everyone knows that in the stilly night we hear things unnoticed in the noise of day. The gentle ticking of the clock, the air circulating through the chimney, the cracking of the chairs in the room, and a thousand other slight noises, impress themselves upon our ear. It is equally well known that in the confused hubbub of the streets, or the clamor of a railway, we may lose not only what our neighbor says to us, but even not hear the sound of our own voice. The stars which are brightest at night are invisible by day; and although we see the moon then, she is far paler than at night. Everyone who has had to deal with weights knows that if to a pound in the hand a second pound be added, the difference is immediately felt; whilst if it be added to a hundred-weight, we are not aware of the difference at all. . . .

"The sound of the clock, the light of the stars, the pressure of the pound, these are all *stimuli* to our senses, and stimuli whose outward amount remains the same. What then do these experiences teach? Evidently nothing but this, that one and the same stimulus, according to the circumstances under which it operates, will be felt either more or less intensely, or not felt at all. Of what sort now is the alteration in the circumstances upon which this alteration in the feeling may depend? On considering the matter closely we see that it is everywhere of one and the same kind. The tick of the clock is a feeble stimulus for our auditory nerve, which we hear plainly when it is alone, but not when it is added to the strong stimulus of the carriage-wheels and other noises of the day. The light of the stars is a stimulus to the eye. But if the stimulation which this light exerts be added to the strong stimulus of daylight, we feel nothing of it, although we feel it distinctly when it unites itself with the feebler stimulation of the twilight. The poundweight is a stimulus to our skin, which we feel when it joins itself to a preceding stimulus of equal strength, but which vanishes when it is combined with a stimulus a thousand times greater in amount.

"We may therefore lay it down as a general rule that a stimulus, in order to be felt, may be so much the smaller if the already preëxisting stimulation of the organ is small, but must be so much the larger, the greater the preëxisting stimulation is. . . . The simplest relation would obviously be that the sensation should increase in identically the same ratio as the stimulus. . . . But if this simplest of all relations prevailed, . . . the light of the stars, e.g., ought to make as great an addition to the daylight as it does to the darkness of the nocturnal sky, and this we know to be not the case. . . . So it is clear that the strength of the sensations does not increase in proportion to the amount of the stimuli, but more slowly. And now comes the question, in what proportion does the increase of the sensation grow less as the increase of the stimulus grows greater? To answer this question, every-day experiences do not suffice. We need exact measurements, both of the amounts of the various stimuli, and of the intensity of the sensations themselves.

"How to execute these measurements, however, is something which daily experience suggests. To measure the strength of sensations is, as we saw, impossible; we can only measure the difference of sensations. Experience showed us what very unequal differences of sensation might come from equal differences of outward stimulus. But all these experiences expressed themselves in one kind of fact, that the same difference of stimulus could in one case be felt, and in another case not felt at all—a pound felt if added to another pound, but not if added to a hundredweight. . . . We can quickest reach a result with our observations if we start with an arbitrary strength of stimulus, notice what sensation it gives us, and then *see how much we can increase the stimulus without making the sensation seem to change*. If we carry out such observations with stimuli of varying absolute amounts, we shall be forced to choose in an equally varying way the amounts of addition to the stimulus which are capable of giving us a just barely perceptible feeling of *more*. A light to be just perceptible in the twilight need not be near as bright as the starlight; it must be far brighter to be just perceived during the day. If now we institute such observations for all possible strengths of the various stimuli, and note for each strength the amount of addition of the latter required to produce a barely perceptible alteration of sensation, we shall have a series of figures in which is immediately expressed the law according to which the sensation alters when the stimulation is increased. . . ."

Observations according to this method are particularly easy to make in the spheres of light, sound, and pressure. Beginning with the latter case,

"We find a surprisingly simple result. *The barely sensible addition to the original weight must stand exactly in the same proportion to it*, be the *same fraction* of it, no matter what the absolute value may be of the weights on which the experiment is made. . . . As the average of a number of experiments, this fraction is found to be about $\frac{1}{3}$; that is, no matter what pressure there may already be made upon the skin, an increase or a diminution of the pressure will be *felt*, as soon as the added or subtracted weight amounts to one third of the weight originally there."

Wundt then describes how differences may be observed in the muscular feelings, in the feelings of heat, in those of light, and in those of sound; and he concludes thus:

"So we have found that all the senses whose stimuli we are enabled to measure accurately, obey a uniform law. However various may be their several delicacies of discrimination, *this* holds true of all, that *the increase of the stimulus necessary to produce an increase of the sensation bears a constant ratio to the total stimulus.* The figures which express this ratio in the several senses may be shown thus in tabular form:

Sensation of light	. . . . $\frac{1}{100}$
Muscular sensation	. . . . $\frac{1}{17}$
Feeling of pressure,	
// // warmth,	. . . . $\frac{1}{8}$
// // sound,	

"These figures are far from giving as accurate a measure as might be desired. But at least they are fit to convey a general notion of the relative discriminative susceptibility of the different senses. . . . The important law which gives in so simple a form the relation of the sensation to the stimulus that calls it forth was first discovered by the physiologist Ernst Heinrich Weber to obtain in special cases."[3]

Fechner's Law.—Another way of expressing Weber's law is to say that to get equal positive additions to the sensation, one must make equal *relative* additions to the stimulus. Professor Fechner of Leipzig founded upon Weber's law a theory of the numerical measurement of sensations, over which much metaphysical discussion has raged. Each just perceptible addition to the sensation, as we gradually let the stimulus increase, was supposed by him to be a *unit* of sensation, and all these units were treated by him as equal, in spite of the fact that *equally perceptible* increments need by no means appear *equally big* when they once are perceived. The many pounds which form the just perceptible addition to a hundredweight feel bigger when added than the few ounces which form the just perceptible addition to a pound. Fechner ignored this fact. He considered that if *n* distinct perceptible steps of increase might be passed through in gradually increasing a stimulus from the threshold-value till the intensity *s* was felt, then the sensation of *s* was composed of *n* units, which were of the same value all along the line.[4] Sensations once represented by numbers, psy-

---

[3] *Vorlesungen über die Menschen- und Thierseele*, Lecture VII.

[4] In other words, S standing for the sensation in general, and Δ for its noticeable increment, we have the equation $\Delta S = $ const. The increment of stimulus which produces ΔS (call it ΔR) meanwhile varies. Fechner calls it the 'differential threshold'; and as its *relative* value to R is always the same, we have the equation $\Delta R / R = $ const.

chology may become, according to Fechner, an 'exact' science, susceptible of mathematical treatment. His general formula for getting at the number of units in any sensation is $S = C \log R$, where S stands for the sensation, R for the stimulus numerically estimated, and C for a constant that must be separately determined by experiment in each particular order of sensibility. The sensation is proportional to the logarithm of the stimulus; and the absolute values, in units, of any series of sensations might be got from the ordinates of the curve in Fig. 2, if it were a correctly drawn logarithmic curve, with the thresholds rightly plotted out from experiments.

Fechner's psycho-physic formula, as he called it, has been attacked on every hand; and as absolutely nothing practical has come of it, it need receive no farther notice here. The main outcome of his book has been to stir up experimental investigation into the validity of Weber's law (which concerns itself merely with the just perceptible increase, and says nothing about the measurement of the sensation as a whole) and to promote discussion of statistical methods. Weber's law, as will appear when we take the senses, *seriatim*, is only approximately verified. The discussion of statistical methods is necessitated by the extraordinary fluctuations of our sensibility from one moment to the next. It is found, namely, when the difference of two sensations approaches the limit of discernibility, that at one moment we discern it and at the next we do not. Our incessant accidental inner alterations make it impossible to tell just what the least discernible increment of the sensation is without taking the average of a large number of appreciations. These *accidental errors* are as likely to increase as to diminish our sensibility, and are eliminated in such an average, for those above and those below the line then neutralize each other in the sum, and the normal sensibility, if there be one (that is, the sensibility due to constant causes as distinguished from these accidental ones), stands revealed. The methods of getting the average all have their difficulties and their snares, and controversy over them has become very subtle indeed. As an instance of how laborious some of the statistical methods are, and how patient German investigators can be, I may say that Fechner himself, in testing Weber's law for weights by the so-called 'method of true and false cases,' tabulated and computed no less than 24,576 separate judgments.

Sensations are not compounds. The fundamental objection to Fechner's whole attempt seems to be this, that although the outer *causes* of our sensations may have many parts, every distinguishable degree, as well as every distinguishable quality, of the *sensation itself* appears to be a unique fact of consciousness. Each sensation is a complete integer. "A strong one," as Dr. Münsterberg says, "is not the multiple of a weak one, or a compound of many weak ones, but rather something entirely new, and as it were incomparable, so that to seek a measurable difference between strong and weak sonorous, luminous, or thermic sensations would seem at first sight as senseless as to try to compute mathematically the difference between salt and sour, or between headache and toothache. It is clear that if in the stronger sensation of light the weaker sensation is not *contained*, it is unpsychological to say that the former differs from the latter by a certain *increment*."[5] Surely our feeling of scarlet is not a feeling of pink with a lot more pink added; it is something quite other than pink. Similarly with our sensation of an electric arc-light: it does not contain that of many smoky tallow candles in itself. Every sensation presents itself as an indivisible unit; and it is quite impossible to read any clear meaning into the notion that they are masses of units combined.

There is no inconsistency between this statement and the fact that, starting with a weak sensation and increasing it, we feel 'more,' 'more,' 'more,' as the increase goes on. It is not more of the same *stuff* added, so to speak; but it is more and more *difference*, more and more *distance*, which we feel between the sensation we start from and the one we compare with it, each being a unit. In the chapter on Discrimination we shall see that Difference can be perceived between simple things. We shall see, too, that *differences themselves differ*—there are *various directions of difference*; and along any one of them a series of things may be arranged so as to increase steadily in that direction. In any such series the end differs more from the beginning than the middle does. Differences of 'intensity' form one such direction of possible increase—so our judgments of more intensity can be expressed without the hypothesis that more units have been added to a growing sum.

The so-called 'Law of Relativity.'—Weber's law seems only one case of the still wider law that the more we have to attend to

[5] *Beiträge zur experimentellen Psychologie,* Heft 3, p. 3.

27

the less capable we are of noticing any one detail. The law is obvious where the things differ in kind. How easily do we forget a bodily discomfort when conversation waxes hot; how little do we notice the noises in the room so long as our work absorbs us! *Ad plura intentus minus est ad singula sensus*, as the old proverb says. One might now add that the homogeneity of what we have to attend to does not alter the result; but that a mind with two strong sensations of the same sort already before it is incapacitated by their amount from noticing the detail of a difference between them which it would immediately be struck by, were the sensations themselves weaker and consequently endowed with less distracting power.

This particular idea may be taken for what it is worth.[6] Meanwhile it is an undoubted general fact that the psychical effect of incoming currents does depend on what other currents may be simultaneously pouring in. Not only the *perceptibility* of the object which the current brings before the mind, but the *quality* of it, is changed by the other currents. "Simultaneous[7] sensations modify each other" is a brief expression for this law. "We feel all things in relation to each other" is Wundt's vaguer formula for this general 'law of relativity,' which in one shape or other has had vogue since Hobbes's time in psychology. Much mystery has been made of it, but although we are of course ignorant of the more intimate processes involved, there seems no ground to doubt that they are physiological, and come from the interference of one current with another. A current interfered with might naturally give rise to a modified sensation.

Examples of the modification in question are easy to find.[8] Notes make each other sweeter in a chord, and so do colors when harmoniously combined. A certain amount of skin dipped in hot water gives the perception of a certain heat. More skin immersed makes the heat much more intense, although of course the water's heat is the same. Similarly there is a *chromatic minimum* of size in objects. The image they cast on the retina must needs excite a

---

[6] I borrow it from Ziehen: *Leitfaden der physiologischen Psychologie*, 1891, p. 36, who quotes Hering's version of it.

[7] Successive ones also; but I consider simultaneous ones only, for simplicity's sake.

[8] The extreme case is where green light and red, *e.g.*, falling simultaneously on the retina, give a sensation of yellow. But I abstract from this because it is not certain that the incoming currents here affect different fibres of the optic nerve.

sufficient number of fibres, or it will give no sensation of color at all. Weber observed that a thaler laid on the skin of the forehead feels heavier when cold than when warm. Urbantschitsch has found that all our sense-organs influence each other's sensations. The hue of patches of color so distant as not to be recognized was immediately, in his patients, perceived when a tuning-fork was sounded close to the ear. Letters too far off to be read could be read when the tuning-fork was heard, etc., etc. The most familiar examples of this sort of thing seem to be the increase of *pain* by noise or light, and the increase of *nausea* by all concomitant sensations.

Effects of Contrast.—The best-known examples of the way in which one nerve-current modifies another are the phenomena of what is known as 'simultaneous color-contrast.' Take a number of sheets of brightly and differently colored papers, lay on each of them a bit of one and the same kind of gray paper, then cover each sheet with some transparent white paper, which softens the look of both the gray paper and the colored ground. The gray patch will appear in each case tinged by the color *complementary* to the ground; and so different will the several pieces appear that no observer, before raising the transparent paper, will believe them all cut out of the same gray. Helmholtz has interpreted these results as being due to a false application of an inveterate habit— that, namely, of making allowance for the color of the medium through which things are seen. The same *thing*, in the blue light of a clear sky, in the reddish-yellow light of a candle, in the dark brown light of a polished mahogany table which may reflect its image, is always judged of its own proper color, which the mind *adds* out of its own knowledge to the appearance, thereby correcting the falsifying medium. In the cases of the papers, according to Helmholtz, the mind believes the color of the ground, subdued by the transparent paper, to be faintly spread *over* the gray patch. But a patch to *look* gray through such a colored film would have really to *be* of the complementary color to the film. Therefore it *is* of the complementary color, we think, and proceed to *see* it of that color.

This theory has been shown to be untenable by Hering. The discussion of the facts is too minute for recapitulation here, but suffice it to say that it proves the phenomenon to be physiological—a case of the way in which, when sensory nerve-currents run in together, the effect of each on consciousness is different from that which it would be if they ran in separately.

'*Successive contrast*' differs from simultaneous contrast and is supposed to be due to fatigue. The facts will be noticed under the head of 'after-images,' in the section on Vision. It must be borne in mind, however, that after-images from previous sensations may coexist with present sensations, and the two may modify each other just as coexisting sensational processes do.

Other senses than sight show phenomena of contrast, but they are much less obvious, so I will not notice them here. We can now pass to a very brief survey of the various senses in detail.

Chapter III

Sight

The Eye's Structure is described in all the books on anatomy. I will only mention the few points which concern the psychologist.[1] It is a flattish sphere formed by a tough white membrane (the

[1] The student can easily verify the coarser features of the eye's anatomy upon a bullock's eye, which any butcher will furnish. Clean it first from fat and muscles and study its shape, etc., and then (following Golding Bird's method) make an incision with a pointed scalpel into the sclerotic half an inch from the edge of the cornea, so that the black choroid membrane comes into view. Next with one blade of a pair of scissors inserted into this aperture, cut through sclerotic, choroid, and retina (avoid wounding the membrane of the vitreous body!) all round the eyeball parallel to the cornea's edge.

The eyeball is thus divided into two parts, the anterior one containing the iris, lens, vitreous body, etc., whilst the posterior one contains most of the retina. The two parts can be separated by immersing the eyeball in water, cornea downwards, and simply pulling off the portion to which the optic nerve is attached. Floating this detached posterior cap in water, the delicate retina will be seen spread out over the choroid (which is partly iridescent in the ox tribe); and by turning the cup inside out, and working under water with a camel's-hair brush, the vessels and nerves of the eyeball may be detected.

The anterior part of the eyeball can then be attacked. Seize with forceps on each side the edge of the sclerotic and choroid (not including the retina), raise the eye with the forceps thus applied and shake it gently till the vitreous body, lens, capsule, ligament, etc., drop out by their weight, and separate from the iris, ciliary processes, cornea, and sclerotic, which remains in the forceps. Examine these latter parts, and get a view of the ciliary muscle which appears as a white line, when with camel's-hair brush and scalpel the choroid membrane is detached from the sclerotic as far forwards as it will go. Turning to the parts that cling to the vitreous body observe the clear ring around the lens, and radiating outside of it the marks made by the ciliary processes before they were torn away from its suspensory ligament. A fine capillary tube may now be used to insufflate the clear ring, just below the letter p in Fig. 3, and thus to reveal the suspensory ligament itself.

All these parts can be seen in section in a frozen eye or one hardened in alcohol.

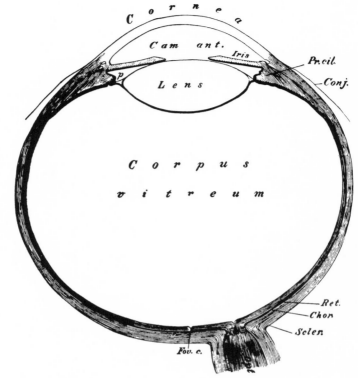

FIG. 3.

sclerotic), which encloses a nervous surface and certain re-
fracting media (lens and 'humors') which cast a picture of the
outer world thereon. It is in fact a little camera obscura, the
essential part of which is the sensitive plate.

The retina is what corresponds to this plate. The optic nerve
pierces the sclerotic shell and spreads its fibres radially in every direction over its inside, forming a thin translucent film (see Fig. 3,
Ret.). The fibres pass into a complicated apparatus of cells, granules, and branches (Fig. 4), and finally end in the so-called rods
and cones (Fig. 4,—9), which are the specific organs for taking up
the influence of the waves of light. Strange to say, these end-
organs are not pointed forwards towards the light as it streams
through the pupil, but backwards towards the sclerotic membrane itself, so that the light-waves traverse the translucent
nerve-fibres, and the cellular and granular layers of the retina,

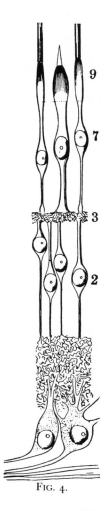

FIG. 4.

before they touch the rods and cones themselves. (See Fig. 5.)

The Blind Spot.—The optic nerve-fibres must thus be unimpressible by light directly. The place where the nerve enters is in fact entirely blind, because nothing but fibres exist there, the other layers of the retina only beginning round about the entrance. Nothing is easier than to prove the existence of this blind spot. Close the right eye and look steadily with the left at the cross in Fig. 6, holding the book vertically in front of the face, and moving it to and fro. It will be found that at about a foot off the black disk disappears; but when the page is nearer or farther, it is

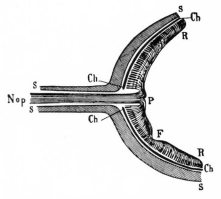

FIG. 5.—Scheme of retinal fibres, after Küss.
Nop, optic nerve; *S*, sclerotic; *Ch*, choroid;
R, retina; *P*, papilla (blind spot); *F*, fovea.

seen. During the experiment the gaze must be kept fixed on the cross. It is easy to show by measurement that this blind spot lies where the optic nerve enters.

The Fovea.—Outside of the blind spot the sensibility of the retina varies. It is greatest at the *fovea*, a little pit lying outwardly from the entrance of the optic nerve, and round which the radiating nerve-fibres bend without passing over it. The other layers also disappear at the fovea, leaving the cones alone to represent the retina there. The sensibility of the retina grows progressively less towards its periphery, by means of which neither colors, shapes, nor number of impressions can be well discriminated.

In the normal use of our two eyes, the eyeballs are rotated so as to cause the two images of any object which catches the attention to fall on the two foveæ, as the spots of acutest vision. This happens involuntarily, as anyone may observe. In fact, it is almost impossible *not* to 'turn the eyes,' the moment any peripherally

FIG. 6.

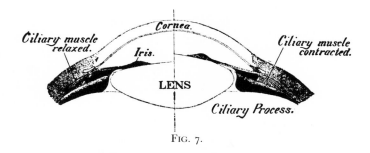

FIG. 7.

lying object does catch our attention, the turning of the eyes being only another name for such rotation of the eyeballs as will bring the foveæ under the object's image.

Accommodation.—The *focussing* or *sharpening* of the image is performed by a special apparatus. In every camera, the farther the object is from the eye the farther forwards, and the nearer the object is to the eye the farther backwards, is its image thrown. In photographers' cameras the back is made to slide, and can be drawn away from the lens when the object that casts the picture is near, and pushed forwards when it is far. The picture is thus kept always sharp. But no such change of length is possible in the eyeball; and the same result is reached in another way. The lens, namely, grows more convex when a near object is looked at, and flatter when the object recedes. This change is due to the antagonism of the circular 'ligament' in which the lens is suspended, and the 'ciliary muscle.' The ligament, when the ciliary muscle is at rest, assumes such a spread-out shape as to keep the lens rather flat. But the lens is highly elastic; and it springs into the more convex form which is natural to it whenever the ciliary muscle, by contracting, causes the ligament to relax its pressure. The contraction of the muscle, by thus rendering the lens more refractive, adapts the eye for near objects ('accommodates' it for them, as we say); and its relaxation, by rendering the lens less refractive, adapts the eye for distant vision. Accommodation for the near is thus the more *active* change, since it involves contraction of the ciliary muscle. When we look far off, we simply let our eyes go passive. We feel this difference in the effort when we compare the two sensations of change.

Convergence accompanies accommodation. The two eyes act as one organ; that is, when an object catches the attention, both eyeballs turn so that its images may fall on the foveæ. When the object is near, this naturally requires them to turn inwards, or converge; and as accommodation then also occurs, the two movements of convergence and accommodation form a naturally associated couple, of which it is difficult to execute either singly. Contraction of the pupil also accompanies the accommodative act. When we come to stereoscopic vision, it will appear that by much practice one can learn to converge with relaxed accommodation, and to accommodate with parallel axes of vision. These are accomplishments which the student of psychological optics will find most useful.

Single Vision by the two Retinæ.—We hear single with two ears, and smell single with two nostrils, and we also see single with two eyes. The difference is that we also *can* see double under certain conditions, whereas under no conditions can we hear or smell double. The main conditions of single vision can be simply expressed.

In the first place, impressions on the two foveæ always appear in the same place. By no artifice can they be made to appear alongside of each other. The result is that one object, casting its images on the foveæ of the two converging eyeballs will necessarily always appear as what it is, namely, one object. Furthermore, if the eyeballs, instead of converging, are kept parallel, and two similar objects, one in front of each, cast their respective images on the foveæ, the two will also appear as one, or (in common parlance) 'their images will fuse.' To verify this, let the reader stare fixedly before him as if through the paper at infinite distance, with the black spots in Fig. 8 in front of his respective eyes. He will then see the two black spots swim together, as it were, and combine into one, which appears situated between their original two positions and as if opposite the root of his nose. This combined spot is the result of the spots opposite both eyes being seen

FIG. 8.

in the same place. But in addition to the combined spot, each eye sees also the spot opposite the *other* eye. To the right eye this appears to the left of the combined spot, to the left eye it appears to the right of it; so that what is seen is *three* spots, of which the middle one is seen by both eyes, and is flanked by two others, each seen by one. That such are the facts can be tested by interposing some small opaque object so as to cut off the vision of either of the spots in the figure from the *other* eye. A vertical partition in the median plane, going from the paper to the nose, will effectually confine each eye's vision to the spot in front of it, and then the single combined spot will be all that appears.[2]

If, instead of two identical spots, we use two different figures, or two differently colored spots, as objects for the two foveæ to look at, they still are seen in the *same place*; but since they cannot appear as a single object, they appear there *alternately* displacing each other from the view. This is the phenomenon called *retinal rivalry*.

As regards the parts of the retinæ round about the foveæ, a similar correspondence obtains. Any impression on the upper half of either retina makes us see an object as below, on the lower half as above, the horizon; and on the right half of either retina, an impression makes us see an object to the left, on the left half one to the right, of the median line. Thus each quadrant of one retina corresponds as a whole to the geometrically *similar* quadrant of the other; and within two similar quadrants, *al* and *ar* for example, there should, if the correspondence were carried out in detail, be geometrically similar points which, if impressed at the same time by light emitted from the same object, should cause that object to appear in the same direction to either eye. Experiment verifies this surmise. If we look at the starry vault with parallel eyes, the stars all seem single; and the laws of perspective show that under the circumstances the parallel light-rays coming from each star must impinge on points within either retina which *are* geometrically similar to each other. Similarly, a pair of spectacles held an inch or so from the eyes seem like one large median glass. Or we may make an experiment like that with the spots. If we take two exactly similar pictures, no larger than those on an ordinary stereoscopic slide, and if we look at one with each eye (a me-

[2] This vertical partition is introduced into stereoscopes, which otherwise would give us three pictures instead of one.

dian partition confining the view) we shall see but one flat picture, all of whose parts appear single. 'Identical retinal points' being impressed, both eyes see their object in the same direction, and the two objects consequently coalesce into one.

Here again retinal rivalry occurs if the pictures differ. And it must be noted that when the experiment is performed for the first time the combined picture is always far from sharp. This is due to the difficulty mentioned on p. 35, of accommodating for anything as near as the surface of the paper, whilst at the same time the convergence is relaxed so that each eye sees the picture in front of itself.

Double Images.—Now it is an immediate consequence of the law of identical location of images falling on geometrically similar points that *images which fall upon geometrically* DISPARATE *points of the two retinæ should be seen in* DISPARATE *directions, and that their objects should consequently appear in* TWO *places, or* LOOK DOUBLE. Take the parallel rays from a star falling upon two eyes which converge upon a near object, O, instead of being parallel as in the previously instanced case. The two foveæ will receive the images of O, which therefore will look single. If then SL and SR in Fig. 10 be the parallel rays, each of them will fall upon the nasal half of the retina which it strikes. But the two nasal halves are disparate, geometrically *symmetrical*, not geometrically *similar*. The star's image on the left eye will therefore appear as if lying to the left of O; its image on the right eye will appear to the right of this point. The star will, in short, be seen double—'homonymously' double.

Conversely, if the star be looked at directly with parallel axes, any near object like O will be seen double, because its images will affect the outer or cheek halves of the two retinæ, instead of one outer and one nasal half. The position of the images will here be reversed from that of the previous case. The right eye's image will now appear to the left, the left eye's to the right; the double images will be 'heteronymous.'

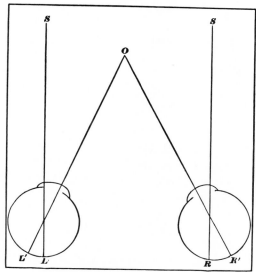

FIG. 10.

The same reasoning and the same result ought to apply where the object's place with respect to the direction of the two optic axes is such as to make its images fall not on non-similar retinal halves, but on non-similar parts of similar halves. Here, of course, the positions seen will be less widely disparate than in the other case, and the double images will appear to lie less widely apart.

Careful experiments made by many observers according to the so-called haploscopic method confirm this law, and show that *corresponding points, of single visual direction*, exist upon the two retinæ. For the detail of these one must consult the special treatises.

Vision of Solidity.—This description of binocular vision follows what is called the theory of identical points. On the whole it formulates the facts correctly. The only odd thing is that we should be so little troubled by the innumerable double images which objects nearer and farther than the point looked at must be constantly producing. The answer to this is that *we have trained ourselves to habits of inattention* in regard to double images. So far as things interest us we turn our foveæ upon them, and they are necessarily seen single; so that if an object impresses disparate points, that may be taken as proof that it is so unimportant for us that we needn't notice whether it appears in one place or in two. By long practice one may acquire great expertness in detecting double

FIG. 11.

images, though, as someone says, it is an art which is not to be learned completely either in one year or in two.

Where the disparity of the images is but slight it is almost impossible to see them as if double. They give rather the perception of a solid object being there. To fix our ideas, take Fig. 11. Suppose we look at the dots in the middle of the lines *a* and *b* just as we looked at the spots in Fig. 8. We shall get the same result—i.e., they will coalesce in the median line. But the entire lines will not coalesce, for, owing to their inclination, their tops fall on the temporal, and their bottoms on the nasal, retinal halves. What we see will be two lines crossed in the middle, thus (Fig. 12):

FIG. 12.   FIG. 13.   FIG. 14.

The moment we attend to the tops of these lines, however, our foveæ tend to abandon the dots and to move upwards, and in doing so, to converge somewhat, following the lines, which then appear coalescing at the top as in Fig. 13.

If we think of the bottom, the eyes descend and diverge, and what we see is Fig. 14.

Running our eyes up and down the lines makes them converge and diverge just as they would were they running up and down some single line whose top was nearer to us than its bottom. Now, if the inclination of the lines be moderate, we may not see them double at all, but single throughout their length, when we look at the dots. Under these conditions their top does look nearer than their bottom—in other words, we see them stereoscopically; and we see them so even when our eyes are rigorously motionless. In other words, the slight disparity in the bottom-ends which *would* draw the foveæ divergently apart makes us see those ends farther, the slight disparity in the top ends which *would* draw them convergently together makes us see these ends nearer, than the point at which we look. The disparities, in short, affect our perception as the actual movements would.[3]

The Perception of Distance.—When we look about us at things, our eyes are incessantly moving, converging, diverging, accommodating, relaxing, and sweeping over the field. The field appears extended in three dimensions, with some of its parts more distant and some more near.

"With one eye our perception of distance is very imperfect, as illustrated by the common trick of holding a ring suspended by a string in front of a person's face, and telling him to shut one eye and pass a rod from one side through the ring. If a penholder be held erect before one eye, while the other is closed, and an attempt be made to touch it with a finger moved across towards it, an error will nearly always be made. . . . In such cases we get the only clue from the amount of effort needed to 'accommodate' the eye to see the object distinctly. When we use both eyes our perception of distance is much better; when we look at an object with two eyes the visual axes are converged on it, and the nearer the object the greater the convergence. We have a pretty accurate knowledge of the degree of muscular effort required to converge the eyes on all tolerably near points. When objects are farther off, their apparent size, and the modifications their retinal images experience by aërial perspective, come in to help. The relative distance of objects is easiest determined by moving the eyes; all stationary objects then appear displaced in the opposite direction (as for example when we look out of the window of a railway car) and those nearest most rapidly; from the different apparent rates of movement we can tell which are farther and which nearer."[4]

Subjectively considered, distance is an altogether peculiar con-

[3] The simplest form of stereoscope is two tin tubes about one and one-half inches calibre, dead black inside and (for normal eyes) ten inches long. Close each end with paper not too opaque, on which an inch-long thick black line is drawn. The tubes can be looked through, one by each eye, and held either parallel or with their farther ends converging. When properly rotated, their images will show every variety of fusion and non-fusion, and stereoscopic effect.

[4] H. Newell Martin: *The Human Body*, p. 530.

tent of consciousness. Convergence, accommodation, binocular disparity, size, degree of brightness, parallax, etc., all give us special feelings which are *signs* of the distance feeling, but not it. They simply suggest it to us. The best way to get it strongly is to go upon some hill-top and invert one's head. The horizon then looks very distant, and draws near as the head erects itself again.

The Perception of Size.—"The dimensions of the retinal image determine primarily the sensations on which conclusions as to size are based; and the larger the visual angle the larger the retinal image: since the visual angle depends on the distance of an object the correct perception of size depends largely upon a correct perception of distance; having formed a judgment, conscious or unconscious, as to that, we conclude as to size from the extent of the retinal region affected. Most people have been surprised now and then to find that what appeared a large bird in the clouds was only a small insect close to the eye; the large apparent size being due to the previous incorrect judgment as to the distance of the object. The presence of an object of tolerably well-known height, as a man, also assists in forming conceptions (by comparison) as to size; artists for this purpose frequently introduce human figures to assist in giving an idea of the size of other objects represented."[5]

Sensations of Color.—The system of colors is a very complex thing. If one take any color, say green, one can pass away from it in more than one direction, through a series of greens more and more yellowish, let us say, towards yellow, or through another series more and more bluish towards blue. The result would be that if we seek to plot out on paper the various distinguishable tints, the arrangement cannot be that of a line, but has to cover a surface. With the tints arranged on a surface we can pass from any one of them to any other by various lines of gradually changing intermediaries. Such an arrangement is represented in Fig. 15. It is a merely classificatory diagram based on degrees of difference simply felt, and has no physical significance. Black is a color, but does not figure on the plane of the diagram. We cannot place it anywhere alongside of the other colors because we need both to represent the straight gradation from untinted white to black, and that from each pure color towards black as well as towards white. The best way is to put black into the third dimension,

[5] *Ibid.*, p. 531.

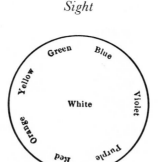

FIG. 15.

beneath the paper, *e.g.*, as is shown perspectively in Fig. 16, then all the transitions can be schematically shown. One can pass straight from black to white, or one can pass round by way of olive, green, and pale green; or one can change from dark blue to yellow through green, or by way of sky-blue, white and straw color; etc., etc. In any case the changes are continuous; and the color system thus forms what Wundt calls a tri-dimensional continuum.

Color-mixture.—Physiologically considered, the colors have this peculiarity, that many pairs of them, when they impress the retina together, produce the sensation of white. The colors which do this are called *complementaries*. Such are spectral red and green-blue, spectral yellow and indigo-blue. Green and purple, again, are complementaries. All the spectral colors added together also make white light, such as we daily experience in the sunshine. Furthermore, both homogeneous ether-waves and heterogeneous ones may make us feel the same color, when they fall on our retina. Thus yellow, which is a simple spectral color, is also felt when green light is added to red; blue is felt when violet and green lights are mixed. Purple, which is not a spectral color at all, results when the waves either of red and of violet or those of blue and of orange are superposed.[6]

---

[6] The ordinary mixing of *pigments* is not an addition, but rather, as Helmholtz has shown, a subtraction, of lights. To *add* one color to another we must either by appropriate glasses throw differently colored beams upon the same reflecting surface; or we must let the eye look at one color through an inclined plate of glass beneath which it lies, whilst the upper surface of the glass reflects into the same eye another color placed alongside—the two lights then mix on the retina; or, finally, we must let the differently colored lights fall in succession upon the retina, so fast that the second is there before the impression made by the first has died away. This is best done by looking at a rapidly rotating disk whose sectors are of the several colors to be mixed.

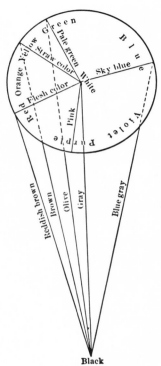

FIG. 16 (after Ziehen).

From all this it follows that there is no particular congruence between our system of color-sensations and the physical stimuli which excite them. Each color-feeling is a 'specific energy' (p. 16) which many different physical causes may arouse. Helmholtz, Hering, and others have sought to simplify the tangle of the facts, by physiological hypotheses which, differing much in detail, agree in principle, since they all postulate a limited number of elementary retinal processes to which, when excited singly, certain 'fundamental' colors severally correspond. When excited in combination, as they may be by the most various physical stimuli, other colors, called 'secondary,' are felt. The secondary color-sensations are often spoken of as if they were compounded of the primary sensations. This is a great mistake. The *sensations as such* are not compounded—yellow, for example, a secondary on Helmholtz's theory, is as unique a quality of feeling as the primaries red and green, which are said to 'compose' it. What are compounded are merely the elementary retinal processes. These, according to their combination, produce diverse results on the brain, and thence the secondary colors result immediately in consciousness. The 'color-theories' are thus physiological, not psychological, hypotheses, and for more information concerning them the reader must consult the physiological books.

The Duration of Luminous Sensations.—"This is greater than that of the stimulus, a fact taken advantage of in making fireworks: an ascending rocket produces the sensation of a trail of light extending far behind the position of the bright part of the rocket itself at the moment, because the sensation aroused by it in a lower part of its course still persists. So, shooting stars appear to have luminous tails behind them. By rotating rapidly before the eye a disk with alternate white and black sectors we get for each point of the retina alternate stimulation (due to the passage of white sector) and rest (when a black sector is passing). If the rotation be rapid enough the sensation aroused is that of a uniform gray, such as would be produced if the white and black were mixed and spread evenly over the disk. In each revolution the eye gets as much light as if that were the case, and is unable to distinguish that this light is made up of separate portions reaching it at intervals: the stimulation due to each lasts until the next begins and so all are fused together. If one turns out suddenly the gas in a room containing no other light, the image of the flame persists a short time after the flame itself is extinguished."[7] If we open our eyes instantaneously upon a scene, and then shroud them in complete darkness, it will be as if we saw the scene in ghostly light through the dark screen. We can read off details in it which were unnoticed whilst the eyes were open. This is the primary positive after-image, so called. According to Helmholtz, one third of a second is the most favorable length of exposure to the light for producing it.

Negative after-images are due to more complex conditions, in which fatigue of the retina is usually supposed to play the chief part.

"The nervous visual apparatus is easily fatigued. Usually we do not observe this because its restoration is also rapid, and in ordinary life our

[7] Martin: *op. cit.*, p. 516.

eyes, when open, are never at rest; we move them to and fro, so that parts of the retina receive light alternately from brighter and darker objects and are alternately excited and rested. How constant and habitual the movement of the eyes is can be readily observed by trying to 'fix' for a short time a small spot without deviating the glance; to do so for even a few seconds is impossible without practice. If any small object is steadily 'fixed' for twenty or thirty seconds it will be found that the whole field of vision becomes grayish and obscure, because the parts of the retina receiving most light get fatigued, and arouse no more sensation than those less fatigued and stimulated by light from less illuminated objects. Or look steadily at a black object, say a blot on a white page, for twenty seconds, and then turn the eye on a white wall; the latter will seem dark gray, with a white patch on it; an effect due to the greater excitability of the retinal parts previously rested by the black, when compared with the sensation aroused elsewhere by light from the white wall acting on the previously stimulated parts of the visual surface. All persons will recall many instances of such phenomena, which are especially noticeable soon after rising in the morning. Similar things may be noticed with colors; after looking at a red patch the eye turned on a white wall sees a blue-green patch; the elements causing red sensations having been fatigued, the white mixed light from the wall now excites on that region of the retina only the other primary color sensations. The blending of colors so as to secure their greatest effect depends on this fact; red and green go well together because each rests the parts of the visual apparatus most excited by the other, and so each appears bright and vivid as the eye wanders to and fro; while red and orange together, each exciting and exhausting mainly the same visual elements, render dull, or in popular phrase 'kill,' one another. . . .

"If we fix steadily for thirty seconds a point between two white squares about 4 mm. ($\frac{1}{6}$ inch) apart on a large black sheet, and then close and cover our eyes, we get a negative after-image in which are seen two dark squares on a brighter surface; this surface is brighter close around the negative after-image of each square, and brightest of all between them. This luminous boundary is called the *corona*, and is explained usually as an effect of simultaneous contrast; the dark after-image of the square it is said makes us mentally err in judgment and think the clear surface close to it brighter than elsewhere; and it is brightest between the two dark squares, just as a middle-sized man between two tall ones looks shorter than if alongside one only. If, however, the after-image be watched it will often be noticed not only that the light band between the squares is intensely white, much more so than the normal idio-retinal light [see below], but, as the image fades away, often the two dark after-images of the squares disappear entirely with all of the corona, except that part between them which is still seen as a bright band on a uniform grayish field. Here there is no *contrast* to produce the error of judgment, and from this and other experiments Hering concludes that light acting on one part of the retina produces inverse changes in all the rest, and that this plays an important part in producing the phenomena of contrasts. Similar phenomena may be observed with colored objects; in their negative after-images each tint is represented by its complementary, as black is by white in colorless vision."[8]

This is one of the facts referred to on p. 29 which have made Hering reject the psychological explanation of simultaneous contrast.

The Intensity of Luminous Objects.—Black is an optical sensation. We have no black except in the field of view; we do not, for instance, see black out of our stomach or out of the palm of our hand. *Pure* black is, however, only an 'abstract idea,' for the retina itself (even in complete objective darkness) seems to be always the seat of internal changes which give some luminous sensation. This is what is meant by the 'idio-retinal light,' spoken of a few lines back. It plays its part in the determination of all after-images with closed eyes. Any objective luminous stimulus, to be perceived, must be strong enough to give a sensible increment of sensation over and above the idio-retinal light. As the objective stimulus increases the perception is of an intenser luminosity; but the perception changes, as we saw on p. 22, more slowly than the stimulus. The latest numerical determinations, by König and Brodhun, were applied to six different colors and ran from an intensity arbitrarily called 1 to one which was 100,000 times as great. From intensity 2000 to 20,000 Weber's law held good; below and above this range discriminative sensibility declined. The relative increment discriminated here was the same for all colors of light, and lay (according to the tables) between 1 and 2 per cent of the stimulus. Previous observers have got different results.

A certain amount of luminous intensity must exist in an object for its color to be discriminated at all. "In the dark all cats are gray." But the colors rapidly become distincter as the light increases, first the blues and last the reds and yellows, up to a certain point of intensity, when they grow indistinct again through the fact that each takes a turn towards white. At the highest bear-

[8] Martin, pp. 524-7.

able intensity of the light all colors are lost in the blinding white dazzle. This again is usually spoken of as a 'mixing' of the sensation white with the original color-sensation. It is no mixing of two sensations, but the replacement of one sensation by another, in consequence of a changed neural process.

Chapter IV

Hearing*

The Ear.—"The auditory organ in man consists of three portions, known respectively as the *external ear*, the *middle ear* or *tympanum*, and the *internal ear* or *labyrinth*; the latter contains the end organs of the auditory nerve. The external ear consists of the expansion seen on the exterior of the head, called the *concha*, *M*, Fig. 17, and a passage leading in from it, the *external auditory meatus*, *G*. This passage is closed at its inner end by the *tympanic* or *drum membrane*, *T*. It is lined by skin, through which numerous small glands, secreting the *wax* of the ear, open.

"*The Tympanum* (*P*, Fig. 17) is an irregular cavity in the temporal bone, closed externally by the drum membrane. From its inner side the *Eustachian tube* (*R*) proceeds and opens into the pharynx. The inner wall of the tympanum is bony except for two small apertures, the *oval* and *round foramens*, *o* and *r*, which lead into the labyrinth. During life the round aperture is closed by the lining mucous membrane, and the oval by the stirrup-bones. The *tympanic membrane*, *T*, stretched across the outer side of the tympanum, forms a shallow funnel with its concavity outwards. It is pressed by the external air on its exterior, and by air entering the tympanic cavity through the Eustachian tube on its inner side. If the tympanum were closed these pressures would not be always

* In teaching the anatomy of the ear, great assistance will be yielded by the admirable model made by Dr. Auzoux, 56 Rue de Vaugirard, Paris, described in the catalogue of the firm as "No. 21—*Oreille, temporal de* 60 cm., nouvelle édition," etc.

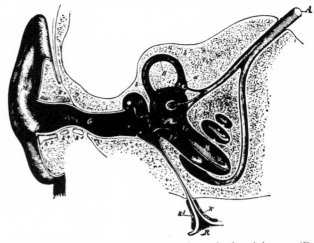

FIG. 17.—Semidiagrammatic section through the right ear (Czermak). *M*, concha; *G*, external auditory meatus; *T*, tympanic membrane; *P*, tympanic cavity; *o*, oval foramen; *r*, round foramen; *R*, pharyngeal opening of Eustachian tube; *V*, vestibule; *B*, a semicircular canal; *S*, the cochlea; *Vt*, scala vestibuli; *Pt*, scala tympani; *A*, auditory nerve.

equal when barometric pressure varied, and the membrane would be bulged in or out according as the external or internal pressure on it were the greater. On the other hand, were the Eustachian tube always open the sounds of our own voices would be loud and disconcerting, so it is usually closed; but every time we swallow it is opened, and thus the air-pressure in the cavity is kept equal to that in the external auditory meatus. On making a balloon ascent or going rapidly down a deep mine, the sudden and great change of aërial pressure outside frequently causes painful tension of the drum membrane, which may be greatly alleviated by frequent swallowing.

The Auditory Ossicles.—"Three small bones lie in the tympanum forming a chain from the drum membrane to the oval foramen. The external bone is the *malleus* or *hammer*; the middle one, the *incus* or *anvil*; and the internal one, the *stapes* or *stirrup*." They are represented in Fig. 18.[1]

Accommodation is provided for in the ear as well as in the eye. One muscle an inch long, the *tensor tympani*, arises in the petrous portion of the temporal bone (running in a canal parallel to the

[1] This description is abridged from Martin's *Human Body*, pp. 535-36.

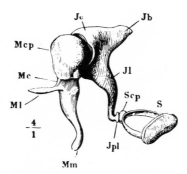

Fig. 18.—*Mcp, Mc, Ml,* and *Mm* stand for different parts of the malleus; *Jc, Jb, Jl, Jpl,* for different parts of the incus. *S* is the stapes.

Eustachian tube) and is inserted into the malleus below its head. When it contracts, it makes the membrane of the tympanum more tense. Another smaller muscle, the *stapedius,* goes to the head of the stirrup-bone. These muscles are by many persons felt distinctly contracting when certain notes are heard, and some can make them contract at will. In spite of this, uncertainty still reigns as to their exact use in hearing, though it is highly probable that they give to the membranes which they influence the degree of tension best suited to take up whatever rates of vibration may fall upon them at the time. In listening, the head and ears in lower animals, and the head alone in man, are turned so as best to receive the sound. This also is a part of the reaction called 'adaptation' of the organ (see the chapter on Attention).

The Internal Ear.—"The labyrinth consists primarily of chambers and tubes hollowed out in the temporal bone and inclosed by it on all sides, except for the oval and round foramens on its exterior, and certain apertures for blood-vessels and the auditory nerve; during life all these are closed water-tight in one way or another. Lying in the *bony labyrinth* thus constituted, are membranous parts, of the same general form but smaller, so that between the two a space is left; this is filled with a watery fluid, called the *perilymph*; and the *membranous internal ear* is filled by a similar liquid, the *endolymph.*

The Bony Labyrinth.—"The bony labyrinth is described in three portions, the *vestibule,* the *semicircular canals,* and the *coch-*

·

51

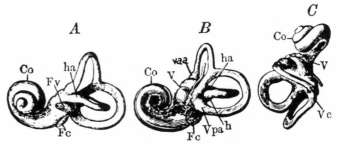

FIG. 19.—Casts of the bony labyrinth. *A*, left labyrinth seen from the outer side; *B*, right labyrinth from the inner side; *C*, left labyrinth from above; *Co*, cochlea; *V*, vestibule; *Fc*, round foramen; *Fv*, oval foramen; *h*, horizontal semicircular canal; *ha*, its ampulla; *vaa*, ampulla of anterior vertical semicircular canal; *vpa*, ampulla of posterior vertical semicircular canal; *vc*, conjoined portion of the two vertical canals.

lea; casts of its interior are represented from different aspects in Fig. 19. The vestibule is the central part and has on its exterior the oval foramen (*Fv*) into which the base of the stirrup-bone fits. Behind the vestibule are three bony semicircular canals, communicating with the back of the vestibule at each end, and dilated near one end to form an *ampulla* . . . . The bony cochlea is a tube coiled on itself somewhat like a snail's shell, and lying in front of the vestibule.

The Membranous Labyrinth.—"The membranous vestibule, lying in the bony, consists of two sacs communicating by a narrow aperture. The posterior is called the *utriculus*, and into it the membranous semicircular canals open. The anterior, called the *sacculus*, communicates by a tube with the membranous cochlea. The membranous semicircular canals much resemble the bony, and each has an ampulla; . . . in the ampulla one side of the membra-

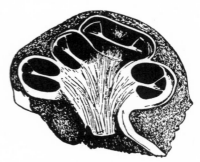

FIG. 20.—A section through the cochlea in the line of its axis.

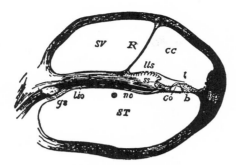

FIG. 21.—Section of one coil of the cochlea, magnified. *SV, scala ves-tibuli*; *R*, membrane of Reissner; *CC*, membranous cochlea (*scala media*); *lls, limbus laminæ spiralis*; *t*, tectorial membrane; *ST*, scala tympani; *lso, spiral lamina*; *Co*, rods of Corti; *b*, basilar membrane.

nous tube is closely adherent to its bony protector; at this point nerves enter the former. The relations of the membranous to the bony cochlea are more complicated. A section through this part of the auditory apparatus (Fig. 20) shows that its osseous portion consists of a tube wound two and a half times around a central bony axis, the *modiolus*. From the axis a shelf, the *lamina spiralis*, projects and partially subdivides the tube, extending farthest across in its lower coils. Attached to the outer edge of this bony plate is the membranous cochlea (*scala media*), a tube triangular in cross-section and attached by its base to the outer side of the bony cochlear spiral. The spiral lamina and the membranous cochlea thus subdivide the cavity of the bony tube (Fig. 21) into an upper portion, the *scala vestibuli*, *SV*, and a lower, the *scala tympani*, *ST*. Between these lie the lamina spiralis (*lso*) and the membranous cochlea (*CC*), the latter being bounded above by the membrane of Reissner (*R*) and below by the basilar membrane (*b*)."[2]

The membranous cochlea does not extend to the tip of the bony cochlea; above its apex the scala vestibuli and scala tympani communicate. Both are filled with perilymph, so that when the stapes is pushed into the oval foramen, *o*, in Fig. 17, by the impact of an air-wave on the tympanic membrane, a wave of perilymph runs up the scala vestibuli to the top, where it turns into the scala tympani, down whose whorls it runs and pushes out the round foramen, *r*, ruffling probably the membrane of Reissner and the basilar membrane on its way up and down.

[2] Martin: *op. cit.*, pp. 538–40.

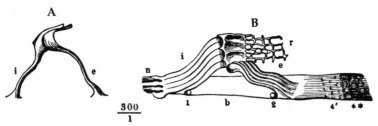

FIG. 22.—The rods of Corti. *A*, a pair of rods separated from the rest; *B*, a bit of the basilar membrane with several rods on it, showing how they cover in the *tunnel of Corti*; *i*, inner, and *e*, outer rods; *b*, basilar membrane; *r*, reticular membrane.

The Terminal Organs.—"The membranous cochlea contains certain solid structures seated on the basilar membrane and forming the *organ of Corti.* . . . This contains the end organs of the cochlear nerves. Lining the sulcus spiralis, a groove in the edge of the bony lamina spiralis, are cuboidal cells; on the inner margin of the basilar membrane they become columnar, and then are succeeded by a row which bear on their upper ends a set of short stiff hairs, and constitute the *inner hair-cells*, which are fixed below by a narrow apex to the basilar membrane; nerve-fibres enter them. To the inner hair-cells succeed the *rods of Corti* (*Co*, Fig. 21), which are represented highly magnified in Fig. 22. These rods are stiff and arranged side by side in two rows, leaned against one another by their upper ends so as to cover in a tunnel; they are known respectively as the *inner* and *outer rods*, the former being nearer the *lamina spiralis.* . . . The inner rods are more numerous than the outer, the numbers being about 6000 and 4500 respectively. Attached to the external sides of the heads of the outer rods is the *reticular membrane* (*r*, Fig. 22), which is stiff and perforated by holes. External to the outer rods come four rows of *outer hair-cells*, connected like the inner row with nerve-fibres; their bristles project into the holes of the reticular membrane. Beyond the outer hair-cells is ordinary columnar epithelium, which passes gradually into cuboidal cells lining most of the membranous cochlea. From the upper lip of the sulcus spiralis projects the *tectorial membrane* (*t*, Fig. 21) which extends over the rods of Corti and the hair-cells."[3]

The hair-cells would thus seem to be the terminal organs for

[3] Martin: *op. cit.*, pp. 540–42.

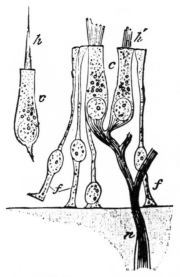

Fig. 23.—Sensory epithelium from ampulla or semicircular canal, and saccule. At *n* a nerve-fibre pierces the wall,
and after branching enters the two hair-cells, *c*. At *h* a
'columnar cell' with a long hair is shown, the nerve-fibre
being broken away from its base. The slender cells at *f*
seem unconnected with nerves.

'picking up' the vibrations which the air-waves communicate
through all the intervening apparatus, solid and liquid, to the basilar membrane. Analogous hair-cells receive the terminal nerve-
filaments in the walls of the saccule, utricle, and ampullæ (see Fig.
23).

The Various Qualities of Sound.—Physically, sounds consist of
vibrations, and these are, generally speaking, *aërial waves*. When
the waves are non-periodic the result is a *noise*; when periodic it is
what is nowadays called a *tone*, or *note*. The *loudness* of a sound depends on the *force* of the waves. When they recur periodically a
peculiar quality called *pitch* is the effect of their *frequency*. In addition to loudness and pitch tones have each their *voice* or *timbre*,
which may differ widely in different instruments giving equally
loud tones of the same pitch. This voice depends on the *form* of the
aërial wave.

Pitch.—A single puff of air, set in motion by no matter what
cause, will give a sensation of sound, but it takes at least four or
five puffs, or more, to convey a sensation of pitch. The pitch of the

note *c*, for instance, is due to 132 vibrations a second, that of its octave *c'* is produced by twice as many, or 264 vibrations; but in neither case is it necessary for the vibrations to go on during a full second for the pitch to be discerned. "Sound vibrations may be too rapid or too slow in succession to produce sonorous sensations, just as the ultra-violet and ultra-red rays of the solar spectrum fail to excite the retina. The highest-pitched audible note answers to about 38,016 vibrations in a second, but it differs in individuals; many persons cannot hear the cry of a bat nor the chirp of a cricket, which lie near this upper audible limit. On the other hand, sounds of vibrational rate about 40 per second are not well heard, and a little below this . . . they produce rather a 'hum' than a true tone sensation, and are only used along with notes of higher octaves to which they give a character of greater depth."[4]

The entire system of pitches forms *a continuum of one dimension*; that is to say, you can pass from one pitch to another only by one set of intermediaries, instead of by more than one, as in the case of colors. (See p. 42.) The whole series of pitches is embraced in and between the terms of what is called the musical scale. The adoption of certain arbitrary points in this scale as 'notes' has an explanation partly historic and partly æsthetic, but too complex for exposition here.

The 'timbre' of a note is due to its *wave-form*. Waves are either simple ('pendular') or compound. Thus if a tuning-fork (which gives waves nearly simple) vibrate 132 times a second, we shall hear the note *c*. If simultaneously a fork of 264 vibrations be struck, giving the next higher octave, *c'*, the aërial movement at any time will be the algebraic sum of the movements due to both forks; whenever both drive the air one way they reinforce one another; when on the contrary the recoil of one fork coincides with the forward stroke of another, they detract from each other's effect. The result is a movement which is still periodic, repeating itself at equal intervals of time, but no longer *pendular*, since it is not alike on the ascending and descending limbs of the curves. We thus get at the fact that non-pendular vibrations may be produced by the fusion of pendular, or, in technical phrase, by their *composition*.

Suppose several musical instruments, as those of an orchestra, to be sounded together. Each produces its own effect on the air-

4 Martin: *op. cit.,* pp. 543-44.

particles, whose movements, being an algebraical sum, must at any given instant be very complex; yet the ear can pick out at will and follow the tones of any one instrument. Now in most musical instruments it is susceptible of physical proof that with every single note that is sounded many upper octaves and other 'harmonics' sound simultaneously in fainter form. On the relative strength of this or that one or more of these Helmholtz has shown that the instrument's peculiar voice depends. The several vowel-sounds in the human voice also depend on the predominance of diverse upper harmonics accompanying the note on which the vowel is sung. When the two tuning-forks of the last paragraph are sounded together the new form of vibration has the same *period* as the lower-pitched fork; yet the ear can clearly distinguish the resultant sound from that of the lower fork alone, as a note of the same pitch but of different timbre; and within the compound sound the two components can by a trained ear be severally heard. Now how can one resultant wave-form make us hear so many sounds at once?

The analysis of compound wave-forms is supposed (after Helmholtz) to be effected through the different rates of sympathetic resonance of the different parts of the membranous cochlea. The basilar membrane is some twelve times broader at the apex of the cochlea than at the base where it begins, and is largely composed of radiating fibres which may be likened to stretched strings. Now the physical principle of sympathetic resonance says that when stretched strings are near a source of vibration those whose own rate agrees with that of the source also vibrate, the others remaining at rest. On this principle, waves of perilymph running down the scala tympani at a certain rate of frequency ought to set certain particular fibres of the basilar membrane vibrating, and ought to leave others unaffected. If then each vibrating fibre stimulated the hair-cell above it, and no others, and each such hair-cell, sending a current to the auditory brain-centre, awakened therein a specific process to which the sensation of one particular pitch was correlated, the physiological condition of our several pitch-sensations would be explained. Suppose now a chord to be struck in which perhaps twenty different physical rates of vibration are found: at least twenty different hair-cells or end-organs will receive the jar; and if the power of mental discrimination be at its maximum, twenty different 'objects' of hearing, in the shape of as many distinct pitches of sound, may appear before the mind.

The rods of Corti are supposed to be *dampers* of the fibres of the basilar membrane, just as the malleus, incus, and stapes are dampers of the tympanic membrane, as well as transmitters of its oscillations to the inner ear. There must be, in fact, an instantaneous *damping* of the physiological vibrations, for there are no such positive after-images, and no such blendings of rapidly successive tones, as the retina shows us in the case of light. Helmholtz's theory of the analysis of sounds is plausible and ingenious. One objection to it is that the keyboard of the cochlea does not seem extensive enough for the number of distinct resonances required. We can discriminate many more degrees of pitch than the 20,000 hair-cells, more or less, will allow for.

The so-called Fusion of Sensations in Hearing.—A very common way of explaining the fact that waves which singly give no feeling of pitch give one when recurrent, is to say that their several sensations *fuse into a compound sensation.* A preferable explanation is that which follows the analogy of muscular contraction. If electric shocks are sent into a frog's sciatic nerve at slow intervals, the muscle which the nerve supplies will give a series of distinct twitches, one for each shock. But if they follow each other at the rate of as many as thirty a second, no distinct twitches are observed, but a steady state of contraction instead. This steady contraction is known as *tetanus*. The experiment proves that there is a physiological cumulation or overlapping of processes in the muscular tissue. It takes a twentieth of a second or more for the latter to relax after the twitch due to the first shock. But the second shock comes in before the relaxation can occur, then the third again, and so on; so that continuous tetanus takes the place of discrete twitching. Similarly in the auditory nerve. One shock of air starts in it a current to the auditory brain-centre, and affects the latter, so that a dry stroke of sound is heard. If other shocks follow slowly, the brain-centre recovers its equilibrium after each, to be again upset in the same way by the next, and the result is that for each shock of air a distinct sensation of sound occurs. But if the shock comes in too quick succession, the later ones reach the brain before the effects of the earlier ones on that organ have died away. There is thus an overlapping of processes in the auditory centre, a physiological condition analogous to the muscle's tetanus, to which new condition a new quality of feeling, that of pitch, directly corresponds. This latter feeling is a new kind of sensation altogether, not a mere 'appearance' due to many sensations of dry stroke being compounded into one. No sensations of dry stroke can exist under these circumstances, for their physiological conditions have been replaced by others. What 'compounding' there is has already taken place in the brain-cells before the threshold of sensation was reached. Just so red light and green light beating on the retina in rapid enough alternation, arouse the central process to which the sensation *yellow* directly corresponds. The sensations of red and of green get no chance, under such conditions, to be born. Just so if the muscle could feel, it would have a certain sort of feeling when it gave a single twitch, but it would undoubtedly have a distinct sort of feeling altogether, when it contracted tetanically; and this feeling of the tetanic contraction would by no means be identical with a multitude of the feelings of twitching.

Harmony and Discord.—When several tones sound together we may get peculiar feelings of pleasure or displeasure designated as consonance and dissonance respectively. A note sounds most consonant with its octave. When with the octave the 'third' and the 'fifth' of the note are sounded, for instance *c—e—g—c'*, we get the 'full chord' or maximum of consonance. The ratios of vibration here are as 4:5:6:8, so that one might think simple ratios were the ground of harmony. But the interval *c—d* is discordant, with the comparatively simple ratio 8:9. Helmholtz explains discord by the overtones making 'beats' together. This gives a subtle grating which is unpleasant. Where the overtones make no 'beats,' or beats too rapid for their effect to be perceptible, there is consonance, according to Helmholtz, which is thus a negative rather than a positive thing. Wundt explains consonance by the presence of strong identical overtones in the notes which harmonize. No one of these explanations of musical harmony can be called quite satisfactory; and the subject is too intricate to be treated farther in this place.

Discriminative Sensibility of the Ear.—Weber's law holds fairly well for the intensity of sounds. If ivory or metal balls are dropped on an ebony or iron plate, they make a sound which is the louder as they are heavier or dropped from a greater height. Experimenting in this way (after others) Merkel found that the just perceptible increment of loudness required an increase of $^3/_{10}$ of the original stimulus everywhere between the intensities marked 20 and 5000 of his arbitrary scale. Below this the fractional increment of stimulus must be larger; above it, no measurements were made.

Discrimination of differences of *pitch* varies in different parts of the scale. Between 200 and 1000 vibrations per second, one fifth of a vibration more or less can make the sound sharp or flat for a good ear. It takes a much greater *relative* alteration to sound sharp or flat elsewhere on the scale. The chromatic scale itself has been used as an illustration of Weber's law. The notes seem to differ equally from each other, yet their vibration-numbers form a series of which each is a certain multiple of the last. This, however, has nothing to do with intensities or just perceptible differences; so the peculiar parallelism between the sensation series and the outer-stimulus series forms here a case all by itself, rather than an instance under Weber's more general law.

Chapter V

Touch, the Temperature Sense, the Muscular Sense, and Pain

Nerve-endings in the Skin.—"Many of the afferent skin-nerves end in connection with hair-bulbs; the fine hairs over most of the cutaneous surface, projecting from the skin, transmit any movement impressed on them, with increased force, to the nerve-fibres at their fixed ends. . . . Fine branches of axis cylinders have also been described as penetrating between epidermic cells and ending there without terminal organs. In or immediately beneath the skin several peculiar forms of nerve end organs have also been described; they are known as (1) *Touch-cells*; (2) *Pacinian corpuscles*; (3) *Tactile corpuscles*; (4) *End-bulbs.*"[1]

These bodies all consist essentially of granules formed of connective tissue, in which or round about which one or more sensory nerve-fibres terminate. They probably magnify impressions just as a grain of sand does in a shoe, or a crumb does in a finger of a glove.

Touch, or the Pressure Sense.—"Through the skin we get several kinds of sensation; touch proper, heat and cold, and pain; and we can with more or less accuracy localize them on the surface of the Body. The interior of the mouth possesses also three sensibilities. Through touch proper we recognize pressure or traction exerted on the skin, and the force of the pressure; the softness or hardness, roughness or smoothness, of the body producing it;

---

[1] Martin: *op. cit.*, p. 556.

61

FIG. 24.—End-bulbs
from the conjunctiva
of the human eye,
magnified.

and the form of this, when not too large to be felt all over. When to learn the form of an object we move the hand over it, muscular sensations are combined with proper tactile, and such a combination of the two sensations is frequent; moreover, we rarely touch anything without at the same time getting temperature sensations; therefore pure tactile feelings are rare. From an evolution point of view, touch is probably the first distinctly differentiated sensation, and this primary position it still largely holds in our mental life."[2]

Objects are most important to us when in direct contact. The chief function of our eyes and ears is to enable us to prepare ourselves for contact with approaching bodies, or to ward such contact off. They have accordingly been characterized as organs of anticipatory touch.

"The delicacy of the tactile sense varies on different parts of the skin; it is greatest on the forehead, temples, and back of the forearm, where a weight of 2 milligr. pressing on an area of 9 sq. millim. can be felt. . . .

"In order that the sense of touch may be excited neighboring skin areas must be differently pressed . . . . When the hand is immersed in a liquid, as mercury, which fits into all its inequalities and presses with practically the same weight on all neighboring immersed areas, the sense of pressure is only felt at a line along the surface, where the immersed and non-immersed parts of the skin meet. . . .

The Localizing Power of the Skin.—"When the eyes are closed and a point of the skin is touched we can with some accuracy indicate the region stimulated; although tactile feelings are in gen-

[2] Martin: *op. cit.*, p. 558.

eral characters alike, they differ in something besides intensity by which we can distinguish them; some sub-sensation quality not rising definitely into prominence in consciousness must be present, comparable to the upper partials determining the timbre of a tone. The accuracy of the localizing power varies widely in different skin regions and is measured by observing the least distance which must separate two objects (as the blunted points of a pair of compasses) in order that they may be felt as two. The following table illustrates some of the differences observed—

Tongue-tip	1.1 mm.	(.04 inch)
Palm side of last phalanx of finger	2.2 mm.	(.08 inch)
Red part of lips	4.4 mm.	(.16 inch)
Tip of nose	6.6 mm.	(.24 inch)
Back of second phalanx of finger	11.0 mm.	(.44 inch)
Heel	22.0 mm.	(.88 inch)
Back of hand	30.8 mm.	(1.23 inches)
Forearm	39.6 mm.	(1.58 inches)
Sternum	44.0 mm.	(1.76 inches)
Back of neck	52.8 mm.	(2.11 inches)
Middle of back	66.0 mm.	(2.64 inches)

The localizing power is a little more acute across the long axis of a limb than in it; and is better when the pressure is only strong enough to just cause a distinct tactile sensation, than when it is more powerful; it is also very readily and rapidly improvable by practice." It seems to be naturally delicate in proportion as the skin which possesses it covers a more movable part of the body.

"It might be thought that this localizing power depended directly on nerve distribution; that each touch-nerve had connection with a special brain-centre at one end (the excitation of which caused a sensation with a characteristic local sign), and at the other end was distributed over a certain skin area, and that the larger this area the farther apart might two points be and still give rise to only one sensation. If this were so, however, the peripheral tactile areas (each being determined by the anatomical distribution of a nerve-fibre) must have definite unchangeable limits, which experiment shows that they do not possess. Suppose the small areas in Fig. 25 to each represent a peripheral area of nerve-distribution. If any two points in *c* were touched we would according to the theory get but a single sensation; but if, while the

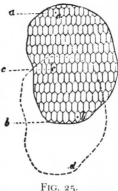

FIG. 25.

compass points remained the same distance apart, or were even approximated, one were placed in *c* and the other on a contiguous area, two fibres would be stimulated and we ought to get two sensations; but such is not the case; on the same skin region the points must be always the same distance apart, no matter how they be shifted, in order to give rise to two just distinguishable sensations.

"It is probable that the nerve areas are much smaller than the tactile; and that several unstimulated must intervene between the excited, in order to produce sensations which shall be distinct. If we suppose twelve unexcited nerve areas must intervene, then, in Fig. 25, *a* and *b* will be just on the limits of a single tactile area; and no matter how the points are moved, so long as eleven, or fewer, unexcited areas come between, we would get a single tactile sensation; in this way we can explain the fact that tactile areas have no fixed boundaries in the skin, although the nerve distribution in any part must be constant. We also see why the back of a knife laid on the surface causes a continuous linear sensation, although it touches many distinct nerve areas; if we could discriminate the excitations of each of these from that of its immediate neighbors we would get the sensation of a series of points touching us, one for each nerve region excited; but in the absence of intervening unexcited nerve areas the sensations are fused together. . . .

The Temperature-sense. Its Terminal Organs.—"By this we mean our faculty of perceiving cold and warmth; and, with the help of these sensations, of perceiving temperature differences in external objects. Its organ is the whole skin, the mucous membrane of mouth and fauces, pharynx and gullet, and the entry of the nares. Direct heating or cooling of a sensory nerve may stimulate it and cause pain, but not a true temperature sensation; . . . hence we assume the presence of temperature end organs. [These have not yet been ascertained anatomically. Physiologically, however, the demonstration of special spots in the skin for feeling heat and cold is one of the most interesting discoveries of recent years. If one draw a pencil-point over the palm or cheek one will notice certain spots of sudden coolness. These are the cold-spots; the heat-spots are less easy to single out. Goldscheider, Blix, and Donaldson have made minute exploration of determinate tracts of skin and found the heat- and cold-spots thickset and permanently distinct. Between them no temperature-sensation is excited by contact with a pointed cold or hot object. Mechanical and faradic irritation also excites in these points their specific feelings respectively.]

The feeling of temperature is relative to the state of the skin. "In a comfortable room we feel at no part of the Body either heat or cold, although different parts of its surface are at different temperatures; the fingers and nose being cooler than the trunk which is covered by clothes, and this, in turn, cooler than the interior of the mouth. The temperature which a given region of the temperature organ has (as measured by a thermometer) when it feels neither heat nor cold is its *temperature-sensation zero*, and is not associated with any one objective temperature; for not only, as we have just seen, does it vary in different parts of the organ, but also on the same part from time to time. Whenever a skin region has a temperature above its sensation zero we feel warmth and *vice versa*; the sensation is more marked the greater the difference, and the more suddenly it is produced; touching a metallic body, which conducts heat rapidly to or from the skin, causes a more marked

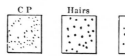

Fig. 26.—The figure marked C P shows the cold-spots, that marked H P the heat-spots, and the middle one the hairs on a certain patch of skin on one of Goldscheider's fingers.

hot or cold sensation than touching a worse conductor, as a piece of wood, of the same temperature.

"The change of temperature in the organ may be brought about by changes in the circulatory apparatus (more blood flowing through the skin warms it and less leads to its cooling), or by temperature changes in gases, liquids, or solids in contact with it. Sometimes we fail to distinguish clearly whether the cause is external or internal; a person coming in from a windy walk often feels a room uncomfortably warm which is not really so; the exercise has accelerated his circulation and tended to warm his skin, but the moving outer air has rapidly conducted off the extra heat; on entering the house the stationary air there does this less quickly, the skin gets hot, and the cause is supposed to be oppressive heat of the room. Hence, frequently, opening of windows and sitting in a draught, with its concomitant risks; whereas keeping quiet for five or ten minutes, until the circulation has returned to its normal rate, would attain the same end without danger.

"The acuteness of the temperature sense is greatest at temperatures within a few degrees of 30° C. (86° F.); at these differences of less than 0.1° C. can be discriminated. As a means of measuring absolute temperatures, however, the skin is very unreliable, on account of the changeability of its sensation zero. We can localize temperature sensations much as tactile, but not so accurately."[3]

Muscular Sensation.—The sensation in the muscle itself cannot well be distinguished from that in the tendon or in its insertion. In muscular fatigue the insertions are the places most painfully felt. In muscular rheumatism, however, the whole muscle grows painful; and violent contraction such as that caused by the faradic current, or known as cramp, produces a severe and peculiar pain felt in the whole mass of muscle affected. Sachs also thought that he had demonstrated, both experimentally and anatomically, the existence of special sensory nerve-fibres, distinct from the motor fibres, in the frog's muscle. The latter end in the 'terminal plates,' the former in a network.

Great importance has been attached to the muscular sense as a factor in our perceptions, not only of weight and pressure, but of the space-relations between things generally. Our eyes and our

[3] Martin: *op. cit.*, pp. 558-63, with omissions.

66

hands, in their explorations of space, move over it and through it. It is usually supposed that without this sense of an intervening motion performed we should not perceive two seen points or two touched points to be separated by an extended interval. I am far from denying the immense participation of experiences of motion in the construction of our space-perceptions. But it is still an open question *how* our muscles help us in these experiences, whether by their own sensations, or by awakening sensations of motion on our skin, retina, and articular surfaces. The latter seems to me the more probable view, and the reader may be of the same opinion after reading Chapter VI.

Sensibility to Weight.—When we wish to estimate accurately the weight of an object we always, when possible, lift it, and so combine muscular and articular with tactile sensations. By this means we can form much better judgments.

Weber found that whereas $\frac{1}{3}$ must be added to a weight resting on the hand for the increase to be felt, the same hand actively 'hefting' the weight could feel an addition of as little as $\frac{1}{17}$. Merkel's recent and very careful experiments, in which the finger pressed down the beam of a balance counterweighted by from 25 to 8020 grams, showed that between 200 and 2000 grams a constant fractional increase of about $\frac{1}{13}$ was felt when there was no movement of the finger, and of about $\frac{1}{19}$ when there was movement. Above and below these limits the discriminative power grew less.

Pain.—The physiology of pain is still an enigma. One might suppose separate afferent fibres with their own end-organs to carry painful impressions to a specific pain-centre. Or one might suppose such a specific centre to be reached by currents of overflow from the other sensory centres when the violence of their inner excitement should have reached a certain pitch. Or again one might suppose a certain extreme degree of inner excitement to produce the feeling of pain in all the centres. It is certain that sensations of every order, which in moderate degrees are rather pleasant than otherwise, become painful when their intensity grows strong. The rate at which the agreeableness and disagreeableness vary with the intensity of a sensation is roughly represented by the dotted curve in Fig. 27. The horizontal line represents the threshold both of sensational and of agreeable sensibility. Below the line is the disagreeable. The continuous

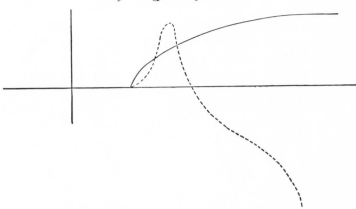

FIG. 27 (after Wundt).

curve is that of Weber's law which we learned to know in Fig. 2, p. 22. With the minimal sensation the agreeableness is *nil*, as the dotted curve shows. It rises at first more slowly than the sensational intensity, then faster; and reaches its maximum before the sensation is near its acme. After its maximum of agreeableness the dotted line rapidly sinks, and soon tumbles below the horizontal into the realm of the disagreeable or painful in which it declines. That all sensations are painful when too strong is a piece of familiar knowledge. Light, sound, odors, the taste of sweet even, cold, heat, and all the skin-sensations, must be moderate to be enjoyed.

The quality of the sensation complicates the question, however, for in some sensations, as bitter, sour, salt, and certain smells, the turning point of the dotted curve must be drawn very near indeed to the beginning of the scale. In the skin the painful quality soon becomes so intense as entirely to overpower the specific quality of the sort of stimulus. Heat, cold, and pressure are indistinguishable when extreme—we only feel the pain. The hypothesis of separate end-organs in the skin receives some corroboration from recent experiments, for both Blix and Goldscheider have found, along with their special heat- and cold-spots, also special 'pain-spots' on the skin. Mixed in with these are spots which are quite feelingless. However it may stand with the terminal pain-spots, separate paths of *conduction* to the brain, for painful and for merely tactile stimulations of the skin, are made probable by certain facts. In the condition termed *analgesia*, a touch is felt, but the most violent pinch, burn, or electric spark destructive of the tissue will awaken no sensation. This may occur in disease of the cord, by suggestion in hypnotism, or in certain stages of ether and chloroform intoxication. "In rabbits a similar state of things was produced by Schiff, by dividing the gray matter of the cord, leaving the posterior white columns intact. If, on the contrary, the latter were divided and the gray substance left, there was increased sensitiveness to pain, and possibly touch proper was lost. Such experiments make it pretty certain that when afferent impulses reach the spinal cord at any level and there enter its gray matter with the posterior root-fibres, they travel on in different tracks to conscious centres; the tactile ones coming soon out of the gray network and coursing on in a readily conducting white fibre, while the painful ones first travel on farther in the gray substance. It is still uncertain if both impulses reach the cord in the same fibres. The gray network conducts nerve impulses, but not easily; they tend soon to be blocked in it. A feeble (tactile) impulse reaching it by an afferent fibre might only spread a short way and then pass out into a single good conducting fibre in a white column, and proceed to the brain; while a stronger (painful) impulse would radiate farther in the gray matter, and perhaps break out of it by many fibres leading to the brain through the white columns, and so give rise to an inco-ordinate and ill localized sensation. That pains are badly localized, and worse the more intense they are, is a well-known fact, which would thus receive an explanation."[4]

Pain also gives rise to ill-coördinated movements of defence. The stronger the pain the more violent the start. Doubtless in low animals pain is almost the only stimulus; and we have preserved the peculiarity in so far that to-day it is the stimulus of our most energetic, though not of our most discriminating, reactions.

Taste, smell, as well as hunger, thirst, nausea, and other so-called 'common' sensations need not be touched on in this book, as almost nothing of psychological interest is known concerning them.

[4] Martin: *op. cit.*, p. 568.

Chapter VI

Sensations of Motion

I treat of these in a separate chapter in order to give them the emphasis which their importance deserves. They are of two orders:

1) Sensations of objects moving over our sensory surfaces; and

2) Sensations of our whole person's translation through space.

1) **The Sensation of Motion over Surfaces.**—This has generally been assumed by physiologists to be impossible until the positions of *terminus a quo* and *terminus ad quem* are severally cognized, and the successive occupancies of these positions by the moving body are perceived to be separated by a distinct interval of time. As a matter of fact, however, we cognize only the very slowest motions in this way. Seeing the hand of a clock at XII and afterwards at VI, I judge that it has moved through the interval. Seeing the sun now in the east and again in the west, I infer it to have passed over my head. But we can only *infer* that which we already generically know in some more direct fashion, and it is experimentally certain that we have the feeling of motion given us as a direct and simple *sensation*. Czermak long ago pointed out the difference between *seeing the motion* of the second-hand of a watch, when we look directly at it, and noticing the fact that it has *altered its position*, whilst our gaze is fixed upon some other point of the dial-plate. In the first case we have a specific quality of sensation which is absent in the second. If the reader will find a portion of his skin—the arm, for example—where a pair of compass-points

an inch apart are felt as one impression, and if he will then trace lines a tenth of an inch long on that spot with a pencil-point, he will be distinctly aware of the point's motion and vaguely aware of the direction of the motion. The perception of the motion here is certainly not derived from a preëxisting knowledge that its starting and ending points are separate positions in space, because positions in space ten times wider apart fail to be discriminated as such when excited by the compass-points. It is the same with the retina. One's fingers when cast upon its peripheral portions cannot be counted—that is to say, the five retinal tracts which they occupy are not distinctly apprehended by the mind as five separate positions in space—and yet the slightest *movement* of the fingers is most vividly perceived as movement and nothing else. It is thus certain that our sense of movement, being so much more delicate than our sense of position, cannot possibly be derived from it.

Vierordt, at almost the same time, called attention to certain persistent illusions, amongst which are these: If another person gently trace a line across our wrist or finger, the latter being stationary, it will feel to us as if the member were moving in the opposite direction to the tracing point. If, on the contrary, we move our limb across a fixed point, it will seem as if the point were moving as well. If the reader will touch his forehead with his forefinger kept motionless, and then rotate the head so that the skin of the forehead passes beneath the finger's tip, he will have an irresistible sensation of the latter being itself in motion in the opposite direction to the head. So in abducting the fingers from each other; some may move and the rest be still, but the still ones will feel as if they were actively separating from the rest. These illusions, according to Vierordt, are survivals of a primitive form of perception, when motion was felt as such, but ascribed to the whole 'content' of consciousness, and not yet distinguished as belonging exclusively to one of its parts. When our perception is fully developed we go beyond the mere relative motion of thing and ground, and can ascribe absolute motion to one of these components of our total object, and absolute rest to another. When, in vision for example, the whole field of view seems to move together, we think it is ourselves or our eyes which are moving; and any object in the foreground which may seem to move relatively to the background is judged by us to be really still. But primitively this discrimination is not perfectly made. The sensation of the motion spreads over all that we see and infects it. Any relative motion of object and retina both makes the object seem to move, and makes us feel ourselves in motion. Even now when our whole field of view really does move we get giddy, and feel as if we too were moving; and we still see an apparent motion of the entire field of view whenever we suddenly jerk our head and eyes or shake them quickly to and fro. Pushing our eyeballs gives the same illusion. We *know* in all these cases what really happens, but the conditions are unusual, so our primitive sensation persists unchecked. So it does when clouds float by the moon. We *know* the moon is still; but we *see* it move faster than the clouds. Even when we slowly move our eyes the primitive sensation persists under the victorious conception. If we notice closely the experience, we find that any object towards which we look appears moving to meet our eye.

But the most valuable contribution to the subject is the paper of G. H. Schneider,[1] who takes up the matter zoölogically, and shows by examples from every branch of the animal kingdom that movement is the quality by which animals most easily attract each other's attention. The instinct of 'shamming death' is no shamming of death at all, but rather a paralysis through fear, which saves the insect, crustacean, or other creature from being *noticed at all* by his enemy. It is paralleled in the human race by the breath-holding stillness of the boy playing 'I spy,' to whom the seeker is near; and its obverse side is shown in our involuntary waving of arms, jumping up and down, and so forth, when we wish to attract someone's attention at a distance. Creatures 'stalking' their prey and creatures hiding from their pursuers alike show how immobility diminishes conspicuity. In the woods, if we are quiet, the squirrels and birds will actually touch us. Flies will light on stuffed birds and stationary frogs. On the other hand, the tremendous shock of feeling the thing we are sitting on begin to move, the exaggerated start it gives us to have an insect unexpectedly pass over our skin, or a cat noiselessly come and snuffle about our hand, the excessive reflex effects of tickling, etc., show how exciting the sensation of motion is *per se*. A kitten cannot help pursuing a moving ball. Impressions too faint to be cognized at all are immediately felt if they move. A fly sitting is unnoticed,—we feel it the moment it crawls. A shadow may be too faint to be per-

[1] *Vierteljahrsschrift für wissenschaftliche Philosophie*, II, 377.

ceived. If we hold a finger between our closed eyelid and the sunshine we do not notice its presence. The moment we move it to and fro, however, we discern it. Such visual perception as this reproduces the conditions of sight among the radiates.

In ourselves, the main function of the peripheral parts of the retina is that of sentinels, which, when beams of light move over them, cry 'Who goes there?' and call the fovea to the spot. Most parts of the skin do but perform the same office for the finger-tips. Of course *movement of surface under object is (for purposes of stimulation) equivalent to movement of object over surface.* In exploring the shapes and sizes of things by either eye or skin the movements of these organs are incessant and unrestrainable. Every such movement draws the points and lines of the object across the surface, imprints them a hundred times more sharply, and drives them home to the attention. The immense part thus played by movements in our perceptive activity is held by many psychologists to prove that the muscles are themselves the space-perceiving organ. Not surface-sensibility, but 'the muscular sense,' is for these writers the original and only revealer of objective extension. But they have all failed to notice with what peculiar intensity muscular movements call surface-sensibilities into play, and how largely the mere discernment of impressions depends on the mobility of the surfaces upon which they fall.

Our *articular surfaces are tactile organs* which become intensely painful when inflamed. Besides pressure, *the only stimulus they receive is their motion upon each other.* To the sensation of this motion more than anything else seems due the perception of the position which our limbs may have assumed. Patients cutaneously and muscularly anæsthetic in one leg can often prove that their articular sensibility remains, by showing (by movements of their well leg) the positions in which the surgeon may place their insensible one. Goldscheider in Berlin caused fingers, arms, and legs to be passively rotated upon their various joints in a mechanical apparatus which registered both the velocity of movement impressed and the amount of angular rotation. The minimal felt amounts of rotation were much less than a single angular degree in all the joints except those of the fingers. Such displacements as these, Goldscheider says, can hardly be detected by the eye. Anæsthesia of the skin produced by induction-currents had no disturbing effect on the perception, nor did the various degrees of pressure of the moving force upon the skin affect it. It became, in fact, all the more distinct in proportion as the concomitant pressure-feelings were eliminated by artificial anæsthesia. When the joints themselves, however, were made artificially anæsthetic, the perception of the movement grew obtuse and the angular rotations had to be much increased before they were perceptible. All these facts prove, according to Herr Goldscheider, that *the joint-surfaces and these alone are the seat of the impressions by which the movements of our members are immediately perceived.*

2) **Sensations of Movement through Space.**—These may be divided into feelings of rotation and feelings of translation. As was stated at the end of the chapter on the ear, the labyrinth (semicircular canals, utricle and saccule) seems to have nothing to do with hearing. It is conclusively established to-day that the semicircular canals are the organs of a sixth special sense, that namely of rotation. When subjectively excited, this sensation is known as *dizziness* or *vertigo*, and rapidly engenders the farther feeling of nausea. Irritative disease of the inner ear causes intense vertigo (Ménière's disease). Traumatic irritation of the canals in birds and mammals makes the animals tumble and throw themselves about in a way best explained by supposing them to suffer from false sensations of falling, etc., which they compensate by reflex muscular acts that throw them the other way. Galvanic irritation of the membranous canals in pigeons causes just the same compensatory movements of head and eye which actual rotations impressed on the creatures produce. Deaf and dumb persons (amongst whom many must have had their auditory nerves or labyrinths destroyed by the same disease which took away their hearing) are in a very large percentage of cases found quite insusceptible of being made dizzy by rotation. Purkinje and Mach have shown that, whatever the organ of the sense of rotation may be, it must have its seat in the head. The body is excluded by Mach's elaborate experiments.

The semicircular canals, being, as it were, six little spirit-levels in three rectangular planes, seem admirably adapted to be organs of a sense of rotation. We need only suppose that when the head turns in the plane of any one of them, the relative inertia of the endolymph momentarily increases its pressure on the nerve-termini in the appropriate ampulla, which pressure starts a current towards the central organ for feeling vertigo. This organ seems to be the cerebellum, and the teleology of the whole business would appear to be the maintenance of the upright position. If a man stand with shut eyes and attend to his body, he will find that he is hardly for a moment in equilibrium. Incipient fallings towards every side in succesion are incessantly repaired by muscular contractions which restore the balance; and although impressions on the tendons, ligaments, foot-soles, joints, etc., doubtless are among the causes of the compensatory contractions, yet the strongest and most special reflex arc would seem to be that which has the sensation of incipient vertigo for its afferent member. This is experimentally proved to be much more easily excited than the other sensations referred to. When the cerebellum is disorganized the reflex response fails to occur properly and loss of equilibrium is the result. Irritation of the cerebellum produces vertigo, loss of balance, and nausea; and galvanic currents through the head produce various forms of vertigo correlated with their direction. It seems probable that direct excitement of the cerebellar centre is responsible for these feelings. In addition to these corporeal reflexes the sense of rotation causes compensatory rollings of the eyeballs in the opposite direction, to which some of the subjective phenomena of *optical vertigo* are due. Steady rotation gives no sensation; it is only starting or stopping, or, more generally speaking, acceleration (positive or negative), which impresses the end-organs in the ampullæ. The sensation always has a little duration, however; and the feeling of reversed movement after whirling violently may last for nearly a minute, slowly fading out.

The cause of the *sense of translation* (movement forwards or backwards) is more open to dispute. The seat of this sensation has been assigned to the semicircular canals when compounding their currents to the brain; and also to the utricle. The latest experimenter, M. Delage, considers that it cannot possibly be in the head, and assigns it rather to the entire body, so far as its parts (blood-vessels, viscera, etc.) are movable against each other and suffer friction or pressure from their relative inertia when a movement of translation begins. M. Delage's exclusion of the labyrinth from this form of sensibility cannot, however, yet be considered definitively established, so the matter may rest with this mention.

Chapter VII

The Structure of the Brain*

Embryological Sketch.—The brain is a sort of *pons asinorum* in anatomy until one gets a certain general conception of it as a clue. Then it becomes a comparatively simple affair. The clue is given by comparative anatomy and especially by embryology. At a certain moment in the development of all the higher vertebrates the cerebro-spinal axis is formed by a hollow tube containing fluid and terminated in front by an enlargement separated by transverse constrictions into three 'cerebral vesicles,' so called (see Fig. 28). The walls of these vesicles thicken in most places, change in others into a thin vascular tissue, and in others again send out processes which produce an appearance of farther subdivision. The middle vesicle or mid-brain (*M-b* in the figures) is the least affected by change. Its upper walls thicken into the optic lobes, or *corpora quadrigemina* as they are named in man; its lower walls become the so-called peduncles or *crura* of the brain; and its cavity dwindles into the aqueduct of Silvius. A section through the adult human mid-brain is shown in Fig. 31.

The anterior and posterior vesicles undergo much more consid-

* This chapter will be understood as a mere sketch for beginners. Models will be found of assistance. The best is the 'Cerveau de Texture de Grande Dimension,' made by Auzoux, 56 Rue de Vaugirard, Paris. It is a wonderful work of art, and costs 300 francs. M. Jules Talrich of No. 97 Boulevard Saint-Germain, Paris, makes a series of five large plaster models, which I have found very useful for class-room purposes. They cost 350 francs, and are far better than any German models which I have seen.

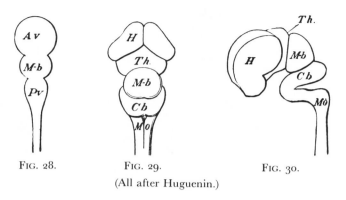

FIG. 28.   FIG. 29.   FIG. 30.

(All after Huguenin.)

erable change. The walls of the posterior vesicle thicken enormously in their foremost portion and form the *cerebellum* on top (*Cb* in all the figures) and the *pons Varolii* below (*P.V.* in Fig. 33). In its hindmost portions the posterior vesicle thickens below into the medulla oblongata (*Mo* in all the figures), whilst on top its walls thin out and melt, so that one can pass a probe into the cavity without breaking through any truly nervous tissue. The cavity which one thus enters from without is named the *fourth ventricle* (4 in Figs. 32 and 33). One can run the probe forwards through it, passing first under the cerebellum and then under a thin sheet of nervous tissue (the *valve of Vieussens*) just anterior thereto, as far as the *aqueduct of Silvius*. Passing through this, the probe emerges forwards into what was once the cavity of the anterior vesicle. But the covering has melted away at this place, and the cavity now forms a deep compressed pit or groove between the two walls of the vesicle, and is called the *third ventricle* (3 in Figs. 32 and 33). The 'aqueduct of Sylvius' is in consequence of this connection often called the *iter a tertio ad quartum ventriculum*. The walls of the vesicle form the *optic thalami* (*Th* in all the figures).

From the anterior vesicle just in front of the thalami there buds out on either side an enlargement, into which the cavity of the vesicle continues, and which becomes the *hemisphere* of that side. In man its walls thicken enormously and form folds, the so-called *convolutions*, on their surface. At the same time they grow backwards rather than forwards of their starting-point just in front of the thalamus, arching over the latter; and growing fastest along their top circumference, they end by bending downwards and forwards again when they have passed the rear end of the thal-

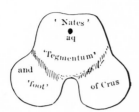

FIG. 31.—The 'nates' are the anterior corpora quadrigemina, the spot above *aq* is a section of the sylvian aqueduct, and the tegmentum and two 'feet' together make the Crura. These are marked *C.C.*, in Fig. 33, and a cross (+) marks the aqueduct, in Fig. 32.

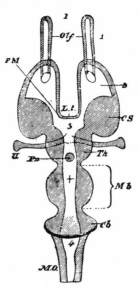

FIG. 32 (after Huxley).

amus. When fully developed in man, they overlay and cover in all the other parts of the brain. Their cavities form the *lateral ventricles*, easier to understand by a dissection than by a description. A probe can be passed into either of them from the third ventricle at its anterior end; and like the third ventricle, their wall is melted down along a certain line, forming a long cleft through which they can be entered without rupturing the nervous tissue. This cleft, on account of the growth of the hemisphere outwards, backwards, and then downwards from its starting point, has got rolled in and tucked away beneath the apparent surface.[1]

At first the two hemispheres are connected only with their respective thalami. But during the fourth and fifth months of embryonic life they become connected with each other above the thalami through the growth between them of a massive system of transverse fibres which crosses the median line like a great bridge and is called the *corpus callosum*. These fibres radiate in the walls of both hemispheres and form a direct connection between the convolutions of the right and of the left side. Beneath the corpus callosum another system of fibres called the *fornix* is formed, between

[1] All the places in the brain at which the cavities come through are filled in during life by prolongations of the membrane called *pia mater*, carrying rich plexuses of blood-vessels in their folds.

78

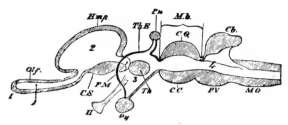

Fig. 33 (after Huxley).

which and the corpus callosum there is a peculiar connection. Just in front of the thalami, where the hemispheres begin their growth, a ganglionic mass called the *corpus striatum* (*C.S.*, Figs. 32 and 33) is formed in their wall. It is complex in structure, consisting of two main parts, called *nucleus lenticularis* and *nucleus caudatus* respectively. The figures, with their respective explanations, will give a better idea of the farther details of structure than any verbal description; so, after some practical directions for dissecting the organ, I will pass to a brief account of the physiological relations of its different parts to each other.

Dissection of Sheep's Brain.—The way really to understand the brain is to dissect it. The brains of mammals differ only in their proportions, and from the sheep's one can learn all that is essential in man's. The student is therefore strongly urged to dissect a sheep's brain. Full directions of the order of procedure are given in the human dissecting books, e.g., Holden's *Practical Anatomy* (Churchill), Morrell's *Student's Manual of Comparative Anatomy, and Guide to Dissection* (Longmans), and Foster and Langley's *Practical Physiology* (Macmillan). For the use of classes who cannot procure these books I subjoin a few practical notes. The instruments needed are a small saw, a chisel with a shoulder, and a hammer with a hook on its handle, all three of which form part of the regular medical autopsy-kit and can be had of surgical-instrument-makers. In addition a scalpel, a pair of scissors, a pair of dissecting-forceps, and a silver probe are required. The solitary student can find home-made substitutes for all these things but the forceps, which he ought to buy.

The first thing is to get off the skull-cap. Make two saw-cuts, through the prominent portion of each condyle (or articular surface bounding the hole at the back of the skull, where the spinal cord enters) and passing forwards to the temples of the animal.

Then make two cuts, one on each side, which cross these and meet in an angle on the frontal bone. By actual trial, one will find the best direction for the saw-cuts. It is hard to saw entirely through the skull-bone without in some places also sawing into the brain. Here is where the chisel comes in—one can break by a smart blow on it with the hammer any parts of the skull not quite sawn through. When the skull-cap is ready to come off one will feel it 'wobble.' Insert then the hook under its forward end and pull firmly. The bony skull-cap alone will come away, leaving the periosteum of the inner surface adhering to that of the base of the skull, enveloping the brain, and forming the so-called *dura mater* or outer one of its 'meninges.' This dura mater should be slit open round the margins, when the brain will be exposed wrapped in its nearest membrane, the *pia mater*, full of blood-vessels whose branches penetrate the tissues.

The brain in its pia mater should now be carefully 'shelled out.' Usually it is best to begin at the forward end, turning it up there and gradually working backwards. The *olfactory lobes* are liable to be torn; they must be carefully scooped from the pits in the base of the skull to which they adhere by the branches which they send through the bone into the nose-cavity. It is well to have a little blunt curved instrument expressly for this purpose. Next the *optic nerves* tie the brain down, and must be cut through—close to the chiasma is easiest. After that comes the *pituitary body*, which has to be left behind. It is attached by a neck, the so-called *infundibulum*, into the upper part of which the cavity of the third ventricle is prolonged downwards for a short distance. It has no known function and is probably a 'rudimentary organ.' Other nerves, into the detail of which I shall not go, must be cut successively. Their places in the human brain are shown in Fig. 34. When they are divided, and the portion of dura mater (tentorium) which projects between the hemispheres and the cerebellum is cut through at its edges, the brain comes readily out.

It is best examined fresh. If numbers of brains have to be prepared and kept, I have found it a good plan to put them first in a solution of chloride of zinc, just dense enough at first to float them, and to leave them for a fortnight or less. This softens the pia mater, which can then be removed in large shreds, after which it is enough to place them in quite weak alcohol to preserve them indefinitely, tough, elastic, and in their natural shape, though

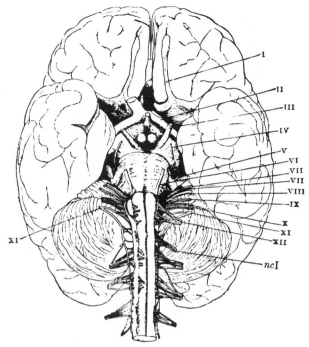

FIG. 34.—The human brain from below, with its nerves numbered (after Henle). I, olfactory; II, optic; III, oculo-motorius; IV, troch-learis; V, trifacial; VI, abducens oculi; VII, facial; VIII, auditory; IX, glosso-pharyngeal; X, pneumogastric; XI, spinal accessory; XII, hypoglossal; *nc*I, first cervical, etc.

bleached to a uniform white color. Before immersion in the chloride all the more superficial adhesions of the parts must be broken through, to bring the fluid into contact with a maximum of surface. If the brain is used fresh, the pia mater had better be removed carefully in most places with the forceps, scalpel, and scissors. Over the grooves between the cerebellum and hemispheres, and between the cerebellum and medulla oblongata, thin cobwebby moist transparent vestiges of the *arachnoid* membrane will be found.

The subdivisions may now be examined in due order. For the convolutions, blood-vessels, and nerves the more special books must be consulted.

First, looked at from above, with the deep *longitudinal fissure* between them, the hemispheres are seen partly overlapping the intricately wrinkled *cerebellum*, which juts out behind, and covers in turn almost all the medulla oblongata. Drawing the hemispheres apart, the brilliant white *corpus callosum* is revealed, some half an inch below their surface. There is no median partition in the cerebellum, but a median elevation instead.

Looking at the brain from below, one still sees the longitudinal fissure in the median line in front, and on either side of it the *olfactory lobes*, much larger than in man; the *optic tracts* and *commissure* or '*chiasma*'; the *infundibulum* cut through just behind them; and behind that the single *corpus albicans* or *mamillare*, whose function is unknown and which is double in man. Next the *crura* appear, converging upon the pons as if carrying fibres back from either side. The *pons* itself succeeds, much less prominent than in man; and finally behind it comes the medulla oblongata, broad and flat and relatively large. The pons looks like a sort of collar uniting the two halves of the cerebellum, and surrounding the medulla, whose fibres by the time they have emerged anteriorly from beneath the collar have divided into the two crura. The inner relations are, however, somewhat less simple than what this description may suggest.

Now turn forwards the cerebellum; pull out the vascular *choroid plexuses* of the pia, which fill the fourth ventricle; and bring the upper surface of the *medulla oblongata* into view. The *fourth ventricle* is a triangular depression terminating in a posterior point called the *calamus scriptorius*. (Here a very fine probe may pass into the central canal of the spinal cord.) The lateral boundary of the ventricle on either side is formed by the *restiform body* or *column*, which runs into the cerebellum, forming its *inferior* or *posterior peduncle* on that side. Including the calamus scriptorius by their divergence, the posterior columns of the spinal cord continue into the medulla as the *fasciculi graciles*. These are at first separated from the broad restiform bodies by a slight groove. But this disappears anteriorly, and the 'slender' and 'ropelike' strands soon become outwardly indistinguishable.

Turn next to the ventral surface of the medulla, and note the *anterior pyramids*, two roundish cords, one on either side of the slight *median groove*. The pyramids are crossed and closed over anteriorly by the *pons Varolii*, a broad transverse band which surrounds them like a collar, and runs up into the cerebellum on either side, forming its *middle peduncles*. The pons has a slight me-

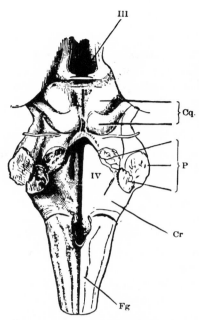

FIG. 35.—Fourth ventricle, etc. (Henle). *III*, third ventricle; *IV*, fourth ventricle; *P*, anterior, middle, and posterior peduncles of cerebellum cut through; *Cr*, restiform body; *Fg*, funiculus gracilis; *Cq*, corpora quadrigemina.

dian depression and its posterior edge is formed by the *trapezium* on either side. The trapezium consists of fibres which, instead of surrounding the pyramid, seem to start from alongside of it. It is not visible in man. The *olivary bodies* are small eminences on the medulla lying just laterally of the pyramids and below the trapezium.

Now cut through the peduncles of the cerebellum, close to their entrance into that organ. They give one surface of section on each side, though they receive contributions from three directions. The posterior and middle portions we have seen: the *anterior peduncles* pass forwards to the *corpora quadrigemina*. The thin white layer of nerve-tissue between them and continuous with them is called the *valve of Vieussens*. It covers part of the canal from the fourth ventricle to the third. The cerebellum being removed, examine it, and cut sections to show the peculiar distribution of white and gray matter, forming an appearance called the *arbor vitæ* in the books.

Now bend up the posterior edge of the hemispheres, exposing

the corpora quadrigemina (of which the anterior pair are dubbed the *nates* and the posterior the *testes*), and noticing the *pineal gland*, a small median organ situated just in front of them and probably, like the pituitary body, a vestige of something useful in premammalian times. The rounded posterior edge of the corpus callosum is visible now passing from one hemisphere to the other. Turn it still farther up, letting the medulla, etc., hang down as much as possible and trace the under surface from this edge forwards. It is broad behind but narrows forwards, becoming continuous with the *fornix*. The anterior stem, so to speak, of this organ plunges down just in front of the *optic thalami*, which now appear with the fornix arching over them, and the median *third ventricle* between them. The margins of the fornix, as they pass backwards, diverge laterally farther than the margins of the corpus callosum, and under the name of *corpora fimbriata* are carried into the lateral ventricles, as will be seen again.

It takes a good topographical mind to understand these ventricles clearly, even when they are followed with eye and hand. A verbal description is absolutely useless. The essential thing to remember is that they are offshoots from the original cavity (now the third ventricle) of the anterior vesicle, and that a great split has occurred in the walls of the hemispheres so that they (the lateral ventricles) now communicate with the exterior along a cleft which appears sickle-shaped, as it were, and folded in.

The student will probably examine the relations of the parts in various ways. But he will do well to begin in any case by cutting horizontal slices off the hemispheres almost down to the level of the corpus callosum, and examining the distribution of gray and white matter on the surfaces of section, any one of which is the so-called *centrum ovale*. Then let him cut down in a fore-and-aft direction along the edge of the corpus callosum, till he comes 'through' and draw the hemispherical margin of the cut outwards—he will see a space which is the ventricle, and which farther cutting along the side and removing of its hemisphere-roof will lay more bare. The most conspicuous object on its floor is the *nucleus caudatus* of the *corpus striatum*.

Cut the corpus callosum transversely through near its posterior edge and bend the anterior portion of it forwards and sideways. The rear edge (*splenium*) left *in situ* bends round and downwards and becomes continuous with the *fornix*. The anterior part is also

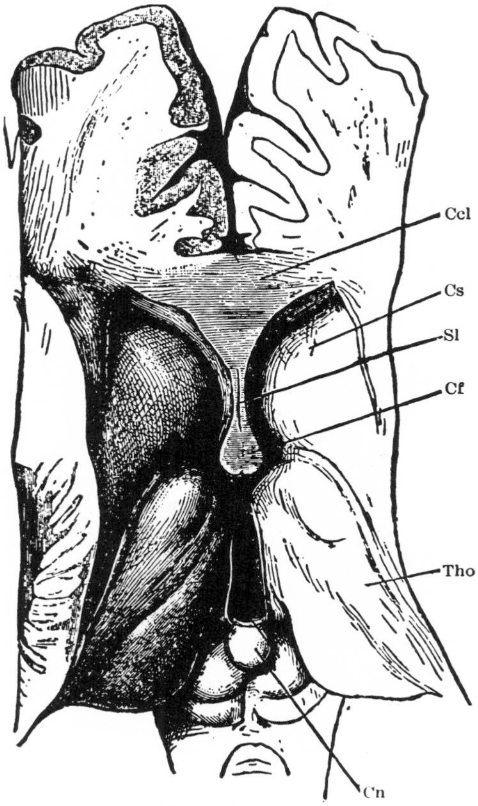

FIG. 36.—Horizontal section of human brain just above the thalami.—*Ccl*, corpus callosum in section; *Cs*, corpus striatum; *Sl*, septum lucidum; *Cf*, columns of the fornix; *Tho*, optic thalami; *Cn*, pineal gland. (After Henle.)

continuous with the fornix, but more along the median line, where a thinnish membrane, the *septum lucidum*, triangular in shape, reaching from the one body to the other, practically forms a sort of partition between the contiguous portion of the lateral ventricles on the two sides. Break through the *septum* if need be and expose the upper surface of the fornix, broad behind and narrow in front where its *anterior pillars* plunge down in front of the third ventricle (from a thickening in whose anterior walls they were originally formed), and finally penetrate the corpus albicans. Cut these pillars through and fold them back, exposing the thalamic portion of the brain, and noting the under surface of the fornix. Its diverging *posterior pillars* run backwards, downwards, and then forwards again, forming with their sharp edges the *corpora fimbriata*, which bound the cleft by which the ventricle lies open. The semi-cylindrical welts behind the *corpora fimbriata* and parallel thereto in the wall of the ventricle are the *hippocampi*. Imagine the fornix and corpus callosum shortened in the fore-and-aft direction to a transverse cord; imagine the hemispheres not having grown backwards and downwards round the thalamus; and the corpus fimbriatum on either side would then be the upper or anterior

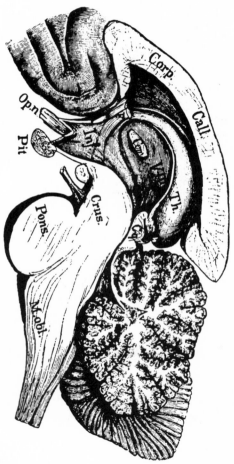

FIG. 37.—Median section of human brain below the hemispheres. *Th.*, thalamus; *Cq*, corpora quadrigemina; *V*^III, third ventricle; *Com*, middle commissure; *F*, columns of fornix; *Inf.*, infundibulum; *Op.n*, optic nerve; *Pit*, pituitary body; *Av.*, arbor vitæ. (After Obersteiner.)

margin of a split in the wall of the hemispheric ventricle of which the lower and posterior margin would be the posterior border of the corpus striatum where it grows out of the thalamus.

The little notches just behind the anterior pillar of the fornix and between them and the thalami are the so-called *foramina of Monro* through which the plexus of vessels, etc., passes from the median to the lateral ventricles.

See the thick *middle commissure* joining the two thalami, just as the corpus callosum and fornix join the hemispheres. These are all embryological aftergrowths. Seek also the *anterior commissure* crossing just in front of the anterior pillars of the fornix, as well as the *posterior commissure* with its lateral prolongations along the thalami, just below the pineal gland.

On a median section, note the thinnish *anterior wall* of the third ventricle and its prolongation downwards into the *infundibulum*.

Turn up or cut off the rear end of one hemisphere so as to see clearly the optic tracts turning upwards towards the rear corner of the thalamus. The *corpora geniculata* to which they also go, distinct in man, are less so in the sheep. The lower ones are visible between the optic-tract band and the 'testes,' however.

The brain's principal parts are thus passed in review. A longitudinal section of the whole organ through the median line will be found most instructive (Fig. 37). The student should also (on a *fresh* brain, or one hardened in bichromate of potash or ammonia

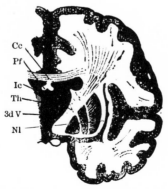

FIG. 38.—Transverse section through right hemisphere (after Gegenbaur). *Cc*, corpus callosum; *Pf*, pillars of fornix; *Ic*, internal capsule; *V*, third ventricle; *Nl*, nucleus lenticularis.

to save the contrast of color between white and gray matter) make transverse sections through the *nates* and *crura*, and through the hemispheres just in front of the corpus albicans. The latter section shows on each side the *nucleus lenticularis* of the corpus striatum, and also the *inner capsule* (see Fig. 38, *Nl*, and *Ic*).

When all is said and done, the fact remains that, for the beginner, the understanding of the brain's structure is not an easy thing. It must be gone over and forgotten and learned again many times before it is definitively assimilated by the mind. But patience and repetition, here as elsewhere, will bear their perfect fruit.

Chapter VIII

The Functions of the Brain

General Idea of Nervous Function.—If I begin chopping the foot of a tree, its branches are unmoved by my act, and its leaves murmur as peacefully as ever in the wind. If, on the contrary, I do violence to the foot of a fellow-man, the rest of his body instantly responds to the aggression by movements of alarm or defence. The reason of this difference is that the man has a nervous system, whilst the tree has none; and the function of the nervous system is to bring each part into harmonious coöperation with every other. The afferent nerves, when excited by some physical irritant, be this as gross in its mode of operation as a chopping axe or as subtle as the waves of light, convey the excitement to the nervous centres. The commotion set up in the centres does not stop there, but discharges through the efferent nerves, exciting movements which vary with the animal and with the irritant applied. These acts of response have usually the common character of being of service. They ward off the noxious stimulus and support the beneficial one; whilst if, in itself indifferent, the stimulus be a sign of some distant circumstance of practical importance, the animal's acts are addressed to this circumstance so as to avoid its perils or secure its benefits, as the case may be. To take a common example, if I hear the conductor calling 'All aboard!' as I enter the station, my heart first stops, then palpitates, and my legs respond to the air-waves falling on my tympanum by quickening their movements. If I stumble as I run, the sensation of falling provokes a movement of the hands towards the direction of the fall, the effect of which is to shield the body from too sudden a shock. If a cinder enter my eye, its lids close forcibly and a copious flow of tears tends to wash it out.

These three responses to a sensational stimulus differ, however, in many respects. The closure of the eye and the lachrymation are quite involuntary, and so is the disturbance of the heart. Such involuntary responses we know as 'reflex' acts. The motion of the arms to break the shock of falling may also be called reflex, since it occurs too quickly to be deliberately intended. It is, at any rate, less automatic than the previous acts, for a man might by conscious effort learn to perform it more skilfully, or even to suppress it altogether. Actions of this kind, into which instinct and volition enter upon equal terms, have been called 'semi-reflex.' The act of running towards the train, on the other hand, has no instinctive element about it. It is purely the result of education, and is preceded by a consciousness of the purpose to be attained and a distinct mandate of the will. It is a 'voluntary act.' Thus the animal's reflex and voluntary performances shade into each other gradually, being connected by acts which may often occur automatically, but may also be modified by conscious intelligence.

The Frog's Nerve-centres.—Let us now look a little more closely at what goes on.

The best way to enter the subject will be to take a lower creature, like a frog, and study by the vivisectional method the functions of his different nerve-centres. The frog's nerve-centres are figured in the diagram over the page, which needs no further explanation. I shall first proceed to state what happens when various amounts of the anterior parts are removed, in different frogs, in the way in which an ordinary student removes them—that is, with no extreme precautions as to the purity of the operation.

If, then, we reduce the frog's nervous system to the spinal cord alone, by making a section behind the base of the skull, between the spinal cord and the medulla oblongata, thereby cutting off the brain from all connection with the rest of the body, the frog will still continue to live, but with a very peculiarly modified activity. It ceases to breathe or swallow; it lies flat on its belly, and does not, like a normal frog, sit up on its fore-paws, though its hind-legs are kept, as usual, folded against its body and immediately resume this position if drawn out. If thrown on its back it lies

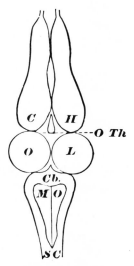

FIG. 39.—*C H*, cerebral hemispheres; *O Th*, optic thalami; *O L*, optic lobes; *Cb.*, cerebellum; *M O*, medulla oblongata; *S C*, spinal cord.

there quietly, without turning over like a normal frog. Locomotion and voice seem entirely abolished. If we suspend it by the nose, and irritate different portions of its skin by acid, it performs a set of remarkable 'defensive' movements calculated to wipe away the irritant. Thus, if the breast be touched, both fore-paws will rub it vigorously; if we touch the outer side of the elbow, the hind-foot of the same side will rise directly to the spot and wipe it. The back of the foot will rub the knee if that be attacked, whilst if the foot be cut away, the stump will make ineffectual movements, and then, in many frogs, a pause will come, as if for deliberation, succeeded by a rapid passage of the opposite unmutilated foot to the acidulated spot.

The most striking character of all these movements, after their teleological appropriateness, is their precision. They vary, in sensitive frogs and with a proper amount of irritation, so little as almost to resemble in their machine-like regularity the performances of a jumping-jack, whose legs must twitch whenever you pull the string. The spinal cord of the frog thus contains arrangements of cells and fibres fitted to convert skin-irritations into movements of defence. We may call it the *centre for defensive movements* in this animal. We may indeed go farther than this, and by cutting the spinal cord in various places find that its separate segments are independent mechanisms, for appropriate activities of the head and of the arms and legs respectively. The segment governing the arms is especially active, in male frogs, in the breeding season; and these members alone, with the breast and back appertaining to them, and everything else cut away, will actively grasp a finger placed between them and remain hanging to it for a considerable time.

Similarly of the medulla oblongata, optic lobes, and other centres between the spinal cord and the hemispheres of the frog. Each of them is proved by experiment to contain a mechanism for the accurate execution, in response to definite stimuli, of certain special acts. Thus with the medulla the animal swallows; with the medulla and cerebellum together he jumps, swims, and turns over from his back; with his optic lobes he croaks when pinched; etc. *A frog which has lost his cerebral hemispheres alone is by an unpractised observer indistinguishable from a normal animal.*

Not only is he capable, on proper instigation, of all the acts already mentioned, but he guides himself by sight, so that if an obstacle be set up between him and the light, and he be forced to move forwards, he either jumps over it or swerves to one side. He manifests sexual passion at the proper season, and, unlike an altogether brainless frog, which embraces anything placed between his arms, postpones this reflex act until a female of his own species is provided. Thus far, as aforesaid, a person unfamiliar with frogs might not suspect a mutilation; but even such a person would soon remark the almost entire absence of spontaneous motion— that is, motion unprovoked by any present incitation of sense. The continued movements of swimming, performed by the creature in the water, seem to be the fatal result of the contact of that fluid with its skin. They cease when a stick, for example, touches his hands. This is a sensible irritant towards which the feet are automatically drawn by reflex action, and on which the animal remains sitting. He manifests no hunger, and will suffer a fly to crawl over his nose unsnapped at. Fear, too, seems to have deserted him. In a word, he is an extremely complex machine whose actions, so far as they go, tend to self-preservation; but still a *machine*, in this sense—that it seems to contain no incalculable element. By applying the right sensory stimulus to him we are almost as certain of getting a fixed response as an organist is of hearing a certain tone when he pulls out a certain stop.

But now if to the lower centres we add the cerebral hemispheres, or if, in other words, we make an intact animal the subject of our observations, all this is changed. In addition to the previous responses to present incitements of sense, our frog now goes through long and complex acts of locomotion *spontaneously*, or as if moved by what in ourselves we should call an idea. His reactions to outward stimuli vary their form, too. Instead of making simple defensive movements with his hind-legs, like a headless frog, if touched; or of giving one or two leaps and then sitting still like a hemisphere-less one, he makes persistent and varied efforts of escape, as if, not the mere contact of the physiologist's hand, but the notion of danger suggested by it were now his spur. Led by the feeling of hunger, too, he goes in search of insects, fish, or smaller frogs, and varies his procedure with each species of victim. The physiologist cannot by manipulating him elicit croaking, crawling up a board, swimming or stopping, at will. His conduct has become incalculable—we can no longer foretell it exactly. Effort to escape is his dominant reaction, but he *may* do anything else, even swell up and become perfectly passive in our hands.

Such are the phenomena commonly observed, and such the impressions which one naturally receives. Certain general conclusions follow irresistibly. First of all the following:

The acts of all the centres involve the use of the same muscles. When a brainless frog's hind-leg wipes the acid, he calls into play all the leg-muscles which a frog with his full medulla oblongata and cerebellum uses when he turns from his back to his belly. Their contractions are, however, *combined* differently in the two cases, so that the results vary widely. We must consequently conclude that specific arrangements of cells and fibres exist in the cord for wiping, in the medulla for turning over, etc. Similarly they exist in the thalami for jumping over seen obstacles and for balancing the moved body; in the optic lobes for creeping backwards, or what not. But in the hemispheres, since the presence of these organs *brings no new elementary form of movement* with it, but only *determines differently the occasions* on which the movements shall occur, making the usual stimuli less fatal and machine-like, we need suppose no such machinery *directly* coördinative of muscular contractions to exist. We may rather assume, when the mandate for a wiping-movement is sent forth by the hemispheres, that a current goes straight to the wiping-arrangement in the spinal cord, exciting this arrangement as a whole. Similarly, if an intact frog wishes to jump, all he need do is to excite from the hemispheres the jumping-centre in the thalami or wherever it may be, and the latter will provide for the details of the execution. It is like a general ordering a colonel to make a certain movement, but not telling him how it shall be done.

The same muscle, then, is repeatedly represented at different heights; and at each it enters into a different combination with other muscles to coöperate in some special form of concerted movement. At each height the movement is discharged by some particular form of sensorial stimulus, whilst the stimuli which discharge the hemispheres would seem not so much to be elementary sorts of sensation, as groups of sensations forming determinate *objects* or *things*.

The Pigeon's Lower Centres.—The results are just the same if, instead of a frog, we take a pigeon, cut out his hemispheres carefully and wait till he recovers from the operation. There is not a movement natural to him which this brainless bird cannot execute; he seems, too, after some days to execute movements from some inner irritation, for he moves spontaneously. But his emotions and instincts exist no longer. In Schrader's striking words:

"The hemisphereless animal moves in a world of bodies which . . . are all of equal value for him. . . . He is, to use Goltz's apt expression, *impersonal*. . . . Every object is for him only a space-occupying mass, he turns out of his path for an ordinary pigeon no otherwise than for a stone. He may try to climb over both. All authors agree that they never found any difference, whether it was an inanimate body, a cat, a dog, or a bird of prey which came in their pigeon's way. The creature knows neither friends nor enemies, in the thickest company it lives like a hermit. The languishing cooing of the male awakens no more impression than the rattling of the peas, or the call-whistle which in the days before the injury used to make the birds hasten to be fed. Quite as little as the earlier observers have I seen hemisphereless she-birds answer the courting of the male. A hemisphereless male will coo all day long and show distinct signs of sexual excitement, but his activity is without any object, it is entirely indifferent to him whether the she-bird be there or not. If one is placed near him, he leaves her unnoticed. . . . As the male pays no attention to the female, so she pays none to her young. The brood may follow the mother ceaselessly calling for food, but they might as well ask it from a stone.... The hemisphereless pigeon is in the highest degree tame, and fears man as little as cat or bird of prey."

General Notion of Hemispheres.—All these facts lead us, when we try to formulate them broadly, to some such conception as this: *The lower centres act from present sensational stimuli alone; the hemispheres act from considerations*, the sensations which they may receive serving only as suggesters of these. But what are considerations but expectations, in the fancy, of sensations which will be felt one way or another according as action takes this course or that? If I step aside on seeing a rattlesnake, from considering how dangerous an animal he is, the mental materials which constitute my prudential reflection are images more or less vivid of the movement of his head, of a sudden pain in my leg, of a state of terror, a swelling of the limb, a chill, delirium, death, etc., etc., and the ruin of my hopes. But all these images are constructed out of my past experiences. They are *reproductions* of what I have felt or witnessed. They are, in short, *remote* sensations; and the main difference between the hemisphereless animal and the whole one may be concisely expressed by saying that *the one obeys absent, the other only present, objects*.

The hemispheres would then seem to be the chief seat of memory. Vestiges of past experience must in some way be stored up in them, and must, when aroused by present stimuli, first appear as representations of distant goods and evils; and then must discharge into the appropriate motor channels for warding off the evil and securing the benefits of the good. If we liken the nervous currents to electric currents, we can compare the nervous system, C, below the hemispheres to a direct circuit from sense-organ to muscle along the line $S \ldots C \ldots M$ of Fig. 40. The hemisphere, H, adds

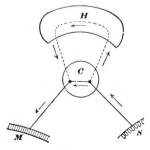

FIG. 40.

95

the long circuit or loop-line through which the current may pass when for any reason the direct line is not used.

Thus, a tired wayfarer on a hot day throws himself on the damp earth beneath a maple-tree. The sensations of delicious rest and coolness pouring themselves through the direct line would naturally discharge into the muscles of complete extension: he would abandon himself to the dangerous repose. But the loop-line being open, part of the current is drafted along it, and awakens rheumatic or catarrhal reminiscences, which prevail over the instigations of sense, and make the man arise and pursue his way to where he may enjoy his rest more safely. Presently we shall examine the manner in which the hemispheric loop-line may be supposed to serve as a reservoir for such reminiscences as these. Meanwhile I will ask the reader to notice some corollaries of its being such a reservoir.

First, no animal without it can deliberate, pause, postpone, nicely weigh one motive against another, or compare. Prudence, in a word, is for such a creature an impossible virtue. Accordingly we see that nature removes those functions in the exercise of which prudence is a virtue from the lower centres and hands them over to the cerebrum. Wherever a creature has to deal with complex features of the environment, prudence is a virtue. The higher animals have so to deal; and the more complex the features, the higher we call the animals. The fewer of his acts, then, can *such* an animal perform without the help of the organs in question. In the frog many acts devolve wholly on the lower centres; in the bird fewer; in the rodent fewer still; in the dog very few indeed; and in apes and men hardly any at all.

The advantages of this are obvious. Take the prehension of food as an example and suppose it to be a reflex performance of the lower centres. The animal will be condemned fatally and irresistibly to snap at it whenever presented, no matter what the circumstances may be; he can no more disobey this prompting than water can refuse to boil when a fire is kindled under the pot. His life will again and again pay the forfeit of his gluttony. Exposure to retaliation, to other enemies, to traps, to poisons, to the dangers of repletion, must be regular parts of his existence. His lack of all thought by which to weigh the danger against the attractiveness of the bait, and of all volition to remain hungry a little while longer, is the direct measure of his lowness in the mental scale.

And those fishes which, like our cunners and sculpins, are no sooner thrown back from the hook into the water than they automatically seize the hook again, would soon expiate the degradation of their intelligence by the extinction of their type, did not their extraordinary fecundity atone for their imprudence. Appetite and the acts it prompts have consequently become in all higher vertebrates functions of the cerebrum. They disappear when the physiologist's knife has left the subordinate centres alone in place. The brainless pigeon will starve though left on a corn-heap.

Take again the sexual function. In birds this devolves exclusively upon the hemispheres. When these are shorn away the pigeon pays no attention to the billings and cooings of its mate. And Goltz found that a bitch in heat would excite no emotion in male dogs who had suffered large loss of cerebral tissue. Those who have read Darwin's *Descent of Man* know what immense importance in the amelioration of the breed in birds this author ascribes to the fact of sexual selection. The sexual act is not performed until every condition of circumstance and sentiment is fulfilled, until time, place, and partner all are fit. But in frogs and toads this passion devolves on the lower centres. They show consequently a machine-like obedience to the present incitement of sense, and an almost total exclusion of the power of choice. Copulation occurs *per fas aut nefas*, occasionally between males, often with dead females, in puddles exposed on the highway, and the male may be cut in two without letting go his hold. Every spring an immense sacrifice of batrachian life takes place from these causes alone.

No one need be told how dependent all human social elevation is upon the prevalence of chastity. Hardly any factor measures more than this the difference between civilization and barbarism. Physiologically interpreted, chastity means nothing more than the fact that present solicitations of sense are overpowered by suggestions of æsthetic and moral fitness which the circumstances awaken in the cerebrum; and that upon the inhibitory or permissive influence of these alone action directly depends.

Within the psychic life due to the cerebrum itself the same general distinction obtains, between considerations of the more immediate and considerations of the more remote. In all ages the man whose determinations are swayed by reference to the most distant ends has been held to possess the highest intelligence. The tramp who lives from hour to hour; the bohemian whose engagements are from day to day; the bachelor who builds but for a single life; the father who acts for another generation; the patriot who thinks of a whole community and many generations; and, finally, the philosopher and saint whose cares are for humanity and for eternity,—these range themselves in an unbroken hierarchy, wherein each successive grade results from an increased manifestation of the special form of action by which the cerebral centres are distinguished from all below them.

The Automaton-Theory.—In the 'loop-line' along which the memories and ideas of the distant are supposed to lie, the action, so far as it is a physical process, must be interpreted after the type of the action in the lower centres. If regarded here as a reflex process, it must be reflex there as well. The current in both places runs out into the muscles only after it has first run in; but whilst the path by which it runs out is determined in the lower centres by reflections few and fixed amongst the cell-arrangements, in the hemispheres the reflections are many and instable. This, it will be seen, is only a difference of degree and not of kind, and does not change the reflex type. The conception of *all* action as conforming to this type is the fundamental conception of modern nerve-physiology. This conception, now, has led to two quite opposite theories about the relation to consciousness of the nervous functions. Some authors, finding that the higher voluntary functions seem to require the guidance of feeling, conclude that over the lowest reflexes some such feeling also presides, though it may be a feeling connected with the spinal cord, of which the higher conscious self connected with the hemispheres remains unconscious. Others, finding that reflex and semi-automatic acts may, notwithstanding their appropriateness, take place with an unconsciousness apparently complete, fly to the opposite extreme and maintain that the appropriateness even of the higher voluntary actions connected with the hemispheres owes nothing to the fact that consciousness attends them. They are, according to these writers, results of physiological mechanism pure and simple.

To comprehend completely this latter doctrine one should apply it to examples. The movements of our tongues and pens, the flashings of our eyes in conversation, are of course events of a physiological order, and as such their causal antecedents may be exclusively mechanical. If we knew thoroughly the nervous system of Shakespeare, and as thoroughly all his environing conditions, we should be able, according to the theory of automatism, to show why at a given period of his life his hand came to trace on certain sheets of paper those crabbed little black marks which we for shortness' sake call the manuscript of *Hamlet*. We should understand the rationale of every erasure and alteration therein, and we should understand all this without in the slightest degree acknowledging the existence of the thoughts in Shakespeare's mind. The words and sentences would be taken, not as signs of anything beyond themselves, but as little outward facts, pure and simple. In like manner, the automaton-theory affirms, we might exhaustively write the biography of those two hundred pounds, more or less, of warmish albuminoid matter called Martin Luther, without ever implying that it felt.

But, on the other hand, nothing in all this could prevent us from giving an equally complete account of either Luther's or Shakespeare's spiritual history, an account in which every gleam of thought and emotion should find its place. The mind-history would run alongside of the body-history of each man, and each point in the one would correspond to, but not react upon, a point in the other. So the melody floats from the harp-string, but neither checks nor quickens its vibrations; so the shadow runs alongside the pedestrian, but in no way influences his steps.

As a mere *conception*, and so long as we confine our view to the nervous centres themselves, few things are more seductive than this radically mechanical theory of their action. And yet our consciousness *is there*, and has in all probability been evolved, like all other functions, for a use—it is to the highest degree improbable *a priori* that it should have no use. Its use *seems* to be that of *selection*; but to select, it must be efficacious. States of consciousness which feel right are held fast to; those which feel wrong are checked. If the 'holding' and the 'checking' of the conscious states severally mean also the efficacious reinforcing or inhibiting of the correlated neural processes, then it would seem as if the presence of the states of mind might help to steer the nervous system and keep it in the path which to the consciousness seemed best. Now on the average what seems best to consciousness is really best for the creature. It is a well-known fact that pleasures are generally associated with beneficial, pains with detrimental, experiences. All the fundamental vital processes illustrate this law. Starvation; suffocation; privation of food, drink, and sleep; work when exhausted; burns, wounds, inflammation; the effects of poison, are as disagreeable as filling the hungry stomach, enjoying rest and sleep after fatigue, exercise after rest, and a sound skin and unbroken bones at all times, are pleasant. Mr. Spencer and others have suggested that these coincidences are due, not to any preëstablished harmony, but to the mere action of natural selection, which would certainly kill off in the long-run any breed of creatures to whom the fundamentally noxious experience seemed enjoyable. An animal that should take pleasure in a feeling of suffocation would, if that pleasure were efficacious enough to make him keep his head under water, enjoy a longevity of four or five minutes. But if conscious pleasure does not reinforce, and conscious pain does not inhibit anything, one does not see (without some such *a priori* rational harmony as would be scouted by the 'scientific' champions of the automaton-theory) why the most noxious acts, such as burning, might not with perfect impunity give thrills of delight, and the most necessary ones, such as breathing, cause agony. The only considerable attempt that has been made to explain the *distribution* of our feelings is that of Mr. Grant Allen in his suggestive little work, *Physiological Æsthetics*; and his reasoning is based exclusively on that causal efficacy of pleasures and pains which the partisans of pure automatism so strenuously deny.

Probability and circumstantial evidence thus run dead against the theory that our actions are *purely* mechanical in their causation. From the point of view of descriptive Psychology (even though we be bound to assume, as on p. 13, that all our feelings have brain-processes for their condition of existence, and can be remotely traced in every instance to currents coming from the outer world) we have no clear reason to doubt that the feelings may react so as to further or to dampen the processes to which they are due. I shall therefore not hesitate in the course of this book to use the language of common-sense. I shall talk as if consciousness kept actively pressing the nerve-centres in the direction of its own ends, and was no mere impotent and paralytic spectator of life's game.

The Localization of Functions in the Hemispheres.—The hemispheres, we lately said, must be the organ of memory, and in some way retain vestiges of former currents, by means of which mental considerations drawn from the past may be aroused before action takes place. The vivisections of physiologists and the observations of physicians have of late years given a concrete confirmation to this notion which the first rough appearances suggest. The various convolutions have had special functions assigned to them in relation to this and that sense-organ, as well as to this or that portion of the muscular system. This book is no place for going over the evidence in detail, so I will simply indicate the conclusions which are most probable at the date of writing.

Mental and Cerebral Elements.—In the first place, there is a very neat parallelism between the analysis of brain-functions by the physiologists and that of mental functions by the 'analytic' psychologists.

The phrenological brain-doctrine divided the brain into 'organs,' each of which stood for the man in a certain partial attitude. The organ of 'Philoprogenitiveness,' with its concomitant consciousness, is an entire man so far as he loves children, that of 'Reverence' is an entire man worshipping, etc. The spiritualistic psychology, in turn, divided the Mind into 'faculties,' which were also entire mental men in certain limited attitudes. But 'faculties' are not mental *elements* any more than 'organs' are brain-elements. Analysis breaks both into more elementary constituents.

Brain and mind alike consist of simple elements, sensory and motor. "All nervous centres," says Dr. J. Hughlings Jackson, "from the lowest to the very highest (the substrata of consciousness), are made up of nothing else than nervous arrangements representing impressions and movements. . . . I do not see of what other 'materials' the rest of the brain *can* be made." Meynert represents the matter similarly when he calls the cortex of the hemispheres the surface of projection for every muscle and every sensitive point of the body. The muscles and the sensitive points are *represented* each by a cortical point, and the Brain is little more than the sum of all these cortical points, to which, on the mental side, as many sensations and *ideas* correspond. The sensations and ideas of sensation and of motion are, in turn, the elements out of which the Mind is built according to the analytic school of psychology. The relations between objects are explained by 'associations' between the ideas; and the emotional and instinctive tendencies, by associations between ideas and movements. The same diagram can symbolize both the inner and the outer world; dots or circles standing indifferently for cells or ideas, and lines joining them, for fibres or associations. The associationist doctrine of 'ideas' may be doubted to be a literal expression of the truth, but it probably will always retain a didactic usefulness. At all events, it is interesting to see how well physiological analysis plays into its hands. To proceed to details.

The Motor Region.—The one thing which is *perfectly* well established is this, that the 'central' convolutions, on either side of the fissure of Rolando, and (at least in the monkey) the callosomarginal convolution (which is continuous with them on the mesial surface where one hemisphere is applied against the other), form the region by which all the motor incitations which leave the cortex pass out, on their way to those executive centres in the region of the pons, medulla, and spinal cord from which the muscular contractions are discharged in the last resort. The existence of this so-called 'motor zone' is established by anatomical as well as vivisectional and pathological evidence.

The accompanying figures (Figs. 41 and 42), from Schäfer and Horsley, show the topographical arrangement of the monkey's motor zone more clearly than any description.

Fig. 43, after Starr, shows how the fibres run downwards. All sensory currents entering the hemispheres run out from the Rolandic region, which may thus be regarded as a sort of funnel of escape, which narrows still more as it plunges beneath the surface,

FIG. 41.—Left hemisphere of monkey's brain. Outer surface.

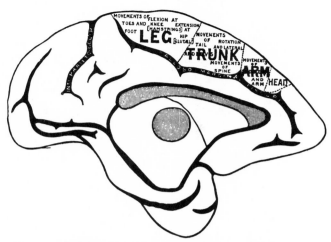

FIG. 42.—Left hemisphere of monkey's brain. Mesial surface.

traversing the inner capsule, pons, and parts below. The dark ellipses on the left half of the diagram stand for hemorrhages or tumors, and the reader can easily trace, by following the course of the fibres, what the effect of them in interrupting motor currents may be.

One of the most instructive proofs of motor localization in the cortex is that furnished by the disease now called aphemia, or *motor aphasia*. Motor aphasia is neither loss of voice nor paralysis of the tongue or lips. The patient's voice is as strong as ever, and all the innervations of his hypoglossal and facial nerves, except those necessary for speaking, may go on perfectly well. He can laugh and cry, and even sing; but he either is unable to utter any words at all; or a few meaningless stock phrases form his only speech; or else he speaks incoherently and confusedly, mispronouncing, misplacing, and misusing his words in various degrees. Sometimes his speech is a mere broth of unintelligible syllables. In cases of pure motor aphasia the patient recognizes his mistakes and suffers acutely from them. Now whenever a patient dies in such a condition as this, and an examination of his brain is permitted, it is found that the lowest frontal gyrus (see Fig. 44) is the seat of injury. Broca first noticed this fact in 1861, and since then the gyrus has gone by the name of Broca's convolution. The injury in right-handed people is found on the left hemisphere, and in left-handed people on the right hemisphere. Most people, in fact, are left-

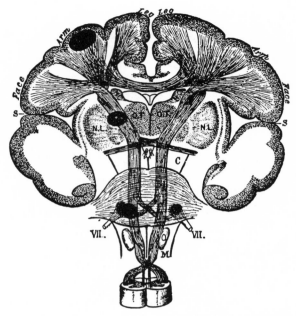

FIG. 43.—Schematic transverse section of the human brain, through the rolandic region. *S*, fissure of Sylvius; *N.C.*, *nucleus caudatus*, and *N.L.*, *nucleus lenticularis*, of the corpus striatum; *O.T.*, thalamus; *C*, crus; *M*, medulla oblongata; *VII.*, the facial nerves passing out from their nucleus in the region of the *pons*. The fibres passing between *O.T.* and *N.L.* constitute the so-called internal capsule.

brained, that is, all their delicate and specialized movements are handed over to the charge of the left hemisphere. The ordinary right-handedness for such movements is only a consequence of that fact, a consequence which shows outwardly on account of that extensive crossing of the fibres from the left hemisphere to the right half of the body only, which is shown in Fig. 43, below the letter *M*. But the left-brainedness might exist and *not* show outwardly. This would happen wherever organs on *both* sides of the body could be governed by the left hemisphere; and just such a case seems offered by the vocal organs, in that highly delicate and special motor service which we call speech. Either hemisphere *can* innervate them bilaterally, just as either seems able to innervate bilaterally the muscles of the trunk, ribs, and diaphragm. Of the special movements of speech, however, it would

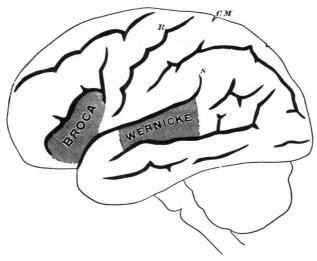

Fig. 44.—Schematic profile of left hemisphere, with the parts shaded whose destruction causes motor ('Broca') and sensory ('Wernicke') aphasia.

appear (from these very facts of aphasia) that the left hemisphere in most persons habitually takes exclusive charge. With that hemisphere thrown out of gear, speech is undone; even though the opposite hemisphere still be there for the performance of less specialized acts, such as the various movements required in eating.

The visual centre is in the *occipital lobes*. This also is proved by all the three kinds of possible evidence. It seems that the fibres from the *left* halves of *both* retinæ go to the *left* hemisphere, those from the right half to the right hemisphere. The consequence is that when the right occipital lobe, for example, is injured, 'hemianopsia' results in both eyes, that is, both retinæ grow blind as to their right halves, and the patient loses the leftward half of his field of view. The diagram on p. 106 will make this matter clear (see Fig. 45).

Quite recently, both Schäfer and Munk, in studying the movements of the eyeball produced by galvanizing the visual cortex in monkeys and dogs, have found reason to plot out an analogous correspondence between the upper and lower portions of the retinæ and certain parts of the visual cortex. If both occipital lobes were destroyed, we should have double hemiopia, or, in other words, total blindness. In human hemiopic blindness there

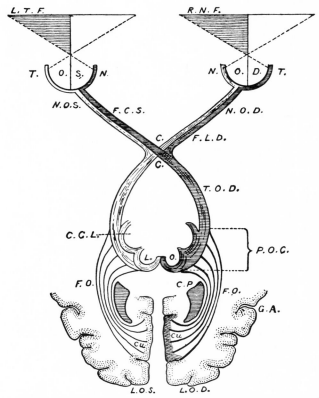

FIG. 45.—Scheme of the mechanism of vision, after Seguin. The *cuneus* convolution (*Cu*) of the right occipital lobe is supposed to be injured, and all the parts which lead to it are darkly shaded to show that they fail to exert their function. *F.O.* are the intra-hemispheric optical fibres. *P.O.C.* is the region of the lower optic centres (corpora geniculata and quadrigemina). *T.O.D.* is the right optic tract; *C.*, the chiasma; *F.L.D.* are the fibres going to the lateral or temporal half *T.* of the right retina, and *F.C.S.* are those going to the central or nasal half of the left retina. *O.D.* is the right, and *O.S.* the left, eyeball. The rightward half of each is therefore blind; in other words, the right nasal field, *R.N.F.*, and the left temporal field, *L.T.F.*, have become invisible to the subject with the lesion at *Cu*.

is insensibility to light on one half of the field of view, but mental images of visible things remain. In *double* hemiopia there is every reason to believe that not only the sensation of light must go, but that all memories and images of a visual order must be annihilated also. The man loses his visual 'ideas.' Only 'cortical' blindness can produce this effect on the ideas. Destruction of the retinæ or of the visual tracts anywhere between the cortex and the eyes impairs the retinal sensibility to light, but not the power of visual imagination.

Mental Blindness.—A most interesting effect of cortical disorder is *mental blindness*. This consists not so much in insensibility to optical impressions, as in *inability to understand them*. Psychologically it is interpretable as *loss of associations* between optical sensations and what they signify; and any interruption of the paths between the optic centres and the centres for other ideas ought to bring it about. Thus, printed letters of the alphabet, or words, signify both certain sounds and certain articulatory movements. But the connection between the articulating or auditory centres and those for sight being ruptured, we ought *a priori* to expect that the sight of words would fail to awaken the idea of their sound, or of the movement for pronouncing them. We ought, in short, to have *alexia,* or inability to read; and this is just what we do have as a complication of *aphasic* disease in many cases of extensive injury about the fronto-temporal regions.

Where an object fails to be recognized by sight, it often happens that the patient will recognize and name it as soon as he touches it with his hand. This shows in an interesting way how numerous are the incoming paths which all end by running out of the brain through the channel of speech. The hand-path is open,

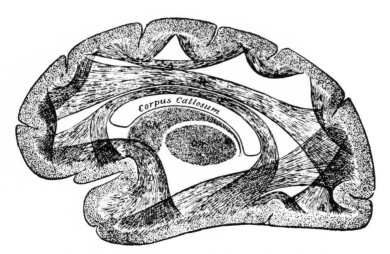

FIG. 46.—Fibres associating the cortical centres together. (Schematic, after Starr.)

though the eye-path be closed. When mental blindness is most complete, neither sight, touch, nor sound avails to steer the patient, and a sort of dementia which has been called *asymbolia* or *apraxia* is the result. The commonest articles are not understood. The patient will put his breeches on one shoulder and his hat upon the other, will bite into the soap and lay his shoes on the table, or take his food into his hand and throw it down again, not knowing what to do with it, etc. Such disorder can only come from extensive brain-injury.

The centre for hearing is situated in man in the upper convolution of the temporal lobe (see the part marked 'Wernicke' in Fig. 44). The phenomena of aphasia show this. We studied motor aphasia a few pages back; we must now consider *sensory aphasia.* Our knowledge of aphasia has had three stages: we may talk of the period of Broca, the period of Wernicke, and the period of Charcot. What Broca's discovery was we have seen. Wernicke was the first to discriminate those cases in which the patient can *not even understand* speech from those in which he can understand, only not talk; and to ascribe the former condition to lesion of the temporal lobe. The condition in question is *word-deafness*, and the disease is *auditory aphasia.* The latest statistical survey of the subject is that by Dr. M. Allen Starr. In the seven cases of *pure* word-deafness which he has collected (cases in which the patient could read, talk, and write, but not understand what was said to him), the lesion was limited to the first and second temporal convolutions in their posterior two thirds. The lesion (in right-handed, i.e., left-brained, persons) is always on the left side, like the lesion in motor aphasia. Crude hearing would not be abolished even were the left centre for it utterly destroyed; the right centre would still provide for that. But the *linguistic use* of hearing appears bound up with the integrity of the left centre more or less exclusively. Here it must be that words heard enter into association with the things which they represent, on the one hand, and with the movements necessary for pronouncing them, on the other. In most of us (as Wernicke said) speech must go on from auditory cues; that is, our visual, tactile, and other ideas probably do not innervate our motor centres directly, but only after first arousing the mental sound of the words. This is the immediate stimulus to articulation; and where the possibility of this is abolished by the destruction of its usual channel in the left temporal lobe, the articulation must suffer. In the few cases in which the channel is abolished with no bad effect on speech we must suppose an idiosyncrasy. The patient must innervate his speech-organs either from the corresponding portion of the other hemisphere or directly from the centres of vision, touch, etc., without leaning on the auditory region. It is the minuter analysis of such individual differences as these which constitutes Charcot's contribution towards clearing up the subject.

Every namable thing has numerous properties, qualities, or aspects. In our minds the properties together with the name form an associated group. If different parts of the brain are severally concerned with the several properties, and a farther part with the hearing, and still another with the uttering, of the name, there must inevitably be brought about (through the law of association which we shall later study) such a connection amongst all these brain-parts that the activity of any one of them will be likely to awaken the activity of all the rest. When we are talking whilst we think, the *ultimate* process is utterance. If the brain-part for *that* be injured, speech is impossible or disorderly, even though all the other brain-parts be intact: and this is just the condition of things which, on p. 103, we found to be brought about by lesion of the convolution of Broca. But back of that last act various orders of succession are possible in the associations of a talking man's ideas. The more usual order is, as aforesaid, from the tactile, visual, or other properties of the things thought-about to the sound of their names, and then to the latter's utterance. But if in a certain individual's mind the *look* of an object or the *look* of its name be what habitually precedes articulation, then the loss of the *hearing* centre will *pro tanto* not affect that individual's speech or reading. He will be mentally deaf, i.e., his *understanding* of the human voice will suffer, but he will not be aphasic. In this way it is possible to explain the seven cases of word-deafness without motor aphasia which figure in Dr. Starr's table.

If this order of association be ingrained and habitual in that individual, injury to his *visual* centres will make him not only word-blind, but aphasic as well. His speech will become confused in consequence of an occipital lesion. Naunyn, consequently, plotting out on a diagram of the hemisphere the 71 irreproachably reported cases of aphasia which he was able to collect, finds that the lesions concentrate themselves in three places: first, on Broca's

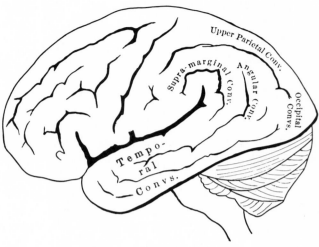

FIG. 47.

centre; second, on Wernicke's; third, on the supra-marginal and angular convolutions under which those fibres pass which connect the visual centres with the rest of the brain (see Fig. 47). With this result Dr. Starr's analysis of purely sensory cases agrees.

In the chapter on Imagination we shall return to these differences in the sensory spheres of different individuals. Meanwhile few things show more beautifully than the history of our knowledge of aphasia how the sagacity and patience of many banded workers are in time certain to analyze the darkest confusion into an orderly display. There is no 'organ' of Speech in the brain any more than there is a 'faculty' of Speech in the mind. The entire mind and the entire brain are more or less at work in a man who uses language. The subjoined diagram, from Ross, shows the four parts most vitally concerned, and, in the light of our text, needs no farther explanation (see Fig. 48, p. 111).

Centres for Smell, Taste, and Touch.—The other sensory centres are less definitely made out. Of smell and taste I will say nothing; and of muscular and cutaneous feeling only this, that it seems most probably seated in the motor zone, and possibly in the convolutions immediately backwards and midwards thereof. The incoming tactile currents must enter the cells of this region by one set of fibres, and the discharges leave them by another, but of these refinements of anatomy we at present know nothing.

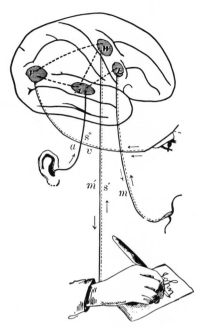

FIG. 48.—*A* is the auditory centre, *V* the visual, *W* the writing,
and *E* that for speech.

Conclusion.—We thus see the postulate of Meynert and Jackson, with which we started on p. 101, to be on the whole most satisfactorily corroborated by objective research. *The highest centres do probably contain nothing but arrangements for representing impressions and movements, and other arrangements for coupling the activity of these arrangements together.* Currents pouring in from the sense-organs first excite some arrangements, which in turn excite others, until at last a discharge downwards of some sort occurs. When this is once clearly grasped there remains little ground for asking whether the motor zone is exclusively motor, or sensitive as well. The whole cortex, inasmuch as currents run through it, is both. All the currents probably have feelings going with them, and sooner or later bring movements about. In one aspect, then, every centre is afferent, in another efferent, even the motor cells of the spinal cord having these two aspects inseparably conjoined. Marique, and Exner and Paneth have shown that by cutting *round* a 'motor' centre and so separating it from the influence of the rest of the cortex, the same disorders are produced as by cutting it out, so that it is really just what I called it, only the funnel through which the stream of innervation, starting from elsewhere, escapes; *consciousness accompanying the stream, and being mainly of things seen if the stream is strongest occipitally, of things heard if it is strongest temporally, of things felt, etc., if the stream occupies most intensely the 'motor zone.'* It seems to me that some broad and vague formulation like this is as much as we can safely venture on in the present state of science— so much at least is not likely to be overturned. But it is obvious how little this tells us of the detail of what goes on in the brain when a certain thought is before the mind. The general forms of relation perceived between things, as their identities, likenesses, or contrasts; the forms of the consciousness itself, as effortless or perplexed, attentive or inattentive, pleasant or disagreeable; the phenomena of interest and selection, etc., etc., are all lumped together as effects correlated with the currents that connect one centre with another. Nothing can be more vague than such a formula. Moreover certain portions of the brain, as the lower frontal lobes, escape formulation altogether. Their destruction gives rise to no local trouble of either motion or sensibility in dogs, and in monkeys neither stimulation nor excision of these lobes produces any symptoms whatever. One monkey of Horsley and Schäfer's was as tame, and did certain tricks as well, after as before the operation.

It is in short obvious that our knowledge of our mental states infinitely exceeds our knowledge of their concomitant cerebral conditions. Without introspective analysis of the mental elements of speech, the doctrine of Aphasia, for instance, which is the most brilliant jewel in Physiology, would have been utterly impossible. Our assumption, therefore (p. 12), that mind-states are absolutely dependent on brain-conditions, must still be understood as a mere postulate. We may have a general faith that it must be true, but any exact insight as to *how* it is true lags wofully behind.

Before taking up the study of conscious states properly so called, I will in a separate chapter speak of two or three aspects of brain-function which have a general importance and which coöperate in the production of all our mental states.

Chapter IX

Some General Conditions of Neural Activity

The Nervous Discharge.—The word discharge is constantly used, and must be used in this book, to designate the escape of a current downwards into muscles or other internal organs. The reader must not understand the word figuratively. From the point of view of dynamics the passage of a current out of a motor cell is probably altogether analogous to the explosion of a gun. The matter of the cell is in a state of internal tension, which the incoming current resolves, tumbling the molecules into a more stable equilibrium and liberating an amount of energy which starts the current of the outgoing fibre. This current is stronger than that of the incoming fibre. When it reaches the muscle it produces an analogous disintegration of pent-up molecules and the result is a stronger effect still. Matteuci found that the work done by a muscle's contraction was 27,000 times greater than that done by the galvanic current which stimulated its motor nerve. When a frog's leg-muscle is made to contract, first directly, by stimulation of its motor nerve, and second reflexly, by stimulation of a sensory nerve, it is found that the reflex way requires a stronger current and is more tardy, but that the contraction is stronger when it does occur. These facts prove that the cells in the spinal cord through which the reflex takes place offer a resistance which has first to be overcome, but that a relatively violent outward current outwards then escapes from them. What is this but an explosive discharge on a minute scale?

Reaction-time.—The measurement of the time required for the discharge is one of the lines of experimental investigation most diligently followed of late years. Helmholtz led the way by discovering the rapidity of the outgoing current in the sciatic nerve of the frog. The methods he used were soon applied to sensory reactions, and the results caused much popular admiration when described as measurements of the 'velocity of thought.' The phrase 'quick as thought' had from time immemorial signified all that was wonderful and elusive of determination in the line of speed; and the way in which Science laid her doomful hand upon this mystery reminded people of the day when Franklin first '*eripuit cœlo fulmen*,' foreshadowing the reign of a newer and colder race of gods. I may say, however, immediately, that the phrase 'velocity of *thought*' is misleading, for it is by no means clear in any of the cases what particular act of thought occurs during the time which is measured. What the times in question really represent is the total duration of certain *reactions upon stimuli*. Certain of the conditions of the reaction are prepared beforehand; they consist in the assumption of those motor and sensory tensions which we name the expectant state. Just what happens during the actual time occupied by the reaction (in other words, just what is added to the preëxistent tensions to produce the actual discharge) is not made out at present, either from the neural or from the mental point of view.

The method is essentially the same in all these investigations. A signal of some sort is communicated to the subject, and at the same instant records itself on a time-registering apparatus. The subject then makes a muscular movement of some sort, which is the 'reaction,' and which also records itself automatically. The time found to have elapsed between the two records is the total time of that reaction. The time-registering instruments are of various types. One type is that of the revolving drum covered with smoked paper, on which one electric pen traces a line which the signal breaks and the 'reaction' draws again; whilst another electric pen (connected with a rod of metal vibrating at a known rate) traces alongside of the former line a 'time-line' of which each undulation or link stands for a certain fraction of a second, and against which the break in the reaction-line can be measured. Compare Fig. 49, where the line is broken by the signal at the first arrow, and continued again by the reaction at the second. The

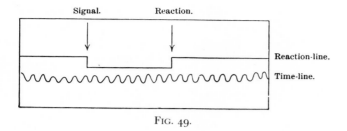

Fig. 49.

machine most often used is Hipp's chronoscopic clock. The hands are placed at zero, the signal starts them (by an electric connection), and the reaction stops them. The duration of their movement, down to 1000ths of a second, is then read off from the dial-plates.

Simple Reactions.—It is found that the reaction-time differs in the same person according to the direction of his expectant attention. If he thinks as little as possible of the movement which he is to make, and concentrates his mind upon the signal to be received, it is longer; if, on the contrary, he bends his mind exclusively upon the muscular response, it is shorter. Lange, who first noticed this fact when working in Wundt's laboratory, found his own 'muscular' reaction-time to average $0''.123$, whilst his 'sensorial' reaction-time averaged as much as $0''.230$. It is obvious that experiments, to have any *comparative* value, must always be made according to the 'muscular' method, which reduces the figure to its minimum and makes it more constant. In general it lies between one and two tenths of a second. It seems to me that under these circumstances the reaction is essentially a reflex act. The preliminary *making-ready* of the muscles for the movement means the excitement of the paths of discharge to a point just short of actual discharge before the signal comes in. In other words, it means the temporary formation of a real 'reflex-arc' in the centres, through which the incoming current instantly can pour out again. But when, on the other hand, the expectant attention is exclusively addressed to the signal, the excitement of the motor tracts can only begin after this latter has come in, and under this condition the reaction takes more time. In the hair-trigger condition in which we stand when making reactions by the 'muscular' method, we sometimes respond to a wrong signal, especially if it be of the same *kind* with the one we expect. The signal is but the spark which touches off a train already laid. There is no thought in the matter; the hand jerks by an involuntary start.

These experiments are thus in no sense measurements of the swiftness of *thought*. Only when we complicate them is there a chance for anything like an intellectual operation to occur. They may be complicated in various ways. The reaction may be withheld until the signal has consciously awakened a distinct idea (Wundt's discrimination-time, association-time), and may then be performed. Or there may be a variety of possible signals, each with a different reaction assigned to it, and the reacter may be uncertain which one he is about to receive. The reaction would then hardly seem to occur without a preliminary recognition and choice. Even here, however, the discrimination and choice are widely different from the intellectual operations of which we are ordinarily conscious under those names. Meanwhile the simple re-action-time remains as the starting point of all these superinduced complications, and its own variations must be briefly passed in review.

The reaction-time varies with the *individual* and his *age*. Old and uncultivated people have it long (nearly a second, in an old pauper observed by Exner). Children have it long (half a second, according to Herzen).

Practice shortens it to a quantity which is for each individual a minimum beyond which no farther reduction can be made. The aforesaid old pauper's time was, after much practice, reduced to 0.1866 sec.

Fatigue lengthens it, and *concentration of attention* shortens it. The *nature of the signal* makes it vary. I here bring together the averages which have been obtained by some observers:

	Hirsch.	Hankel.	Exner.	Wundt.
Sound	0.149	0.1505	0.1360	0.167
Light	0.200	0.2246	0.1506	0.222
Touch	0.182	0.1546	0.1337	0.213

It will be observed that *sound* is more promptly reacted on than either *sight* or *touch*. *Taste* and *smell* are slower than either. The *intensity of the signal* makes a difference. The intenser the stimulus the shorter the time. Herzen compared the reaction from a *corn* on the toe with that from the skin of the hand of the same subject.

The two places were stimulated simultaneously, and the subject tried to react simultaneously with both hand and foot, but the foot always went quickest. When the sound skin of the foot was touched instead of the corn, it was the hand which always reacted first. *Intoxicants* on the whole lengthen the time, but much depends on the dose.

Complicated Reactions.—These occur when some kind of intellectual operation accompanies the reaction. The rational place in which to report of them would be under the head of the various intellectual operations concerned. But certain persons prefer to see all these measurements bunched together regardless of context; so, to meet their views, I give the complicated reactions here.

When we have to think before reacting it is obvious that there is no definite reaction-time of which we can talk—it all depends on how long we think. The only times we can measure are the *minimum* times of certain determinate and very simple intellectual operations. The *time required for discrimination* has thus been made a subject of experimental measurement. Wundt calls it *Unterscheidungszeit*. His subjects (whose simple reaction-time had previously been determined) were required to make a movement, always the same, the instant they discerned *which* of two or more signals they received. The *excess* of time occupied by these reactions *over the simple reaction-time*, in which only one signal was used and known in advance, measured, according to Wundt, the time required for the act of discrimination. It was found longer when four different signals were irregularly used than when only two were used. When two were used (the signals being the sudden appearance of a black or of a white object), the average times of three observers were respectively (in seconds)

0.050   0.047   0.079.

When four signals were used, a red and a green light being added to the others, it became, for the same observers,

0.157   0.073   0.132.

Prof. Cattell found he could get no results by this method, and reverted to one used by observers previous to Wundt and which Wundt had rejected. This is the *einfache Wahlmethode*, as Wundt calls it. The reacter awaits the signal and reacts if it is of one sort, but omits to act if it is of another sort. The reaction thus occurs after discrimination; the motor impulse cannot be sent to the hand until the subject knows what the signal is. Reacting in this way, Prof. Cattell found the increment of time required for distinguishing a white signal from no signal to be, in two observers,

0.030 and 0.050;

that for distinguishing one color from another was similarly,

0.100 and 0.110;

that for distinguishing a certain color from ten other colors,

0.105 and 0.117;

that for distinguishing the letter A in ordinary print from the letter Z,

0.142 and 0.137;

that for distinguishing a given letter from all the rest of the alphabet (not reacting until that letter appeared),

0.119 and 0.116;

that for distinguishing a word from any of twenty-five other words, from

0.118 to 0.158 sec.

—the difference depending on the length of the words and the familiarity of the language to which they belonged.

Prof. Cattell calls attention to the fact that the time for distinguishing a word is often but little more than that for distinguishing a letter: "We do not therefore," he says, "perceive separately the letters of which a word is composed, but the word as a whole. The application of this to teaching children to read is evident."

He also finds a great difference in the time with which various letters are distinguished, E being particularly bad.

The time required for association of one idea with another has been measured. Galton, using a very simple apparatus, found that the sight of an unforeseen word would awaken an associated 'idea' in about 5/6 of a second. Wundt next made determinations in which the 'cue' was given by single-syllabled words called out by an assistant. The person experimented on had to press a key as soon as the sound of the word awakened an associated idea. Both word and reaction were chronographically registered, and the total time-interval between the two amounted, in four observers, to 1.009, 0.896, 1.037, and 1.154 seconds respectively. From this the simple reaction-time and the time of merely identifying the word's sound (the 'apperception-time,' as Wundt calls it) must be subtracted, to get the exact time required for the associated idea to arise. These times were separately determined and subtracted. The difference, called by Wundt *association-time*, amounted, in the same four persons, to 706, 723, 752, and 874 thousandths of a second respectively. The length of the last figure is due to the fact that the person reacting was an American, whose associations with German words would naturally be slower than those of natives. The shortest association-time noted was when the word 'Sturm' suggested to Wundt the word 'Wind' in 0.341 second. Prof. Cattell made some interesting observations upon the association-time between the look of letters and their names. "I pasted letters," he says, "on a revolving drum, and determined at what rate they could be read aloud, as they passed by a slit in a screen." He found it to vary according as one, or more than one, letter was visible at a time through the slit, and gives half a second as about the time which it takes to see and name a single letter seen alone. The rapidity of a man's *reading* is of course a measure of that of his associations, since each seen word must call up its name, at least, ere it is read. "I find," says Prof. Cattell, "that it takes about twice as long to read (aloud, as fast as possible) words which have no connexion as words which make sentences, and letters which have no connexion as letters which make words. When the words make sentences and the letters words, not only do the processes of seeing and naming overlap, but by one mental effort the subject can recognise a whole group of words or letters, and by one will-act choose the motions to be made in naming them, so that the rate at which the words and letters are read is really only limited by the maximum rapidity at which the speech-organs can be moved. . . . For example, when reading as fast as possible the writer's rate was, English 138, French 167, German 250, Italian 327, Latin 434 and Greek 484; the figures giving the thousandths of a second taken to read each word. Experiments made on others strikingly confirm these results. The subject does not know that he is reading the foreign language more slowly than his own; this explains why foreigners seem to talk so fast. . . .

"The time required to see and name colours and pictures of objects was determined in the same way. The time was found to be about the same (over ½ sec.) for colours as for pictures, and about twice as long as for words and letters. Other experiments I have made show that we can recognise a single colour or picture in a slightly shorter time than a word or letter, but take longer to name it. This is because in the case of words and letters the association between the idea and name has taken place so often that the process has become automatic, whereas in the case of colours and pictures we must by a voluntary effort choose the name."

Dr. Romanes has found "astonishing differences in the *maximum* rate of reading which is possible to different individuals, all of whom have been accustomed to extensive reading. That is to say, the difference may amount to 4 to 1; or, otherwise stated, in a given time one individual may be able to read four times as much as another. Moreover, it appeared that there was no relationship between slowness of reading and power of assimilation; on the contrary, when all the efforts are directed to assimilating as much as possible in a given time, the rapid readers (as shown by their written notes) usually give a better account of the portions of the paragraph which has been compassed by the slow readers than the latter are able to give; and the most rapid reader whom I have found is also the best at assimilating. I should further say," Dr. R. continues, "that there is no relationship between rapidity of perception as thus tested and intellectual activity as tested by the general results of intellectual work; for I have tried the experiment with several highly distinguished men in science and literature, most of whom I found to be slow readers."

The degree of concentration of the attention has much to do with determining the reaction-time. Anything which baffles or distracts us beforehand, or startles us in the signal, makes the time proportionally long.

The Summation of Stimuli.—Throughout the nerve-centres it is a law that *a stimulus which would be inadequate by itself to excite a nerve-centre to effective discharge may, by acting with one or more other stimuli (equally ineffectual by themselves alone), bring the discharge about.* The natural way to consider this is as a summation of tensions which at last overcome a resistance. The first of them produce a 'latent excitement' or a 'heightened irritability'—the phrase is immaterial so far as practical consequences go;—the last is the straw which breaks the camel's back.

This is proved by many physiological experiments which cannot here be detailed; but outside of the laboratory we constantly apply the law of summation in our practical appeals. If a car-horse balks, the final way of starting him is by applying a number of customary incitements at once. If the driver uses reins and voice, if one bystander pulls at his head, another lashes his hindquarters, the conductor rings the bell, and the dismounted passengers shove the car, all at the same moment, his obstinacy generally yields, and he goes on his way rejoicing. If we are striving to remember a lost name or fact, we think of as many 'cues' as possible, so that by their joint action they may recall what no one of them can recall alone. The sight of a dead prey will often not stimulate a beast to pursuit, but if the sight of movement be added to that of form, pursuit occurs. "Brücke noticed that his brainless hen, which made no attempt to peck at the grain under her very eyes, began pecking if the grain were thrown on the ground with force, so as to produce a rattling sound." "Dr. Allen Thomson ... hatched out some chickens on a carpet, where he kept them for several days. They showed no inclination to scrape, ... but when Dr. Thomson sprinkled a little gravel on the carpet, ... the chickens immediately began their scraping movements." A strange person, and darkness, are both of them stimuli to fear and mistrust in dogs (and for the matter of that, in men). Neither circumstance alone may awaken outward manifestations, but together, i.e., when the strange man is met in the dark, the dog will be excited to violent defiance. Street hawkers well know the efficacy of summation, for they arrange themselves in a line on the sidewalk, and the passer often buys from the last one of them, through the effect of the reiterated solicitation, what he refused to buy from the first in the row.

Cerebral Blood-supply.—All parts of the cortex, when electrically excited, produce alterations both of respiration and circulation. The blood-pressure somewhat rises, as a rule, all over the body, no matter where the cortical irritation is applied, though the motor zone is the most sensitive region for the purpose. Slowing and quickening of the heart are also observed. Mosso, using his 'plethysmograph' as an indicator, discovered that the blood-supply to the arms diminished during intellectual activity, and found furthermore that the arterial tension (as shown by the sphygmograph) was increased in these members (see Fig. 50). So slight an emotion as that produced by the entrance of Professor Ludwig into the laboratory was instantly followed by a shrinkage of the arms. The brain itself is an excessively vascular organ, a sponge full of blood, in fact; and another of Mosso's inventions showed that when less blood went to the legs, more went to the head. The subject to be observed lay on a delicately balanced table which could tip downwards either at the head or at the foot

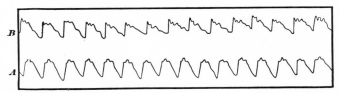

Fig. 50.—Sphygmographic pulse-tracing. *A*, during intellectual repose; *B*, during intellectual activity. (Mosso.)

if the weight of either end were increased. The moment emotional or intellectual activity began in the subject, down went the head-end, in consequence of the redistribution of blood in his system. But the best proof of the immediate afflux of blood to the brain during mental activity is due to Mosso's observations on three persons whose brain had been laid bare by lesion of the skull. By means of apparatus described in his book, this physiologist was enabled to let the brain-pulse record itself directly by a tracing. The intra-cranial blood-pressure rose immediately whenever the subject was spoken to, or when he began to think actively, as in solving a problem in mental arithmetic. Mosso gives in his work a large number of reproductions of tracings which show the instantaneity of the change of blood-supply, whenever the mental activity was quickened by any cause whatever, intellectual or emotional. He relates of his female subject that one day whilst tracing her brain-pulse he observed a sudden rise with no apparent outer or inner cause. She however confessed to him afterwards that at that moment she had caught sight of a *skull* on top of a piece of furniture in the room, and that this had given her a slight emotion.

Cerebral Thermometry.—*Brain-activity seems accompanied by a local disengagement of heat.* The earliest careful work in this direction was by Dr. J. S. Lombard in 1867. He noted the changes in delicate thermometers and electric piles placed against the scalp in human beings, and found that any intellectual effort, such as computing, composing, reciting poetry silently or aloud, and especially that emotional excitement such as an angry fit, caused a general rise of temperature, which rarely exceeded a degree Fahrenheit. In 1870 the indefatigable Schiff took up the subject, experimenting on live dogs and chickens by plunging thermo-electric needles into the substance of their brain. After habituation was established, he tested the animals with various sensations, tactile, optic, olfactory, and auditory. He found very regularly an abrupt alteration of the intra-cerebral temperature. When, for instance, he presented an empty roll of paper to the nose of his dog as it lay motionless, there was a small deflection, but when a piece of meat was in the paper the deflection was much greater. Schiff concluded from these and other experiments that sensorial activity heats the brain-tissue, but he did not try to localize the increment of heat beyond finding that it was in both hemispheres, whatever might be the sensation applied. Dr. Amidon in 1880 made a farther step forwards, in localizing the heat produced by voluntary muscular contractions. Applying a number of delicate surface-thermometers simultaneously against the scalp, he found that when different muscles of the body were made to contract vigorously for ten minutes or more, different regions of the scalp rose in temperature, that the regions were well focalized, and that the rise of temperature was often considerably over a Fahrenheit degree. To a large extent these regions correspond to the centres for the same movements assigned by Ferrier and others on other grounds; only they cover more of the skull.

Phosphorus and Thought.—Considering the large amount of popular nonsense which passes current on this subject I may be pardoned for a brief mention of it here. '*Ohne Phosphor, kein Gedanke*,' was a noted war-cry of the 'materialists' during the excitement on that subject which filled Germany in the '60s. The brain, like every other organ of the body, contains phosphorus, and a score of other chemicals besides. Why the phosphorus should be picked out as its essence, no one knows. It would be equally true to say, 'Ohne Wasser, kein Gedanke,' or 'Ohne Kochsalz, kein Gedanke'; for thought would stop as quickly if the brain should dry up or lose its NaCl as if it lost its phosphorus. In America the phosphorus-delusion has twined itself round a saying quoted (rightly or wrongly) from Professor L. Agassiz, to the effect that fishermen are more intelligent than farmers because they eat so much fish, which contains so much phosphorus. All the alleged facts may be doubted.

The only straight way to ascertain the importance of phosphorus to thought would be to find whether more is excreted by the brain during mental activity than during rest. Unfortunately we cannot do this directly, but can only gauge the amount of PO_5 in the urine, and this procedure has been adopted by a variety of observers, some of whom found the phosphates in the urine diminished, whilst others found them increased, by intellectual work. On the whole, it is impossible to trace any constant relation. In maniacal excitement less phosphorus than usual seems to be excreted. More is excreted during sleep. The fact that phosphorus-preparations may do good in nervous exhaustion proves nothing as to the part played by phosphorus in mental activity. Like iron, arsenic, and other remedies it is a stimulant or tonic, of whose intimate workings in the system we know absolutely nothing, and which moreover does good in an extremely small number of the cases in which it is prescribed.

The phosphorus-philosophers have often compared thought to a secretion. "The brain secretes thought, as the kidneys secrete urine, or as the liver secretes bile," are phrases which one sometimes hears. The lame analogy need hardly be pointed out. The materials which the brain *pours into the blood* (cholesterin, creatin, xanthin, or whatever they may be) are the analogues of the urine and the bile, being in fact real material excreta. As far as these matters go, the brain is a ductless gland. But we know of nothing connected with liver- and kidney-activity which can be in the remotest degree compared with the stream of thought that accompanies the brain's material secretions.

Chapter X

Habit

Its Importance for Psychology.—There remains a condition of general neural activity so important as to deserve a chapter by itself—I refer to the aptitude of the nerve-centres, especially of the hemispheres, for acquiring habits. *An acquired habit, from the physiological point of view, is nothing but a new pathway of discharge formed in the brain, by which certain incoming currents ever after tend to escape.* That is the thesis of this chapter; and we shall see in the later and more psychological chapters that such functions as the association of ideas, perception, memory, reasoning, the education of the will, etc. etc., can best be understood as results of the formation *de novo* of just such pathways of discharge.

Habit has a physical basis. The moment one tries to define what habit is, one is led to the fundamental properties of matter. The laws of Nature are nothing but the immutable habits which the different elementary sorts of matter follow in their actions and reactions upon each other. In the organic world, however, the habits are more variable than this. Even instincts vary from one individual to another of a kind; and are modified in the same individual, as we shall later see, to suit the exigencies of the case. On the principles of the atomistic philosophy the habits of an elementary particle of matter cannot change, because the particle is itself an unchangeable thing; but those of a compound mass of matter can change, because they are in the last instance due to the structure of the compound, and either outward forces or inward tensions can, from one hour to another, turn that structure into something different from what it was. That is, they can do so if the body be plastic enough to maintain its integrity, and be not disrupted when its structure yields. The change of structure here spoken of need not involve the outward shape; it may be invisible and molecular, as when a bar of iron becomes magnetic or crystalline through the action of certain outward causes, or india-rubber becomes friable, or plaster 'sets.' All these changes are rather slow; the material in question opposes a certain resistance to the modifying cause, which it takes time to overcome, but the gradual yielding whereof often saves the material from being disintegrated altogether. When the structure has yielded, the same inertia becomes a condition of its comparative permanence in the new form, and of the new habits the body then manifests. *Plasticity*, then, in the wide sense of the word, means the possession of a structure weak enough to yield to an influence, but strong enough not to yield all at once. Each relatively stable phase of equilibrium in such a structure is marked by what we may call a new set of habits. Organic matter, especially nervous tissue, seems endowed with a very extraordinary degree of plasticity of this sort; so that we may without hesitation lay down as our first proposition the following: that *the phenomena of habit in living beings are due to the plasticity of the organic materials of which their bodies are composed.*

The philosophy of habit is thus, in the first instance, a chapter in physics rather than in physiology or psychology. That it is at bottom a physical principle is admitted by all good recent writers on the subject. They call attention to analogues of acquired habits exhibited by dead matter. Thus, M. Léon Dumont writes:

"Everyone knows how a garment, after having been worn a certain time, clings to the shape of the body better than when it was new; there has been a change in the tissue, and this change is a new habit of cohesion. A lock works better after being used some time; at the outset more force was required to overcome certain roughnesses in the mechanism. The overcoming of their resistance is a phenomenon of habituation. It costs less trouble to fold a paper when it has been folded already; . . . and just so the impressions of outer objects fashion for themselves in the nervous system more and more appropriate paths, and these vital phenomena recur under similar excitements from without, when they have been interrupted a certain time."

Not in the nervous system alone. A scar anywhere is a *locus minoris resistentiæ*, more liable to be abraded, inflamed, to suffer pain and cold, than are the neighboring parts. A sprained ankle, a dislocated arm, are in danger of being sprained or dislocated again; joints that have once been attacked by rheumatism or gout, mucous membranes that have been the seat of catarrh, are with each fresh recurrence more prone to a relapse, until often the morbid state chronically substitutes itself for the sound one. And in the nervous system itself it is well known how many so-called functional diseases seem to keep themselves going simply because they happen to have once begun; and how the forcible cutting short by medicine of a few attacks is often sufficient to enable the physiological forces to get possession of the field again, and to bring the organs back to functions of health. Epilepsies, neuralgias, convulsive affections of various sorts, insomnias, are so many cases in point. And, to take what are more obviously habits, the success with which a 'weaning' treatment can often be applied to the victims of unhealthy indulgence of passion, or of mere complaining or irascible disposition, shows us how much the morbid manifestations themselves were due to the mere inertia of the nervous organs, when once launched on a false career.

Habits are due to pathways through the nerve-centres. If habits are due to the plasticity of materials to outward agents, we can immediately see to what outward influences, if to any, the brain-matter is plastic. Not to mechanical pressures, not to thermal changes, not to any of the forces to which all the other organs of our body are exposed; for, as we saw on p. 15, Nature has so blanketed and wrapped the brain about that the only impressions that can be made upon it are through the blood, on the one hand, and the sensory nerve-roots, on the other; and it is to the infinitely attenuated currents that pour in through these latter channels that the hemispherical cortex shows itself to be so peculiarly susceptible. The currents, once in, must find a way out. In getting out they leave their traces in the paths which they take. The only thing they *can* do, in short, is to deepen old paths or to make new ones; and the whole plasticity of the brain sums itself up in two words when we call it an organ in which currents pouring in from the sense-organs make with extreme facility paths which do not easily disappear. For, of course, a simple habit, like every other nervous event—the habit of snuffling, for example, or of putting one's hands into one's pockets, or of biting one's nails—is, mechanically, nothing but a reflex discharge; and its anatomical substratum must be a path in the system. The most complex habits, as we shall presently see more fully, are, from the same point of view, nothing but *concatenated* discharges in the nerve-centres, due to the presence there of systems of reflex paths, so organized as to wake each other up successively—the impression produced by one muscular contraction serving as a stimulus to provoke the next, until a final impression inhibits the process and closes the chain.

It must be noticed that the growth of structural modification in living matter may be more rapid than in any lifeless mass, because the incessant nutritive renovation of which the living matter is the seat tends often to corroborate and fix the impressed modification, rather than to counteract it by renewing the original constitution of the tissue that has been impressed. Thus, we notice after exercising our muscles or our brain in a new way, that we can do so no longer at that time; but after a day or two of rest, when we resume the discipline, our increase in skill not seldom surprises us. I have often noticed this in learning a tune; and it has led a German author to say that we learn to swim during the winter, and to skate during the summer.

Practical Effects of Habit.—First, habit simplifies our movements, makes them accurate, and diminishes fatigue.

Man is born with a tendency to do more things than he has ready-made arrangements for in his nerve-centres. Most of the performances of other animals are automatic. But in him the number of them is so enormous that most of them must be the fruit of painful study. If practice did not make perfect, nor habit economize the expense of nervous and muscular energy, he would be in a sorry plight. As Dr. Maudsley says:[1]

"If an act became no easier after being done several times, if the careful direction of consciousness were necessary to its accomplishment on each occasion, it is evident that the whole activity of a lifetime might be confined to one or two deeds—that no progress could take place in development. A man might be occupied all day in dressing and undressing himself; the attitude of his body would absorb all his attention and energy; the washing of his hands or the fastening of a button would be as difficult to him on

[1] *The Physiology of Mind*, p. 154.

each occasion as to the child on its first trial; and he would furthermore be completely exhausted by his exertions. Think of the pains necessary to teach a child to stand, of the many efforts which it must make, and of the ease with which it at last stands, unconscious even of an effort. For while secondary automatic acts are accomplished with comparatively little weariness—in this regard approaching the organic movements, or the original reflex movements—the conscious efforts of the will soon produce exhaustion. A spinal cord without . . . memory would simply be an idiotic spinal cord . . . . It is impossible for an individual to realise how much he owes to its automatic agency until disease has impaired its functions."

Secondly, *habit diminishes the conscious attention with which our acts are performed.*

One may state this abstractly thus: If an act require for its execution a chain, A,B,C,D,E,F,G, etc., of successive nervous events, then in the first performances of the action the conscious will must choose each of these events from a number of wrong alternatives that tend to present themselves; but habit soon brings it about that each event calls up its own appropriate successor without any alternative offering itself, and without any reference to the conscious will, until at last the whole chain, A,B,C,D,E,F,G, rattles itself off as soon as A occurs, just as if A and the rest of the chain were fused into a continuous stream. Whilst we are learning to walk, to ride, to swim, skate, fence, write, play, or sing, we interrupt ourselves at every step by unnecessary movements and false notes. When we are proficients, on the contrary, the results follow not only with the very minimum of muscular action requisite to bring them forth, but they follow from a single instantaneous 'cue.' The marksman sees the bird, and, before he knows it, he has aimed and shot. A gleam in his adversary's eye, a momentary pressure from his rapier, and the fencer finds that he has instantly made the right parry and return. A glance at the musical hieroglyphics, and the pianist's fingers have rippled through a shower of notes. And not only is it the right thing at the right time that we thus involuntarily do, but the wrong thing also, if it be an habitual thing. Who is there that has never wound up his watch on taking off his waistcoat in the daytime, or taken his latch-key out on arriving at the door-step of a friend? Persons in going to their bedroom to dress for dinner have been known to take off one garment after another and finally to get into bed, merely because that was the habitual issue of the first few movements when performed at a later hour. We all have a definite routine manner of performing certain daily offices connected with the toilet, with the opening and shutting of familiar cupboards, and the like. But our higher thought-centres know hardly anything about the matter. Few men can tell off-hand which sock, shoe, or trousers-leg they put on first. They must first mentally rehearse the act; and even that is often insufficient—the act must be *performed*. So of the questions, Which valve of the shutters opens first? Which way does my door swing? etc. I cannot *tell* the answer; yet my *hand* never makes a mistake. No one can *describe* the order in which he brushes his hair or teeth; yet it is likely that the order is a pretty fixed one in all of us.

These results may be expressed as follows:

In action grown habitual, what instigates each new muscular contraction to take place in its appointed order is not a thought or a perception, but the *sensation occasioned by the muscular contraction just finished*. A strictly voluntary act has to be guided by idea, perception, and volition, throughout its whole course. In habitual action, mere sensation is a sufficient guide, and the upper regions of brain and mind are set comparatively free. A diagram will make the matter clear:

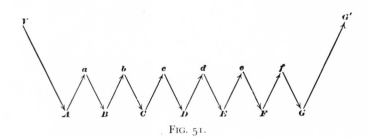

FIG. 51.

Let *A,B,C,D,E,F,G* represent an habitual chain of muscular contractions, and let *a,b,c,d,e,f* stand for the several sensations which these contractions excite in us when they are successively performed. Such sensations will usually be in the parts moved, but they may also be effects of the movement upon the eye or the ear. Through them, and through them alone, we are made aware whether or not the contraction has occurred. When the series, *A,B,C,D,E,F,G*, is being learned, each of these sensations becomes the object of a separate act of attention by the mind. We test each movement intellectually, to see if it have been rightly performed, before advancing to the next. We hesitate, compare, choose, revoke, reject, etc.; and the order by which the next movement is discharged is an express order from the ideational centres after this deliberation has been gone through.

In habitual action, on the contrary, the only impulse which the intellectual centres need send down is that which carries the command to *start*. This is represented in the diagram by V; it may be a thought of the first movement or of the last result, or a mere perception of some of the habitual conditions of the chain, the presence, e.g., of the keyboard near the hand. In the present example, no sooner has this conscious thought or volition instigated movement A, than A, through the sensation a of its own occurrence, awakens B reflexly; B then excites C through b, and so on till the chain is ended, when the intellect generally takes cognizance of the final result. The intellectual perception at the end is indicated in the diagram by the sensible effect of the movement G being represented at G', in the ideational centres above the merely sensational line. The sensational impressions, a,b,c,d,e,f, are all supposed to have their seat below the ideational level.

Habits depend on sensations not attended to. We have called a,b,c,d,e,f by the name of 'sensations.' If sensations, they are sensations to which we are usually inattentive; but that they are more than unconscious nerve-currents seems certain, for they catch our attention if they go wrong. Schneider's account of these sensations deserves to be quoted. In the act of walking, he says, even when our attention is entirely absorbed elsewhere, "it is doubtful whether we could preserve equilibrium if no sensation of our body's attitude were there, and doubtful whether we should advance our leg if we had no sensation of its movement as executed, and not even a minimal feeling of impulse to set it down. Knitting appears altogether mechanical, and the knitter keeps up her knitting even while she reads or is engaged in lively talk. But if we ask her how this is possible, she will hardly reply that the knitting goes on of itself. She will rather say that she has a feeling of it, that she feels in her hands that she knits and how she must knit, and that therefore the movements of knitting are called forth and regulated by the sensations associated therewith, even when the attention is called away. . . ." Again: "When a pupil begins to play on the violin, to keep him from raising his right elbow in playing a book is placed under his right armpit, which he is ordered to hold fast by keeping the upper arm tight against his body. The muscular feelings, and feelings of contact connected with the book, provoke an impulse to press it tight. But often it happens that the beginner, whose attention gets absorbed in the production of the notes, lets drop the book. Later, however, this never happens; the faintest sensations of contact suffice to awaken the impulse to keep it in its place, and the attention may be wholly absorbed by the notes and the fingering with the left hand. *The simultaneous combination of movements is thus in the first instance conditioned by the facility with which in us, alongside of intellectual processes, processes of inattentive feeling may still go on.*"

Ethical and Pedagogical Importance of the Principle of Habit.—"Habit a second nature! Habit is ten times nature," the Duke of Wellington is said to have exclaimed; and the degree to which this is true no one probably can appreciate as well as one who is a veteran soldier himself. The daily drill and the years of discipline end by fashioning a man completely over again, as to most of the possibilities of his conduct.

"There is a story," says Prof. Huxley, "which is credible enough, though it may not be true, of a practical joker, who, seeing a discharged veteran carrying home his dinner, suddenly called out 'Attention!' whereupon the man instantly brought his hands down, and lost his mutton and potatoes in the gutter. The drill had been thorough, and its effects had become embodied in the man's nervous structure."

Riderless cavalry-horses, at many a battle, have been seen to come together and go through their customary evolutions at the sound of the bugle-call. Most domestic beasts seem machines almost pure and simple, undoubtingly, unhesitatingly doing from minute to minute the duties they have been taught, and giving no sign that the possibility of an alternative ever suggests itself to their mind. Men grown old in prison have asked to be readmitted after being once set free. In a railroad accident a menagerie-tiger, whose cage had broken open, is said to have emerged, but presently crept back again, as if too much bewildered by his new responsibilities, so that he was without difficulty secured.

Habit is thus the enormous fly-wheel of society, its most precious conservative agent. It alone is what keeps us all within the bounds of ordinance, and saves the children of fortune from the envious uprisings of the poor. It alone prevents the hardest and most repulsive walks of life from being deserted by those brought up to tread therein. It keeps the fisherman and the deck-hand at sea through the winter; it holds the miner in his darkness, and nails the countryman to his log-cabin and his lonely farm through all the months of snow; it protects us from invasion by the natives of the desert and the frozen zone. It dooms us all to fight out the battle of life upon the lines of our nurture or our early choice, and to make the best of a pursuit that disagrees, because there is no other for which we are fitted, and it is too late to begin again. It keeps different social strata from mixing. Already at the age of twenty-five you see the professional mannerism settling down on the young commercial traveller, on the young doctor, on the young minister, on the young counsellor-at-law. You see the little lines of cleavage running through the character, the tricks of thought, the prejudices, the ways of the 'shop,' in a word, from which the man can by-and-by no more escape than his coat-sleeve can suddenly fall into a new set of folds. On the whole, it is best he should not escape. It is well for the world that in most of us, by the age of thirty, the character has set like plaster, and will never soften again.

If the period between twenty and thirty is the critical one in the formation of intellectual and professional habits, the period below twenty is more important still for the fixing of *personal* habits, properly so called, such as vocalization and pronunciation, gesture, motion, and address. Hardly ever is a language learned after twenty spoken without a foreign accent; hardly ever can a youth transferred to the society of his betters unlearn the nasality and other vices of speech bred in him by the associations of his growing years. Hardly ever, indeed, no matter how much money there be in his pocket, can he even learn to *dress* like a gentleman-born. The merchants offer their wares as eagerly to him as to the veriest 'swell,' but he simply *cannot* buy the right things. An invisible law, as strong as gravitation, keeps him within his orbit, arrayed this year as he was the last; and how his better-clad acquaintances contrive to get the things they wear will be for him a mystery till his dying day.

The great thing, then, in all education, is to *make our nervous system our ally instead of our enemy*. It is to fund and capitalize our acquisitions, and live at ease upon the interest of the fund. *For this we must make automatic and habitual, as early as possible, as many useful actions as we can,* and guard against the growing into ways that are likely to be disadvantageous to us, as we should guard against the plague. The more of the details of our daily life we can hand over to the effortless custody of automatism, the more our higher powers of mind will be set free for their own proper work. There is no more miserable human being than one in whom nothing is habitual but indecision, and for whom the lighting of every cigar, the drinking of every cup, the time of rising and going to bed every day, and the beginning of every bit of work, are subjects of express volitional deliberation. Full half the time of such a man goes to the deciding, or regretting, of matters which ought to be so ingrained in him as practically not to exist for his consciousness at all. If there be such daily duties not yet ingrained in any one of my readers, let him begin this very hour to set the matter right.

In Professor Bain's chapter on "The Moral Habits" there are some admirable practical remarks laid down. Two great maxims emerge from his treatment. The first is that in the acquisition of a new habit, or the leaving off of an old one, we must take care to *launch ourselves with as strong and decided an initiative as possible.* Accumulate all the possible circumstances which shall re-enforce the right motives; put yourself assiduously in conditions that encourage the new way; make engagements incompatible with the old; take a public pledge, if the case allows; in short, envelop your resolution with every aid you know. This will give your new beginning such a momentum that the temptation to break down will not occur as soon as it otherwise might; and every day during which a breakdown is postponed adds to the chances of its not occurring at all.

The second maxim is: *Never suffer an exception to occur till the new habit is securely rooted in your life.* Each lapse is like the letting fall of a ball of string which one is carefully winding up; a single slip undoes more than a great many turns will wind again. *Continuity* of training is the great means of making the nervous system act infallibly right. As Professor Bain says:

"The peculiarity of the moral habits, contra-distinguishing them from the intellectual acquisitions, is the presence of two hostile powers, one to be gradually raised into the ascendant over the other. It is necessary, above all things, in such a situation, never to lose a battle. Every gain on the wrong side undoes the effect of many conquests on the right. The essential precaution, therefore, is, so to regulate the two opposing powers that the one may have a series of uninterrupted successes, until repetition has fortified it to such a degree as to enable it to cope with the opposition, under any circumstances. This is the theoretically best career of mental progress."

The need of securing success at the *outset* is imperative. Failure at first is apt to damp the energy of all future attempts, whereas past experiences of success nerve one to future vigor. Goethe says to a man who consulted him about an enterprise but mistrusted his own powers: "Ach! you need only blow on your hands!" And the remark illustrates the effect on Goethe's spirits of his own habitually successful career.

The question of 'tapering-off,' in abandoning such habits as drink and opium-indulgence, comes in here, and is a question about which experts differ within certain limits, and in regard to what may be best for an individual case. In the main, however, all expert opinion would agree that abrupt acquisition of the new habit is the best way, *if there be a real possibility of carrying it out.* We must be careful not to give the will so stiff a task as to insure its defeat at the very outset; but, *provided one can stand it,* a sharp period of suffering, and then a free time, is the best thing to aim at, whether in giving up a habit like that of opium, or in simply changing one's hours of rising or of work. It is surprising how soon a desire will die of inanition if it be *never* fed.

"One must first learn, unmoved, looking neither to the right nor left, to walk firmly on the straight and narrow path, before one can begin 'to make one's self over again.' He who every day makes a fresh resolve is like one who, arriving at the edge of the ditch he is to leap, forever stops and returns for a fresh run. Without *unbroken* advance there is no such thing as *accumulation* of the ethical forces possible, and to make this possible, and to exercise us and habituate us in it, is the sovereign blessing of regular work."[2]

A third maxim may be added to the preceding pair: *Seize the very first possible opportunity to act on every resolution you make, and on every emotional prompting you may experience in the direction of the habits*

---

[2] J. Bahnsen: *Beiträge zur Charakterologie* (1867), vol. I, p. 209.

you aspire to gain. It is not in the moment of their forming, but in the moment of their producing *motor effects*, that resolves and aspirations communicate the new 'set' to the brain. As the author last quoted remarks:

"The actual presence of the practical opportunity alone furnishes the fulcrum upon which the lever can rest, by means of which the moral will may multiply its strength, and raise itself aloft. He who has no solid ground to press against will never get beyond the stage of empty gesture-making."

No matter how full a reservoir of *maxims* one may possess, and no matter how good one's *sentiments* may be, if one have not taken advantage of every concrete opportunity to *act*, one's character may remain entirely unaffected for the better. With mere good intentions, hell is proverbially paved. And this is an obvious consequence of the principles we have laid down. A 'character,' as J. S. Mill says, 'is a completely fashioned will'; and a will, in the sense in which he means it, is an aggregate of tendencies to act in a firm and prompt and definite way upon all the principal emergencies of life. A tendency to act only becomes effectively ingrained in us in proportion to the uninterrupted frequency with which the actions actually occur, and the brain 'grows' to their use. When a resolve or a fine glow of feeling is allowed to evaporate without bearing practical fruit it is worse than a chance lost; it works so as positively to hinder future resolutions and emotions from taking the normal path of discharge. There is no more contemptible type of human character than that of the nerveless sentimentalist and dreamer, who spends his life in a weltering sea of sensibility and emotion, but who never does a manly concrete deed. Rousseau, inflaming all the mothers of France, by his eloquence, to follow Nature and nurse their babies themselves, while he sends his own children to the foundling hospital, is the classical example of what I mean. But every one of us in his measure, whenever, after glowing for an abstractly formulated Good, he practically ignores some actual case, among the squalid 'other particulars' of which that same Good lurks disguised, treads straight on Rousseau's path. All Goods are disguised by the vulgarity of their concomitants, in this work-a-day world; but woe to him who can only recognize them when he thinks them in their pure and abstract form! The habit of excessive novel-reading and theatre-going will produce true monsters in this line. The weeping of the Russian lady over the fictitious personages in the play, while her coachman is freezing to death on his seat outside, is the sort of thing that everywhere happens on a less glaring scale. Even the habit of excessive indulgence in music, for those who are neither performers themselves nor musically gifted enough to take it in a purely intellectual way, has probably a relaxing effect upon the character. One becomes filled with emotions which habitually pass without prompting to any deed, and so the inertly sentimental condition is kept up. The remedy would be, never to suffer one's self to have an emotion at a concert, without expressing it afterwards in *some* active way. Let the expression be the least thing in the world—speaking genially to one's grandmother, or giving up one's seat in a horse-car, if nothing more heroic offers—but let it not fail to take place.

These latter cases make us aware that it is not simply *particular lines* of discharge, but also *general forms* of discharge, that seem to be grooved out by habit in the brain. Just as, if we let our emotions evaporate, they get into a way of evaporating; so there is reason to suppose that if we often flinch from making an effort, before we know it the effort-making capacity will be gone; and that, if we suffer the wandering of our attention, presently it will wander all the time. Attention and effort are, as we shall see later, but two names for the same psychic fact. To what brain-processes they correspond we do not know. The strongest reason for believing that they do depend on brain-processes at all, and are not pure acts of the spirit, is just this fact, that they seem in some degree subject to the law of habit, which is a material law. As a final practical maxim, relative to these habits of the will, we may, then, offer something like this: *Keep the faculty of effort alive in you by a little gratuitous exercise every day.* That is, be systematically ascetic or heroic in little unnecessary points, do every day or two something for no other reason than that you would rather not do it, so that when the hour of dire need draws nigh, it may find you not unnerved and untrained to stand the test. Asceticism of this sort is like the insurance which a man pays on his house and goods. The tax does him no good at the time, and possibly may never bring him a return. But if the fire *does* come, his having paid it will be his salvation from ruin. So with the man who has daily inured himself to habits of concentrated attention, energetic volition, and self-denial in unnecessary things. He will stand like a tower when everything rocks around him, and when his softer fellow-mortals are winnowed like chaff in the blast.

The physiological study of mental conditions is thus the most powerful ally of hortatory ethics. The hell to be endured hereafter, of which theology tells, is no worse than the hell we make for ourselves in this world by habitually fashioning our characters in the wrong way. Could the young but realize how soon they will become mere walking bundles of habits, they would give more heed to their conduct while in the plastic state. We are spinning our own fates, good or evil, and never to be undone. Every smallest stroke of virtue or of vice leaves its never so little scar. The drunken Rip Van Winkle, in Jefferson's play, excuses himself for every fresh dereliction by saying, 'I won't count this time!' Well! he may not count it, and a kind Heaven may not count it; but it is being counted none the less. Down among his nerve-cells and fibres the molecules are counting it, registering and storing it up to be used against him when the next temptation comes. Nothing we ever do is, in strict scientific literalness, wiped out. Of course this has its good side as well as its bad one. As we become permanent drunkards by so many separate drinks, so we become saints in the moral, and authorities and experts in the practical and scientific spheres, by so many separate acts and hours of work. Let no youth have any anxiety about the upshot of his education, whatever the line of it may be. If he keep faithfully busy each hour of the working day, he may safely leave the final result to itself. He can with perfect certainty count on waking up some fine morning, to find himself one of the competent ones of his generation, in whatever pursuit he may have singled out. Silently, between all the details of his business, the *power of judging* in all that class of matter will have built itself up within him as a possession that will never pass away. Young people should know this truth in advance. The ignorance of it has probably engendered more discouragement and faint-heartedness in youths embarking on arduous careers than all other causes put together.

Chapter XI

The Stream of Consciousness

The order of our study must be analytic. We are now prepared to begin the introspective study of the adult consciousness itself. Most books adopt the so-called synthetic method. Starting with 'simple ideas of sensation,' and regarding these as so many atoms, they proceed to build up the higher states of mind out of their 'association,' 'integration,' or 'fusion,' as houses are built by the agglutination of bricks. This has the didactic advantages which the synthetic method usually has. But it commits one beforehand to the very questionable theory that our higher states of consciousness are compounds of units; and instead of starting with what the reader directly knows, namely his total concrete states of mind, it starts with a set of supposed 'simple ideas' with which he has no immediate acquaintance at all, and concerning whose alleged interactions he is much at the mercy of any plausible phrase. On every ground, then, the method of advancing from the simple to the compound exposes us to illusion. All pedants and abstractionists will naturally hate to abandon it. But a student who loves the fulness of human nature will prefer to follow the 'analytic' method, and to begin with the most concrete facts, those with which he has a daily acquaintance in his own inner life. The analytic method will discover in due time the elementary parts, if such exist, without danger of precipitate assumption. The reader will bear in mind that our own chapters on sensation have dealt mainly with the physiological conditions thereof. They were put first as a mere matter of convenience, because incoming currents come first. *Psychologically* they might better have come last. Pure sensations were described on page 18 as processes which in adult life are well-nigh unknown, and nothing was said which could for a moment lead the reader to suppose that they were the *elements of composition* of the higher states of mind.

The Fundamental Fact.—The first and foremost concrete fact which everyone will affirm to belong to his inner experience is the fact that *consciousness of some sort goes on. 'States of mind' succeed each other in him.* If we could say in English 'it thinks,' as we say 'it rains' or 'it blows,' we should be stating the fact most simply and with the minimum of assumption. As we cannot, we must simply say that *thought goes on.*

Four Characters in Consciousness.—How does it go on? We notice immediately four important characters in the process, of which it shall be the duty of the present chapter to treat in a general way:

1) Every 'state' tends to be part of a personal consciousness.

2) Within each personal consciousness states are always changing.

3) Each personal consciousness is sensibly continuous.

4) It is interested in some parts of its object to the exclusion of others, and welcomes or rejects—*chooses* from among them, in a word—all the while.

In considering these four points successively, we shall have to plunge *in medias res* as regards our nomenclature and use psychological terms which can only be adequately defined in later chapters of the book. But everyone knows what the terms mean in a rough way; and it is only in a rough way that we are now to take them. This chapter is like a painter's first charcoal sketch upon his canvas, in which no niceties appear.

When I say *every 'state' or 'thought' is part of a personal consciousness,* 'personal consciousness' is one of the terms in question. Its meaning we know so long as no one asks us to define it, but to give an accurate account of it is the most difficult of philosophic tasks. This task we must confront in the next chapter; here a preliminary word will suffice.

In this room—this lecture-room, say—there are a multitude of thoughts, yours and mine, some of which cohere mutually, and some not. They are as little each-for-itself and reciprocally independent as they are all-belonging-together. They are neither: no one of them is separate, but each belongs with certain others and with none beside. My thought belongs with *my* other thoughts, and your thought with *your* other thoughts. Whether anywhere in the room there be a *mere* thought, which is nobody's thought, we have no means of ascertaining, for we have no experience of its like. The only states of consciousness that we naturally deal with are found in personal consciousnesses, minds, selves, concrete particular I's and you's.

Each of these minds keeps its own thoughts to itself. There is no giving or bartering between them. No thought even comes into direct *sight* of a thought in another personal consciousness than its own. Absolute insulation, irreducible pluralism, is the law. It seems as if the elementary psychic fact were not *thought* or *this thought* or *that thought*, but *my thought*, every thought being *owned*. Neither contemporaneity, nor proximity in space, nor similarity of quality and content are able to fuse thoughts together which are sundered by this barrier of belonging to different personal minds. The breaches between such thoughts are the most absolute breaches in nature. Everyone will recognize this to be true, so long as the existence of *something* corresponding to the term 'personal mind' is all that is insisted on, without any particular view of its nature being implied. On these terms the personal self rather than the thought might be treated as the immediate datum in psychology. The universal conscious fact is not 'feelings and thoughts exist,' but 'I think' and 'I feel.' No psychology, at any rate, can question the *existence* of personal selves. Thoughts connected as we feel them to be connected are *what we mean* by personal selves. The worst a psychology can do is so to interpret the nature of these selves as to rob them of their *worth*.

Consciousness is in constant change. I do not mean by this to say that no one state of mind has any duration—even if true, that would be hard to establish. What I wish to lay stress on is this, that *no state once gone can recur and be identical with what it was before.* Now we are seeing, now hearing; now reasoning, now willing; now recollecting, now expecting; now loving, now hating; and in a hundred other ways we know our minds to be alternately engaged. But all these are complex states, it may be said, produced by combination of simpler ones;—do not the simpler ones follow a different law? Are not the *sensations* which we get from the same object, for example, always the same? Does not the same piano-key, struck with the same force, make us hear in the same way? Does not the same grass give us the same feeling of green, the same sky the same feeling of blue, and do we not get the same olfactory sensation no matter how many times we put our nose to the same flask of cologne? It seems a piece of metaphysical sophistry to suggest that we do not; and yet a close attention to the matter shows that *there is no proof that an incoming current ever gives us just the same bodily sensation twice.*

What is got twice is the same OBJECT. We hear the same *note* over and over again; we see the same *quality* of green, or smell the same objective perfume, or experience the same *species* of pain. The realities, concrete and abstract, physical and ideal, whose permanent existence we believe in, seem to be constantly coming up again before our thought, and lead us, in our carelessness, to suppose that our 'ideas' of them are the same ideas. When we come, some time later, to the chapter on Perception, we shall see how inveterate is our habit of simply using our sensible impressions as stepping-stones to pass over to the recognition of the realities whose presence they reveal. The grass out of the window now looks to me of the same green in the sun as in the shade, and yet a painter would have to paint one part of it dark brown, another part bright yellow, to give its real sensational effect. We take no heed, as a rule, of the different way in which the same things look and sound and smell at different distances and under different circumstances. The sameness of the *things* is what we are concerned to ascertain; and any sensations that assure us of that will probably be considered in a rough way to be the same with each other. This is what makes off-hand testimony about the subjective identity of different sensations well-nigh worthless as a proof of the fact. The entire history of what is called Sensation is a commentary on our inability to tell whether two sensible qualities received apart are exactly alike. What appeals to our attention far more than the absolute quality of an impression is its *ratio* to whatever other impressions we may have at the same time. When everything is dark a somewhat less dark sensation makes us see an object white. Helmholtz calculates that the white marble painted in a picture representing an architectural view by moonlight is, when seen by daylight, from ten to twenty thousand times brighter than the real moonlit marble would be, yet the latter looks white.

Such a difference as this could never have been *sensibly* learned; it had to be inferred from a series of indirect considerations. These make us believe that our sensibility is altering all the time, so that the same object cannot easily give us the same sensation over again. We feel things differently accordingly as we are sleepy or awake, hungry or full, fresh or tired; differently at night and in the morning, differently in summer and in winter; and above all, differently in childhood, manhood, and old age. And yet we never doubt that our feelings reveal the same world, with the same sensible qualities and the same sensible things occupying it. The difference of the sensibility is shown best by the difference of our emotion about the things from one age to another, or when we are in different organic moods. What was bright and exciting becomes weary, flat, and unprofitable. The bird's song is tedious, the breeze is mournful, the sky is sad.

To these indirect presumptions that our sensations, following the mutations of our capacity for feeling, are always undergoing an essential change, must be added another presumption, based on what must happen in the brain. Every sensation corresponds to some cerebral action. For an identical sensation to recur it would have to occur the second time *in an unmodified brain.* But as this, strictly speaking, is a physiological impossibility, so is an unmodified feeling an impossibility; for to every brain-modification, however small, we suppose that there must correspond a change of equal amount in the consciousness which the brain subserves.

But if the assumption of 'simple sensations' recurring in immutable shape is so easily shown to be baseless, how much more baseless is the assumption of immutability in the larger masses of our thought!

For there it is obvious and palpable that our state of mind is never precisely the same. Every thought we have of a given fact is, strictly speaking, unique, and only bears a resemblance of kind with our other thoughts of the same fact. When the identical fact recurs, we *must* think of it in a fresh manner, see it under a somewhat different angle, apprehend it in different relations from those in which it last appeared. And the thought by which we cognize it is the thought of it-in-those-relations, a thought suffused with the consciousness of all that dim context. Often we are ourselves struck at the strange differences in our successive views of the same thing. We wonder how we ever could have opined as we did last month about a certain matter. We have outgrown the possibility of that state of mind, we know not how. From one year to another we see things in new lights. What was unreal has grown real, and what was exciting is insipid. The friends we used to care the world for are shrunken to shadows; the women once so divine, the stars, the woods, and the waters, how now so dull and common!—the young girls that brought an aura of infinity, at present hardly distinguishable existences; the pictures so empty; and as for the books, what *was* there to find so mysteriously significant in Goethe, or in John Mill so full of weight? Instead of all this, more zestful than ever is the work, the work; and fuller and deeper the import of common duties and of common goods.

I am sure that this concrete and total manner of regarding the mind's changes is the only true manner, difficult as it may be to carry it out in detail. If anything seems obscure about it, it will grow clearer as we advance. Meanwhile, if it be true, it is certainly also true that no two 'ideas' are ever exactly the same, which is the proposition we started to prove. The proposition is more important theoretically than it at first sight seems. For it makes it already impossible for us to follow obediently in the footprints of either the Lockian or the Herbartian school, schools which have had almost unlimited influence in Germany and among ourselves. No doubt it is often *convenient* to formulate the mental facts in an atomistic sort of way, and to treat the higher states of consciousness as if they were all built out of unchanging simple ideas which 'pass and turn again.' It is convenient often to treat curves as if they were composed of small straight lines, and electricity and nerve-force as if they were fluids. But in the one case as in the other we must never forget that we are talking symbolically, and that there is nothing in nature to answer to our words. *A permanently existing 'Idea' which makes its appearance before the footlights of consciousness at periodical intervals is as mythological an entity as the Jack of Spades.*

Within each personal consciousness, thought is sensibly continuous. I can only define 'continuous' as that which is without breach, crack, or division. The only breaches that can well be conceived to occur within the limits of a single mind would either be *interruptions*, *time*-gaps during which the consciousness went out; or they would be breaks in the content of the thought, so abrupt that what followed had no connection whatever with what went before. The proposition that consciousness feels continuous, means two things:

a. That even where there is a time-gap the consciousness after it feels as if it belonged together with the consciousness before it, as another part of the same self;

b. That the changes from one moment to another in the quality of the consciousness are never absolutely abrupt.

The case of the time-gaps, as the simplest, shall be taken first.

a. When Paul and Peter wake up in the same bed, and recognize that they have been asleep, each one of them mentally reaches back and makes connection with but *one* of the two streams of thought which were broken by the sleeping hours. As the current of an electrode buried in the ground unerringly finds its way to its own similarly buried mate, across no matter how much intervening earth; so Peter's present instantly finds out Peter's past, and never by mistake knits itself on to that of Paul. Paul's thought in turn is as little liable to go astray. The past thought of Peter is appropriated by the present Peter alone. He may have a *knowledge*, and a correct one too, of what Paul's last drowsy states of mind were as he sank into sleep, but it is an entirely different sort of knowledge from that which he has of his own last states. He *remembers* his own states, whilst he only *conceives* Paul's. Remembrance is like direct feeling; its object is suffused with a warmth and intimacy to which no object of mere conception ever attains. This quality of warmth and intimacy and immediacy is what Peter's *present* thought also possesses for itself. So sure as this present is me, is mine, it says, so sure is anything else that comes with the same warmth and intimacy and immediacy, me and mine. What the qualities called warmth and intimacy may in themselves be will have to be matter for future consideration. But whatever past states appear with those qualities must be admitted to receive the greeting of the present mental state, to be owned by it, and accepted as belonging together with it in a common self. This community of self is what the time-gap cannot break in twain, and is why a present thought, although not ignorant of the time-gap, can still regard itself as continuous with certain chosen portions of the past.

Consciousness, then, does not appear to itself chopped up in bits. Such words as 'chain' or 'train' do not describe it fitly as it presents itself in the first instance. It is nothing jointed; it flows. A 'river' or a 'stream' are the metaphors by which it is most naturally described. *In talking of it hereafter, let us call it the stream of thought, of consciousness, or of subjective life.*

b. But now there appears, even within the limits of the same self, and between thoughts all of which alike have this same sense of belonging together, a kind of jointing and separateness among the parts, of which this statement seems to take no account. I refer to the breaks that are produced by sudden *contrasts in the quality* of the successive segments of the stream of thought. If the words 'chain' and 'train' had no natural fitness in them, how came such words to be used at all? Does not a loud explosion rend the consciousness upon which it abruptly breaks, in twain? No; for even into our awareness of the thunder the awareness of the previous silence creeps and continues; for what we hear when the thunder crashes is not thunder *pure*, but thunder-breaking-upon-silence-and-contrasting-with-it. Our feeling of the same objective thunder, coming in this way, is quite different from what it would be were the thunder a continuation of previous thunder. The thunder itself we believe to abolish and exclude the silence; but the *feeling* of the thunder is also a feeling of the silence as just gone; and it would be difficult to find in the actual concrete consciousness of man a feeling so limited to the present as not to have an inkling of anything that went before.

'Substantive' and 'Transitive' States of Mind.—When we take a general view of the wonderful stream of our consciousness, what strikes us first is the different pace of its parts. Like a bird's life, it seems to be an alternation of flights and perchings. The rhythm of language expresses this, where every thought is expressed in a sentence, and every sentence closed by a period. The resting-places are usually occupied by sensorial imaginations of some sort, whose peculiarity is that they can be held before the mind for an indefinite time, and contemplated without changing; the places of flight are filled with thoughts of relations, static or dynamic, that for the most part obtain between the matters contemplated in the periods of comparative rest.

Let us call the resting-places the 'substantive parts,' and the places of flight the 'transitive parts,' of the stream of thought. It then appears that our thinking tends at all times towards some other substantive part than the one from which it has just been dislodged. And we may say that the main use of the transitive parts is to lead us from one substantive conclusion to another.

Now it is very difficult, introspectively, to see the transitive parts for what they really are. If they are but flights to a conclusion, stopping them to look at them before the conclusion is reached is really annihilating them. Whilst if we wait till the conclusion *be* reached, it so exceeds them in vigor and stability that it quite eclipses and swallows them up in its glare. Let anyone try to cut a thought across in the middle and get a look at its section, and he will see how difficult the introspective observation of the transitive tracts is. The rush of the thought is so headlong that it almost always brings us up at the conclusion before we can arrest it. Or if our purpose is nimble enough and we do arrest it, it ceases forthwith to be itself. As a snowflake caught in the warm hand is no longer a flake but a drop, so, instead of catching the feeling of relation moving to its term, we find we have caught some substantive thing, usually the last word we were pronouncing, statically taken, and with its function, tendency, and particular meaning in the sentence quite evaporated. The attempt at introspective analysis in these cases is in fact like seizing a spinning top to catch its motion, or trying to turn up the gas quickly enough to see how the darkness looks. And the challenge to *produce* these transitive states of consciousness, which is sure to be thrown by doubting psychologists at anyone who contends for their existence, is as unfair as Zeno's treatment of the advocates of motion, when, asking them to point out in what place an arrow *is* when it moves, he argues the falsity of their thesis from their inability to make to so preposterous a question an immediate reply.

The results of this introspective difficulty are baleful. If to hold fast and observe the transitive parts of thought's stream be so hard, then the great blunder to which all schools are liable must be the failure to register them, and the undue emphasizing of the more substantive parts of the stream. Now the blunder has historically worked in two ways. One set of thinkers have been led by it to *Sensationalism.* Unable to lay their hands on any substantive feelings corresponding to the innumerable relations and forms of connection between the sensible things of the world, finding no *named* mental states mirroring such relations, they have for the most part denied that any such states exist; and many of them, like Hume, have gone on to deny the reality of most relations *out* of the mind as well as in it. Simple substantive 'ideas,' sensations and their copies, juxtaposed like dominoes in a game, but really separate, everything else verbal illusion,—such is the upshot of this view. The *Intellectualists,* on the other hand, unable to give up the reality of relations *extra mentem*, but equally unable to point to any distinct substantive feelings in which they were known, have made the same admission that such feelings do not exist. But they have drawn an opposite conclusion. The relations must be known, they say, in something that is no feeling, no mental 'state,' continuous and consubstantial with the subjective tissue out of which sensations and other substantive conditions of consciousness are made. They must be known by something that lies on an entirely different plane, by an *actus purus* of Thought, Intellect, or Reason, all written with capitals and considered to mean something unutterably superior to any passing perishing fact of sensibility whatever.

But from our point of view both Intellectualists and Sensationalists are wrong. If there be such things as feelings at all, *then so surely as relations between objects exist* in rerum naturâ, *so surely, and more surely, do feelings exist to which these relations are known.* There is not a conjunction or a preposition, and hardly an adverbial phrase, syntactic form, or inflection of voice, in human speech, that does not express some shading or other of relation which we at some moment actually feel to exist between the larger objects of our thought. If we speak objectively, it is the real relations that appear revealed; if we speak subjectively, it is the stream of consciousness that matches each of them by an inward coloring of its own. In either case the relations are numberless, and no existing language is capable of doing justice to all their shades.

We ought to say a feeling of *and*, a feeling of *if*, a feeling of *but*, and a feeling of *by*, quite as readily as we say a feeling of *blue* or a feeling of *cold*. Yet we do not: so inveterate has our habit become of recognizing the existence of the substantive parts alone, that language almost refuses to lend itself to any other use. Consider once again the analogy of the brain. We believe the brain to be an organ whose internal equilibrium is always in a state of change—the change affecting every part. The pulses of change are doubtless more violent in one place than in another, their rhythm more rapid at this time than at that. As in a kaleidoscope revolving at a uniform rate, although the figures are always rearranging themselves, there are instants during which the transformation seems minute and interstitial and almost absent, followed by others when it shoots with magical rapidity, relatively stable forms thus alternating with forms we should not distinguish if seen again; so in the brain the perpetual rearrangement must result in some forms of tension lingering relatively long, whilst others simply come and pass. But if consciousness corresponds to the fact of rearrangement itself, why, if the rearrangement stop not, should the consciousness ever cease? And if a lingering rearrangement brings with it one kind of consciousness, why should not a swift rearrangement bring another kind of consciousness as peculiar as the rearrangement itself?

The object before the mind always has a 'Fringe.' There are other unnamed modifications of consciousness just as important as the transitive states, and just as cognitive as they. Examples will show what I mean.

Suppose three successive persons say to us: 'Wait!' 'Hark!' 'Look!' Our consciousness is thrown into three quite different attitudes of expectancy, although no definite object is before it in any one of the three cases. Probably no one will deny here the existence of a real conscious affection, a sense of the direction from which an impression is about to come, although no positive impression is yet there. Meanwhile we have no names for the psychoses in question but the names hark, look, and wait.

Suppose we try to recall a forgotten name. The state of our consciousness is peculiar. There is a gap therein; but no mere gap. It is a gap that is intensely active. A sort of wraith of the name is in it, beckoning us in a given direction, making us at moments tingle with the sense of our closeness, and then letting us sink back without the longed-for term. If wrong names are proposed to us, this singularly definite gap acts immediately so as to negate them. They do not fit into its mould. And the gap of one word does not feel like the gap of another, all empty of content as both might seem necessarily to be when described as gaps. When I vainly try to recall the name of Spalding, my consciousness is far removed from what it is when I vainly try to recall the name of Bowles. There are innumerable consciousnesses of *want*, no one of which taken in itself has a name, but all different from each other. Such a feeling of want is *toto cœlo* other than a want of feeling: it is an intense feeling. The rhythm of a lost word may be there without a sound to clothe it; or the evanescent sense of something which is the initial vowel or consonant may mock us fitfully, without growing more distinct. Everyone must know the tantalizing effect of the blank rhythm of some forgotten verse, restlessly dancing in one's mind, striving to be filled out with words.

What is that first instantaneous glimpse of someone's meaning which we have, when in vulgar phrase we say we 'twig' it? Surely an altogether specific affection of our mind. And has the reader never asked himself what kind of a mental fact is his *intention of saying a thing* before he has said it? It is an entirely definite intention, distinct from all other intentions, an absolutely distinct state of consciousness, therefore; and yet how much of it consists of definite sensorial images, either of words or of things? Hardly anything! Linger, and the words and things come into the mind; the anticipatory intention, the divination is there no more. But as the words that replace it arrive, it welcomes them successively and calls them right if they agree with it, it rejects them and calls them wrong if they do not. The intention *to-say-so-and-so* is the only name it can receive. One may admit that a good third of our psychic life consists in these rapid premonitory perspective views of schemes of thought not yet articulate. How comes it about that a man reading something aloud for the first time is able immediately to emphasize all his words aright, unless from the very first he have a sense of at least the form of the sentence yet to come, which sense is fused with his consciousness of the present word, and modifies its emphasis in his mind so as to make him give it the proper accent as he utters it? Emphasis of this kind almost altogether depends on grammatical construction. If we read 'no more,' we expect presently a 'than'; if we read 'however,' it is a 'yet,' a 'still,' or a 'nevertheless,' that we expect. And this foreboding of the coming verbal and grammatical scheme is so practically accurate that a reader incapable of understanding four ideas of the book he is reading aloud can nevertheless read it with the most delicately modulated expression of intelligence.

It is, the reader will see, the reinstatement of the vague and inarticulate to its proper place in our mental life which I am so anxious to press on the attention. Mr. Galton and Prof. Huxley have, as we shall see in the chapter on Imagination, made one step in advance in exploding the ridiculous theory of Hume and Berkeley that we can have no images but of perfectly definite things. Another is made if we overthrow the equally ridiculous notion that, whilst simple objective qualities are revealed to our knowledge in 'states of consciousness,' relations are not. But these reforms are not half sweeping and radical enough. What must be admitted is that the definite images of traditional psychology form but the very smallest part of our minds as they actually live.

The traditional psychology talks like one who should say a river consists of nothing but pailsful, spoonsful, quartpotsful, barrelsful, and other moulded forms of water. Even were the pails and the pots all actually standing in the stream, still between them the free water would continue to flow. It is just this free water of consciousness that psychologists resolutely overlook. Every definite image in the mind is steeped and dyed in the free water that flows round it. With it goes the sense of its relations, near and remote, the dying echo of whence it came to us, the dawning sense of whither it is to lead. The significance, the value, of the image is all in this halo or penumbra that surrounds and escorts it,—or rather that is fused into one with it and has become bone of its bone and flesh of its flesh; leaving it, it is true, an image of the same *thing* it was before, but making it an image of that thing newly taken and freshly understood.

Let us call the consciousness of this halo of relations around the image by the name of 'psychic overtone' or 'fringe.'

Cerebral Conditions of the 'Fringe.'—Nothing is easier than to symbolize these facts in terms of brain-action. Just as the echo of the *whence*, the sense of the starting point of our thought, is probably due to the dying excitement of processes but a moment since vividly aroused; so the sense of the whither, the foretaste of the terminus, must be due to the waxing excitement of tracts or processes whose psychical correlative will a moment hence be the vividly present feature of our thought. Represented by a curve, the neurosis underlying consciousness must at any moment be like this:

Let the horizontal in Fig. 52 be the line of time, and let the three curves beginning at *a, b,* and *c* respectively stand for the neural processes correlated with the thoughts of those three letters.

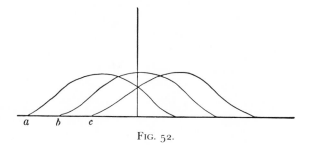

FIG. 52.

Each process occupies a certain time during which its intensity waxes, culminates, and wanes. The process for *a* has not yet died out, the process for *c* has already begun, when that for *b* is culminating. At the time-instant represented by the vertical line all three processes are *present*, in the intensities shown by the curve. Those before *c*'s apex *were* more intense a moment ago; those after it *will be* more intense a moment hence. If I recite *a,b,c*, then, at the moment of uttering *b*, neither *a* nor *c* is out of my consciousness altogether, but both, after their respective fashions, 'mix their dim lights' with the stronger *b*, because their processes are both awake in some degree.

It is just like 'overtones' in music: they are not separately heard by the ear; they blend with the fundamental note, and suffuse it, and alter it; and even so do the waxing and waning brain-processes at every moment blend with and suffuse and alter the psychic effect of the processes which are at their culminating point.

The 'Topic' of the Thought.—If we then consider the *cognitive function* of different states of mind, we may feel assured that the difference between those that are mere 'acquaintance' and those that are 'knowledges-*about*' is reducible almost entirely to the absence or presence of psychic fringes or overtones. Knowledge *about* a thing is knowledge of its relations. Acquaintance with it is limitation to the bare impression which it makes. Of most of its relations we are only aware in the penumbral nascent way of a 'fringe' of unarticulated affinities about it. And, before passing to the next topic in order, I must say a little of this sense of affinity, as itself one of the most interesting features of the subjective stream.

Thought may be equally rational in any sort of terms. *In all our voluntary thinking there is some* TOPIC *or* SUBJECT about which all the members of the thought revolve. Relation to this topic or interest is constantly felt in the fringe, and particularly the relation of harmony and discord, of furtherance or hindrance of the topic. Any thought the quality of whose fringe lets us feel ourselves 'all right,' may be considered a thought that furthers the topic. Provided we only feel its object to have a place in the scheme of relations in which the topic also lies, that is sufficient to make of it a relevant and appropriate portion of our train of ideas.

Now we may think about our topic mainly in words, or we may think about it mainly in visual or other images, but this need make no difference as regards the furtherance of our knowledge of the topic. If we only feel in the terms, whatever they be, a fringe of affinity with each other and with the topic, and if we are conscious of approaching a conclusion, we feel that our thought is rational and right. The words in every language have contracted by long association fringes of mutual repugnance or affinity with each other and with the conclusion, which run exactly parallel with like fringes in the visual, tactile and other ideas. The most important element of these fringes is, I repeat, the mere feeling of harmony or discord, of a right or wrong direction in the thought.

If we know English and French and begin a sentence in French, all the later words that come are French; we hardly ever drop into English. And this affinity of the French words for each other is not something merely operating mechanically as a brain-law, it is something we feel at the time. Our understanding of a French sentence heard never falls to so low an ebb that we are not aware that the words linguistically belong together. Our attention can hardly so wander that if an English word be suddenly introduced we shall not start at the change. Such a vague sense as this of the words belonging together is the very minimum of fringe that can accompany them, if 'thought' at all. Usually the vague perception that all the words we hear belong to the same language and to the same special vocabulary in that language, and that the grammatical sequence is familiar, is practically equivalent to an admission that what we hear is sense. But if an unusual foreign word be introduced, if the grammar trip, or if a term from an incongruous vocabulary suddenly appear, such as 'rat-trap' or 'plumber's bill' in a philosophical discourse, the sentence detonates as it were, we receive a shock from the incongruity, and the drowsy assent is gone. The feeling of rationality in these cases seems rather a negative than a positive thing, being the mere absence of shock, or sense of discord, between the terms of thought.

Conversely, if words do belong to the same vocabulary, and if the grammatical structure is correct, sentences with absolutely no meaning may be uttered in good faith and pass unchallenged. Discourses at prayer-meetings, reshuffling the same collection of cant phrases, and the whole genus of penny-a-line-isms and newspaper-reporter's flourishes give illustrations of this. "The birds filled the tree-tops with their morning song, making the air moist, cool, and pleasant," is a sentence I remember reading once in a report of some athletic exercises in Jerome Park. It was probably written unconsciously by the hurried reporter, and read uncritically by many readers.

We see, then, that it makes little or no difference in what sort of mind-stuff, in what quality of imagery, our thinking goes on. The only images *intrinsically* important are the halting-places, the substantive conclusions, provisional or final, of the thought. Throughout all the rest of the stream, the feelings of relation are everything, and the terms related almost naught. These feelings of relation, these psychic overtones, halos, suffusions, or fringes about the terms, may be the same in very different systems of imagery. A diagram may help to accentuate this indifference of the mental means where the end is the same. Let A be some experience from which a number of thinkers start. Let Z be the practical conclusion rationally inferrible from it. One gets to this conclusion by one line, another by another; one follows a course of English, another of German, verbal imagery. With one, visual images predominate; with another, tactile. Some trains are tinged with emotions, others not; some are very abridged, synthetic and rapid; others, hesitating and broken into many steps. But when the penultimate terms of all the trains, however differing *inter se*, finally shoot into the same conclusion, we say, and rightly say, that all the thinkers have had substantially the same thought. It would probably astound each of them beyond measure to be let into his neighbor's mind and to find how different the scenery there was from that in his own.

The last peculiarity to which attention is to be drawn in this first rough description of thought's stream is that—

Consciousness is always interested more in one part of its object than in another, and welcomes and rejects, or chooses, all the while it thinks.

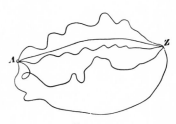

FIG. 53.

The phenomena of selective attention and of deliberative will are of course patent examples of this choosing activity. But few of us are aware how incessantly it is at work in operations not ordinarily called by these names. Accentuation and Emphasis are present in every perception we have. We find it quite impossible to disperse our attention impartially over a number of impressions. A monotonous succession of sonorous strokes is broken up into rhythms, now of one sort, now of another, by the different accent which we place on different strokes. The simplest of these rhythms is the double one, tick-tóck, tick-tóck, tick-tóck. Dots dispersed on a surface are perceived in rows and groups. Lines separate into diverse figures. The ubiquity of the distinctions, *this* and *that*, *here* and *there*, *now* and *then*, in our minds is the result of our laying the same selective emphasis on parts of place and time.

But we do far more than emphasize things, and unite some, and keep others apart. We actually *ignore* most of the things before us. Let me briefly show how this goes on.

To begin at the bottom, what are our very senses themselves, as we saw on pp. 15–17, but organs of selection? Out of the infinite chaos of movements, of which physics teaches us that the outer world consists, each sense-organ picks out those which fall within certain limits of velocity. To these it responds, but ignores the rest as completely as if they did not exist. Out of what is in itself an undistinguishable, swarming *continuum*, devoid of distinction or emphasis, our senses make for us, by attending to this motion and ignoring that, a world full of contrasts, of sharp accents, of abrupt changes, of picturesque light and shade.

If the sensations we receive from a given organ have their causes thus picked out for us by the conformation of the organ's termination, Attention, on the other hand, out of all the sensations yielded, picks out certain ones as worthy of its notice and suppresses all the rest. We notice only those sensations which are signs to us of *things* which happen practically or æsthetically to interest us, to which we therefore give substantive names, and which we exalt to this exclusive status of independence and dignity. But in itself, apart from my interest, a particular dust-wreath on a windy day is just as much of an individual *thing*, and just as much or as little deserves an individual name, as my own body does.

And then, among the sensations we get from each separate

155

thing, what happens? The mind selects again. It chooses certain of the sensations to represent the thing most *truly*, and considers the rest as its appearances, modified by the conditions of the moment. Thus my table-top is named *square*, after but one of an infinite number of retinal sensations which it yields, the rest of them being sensations of two acute and two obtuse angles; but I call the latter *perspective* views, and the four right angles the *true* form of the table, and erect the attribute squareness into the table's essence, for æsthetic reasons of my own. In like manner, the real form of the circle is deemed to be the sensation it gives when the line of vision is perpendicular to its centre—all its other sensations are *signs* of this sensation. The real sound of the cannon is the sensation it makes when the ear is close by. The real color of the brick is the sensation it gives when the eye looks squarely at it from a near point, out of the sunshine and yet not in the gloom; under other circumstances it gives us other color-sensations which are but signs of this—we then see it looks pinker or bluer than it really is. The reader knows no object which he does not represent to himself by preference as in some typical attitude, of some normal size, at some characteristic distance, of some standard tint, etc., etc. But all these essential characteristics, which together form for us the genuine objectivity of the thing and are contrasted with what we call the subjective sensations it may yield us at a given moment, are mere sensations like the latter. The mind chooses to suit itself, and decides what particular sensation shall be held more real and valid than all the rest.

Next, in a world of objects thus individualized by our mind's selective industry, what is called our 'experience' is almost entirely determined by our habits of attention. A thing may be present to a man a hundred times, but if he persistently fails to notice it, it cannot be said to enter into his experience. We are all seeing flies, moths, and beetles by the thousand, but to whom, save an entomologist, do they say anything distinct? On the other hand, a thing met only once in a lifetime may leave an indelible experience in the memory. Let four men make a tour in Europe. One will bring home only picturesque impressions—costumes and colors, parks and views and works of architecture, pictures and statues. To another all this will be non-existent; and distances and prices, populations and drainage-arrangements, door- and window-fastenings, and other useful statistics will take their place.

A third will give a rich account of the theatres, restaurants, and public balls, and naught beside; whilst the fourth will perhaps have been so wrapped in his own subjective broodings as to be able to tell little more than a few names of places through which he passed. Each has selected, out of the same mass of presented objects, those which suited his private interest and has made his experience thereby.

If now, leaving the empirical combination of objects, we ask how the mind proceeds *rationally* to connect them, we find selection again to be omnipotent. In a future chapter we shall see that all Reasoning depends on the ability of the mind to break up the totality of the phenomenon reasoned about, into parts, and to pick out from among these the particular one which, in the given emergency, may lead to the proper conclusion. The man of genius is he who will always stick in his bill at the right point, and bring it out with the right element—'reason' if the emergency be theoretical, 'means' if it be practical—transfixed upon it.

If now we pass to the æsthetic department, our law is still more obvious. The artist notoriously selects his items, rejecting all tones, colors, shapes, which do not harmonize with each other and with the main purpose of his work. That unity, harmony, 'convergence of characters,' as M. Taine calls it, which gives to works of art their superiority over works of nature, is wholly due to *elimination*. Any natural subject will do, if the artist has wit enough to pounce upon some one feature of it as characteristic, and suppress all merely accidental items which do not harmonize with this.

Ascending still higher, we reach the plane of Ethics, where choice reigns notoriously supreme. An act has no ethical quality whatever unless it be chosen out of several all equally possible. To sustain the arguments for the good course and keep them ever before us, to stifle our longing for more flowery ways, to keep the foot unflinchingly on the arduous path, these are characteristic ethical energies. But more than these; for these but deal with the means of compassing interests already felt by the man to be supreme. The ethical energy *par excellence* has to go farther and choose which *interest* out of several, equally coercive, shall become supreme. The issue here is of the utmost pregnancy, for it decides a man's entire career. When he debates, Shall I commit this crime? choose that profession? accept that office, or marry this fortune?—his choice really lies between one of several equally possible future Characters. What he shall *become* is fixed by the conduct of this moment. Schopenhauer, who enforces his determinism by the argument that with a given fixed character only one reaction is possible under given circumstances, forgets that, in these critical ethical moments, what consciously *seems* to be in question is the complexion of the character itself. The problem with the man is less what act he shall now resolve to do than what being he shall now choose to become.

Taking human experience in a general way, the choosings of different men are to a great extent the same. The race as a whole largely agrees as to what it shall notice and name; and among the noticed parts we select in much the same way for accentuation and preference, or subordination and dislike. There is, however, one entirely extraordinary case in which no two men ever are known to choose alike. One great splitting of the whole universe into two halves is made by each of us; and for each of us almost all of the interest attaches to one of the halves; but we all draw the line of division between them in a different place. When I say that we all call the two halves by the same names, and that those names are '*me*' and '*not-me*' respectively, it will at once be seen what I mean. The altogether unique kind of interest which each human mind feels in those parts of creation which it can call *me* or *mine* may be a moral riddle, but it is a fundamental psychological fact. No mind can take the same interest in his neighbor's *me* as in his own. The neighbor's me falls together with all the rest of things in one foreign mass against which his own *me* stands out in startling relief. Even the trodden worm, as Lotze somewhere says, contrasts his own suffering self with the whole remaining universe, though he have no clear conception either of himself or of what the universe may be. He is for me a mere part of the world; for him it is I who am the mere part. Each of us dichotomizes the Kosmos in a different place.

Descending now to finer work than this first general sketch, let us in the next chapter try to trace the psychology of this fact of self-consciousness to which we have thus once more been led.

Chapter XII

The Self

The Me and the I.—Whatever I may be thinking of, I am always at the same time more or less aware of *myself*, of my *personal existence*. At the same time it is *I* who am aware; so that the total self of me, being as it were duplex, partly known and partly knower, partly object and partly subject, must have two aspects discriminated in it, of which for shortness we may call one the *Me* and the other the *I*. I call these 'discriminated aspects,' and not separate things, because the identity of *I* with *me*, even in the very act of their discrimination, is perhaps the most ineradicable dictum of common-sense, and must not be undermined by our terminology here at the outset, whatever we may come to think of its validity at our inquiry's end.

I shall therefore treat successively of A) the self as known, or the *me*, the 'empirical ego' as it is sometimes called; and of B) the self as knower, or the I, the 'pure ego' of certain authors.

A) The Self as Known

The Empirical Self or Me.—Between what a man calls *me* and what he simply calls *mine* the line is difficult to draw. We feel and act about certain things that are ours very much as we feel and act about ourselves. Our fame, our children, the work of our hands, may be as dear to us as our bodies are, and arouse the same feelings and the same acts of reprisal if attacked. And our bodies themselves, are they simply ours, or are they *us*? Certainly men have been ready to disown their very bodies and to regard them as mere vestures, or even as prisons of clay from which they should some day be glad to escape.

We see then that we are dealing with a fluctuating material; the same object being sometimes treated as a part of me, at other times as simply mine, and then again as if I had nothing to do with it at all. *In its widest possible sense,* however, *a man's Me is the sum total of all that he* CAN *call his*, not only his body and his psychic powers, but his clothes and his house, his wife and children, his ancestors and friends, his reputation and works, his lands and horses, and yacht and bank-account. All these things give him the same emotions. If they wax and prosper, he feels triumphant; if they dwindle and die away, he feels cast down,—not necessarily in the same degree for each thing, but in much the same way for all. Understanding the Me in this widest sense, we may begin by dividing the history of it into three parts, relating respectively to—

a. Its constituents;

b. The feelings and emotions they arouse,—*self-appreciation*;

c. The acts to which they prompt,—*self-seeking and self-preservation.*

a. The constituents of the Me may be divided into three classes, those which make up respectively—

> The material me;
> The social me; and
> The spiritual me.

The Material Me.—The *body* is the innermost part of the material me in each of us; and certain parts of the body seem more intimately ours than the rest. The clothes come next. The old saying that the human person is composed of three parts—soul, body and clothes—is more than a joke. We so appropriate our clothes and identify ourselves with them that there are few of us who, if asked to choose between having a beautiful body clad in raiment perpetually shabby and unclean, and having an ugly and blemished form always spotlessly attired, would not hesitate a moment before making a decisive reply. Next, our immediate family is a part of ourselves. Our father and mother, our wife and babes, are bone of our bone and flesh of our flesh. When they die, a part of our very selves is gone. If they do anything wrong, it is our shame. If they are insulted, our anger flashes forth as readily as if we stood in their place. Our home comes next. Its scenes are part of our life; its aspects awaken the tenderest feelings of affection; and we do not easily forgive the stranger who, in visiting it, finds fault with its arrangements or treats it with contempt. All these different things are the objects of instinctive preferences coupled with the most important practical interests of life. We all have a blind impulse to watch over our body, to deck it with clothing of an ornamental sort, to cherish parents, wife and babes, and to find for ourselves a house of our own which we may live in and 'improve.'

An equally instinctive impulse drives us to collect property; and the collections thus made become, with different degrees of intimacy, parts of our empirical selves. The parts of our wealth most intimately ours are those which are saturated with our labor. There are few men who would not feel personally annihilated if a life-long construction of their hands or brains—say an entomological collection or an extensive work in manuscript—were suddenly swept away. The miser feels similarly towards his gold; and although it is true that a part of our depresssion at the loss of possessions is due to our feeling that we must now go without certain goods that we expected the possessions to bring in their train, yet in every case there remains, over and above this, a sense of the shrinkage of our personality, a partial conversion of ourselves to nothingness, which is a psychological phenomenon by itself. We are all at once assimilated to the tramps and poor devils whom we so despise, and at the same time removed farther than ever away from the happy sons of earth who lord it over land and sea and men in the full-blown lustihood that wealth and power can give, and before whom, stiffen ourselves as we will by appealing to anti-snobbish first principles, we cannot escape an emotion, open or sneaking, of respect and dread.

The Social Me.—A man's social me is the recognition which he gets from his mates. We are not only gregarious animals, liking to be in sight of our fellows, but we have an innate propensity to get ourselves noticed, and noticed favorably, by our kind. No more fiendish punishment could be devised, were such a thing physically possible, than that one should be turned loose in society and remain absolutely unnoticed by all the members thereof. If no one turned round when we entered, answered when we spoke, or minded what we did, but if every person we met 'cut us dead,' and acted as if we were non-existing things, a kind of rage and impotent despair would ere long well up in us, from which the cruellest bodily tortures would be a relief; for these would make us feel that, however bad might be our plight, we had not sunk to such a depth as to be unworthy of attention at all.

Properly speaking, *a man has as many social selves as there are individuals who recognize him* and carry an image of him in their mind. To wound any one of these his images is to wound him. But as the individuals who carry the images fall naturally into classes, we may practically say that he has as many different social selves as there are distinct *groups* of persons about whose opinion he cares. He generally shows a different side of himself to each of these different groups. Many a youth who is demure enough before his parents and teachers, swears and swaggers like a pirate among his 'tough' young friends. We do not show ourselves to our children as to our club-companions, to our customers as to the laborers we employ, to our own masters and employers as to our intimate friends. From this there results what practically is a division of the man into several selves; and this may be a discordant splitting, as where one is afraid to let one set of his acquaintances know him as he is elsewhere; or it may be a perfectly harmonious division of labor, as where one tender to his children is stern to the soldiers or prisoners under his command.

The most peculiar social self which one is apt to have is in the mind of the person one is in love with. The good or bad fortunes of this self cause the most intense elation and dejection—unreasonable enough as measured by every other standard than that of the organic feeling of the individual. To his own consciousness he *is* not, so long as this particular social self fails to get recognition, and when it is recognized his contentment passes all bounds.

A man's *fame*, good or bad, and his *honor* or dishonor, are names for one of his social selves. The particular social self of a man called his honor is usually the result of one of those splittings of which we have spoken. It is his image in the eyes of his own 'set,' which exalts or condemns him as he conforms or not to certain requirements that may not be made of one in another walk of life. Thus a layman may abandon a city infected with cholera; but a priest or a doctor would think such an act incompatible with his honor. A soldier's honor requires him to fight or to die under circumstances where another man can apologize or run away with no stain upon his social self. A judge, a statesman, are in like manner debarred by the honor of their cloth from entering into pecuniary relations perfectly honorable to persons in private life. Nothing is commoner than to hear people discriminate between their different selves of this sort: "As a man I pity you, but as an official I must show you no mercy"; "As a politician I regard him as an ally, but as a moralist I loathe him"; etc., etc. What may be called 'club-opinion' is one of the very strongest forces in life. The thief must not steal from other thieves; the gambler must pay his gambling-debts, though he pay no other debts in the world. The code of honor of fashionable society has throughout history been full of permissions as well as of vetoes, the only reason for following either of which is that so we best serve one of our social selves. You must not lie in general, but you may lie as much as you please if asked about your relations with a lady; you must accept a challenge from an equal, but if challenged by an inferior you may laugh him to scorn: these are examples of what is meant.

The Spiritual Me.—By the 'spiritual me,' so far as it belongs to the empirical self, I mean no one of my passing states of consciousness. I mean rather the entire collection of my states of consciousness, my psychic faculties and dispositions taken concretely. This collection can at any moment become an object to my thought at that moment and awaken emotions like those awakened by any of the other portions of the Me. When we *think of ourselves as thinkers*, all the other ingredients of our Me seem relatively external possessions. Even within the spiritual *Me* some ingredients seem more external than others. Our capacities for sensation, for example, are less intimate possessions, so to speak, than our emotions and desires; our intellectual processes are less intimate than our volitional decisions. The more *active-feeling* states of consciousness are thus the more central portions of the spiritual Me. The very core and nucleus of our self, as we know it, the very sanctuary of our life, is the sense of activity which certain inner states possess. This sense of activity is often held to be a direct revelation of the living substance of our Soul. Whether this be so or not is an ulterior question. I wish now only to lay down the peculiar *internality* of whatever states possess this quality of seeming to be active. It is as if they *went out to meet* all the other elements of our experience. In thus feeling about them probably all men agree.

b. The feelings and emotions of self come after the constituents.

Self-appreciation.—This is of two sorts, *self-complacency* and *self-dissatisfaction*. 'Self-love' more properly belongs under the division *C*, of *acts*, since what men mean by that name is rather a set of motor tendencies than a kind of feeling properly so called.

Language has synonyms enough for both kinds of self-appreciation. Thus pride, conceit, vanity, self-esteem, arrogance, vainglory, on the one hand; and on the other modesty, humility, confusion, diffidence, shame, mortification, contrition, the sense of obloquy, and personal despair. These two opposite classes of affection seem to be direct and elementary endowments of our nature. Associationists would have it that they are, on the other hand, secondary phenomena arising from a rapid computation of the sensible pleasures or pains to which our prosperous or debased personal predicament is likely to lead, the sum of the represented pleasures forming the self-satisfaction, and the sum of the represented pains forming the opposite feeling of shame. No doubt, when we are self-satisfied, we do fondly rehearse all possible rewards for our desert, and when in a fit of self-despair we forebode evil. But the mere expectation of reward *is* not the self-satisfaction, and the mere apprehension of the evil *is* not the self-despair; for there is a certain average tone of self-feeling which each one of us carries about with him, and which is independent of the objective reasons we may have for satisfaction or discontent. That is, a very meanly-conditioned man may abound in unfaltering conceit, and one whose success in life is secure, and who is esteemed by all, may remain diffident of his powers to the end.

One may say, however, that the normal *provocative* of self-feeling is one's actual success or failure, and the good or bad actual position one holds in the world. "He put in his thumb and pulled out a plum, and said, 'What a good boy am I!' " A man with a broadly extended empirical Ego, with powers that have uniformly brought him success, with place and wealth and friends and fame, is not likely to be visited by the morbid diffidences and doubts about himself which he had when he was a boy. "Is not this great Babylon, which I have planted?" Whereas he who has made one blunder after another, and still lies in middle life among the failures at the foot of the hill, is liable to grow all sicklied o'er with self-distrust, and to shrink from trials with which his powers can really cope.

The emotions themselves of self-satisfaction and abasement are of a unique sort, each as worthy to be classed as a primitive emotional species as are, for example, rage or pain. Each has its own peculiar physiognomical expression. In self-satisfaction the extensor muscles are innervated, the eye is strong and glorious, the gait rolling and elastic, the nostril dilated, and a peculiar smile plays upon the lips. This whole complex of symptoms is seen in an exquisite way in lunatic asylums, which always contain some patients who are literally mad with conceit, and whose fatuous expression and absurdly strutting or swaggering gait is in tragic contrast with their lack of any valuable personal quality. It is in these same castles of despair that we find the strongest examples of the opposite physiognomy, in good people who think they have committed 'the unpardonable sin' and are lost forever, who crouch and cringe and slink from notice, and are unable to speak aloud or look us in the eye. Like fear and like anger, in similar morbid conditions, these opposite feelings of Self may be aroused with no adequate exciting cause. And in fact we ourselves know how the barometer of our self-esteem and confidence rises and falls from one day to another through causes that seem to be visceral and organic rather than rational, and which certainly answer to no corresponding variations in the esteem in which we are held by our friends.

c. Self-seeking and self-preservation come next.

These words cover a large number of our fundamental instinctive impulses. We have those of *bodily self-seeking*, those of *social self-seeking*, and those of *spiritual self-seeking*.

Bodily Self-seeking.—All the ordinary useful reflex actions and movements of alimentation and defence are acts of bodily self-preservation. Fear and anger prompt to acts that are useful in the same way. Whilst if by self-seeking we mean the providing for the future as distinguished from maintaining the present, we must class both anger and fear, together with the hunting, the acquisitive, the home-constructing and the tool-constructing instincts, as impulses to self-seeking of the bodily kind. Really, however, these latter instincts, with amativeness, parental fondness, curiosity and emulation, seek not only the development of the bodily Me, but that of the material Me in the widest possible sense of the word.

Our **social self-seeking**, in turn, is carried on directly through our amativeness and friendliness, our desire to please and attract notice and admiration, our emulation and jealousy, our love of glory, influence, and power, and indirectly through whichever of the material self-seeking impulses prove serviceable as means to social ends. That the direct social self-seeking impulses are probably pure instincts is easily seen. The noteworthy thing about the desire to be 'recognized' by others is that its strength has so little to do with the worth of the recognition computed in sensational or rational terms. We are crazy to get a visiting-list which shall be large, to be able to say when anyone is mentioned, "Oh! I know him well," and to be bowed to in the street by half the people we meet. Of course distinguished friends and admiring recognition are the most desirable—Thackeray somewhere asks his readers to confess whether it would not give each of *them* an exquisite pleasure to be met walking down Pall Mall with a duke on either arm. But in default of dukes and envious salutations almost anything will do for some of us; and there is a whole race of beings to-day whose passion is to keep their names in the newspapers, no matter under what heading, 'arrivals and departures,' 'personal paragraphs,' 'interviews,'—gossip, even scandal, will suit them if nothing better is to be had. Guiteau, Garfield's assassin, is an example of the extremity to which this sort of craving for the notoriety of print may go in a pathological case. The newspapers bounded his mental horizon; and in the poor wretch's prayer on the scaffold, one of the most heart-felt expressions was: "The newspaper press of this land has a big bill to settle with thee, O Lord!"

Not only the people but the places and things I know enlarge my Self in a sort of metaphoric social way. '*Ça me connaît*,' as the French workman says of the implement he can use well. So that it comes about that persons for whose *opinion* we care nothing are nevertheless persons whose notice we woo; and that many a man truly great, many a woman truly fastidious in most respects, will take a deal of trouble to dazzle some insignificant cad whose whole personality they heartily despise.

Under the head of **spiritual self-seeking** ought to be included every impulse towards psychic progress, whether intellectual, moral, or spiritual in the narrow sense of the term. It must be admitted, however, that much that commonly passes for spiritual self-seeking in this narrow sense is only material and social self-seeking beyond the grave. In the Mohammedan desire for paradise and the Christian aspiration not to be damned in hell, the materiality of the goods sought is undisguised. In the more positive and refined view of heaven, many of its goods, the fellowship of the saints and of our dead ones, and the presence of God, are but social goods of the most exalted kind. It is only the search of the redeemed inward nature, the spotlessness from sin, whether here or hereafter, that can count as spiritual self-seeking pure and undefiled.

But this broad external review of the facts of the life of the Me will be incomplete without some account of the

Rivalry and Conflict of the Different Mes.—With most objects of desire, physical nature restricts our choice to but one of many represented goods, and even so it is here. I am often confronted by the necessity of standing by one of my empirical selves and relinquishing the rest. Not that I would not, if I could, be both handsome and fat and well dressed, and a great athlete, and make a million a year, be a wit, a *bon-vivant*, and a lady-killer, as well as a philosopher; a philanthropist, statesman, warrior, and African explorer, as well as a 'tone-poet' and saint. But the thing is simply impossible. The millionaire's work would run counter to the saint's; the *bon-vivant* and the philanthropist would trip each other up; the philosopher and the lady-killer could not well keep house in the same tenement of clay. Such different characters may conceivably at the outset of life be alike *possible* to a man. But to make any one of them actual, the rest must more or less be suppressed. So the seeker of his truest, strongest, deepest self must review the list carefully, and pick out the one on which to stake his salvation. All other selves thereupon become unreal, but the fortunes of this self are real. Its failures are real failures, its triumphs real triumphs, carrying shame and gladness with them. This is as strong an example as there is of that selective industry of the mind on which I insisted some pages back (p. 156 ff.). Our thought, incessantly deciding, among many things of a kind, which ones for it shall be realities, here chooses one of many possible selves or characters, and forthwith reckons it no shame to fail in any of those not adopted expressly as its own.

So we have the paradox of a man shamed to death because he is only the second pugilist or the second oarsman in the world. That he is able to beat the whole population of the globe minus one is nothing; he has 'pitted' himself to beat that one; and as long as he doesn't do that nothing else counts. He is to his own regard as if he were not, indeed he *is* not. Yonder puny fellow, however, whom everyone can beat, suffers no chagrin about it, for he has long ago abandoned the attempt to 'carry that line,' as the merchants say, of self at all. With no attempt there can be no failure; with no failure, no humiliation. So our self-feeling in this world depends entirely on what we *back* ourselves to be and do. It is determined by the ratio of our actualities to our supposed potentialities; a fraction of which our pretensions are the denominator and the numerator our success: thus,

$$\text{Self-esteem} = \frac{\text{Success}}{\text{Pretensions}}.$$

Such a fraction may be increased as well by diminishing the denominator as by increasing the numerator. To give up pretensions is as blessed a relief as to get them gratified; and where disappointment is incessant and the struggle unending, this is what men will always do. The history of evangelical theology, with its conviction of sin, its self-despair, and its abandonment of salvation by works, is the deepest of possible examples, but we meet others in every walk of life. There is the strangest lightness about the heart when one's nothingness in a particular line is once accepted in good faith. *All* is not bitterness in the lot of the lover sent away by the final inexorable 'No.' Many Bostonians, *crede experto* (and inhabitants of other cities, too, I fear), would be happier women and men to-day, if they could once for all abandon the notion of keeping up a Musical Self, and without shame let people hear them call a symphony a nuisance. How pleasant is the day when we give up striving to be young,—or slender! Thank God! we say, *those* illusions are gone. Everything added to the Self is a burden as well as a pride. A certain man who lost every penny during our civil war went and actually rolled in the dust, saying he had not felt so free and happy since he was born.

Once more, then, our self-feeling is in our power. As Carlyle says: "Make thy claim of wages a zero, then; thou hast the world under thy feet. Well did the wisest of our time write: 'It is only with *renunciation* that life, properly speaking, can be said to begin.'"

Neither threats nor pleadings can move a man unless they touch some one of his potential or actual selves. Only thus can we, as a rule, get a 'purchase' on another's will. The first care of diplomatists and monarchs and all who wish to rule or influence is, accordingly, to find out their victim's strongest principle of self-regard, so as to make that the fulcrum of all appeals. But if a man has given up those things which are subject to foreign fate, and ceased to regard them as parts of himself at all, we are well-nigh powerless over him. The Stoic receipt for contentment was to dispossess yourself in advance of all that was out of your own power,—then fortune's shocks might rain down unfelt. Epictetus exhorts us, by thus narrowing and at the same time solidifying our Self to make it invulnerable: "I must die; well, but must I die groaning too? . . . I will speak what appears to be right, and if the despot says, 'Then I will put you to death,' I will reply, 'When did I ever tell you that I was immortal? You will do your part, and I mine: it is yours to kill and mine to die intrepid; yours to banish, mine to depart untroubled.' . . . How do we act in a voyage? We choose the pilot, the sailors, the hour. Afterwards comes a storm. What have I to care for? My part is performed. This matter belongs to the pilot. But the ship is sinking; what then have I to do? That which alone I can do; submit to being drowned, without fear, without clamor, or accusing of God; but as one who knows, that what is born, must likewise die."

This Stoic fashion, though efficacious and heroic enough in its place and time, is, it must be confessed, only possible as an habitual mood of the soul to narrow and unsympathetic characters. It proceeds altogether by exclusion. If I am a Stoic, the goods I cannot appropriate cease to be *my* goods, and the temptation lies very near to deny that they are goods at all. We find this mode of protecting the Self by exclusion and denial very common among people who are in other respects not Stoics. All narrow people *intrench* their Me, they *retract* it,—from the region of what they cannot securely possess. People who don't resemble them, or who treat them with indifference, people over whom they gain no influence, are people on whose existence, however meritorious it may intrinsically be, they look with chill negation, if not with positive hate. Who will not be mine I will exclude from existence altogether; that is, as far as I can make it so, such people shall be as if they were not. Thus may a certain absoluteness and definiteness in the outline of my Me console me for the smallness of its content.

Sympathetic people, on the contrary, proceed by the entirely opposite way of expansion and inclusion. The outline of their self often gets uncertain enough, but for this the spread of its content more than atones. *Nil humani a me alienum.* Let them despise this little person of mine, and treat me like a dog, *I* shall not negate *them* so long as I have a soul in my body. They are realities as much as I am. What positive good is in them shall be mine too, etc., etc. The magnanimity of these expansive natures is often touching indeed. Such persons can feel a sort of delicate rapture in thinking that, however sick, ill-favored, mean-conditioned, and generally forsaken they may be, they yet are integral parts of the whole of this brave world, have a fellow's share in the strength of the dray-horses, the happiness of the young people, the wisdom of the wise ones, and are not altogether without part or lot in the good fortunes of the Vanderbilts and the Hohenzollerns themselves. Thus either by negating or by embracing, the Ego may seek to establish itself in reality. He who, with Marcus Aurelius, can truly say, "O Universe, I wish all that thou wishest," has a self from which every trace of negativeness and obstructiveness has been removed—no wind can blow except to fill its sails.

The Hierarchy of the Mes.—A tolerably unanimous opinion ranges the different selves of which a man may be 'seized and possessed,' and the consequent different orders of his self-regard, in an *hierarchical scale, with the bodily me at the bottom, the spiritual me at top, and the extra-corporeal material selves and the various social selves between.* Our merely natural self-seeking would lead us to aggrandize all these selves; we give up deliberately only those among them which we find we cannot keep. Our unselfishness is thus apt to be a 'virtue of necessity'; and it is not without all show of reason that cynics quote the fable of the fox and the grapes in describing our progress therein. But this is the moral education of the race; and if we agree in the result that on the whole the selves we can keep are the intrinsically best, we need not complain of being led to the knowledge of their superior worth in such a tortuous way.

Of course this is not the only way in which we learn to subordinate our lower selves to our higher. A direct ethical judgment unquestionably also plays its part, and last, not least, we apply to our own persons judgments originally called forth by the acts of others. It is one of the strangest laws of our nature that many things which we are well satisfied with in ourselves disgust us when seen in others. With another man's bodily 'hoggishness' hardly anyone has any sympathy; almost as little with his cupidity, his social vanity and eagerness, his jealousy, his despotism, and his pride. Left absolutely to myself I should probably allow all these spontaneous tendencies to luxuriate in me unchecked, and it would be long before I formed a distinct notion of the order of their subordination. But having constantly to pass judgment on my associates, I come ere long to see, as Herr Horwicz says, my own lusts in the mirror of the lusts of others, and to *think* about them in a very different way from that in which I simply *feel*. Of course, the moral generalities which from childhood have been instilled into me accelerate enormously the advent of this reflective judgment on myself.

So it comes to pass that, as aforesaid, men have arranged the various selves which they may seek in an hierarchical scale according to their worth. A certain amount of bodily selfishness is required as a basis for all the other selves. But too much sensuality is despised, or at best condoned on account of the other qualities of the individual. The wider material selves are regarded as higher than the immediate body. He is esteemed a poor creature who is unable to forego a little meat and drink and warmth and sleep for the sake of getting on in the world. The social self as a whole, again, ranks higher than the material self as a whole. We must care more for our honor, our friends, our human ties, than for a sound skin or wealth. And the spiritual self is so supremely precious that, rather than lose it, a man ought to be willing to give up friends and good fame, and property, and life itself.

In each kind of Me, material, social, and spiritual, men distinguish between the immediate and actual, and the remote and potential, between the narrower and the wider view, to the detriment of the former and the advantage of the latter. One must forego a present bodily enjoyment for the sake of one's general health; one must abandon the dollar in the hand for the sake of the hundred dollars to come;

one must make an enemy of his present interlocutor if thereby one makes friends of a more valued circle; one must go without learning and grace and wit, the better to compass one's soul's salvation.

Of all these wider, more potential selves, *the potential social Me* is the most interesting, by reason of certain apparent paradoxes to which it leads in conduct, and by reason of its connection with our moral and religious life. When for motives of honor and conscience I brave the condemnation of my own family, club, and 'set'; when, as a Protestant, I turn Catholic; as a Catholic, free-thinker; as a 'regular practitioner,' homœopath, or what not, I am always inwardly strengthened in my course and steeled against the loss of my actual social self by the thought of other and better *possible* social judges than those whose verdict goes against me now. The ideal social self which I thus seek in appealing to their decision may be very remote: it may be represented as barely possible. I may not hope for its realization during my lifetime; I may even expect the future generations, which would approve me if they knew me, to know nothing about me when I am dead and gone. Yet still the emotion that beckons me on is indubitably the pursuit of an ideal social self, of a self that is at least *worthy* of approving recognition by the highest *possible* judging companion, if such companion there be. This self is the true, the intimate, the ultimate, the permanent me which I seek. This judge is God, the Absolute Mind, the 'Great Companion.' We hear, in these days of scientific enlightenment, a great deal of discussion about the efficacy of prayer; and many reasons are given us why we should not pray, whilst others are given us why we should. But in all this very little is said of the reason why we *do* pray, which is simply that we cannot help praying. It seems probable that, in spite of all that 'science' may do to the contrary, men will continue to pray to the end of time, unless their mental nature changes in a manner which nothing we know should lead us to expect. The impulse to pray is a necessary consequence of the fact that whilst the innermost of the empirical selves of a man is a Self of the *social* sort, it yet can find its only adequate *Socius* in an ideal world.

All progress in the social Self is the substitution of higher tribunals for lower; this ideal tribunal is the highest; and most men, either continually or occasionally, carry a reference to it in their breast. The humblest outcast on this earth can feel himself to be real and valid by means of this higher recognition. And, on the other hand, for most of us, a world with no such inner refuge when the outer social self failed and dropped from us would be the abyss of horror. I say 'for most of us,' because it is probable that individuals differ a good deal in the degree in which they are haunted by this sense of an ideal spectator. It is a much more essential part of the consciousness of some men than of others. Those who have the most of it are possibly the most *religious* men. But I am sure that even those who say they are altogether without it deceive themselves, and really have it in some degree. Only a non-gregarious animal could be completely without it. Probably no one can make sacrifices for 'right,' without to some degree personifying the principle of right for which the sacrifice is made, and expecting thanks from it. *Complete* social unselfishness, in other words, can hardly exist; *complete* social suicide hardly occur to a man's mind. Even such texts as Job's, "Though He slay me, yet will I trust in Him," or Marcus Aurelius's, "If gods hate me and my children, there is a reason for it," can least of all be cited to prove the contrary. For beyond all doubt Job revelled in the thought of Jehovah's recognition of the worship after the slaying should have been done; and the Roman emperor felt sure the Absolute Reason would not be all indifferent to his acquiescence in the gods' dislike. The old test of piety, "Are you willing to be damned for the glory of God?" was probably never answered in the affirmative except by those who felt sure in their heart of hearts that God would 'credit' them with their willingness, and set more store by them thus than if in His unfathomable scheme He had not damned them at all.

Teleological Uses of Self-interest.—On zoölogical principles it is easy to see why we have been endowed with impulses of self-seeking and with emotions of self-satisfaction and the reverse. Unless our consciousness were something more than cognitive, unless it experienced a partiality for certain of the objects, which, in succession, occupy its ken, it could not long maintain itself in existence; for, by an inscrutable necessity, each human mind's appearance on this earth is conditioned upon the integrity of the body with which it belongs, upon the treatment which that body gets from others, and upon the spiritual dispositions which use it as their tool, and lead it either towards longevity or to destruction. *Its own body, then, first of all, its friends next, and finally its spiritual dispositions,* MUST *be the supremely interesting objects for each human*

173

mind. Each mind, to begin with, must have a certain minimum of selfishness in the shape of instincts of bodily self-seeking in order to exist. This minimum must be there as a basis for all farther conscious acts, whether of self-negation or of a selfishness more subtle still. All minds must have come, by the way of the survival of the fittest, if by no directer path, to take an intense interest in the bodies to which they are yoked, altogether apart from any interest in the pure Ego which they also possess.

And similarly with the images of their person in the minds of others. I should not be extant now had I not become sensitive to looks of approval or disapproval on the faces among which my life is cast. Looks of contempt cast on other persons need affect me in no such peculiar way. My spiritual powers, again, must interest me more than those of other people, and for the same reason. I should not be here at all unless I had cultivated them and kept them from decay. And the same law which made me once care for them makes me care for them still.

All these three things form the *natural Me.* But all these things are *objects*, properly so called, to the thought which at any time may be doing the thinking; and if the zoölogical and evolutionary point of view is the true one, there is no reason why one object *might* not arouse passion and interest as primitively and instinctively as any other. The phenomenon of passion is in origin and essence the same, whatever be the target upon which it is discharged; and what the target actually happens to be is solely a question of fact. I might conceivably be as much fascinated, and as primitively so, by the care of my neighbor's body as by the care of my own. I *am* thus fascinated by the care of my child's body. The only check to such exuberant non-egoistic interests is natural selection, which would weed out such as were very harmful to the individual or to his tribe. Many such interests, however, remain unweeded out—the interest in the opposite sex, for example, which seems in mankind stronger than is called for by its utilitarian need; and alongside of them remain interests, like that in alcoholic intoxication, or in musical sounds, which, for aught we can see, are without any utility whatever. The sympathetic instincts and the egoistic ones are thus coördinate. They arise, so far as we can tell, on the same psychologic level. The only difference between them is that the instincts called egoistic form much the larger mass.

Summary.—The following table may serve for a summary of what has been said thus far. The empirical life of Self is divided, as below, into

	MATERIAL	SOCIAL	SPIRITUAL
SELF-SEEKING	Bodily Appetites and Instincts. Love of Adornment, Foppery, Acquisitiveness, Constructiveness. Love of Home, etc.	Desire to Please, be Noticed, Admired, etc. Sociability, Emulation, Envy, Love, Pursuit of Honor, Ambition, etc.	Intellectual, Moral and Religious Aspirations, Conscientiousness.
SELF-ESTIMATION	Personal Vanity, Modesty, etc. Pride of Wealth, Fear of Poverty.	Social and Family Pride, Vainglory, Snobbery, Humility, Shame, etc.	Sense of Moral or Mental Superiority, Purity, etc. Sense of Inferiority or of Guilt.

B) THE SELF AS KNOWER

The I, or 'pure ego,' is a very much more difficult subject of inquiry than the Me. It is that which at any given moment *is* conscious, whereas the Me is only one of the things which it is conscious *of*. In other words, it is the *Thinker*; and the question immediately comes up, *what* is the thinker? Is it the passing state of consciousness itself, or is it something deeper and less mutable? The passing state we have seen to be the very embodiment of change (see p. 143 ff.). Yet each of us spontaneously considers that by 'I,' he means something always the same. This has led most philosophers to postulate behind the passing state of consciousness a permanent Substance or Agent whose modification or act it is. This Agent is the thinker; the 'state' is only its instrument or means. 'Soul,' 'transcendental Ego,' 'Spirit,' are so many names for this more permanent sort of Thinker. Not discriminating them just yet, let us proceed to define our idea of the passing state of consciousness more clearly.

The Unity of the Passing Thought.—Already, in speaking of 'sensations,' from the point of view of Fechner's idea of measuring them, we saw that there was no ground for calling them compounds. But what is true of sensations cognizing simple qualities is also true of thoughts with complex objects composed of many parts. This proposition unfortunately runs counter to a widespread prejudice, and will have to be defended at some length. Common-sense, and psychologists of almost every school, have agreed that whenever an object of thought contains many elements, the thought itself must be made up of just as many ideas, one idea for each element, all fused together in appearance, but really separate.

"There can be no difficulty in admitting that association *does* form the ideas of an indefinite number of individuals into one complex idea," says James Mill, "because it is an acknowledged fact. Have we not the idea of an army? And is not that precisely the ideas of an indefinite number of men formed into one idea?"

Similar quotations might be multiplied, and the reader's own first impressions probably would rally to their support. Suppose, for example, he thinks that "the pack of cards is on the table." If he begins to reflect, he is as likely as not to say: "Well, isn't that a thought of the pack of cards? Isn't it of the cards as included in the pack? Isn't it of the table? And of the legs of the table as well? Hasn't my thought, then, all these parts—one part for the pack and another for the table? And within the pack-part a part for each card, as within the table-part a part for each leg? And isn't each of these parts an idea? And can thought, then, be anything but an assemblage or pack of ideas, each answering to some element of what it knows?"

Plausible as such considerations may seem, it is astonishing how little force they have. In assuming a pack of ideas, each cognizant of some one element of the fact one has assumed, nothing has been assumed which knows the whole fact *at once*. The idea which, on the hypothesis of the pack of ideas, knows, *e.g.*, the ace of spades must be ignorant of the leg of the table, since to account for that knowledge another special idea is by the same hypothesis invoked; and so on with the rest of the ideas, all equally ignorant of each other's objects. And yet in the actual living human mind what knows the cards also knows the table, its legs, etc., for all these things are known in relation to each other and at once. Our notion of the abstract numbers eight, four, two is as truly one feeling in the mind as our notion of simple unity. Our idea of a couple is not a couple of ideas. "But," the reader may say, "is not the taste of lemonade composed of that of lemon *plus* that of sugar?" No! I reply, this is taking the combining of objects for that of feelings. The physical lemonade contains both the lemon

176

and the sugar, but its taste does not contain their tastes; for if there are any two things which are certainly *not* present in the taste of lemonade, those are the pure lemon-sour on the one hand and the pure sugar-sweet on the other. These tastes are absent utterly. A taste somewhat *like* both of them is there, but that is a distinct state of mind altogether.

Distinct mental states cannot 'fuse.' But not only is the notion that our ideas are combinations of smaller ideas improbable, it is logically unintelligible; it leaves out the essential features of all the 'combinations' which we actually know.

All the 'combinations' which we actually know are EFFECTS, *wrought by the units said to be 'combined,'* UPON SOME ENTITY OTHER THAN THEMSELVES. Without this feature of a medium or vehicle, the notion of combination has no sense.

In other words, no possible number of entities (call them as you like, whether forces, material particles, or mental elements) can sum *themselves* together. Each remains, in the sum, what it always was; and the sum itself exists only *for a bystander* who happens to overlook the units and to apprehend the sum as such; or else it exists in the shape of some other effect on an entity external to the sum itself. When H_2 and O are said to combine into 'water,' and thenceforward to exhibit new properties, the 'water' is just the old atoms in the new position, H–O–H; the 'new properties' are just their combined *effects*, when in this position, upon external media, such as our sense-organs and the various reagents on which water may exert its properties and be known. Just so, the strength of many men may combine when they pull upon one rope, of many muscular fibres when they pull upon one tendon.

In the parallelogram of forces, the 'forces' do not combine *themselves* into the diagonal resultant; a *body* is needed on which they may impinge, to exhibit their resultant effect. No more do musical sounds combine *per se* into concords or discords. Concord and discord are names for their combined effects on that external medium, the *ear*.

Where the elemental units are supposed to be feelings, the case is in no wise altered. Take a hundred of them, shuffle them and pack them as close together as you can (whatever that may mean); still each remains the same feeling it always was, shut in its own skin, windowless, ignorant of what the other feelings are and mean. There would be a hundred-and-first feeling there, if, when a group or series of such feelings were set up, a consciousness *belonging to the group as such* should emerge; and this one hundred and first feeling would be a totally new fact. The one hundred original feelings might, by a curious physical law, be a signal for its *creation*, when they came together—we often have to learn things separately before we know them as a sum—but they would have no substantial identity with the new feeling, nor it with them; and one could never deduce the one from the others, or (in any intelligible sense) say that they *evolved* it out of themselves.

Take a sentence of a dozen words, and take twelve men and tell to each one word. Then stand the men in a row or jam them in a bunch, and let each think of his word as intently as he will: nowhere will there be a consciousness of the whole sentence. We talk, it is true, of the 'spirit of the age,' and the 'sentiment of the people,' and in various ways we hypostatize 'public opinion.' But we know this to be symbolic speech, and never dream that the spirit, opinion, or sentiment constitutes a consciousness other than, and additional to, that of the several individuals whom the words 'age,' 'people,' or 'public' denote. The private minds do not agglomerate into a higher compound mind. This has always been the invincible contention of the spiritualists against the associationists in Psychology. The associationists say the mind is constituted by a multiplicity of distinct 'ideas' *associated* into a unity. There is, they say, an idea of *a*, and also an idea of *b*. *Therefore*, they say, there is an idea of *a+b*, or of *a* and *b* together. Which is like saying that the mathematical square of *a* plus that of *b* is equal to the square of *a+b*, a palpable untruth. Idea of *a*, plus idea of *b*, are *not* identical with idea of *(a+b)*. It is one, they are two; in it, what knows *a* also knows *b*; in them, what knows *a* is expressly posited as not knowing *b*; etc. In short, the two separate ideas can never by any logic be made to figure as one idea. If one idea (of *a+b*, for example) come as a matter of fact after the two separate ideas (of *a* and of *b*), then we must hold it to be as direct a product of the later conditions as the two separate ideas were of the earlier conditions.

The simplest thing, therefore, if we are to assume the existence of a stream of consciousness at all, would be to suppose that things that are known together are known in single pulses of that stream. The things may be many, and may occasion many currents in the brain. But the psychic phenomenon correlative to these many currents is one integral 'state,' transitive or substantive (see p. 146), to which the many things appear.

The Soul as a Combining Medium.—The spiritualists in philosophy have been prompt to see that things which are known together are known by one *something*, but that something, they say, is no mere passing thought, but a simple and permanent spiritual being on which many ideas combine their effects. It makes no difference in this connection whether this being be called Soul, Ego, or Spirit, in either case its chief function is that of a combining medium. This is a different vehicle of knowledge from that in which we just said that the mystery of knowing things together might be most simply lodged. Which is the real knower, this permanent being, or our passing state? If we had other grounds, not yet considered, for admitting the Soul into our psychology, then getting there on those grounds, she might turn out to be the knower too. But if there be no *other* grounds for admitting the Soul, we had better cling to our passing 'states' as the exclusive agents of knowledge; for we have to assume their existence anyhow in psychology, and the knowing of many things together is just as well accounted for when we call it one of their functions as when we call it a reaction of the Soul. *Explained* it is not by either conception, and has to figure in psychology as a datum that is ultimate.

But there are other alleged grounds for admitting the Soul into psychology, and the chief of them is

The Sense of Personal Identity.—In the last chapter it was stated (see p. 141) that the thoughts which we actually know to exist do not fly about loose, but seem each to belong to some one thinker and not to another. Each thought, out of a multitude of other thoughts of which it may think, is able to distinguish those which belong to it from those which do not. The former have a warmth and intimacy about them of which the latter are completely devoid, and the result is a Me of yesterday, judged to be in some peculiarly subtle sense the *same* with the I who now make the judgment. As a mere subjective phenomenon the judgment presents no special mystery. It belongs to the great class of judgments of sameness; and there is nothing more remarkable in making a judgment of sameness in the first person than in the second or the third. The intellectual operations seem essentially alike, whether I say 'I am the same as I was,' or whether I say 'the pen is the same as it was, yesterday.' It is as easy to think this as to think the opposite and say 'neither of us is the same.' The only question which we have to consider is whether it be a right judgment. *Is the sameness predicated really there?*

Sameness in the Self as Known.—If in the sentence "I am the same that I was yesterday," we take the 'I' broadly, it is evident that in many ways I am *not* the same. As a concrete Me, I am somewhat different from what I was: then hungry, now full; then walking, now at rest; then poorer, now richer; then younger, now older; etc. And yet in other ways I *am* the same, and we may call these the essential ways. My name and profession and relations to the world are identical, my face, my faculties and store of memories, are practically indistinguishable, now and then. Moreover the Me of now and the Me of then are *continuous*: the alterations were gradual and never affected the whole of me at once. So far, then, my personal identity is just like the sameness predicated of any other aggregate thing. It is a conclusion grounded either on the resemblance in essential respects, or on the continuity of the phenomena compared. And it must not be taken to mean more than these grounds warrant, or treated as a sort of metaphysical or absolute Unity in which all differences are overwhelmed. The past and present selves compared are the same just so far as they *are* the same, and no farther. They are the same in *kind*. But this generic sameness coexists with generic differences just as real; and if from the one point of view I am one self, from another I am quite as truly many. Similarly of the attribute of continuity: it gives to the self the unity of mere connectedness, or unbrokenness, a perfectly definite phenomenal thing—but it gives not a jot or tittle more.

Sameness in the Self as Knower.—But all this is said only of the Me, or Self as known. In the judgment 'I am the same,' etc., the 'I' was taken broadly as the concrete person. Suppose, however, that we take it narrowly, as the *Thinker*, as '*that to which*' all the concrete determinations of the Me belong and are known: does there not then appear an absolute identity at different times? That something which at every moment goes out and knowingly appropriates the *Me* of the past, and discards the non-me as foreign, is it not a permanent abiding principle of spiritual activity identical with itself wherever found?

That it is such a principle is the reigning doctrine both of philosophy and common-sense, and yet reflection finds it difficult to justify the idea. *If there were no passing states of consciousness*, then indeed we might suppose an abiding principle, absolutely one with itself, to be the ceaseless thinker in each one of us. But if the states of consciousness be accorded as realities, no such 'substantial' identity in the thinker need be supposed. Yesterday's and to-day's states of consciousnesses have no *substantial* identity, for when one is here the other is irrevocably dead and gone. But they have a *functional* identity, for both know the same objects, and so far as the by-gone me is one of those objects, they react upon it in an identical way, greeting it and calling it *mine*, and opposing it to all the other things they know. This functional identity seems really the only sort of identity in the thinker which the facts require us to suppose. Successive thinkers, numerically distinct, but all aware of the same past in the same way, form an adequate vehicle for all the experience of personal unity and sameness which we actually have. And just such a train of successive thinkers is the stream of mental states (each with its complex object cognized and emotional and selective reaction thereupon) which psychology treated as a natural science has to assume (see p. 10).

The logical conclusion seems then to be that *the states of consciousness are all that psychology needs to do her work with. Metaphysics or theology may prove the Soul to exist; but for psychology the hypothesis of such a substantial principle of unity is superfluous.*

How the I appropriates the Me.—But *why* should each successive mental state appropriate the same past Me? I spoke a while ago of my own past experiences appearing to me with a 'warmth and intimacy' which the experiences thought of by me as having occurred to other people lack. This leads us to the answer sought. My present Me is felt with warmth and intimacy. The heavy warm mass of my body is there, and the nucleus of the 'spiritual me,' the sense of intimate activity (p. 163), is there. We cannot realize our present self without simultaneously feeling one or other of these two things. Any other object of thought which brings these two things with it into consciousness will be thought with a warmth and an intimacy like those which cling to the present me.

Any *distant* object which fulfils this condition will be thought with such warmth and intimacy. But which distant objects *do* fulfil the condition, when represented?

Obviously those, and only those, which fulfilled it when they were alive. *Them* we shall still represent with the animal warmth upon them; to them may possibly still cling the flavor of the inner activity taken in the act. And by a natural consequence, we shall assimilate them to each other and to the warm and intimate self we now feel within us as we think, and separate them as a collection from whatever objects have not this mark, much as out of a herd of cattle let loose for the winter on some wide Western prairie the owner picks out and sorts together, when the round-up comes in the spring, all the beasts on which he finds his own particular brand. Well, just such objects are the past experiences which I now call mine. Other men's experiences, no matter how much I may know about them, never bear this vivid, this peculiar brand. This is why Peter, awakening in the same bed with Paul, and recalling what both had in mind before they went to sleep, reidentifies and appropriates the 'warm' ideas as his, and is never tempted to confuse them with those cold and pale-appearing ones which he ascribes to Paul. As well might he confound Paul's body, which he only sees, with his own body, which he sees but also feels. Each of us when he awakens says, Here's the same old Me again, just as he says, Here's the same old bed, the same old room, the same old world.

And similarly in our waking hours, though each pulse of consciousness dies away and is replaced by another, yet that other, among the things it knows, knows its own predecessor, and finding it 'warm,' in the way we have described, greets it, saying: "Thou art *mine*, and part of the same self with me." Each later thought, knowing and including thus the thoughts that went before, is the final receptacle—and appropriating them is the final owner—of all that they contain and own. As Kant says, it is as if elastic balls were to have not only motion but knowledge of it, and a first ball were to transmit both its motion and its consciousness to a second, which took both up into *its* consciousness and passed them to a third, until the last ball held all that the other balls had held, and realized it as its own. It is this trick which the nascent thought has of immediately taking up the expiring thought and 'adopting' it, which leads to the appropriation of most of the remoter constituents of the self. Who owns the last self owns the self before the last, for what possesses the possessor possesses the possessed. It is impossible to discover any *verifiable* features in personal identity which this sketch does not contain, impossible to imagine how any transcendent principle of Unity (were such a principle there) could shape matters to any other result, or be known by any other fruit, than just this production of a stream of consciousness each successive part of which should know, and knowing, hug to itself and adopt, all those that went before,—thus standing as the *representative* of an entire past stream with which it is in no wise to be identified.

Mutations and Multiplications of the Self.—The Me, like every other aggregate, changes as it grows. The passing states of consciousness, which should preserve in their succession an identical knowledge of its past, wander from their duty, letting large portions drop from out of their ken, and representing other portions wrong. The identity which we recognize as we survey the long procession can only be the relative identity of a slow shifting in which there is always some common ingredient retained. The commonest element of all, the most uniform, is the possession of some common memories. However different the man may be from the youth, both look back on the same childhood and call it their own.

Thus the identity found by the *I* in its *Me* is only a loosely construed thing, an identity 'on the whole,' just like that which any outside observer might find in the same assemblage of facts. We often say of a man 'he is so changed one would not know him'; and so does a man, less often, speak of himself. These changes in the *Me*, recognized by the I, or by outside observers, may be grave or slight. They deserve some notice here.

The mutations of the Self may be divided into two main classes:

a. Alterations of memory; and

b. Alterations in the present bodily and spiritual selves.

a. Of the alterations of memory little need be said—they are so familiar. Losses of memory are a normal incident in life, especially in advancing years, and the person's *me*, as 'realized,' shrinks *pari passu* with the facts that disappear. The memory of dreams and of experiences in the hypnotic trance rarely survives.

False memories, also, are by no means rare occurrences, and whenever they occur they distort our consciousness of our Me. Most people, probably, are in doubt about certain matters ascribed to their past. They may have seen them, may have said them, done them, or they may only have dreamed or imagined they did so. The content of a dream will oftentimes insert itself into the stream of real life in a most perplexing way. The most frequent source of false memory is the accounts we give to others of our experiences. Such accounts we almost always make both more simple and more interesting than the truth. We quote what we should have said or done, rather than what we really said or did; and in the first telling we may be fully aware of the distinction. But ere long the fiction expels the reality from memory and reigns in its stead alone. This is one great source of the fallibility of testimony meant to be quite honest. Especially where the marvellous is concerned, the story takes a tilt that way, and the memory follows the story.

b. When we pass beyond alterations of memory to abnormal *alterations in the present self* we have graver disturbances. These alterations are of three main types, but our knowledge of the elements and causes of these changes of personality is so slight that the division into types must not be regarded as having any profound significance. The types are:

α. Insane delusions;
β. Alternating selves;
γ. Mediumships or possessions.

α. In insanity we often have delusions projected into the past, which are melancholic or sanguine according to the character of the disease. But the worst alterations of the self come from present perversions of sensibility and impulse which leave the past undisturbed, but induce the patient to think that the present *Me* is an altogether new personage. Something of this sort happens normally in the rapid expansion of the whole character, intellectual as well as volitional, which takes place after the time of puberty. The pathological cases are curious enough to merit longer notice.

The basis of our personality, as M. Ribot says, is that feeling of our vitality which, because it is so perpetually present, remains in the background of our consciousness.

"It is the basis because, always present, always acting, without peace or rest, it knows neither sleep nor fainting, and lasts as long as life itself, of which it is one form. It serves as a support to that self-conscious *me* which memory constitutes, it is the medium of association among its other parts. . . . Suppose now that it were possible at once to change our body and put another into its place: skeleton, vessels, viscera, muscles, skin, everything made new, except the nervous system with its stored-up memory of the past. There can be no doubt that in such a case the afflux of un-accustomed vital sensations would produce the gravest disorders. Between the old sense of existence engraved on the nervous system, and the new one acting with all the intensity of its reality and novelty, there would be irreconcilable contradiction."

What the particular perversions of the bodily sensibility may be which give rise to these contradictions is, for the most part, impossible for a sound-minded person to conceive. One patient has another self that repeats all his thoughts for him. Others, amongst whom are some of the first characters in history, have internal dæmons who speak with them and are replied to. Another feels that someone 'makes' his thoughts for him. Another has two bodies, lying in different beds. Some patients feel as if they had lost parts of their bodies, teeth, brain, stomach, etc. In some it is made of wood, glass, butter, etc. In some it does not exist any longer, or is dead, or is a foreign object quite separate from the speaker's self. Occasionally, parts of the body lose their connection for consciousness with the rest, and are treated as belonging to another person and moved by a hostile will. Thus the right hand may fight with the left as with an enemy. Or the cries of the patient himself are assigned to another person with whom the patient expresses sympathy. The literature of insanity is filled with narratives of such illusions as these. M. Taine quotes from a patient of Dr. Krishaber an account of sufferings, from which it will be seen how completely aloof from what is normal a man's experience may suddenly become:

"After the first or second day it was for some weeks impossible to observe or analyze myself. The suffering—angina pectoris—was too overwhelming. It was not till the first days of January that I could give an account to myself of what I experienced. . . . Here is the first thing of which I retain a clear remembrance. I was alone, and already a prey to permanent visual trouble, when I was suddenly seized with a visual trouble infinitely more pro-nounced. Objects grew small and receded to infinite distances—men and things together. I was myself immeasurably far away. I looked about me with terror and astonishment; *the world was escaping from me*. . . . I remarked at the same time that my voice was extremely far away from me, that it sounded no longer as if mine. I struck the ground with my foot, and perceived its resistance; but this resistance seemed illusory—not that the soil was soft, but that the weight of my body was reduced to almost nothing. . . . I had the feeling of being without weight. . . ." In addition to being so distant, "objects appeared to me *flat*. When I spoke with anyone, I saw him like an image cut out of paper with no relief. . . . This sensation lasted intermittently for two years. . . . Constantly it seemed as if my legs did not belong to me. It was almost as bad with my arms. As for my head, it seemed no longer to exist. . . . I appeared to myself to act automatically, by an impulsion foreign to myself. . . . There was inside of me a new being, and another part of myself, the old being, which took no interest in the new-comer. I distinctly remember saying to myself that the sufferings of this new being were to me indifferent. I was never really dupe of these illusions, but my mind grew often tired of incessantly correcting the new impressions, and I let myself go and live the unhappy life of this new entity. I had an ardent desire to see my old world again, to get back to my old self. This desire kept me from killing myself. . . . I was another, and I hated, I despised this other; he was perfectly odious to me; it was certainly another who had taken my form and assumed my functions."[1]

In cases like this, it is as certain that the *I* is unaltered as that the *Me* is changed. That is to say, the present Thought of the patient is cognitive of both the old Me and the new, so long as its memory holds good. Only, within that objective sphere which formerly lent itself so simply to the judgment of recognition and of egoistic appropriation, strange perplexities have arisen. The present and the past, both seen therein, will not unite. Where is my old Me? What is this new one? Are they the same? Or have I two? Such questions, answered by whatever theory the patient is able to conjure up as plausible, form the beginning of his insane life.

β. The phenomenon of *alternating personality* in its simplest phases seems based on lapses of memory. Any man becomes, as we say, *inconsistent* with himself if he forgets his engagements, pledges, knowledges, and habits; and it is merely a question of degree at what point we shall say that his personality is changed. But in the pathological cases known as those of double or alternate personal-

[1] *De l'intelligence*, 3me édition (1878), vol. II, p. 461, note.

ity the loss of memory is abrupt, and is usually preceded by a period of unconsciousness or syncope lasting a variable length of time. In the hypnotic trance we can easily produce an alteration of the personality, either by telling the subject to forget all that has happened to him since such or such a date, in which case he becomes (it may be) a child again, or by telling him he is another altogether imaginary personage, in which case all facts about himself seem for the time being to lapse from out his mind, and he throws himself into the new character with a vivacity proportionate to the amount of histrionic imagination which he possesses. But in the pathological cases the transformation is spontaneous. The most famous case, perhaps, on record is that of Félida X., reported by Dr. Azam of Bordeaux. At the age of fourteen this woman began to pass into a 'secondary' state characterized by a change in her general disposition and character, as if certain 'inhibitions,' previously existing, were suddenly removed. During the secondary state she remembered the first state, but on emerging from it into the first state she remembered nothing of the second. At the age of forty-four the duration of the secondary state (which was on the whole superior in quality to the original state) had gained upon the latter so much as to occupy most of her time. During it she remembers the events belonging to the original state, but her complete oblivion of the secondary state when the original state recurs is often very distressing to her, as, for example, when the transition takes place in a carriage on her way to a funeral, and she has no idea which one of her friends may be dead. She actually became pregnant during one of her early secondary states, and during her first state had no knowledge of how it had come to pass. Her distress at these blanks of memory is sometimes intense and once drove her to attempt suicide.

M. Pierre Janet describes a still more remarkable case as follows: "Léonie B., whose life sounds more like an improbable romance than a genuine history, has had attacks of natural somnambulism since the age of three years. She has been hypnotized constantly by all sorts of persons from the age of sixteen upwards, and she is now forty-five. Whilst her normal life developed in one way in the midst of her poor country surroundings, her second life was passed in drawing-rooms and doctors' offices, and naturally took an entirely different direction. To-day, when in her normal state, this poor peasant woman is a serious and rather sad person, calm and slow, very mild with everyone, and extremely timid: to look at her one would never suspect the personage which she contains. But hardly is she put to sleep hypnotically when a metamorphosis occurs. Her face is no longer the same. She keeps her eyes closed, it is true, but the acuteness of her other senses supplies their place. She is gay, noisy, restless, sometimes insupportably so. She remains good-natured, but has acquired a singular tendency to irony and sharp jesting. Nothing is more curious than to hear her after a sitting when she has received a visit from strangers who wished to see her asleep. She gives a word-portrait of them, apes their manners, claims to know their little ridiculous aspects and passions, and for each invents a romance. To this character must be added the possession of an enormous number of recollections, whose existence she does not even suspect when awake, for her amnesia is then complete. . . . She refuses the name of Léonie and takes that of Léontine (Léonie 2) to which her first magnetizers had accustomed her. 'That good woman is not myself,' she says, 'she is too stupid!' To herself, Léontine, or Léonie 2, she attributes all the sensations and all the actions, in a word all the conscious experiences, which she has undergone *in somnambulism*, and knits them together to make the history of her already long life. To Léonie 1 [as M. Janet calls the waking woman], on the other hand, she exclusively ascribes the events lived through in waking hours. I was at first struck by an important exception to the rule, and was disposed to think that there might be something arbitrary in this partition of her recollections. In the normal state Léonie has a husband and children; but Léonie 2, the somnambulist, whilst acknowledging the children as her own, attributes the husband to 'the other.' This choice was perhaps explicable, but it followed no rule. It was not till later that I learned that her magnetizers in early days, as audacious as certain hypnotizers of recent date, had somnambulized her for her first *accouchements*, and that she had lapsed into that state spontaneously in the later ones. Léonie 2 was thus quite right in ascribing to herself the children—it was she who had had them, and the rule that her first trance-state forms a different personality was not broken. But it is the same with her second or deepest state of trance. When after the renewed passes, syncope, etc., she reaches the condition which I have called Léonie 3, she is another person still. Serious and grave, instead of being a restless child, she speaks slowly and moves but little. Again she separates herself from the waking

Léonie 1. 'A good but rather stupid woman,' she says, 'and not me.' And she also separates herself from Léonie 2: 'How can you see anything of me in that crazy creature?' she says. 'Fortunately I am nothing for her.'"

γ. In *'mediumships'* or *'possessions'* the invasion and the passing away of the secondary state are both relatively abrupt, and the duration of the state is usually short—i.e., from a few minutes to a few hours. Whenever the secondary state is well developed, no memory for aught that happened during it remains after the primary consciousness comes back. The subject during the secondary consciousness speaks, writes, or acts as if animated by a foreign person, and often names this foreign person and gives his history. In old times the foreign 'control' was usually a demon, and is so now in communities which favor that belief. With us he gives himself out at the worst for an Indian or other grotesquely speaking but harmless personage. Usually he purports to be the spirit of a dead person known or unknown to those present, and the subject is then what we call a 'medium.' Mediumistic possession in all its grades seems to form a perfectly natural special type of alternate personality, and the susceptibility to it in some form is by no means an uncommon gift, in persons who have no other obvious nervous anomaly. The phenomena are very intricate, and are only just beginning to be studied in a proper scientific way. The lowest phase of mediumship is automatic writing, and the lowest grade of that is where the Subject knows what words are coming, but feels impelled to write them as if from without. Then comes writing unconsciously, even whilst engaged in reading or talk. Inspirational speaking, playing on musical instruments, etc., also belong to the relatively lower phases of possession, in which the normal self is not excluded from conscious participation in the performance, though their initiative seems to come from elsewhere. In the highest phase the trance is complete, the voice, language, and everything are changed, and there is no after-memory whatever until the next trance comes. One curious thing about trance-utterances is their generic similarity in different individuals. The 'control' here in America is either a grotesque, slangy, and flippant personage ('Indian' controls, calling the ladies 'squaws,' the men 'braves,' the house a 'wigwam,' etc., etc., are excessively common); or, if he ventures on higher intellectual flights, he abounds in a curiously vague optimistic philosophy-and-water, in which phrases about spirit, harmony, beauty, law, progression, development, etc., keep recurring. It seems exactly as if one author composed more than half of the trance-messages, no matter by whom they are uttered. Whether all sub-conscious selves are peculiarly susceptible to a certain stratum of the *Zeitgeist*, and get their inspiration from it, I know not; but this is obviously the case with the secondary selves which become 'developed' in spiritualist circles. There the beginnings of the medium trance are indistinguishable from effects of hypnotic suggestion. The subject assumes the rôle of a medium simply because opinion expects it of him under the conditions which are present; and carries it out with a feebleness or a vivacity proportionate to his histrionic gifts. But the odd thing is that persons unexposed to spiritualist traditions will so often act in the same way when they become entranced, speak in the name of the departed, go through the motions of their several death-agonies, send messages about their happy home in the summer-land, and describe the ailments of those present.

I have no theory to publish of these cases, the actual beginning of several of which I have personally seen. I am, however, persuaded by abundant acquaintance with the trances of one medium that the 'control' may be altogether different from any *actual* waking self of the person. In the case I have in mind, it professes to be a certain departed French doctor; and is, I am convinced, acquainted with facts about the circumstances, and the living and dead relatives and acquaintances, of numberless sitters whom the medium never met before, and of whom she has never heard the names. I record my bare opinion here unsupported by the evidence, not, of course, in order to convert anyone to my view, but because I am persuaded that a serious study of these trance-phenomena is one of the greatest needs of psychology, and think that my personal confession may possibly draw a reader or two into a field which the *soi-disant* 'scientist' usually refuses to explore.[2]

Review, and Psychological Conclusion.—To sum up this long chapter:—The consciousness of Self involves a stream of thought,

---

[2] Some of the evidence for this medium's supernormal powers is given in *The Proceedings of the Society for Psychical Research*, vol. VI, p. 436, and in the first Part of vol. VIII (1892).

each part of which as 'I' can remember those which went before, know the things they knew, and care paramountly for certain ones among them as '*Me*,' and *appropriate to these* the rest. This Me is an empirical aggregate of things objectively known. The *I* which knows them cannot itself be an aggregate; neither for psychological purposes need it be an unchanging metaphysical entity like the Soul, or a principle like the transcendental Ego, viewed as 'out of time.' It is a *thought*, at each moment different from that of the last moment, but *appropriative* of the latter, together with all that the latter called its own. All the experiential facts find their place in this description, unencumbered with any hypothesis save that of the existence of passing thoughts or states of mind.

If passing thoughts be the directly verifiable existents which no school has hitherto doubted them to be, then they are the only 'Knower' of which Psychology, treated as a natural science, need take any account. The only pathway that I can discover for bringing in a more transcendental Thinker would be to deny that we have any such *direct* knowledge of the existence of our 'states of consciousness' as common-sense supposes us to possess. The existence of the 'states' in question would then be a mere hypothesis, or one way of asserting that there *must be* a knower correlative to all this known; but the problem *who that knower is* would have become a metaphysical problem. With the question once stated in these terms, the notion either of a Spirit of the world which thinks through us, or that of a set of individual substantial souls, must be considered as *primâ facie* on a par with our own 'psychological' solution, and discussed impartially. I myself believe that room for much future inquiry lies in this direction. The 'states of mind' which every psychologist believes in are by no means clearly apprehensible, if distinguished from their objects. But to doubt them lies beyond the scope of our natural-science (see p. 9) point of view. And in this book the provisional solution which we have reached must be the final word: the thoughts themselves are the thinkers.

Chapter XIII

Attention

The Narrowness of Consciousness.—One of the most extraordinary facts of our life is that, although we are besieged at every moment by impressions from our whole sensory surface, we notice so very small a part of them. The sum total of our impressions never enters into our *experience*, consciously so called, which runs through this sum total like a tiny rill through a broad flowery mead. Yet the physical impressions which do not count are *there* as much as those which do, and affect our sense-organs just as energetically. Why they fail to pierce the mind is a mystery, which is only named and not explained when we invoke *die Enge des Bewusstseins*, 'the narrowness of consciousness,' as its ground.

Its Physiological Ground.—Our consciousness certainly is narrow, when contrasted with the breadth of our sensory surface and the mass of incoming currents which are at all times pouring in. Evidently no current can be recorded in conscious experience unless it succeed in penetrating to the hemispheres and filling their pathways by the processes set up. When an incoming current thus occupies the hemispheres with its consequences, other currents are for the time kept out. They may show their faces at the door, but are turned back until the actual possessors of the place are tired. Physiologically, then, the narrowness of consciousness seems to depend on the fact that the activity of the hemispheres tends at all times to be a consolidated and unified affair, determinable now by this current and now by that, but determinable only as a whole. The ideas correlative to the reigning system of processes are those which are said to 'interest' us at the time; and thus that selective character of our attention on which so much stress was laid on pp. 156 ff. appears to find a physiological ground. At all times, however, there is a liability to disintegration of the reigning system. The consolidation is seldom quite complete, the excluded currents are not wholly abortive, their presence affects the 'fringe' and margin of our thought.

Dispersed Attention.—Sometimes, indeed, the normal consolidation seems hardly to exist. At such moments it is possible that cerebral activity sinks to a minimum. Most of us probably fall several times a day into a fit somewhat like this: The eyes are fixed on vacancy, the sounds of the world melt into confused unity, the attention is dispersed so that the whole body is felt, as it were, at once, and the foreground of consciousness is filled, if by anything, by a sort of solemn sense of surrender to the empty passing of time. In the dim background of our mind we know meanwhile what we ought to be doing: getting up, dressing ourselves, answering the person who has spoken to us, trying to make the next step in our reasoning. But somehow we cannot *start*; the *pensée de derrière la tête* fails to pierce the shell of lethargy that wraps our state about. Every moment we expect the spell to break, for we know no reason why it should continue. But it does continue, pulse after pulse, and we float with it, until—also without reason that we can discover—an energy is given, something—we know not what—enables us to gather ourselves together, we wink our eyes, we shake our heads, the background-ideas become effective, and the wheels of life go round again.

This is the extreme of what is called dispersed attention. Between this extreme and the extreme of concentrated attention, in which absorption in the interest of the moment is so complete that grave bodily injuries may be unfelt, there are intermediate degrees, and these have been studied experimentally. The problem is known as that of

The Span of Consciousness.—How many objects can we attend to at once when they are not embraced in one conceptual system? Prof. Cattell experimented with combinations of letters exposed to the eye for so short a fraction of a second that attention to them in succession seemed to be ruled out. When the letters formed familiar words, three times as many of them could be named as when their combination was meaningless. If the words formed a sentence, twice as many could be caught as when they had no connection. "The sentence was then apprehended as a whole. If not apprehended thus, almost nothing is apprehended of the several words; but if the sentence as a whole is apprehended, then the words appear very distinct."

A word is a conceptual system in which the letters do not enter consciousness separately, as they do when apprehended alone. A sentence flashed at once upon the eye is such a system relatively to its words. A conceptual system may *mean* many sensible objects, may be translated later into them, but as an actual existent mental state, it does not *consist of* the consciousnesses of these objects. When I think of the word *man* as a whole, for instance, what is in my mind is something different from what is there when I think of the letters *m*, *a*, and *n*, as so many disconnected data.

When data are so disconnected that we have no conception which embraces them together it is much harder to apprehend several of them at once, and the mind tends to let go of one whilst it attends to another. Still, within limits this can be avoided. M. Paulhan has experimented on the matter by declaiming one poem aloud whilst he repeated a different one mentally, or by writing one sentence whilst speaking another, or by performing calculations on paper whilst reciting poetry. He found that "the most favorable condition for the doubling of the mind was its simultaneous application to two easy and heterogeneous operations. Two operations of the same sort, two multiplications, two recitations, or the reciting one poem and writing another, render the process more uncertain and difficult."

M. Paulhan compared the time occupied by the same two operations done simultaneously or in succession, and found that there was often a considerable gain of time from doing them simultaneously. For instance:

"I multiply 421 312 212 by 2; the operation takes 6 seconds; the recitation of four verses also takes 6 seconds. But the two operations done at once only take 6 seconds, so that there is no loss of time from combining them."

If, then, by the original question, how many objects can we attend to at once, be meant how many entirely disconnected systems or processes can go on simultaneously, the answer is, *not easily more than one, unless the processes are very habitual; but then two, or even three*, without very much oscillation of the attention. Where, however, the processes are less automatic, as in the story of Julius Cæsar dictating four letters whilst he writes a fifth, there must be a rapid oscillation of the mind from one to the next, and no consequent gain of time.

When the things to be attended to are minute sensations, and when the effort is to be exact in noting them, it is found that attention to one interferes a good deal with the perception of the other. A good deal of fine work has been done in this field by Professor Wundt. He tried to note the exact position on a dial of a rapidly revolving hand, at the moment when a bell struck. Here were two disparate sensations, one of vision, the other of sound, to be noted together. But it was found that in a long and patient research, the eye-impression could seldom or never be noted at the exact moment when the bell actually struck. An earlier or a later point were all that could be seen.

The Varieties of Attention.—Attention may be divided into kinds in various ways. It is either to

a) Objects of sense (sensorial attention); or to

b) Ideal or represented objects (intellectual attention). It is either

c) Immediate; or

d) Derived: immediate, when the topic or stimulus is interesting in itself, without relation to anything else; derived, when it owes its interest to association with some other immediately interesting thing. What I call derived attention has been named 'apperceptive' attention. Furthermore, Attention may be either

e) Passive, reflex, involuntary, effortless; or

f) Active and voluntary.

Voluntary attention is always derived; we never make an *effort* to attend to an object except for the sake of some *remote* interest which the effort will serve. But both sensorial and intellectual attention may be either passive or voluntary.

In *involuntary attention* of the *immediate sensorial* sort the stimulus is either a sense-impression, very intense, voluminous, or sudden; or it is an *instinctive* stimulus, a perception which, by reason of its nature rather than its mere force, appeals to some one of our congenital impulses and has a directly exciting quality. In the chapter on Instinct we shall see how these stimuli differ from one animal to another, and what most of them are in man: strange things, moving things, wild animals, bright things, pretty things, metallic things, words, blows, blood, etc., etc., etc.

Sensitiveness to immediately exciting sensorial stimuli characterizes the attention of childhood and youth. In mature age we have generally selected those stimuli which are connected with one or more so-called permanent interests, and our attention has grown irresponsive to the rest. But childhood is characterized by great active energy, and has few organized interests by which to meet new impressions and decide whether they are worthy of notice or not, and the consequence is that extreme mobility of the attention with which we are all familiar in children, and which makes of their first lessons such chaotic affairs. Any strong sensation whatever produces accommodation of the organs which perceive it, and absolute oblivion, for the time being, of the task in hand. This reflex and passive character of the attention which, as a French writer says, makes the child seem to belong less to himself than to every object which happens to catch his notice, is the first thing which the teacher must overcome. It never is overcome in some people, whose work, to the end of life, gets done in the interstices of their mind-wandering.

The passive sensorial attention is *derived* when the impression, without being either strong or of an instinctively exciting nature, is connected by previous experience and education with things that are so. These things may be called the *motives* of the attention. The impression draws an interest from them, or perhaps it even fuses into a single complex object with them; the result is that it is brought into the focus of the mind. A faint tap *per se* is not an interesting sound; it may well escape being discriminated from the general rumor of the world. But when it is a signal, as that of a lover on the window-pane, hardly will it go unperceived. Herbart writes:

"How a bit of bad grammar wounds the ear of the purist! How a false note hurts the musician! or an offence against good manners the man of the world! How rapid is progress in a science when its first principles have been so well impressed upon us that we reproduce them mentally with perfect distinctness and ease! How slow and uncertain, on the other hand, is our learning of the principles themselves, when familiarity with the still more elementary percepts connected with the subject has not given us an adequate predisposition!—Apperceptive attention may be plainly observed in very small children when, hearing the speech of their elders, as yet unintelligible to them, they suddenly catch a single known word here and there, and repeat it to themselves; yes! even in the dog who looks round at us when we speak of him and pronounce his name. Not far removed is the talent which mind-wandering school-boys display during the hours of instruction, of noticing every moment in which the teacher tells a story. I remember classes in which, instruction being uninteresting, and discipline relaxed, a buzzing murmur was always to be heard, which invariably stopped for as long a time as an anecdote lasted. How could the boys, since they seemed to hear nothing, notice when the anecdote began? Doubtless most of them always heard something of the teacher's talk; but most of it had no connection with their previous knowledge and occupations, and therefore the separate words no sooner entered their consciousness than they fell out of it again; but, on the other hand, no sooner did the words awaken old thoughts, forming strongly-connected series with which the new impression easily combined, than out of new and old together a total interest resulted which drove the vagrant ideas below the threshold of consciousness, and brought for a while settled attention into their place."

Involuntary intellectual attention is immediate when we follow in thought a train of images exciting or interesting *per se*; derived, when the images are interesting only as means to a remote end, or merely because they are associated with something which makes them dear. The brain-currents may then form so solidly unified a system, and the absorption in their object be so deep, as to banish not only ordinary sensations, but even the severest pain. Pascal, Wesley, Robert Hall, are said to have had this capacity. Dr. Carpenter says of himself that "he has frequently begun a lecture, whilst suffering neuralgic pain so severe as to make him apprehend that he would find it impossible to proceed; yet no sooner has he, by a determined effort, fairly launched himself into the stream of thought, than he has found himself continuously borne along without the least distraction, until the end has come, and the attention has been released; when the pain has recurred with a force that has over-mastered all resistance, making him wonder how he could have ever ceased to feel it."[1]

Voluntary Attention.—Dr. Carpenter speaks of launching himself by a determined *effort*. This effort characterizes what we

---

[1] *Mental Physiology*, § 124. The oft-cited case of soldiers in battle not perceiving that they are wounded is of an analogous sort.

called *active or voluntary attention*. It is a feeling which everyone knows, but which most people would call quite indescribable. We get it in the sensorial sphere whenever we seek to catch an impression of extreme *faintness*, be it of sight, hearing, taste, smell, or touch; we get it whenever we seek to *discriminate* a sensation merged in a mass of others that are similar; we get it whenever we *resist the attractions* of more potent stimuli and keep our mind occupied with some object that is naturally unimpressive. We get it in the intellectual sphere under exactly similar conditions: as when we strive to sharpen and make distinct an idea which we but vaguely seem to have; or painfully discriminate a shade of meaning from its similars; or resolutely hold fast to a thought so discordant with our impulses that, if left unaided, it would quickly yield place to images of an exciting and impassioned kind. All forms of attentive effort would be exercised at once by one whom we might suppose at a dinner-party resolutely to listen to a neighbor giving him insipid and unwelcome advice in a low voice, whilst all around the guests were loudly laughing and talking about exciting and interesting things.

There is no such thing as voluntary attention sustained for more than a few seconds at a time. What is called sustained voluntary attention is a repetition of successive efforts which bring back the topic to the mind. The topic once brought back, if a congenial one, *develops*; and if its development is interesting it engages the attention passively for a time. Dr. Carpenter, a moment back, described the stream of thought, once entered, as 'bearing him along.' This passive interest may be short or long. As soon as it flags, the attention is diverted by some irrelevant thing, and then a voluntary effort may bring it back to the topic again; and so on, under favorable conditions, for hours together. During all this time, however, note that it is not an identical *object* in the psychological sense, but a succession of mutually related objects forming an identical *topic* only, upon which the attention is fixed. *No one can possibly attend continuously to an object that does not change.*

Now there are always some objects that for the time being *will not develop*. They simply *go out*; and to keep the mind upon anything related to them requires such incessantly renewed effort that the most resolute Will ere long gives out and lets its thoughts follow the more stimulating solicitations after it has withstood them for what length of time it can. There are topics known to every man from which he shies like a frightened horse, and which to get a glimpse of is to shun. Such are his ebbing assets to the spendthrift in full career. But why single out the spendthrift, when to every man actuated by passion the thought of interests which negate the passion can hardly for more than a fleeting instant stay before the mind? It is like 'memento mori' in the heyday of the pride of life. Nature rises at such suggestions, and excludes them from the view:—How long, O healthy reader, can you now continue thinking of your tomb?—In milder instances the difficulty is as great, especially when the brain is fagged. One snatches at any and every passing pretext, no matter how trivial or external, to escape from the odiousness of the matter in hand. I know a person, for example, who will poke the fire, set chairs straight, pick dust-specks from the floor, arrange his table, snatch up the newspaper, take down any book which catches his eye, trim his nails, waste the morning *anyhow*, in short, and all without premeditation,—simply because the only thing he *ought* to attend to is the preparation of a noonday lesson in formal logic which he detests. Anything but *that*!

Once more, the object must change. When it is one of sight, it will actually become invisible; when of hearing, inaudible,—if we attend to it too unmovingly. Helmholtz, who has put his sensorial attention to the severest tests, by using his eyes on objects which in common life are expressly overlooked, makes some interesting remarks on this point in his section on retinal rivalry. The phenomenon called by that name is this, that if we look with each eye upon a different picture (as in the annexed stereoscopic slide), sometimes one picture, sometimes the other, or parts of both, will

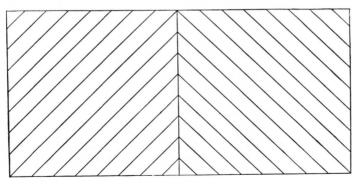

FIG. 54.

come to consciousness, but hardly ever both combined. Helmholtz now says:

"I find that I am able to attend voluntarily, now to one and now to the other system of lines; and that then this system remains visible alone for a certain time, whilst the other completely vanishes. This happens, for example, whenever I try to count the lines first of one and then of the other system. . . . But it is extremely hard to chain the attention down to one of the systems for long, unless we associate with our looking some distinct purpose which keeps the activity of the attention perpetually renewed. Such a one is counting the lines, comparing their intervals, or the like. An equilibrium of the attention, persistent for any length of time, is under no circumstances attainable. The natural tendency of attention when left to itself is to wander to ever new things; and so soon as the interest of its object is over, so soon as nothing new is to be noticed there, it passes, in spite of our will, to something else. *If we wish to keep it upon one and the same object, we must seek constantly to find out something new about the latter*, especially if other powerful impressions are attracting us away."

These words of Helmholtz are of fundamental importance. And if true of sensorial attention, how much more true are they of the intellectual variety! The *conditio sine quâ non* of sustained attention to a given topic of thought is that we should roll it over and over incessantly and consider different aspects and relations of it in turn. Only in pathological states will a fixed and ever monotonously recurring idea possess the mind.

Genius and Attention.—And now we can see why it is that what is called sustained attention is the easier, the richer in acquisitions and the fresher and more original the mind. In such minds, subjects bud and sprout and grow. At every moment, they please by a new consequence and rivet the attention afresh. But an intellect unfurnished with materials, stagnant, unoriginal, will hardly be likely to consider any subject long. A glance exhausts its possibilities of interest. Geniuses are commonly believed to excel other men in their power of sustained attention. In most of them, it is to be feared, the so-called 'power' is of the passive sort. Their ideas coruscate, every subject branches infinitely before their fertile minds, and so for hours they may be rapt. *But it is their genius making them attentive, not their attention making geniuses of them.* And, when we come down to the root of the matter, we see that they differ from ordinary men less in the character of their attention than in the nature of the objects upon which it is successively bestowed. In the genius, these form a concatenated series, suggesting each other mutually by some rational law. Therefore we call the attention 'sustained' and the topic of meditation for hours 'the same.' In the common man the series is for the most part incoherent, the objects have no rational bond, and we call the attention wandering and unfixed.

It is probable that genius tends actually to prevent a man from acquiring habits of voluntary attention, and that moderate intellectual endowments are the soil in which we may best expect, here as elsewhere, the virtues of the will, strictly so called, to thrive. But, whether the attention come by grace of genius or by dint of will, the longer one does attend to a topic the more mastery of it one has. And the faculty of voluntarily bringing back a wandering attention over and over again is the very root of judgment, character, and will. No one is *compos sui* if he have it not. An education which should improve this faculty would be *the* education *par excellence.* But it is easier to define this ideal than to give practical directions for bringing it about. The only general pedagogic maxim bearing on attention is that the more interests the child has in advance in the subject, the better he will attend. Induct him therefore in such a way as to knit each new thing on to some acquisition already there; and if possible awaken curiosity, so that the new thing shall seem to come as an answer, or part of an answer, to a question preëxisting in his mind.

The Physiological Conditions of Attention.—These seem to be the following:

1) *The appropriate cortical centre must be excited ideationally as well as sensorially, before attention to an object can take place.*

2) *The sense-organ must then adapt itself to clearest reception of the object, by the adjustment of its muscular apparatus.*

3) *In all probability a certain afflux of blood to the cortical centre must ensue.*

Of this third condition I will say no more, since we have no proof of it in detail, and I state it on the faith of general analogies. Conditions 1) and 2), however, are verifiable; and the best order will be to take the latter first.

The Adaptation of the Sense-organ.—This occurs not only in sensorial but also in intellectual attention to an object.

That it is present when we attend to *sensible* things is obvious. When we look or listen we accommodate our eyes and ears involuntarily, and we turn our head and body as well; when we taste or smell we adjust the tongue, lips, and respiration to the object; in feeling a surface we move the palpatory organ in a suitable way; in all these acts, besides making involuntary muscular contractions of a positive sort, we inhibit others which might interfere with the result—we close the eyes in tasting, suspend the respiration in listening, etc. The result is a more or less massive organic feeling that attention is going on. This organic feeling we usually treat as part of the sense of our *own activity*, although it comes in to us from our organs after they are accommodated. Any object, then, if *immediately* exciting, causes a reflex accommodation of the sense-organ, which has two results—first, the feeling of activity in question; and second, the object's increase in clearness.

But in *intellectual* attention similar feelings of activity occur. Fechner was the first, I believe, to analyze these feelings, and discriminate them from the stronger ones just named. He writes:

"When we transfer the attention from objects of one sense to those of another, we have an indescribable feeling (though at the same time one perfectly determinate, and reproducible at pleasure), of altered *direction* or differently localized tension (*Spannung*). We feel a strain forwards in the eyes, one directed sidewise in the ears, increasing with the degree of our attention, and changing according as we look at an object carefully, or listen to something attentively; and we speak accordingly of *straining the attention*. The difference is most plainly felt when the attention oscillates rapidly between eye and ear; and the feeling localizes itself with most decided difference in regard to the various sense-organs, according as we wish to discriminate a thing delicately by touch, taste, or smell.

"But now I have, when I try to vividly recall a picture of memory or fancy, a feeling perfectly analogous to that which I experience when I seek to apprehend a thing keenly by eye or ear; and this analogous feeling is very differently localized. While in sharpest possible attention to real objects (as well as to after-images) the strain is plainly forwards, and (when the attention changes from one sense to another) only alters its direction between the several external sense-organs, leaving the rest of the head free from strain, the case is different in memory or fancy, for here the feeling withdraws entirely from the external sense-organs, and seems rather to take refuge in that part of the head which the brain fills. If I wish, for example, to *recall* a place or person, it will arise before me with vividness, not according as I strain my attention forwards, but rather in proportion as I, so to speak, retract it backwards."

In myself the 'backward retraction' which is felt during attention to ideas of memory, etc., seems to be principally constituted by the feeling of an actual rolling outwards and upwards of the eyeballs, such as occurs in sleep, and is the exact opposite of their behavior when we look at a physical thing.

This accommodation of the sense-organ is not, however, the *essential* process, even in sensorial attention. It is a secondary result which may be prevented from occurring, as certain observations show. Usually, it is true that no object lying in the marginal portions of the field of vision can catch our attention without at the same time 'catching our eye'—that is, fatally provoking such movements of rotation and accommodation as will focus its image on the fovea, or point of greatest sensibility. Practice, however, enables us, *with effort*, to attend to a marginal object whilst keeping the eyes immovable. The object under these circumstances never becomes perfectly distinct—the place of its image on the retina makes distinctness impossible—but (as anyone can satisfy himself by trying) we become more vividly conscious of it than we were before the effort was made. Teachers thus notice the acts of children in the school-room at whom they appear not to be looking. Women in general train their peripheral visual attention more than men. Helmholtz states the fact so strikingly that I will quote his observation in full. He was trying to combine in a single solid percept pairs of stereoscopic pictures illuminated instantaneously by the electric spark. The pictures were in a dark box which the spark from time to time lighted up; and, to keep the eyes from wandering betweenwhiles, a pin-hole was pricked through the middle of each picture, through which the light of the room came, so that each eye had presented to it during the dark intervals a single bright point. With parallel optical axes these points combined into a single image; and the slightest movement of the eyeballs was betrayed by this image at once becoming double. Helmholtz now found that simple linear figures could, when the eyes were thus kept immovable, be perceived as solids at a single flash of the spark. But when the figures were complicated photographs, many successive flashes were required to grasp their totality.

"Now it is interesting," he says, "to find that, although we keep steadily fixating the pin-holes and never allow their combined image to break into two, we can nevertheless, before the spark comes, keep our attention voluntarily turned to any particular portion we please of the dark field, so as then, when the spark comes, to receive an impression only from such parts of the picture as lie in this region. In this respect, then, our attention is quite independent of the position and accommodation of the eyes, and of any known alteration in these organs, and free to direct itself by a conscious and voluntary effort upon any selected portion of a dark and undifferenced field of view. This is one of the most important observations for a future theory of attention."[2]

The Ideational Excitement of the Centre.—But if the peripheral part of the picture in this experiment be not physically accommodated for, what is meant by its sharing our attention? What happens when we 'distribute' or 'disperse' the latter upon a thing for which we remain unwilling to 'adjust'? This leads us to that second feature in the process, the *'ideational excitement'* of which we spoke. *The effort to attend to the marginal region of the picture consists in nothing more nor less than the effort to form as clear an* IDEA *as is possible of what is there portrayed.* The idea is to come to the help of the sensation and make it more distinct. It may come with effort, and such a mode of coming is the remaining part of what we know as our attention's 'strain' under the circumstances. Let us show how universally present in our acts of attention is this anticipatory thinking of the thing to which we attend. Mr. Lewes's name of *preperception* seems the best possible designation for this imagining of an experience before it occurs.

It must as a matter of course be present when the attention is of the intellectual variety, for the thing attended to then *is* nothing but an idea, an inward reproduction or conception. If then we prove ideal construction of the object to be present in *sensorial* attention, it will be present everywhere. When, however, sensorial attention is at its height, it is impossible to tell how much of the percept comes from without and how much from within; but if we find that the *preparation* we make for it always partly consists of

[2] *Physiologische Optik*, p. 741.

the creation of an imaginary duplicate of the object in the mind, that will be enough to establish the point in dispute.

In reaction-time experiments, keeping our mind intent upon the motion about to be made shortens the time. This shortening we ascribed in Chapter IX to the fact that the signal when it comes finds the motor-centre already charged almost to the explosion-point in advance. Expectant attention to a reaction thus goes with sub-excitement of the centre concerned.

Where the impression to be caught is very weak, the way not to miss it is to sharpen our attention for it by preliminary contact with it in a stronger form. Helmholtz says: "If we wish to begin to observe overtones, it is advisable, just before the sound which is to be analyzed, to sound very softly the note of which we are in search . . . . If you place the resonator which corresponds to a certain overtone, for example *g'* of the sound *c*, against your ear, and then make the note *c* sound, you will hear *g'* much strengthened by the resonator. . . . This strengthening by the resonator can be used to make the naked ear attentive to the sound which it is to catch. For when the resonator is gradually removed, the *g'* grows weaker; but the attention, once directed to it, holds it now more easily fast, and the observer hears the tone *g'* now in the natural unaltered sound of the note with his unaided ear."

Wundt, commenting on experiences of this sort, says that "The same thing is to be noticed in weak or fugitive visual impressions. Illuminate a drawing by electric sparks separated by considerable intervals, and after the first, and often after the second and third spark, hardly anything will be recognized. But the confused image is held fast in memory; each successive illumination completes it; and so at last we attain to a clearer perception. The primary motive to this inward activity proceeds usually from the outer impression itself. We hear a sound in which, from certain associations, we suspect a certain overtone; the next thing is to recall the overtone in memory; and finally we catch it in the sound we hear. Or perhaps we see some mineral substance we have met before; the impression awakens the memory-image, which again more or less completely melts with the impression itself. . . . Different qualities of impression require disparate adaptations. And we remark that our feeling of the *strain* of our inward attentiveness increases with every increase in the strength of the impressions on whose perception we are intent."

The natural way of conceiving all this is under the symbolic form of a brain-cell played upon from two directions. Whilst the object excites it from without, other brain-cells arouse it from within. *The plenary energy of the brain-cell demands the coöperation of both factors*: not when merely present, but when both present and inwardly imagined, is the object fully attended to and perceived.

A few additional experiences will now be perfectly clear. Helmholtz, for instance, adds this observation concerning the stereoscopic pictures lit by the electric spark. "In pictures," he says, "so simple that it is relatively difficult for me to see them double, I can succeed in seeing them double, even when the illumination is only instantaneous, the moment I strive to *imagine in a lively way how they ought then to look.* The influence of attention is here pure; for all eye-movements are shut out."

Again, writing of retinal rivalry, Helmholtz says:

"It is not a trial of strength between two sensations, but depends upon our fixing or failing to fix the attention. Indeed there is scarcely any phenomenon so well fitted for the study of the causes which are capable of determining the attention. It is not enough to form the conscious intention of seeing first with one eye and then with the other; *we must form as clear a notion as possible of what we expect to see. Then it will actually appear.*"

In Figs. 55 and 56, where the result is ambiguous, we can make the change from one apparent form to the other by imagining strongly in advance the form we wish to see. Similarly in those puzzles where certain lines in a picture form by their combination an object that has no connection with what the picture obviously represents; or indeed in every case where an object is inconspicuous and hard to discern from the background; we may not be able to see it for a long time; but, having once seen it, we can attend to

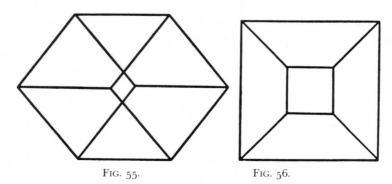

Fig. 55.   Fig. 56.

it again whenever we like, on account of the mental duplicate of it which our imagination now bears. In the meaningless French words '*pas de lieu Rhône que nous*,' who can recognize immediately the English 'paddle your own canoe'? But who that has once noticed the identity can fail to have it arrest his attention again? When watching for the distant clock to strike, our mind is so filled with its image that at every moment we think we hear the longed-for or dreaded sound. So of an awaited footstep. Every stir in the wood is for the hunter his game; for the fugitive his pursuers. Every bonnet in the street is momentarily taken by the lover to enshroud the head of his idol. The image in the mind *is* the attention; the preperception is half of the perception of the looked-for thing.

It is for this reason that men have no eyes but for those aspects of things which they have already been taught to discern. Any one of us can notice a phenomenon after it has once been pointed out, which not one in ten thousand could ever have discovered for himself. Even in poetry and the arts, someone has to come and tell us what aspects to single out, and what effects to admire, before our æsthetic nature can 'dilate' to its full extent and never 'with the wrong emotion.' In kindergarten-instruction one of the exercises is to make the children see how many features they can point out in such an object as a flower or a stuffed bird. They readily name the features they know already, such as leaves, tail, bill, feet. But they may look for hours without distinguishing nostrils, claws, scales, etc., until their attention is called to these details; thereafter, however, they see them every time. In short, *the only things which we commonly see are those which we preperceive*, and the only things which we preperceive are those which have been labelled for us, and the labels stamped into our mind. If we lost our stock of labels we should be intellectually lost in the midst of the world.

Educational Corollaries.—First, to *strengthen attention in children* who care nothing for the subject they are studying and let their wits go wool-gathering. The interest here must be 'derived' from something that the teacher associates with the task, a reward or a punishment if nothing more internal comes to mind. If a topic awakens no spontaneous attention it must borrow an interest from elsewhere. But the best interest is internal, and we must always try, in teaching a class, to knit our novelties by rational links on to things of which they already have preperceptions. The old and familiar is readily attended to by the mind and helps to hold in turn the new, forming, in Herbartian phraseology, an '*Apperceptionsmasse*' for it. Of course the teacher's talent is best shown by knowing what 'Apperceptionsmasse' to use. Psychology can only lay down the general rule.

Second, take that mind-wandering which at a later age may trouble us *whilst reading or listening to a discourse*. If attention be the reproduction of the sensation from within, the habit of reading not merely with the eye, and of listening not merely with the ear, but of articulating to one's self the words seen or heard, ought to deepen one's attention to the latter. Experience shows that this is the case. I can keep my wandering mind a great deal more closely upon a conversation or a lecture if I actively re-echo to myself the words than if I simply hear them; and I find a number of my students who report benefit from voluntarily adopting a similar course.

Attention and Free-Will.—I have spoken as if our attention were wholly determined by neural conditions. I believe that the array of *things* we can attend to is so determined. No object can *catch* our attention except by the neural machinery. But the *amount* of the attention which an object receives after it has caught our mental eye is another question. It often takes effort to keep the mind upon it. We feel that we can make more or less of the effort as we choose. If this feeling be not deceptive, if our effort be a spiritual force, and an indeterminate one, then of course it contributes coequally with the cerebral conditions to the result. Though it *introduce* no new idea, it will deepen and prolong the stay in consciousness of innumerable ideas which else would fade more quickly away. The delay thus gained might not be more than a second in duration—but that second may be *critical*; for in the constant rising and falling of considerations in the mind, where two associated systems of them are nearly in equilibrium it is often a matter of but a second more or less of attention at the outset, whether one system shall gain force to occupy the field and develop itself, and exclude the other, or be excluded itself by the other. When developed, it may make us act; and that act may seal our doom. When we come to the chapter on the Will, we shall see that the whole drama of the voluntary life hinges on the amount of attention, slightly more or slightly less, which rival motor ideas may receive. But the whole feeling of reality, the whole sting and excitement of our voluntary life, depends on our sense that in it things are *really being decided* from one moment to another, and that it is not the dull rattling-off of a chain that was forged innumerable ages ago. This appearance, which makes life and history tingle with such a tragic zest, *may* not be an illusion. Effort may be an original force and not a mere effect, and it may be indeterminate in amount. The last word of sober insight here is ignorance, for the forces engaged are too delicate ever to be measured in detail. Psychology, however, as a would-be 'Science,' must, like every other Science, *postulate* complete determinism in its facts, and abstract consequently from the effects of free-will, even if such a force exist. I shall do so in this book like other psychologists; well knowing, however, that such a procedure, although a methodical device justified by the subjective need of arranging the facts in a simple and 'scientific' form, does not settle the ultimate truth of the free-will question one way or the other.

Chapter XIV

Conception

Different states of mind can mean the same. The function by which we mark off, discriminate, draw a line round, and identify a numerically distinct subject of discourse is called *conception*. It is plain that whenever one and the same mental state thinks of many things, it must be the vehicle of many conceptions. If it has such a multiple conceptual function, it may be called a state of compound conception.

We may conceive realities supposed to be extra-mental, as steam-engine; fictions, as mermaid; or mere *entia rationis*, like difference or nonentity. But whatever we do conceive, our conception is of that and nothing else—nothing else, that is, *instead* of that, though it may be of much else *in addition* to that. Each act of conception results from our attention's having singled out some one part of the mass of matter-for-thought which the world presents, and from our holding fast to it, without confusion. Confusion occurs when we do not know whether a certain object proposed to us is *the same* with one of our meanings or not; so that the conceptual function requires, to be complete, that the thought should not only say 'I mean this,' but also say 'I don't mean that.'

Each conception thus eternally remains what it is, and never can become another. The mind may change its states, and its meanings, at different times; may drop one conception and take up another: but the dropped conception itself can in no intelligible sense be said to *change into* its successor. The paper, a moment ago white, I may now see to be scorched black. But my *conception* 'white' does not change into my *conception* 'black.' On the contrary, it stays alongside of the objective blackness, as a different meaning in my mind, and by so doing lets me judge the blackness as the paper's change. Unless it stayed, I should simply say 'blackness' and know no more. Thus, amid the flux of opinions and of physical things, the world of conceptions, or things intended to be thought about, stands stiff and immutable, like Plato's Realm of Ideas.

Some conceptions are of things, some of events, some of qualities. Any fact, be it thing, event, or quality, may be conceived sufficiently for purposes of identification, if only it be singled out and marked so as to separate it from other things. Simply calling it 'this' or 'that' will suffice. To speak in technical language, a subject may be conceived by its *denotation*, with no *connotation*, or a very minimum of connotation, attached. The essential point is that it should be re-identified by us as that which the talk is about; and no full representation of it is necessary for this, even when it is a fully representable thing.

In this sense, creatures extremely low in the intellectual scale may have conception. All that is required is that they should recognize the same experience again. A polyp would be a conceptual thinker if a feeling of 'Hollo! thingumbob again!' ever flitted through its mind. This sense of sameness is the very keel and backbone of our consciousness. The same matters can be thought of in different states of mind, and some of these states can know that they mean the same matters which the other states meant. In other words, *the mind can always intend, and know when it intends, to think the Same*.

Conceptions of Abstract, of Universal, and of Problematic Objects.—The sense of our meaning is an entirely peculiar element of the thought. It is one of those evanescent and 'transitive' facts of mind which introspection cannot turn round upon, and isolate and hold up for examination, as an entomologist passes round an insect on a pin. In the (somewhat clumsy) terminology I have used, it has to do with the 'fringe' of the object, and is a 'feeling of tendency,' whose neural counterpart is undoubtedly a lot of dawning and dying processes too faint and complex to be traced. (See p. 154.) The geometer, with his one definite figure before him, knows perfectly that his thoughts apply to countless other figures as well, and that although he *sees* lines of a certain special bigness, direction, color, etc., he *means* not one of these details. When I use the word *man* in two different sentences, I may have both times exactly the same sound upon my lips and the same picture in my mental eye, but I may mean, and at the very moment of uttering the word and imagining the picture know that I mean, two entirely different things. Thus when I say: "What a wonderful man Jones is!" I am perfectly aware that I mean by man to exclude Napoleon Bonaparte or Smith. But when I say: "What a wonderful thing Man is!" I am equally well aware that I mean no such exclusion. This added consciousness is an absolutely positive sort of feeling, transforming what would otherwise be mere noise or vision into something *understood*; and determining the sequel of my thinking, the later words and images, in a perfectly definite way.

No matter how definite and concrete the habitual imagery of a given mind may be, the things represented appear always surrounded by their fringe of relations, and this is as integral a part of the mind's object as the things themselves are. We come, by steps with which everyone is sufficiently familiar, to think of whole classes of things as well as of single specimens; and to think of the special qualities or attributes of things as well as of the complete things—in other words, we come to have *universals* and *abstracts*, as the logicians call them, for our objects. We also come to think of objects which are only *problematic*, or not yet definitely representable, as well as of objects imagined in all their details. An object which is problematic is defined by its relations only. We think of a thing *about* which certain facts must obtain. But we do not yet know how the thing will look when realized—that is, although conceiving it we cannot *imagine* it. We have in the relations, however, enough to individualize our topic and distinguish it from all the other meanings of our mind. Thus, for example, we may conceive of a perpetual-motion machine. Such a machine is a *quæsitum* of a perfectly definite kind,—we can tell whether the actual machines offered us do or do not agree with what we mean by it. The natural possibility or impossibility of the thing never touches the question of its conceivability in this problematic way. 'Round-square,' again, or 'black-white-thing,' are absolutely definite conceptions; it is a mere accident, as far as conception goes, that they happen to stand for things which nature never shows us, and of which we consequently can make no picture.

The nominalists and conceptualists carry on a great quarrel over the question whether "the mind can frame abstract or universal ideas." Ideas, it should be said, of abstract or universal objects. But truly in comparison with the wonderful fact that our thoughts, however different otherwise, can still be of *the same*, the question whether that same be a single thing, a whole class of things, an abstract quality or something unimaginable, is an insignificant matter of detail. Our meanings are of singulars, particulars, indefinites, problematics, and universals, mixed together in every way. A singular individual is as much *conceived* when he is isolated and identified away from the rest of the world in my mind, as is the most rarefied and universally applicable quality he may possess—*being*, for example, when treated in the same way. From every point of view, the overwhelming and portentous character ascribed to universal conceptions is surprising. Why, from Socrates downwards, philosophers should have vied with each other in scorn of the knowledge of the particular, and in adoration of that of the general, is hard to understand, seeing that the more adorable knowledge ought to be that of the more adorable things, and that the *things* of worth are all concretes and singulars. The only value of universal characters is that they help us, by reasoning, to know new truths about individual things. The restriction of one's meaning, moreover, to an individual thing, probably requires even more complicated brain-processes than its extension to all the instances of a kind; and the mere mystery, as such, of the knowledge, is equally great, whether generals or singulars be the things known. In sum, therefore, the traditional Universal-worship can only be called a bit of perverse sentimentalism, a philosophic 'idol of the cave.'

Nothing can be conceived as the same without being conceived in a novel state of mind. It seems hardly necessary to add this, after what was said on p. 143. Thus, my arm-chair is one of the things of which I have a conception; I knew it yesterday and recognized it when I looked at it. But if I think of it to-day as the same arm-chair which I looked at yesterday, it is obvious that the very conception of it *as* the same is an additional complication to the thought, whose inward constitution must alter in consequence. In short, it is logically impossible that the same thing should be *known as the same* by two successive copies of the same thought. As a matter of fact, the thoughts by which we know that we mean the same thing are apt to be very different indeed from each other. We think the thing now substantively, now transitively; now in a direct image, now in one symbol, and now in another symbol; but nevertheless we somehow always *do* know which of all possible subjects we have in mind. Introspective psychology must here throw up the sponge; the fluctuations of subjective life are too exquisite to be described by its coarse terms. It must confine itself to bearing witness to the fact that all sorts of different subjective states do form the vehicle by which the same is known; and it must contradict the opposite view.

Chapter XV

Discrimination

Discrimination versus Association.—On p. 20 I spoke of the baby's first object being the germ out of which his whole later universe develops by the addition of new parts from without and the discrimination of others within. Experience, in other words, is trained *both* by association and dissociation, and psychology must be writ *both* in synthetic and in analytic terms. Our original sensible totals are, on the one hand, subdivided by discriminative attention, and, on the other, united with other totals,—either through the agency of our own movements, carrying our senses from one part of space to another, or because new objects come successively and replace those by which we were at first impressed. The 'simple impression' of Hume, the 'simple idea' of Locke are abstractions, never realized in experience. Life, from the very first, presents us with concreted objects, vaguely continuous with the rest of the world which envelops them in space and time, and potentially divisible into inward elements and parts. These objects we break asunder and reunite. We must do both for our knowledge of them to grow; and it is hard to say, on the whole, which we do most. But since the elements with which the traditional associationism performs its constructions—'simple sensations,' namely—are all products of discrimination carried to a high pitch, it seems as if we ought to discuss the subject of analytic attention and discrimination first.

Discrimination defined.—The noticing of any *part* whatever of our object is an act of discrimination. Already on p. 193 I have described the manner in which we often spontaneously lapse into the undiscriminating state, even with regard to objects which we have already learned to distinguish. Such anæsthetics as chloroform, nitrous oxide, etc., sometimes bring about transient lapses even more total, in which numerical discrimination especially seems gone; for one sees light and hears sound, but whether one or many lights and sounds is quite impossible to tell. Where the parts of an object have already been discerned, and each made the object of a special discriminative act, we can with difficulty feel the object again in its pristine unity; and so prominent may our consciousness of its composition be, that we may hardly believe that it ever could have appeared undivided. But this is an erroneous view, the undeniable fact being that *any number of impressions, from any number of sensory sources, falling simultaneously on a mind* WHICH HAS NOT YET EXPERIENCED THEM SEPARATELY, *will yield a single undivided object to that mind.* The law is that all things fuse that *can* fuse, and that nothing separates except what must. What makes impressions separate is what we have to study in this chapter.

Conditions which favor Discrimination.—I will treat successively of differences:

1) So far as they are directly *felt*;
2) So far as they are *inferred*;
3) So far as they are *singled out in compounds.*

Differences directly felt.—The first condition is that *the things to be discriminated must* BE *different,* either in time, place, or quality. In other words, and physiologically speaking, they must awaken neural processes which are *distinct.* But this, as we have just seen, though an indispensable condition, is not a sufficient condition. To begin with, the several neural processes must be distinct *enough.* No one can help singling out a black stripe on a white ground, or feeling the contrast between a bass note and a high one sounded immediately after it. Discrimination is here *involuntary.* But where the objective difference is less, discrimination may require considerable effort of attention to be performed at all.

Secondly, *the sensations excited by the differing objects must not fall simultaneously, but must fall in immediate* SUCCESSION *upon the same organ.* It is easier to compare successive than simultaneous sounds, easier to compare two weights or two temperatures by testing one after the other with the same hand, than by using both hands and comparing both at once. Similarly it is easier to discriminate shades of light or color by moving the eye from one to the other, so that they successively stimulate the same retinal tract. In testing the local discrimination of the skin, by applying compass-points, it is found that they are felt to touch different spots much more readily when set down one after the other than when both are applied at once. In the latter case they may be two or three inches apart on the back, thighs, etc., and still feel as if they were set down in one spot. Finally, in the case of smell and taste it is well-nigh impossible to compare simultaneous impressions at all. The reason why successive impression so much favors the result seems to be that there is a real *sensation of difference*, aroused by the shock of transition from one perception to another which is unlike the first. This sensation of difference has its own peculiar quality, no matter what the terms may be, between which it obtains. It is, in short, one of those transitive feelings, or feelings of relation, of which I treated in a former place (p. 147); and, when once aroused, its object lingers in the memory along with the substantive terms which precede and follow, and enables our *judgments of comparison* to be made.

Where the difference between the successive sensations is but slight, the transition between them must be made as immediate as possible, and both must be compared *in memory*, in order to get the best results. One cannot judge accurately of the difference between two similar wines whilst the second is still in one's mouth. So of sounds, warmths, etc.—we must get the dying phases of both sensations of the pair we are comparing. Where, however, the difference is strong, this condition is immaterial, and we can then compare a sensation actually felt with another carried in memory only. The longer the interval of time between the sensations, the more uncertain is their discrimination.

The difference, thus immediately felt between two terms, is independent of our ability to say anything *about* either of the terms by itself. I can feel two distinct spots to be touched on my skin, yet not know which is above and which below. I can observe two neighboring musical tones to differ, and still not know which of the two is the higher in pitch. Similarly I may discriminate two neighboring tints, whilst remaining uncertain which is the bluer or the yellower, or *how* either differs from its mate.

I said that in the immediate succession of *m* upon *n* the shock of their difference is *felt*. It is felt *repeatedly* when we go back and

forth from *m* to *n*; and we make a point of getting it thus repeatedly (by alternating our attention at least) whenever the shock is
so slight as to be with difficulty perceived. But in addition to
being felt at the brief instant of transition, the difference also feels
as if incorporated and taken up into the second term, which feels
'different-from-the-first' even while it lasts. It is obvious that the
'second term' of the mind in this case is not bald *n*, but a very
complex object; and that the sequence is not simply first '*m*,' then
'*difference*,' then '*n*'; but first '*m*,' then '*difference*,' then '*n-different-
from-m.*' The first and third states of mind are substantive, the second transitive. As our brains and minds are actually made, it is
impossible to get certain *m*'s and *n*'s in immediate sequence and to
keep them *pure*. If kept pure, it would mean that they remained
uncompared. With us, inevitably, by a mechanism which we as
yet fail to understand, the shock of difference is felt between them,
and the second object is not *n* pure, but *n-as-different-from-m*. The
pure idea of *n* is *never in the mind at all* when *m* has gone before.

Differences inferred.—With such direct perceptions of difference as this, we must not confound those entirely unlike cases in
which we *infer* that two things must differ because we know
enough *about* each of them taken by itself to warrant our classing
them under distinct heads. It often happens, when the interval is
long between two experiences, that our judgments are guided, not
so much by a positive image or copy of the earlier one, as by our
recollection of certain facts about it. Thus I know that the sunshine to-day is less bright than on a certain day last week, because
I then said it was quite dazzling, a remark I should not now care
to make. Or I know myself to feel livelier now than I did last
summer, because I can now psychologize, and then I could not.
We are constantly comparing feelings with whose quality our
imagination has no sort of *acquaintance* at the time—pleasures, or
pains, for example. It is notoriously hard to conjure up in imagination a lively image of either of these classes of feeling. The associationists may prate of an idea of pleasure being a pleasant idea,
of an idea of pain being a painful one, but the unsophisticated
sense of mankind is against them, agreeing with Homer that the
memory of griefs when past may be a joy, and with Dante that
there is no greater sorrow than, in misery, to recollect one's happier time.

The 'Singling out' of Elements in a Compound.—It is safe to
lay it down as a fundamental principle that *any total impression*

made on the mind must be unanalyzable so long as its elements have never been experienced apart or in other combinations elsewhere. The components of an absolutely changeless group of not-elsewhere-occurring attributes could never be discriminated. If all cold things were wet, and all wet things cold; if all hard things pricked our skin, and no other things did so; is it likely that we should discriminate between coldness and wetness, and hardness and pungency, respectively? If all liquids were transparent and no non-liquid were transparent, it would be long before we had separate names for liquidity and transparency. If heat were a function of position above the earth's surface, so that the higher a thing was the hotter it became, one word would serve for hot and high. We have, in fact, a number of sensations whose concomitants are invariably the same, and we find it, accordingly, impossible to analyze them out from the totals in which they are found. The contraction of the diaphragm and the expansion of the lungs, the shortening of certain muscles and the rotation of certain joints, are examples. We learn that the *causes* of such groups of feelings are multiple, and therefore we frame theories about the composition of the feelings themselves, by 'fusion,' 'integration,' 'synthesis,' or what not. But by direct introspection no analysis of the feelings is ever made. A conspicuous case will come to view when we treat of the emotions. Every emotion has its 'expression,' of quick breathing, palpitating heart, flushed face, or the like. The expression gives rise to bodily feelings; and the emotion is thus necessarily and invariably accompanied by these bodily feelings. The consequence is that it is impossible to apprehend it as a spiritual state by itself, or to analyze it away from the lower feelings in question. It is in fact impossible to prove that it exists as a distinct psychic fact. The present writer strongly doubts that it does so exist.

In general, then, if an object affects us simultaneously in a number of ways, *abcd*, we get a peculiar integral impression, which thereafter characterizes to our mind the individuality of that object, and becomes the sign of its presence; and which is only resolved into *a*, *b*, *c*, and *d*, respectively, by the aid of farther experiences. These we now may turn to consider.

If any single quality or constituent, a, of such an object have previously been known by us isolatedly, or have in any other manner already become an object of separate acquaintance on our part, so that we have an image of it, distinct or vague, in our mind, disconnected with *bcd, then that constituent a may be analyzed out from the total impres-*

sion. Analysis of a thing means separate attention to each of its parts. In Chapter XIII we saw that one condition of attending to a thing was the formation from within of a separate image of that thing, which should, as it were, go out to meet the impression received. Attention being the condition of analysis, and separate imagination being the condition of attention, it follows also that separate imagination is the condition of analysis. *Only such elements as we are acquainted with, and can imagine separately, can be discriminated within a total sense-impression.* The image seems to welcome its own mate from out of the compound, and to separate it from the other constituents; and thus the compound becomes broken for our consciousness into parts.

All the facts cited in Chapter XIII to prove that attention involves inward reproduction prove that discrimination involves it as well. In looking for any object in a room, for a book in a library, for example, we detect it the more readily if, in addition to merely knowing its name, etc., we carry in our mind a distinct image of its appearance. The assafœtida in 'Worcestershire sauce' is not obvious to anyone who has not tasted assafœtida *per se*. In a 'cold' color an artist would never be able to analyze out the pervasive presence of *blue*, unless he had previously made acquaintance with the color blue by itself. All the colors we actually experience are mixtures. Even the purest primaries always come to us with some white. Absolutely pure red or green or violet is never experienced, and so can never be discerned in the so-called primaries with which we have to deal: the latter consequently pass for pure.—The reader will remember how an overtone can only be attended to in the midst of its consorts in the voice of a musical instrument, by sounding it previously alone. The imagination, being then full of it, hears the like of it in the compound tone.

Non-isolable elements may be discriminated, provided their concomitants change. Very few elements of reality are experienced by us in absolute isolation. The most that usually happens to a constituent *a* of a compound phenomenon *abcd* is that its *strength* relatively to *bcd* varies from a maximum to a minimum; or that it appears linked with *other* qualities, in other compounds, as *aefg* or *ahik*. Either of these vicissitudes in the mode of our experiencing *a* may, under favorable circumstances, lead us to feel the difference between it and its concomitants, and to single it out—not absolutely, it is true, but approximately—and so to analyze the compound of which it is a part. The act of singling out is then called *abstraction*, and the element disengaged is an *abstract*.

Fluctuation in a quality's intensity is a less efficient aid to our abstracting of it than variety in the combinations in which it appears. *What is associated now with one thing and now with another tends to become dissociated from either, and to grow into an object of abstract contemplation by the mind.* One might call this the *law of dissociation by varying concomitants.* The practical result of this law is that a mind which has once dissociated and abstracted a character by its means can analyze it out of a total whenever it meets with it again.

Dr. Martineau gives a good example of the law: "When a red ivory-ball, seen for the first time, has been withdrawn, it will leave a mental representation of itself, in which all that it simultaneously gave us will indistinguishably co-exist. Let a white ball succeed to it; now, and not before, will an attribute detach itself, and the *color*, by force of contrast, be shaken out into the foreground. Let the white ball be replaced by an egg: and this new difference will bring the *form* into notice from its previous slumber. And thus, that which began by being simply an object, cut out from the surrounding scene, becomes for us first a *red* object, and then a *red round* object; and so on."

Why the repetition of the character in combination with different wholes will cause it thus to break up its adhesion with any one of them, and roll out, as it were, alone upon the table of consciousness, is a little of a mystery, but one which need not be considered here.

Practice improves Discrimination.—Any personal or practical interest in the results to be obtained by distinguishing, makes one's wits amazingly sharp to detect differences. And long training and practice in distinguishing has the same effect as personal interest. Both of these agencies give to small amounts of objective difference the same effectiveness upon the mind that, under other circumstances, only large ones would have.

That 'practice makes perfect' is notorious in the field of motor accomplishments. But motor accomplishments depend in part on sensory discrimination. Billiard-playing, rifle-shooting, tight-rope-dancing demand the most delicate appreciation of minute disparities of sensation, as well as the power to make accurately graduated muscular response thereto. In the purely sensorial field we have the well-known virtuosity displayed by the professional buyers and testers of various kinds of goods. One man will distinguish by taste between the upper and the lower half of a bottle of old Madeira. Another will recognize, by feeling the flour in a barrel, whether the wheat was grown in Iowa or Tennessee. The blind deaf-mute, Laura Bridgman, so improved her touch as to recognize, after a year's interval, the hand of a person who once had shaken hers; and her sister in misfortune, Julia Brace, is said to have been employed in the Hartford Asylum to sort the linen of its multitudinous inmates, after it came from the wash, by her wonderfully educated sense of smell.

Chapter XVI

Association

The Order of our Ideas.—After discrimination, association! It is obvious that all advance in knowledge must consist of both operations; for in the course of our education, objects at first appearing as wholes are analyzed into parts, and objects appearing separately are brought together and appear as new compound wholes to the mind. Analysis and synthesis are thus the incessantly alternating mental activities, a stroke of the one preparing the way for a stroke of the other, much as, in walking, a man's two legs are alternately brought into use, both being indispensable for any orderly advance.

The manner in which trains of imagery and consideration follow each other through our thinking, the restless flight of one idea before the next, the transitions our minds make between things wide as the poles asunder, transitions which at first sight startle us by their abruptness, but which, when scrutinized closely, often reveal intermediating links of perfect naturalness and propriety—all this magical, imponderable streaming has from time immemorial excited the admiration of all whose attention happened to be caught by its omnipresent mystery. And it has furthermore challenged the race of philosophers to banish something of the mystery by formulating the process in simpler terms. The problem which the philosophers have set themselves is that of ascertaining, between the thoughts which thus appear to sprout one out of the other, *principles of connection* whereby their peculiar succession or coexistence may be explained.

But immediately an ambiguity arises: which sort of connection is meant? connection *thought-of*, or connection *between the things thought of?* These are two entirely different things, and only in the case of one of them is there any hope of finding 'principles.' The jungle of connections *thought of* can never be formulated simply. Every conceivable connection may be thought of—of coexistence, succession, resemblance, contrast, contradiction, cause and effect, means and end, genus and species, part and whole, substance and property, early and late, large and small, landlord and tenant, master and servant,—Heaven knows what, for the list is literally inexhaustible. The only simplification which could possibly be aimed at would be the reduction of the relations to a small number of *types*, like those which some authors call the 'categories' of the understanding. According as we followed one category or another we should sweep, from any object with our thought, in this way or in that, to others. Were *this* the sort of connection sought between one moment of our thinking and another, our chapter might end here. For the only summary description of these categories is that they are all thinkable relations, and that the mind proceeds from one object to another by some intelligible path.

Is it determined by any laws? But as a matter of fact, What determines the particular path? Why do we at a given time and place proceed to think of *b* if we have just thought of *a*, and at another time and place why do we think, not of *b*, but of *c*? Why do we spend years straining after a certain scientific or practical problem, but all in vain—our thought unable to evoke the solution we desire? And why, some day, walking in the street with our attention miles away from that quest, does the answer saunter into our minds as carelessly as if it had never been called for— suggested, possibly, by the flowers on the bonnet of the lady in front of us, or possibly by nothing that we can discover?

The truth must be admitted that thought works under strange conditions. Pure 'reason' is only one out of a thousand possibilities in the thinking of each of us. Who can count all the silly fancies, the grotesque suppositions, the utterly irrelevant reflections he makes in the course of a day? Who can swear that his prejudices and irrational opinions constitute a less bulky part of his mental furniture than his clarified beliefs? And yet, the *mode of genesis* of the worthy and the worthless in our thinking seems the same.

The laws are cerebral laws. *There seem to be mechanical conditions on which thought depends, and which,* to say the least, *determine the order* *in which the objects for her comparisons and selections are presented.* It is a suggestive fact that Locke, and many more recent Continental psychologists, have found themselves obliged to invoke a mechanical process to account for the *aberrations* of thought, the obstructive prepossessions, the frustrations of reason. This they found in the law of habit, or what we now call association by contiguity. But it never occurred to these writers that a process which could go the length of actually producing some ideas and sequences in the mind might safely be trusted to produce others too; and that those habitual associations which further thought may also come from the same mechanical source as those which hinder it. Hartley accordingly suggested habit as a sufficient explanation of the sequence of our thoughts, and in so doing planted himself squarely upon the properly *causal* aspect of the problem, and sought to treat both rational and irrational associations from a single point of view. How does a man come, after having the thought of A, to have the thought of B the next moment? or how does he come to think A and B always together? These were the phenomena which Hartley undertook to explain by cerebral physiology. I believe that he was, in essential respects, on the right track, and I propose simply to revise his conclusions by the aid of distinctions which he did not make.

Objects are associated, not ideas. We shall avoid confusion if we consistently speak as if *association*, so far as the word stands for an *effect, were between* THINGS THOUGHT OF—*as if it were* THINGS, *not ideas, which are associated in the mind.* We shall talk of the association of *objects*, not of the association of *ideas*. And so far as association stands for a *cause*, it is between *processes in the brain*—it is these which, by being associated in certain ways, determine what successive objects shall be thought.

The Elementary Principle.—I shall now try to show that there is no other *elementary* causal law of association than the law of neural habit. All the *materials* of our thought are due to the way in which one elementary process of the cerebral hemispheres tends to excite whatever other elementary process it may have excited at some former time. The number of elementary processes at work, however, and the nature of those which at any time are fully effective in rousing the others, determine the character of the total brain-action, and, as a consequence of this, they determine the object thought of at the time. According as this resultant object is one thing or another, we call it a product of association by contiguity or of association by similarity, or contrast, or whatever other sorts we may have recognized as ultimate. Its *production*, however, is, in each one of these cases, to be explained by a merely quantitative variation in the elementary brain-processes momentarily at work under the law of habit.

My thesis, stated thus briefly, will soon become more clear; and at the same time certain disturbing factors, which coöperate with the law of neural habit, will come to view.

Let us then assume as the basis of all our subsequent reasoning this law: *When two elementary brain-processes have been active together or in immediate succession, one of them, on re-occurring, tends to propagate its excitement into the other.*

But, as a matter of fact, every elementary process has unavoidably found itself at different times excited in conjunction with *many* other processes. Which of these others it shall awaken now becomes a problem. Shall *b* or *c* be aroused next by the present *a*? To answer this, we must make a further postulate, based on the fact of *tension* in nerve-tissue, and on the fact of summation of excitements, each incomplete or latent in itself, into an open resultant (see p. 120). The process *b*, rather than *c*, will awake, if in addition to the vibrating tract *a* some other tract *d* is in a state of sub-excitement, and formerly was excited with *b* alone and not with *a*. In short, we may say:

The amount of activity at any given point in the brain-cortex is the sum of the tendencies of all other points to discharge into it, such tendencies being proportionate (1) *to the number of times the excitement of each other point may have accompanied that of the point in question;* (2) *to the intensity of such excitements; and* (3) *to the absence of any rival point functionally disconnected with the first point, into which the discharges might be diverted.*

Expressing the fundamental law in this most complicated way leads to the greatest ultimate simplification. Let us, for the present, only treat of spontaneous trains of thought and ideation, such as occur in revery or musing. The case of voluntary thinking towards a certain end shall come up later.

Spontaneous Trains of Thought.—Take, to fix our ideas, the two verses from "Locksley Hall":

"I the heir of all *the ages*, in the foremost files of time,"
and—

"Yet I doubt not through *the ages* one increasing purpose runs."

Why is it that when we recite from memory one of these lines, and get as far as *the ages*, that portion of the *other* line which follows and, so to speak, sprouts out of *the ages* does not also sprout out of our memory and confuse the sense of our words? Simply because the word that follows *the ages* has its brain-process awakened not simply by the brain-process of *the ages* alone, but by it *plus* the brain-processes of all the words preceding *the ages*. The word *ages* at its moment of strongest activity would, *per se*, indifferently discharge into either 'in' or 'one.' So would the previous words (whose tension is momentarily much less strong than that of *ages*) each of them indifferently discharge into either of a large number of other words with which they have been at different times combined. But when the processes of '*I the heir of all the ages*,' simultaneously vibrate in the brain, the last one of them in a maximal, the others in a fading, phase of excitement; then the strongest line of discharge will be that which they *all alike* tend to take. '*In*' and not '*one*' or any other word will be the next to awaken, for its brain-process has previously vibrated in unison not only with that of *ages*, but with that of all those other words whose activity is dying away. It is a good case of the effectiveness over thought of what we called on p. 153 a 'fringe.'

But if some one of these preceding words—'heir,' for example—had an intensely strong association with some brain-tracts entirely disjoined in experience from the poem of "Locksley Hall"—if the reciter, for instance, were tremulously awaiting the opening of a will which might make him a millionaire—it is probable that the path of discharge through the words of the poem would be suddenly interrupted at the word 'heir.' His *emotional interest in that word* would be such that its *own special associations would prevail* over the combined ones of the other words. He would, as we say, be abruptly reminded of his personal situation, and the poem would lapse altogether from his thoughts.

The writer of these pages has every year to learn the names of a large number of students who sit in alphabetical order in a lecture-room. He finally learns to call them by name, as they sit in their accustomed places. On meeting one in the street, however, early in the year, the face hardly ever recalls the name, but it may recall the place of its owner in the lecture-room, his neighbors' faces, and consequently his general alphabetical position; and then, usually as the common associate of all these combined data, the student's name surges up in his mind.

A father wishes to show to some guests the progress of his rather dull child in kindergarten-instruction. Holding the knife upright on the table, he says, "What do you call that, my boy?" "I calls it a *knife*, I does," is the sturdy reply, from which the child cannot be induced to swerve by any alteration in the form of question, until the father, recollecting that in the kindergarten a pencil was used and not a knife, draws a long one from his pocket, holds it in the same way, and then gets the wished-for answer, "I calls it *vertical*." All the concomitants of the kindergarten experience had to recombine their effect before the word 'vertical' could be reawakened.

Total Recall.—The ideal working of the law of compound association, as Prof. Bain calls it, were it unmodified by any extraneous influence, would be such as to keep the mind in a perpetual treadmill of concrete reminiscences from which no detail could be omitted. Suppose, for example, we begin by thinking of a certain dinner-party. The only thing which all the components of the dinner-party could combine to recall would be the first concrete occurrence which ensued upon it. All the details of this occurrence could in turn only combine to awaken the next following occurrence, and so on. If a, b, c, d, e, for instance, be the elementary nerve-tracts excited by the last act of the dinner-party, call this act A, and l, m, n, o, p be those of walking home through the frosty night, which we may call B, then the thought of A must awaken that of B, because a, b, c, d, e will each and all discharge into l through the paths by which their original discharge took place. Similarly they will discharge into m, n, o, and p; and these latter tracts will also each reinforce the other's action because, in the experience B, they have already vibrated in unison. The lines in Fig. 57 symbolize the summation of discharges into each of the components of B, and the consequent strength of the combination of influences by which B in its totality is awakened.

Hamilton first used the word 'redintegration' to designate all association. Such processes as we have just described might in an emphatic sense be termed redintegrations, for they would necessarily lead, if unobstructed, to the reinstatement in thought of the *entire* content of large trains of past experience. From this complete redintegration there could be no escape save through the ir-

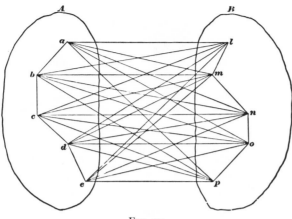

FIG. 57.

ruption of some new and strong present impression of the senses, or through the excessive tendency of some one of the elementary brain-tracts to discharge independently into an aberrant quarter of the brain. Such was the tendency of the word 'heir' in the verse from "Locksley Hall," which was our first example. How such tendencies are constituted we shall have soon to inquire with some care. Unless they are present, the panorama of the past, once opened, must unroll itself with fatal literality to the end, unless some outward sound, sight, or touch divert the current of thought.

Let us call this process *impartial redintegration*, or, still better, *total recall*. Whether it ever occurs in an absolutely complete form is doubtful. We all immediately recognize, however, that in some minds there is a much greater tendency than in others for the flow of thought to take this form. Those insufferably garrulous old women, those dry and fanciless beings who spare you no detail, however petty, of the facts they are recounting, and upon the thread of whose narrative all the irrelevant items cluster as pertinaciously as the essential ones, the slaves of literal fact, the stumblers over the smallest abrupt step in thought, are figures known to all of us. Comic literature has made her profit out of them. Juliet's nurse is a classical example. George Eliot's village characters and some of Dickens's minor personages supply excellent instances.

Perhaps as successful a rendering as any of this mental type is the character of Miss Bates in Miss Austen's *Emma*. Hear how she redintegrates:

" 'But where could *you* hear it?' cried Miss Bates. 'Where could you possibly hear it, Mr. Knightley? For it is not five minutes since I received Mrs. Cole's note—no, it cannot be more than five—or at least ten—for I had got my bonnet and spencer on, just ready to come out—I was only gone down to speak to Patty again about the pork—Jane was standing in the passage—were not you, Jane?—for my mother was so afraid that we had not any salting-pan large enough. So I said, I would go down and see, and Jane said, "Shall I go down instead? for I think you have a little cold, and Patty has been washing the kitchen."—"Oh, my dear," said I—well, and just then came the note. A Miss Hawkins— that's all I know—a Miss Hawkins of Bath. But, Mr. Knightley, how could you possibly have heard it? for the very moment Mr. Cole told Mrs. Cole of it, she sat down and wrote to me. A Miss Hawkins—' "

Partial Recall.—This case helps us to understand why it is that the ordinary spontaneous flow of our ideas does not follow the law of total recall. *In no revival of a past experience are all the items of our thought equally operative in determining what the next thought shall be. Always some ingredient is prepotent over the rest.* Its special suggestions or associations in this case will often be different from those which it has in common with the whole group of items; and its tendency to awaken these outlying associates will deflect the path of our revery. Just as in the original sensible experience our attention focalized itself upon a few of the impressions of the scene before us, so here in the reproduction of those impressions an equal partiality is shown, and some items are emphasized above the rest. What these items shall be is, in most cases of spontaneous revery, hard to determine beforehand. In subjective terms we say that *the prepotent items are those which appeal most to our* INTEREST.

Expressed in brain-terms, the law of interest will be: *some one brain-process is always prepotent above its concomitants in arousing action elsewhere.*

"Two processes," says Mr. Hodgson, "are constantly going on in redintegration, the one a process of corrosion, melting, decay, and the other a process of renewing, arising, becoming . . . no object of representation remains long before consciousness in the same state, but fades, decays, and becomes indistinct. Those parts of the object, however, which possess an interest resist this tendency to gradual decay of the whole object. . . . This inequality in the object, some parts, the uninteresting, submitting to decay, others, the interesting parts, resisting it, when it has continued for a certain time, ends in becoming a new object."

Only where the interest is diffused equally over all the parts is this law departed from. It will be least obeyed by those minds which have the smallest variety and intensity of interests—those who, by the general flatness and poverty of their æsthetic nature, are kept for ever rotating among the literal sequences of their local and personal history.

Most of us, however, are better organized than this, and our musings pursue an erratic course, swerving continually into some new direction traced by the shifting play of interest as it ever falls on some partial item in each complex representation that is evoked. Thus it so often comes about that we find ourselves thinking at two nearly adjacent moments of things separated by the whole diameter of space and time. Not till we carefully recall each step of our cogitation do we see how naturally we came by Hodgson's law to pass from one to the other. Thus, for instance, after looking at my clock just now (1879), I found myself thinking of a recent resolution in the Senate about our legal-tender notes. The clock had called up the image of the man who had repaired its gong. He had suggested the jeweller's shop where I had last seen him; that shop, some shirt-studs which I had bought there; they, the value of gold and its recent decline; the latter, the equal value of greenbacks, and this, naturally, the question of how long they were to last, and of the Bayard proposition. Each of these images offered various points of interest. Those which formed the turning-points of my thought are easily assigned. The gong was momentarily the most interesting part of the clock, because, from having begun with a beautiful tone, it had become discordant and aroused disappointment. But for this the clock might have suggested the friend who gave it to me, or any one of a thousand circumstances connected with clocks. The jeweller's shop suggested the studs, because they alone of all its contents were tinged with the egoistic interest of possession. This interest in the studs, their value, made me single out the material as its chief source, etc., to the end. Every reader who will arrest himself at any moment and say, "How came I to be thinking of just this?" will be sure to trace a train of representations linked together by lines of contiguity and points of interest inextricably combined. This is the ordinary process of the association of ideas as it spontaneously goes on in average minds. *We may call it ordinary, or mixed, association,* or, if we like better, *partial recall.*

Which Associates come up, in Partial Recall?—Can we determine, now, when a certain portion of the going thought has, by dint of its interest, become so prepotent as to make its own exclusive associates the dominant features of the coming thought—can we, I say, determine *which* of its own associates shall be evoked? For they are many. As Hodgson says:

"The interesting parts of the decaying object are free to combine again with any objects, or parts of objects, with which they have at any time been combined before. All the former combinations of these parts may come back into consciousness; one must; but which will?"

Mr. Hodgson replies:

"There can be but one answer; That which has been most *habitually* combined with them before. This new object begins at once to form itself in consciousness, and to group its parts round the part still remaining from the former object; part after part comes out and arranges itself in its old position; but scarcely has the process begun, when the original law of interest begins to operate on this new formation, seizes on the interesting parts and impresses them on the attention to the exclusion of the rest, and the whole process is repeated again with endless variety. I venture to propose this as a complete and true account of the whole process of spontaneous redintegration."

In restricting the discharge from the interesting item into that channel which is simply most *habitual* in the sense of most frequent, Hodgson's account is assuredly imperfect. An image by no means always revives its most frequent associate, although frequency is certainly one of the most potent determinants of revival. If I abruptly utter the word *swallow,* the reader, if by habit an ornithologist, will think of a bird; if a physiologist or a medical specialist in throat-diseases, he will think of deglutition. If I say *date,* he will, if a fruit-merchant or an Arabian traveller, think of the produce of the palm; if an habitual student of history, figures with A.D. or B.C. before them will rise in his mind. If I say *bed, bath, morning,* his own daily toilet will be invincibly suggested by the combined names of three of its habitual associates. But frequent lines of transition are often set at naught. The sight of a certain book has most frequently awakened in me thoughts of the opinions therein propounded. The idea of suicide has never been connected with the volume. But a moment since, as my eye fell upon it, suicide was the thought that flashed into my mind. Why? Because but yesterday I received a letter informing me that the author's recent death was an act of self-destruction. Thoughts tend, then, to awaken their most recent as well as their most habitual associates. This is a matter of notorious experience, too notorious, in fact, to need illustration. If we have seen our friend this morning, the mention of his name now recalls the circumstances of that interview, rather than any more remote details concerning him. If Shakespeare's plays are mentioned, and we were last night reading *Richard II.*, vestiges of that play rather than of *Hamlet* or *Othello* float through our mind. Excitement of peculiar tracts, or peculiar modes of general excitement in the brain, leave a sort of tenderness or exalted sensibility behind them which takes days to die away. As long as it lasts, those tracts or those modes are liable to have their activities awakened by causes which at other times might leave them in repose. Hence, *recency* in experience is a prime factor in determining revival in thought.[1]

Vividness in an original experience may also have the same effect as habit or recency in bringing about likelihood of revival. If we have once witnessed an execution, any subsequent conversation or reading about capital punishment will almost certainly suggest images of that particular scene. Thus it is that events lived through only once, and in youth, may come in after-years, by reason of their exciting quality or emotional intensity, to serve as types or instances used by our mind to illustrate any and every occurring topic whose interest is most remotely pertinent to theirs. If a man in his boyhood once talked with Napoleon, any mention of great men or historical events, battles or thrones, or the whirligig of fortune, or islands in the ocean, will be apt to draw to his lips the incidents of that one memorable interview. If the word *tooth* now suddenly appears on the page before the reader's eye,

---

[1] I refer to a recency of a few hours. Mr. Galton found that experiences from boyhood and youth were more likely to be suggested by words seen at random than experiences of later years. See his highly interesting account of experiments in his *Inquiries into Human Faculty*, pp. 191–203.

there are fifty chances out of a hundred that, if he gives it time to awaken any image, it will be an image of some operation of dentistry in which he has been the sufferer. Daily he has touched his teeth and masticated with them; this very morning he brushed, used, and picked them; but the rarer and remoter associations arise more promptly because they were so much more intense.

A fourth factor in tracing the course of reproduction is *congruity in emotional tone* between the reproduced idea and our mood. The same objects do not recall the same associates when we are cheerful as when we are melancholy. Nothing, in fact, is more striking than our inability to keep up trains of joyous imagery when we are depressed in spirits. Storm, darkness, war, images of disease, poverty, perishing, and dread afflict unremittingly the imaginations of melancholiacs. And those of sanguine temperament, when their spirits are high, find it impossible to give any permanence to evil forebodings or to gloomy thoughts. In an instant the train of association dances off to flowers and sunshine, and images of spring and hope. The records of Arctic or African travel perused in one mood awaken no thoughts but those of horror at the malignity of Nature; read at another time they suggest only enthusiastic reflections on the indomitable power and pluck of man. Few novels so overflow with joyous animal spirits as *The Three Guardsmen* of Dumas. Yet it may awaken in the mind of a reader depressed with sea-sickness (as the writer can personally testify) a most woful consciousness of the cruelty and carnage of which heroes like Athos, Porthos, and Aramis make themselves guilty.

Habit, recency, vividness, and emotional congruity are, then, all reasons why one representation rather than another should be awakened by the interesting portion of a departing thought. We may say with truth that *in the majority of cases the coming representation will have been either habitual, recent, or vivid, and will be congruous.* If all these qualities unite in any one absent associate, we may predict almost infallibly that that associate of the going object will form an important ingredient in the object which comes next. In spite of the fact, however, that the succession of representations is thus redeemed from perfect indeterminism and limited to a few classes whose characteristic quality is fixed by the nature of our past experience, it must still be confessed that an immense number of terms in the linked chain of our representations fall outside of all assignable rule. To take the instance of the clock given on page

231. Why did the jeweller's shop suggest the shirt-studs rather than a chain which I had bought there more recently, which had cost more, and whose sentimental associations were much more interesting? Any reader's experience will easily furnish similar instances. So we must admit that to a certain extent, even in those forms of ordinary mixed association which lie nearest to impartial redintegration, *which* associate of the interesting item shall emerge must be called largely a matter of accident—accident, that is, for our intelligence. No doubt it is determined by cerebral causes, but they are too subtle and shifting for our analysis.

Focalized Recall, or Association by Similarity.—In partial or mixed association we have all along supposed the interesting portion of the disappearing thought to be of considerable extent, and to be sufficiently complex to constitute by itself a concrete object. Sir William Hamilton relates, for instance, that after thinking of Ben Lomond he found himself thinking of the Prussian system of education, and discovered that the links of association were a German gentleman whom he had met on Ben Lomond, Germany, etc. The interesting part of Ben Lomond as he had experienced it, the part operative in determining the train of his ideas, was the complex image of a particular man. But now let us suppose that the interested attention refines itself still further and accentuates a portion of the passing object, so small as to be no longer the image of a concrete thing, but only of an abstract quality or property. Let us moreover suppose that the part thus accentuated persists in consciousness (or, in cerebral terms, has its brain-process continue) after the other portions of the object have faded. *This small surviving portion will then surround itself with its own associates* after the fashion we have already seen, and the relation between the new thought's object and the object of the faded thought will be a *relation of similarity*. The pair of thoughts will form an instance of what is called '*association by similarity*.'

The similars which are here associated, or of which the first is followed by the second in the mind, are seen to be *compounds*. Experience proves that this is always the case. *There is no tendency on the part of* SIMPLE '*ideas,' attributes, or qualities to remind us of their like.* The thought of one shade of blue does not summon up that of another shade of blue, etc., unless indeed we have in mind some general purpose of nomenclature or comparison which requires a review of several blue tints.

Now two compound things are similar when some one quality

or group of qualities is shared alike by both, although as regards their other qualities they may have nothing in common. The moon is similar to a gas-jet, it is also similar to a foot-ball; but a gas-jet and a foot-ball are not similar to each other. When we affirm the similarity of two compound things, we should always say *in what respect it obtains.* Moon and gas-jet are similar in respect of luminosity, and nothing else; moon and foot-ball in respect of rotundity, and nothing else. Foot-ball and gas-jet are in no respect similar—that is, they possess no common point, no identical attribute. *Similarity, in compounds, is partial identity.* When the *same* attribute appears in two phenomena, though it be their only common property, the two phenomena are similar in so far forth. To return now to our associated representations. If the thought of the moon is succeeded by the thought of a foot-ball, and that by the thought of one of Mr. X's railroads, it is because the attribute rotundity in the moon broke away from all the rest and surrounded itself with an entirely new set of companions—elasticity, leathery integument, swift mobility in obedience to human caprice, etc.; and because the last-named attribute in the foot-ball in turn broke away from its companions, and, itself persisting, surrounded itself with such new attributes as make up the notions of a 'railroad king,' of a rising and falling stock-market, and the like.

The gradual passage from total to focalized, through what we have called ordinary partial, recall may be symbolized by diagrams. Fig. 58 is total, Fig. 59 is partial, and Fig. 60 focalized, recall. *A* in each is the passing, *B* the coming, thought. In 'total recall,' all parts of *A* are equally operative in calling up *B*. In 'partial recall,' most parts of *A* are inert. The part *M* alone breaks out and awakens *B*. In similar association or 'focalized recall,' the part *M* is much smaller than in the previous case, and after awak-

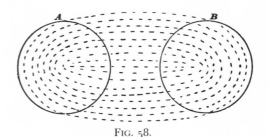

FIG. 58.

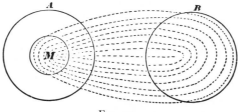

FIG. 59.

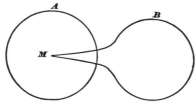

FIG. 60.

ening its new set of associates, instead of fading out itself, it continues persistently active along with them, forming an identical
part in the two ideas, and making these, *pro tanto*, resemble each
other.[2]

Why a single portion of the passing thought should break out
from its concert with the rest and act, as we say, on its own hook,
why the other parts should become inert, are mysteries which we

---

[2] Miss M. W. Calkins (*Philosophical Review*, I, 389, 1892) points out that the persistent feature of the going thought, on which the association in cases of similarity
hinges, is by no means always so slight as to warrant the term 'focalized.' "If the sight
of the whole breakfast-room be followed by the visual image of yesterday's breakfast-table, with the same setting and in the same surroundings, the association is
practically total," and yet the case is one of similarity. For Miss Calkins, accordingly,
the more important distinction is that between what she calls *desistent* and *persistent*
association. In 'desistent' association all parts of the going thought fade out and are
replaced. In 'persistent' association some of them remain, and form a bond of similarity between the mind's successive objects; but only where this bond is extremely
delicate (as in the case of an abstract relation or quality) is there need to call the
persistent process 'focalized.' I must concede the justice of Miss Calkins's criticism,
and think her new pair of terms a useful contribution. Wundt's division of associations into the two classes of *external* and *internal* is congruent with Miss Calkins's division. Things associated internally must have some element in common; and Miss
Calkins's word 'persistent' suggests how this may cerebrally come to pass. 'Desistent,'
on the other hand, suggests the process by which the successive ideas become external to each other or preserve no inner tie.

can ascertain but not explain. Possibly a minuter insight into the laws of neural action will some day clear the matter up; possibly neural laws will not suffice, and we shall need to invoke a dynamic reaction of the consciousness itself. But into this we cannot enter now.

Voluntary Trains of Thought.—Hitherto we have assumed the process of suggestion of one object by another to be spontaneous. The train of imagery wanders at its own sweet will, now trudging in sober grooves of habit, now with a hop, skip, and jump, darting across the whole field of time and space. This is revery, or musing; but great segments of the flux of our ideas consist of something very different from this. They are guided by a distinct purpose or conscious interest; and the course of our ideas is then called *voluntary*.

Physiologically considered, we must suppose that a purpose means the persistent activity of certain rather definite brain-processes throughout the whole course of thought. Our most usual cogitations are not pure reveries, absolute driftings, but revolve about some central interest or topic to which most of the images are relevant, and towards which we return promptly after occasional digressions. This interest is subserved by the persistently active brain-tracts we have supposed. In the mixed associations which we have hitherto studied, the parts of each object which form the pivots on which our thoughts successively turn have their interest largely determined by their connection with some *general interest* which for the time has seized upon the mind. If we call Z the brain-tract of general interest, then, if the object abc turns up, and b has more associations with Z than have either a or c, b will become the object's interesting, pivotal portion, and will call up its own associates exclusively. For the energy of b's brain-tract will be augmented by Z's activity,—an activity which, from lack of previous connection between Z and a and Z and c, does not influence a or c. If, for instance, I think of Paris whilst I am *hungry*, I shall not improbably find that its *restaurants* have become the pivot of my thought, etc., etc.

Problems.—But in the theoretic as well as in the practical life there are interests of a more acute sort, taking the form of definite images of some achievement which we desire to effect. The train of ideas arising under the influence of such an interest constitutes usually the thought of the *means* by which the end shall be attained. If the end by its simple presence does not instantaneously suggest the means, the search for the latter becomes a *problem*; and the discovery of the means forms a new sort of end, of an entirely peculiar nature—an end, namely, which we intensely desire before we have attained it, but of the nature of which, even whilst most strongly craving it, we have no distinct imagination whatever (compare p. 212).

The same thing occurs whenever we seek to recall something forgotten, or to state the reason for a judgment which we have made intuitively. The desire strains and presses in a direction which it feels to be right, but towards a point which it is unable to see. In short, the *absence of an item* is a determinant of our representations quite as positive as its presence can ever be. The gap becomes no mere void, but what is called an *aching* void. If we try to explain in terms of brain-action how a thought which only potentially exists can yet be effective, we seem driven to believe that the brain-tract thereof must actually be excited, but only in a minimal and sub-conscious way. Try, for instance, to symbolize what goes on in a man who is racking his brains to remember a thought which occurred to him last week. The associates of the thought are there, many of them at least, but they refuse to awaken the thought itself. We cannot suppose that they do not irradiate *at all* into its brain-tract, because his mind quivers on the very edge of its recovery. Its actual rhythm sounds in his ears; the words seem on the imminent point of following, but fail (see p. 149). Now the only difference between the effort to recall things forgotten and the search after the means to a given end is that the latter have not, whilst the former have, already formed a part of our experience. If we first study *the mode of recalling a thing forgotten*, we can take up with better understanding the voluntary quest of the unknown.

Their Solution.—The forgotten thing is felt by us as a gap in the midst of certain other things. We possess a dim idea of where we were and what we were about when it last occurred to us. We recollect the general subject to which it pertains. But all these details refuse to shoot together into a solid whole, for the lack of the missing thing, so we keep running over them in our mind, dissatisfied, craving something more. From each detail there radiate lines of association forming so many tentative guesses. Many of these are immediately seen to be irrelevant, are therefore void of interest, and lapse immediately from consciousness. Others are associated with the other details present, and with the missing thought as well. When *these* surge up, we have a peculiar feeling that we are 'warm,' as the children say when they play hide and seek; and such associates as these we clutch at and keep before the attention. Thus we recollect successively that when we last were considering the matter in question we were at the dinner-table; then that our friend J. D. was there; then that the subject talked about was so and so; finally, that the thought came *a propos* of a certain anecdote, and then that it had something to do with a French quotation. Now all these added associates *arise independently of the will,* by the spontaneous processes we know so well. *All that the will does is to emphasize and linger over those which seem pertinent, and ignore the rest.* Through this hovering of the attention in the neighborhood of the desired object, the accumulation of associates becomes so great that the combined tensions of their neural processes break through the bar, and the nervous wave pours into the tract which has so long been awaiting its advent. And as the expectant, sub-conscious itching, so to speak, bursts into the fulness of vivid feeling, the mind finds an inexpressible relief.

The whole process can be rudely symbolized in a diagram. Call the forgotten thing Z, the first facts with which we felt it was related a, b, and c, and the details finally operative in calling it up l, m, and n. Each circle will then stand for the brain-process principally concerned in the thought of the fact lettered within it. The activity in Z will at first be a mere tension; but as the activities in a, b, and c little by little irradiate into l, m, and n, and as *all* these processes are somehow connected with Z, their combined irradia-

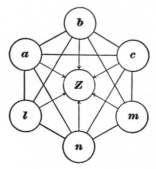

Fig. 61.

240

tions upon *Z*, represented by the centripetal arrows, succeed in rousing *Z* also to full activity.

Turn now to the case of finding the unknown means to a distinctly conceived end. The end here stands in the place of *a*, *b*, *c*, in the diagram. It is the starting-point of the irradiations of suggestion; and here, as in that case, what the voluntary attention does is only to dismiss some of the suggestions as irrelevant, and hold fast to others which are felt to be more pertinent—let these be symbolized by *l*, *m*, *n*. These latter at last accumulate sufficiently to discharge all together into *Z*, the excitement of which process is, in the mental sphere, equivalent to the solution of our problem. The only difference between this and the previous case is that in this one there need be no original sub-excitement in *Z*, coöperating from the very first. In the solving of a problem, all that we are aware of in advance seems to be its *relations*. It must be a cause, or it must be an effect, or it must contain an attribute, or it must be a means, or what not. We know, in short, a lot *about* it, whilst as yet we have no *acquaintance* with it. Our perception that one of the objects which turn up is, at last, our *quæsitum*, is due to our recognition that its relations are identical with those we had in mind, and this may be a rather slow act of judgment. Everyone knows that an object may be for some time present to his mind before its relations to other matters are perceived. Just so the relations may be there before the object is.

From the guessing of newspaper enigmas to the plotting of the policy of an empire there is no other process than this. We must trust to the laws of cerebral nature to present us spontaneously with the appropriate idea, but we must know it for the right one when it comes.

It is foreign to my purpose here to enter into any detailed analysis of the different classes of mental pursuit. In a scientific research we get perhaps as rich an example as can be found. The inquirer starts with a fact of which he seeks the reason, or with an hypothesis of which he seeks the proof. In either case he keeps turning the matter incessantly in his mind until, by the arousal of associate upon associate, some habitual, some similar, one arises which he recognizes to suit his need. This, however, may take years. No rules can be given by which the investigator may proceed straight to his result; but both here and in the case of reminiscence the accumulation of helps in the way of associations may advance more rapidly by the use of certain routine methods. In striving to recall a thought, for example, we may of set purpose run through the successive classes of circumstance with which it may possibly have been connected, trusting that when the right member of the class has turned up it will help the thought's revival. Thus we may run through all the *places* in which we may have had it. We may run through the *persons* whom we remember to have conversed with, or we may call up successively all the *books* we have lately been reading. If we are trying to remember a person we may run through a list of streets or of professions. Some item out of the lists thus methodically gone over will very likely be associated with the fact we are in need of, and may suggest it or help to do so. And yet the item might never have arisen without such systematic procedure. In scientific research this accumulation of associates has been methodized by Mill under the title of "The Four Methods of Experimental Inquiry." By the 'method of agreement,' by that of 'difference,' by those of 'residues' and 'concomitant variations' (which cannot here be more nearly defined), we make certain lists of cases; and by ruminating these lists in our minds the cause we seek will be more likely to emerge. But the final stroke of discovery is only prepared, not effected, by them. The brain-tracts must, of their own accord, shoot the right way at last, or we shall still grope in darkness. That in some brains the tracts *do* shoot the right way much oftener than in others, and that we cannot tell why,—these are ultimate facts to which we must never close our eyes. Even in forming our lists of instances according to Mill's methods, we are at the mercy of the spontaneous workings of Similarity in our brain. How are a number of facts, resembling the one whose cause we seek, to be brought together in a list unless one will rapidly suggest another through association by similarity?

Similarity no Elementary Law.—Such is the analysis I propose, first of the three main types of spontaneous, and then of voluntary, trains of thought. It will be observed that the *object called up may bear any logical relation whatever to the one which suggested it.* The law requires only that one condition should be fulfilled. The fading object must be due to a brain-process some of whose elements awaken through habit some of the elements of the brain-process of the object which comes to view. This awakening is the causal agency in the kind of association called Similarity, as in any other sort. The similarity *itself* between the objects has no causal agency in carrying us from one to the other. It is but a result—the effect of the usual causal agent when this happens to work in a certain way. Ordinary writers talk as if the similarity of the objects were itself an agent, coördinate with habit, and independent of it, and like it able to push objects before the mind. This is quite unintelligible. The similarity of two things does not exist till both things are there—it is meaningless to talk of it as an *agent of production* of anything, whether in the physical or the psychical realms. It is a relation which the mind perceives after the fact, just as it may perceive the relations of superiority, of distance, of causality, of container and content, of substance and accident, or of contrast, between an object and some second object which the associative machinery calls up.

Conclusion.—To sum up, then, we see that *the difference between the three kinds of association reduces itself to a simple difference in the amount of that portion of the nerve-tract supporting the going thought which is operative in calling up the thought which comes.* But the *modus operandi* of this active part is the same, be it large or be it small. The items constituting the coming object waken in every instance because their nerve-tracts once were excited continuously with those of the going object or its operative part. This ultimate physiological law of habit among the neural elements is what *runs* the train. The direction of its course and the form of its transitions are due to the unknown conditions by which in some brains action tends to focalize itself in small spots, while in others it fills patiently its broad bed. What these differing conditions are, it seems impossible to guess. Whatever they are, they are what separate the man of genius from the prosaic creature of habit and routine thinking. In the chapter on Reasoning we shall need to recur again to this point. I trust that the student will now feel that the way to a deeper understanding of the order of our ideas lies in the direction of cerebral physiology. The *elementary* process of revival can be nothing but the law of habit. Truly the day is distant when physiologists shall actually trace from cell-group to cell-group the irradiations which we have hypothetically invoked. Probably it will never arrive. The schematism we have used is, moreover, taken immediately from the analysis of objects into their elementary parts, and only extended by analogy to the brain. And yet it is only as incorporated in the brain that such a schematism can represent anything *causal*. This is, to my mind, the conclusive reason for saying that the order of *presentation of the mind's materials* is due to cerebral physiology alone.

The law of accidental prepotency of certain processes over others falls also within the sphere of cerebral probabilities. Granting such instability as the brain-tissue requires, certain points must always discharge more quickly and strongly than others; and this prepotency would shift its place from moment to moment by accidental causes, giving us a perfect mechanical diagram of the capricious play of similar association in the most gifted mind. A study of dreams confirms this view. The usual abundance of paths of irradiation seems, in the dormant brain, reduced. A few only are pervious, and the most fantastic sequences occur because the currents run—'like sparks in burnt-up paper'—wherever the nutrition of the moment creates an opening, but nowhere else.

The *effects of interested attention and volition* remain. These activities seem to hold fast to certain elements and, by emphasizing them and dwelling on them, to make their associates the only ones which are evoked. *This* is the point at which an anti-mechanical psychology must, if anywhere, make its stand in dealing with association. Everything else is pretty certainly due to cerebral laws. My own opinion on the question of active attention and spiritual spontaneity is expressed elsewhere (see p. 208). But even though there be a mental spontaneity, it can certainly not create ideas or summon them *ex abrupto*. Its power is limited to *selecting* amongst those which the associative machinery introduces. If it can emphasize, reinforce, or protract for half a second either one of these, it can do all that the most eager advocate of free-will need demand; for it then decides the direction of the *next* associations by making them hinge upon the emphasized term; and determining in this wise the course of the man's thinking, it also determines his acts.

Chapter XVII

The Sense of Time

The sensible present has duration. Let anyone try, I will not say to arrest, but to notice or attend to, the *present* moment of time. One of the most baffling experiences occurs. Where is it, this present? It has melted in our grasp, fled ere we could touch it, gone in the instant of becoming. As a poet, quoted by Mr. Hodgson, says,

> "Le moment où je parle est déjà loin de moi,"

and it is only as entering into the living and moving organization of a much wider tract of time that the strict present is apprehended at all. It is, in fact, an altogether ideal abstraction, not only never realized in sense, but probably never even conceived of by those unaccustomed to philosophic meditation. Reflection leads us to the conclusion that it *must* exist, but that it *does* exist can never be a fact of our immediate experience. The only fact of our immediate experience is what has been well called 'the specious' present, a sort of saddle-back of time with a certain length of its own, on which we sit perched, and from which we look in two directions into time. The unit of composition of our perception of time is a *duration*, with a bow and a stern, as it were—a rearward- and a forward-looking end. It is only as parts of this *duration-block* that the relation of *succession* of one end to the other is perceived. We do not first feel one end and then feel the other after it, and from the perception of the succession infer an interval of time between, but we seem to feel the interval of time as a whole, with its two ends embedded in it. The experience is from the outset a synthetic datum, not a simple one; and to sensible perception its elements are inseparable, although attention looking back may easily decompose the experience, and distinguish its beginning from its end.

The moment we pass beyond a very few seconds our consciousness of duration ceases to be an immediate perception and becomes a construction more or less symbolic. To realize even an hour, we must count 'now! now! now! now!' indefinitely. Each 'now' is the feeling of a separate *bit* of time, and the exact sum of the bits never makes a clear impression on our mind. The *longest bit of duration* which we can apprehend at once so as to discriminate it from longer and shorter bits of time would seem (from experiments made for another purpose in Wundt's laboratory) to be about 12 seconds. *The shortest interval* which we can feel as time at all would seem to be $\frac{1}{500}$ of a second. That is, Exner recognized two electric sparks to be successive when the second followed the first at that interval.

We have no sense for empty time. Let one sit with closed eyes and, abstracting entirely from the outer world, attend exclusively to the passage of time, like one who wakes, as the poet says, "to hear time flowing in the middle of the night, and all things creeping to a day of doom." There seems under such circumstances as these no variety in the material content of our thought, and what we notice appears, if anything, to be the pure series of durations budding, as it were, and growing beneath our indrawn gaze. Is this really so or not? The question is important; for, if the experience be what it roughly seems, we have a sort of special sense for pure time—a sense to which empty duration is an adequate stimulus; while if it be an illusion, it must be that our perception of time's flight, in the experiences quoted, is due to the *filling* of the time, and to our *memory* of a content which it had a moment previous, and which we feel to agree or disagree with its content now.

It takes but a small exertion of introspection to show that the latter alternative is the true one, and that *we can no more perceive a duration than we can perceive an extension, devoid of all sensible content.* Just as with closed eyes we see a dark visual field in which a curdling play of obscurest luminosity is always going on; so, be we never so abstracted from distinct outward impressions, we are always inwardly immersed in what Wundt has somewhere called the twilight of our general consciousness. Our heart-beats, our breathing, the pulses of our attention, fragments of words or sentences that pass through our imagination, are what people this dim habitat. Now, all these processes are rhythmical, and are apprehended by us, as they occur, in their totality; the breathing and pulses of attention, as coherent successions, each with its rise and fall; the heart-beats similarly, only relatively far more brief; the words not separately, but in connected groups. In short, empty our minds as we may, some form of *changing process* remains for us to feel, and cannot be expelled. And along with the sense of the process and its rhythm goes the sense of the length of time it lasts. Awareness of *change* is thus the condition on which our perception of time's flow depends; but there exists no reason to suppose that empty time's own changes are sufficient for the awareness of change to be aroused. The change must be of some concrete sort.

Appreciation of Longer Durations.—In the experience of watching empty time flow—'empty' to be taken hereafter in the relative sense just set forth—we tell it off in pulses. We say 'now! now! now!' or we count 'more! more! more!' as we feel it bud. This composition out of units of duration is called the law of time's *discrete flow*. The discreteness is, however, merely due to the fact that our successive acts of *recognition* or *apperception* of *what* it is are discrete. The sensation is as continuous as any sensation can be. All continuous sensations are *named* in beats. We notice that a certain finite 'more' of them is passing or already past. To adopt Hodgson's image, the sensation is the measuring-tape, the perception the dividing-engine which stamps its length. As we listen to a steady sound, we *take it in* in discrete pulses of recognition, calling it successively 'the same! the same! the same!' The case stands no otherwise with time.

After a small number of beats our impression of the amount we have told off becomes quite vague. Our only way of knowing it accurately is by counting, or noticing the clock, or through some other symbolic conception. When the times exceed hours or days, the conception is absolutely symbolic. We think of the amount we mean either solely as a *name*, or by running over a few salient *dates* therein, with no pretence of imagining the full durations that lie between them. No one has anything like a *perception* of the greater length of the time between now and the first century than of that between now and the tenth. To an historian, it is true, the longer interval will suggest a host of additional dates and events, and so appear a more *multitudinous* thing. And for the same reason most people will think they directly perceive the length of the past fortnight to exceed that of the past week. But there is properly no comparative time-*intuition* in these cases at all. It is but dates and events representing time, their abundance symbolizing its length. I am sure that this is so, even where the times compared are no more than an hour or so in length. It is the same with spaces of many miles, which we always compare with each other by the numbers that measure them.

From this we pass naturally to speak of certain familiar variations in our estimation of lengths of time. *In general, a time filled with varied and interesting experiences seems short in passing, but long as we look back. On the other hand, a tract of time empty of experiences seems long in passing, but in retrospect short.* A week of travel and sight-seeing may subtend an angle more like three weeks in the memory; and a month of sickness yields hardly more memories than a day. The length in retrospect depends obviously on the multitudinousness of the memories which the time affords. Many objects, events, changes, many subdivisions, immediately widen the view as we look back. Emptiness, monotony, familiarity, make it shrivel up.

The same space of time seems shorter as we grow older—that is, the days, the months, and the years do so; whether the hours do so is doubtful, and the minutes and seconds to all appearance remain about the same. An old man probably does not *feel* his past life to be any longer than he did when he was a boy, though it may be a dozen times as long. In most men all the events of manhood's years are of such familiar *sorts* that the individual impressions do not last. At the same time more and more of the earlier events get forgotten, the result being that no greater multitude of distinct objects remains in the memory.

So much for the apparent shortening of tracts of time in *retrospect*. They shorten *in passing* whenever we are so fully occupied with their content as not to note the actual time itself. A day full of excitement, with no pause, is said to pass 'ere we know it.' On the contrary, a day full of waiting, of unsatisfied desire for change, will seem a small eternity. *Tædium, ennui, Langweile, boredom,* are words for which, probably, every language known to man has its equivalent. It comes about whenever, from the relative emptiness of content of a tract of time, we grow attentive to the passage of the time itself. Expecting, and being ready for, a new impression to succeed; when it fails to come, we get an empty time instead of it; and such experiences, ceaselessly renewed, make us most formidably aware of the extent of the mere time itself. Close your eyes and simply wait to hear somebody tell you that a minute has elapsed, and the full length of your leisure with it seems incredible. You engulf yourself into its bowels as into those of that interminable first week of an ocean voyage, and find yourself wondering that history can have overcome many such periods in its course. All because you attend so closely to the mere feeling of the time *per se*, and because your attention to that is susceptible of such fine-grained successive subdivision. The *odiousness* of the whole experience comes from its insipidity; for *stimulation* is the indispensable requisite for pleasure in an experience, and the feeling of bare time is the least stimulating experience we can have. The sensation of tedium is a *protest*, says Volkmann, against the entire present.

The feeling of past time is a present feeling. In reflecting on the *modus operandi* of our consciousness of time, we are at first tempted to suppose it the easiest thing in the world to understand. Our inner states succeed each other. They know themselves as they are; then of course, we say, they must know their own succession. But this philosophy is too crude; for between the mind's own changes *being* successive, and *knowing their own succession*, lies as broad a chasm as between the object and subject of any case of cognition in the world. *A succession of feelings, in and of itself, is not a feeling of succession. And since, to our successive feelings, a feeling of their succession is added, that must be treated as an additional fact requiring its own special elucidation*, which this talk about the feelings knowing their time-relations as a matter of course leaves all untouched.

If we represent the actual time-stream of our thinking by an horizontal line, the thought *of* the stream or of any segment of its length, past, present, or to come, might be figured in a perpendicular raised upon the horizontal at a certain point. The length of this perpendicular stands for a certain object or content, which in this case is the time thought of at the actual moment of the stream upon which the perpendicular is raised.

There is thus a sort of *perspective projection* of past objects upon present consciousness, similar to that of wide landscapes upon a camera-screen.

And since we saw a while ago that our maximum distinct *perception* of duration hardly covers more than a dozen seconds (while our maximum vague perception is probably not more than that of a minute or so), we must suppose that *this amount of duration is pictured fairly steadily in each passing instant of consciousness* by virtue of some fairly constant feature in the brain-process to which the consciousness is tied. *This feature of the brain-process, whatever it be, must be the cause of our perceiving the fact of time at all.* The duration thus steadily perceived is hardly more than the 'specious present,' as it was called a few pages back. Its *content* is in a constant flux, events dawning into its forward end as fast as they fade out of its rearward one, and each of them changing its time-coefficient from 'not yet,' or 'not quite yet,' to 'just gone,' or 'gone,' as it passes by. Meanwhile, the specious present, the intuited duration, stands permanent, like the rainbow on the waterfall, with its own quality unchanged by the events that stream through it. Each of these, as it slips out, retains the power of being reproduced; and when reproduced, is reproduced with the duration and neighbors which it originally had. Please observe, however, that the reproduction of an event, *after* it has once completely dropped out of the rearward end of the specious present, is an entirely different psychic fact from its direct perception in the specious present as a thing immediately past. A creature might be entirely devoid of *reproductive* memory, and yet have the time-sense; but the latter would be limited, in his case, to the few seconds immediately passing by. In the next chapter, assuming the sense of time as given, we will turn to the analysis of what happens in reproductive memory, the recall of *dated* things.

Chapter XVIII

Memory

Analysis of the Phenomenon of Memory.—Memory proper, or secondary memory as it might be styled, is the knowledge of a former state of mind after it has already once dropped from consciousness; or rather *it is the knowledge of an event, or fact, of which meantime we have not been thinking, with the additional consciousness that we have thought or experienced it before.*

The first element which such a knowledge involves would seem to be the revival in the mind of an image or copy of the original event. And it is an assumption made by many writers that such revival of an image is all that is needed to constitute the memory of the original occurrence. But such a revival is obviously not a *memory*, whatever else it may be; it is simply a duplicate, a second event, having absolutely no connection with the first event except that it happens to resemble it. The clock strikes to-day; it struck yesterday; and may strike a million times ere it wears out. The rain pours through the gutter this week; it did so last week; and will do so *in sæcula sæculorum*. But does the present clock-stroke become aware of the past ones, or the present stream recollect the past stream, because they repeat and resemble them? Assuredly not. And let it not be said that this is because clock-strokes and gutters are physical and not psychical objects; for psychical objects (sensations, for example) simply recurring in successive editions will remember each other *on that account* no more than clock-strokes do. No memory is involved in the mere fact of recurrence.

The successive editions of a feeling are so many independent events, each snug in its own skin. Yesterday's feeling is dead and buried; and the presence of to-day's is no reason why it should resuscitate along with to-day's. A farther condition is required before the present image can be held to stand for a *past original*.

That condition is that the fact imaged be *expressly referred to the past*, thought as *in the past*. But how can we think a thing as in the past, except by thinking of the past together with the thing, and of the relation of the two? And how can we think of the past? In the chapter on Time-perception we have seen that our intuitive or immediate consciousness of pastness hardly carries us more than a few seconds backwards of the present instant of time. Remoter dates are conceived, not perceived; known symbolically by names, such as 'last week,' '1850'; or thought of by events which happened in them, as the year in which we attended such a school, or met with such a loss. So that if we wish to think of a particular past epoch, we must think of a name or other symbol, or else of certain concrete events, associated therewithal. Both must be thought of, to think the past epoch adequately. And to 'refer' any special fact to the past epoch is to think that fact *with* the names and events which characterize its date, to think it, in short, with a lot of contiguous associates.

But even this would not be memory. Memory requires more than mere dating of a fact in the past. It must be dated in *my* past. In other words, I must think that I directly experienced its occurrence. It must have that 'warmth and intimacy' which were so often spoken of in the chapter on the Self, as characterizing all experiences 'appropriated' by the thinker as his own.

A general feeling of the past direction in time, then, a particular date conceived as lying along that direction, and defined by its name or phenomenal contents, an event imagined as located therein, and owned as part of my experience,—such are the elements of every object of memory.

Retention and Recall.—Such being the phenomenon of memory, or the analysis of its object, can we see how it comes to pass? can we lay bare its causes?

Its complete exercise presupposes two things:

1) The *retention* of the remembered fact; and

2) Its *reminiscence, recollection, reproduction*, or *recall*.

Now *the cause both of retention and of recollection is the law of habit in the nervous system, working as it does in the 'association of ideas.'*

Association explains Recall.—Associationists have long explained *recollection* by association. James Mill gives an account of it which I am unable to improve upon, unless it might be by translating his word 'idea' into 'thing thought of,' or 'object.'

"There is," he says, "a state of mind familiar to all men, in which we are said to try to remember. In this state, it is certain that we have not in the mind the idea which we are trying to have in it. How then is it, that we proceed in the course of our endeavour, to procure its introduction into the mind? If we have not the idea itself, we have certain ideas connected with it. We run over those ideas, one after another, in hopes that some one of them will suggest the idea we are in quest of; and if any one of them does, it is always one so connected with it, as to call it up in the way of association. I meet an old acquaintance, whose name I do not remember, and wish to recollect. I run over a number of names, in hopes that some of them may be associated with the idea of the individual. I think of all the circumstances in which I have seen him engaged; the time when I knew him, the persons along with whom I knew him, the things he did, or the things he suffered; and, if I chance upon any idea with which the name is associated, then immediately I have the recollection; if not, my pursuit of it is in vain. There is another set of cases, very familiar, but affording very important evidence on the subject. It frequently happens, that there are matters which we desire not to forget. What is the contrivance to which we have recourse for preserving the memory; that is, for making sure that it will be called into existence, when it is our wish that it should. All men, invariably employ the same expedient. They endeavour to form an association between the idea of the thing to be remembered, and some sensation, or some idea, which they know beforehand will occur at or near the time when they wish the remembrance to be in their minds. If this association is formed, and the sensation or the idea, with which it has been formed, occurs; the sensation, or idea, calls up the remembrance; and the object of him who formed the association is attained. To use a vulgar instance: a man receives a commission from his friend, and, that he may not forget it, ties a knot on his handkerchief. How is this fact to be explained? First of all, the idea of the commission is associated with the making of the knot. Next, the handkerchief is a thing which it is known beforehand will be frequently seen, and of course at no great distance of time from the occasion on which the memory is desired. The handkerchief being seen, the knot is seen, and this sensation recalls the idea of the commission, between which and itself, the association had been purposely formed."

In short, we make search in our memory for a forgotten idea, just as we rummage our house for a lost object. In both cases we visit what seems to us the probable *neighborhood* of that which we miss. We turn over the things under which, or within which, or alongside of which, it may possibly be; and if it lies near them, it soon comes to view. But these matters, in the case of a mental object sought, are nothing but its *associates*. The machinery of recall is thus the same as the machinery of association, and the machinery of association, as we know, is nothing but the elementary law of habit in the nerve-centres.

It also explains retention. And this same law of habit is the machinery of retention also. Retention means *liability* to recall, and it means nothing more than such liability. The only proof of there being retention is that recall actually takes place. The retention of an experience is, in short, but another name for the *possibility* of thinking it again, or the *tendency* to think it again, with its past surroundings. Whatever accidental cue may turn this tendency into an actuality, the permanent *ground* of the tendency itself lies in the organized neural paths by which the cue calls up the memorable experience, the past associates, the sense that the self was there, the belief that it all really happened, etc., as previously described. When the recollection is of the 'ready' sort, the resuscitation takes place the instant the cue arises; when it is slow, resuscitation comes after delay. But be the recall prompt or slow, the condition which makes it possible at all (or, in other words, the 'retention' of the experience) is neither more nor less than the brain-paths which *associate* the experience with the occasion and cue of the recall. *When slumbering, these paths are the condition of retention; when active, they are the condition of recall.*

Brain-scheme.—A simple scheme will now make the whole cause of memory plain. Let n be a past event, o its 'setting' (concomitants, date, self present, warmth and intimacy, etc., etc., as already set forth), and m some present thought or fact which may appropriately become the occasion of its recall. Let the nerve-centres, active in the thought of m, n, and o, be represented by M, N, and O, respectively; then the *existence* of the *paths* symbolized by the lines between M and N and N and O will be the fact indicated

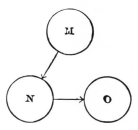

FIG. 62.

by the phrase 'retention of the event *n* in the memory,' and the *excitement* of the brain along these paths will be the condition of the event *n*'s actual recall. The *retention* of *n*, it will be observed, is no mysterious storing up of an 'idea' in an unconscious state. It is not a fact of the mental order at all. It is a purely physical phenomenon, a morphological feature, the presence of these 'paths,' namely, in the finest recesses of the brain's tissue. The recall or recollection, on the other hand, is a *psycho-physical* phenomenon, with both a bodily and a mental side. The bodily side is the excitement of the paths in question; the mental side is the conscious representation of the past occurrence, and the belief that we experienced it before.

The only hypothesis, in short, to which the facts of inward experience give countenance is that *the brain-tracts excited by the event proper, and those excited in its recall, are in part* DIFFERENT *from each other.* If we could revive the past event without any associates we should exclude the possibility of memory, and simply dream that we were undergoing the experience as if for the first time. Wherever, in fact, the recalled event does appear without a definite setting, it is hard to distinguish it from a mere creation of fancy. But in proportion as its image lingers and recalls associates which gradually become more definite, it grows more and more distinctly into a remembered thing. For example, I enter a friend's room and see on the wall a painting. At first I have the strange, wondering consciousness, 'Surely I have seen that before,' but when or how does not become clear. There only clings to the picture a sort of penumbra of familiarity,—when suddenly I exclaim: "I have it! It is a copy of part of one of the Fra Angelicos in the Florentine Academy—I recollect it there." Only when the image of the Academy arises does the picture become remembered, as well as seen.

The Conditions of Goodness in Memory.—The remembered fact being *n*, then, the path N—O is what arouses for *n* its setting when it *is* recalled, and makes it other than a mere imagination. The path M—N, on the other hand, gives the cue or occasion of its being recalled at all. *Memory being thus altogether conditioned on brain-paths, its excellence in a given individual will depend partly on the* NUMBER *and partly on the* PERSISTENCE *of these paths.*

The persistence or permanence of the paths is a physiological property of the brain-tissue of the individual, whilst their number is altogether due to the facts of his mental experience. Let the quality of permanence in the paths be called the native tenacity, or physiological retentiveness. This tenacity differs enormously from infancy to old age, and from one person to another. Some minds are like wax under a seal—no impression, however disconnected with others, is wiped out. Others, like a jelly, vibrate to every touch, but under usual conditions retain no permanent mark. These latter minds, before they can recollect a fact, must weave it into their permanent stores of knowledge. They have no *desultory* memory. Those persons, on the contrary, who retain names, dates and addresses, anecdotes, gossip, poetry, quotations, and all sorts of miscellaneous facts, without an effort, have desultory memory in a high degree, and certainly owe it to the unusual tenacity of their brain-substance for any path once formed therein. No one probably was ever effective on a voluminous scale without a high degree of this physiological retentiveness. In the practical as in the theoretic life, the man whose acquisitions *stick* is the man who is always achieving and advancing, whilst his neighbors, spending most of their time in relearning what they once knew but have forgotten, simply hold their own. A Charlemagne, a Luther, a Leibnitz, a Walter Scott, any example, in short, of your quarto or folio editions of mankind, must needs have amazing retentiveness of the purely physiological sort. Men without this retentiveness may excel in the *quality* of their work at this point or at that, but will never do such mighty sums of it, or be influential contemporaneously on such a scale.

But there comes a time of life for all of us when we can do no more than hold our own in the way of acquisitions, when the old paths fade as fast as the new ones form in our brain, and when we forget in a week quite as much as we can learn in the same space of time. This equilibrium may last many, many years. In extreme old age it is upset in the reverse direction, and forgetting prevails over acquisition, or rather there is no acquisition. Brain-paths are so transient that in the course of a few minutes of conversation the same question is asked and its answer forgotten half a dozen times. Then the superior tenacity of the paths formed in childhood becomes manifest: the dotard will retrace the facts of his earlier years after he has lost all those of later date.

So much for the permanence of the paths. Now for their number.

It is obvious that the more there are of such paths as M—N in the brain, and the more of such possible cues or occasions for the recall of *n* in the mind, the prompter and surer, on the whole, the memory of *n* will be, the more frequently one will be reminded of it, the more avenues of approach to it one will possess. In mental terms, *the more other facts a fact is associated with in the mind, the better possession of it our memory retains.* Each of its associates becomes a hook to which it hangs, a means to fish it up by when sunk beneath the surface. Together, they form a network of attachments by which it is woven into the entire tissue of our thought. The 'secret of a good memory' is thus the secret of forming diverse and multiple associations with every fact we care to retain. But this forming of associations with a fact, what is it but *thinking about* the fact as much as possible? Briefly, then, of two men with the same outward experiences and the same amount of mere native tenacity, *the one who* THINKS *over his experiences most, and weaves them into systematic relations with each other, will be the one with the best memory.* We see examples of this on every hand. Most men have a good memory for facts connected with their own pursuits. The college athlete who remains a dunce at his books will astonish you by his knowledge of men's 'records' in various feats and games, and will be a walking dictionary of sporting statistics. The reason is that he is constantly going over these things in his mind, and comparing and making series of them. They form for him not so many odd facts, but a concept-system—so they stick. So the merchant remembers prices, the politician other politicians' speeches and votes, with a copiousness which amazes outsiders, but which the amount of thinking they bestow on these subjects easily explains. The great memory for facts which a Darwin and a Spencer reveal in their books is not incompatible with the possession on their part of a brain with only a middling degree of physiological retentiveness. Let a man early in life set himself the task of verifying such a theory as that of evolution, and facts will soon cluster and cling to him like grapes to their stem. Their relations to the theory will hold them fast; and the more of these the mind is able to discern, the greater the erudition will become. Meanwhile the theorist may have little, if any, desultory memory. Unutilizable facts may be unnoted by him and forgotten as soon as heard. An ignorance almost as encyclopædic as his erudition may coexist with the latter, and hide, as it were, in the interstices of its web. Those who have had much to do with scholars and *savants* will readily think of examples of the class of mind I mean.

In a system, every fact is connected with every other by some thought-relation. The consequence is that every fact is retained by the combined suggestive power of all the other facts in the system, and forgetfulness is well-nigh impossible.

The reason why cramming is such a bad mode of study is now made clear. I mean by cramming that way of preparing for examinations by committing 'points' to memory during a few hours or days of intense application immediately preceding the final ordeal, little or no work having been performed during the previous course of the term. Things learned thus in a few hours, on one occasion, for one purpose, cannot possibly have formed many associations with other things in the mind. Their brain-processes are led into by few paths, and are relatively little liable to be awakened again. Speedy oblivion is the almost inevitable fate of all that is committed to memory in this simple way. Whereas, on the contrary, the same materials taken in gradually, day after day, recurring in different contexts, considered in various relations, associated with other external incidents, and repeatedly reflected on, grow into such a system, form such connections with the rest of the mind's fabric, lie open to so many paths of approach, that they remain permanent possessions. This is the *intellectual* reason why habits of continuous application should be enforced in educational establishments. Of course there is no moral turpitude in cramming. Did it lead to the desired end of secure learning, it were infinitely the best method of study. But it does not; and students themselves should understand the reason why.

One's native retentiveness is unchangeable. It will now appear clear that *all improvement of the memory lies in the line of* ELABORATING THE ASSOCIATES of each of the several things to be remembered.

No amount of culture would seem capable of modifying a man's GENERAL *retentiveness.* This is a physiological quality, given once for all with his organization, and which he can never hope to change. It differs no doubt in disease and health; and it is a fact of observation that it is better in fresh and vigorous hours than when we are fagged or ill. We may say, then, that a man's native tenacity will fluctuate somewhat with his hygiene, and that whatever is good for his tone of health will also be good for his memory. We may even say that whatever amount of intellectual exercise is bracing to the general tone and nutrition of the brain will also be profitable to the general retentiveness. But more than this we cannot say; and this, it is obvious, is far less than most people believe.

It is, in fact, commonly thought that certain exercises, systematically repeated, will strengthen, not only a man's remembrance of the particular facts used in the exercises, but his faculty for remembering facts at large. And a plausible case is always made out by saying that practice in learning words by heart makes it easier to learn new words in the same way. If this be true, then what I have just said is false, and the whole doctrine of memory as due to 'paths' must be revised. But I am disposed to think the alleged fact untrue. I have carefully questioned several mature actors on the point, and all have denied that the practice of learning parts has made any such difference as is alleged. What it has done for them is to improve their power of *studying* a part systematically. Their mind is now full of precedents in the way of intonation, emphasis, gesticulation; the new words awaken distinct suggestions and decisions; are caught up, in fact, into a preëxisting network, like the merchant's prices, or the athlete's store of 'records,' and are recollected easier, although the mere native tenacity is not a whit improved, and is usually, in fact, impaired by age. It is a case of better remembering by better *thinking*. Similarly when schoolboys improve by practice in ease of learning by heart, the improvement will, I am sure, be always found to reside in the *mode of study of the particular piece* (due to the greater interest, the greater suggestiveness, the generic similarity with other pieces, the more sustained attention, etc., etc.), and not at all to any enhancement of the brute retentive power.

The error I speak of pervades an otherwise useful and judicious book, *How to Strengthen the Memory*, by Dr. M. L. Holbrook of New York. The author fails to distinguish between the general physiological retentiveness and the retention of particular things, and talks as if both must be benefited by the same means.

"I am now treating," he says, "a case of loss of memory in a person advanced in years, who did not know that his memory had failed most remarkably till I told him of it. He is making vigorous effort to bring it back again, and with partial success. The method pursued is to spend two hours daily, one in the morning and one in the evening, in exercising this faculty. The patient is instructed to give the closest attention to all that he learns, so that it shall be impressed on his mind clearly. He is asked to recall every evening all the facts and experiences of the day, and again the next morning. Every name heard is written down and impressed on his mind clearly, and an effort made to recall it at intervals. Ten names from among public men are ordered to be committed to memory every week. A verse of poetry is to be learned, also a verse from the Bible, daily. He is asked to remember the number of the page in any book where any interesting fact is recorded. These and other methods are slowly resuscitating a failing memory."

I find it very hard to believe that the memory of the poor old gentleman is a bit the better for all this torture except in respect of the particular facts thus wrought into it, and other matters that may have been connected therewithal.

Improving the Memory.—All improvement of memory consists, then, in the improvement of one's *habitual methods of recording facts.* Methods have been divided into the mechanical, the ingenious, and the judicious.

The *mechanical methods* consist in the intensification, prolongation, and *repetition* of the impression to be remembered. The modern method of teaching children to read by blackboard work, in which each word is impressed by the fourfold channel of eye, ear, voice, and hand, is an example of an improved mechanical method of memorizing.

Judicious methods of remembering things are nothing but logical ways of conceiving them and working them into rational systems, classifying them, analyzing them into parts, etc., etc. All the sciences are such methods.

Of *ingenious methods* many have been invented, under the name of technical memories. By means of these systems it is often possible to retain entirely disconnected facts, lists of names, numbers, and so forth, so multitudinous as to be entirely unrememberable in a natural way. The method consists usually in a framework learned mechanically, of which the mind is supposed to remain in secure and permanent possession. Then, whatever is to be remembered is deliberately associated by some fanciful analogy or connection with some part of this framework, and this connection thenceforward helps its recall. The best known and most used of these devices is the figure-alphabet. To remember numbers, e.g., a figure-alphabet is first formed, in which each numerical digit is represented by one or more letters. The number is then translated into such letters as will best make a word, if possible a word suggestive of the object to which the number belongs. The word will then be remembered when the numbers alone might be forgotten.[1] The recent system of Loisette is a method, much less mechanical, of weaving the thing into associations which may aid its recall.

Recognition.—If, however, a phenomenon be met with too often, and with too great a variety of contexts, although its image is retained and reproduced with correspondingly great facility, it fails to come up with any one particular setting, and the projection of it backwards to a particular past date consequently does not come about. We *recognize* but do not *remember* it—its associates form too confused a cloud. A similar result comes about when a definite setting is only nascently aroused. We then feel that we have seen the object already, but when or where we cannot say, though we may seem to ourselves to be on the brink of saying it. That nascent cerebral excitations can thus affect consciousness is obvious from what happens when we seek to remember a name. It tingles, it trembles on the verge, but does not come. Just such a tingling and trembling of unrecovered associates is the penumbra of recognition that may surround any experience and make it seem familiar, though we know not why.

There is a curious experience which everyone seems to have had—the feeling that the present moment in its completeness has been experienced before—we were saying just this thing, in just

---

[1] A common figure-alphabet is this:

1	2	3	4	5	6	7	8	9	0
t	n	m	r	l	sh	g	f	b	s
d					j	k	v	p	c
					ch	c			z
					g	qu			

this place, to just these people, etc. This 'sense of preëxistence' has been treated as a great mystery and occasioned much speculation. Dr. Wigan considered it due to a dissociation of the action of the two hemispheres, one of them becoming conscious a little later than the other, but both of the same fact. I must confess that the quality of mystery seems to me here a little strained. I have over and over again in my own case succeeded in resolving the phenomenon into a case of memory, so indistinct that whilst some past circumstances are presented again, the others are not. The dissimilar portions of the past do not arise completely enough at first for the date to be identified. All we get is the present scene with a general suggestion of pastness about it. That faithful observer, Prof. Lazarus, interprets the phenomenon in the same way; and it is noteworthy that just as soon as the past context grows complete and distinct the emotion of weirdness fades from the experience.

Forgetting.—In the practical use of our intellect, forgetting is as important a function as remembering. 'Total recall' (see p. 229) we saw to be comparatively rare in association. If we remembered everything, we should on most occasions be as ill off as if we remembered nothing. It would take as long for us to recall a space of time as it took the original time to elapse, and we should never get ahead with our thinking. All recollected times undergo, accordingly, what M. Ribot calls foreshortening; and this foreshortening is due to the omission of an enormous number of the facts which filled them. "We thus reach the paradoxical result," says M. Ribot, "that one condition of remembering is that we should forget. Without totally forgetting a prodigious number of states of consciousness, and momentarily forgetting a large number, we could not remember at all. Oblivion, except in certain cases, is thus no malady of memory, but a condition of its health and its life."

Pathological Conditions.—Hypnotic subjects as a rule forget all that has happened in their trance. But in a succeeding trance they will often remember the events of a past one. This is like what happens in those cases of 'double personality' in which no recollection of one of the lives is to be found in the other. The sensibility in these cases often differs from one of the alternate personalities to another, the patient being often anæsthetic in certain respects in one of the secondary states. Now the memory may come and go with the sensibility. M. Pierre Janet proved in various ways that what his patients forgot when anæsthetic they remembered when the sensibility returned. For instance, he restored their tactile sense temporarily by means of electric currents, passes, etc., and then made them handle various objects, such as keys and pencils, or make particular movements, like the sign of the cross. The moment the anæsthesia returned they found it impossible to recollect the objects or the acts. "They had had nothing in their hands, they had done nothing," etc. The next day, however, sensibility being again restored by similar processes, they remembered perfectly the circumstance, and told what they had handled or done.

All these pathological facts are showing us that the sphere of possible recollection may be wider than we think, and that in certain matters apparent oblivion is no proof against possible recall under other conditions. They give no countenance, however, to the extravagant opinion that absolutely no part of our experience can be forgotten.

Chapter XIX

Imagination

What it is.—*Sensations, once experienced, modify the nervous organism, so that copies of them arise again in the mind after the original outward stimulus is gone.* No mental copy, however, can arise in the mind, of any kind of sensation which has never been directly excited from without.

The blind may dream of sights, the deaf of sounds, for years after they have lost their vision or hearing; but the man *born* deaf can never be made to imagine what sound is like, nor can the man *born* blind ever have a mental vision. In Locke's words, already quoted, "the mind can frame unto itself no one new simple idea." The originals of them all must have been given from without. Fantasy, or Imagination, are the names given to the faculty of reproducing copies of originals once felt. The imagination is called 'reproductive' when the copies are literal; 'productive' when elements from different originals are recombined so as to make new wholes.

When represented with surroundings concrete enough to constitute a *date*, these pictures, when they revive, form *recollections*. We have just studied the machinery of recollection. When the mental pictures are of data freely combined, and reproducing no past combination exactly, we have acts of imagination properly so called.

Men differ in visual imagination. Our ideas or images of past sensible experiences may be either distinct and adequate or dim, blurred, and incomplete. It is likely that the different degrees in which different men are able to make them sharp and complete has had something to do with keeping up such philosophic disputes as that of Berkeley with Locke over abstract ideas. Locke had spoken of our possessing 'the general idea of a triangle' which "must be neither oblique, nor rectangle, neither equilateral, equicrural, nor scalenon; but all and none of these at once." Berkeley says: "If any man has the faculty of framing in his mind such an idea of a triangle as is here described, it is in vain to pretend to dispute him out of it, nor would I go about it. All I desire is that the reader would fully and certainly inform himself whether *he* has such an idea or no."

Until very recent years it was supposed by philosophers that there was a typical human mind which all individual minds were like, and that propositions of universal validity could be laid down about such faculties as 'the Imagination.' Lately, however, a mass of revelations have poured in which make us see how false a view this is. There are imaginations, not 'the Imagination,' and they must be studied in detail.

Mr. Galton in 1880 began a statistical inquiry which may be said to have made an era in descriptive psychology. He addressed a circular to large numbers of persons asking them to describe the image in their mind's eye of their breakfast-table on a given morning. The variations were found to be enormous; and, strange to say, it appeared that eminent scientific men on the average had less visualizing power than younger and more insignificant persons.

The reader will find details in Mr. Galton's *Inquiries into Human Faculty*, pp. 83–114. I have myself for many years collected from each and all of my psychology-students descriptions of their own visual imagination; and found (together with some curious idiosyncrasies) corroboration of all the variations which Mr. Galton reports. As examples, I subjoin extracts from two cases near the ends of the scale. The writers are first cousins, grandsons of a distinguished man of science. The one who is a good visualizer says:

"This morning's breakfast-table is both dim and bright; it is dim if I try to think of it when my eyes are open upon any object; it is perfectly clear and bright if I think of it with my eyes closed.—All the objects are clear at once, yet when I confine my attention to any one object it becomes far more distinct.—I have more power to recall color than any other one thing: if, for example, I were to recall a plate decorated with flowers I could reproduce in a drawing the exact tone, etc. The color of anything that was on the table is perfectly vivid.—There is very little limitation to the extent of my images: I can see all four sides of a room, I can see all four sides of two, three, four, even more rooms with such distinctness that if you should ask me what was in any particular place in any one, or ask me to count the chairs, etc., I could do it without the least hesitation.—The more I learn by heart the more clearly do I see images of my pages. Even before I can recite the lines I see them so that I could give them very slowly word for word, but my mind is so occupied in looking at my printed image that I have no idea of what I am saying, of the sense of it, etc. When I first found myself doing this I used to think it was merely because I knew the lines imperfectly; but I have quite convinced myself that I really do see an image. The strongest proof that such is really the fact is, I think, the following:

"I can look down the mentally seen page and see the words that *commence* all the lines, and from any one of these words I can continue the line. I find this much easier to do if the words begin in a straight line than if there are breaks. Example:

> *Étant fait* . . . . .
> *Tous* . . . . .
> *A des* . . . . .
> *Que fit* . . . . .
> *Céres* . . . . .
>   *Avec* . . . . .
> *Un fleuve* . . . . .
>   *Comme* . . . . .
> (La Fontaine 8, iv.)"

The poor visualizer says:

"My ability to form mental images seems, from what I have studied of other people's images, to be defective and somewhat peculiar. The process by which I seem to remember any particular event is not by a series of distinct images, but a sort of panorama, the faintest impressions of which are perceptible through a thick fog.—I cannot shut my eyes and get a distinct image of anyone, although I used to be able to a few years ago, and the faculty seems to have gradually slipped away.—In my most vivid dreams, where the events appear like the most real facts, I am often troubled with a dimness of sight which causes the images to appear indistinct.—To come to the question of the breakfast-table, there is nothing definite about it. Everything is vague. I cannot say *what* I see. I could not possibly count the chairs, but I happen to know that there are ten. I see nothing in detail.—The chief thing is a general impression that I cannot tell exactly what I do see. The coloring is about the same, as far as I can recall it, only very much washed out. Perhaps the only color I can see at all distinctly is that of the table-cloth, and I could probably see the color of the wall-paper if I could remember what color it was."

A person whose visual imagination is strong finds it hard to understand how those who are without the faculty can think at all. *Some people undoubtedly have no visual images at all worthy of the name,* and instead of *seeing* their breakfast-table, they tell you that they *remember* it or *know* what was on it. The 'mind-stuff' of which this 'knowing' is made seems to be verbal images exclusively. But if the words 'coffee,' 'bacon,' 'muffins,' and 'eggs' lead a man to speak to his cook, to pay his bills, and to take measures for the morrow's meal exactly as visual and gustatory memories would, why are they not, for all practical intents and purposes, as good a kind of material in which to think? In fact, we may suspect them to be for most purposes better than terms with a richer imaginative coloring. The scheme of relationship and the conclusion being the essential things in thinking, that kind of mind-stuff which is handiest will be the best for the purpose. Now words, uttered or unexpressed, are the handiest mental elements we have. Not only are they very *rapidly* revivable, but they are revivable as actual sensations more easily than any other items of our experience. Did they not possess some such advantage as this, it would hardly be the case that the older men are and the more effective as thinkers, the more, as a rule, they have lost their visualizing power, as Mr. Galton found to be the case with members of the Royal Society.

Images of Sounds.—These also differ in individuals. Those who think by preference in auditory images are called *audiles* by Mr. Galton. *This type*, says M. Binet, *"appears to be rarer than the visual.* Persons of this type imagine what they think of in the language of sound. In order to remember a lesson they impress upon their mind, not the look of the page, but the sound of the words.

They reason, as well as remember, by ear. In performing a mental addition they repeat verbally the names of the figures, and add, as it were, the sounds, without any thought of the graphic signs. Imagination also takes the auditory form. 'When I write a scene,' said Legouvé to Scribe, 'I *hear*; but you *see*. In each phrase which I write, the voice of the personage who speaks strikes my ear. *Vous, qui êtes le théâtre même*, your actors walk, gesticulate before your eyes; I am a *listener*, you a *spectator*.'—'Nothing more true,' said Scribe; 'do you know where I am when I write a piece? In the middle of the parterre.' It is clear that the *pure audile*, seeking to develop only a single one of his faculties, may, like the pure visualizer, perform astounding feats of memory—Mozart, for example, noting from memory the *Miserere* of the Sistine Chapel after two hearings; the deaf Beethoven, composing and inwardly repeating his enormous symphonies. On the other hand, the man of auditory type, like the visual, is exposed to serious dangers; for if he lose his auditory images, he is without resource and breaks down completely."

Images of Muscular Sensations.—Professor Stricker of Vienna, who seems to be a 'motile' or to have this form of imagination developed in unusual strength, has given a careful analysis of his own case. His recollections both of his own movements and of those of other things are accompanied invariably by distinct muscular feelings in those parts of his body which would naturally be used in effecting or in following the movement. In thinking of a soldier marching, for example, it is as if he were helping the image to march by marching himself in his rear. And if he suppresses this sympathetic feeling in his own legs and concentrates all his attention on the imagined soldier, the latter becomes, as it were, paralyzed. In general his imagined movements, of whatsoever objects, seem paralyzed, the moment no feelings of movement either in his own eyes or in his own limbs accompany them. The movements of articulate speech play a predominant part in his mental life. "When after my experimental work," he says, "I proceed to its description, as a rule I reproduce in the first instance only words which I had already associated with the perception of the various details of the observation whilst the latter was going on. For speech plays in all my observing so important a part that I ordinarily clothe phenomena in words as fast as I observe them."

Most persons, on being asked *in what sort of terms they imagine words*, will say, 'In terms of hearing.' It is not until their attention is expressly drawn to the point that they find it difficult to say whether auditory images or motor images connec‍ted with the organs of articulation predominate. A good way of bringing the difficulty to consciousness is that proposed by Stricker: Partly open your mouth and then imagine any word with labials or dentals in it, such as 'bubble,' 'toddle.' Is your image under these conditions distinct? To most people the image is at first 'thick,' as the sound of the word would be if they tried to pronounce it with the lips parted. Many can never imagine the words clearly with the mouth open; others succeed after a few preliminary trials. The experiment proves how dependent our verbal imagination is on actual feelings in lips, tongue, throat, larynx, etc. Prof. Bain says that "a *suppressed articulation is in fact the material of our recollection*, the intellectual manifestation, the *idea* of speech." In persons whose auditory imagination is weak, the articulatory image does indeed seem to constitute the whole material for verbal thought. Professor Stricker says that in his own case no auditory image enters into the words of which he thinks.

Images of Touch.—These are very strong in some people. The most vivid touch-images come when we ourselves barely escape local injury, or when we see another injured. The place may then actually tingle with the imaginary sensation—perhaps not altogether imaginary, since goose-flesh, paling or reddening, and other evidences of actual muscular contraction in the spot, may result.

"An educated man," says Herr G. H. Meyer, "told me once that on entering his house one day he received a shock from crushing the finger of one of his little children in the door. At the moment of his fright he felt a violent pain in the corresponding finger of his own body, and this pain abode with him three days."

The imagination of a blind deaf-mute like Laura Bridgman must be confined entirely to tactile and motor material. *All blind persons must belong to the 'tactile' and 'motile' types* of the French authors. When the young man whose cataracts were removed by Dr. Franz was shown different geometric figures, he said he "had not been able to form from them the idea of a square and a disc, until he perceived a sensation of what he saw in the points of his fingers, as if he really touched the objects."

Pathological Differences.—The study of Aphasia (see p. 108) has of late years shown how unexpectedly individuals differ in the use of their imagination. In some the habitual 'thought-stuff,' if one may so call it, is visual; in others it is auditory, articulatory, or motor; in most, perhaps, it is evenly mixed. These are the "indifferents" of Charcot. The same local cerebral injury must needs work different practical results in persons who differ in this way. In one what is thrown out of gear is a much-used brain-tract; in the other an unimportant region is affected. A particularly instructive case was published by Charcot in 1883. The patient was a merchant, an exceedingly accomplished man, but a visualizer of the most exclusive type. Owing to some intra-cerebral accident he suddenly lost all his visual images, and with them much of his intellectual power, without any other perversion of faculty. He soon discovered that he could carry on his affairs by using his memory in an altogether new way, and described clearly the difference between his two conditions. "Every time he returns to A., from which place business often calls him, he seems to himself as if entering a strange city. He views the monuments, houses, and streets with the same surprise as if he saw them for the first time. When asked to describe the principal public place of the town, he answered, 'I know that it is there, but it is impossible to imagine it, and I can tell you nothing about it.'

"He can no more remember his wife's and children's faces than he can remember A. Even after being with them some time they seem unusual to him. He forgets his own face, and once spoke to his image in a mirror, taking it for a stranger. He complains of his loss of feeling for colors. 'My wife has black hair, this I know; but I can no more recall its color than I can her person and features.' This visual amnesia extends to objects dating from his childhood's years—paternal mansion, etc., forgotten. No other disturbances but this loss of visual images. Now when he seeks something in his correspondence, he must rummage among the letters like other men, until he meets the passage. He can recall only the first few verses of the *Iliad*, and must *grope* to recite Homer, Virgil, and Horace. Figures which he adds he must now whisper to himself. He realizes clearly that he must help his memory out with auditory images, which he does with effort. *The words and expressions which he recalls seem now to echo in his ear, an altogether novel sensation for him.* If he wishes to learn by heart anything, a series of phrases for example, he must *read them several times aloud*, so as to impress his ear. When later he repeats the thing in question, the sensation of inward hearing which precedes articulation rises up in his mind. This feeling was formerly unknown to him."

Such a man would have suffered relatively little inconvenience if his images for hearing had been those suddenly destroyed.

The Neural Process in Imagination.—Most medical writers assume that the cerebral activity on which imagination depends occupies a different *seat* from that subserving sensation. It is, however, a simpler interpretation of the facts to suppose that *the same nerve-tracts are concerned in the two processes.* Our mental images are aroused always by way of association; some previous idea or sensation must have 'suggested' them. Association is surely due to currents from one cortical centre to another. Now all we need suppose is that these intra-cortical currents are unable to produce in the cells the strong explosions which currents from the sense-organs occasion, to account for the subjective difference between images and sensations, without supposing any difference in their local seat. To the strong degree of explosion corresponds the character of 'vividness' or sensible presence, in the object of thought; to the weak degree, that of 'faintness' or outward unreality.

If we admit that sensation and imagination are due to the activity of the same parts of the cortex, we can see a very good teleological reason why they should correspond to discrete kinds of process in these centres, and why the process which gives the sense that the object is really there ought normally to be arousable only by currents entering from the periphery and not by currents from the neighboring cortical parts. We can see, in short, why *the sensational process* OUGHT TO *be discontinuous with all normal ideational processes, however intense.* For, as Dr. Münsterberg justly observes, "Were there not this peculiar arrangement we should not distinguish reality and fantasy, our conduct would not be accommodated to the facts about us, but would be inappropriate and senseless, and we could not keep ourselves alive."

Sometimes, by exception, the deeper sort of explosion may take place from intra-cortical excitement alone. In the sense of hearing, sensation and imagination *are* hard to discriminate where the sensation is so weak as to be just perceptible. At night, hearing a very faint striking of the hour by a far-off clock, our imagination reproduces both rhythm and sound, and it is often difficult to tell which was the last real stroke. So of a baby crying in a distant part of the house, we are uncertain whether we still hear it, or only imagine the sound. Certain violin-players take advantage of this in diminuendo terminations. After the pianissimo has been reached they continue to bow as if still playing, but are careful not to touch the strings. The listener hears in imagination a degree of sound fainter than the pianissimo. *Hallucinations*, whether of sight or hearing, are another case in point, to be touched on in the next chapter. I may mention as a fact still unexplained that several observers (Herr G. H. Meyer, M. Charles Féré, Professor Scott of Ann Arbor, and Mr. T. C. Smith, one of my students) have noticed negative after-images of objects which they had been imagining with the mind's eye. It is as if the retina itself were locally fatigued by the act.

Chapter XX

Perception

Perception and Sensation compared.—A pure sensation we saw above, p. 17, to be an abstraction never realized in adult life. Anything which affects our sense-organs does also more than that: it arouses processes in the hemispheres which are partly due to the organization of that organ by past experiences, and the results of which in consciousness are described as ideas which the sensation suggests. The first of these ideas is that of the *thing* to which the sensible quality belongs. *The consciousness of particular material things present to sense* is nowadays called *perception*. The consciousness of such things may be more or less complete; it may be of the mere name of the thing and its other essential attributes, or it may be of the thing's various remoter relations. It is impossible to draw any sharp line of distinction between the barer and the richer consciousness, because the moment we get beyond the first crude sensation all our consciousness is of what is *suggested*, and the various suggestions shade gradually into each other, being one and all products of the same psychological machinery of association. In the directer consciousness fewer, in the remoter more, associative processes are brought into play.

Sensational and reproductive brain-processes combined, then, are what give us the content of our perceptions. Every concrete particular material thing is a conflux of sensible qualities, with which we have become acquainted at various times. Some of these qualities, since they are more constant, interesting, or practically important, we regard as essential constituents of the thing. In a general way, such are the tangible shape, size, mass, etc. Other properties,

273

being more fluctuating, we regard as more or less accidental or inessential. We call the former qualities the reality, the latter its appearances. Thus, I hear a sound, and say 'a horse-car'; but the sound is not the horse-car, it is one of the horse-car's least important manifestations. The real horse-car is a feelable, or at most a feelable and visible, thing which in my imagination the sound calls up. So when I get, as now, a brown eye-picture with lines not parallel, and with angles unlike, and call it my big solid rectangular walnut library-table, that picture is not the table. It is not even like the table as the table is for vision, when rightly seen. It is a distorted perspective view of three of the sides of what I mentally *perceive* (more or less) in its totality and undistorted shape. The back of the table, its square corners, its size, its heaviness, are features of which I am conscious when I look, almost as I am conscious of its name. The suggestion of the name is of course due to mere custom. But no less is that of the back, the size, weight, squareness, etc.

Nature, as Reid says, is frugal in her operations, and will not be at the expense of a particular instinct to give us that knowledge which experience and habit will soon produce. Reproduced attributes tied together with presently felt attributes in the unity of a *thing* with a name, these are the materials out of which my actually perceived table is made. Infants must go through a long education of the eye and ear before they can perceive the realities which adults perceive. *Every perception is an acquired perception.*

The Perceptive State of Mind is not a Compound.—There is no reason, however, for supposing that this involves a 'fusion' of separate sensations and ideas. The thing perceived is the object of a unique state of thought; due no doubt in part to sensational, and in part to ideational currents, but in no wise 'containing' psychically the identical 'sensations' and images which these currents would severally have aroused if the others were not simultaneously there. We can often directly notice a sensible difference in the consciousness, between the latter case and the former. The sensible quality changes under our very eye. Take the already-quoted catch, *Pas de lieu Rhône que nous*: one may read this over and over again without recognizing the sounds to be identical with those of the words *paddle your own canoe*. As the English associations arise, the sound itself appears to change. Verbal sounds are usually perceived with their meaning at the moment of being

heard. Sometimes, however, the associative irradiations are inhibited for a few moments (the mind being preoccupied with other
thoughts) whilst the words linger on the ear as mere echoes of
acoustic sensation. Then, usually, their interpretation suddenly
occurs. But at that moment one may often surprise a change in
the very *feel* of the word. Our own language would sound very different to us if we heard it without understanding, as we hear a foreign tongue. Rises and falls of voice, odd sibilants and other con-
sonants, would fall on our ear in a way of which we can now form
no notion. Frenchmen say that English sounds to them like the
gazouillement des oiseaux—an impression which it certainly makes
on no native ear. Many of us English would describe the sound of
Russian in similar terms. All of us are conscious of the strong in-
flections of voice and explosives and gutturals of German speech
in a way in which no German can be conscious of them.

This is probably the reason why, if we look at an isolated
printed word and repeat it long enough, it ends by assuming an
entirely unnatural aspect. Let the reader try this with any word
on this page. He will soon begin to wonder if it can possibly be the
word he has been using all his life with that meaning. It stares at
him from the paper like a glass eye, with no speculation in it. Its
body is indeed there, but its soul is fled. It is reduced, by this new
way of attending to it, to its sensational nudity. We never before
attended to it in this way, but habitually got it clad with its
meaning the moment we caught sight of it, and rapidly passed
from it to the other words of the phrase. We apprehended it, in
short, with a cloud of associates, and thus perceiving it, we felt it
quite otherwise than as we feel it now divested and alone.

Another well-known change is when we look at a landscape
with our head upside-down. Perception is to a certain extent baf-
fled by this manœuvre; gradations of distance and other space-de-
terminations are made uncertain; the reproductive or associative
processes, in short, decline; and, simultaneously with their diminution, the colors grow richer and more varied, and the contrasts
of light and shade more marked. The same thing occurs when we
turn a painting bottom-upward. We lose much of its meaning,
but, to compensate for the loss, we feel more freshly the value of
the mere tints and shadings, and become aware of any lack of
purely sensible harmony or balance which they may show. Just
so, if we lie on the floor and look up at the mouth of a person

talking behind us. His lower lip here takes the habitual place of the upper one upon our retina, and seems animated by the most extraordinary and unnatural mobility, a mobility which now strikes us because (the associative processes being disturbed by the unaccustomed point of view) we get it as a naked sensation and not as part of a familiar object perceived.

Once more, then, we find ourselves driven to admit that when qualities of an object impress our sense and we thereupon perceive the object, the pure sensation as such of those qualities does not still exist inside of the perception and form a constituent thereof. The pure sensation is one thing and the perception another, and neither can take place at the same time with the other, because their cerebral conditions are not the same. They may *resemble* each other, but in no respect are they identical states of mind.

Perception is of Definite and Probable Things.—The chief cerebral conditions of perception are old paths of association radiating from the sense-impression. If a certain impression be strongly associated with the attributes of a certain thing, that thing is almost sure to be perceived when we get the impression. Examples of such things would be familiar people, places, etc., which we recognize and name at a glance. But *where the impression is associated with more than one reality*, so that either of two discrepant sets of residual properties may arise, the perception is doubtful and vacillating, and *the most that can then be said of it is that it will be of a* PROBABLE *thing*, of the thing which would most usually have given us that sensation.

In these ambiguous cases it is interesting to note that perception is rarely abortive; *some* perception takes place. The two discrepant sets of associates do not neutralize each other or mix and make a blur. What we more commonly get is first one object in its completeness, and then the other in its completeness. In other words, *all brain-processes are such as give rise to what we may call* FIGURED *consciousness*. If paths are shot-through at all, they are shot-through in consistent systems, and occasion thoughts of definite objects, not mere hodge-podges of elements. Even where the brain's functions are half thrown out of gear, as in aphasia or dropping asleep, this law of figured consciousness holds good. A person who suddenly gets sleepy whilst reading aloud will read wrong; but instead of emitting a mere broth of syllables, he will make such mistakes as to read 'supper-time' instead of 'sovereign,' 'overthrow' instead of 'opposite,' or indeed utter entirely imaginary phrases, composed of several definite words, instead of phrases of the book. So in aphasia: where the disease is mild the patient's mistakes consist in using entire wrong words instead of right ones. It is only in the gravest lesions that he becomes quite inarticulate. These facts show how subtle is the associative link; how delicate yet how strong that connection among brain-paths which makes any number of them, once excited together, thereafter tend to vibrate as a systematic whole. A small group of elements, '*this*,' common to two systems, *A* and *B*, may touch off *A* or *B* according as accident decides the next step (see Fig. 63). If it

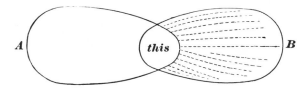

FIG. 63.

happen that a single point leading from '*this*' to *B* is momentarily a little more pervious than any leading from '*this*' to *A*, then that little advantage will upset the equilibrium in favor of the entire system *B*. The currents will sweep first through that point and thence into all the paths of *B*, each increment of advance making *A* more and more impossible. The thoughts correlated with *A* and *B*, in such a case, will have objects different, though similar. The similarity will, however, consist in some very limited feature if the '*this*' be small. *Thus the faintest sensations will give rise to the perception of definite things if only they resemble sensations which the things are wont to arouse.*

Illusions.—Let us now, for brevity's sake, treat *A* and *B* in Fig. 63 as if they stood for objects instead of brain-processes. And let us furthermore suppose that *A* and *B* are, both of them, objects which might probably excite the sensation which I have called '*this*,' but that on the present occasion *A* and not *B* is the one which actually does so. If, then, on this occasion '*this*' suggests *A* and not *B*, the result is a *correct perception*. But if, on the contrary, '*this*' suggests *B* and not *A*, the result is a *false perception*, or, as it is technically called, an *illusion*. But the *process* is the same, whether the perception be true or false.

Note that in every illusion what is false is what is inferred, not what is immediately given. The 'this,' if it were felt by itself alone, would be all right; it only becomes misleading by what it suggests. If it is a sensation of sight, it may suggest a tactile object, for example, which later tactile experiences prove to be not there. *The so-called 'fallacy of the senses,' of which the ancient sceptics made so much account, is not fallacy of the senses proper, but rather of the intellect, which interprets wrongly what the senses give.*[1]

So much premised, let us look a little closer at these illusions. They are due to two main causes. *The wrong object is perceived either because*

1) *Although not on this occasion the real cause, it is yet the habitual, inveterate, or most probable cause of 'this'*; or because

2) *The mind is temporarily full of the thought of that object, and therefore 'this' is peculiarly prone to suggest it at this moment.*

I will give briefly a number of examples under each head. The first head is the more important, because it includes a number of constant illusions to which all men are subject, and which can only be dispelled by much experience.

Illusions of the First Type.—One of the oldest instances dates from Aristotle. Cross two fingers and roll a pea, penholder, or other small object between them. It will seem double. Professor Croom Robertson has given the clearest analysis of this illusion. He observes that if the object be brought into contact first with the forefinger and next with the second finger, the two contacts seem to come in at different points of space. The forefinger-touch seems higher, though the finger is really lower; the second-finger-touch seems lower, though the finger is really higher. "We perceive the contacts as double because we refer them to two distinct parts of space." The touched sides of the two fingers are normally not together in space, and customarily never do touch one thing; the one thing which now touches them, therefore, seems in two places, i.e., seems two things.

There is a whole batch of illusions which come from optical

[1] In *Mind*, IX, 206, M. Binet points out the fact that what is fallaciously inferred is always an object of some other sense than the 'this.' 'Optical illusions' are generally errors of touch and muscular sensibility, and the fallaciously perceived object and the experiences which correct it are both tactile in these cases.

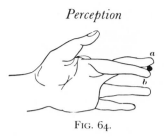

FIG. 64.

sensations interpreted by us in accordance with our usual rule, although they are now produced by an unusual object. The *stereoscope* is an example. The eyes see a picture apiece, and the two pictures are a little disparate, the one seen by the right eye being a view of the object taken from a point slightly to the right of that from which the left eye's picture is taken. Pictures thrown on the two eyes by solid objects present this sort of disparity, so that we react on the sensation in our usual way, and perceive a solid. If the pictures be exchanged we perceive a hollow mould of the object, for a hollow mould would cast just such disparate pictures as these. Wheatstone's instrument, the *pseudoscope*, allows us to look at solid objects and see with each eye the other eye's picture. We then perceive the solid object hollow, *if it be an object which might probably be hollow*, but not otherwise. Thus the perceptive process is true to its law, which is *always to react on the sensation in a determinate and figured fashion if possible, and in as probable a fashion as the case admits.* A human face, e.g., never appears hollow to the pseudoscope, for to couple faces and hollowness violates all our habits. For the same reason it is very easy to make an intaglio cast of a face, or the painted inside of a pasteboard mask, look convex, instead of concave as they are.

Curious illusions of movement in objects occur whenever the eyeballs move without our intending it. We have learned in an earlier chapter (p. 71) that the original visual feeling of movement is produced by any image passing over the retina. Originally, however, this sensation is definitely referred neither to the object nor to the eyes. Such definite reference grows up later, and obeys certain simple laws. For one thing, we believe *objects* to move whenever we get the retinal movement-feeling, but think our *eyes* are still. This gives rise to an illusion when, after whirling on our heel, we stand still; for then objects appear to continue whirling in the same direction in which, a moment previous, our body actually whirled. The reason is that our *eyes* are animated, under

279

these conditions, by an involuntary *nystagmus* or oscillation in their orbits, which may easily be observed in anyone with vertigo after whirling. As these movements are unconscious, the retinal movement-feelings which they occasion are naturally referred to the objects seen. The whole phenomenon fades out after a few seconds. And it ceases if we voluntarily fix our eyes upon a given point.

There is an illusion of movement of the opposite sort, with which everyone is familiar at *railway stations*. Habitually, when we ourselves move forwards, our entire field of view glides backwards over our retina. When our movement is due to that of the windowed carriage, car, or boat in which we sit, all stationary objects visible through the window give us a sensation of gliding in the opposite direction. Hence, whenever we get this sensation, of a window with *all* objects visible through it moving in one direction, we react upon it in our customary way, and perceive a stationary field of view, over which the window, and we ourselves inside of it, are passing by a motion of our own. Consequently when another train comes alongside of ours in a station, and fills the entire window, and, after standing still awhile, begins to glide away, we judge that it is *our* train which is moving, and that the other train is still. If, however, we catch a glimpse of any part of the station through the windows, or between the cars, of the other train, the illusion of our own movement instantly disappears, and we perceive the other train to be the one in motion. This, again, is but making the usual and probable inference from our sensation.

Another illusion due to movement is explained by Helmholtz. Most wayside objects, houses, trees, etc., look small when seen from the windows of a swift train. This is because we perceive them in the first instance unduly near. And we perceive them unduly near because of their extraordinarily rapid parallactic flight backwards. When we ourselves move forwards all objects glide backwards, as aforesaid; but the nearer they are, the more rapid is this apparent translocation. Relative rapidity of passage backwards is thus so familiarly associated with nearness that when we feel it we perceive nearness. But with a given size of retinal image the nearer an object is, the smaller do we judge its actual size to be. Hence in the train, the faster we go, the nearer do the trees and houses seem; and the nearer they seem, the smaller (with that size of retinal image) must they look.

The feelings of our eyes' convergence, of their accommodation, the size of the retinal image, etc., may give rise to illusions about the size and distance of objects, which also belong to this first type.

Illusions of the Second Type.—In this type we perceive a wrong object because our mind is full of the thought of it at the time, and any sensation which is in the least degree connected with it touches off, as it were, a train already laid, and gives us a sense that the object is really before us. Here is a familiar example:

"If a sportsman while shooting woodcock in cover sees a bird about the size and colour of a woodcock get up and fly through the foliage, not having time to see more than that it is a bird of such a size and colour, he immediately supplies by inference the other qualities of a woodcock, and is afterwards disgusted to find that he has shot a thrush. I have done so myself, and could hardly believe that the thrush was the bird I had fired at, so complete was my mental supplement to my visual perception."[2]

As with game, so with enemies, ghosts, and the like. Anyone waiting in a dark place and expecting or fearing strongly a certain object will interpret any abrupt sensation to mean that object's presence. The boy playing 'I spy,' the criminal skulking from his pursuers, the superstitious person hurrying through the woods or past the churchyard at midnight, the man lost in the woods, the girl who tremulously has made an evening appointment with her swain, all are subject to illusions of sight and sound which make their hearts beat till they are dispelled. Twenty times a day the lover, perambulating the streets with his preoccupied fancy, will think he perceives his idol's bonnet before him.

The Proof-reader's Illusion.—I remember one night in Boston, whilst waiting for a 'Mount Auburn' car to bring me to Cambridge, reading most distinctly that name upon the signboard of a car on which (as I afterwards learned) 'North Avenue' was painted. The illusion was so vivid that I could hardly believe my eyes had deceived me. All reading is more or less performed in this way.

"Practised novel- or newspaper-readers could not possibly get on so fast if they had to see accurately every single letter of every

---

[2] Romanes: *Mental Evolution in Animals*, p. 324.

word in order to perceive the words. More than half of the words come out of their mind, and hardly half from the printed page. Were this not so, did we perceive each letter by itself, typographic errors in well-known words would never be overlooked. Children, whose ideas are not yet ready enough to perceive words at a glance, read them wrong if they are printed wrong, that is, right according to the way of printing. In a foreign language, although it may be printed with the same letters, we read by so much the more slowly as we do not understand, or are unable promptly to perceive, the words. But we notice misprints all the more readily. For this reason Latin and Greek, and still better Hebrew, works are more correctly printed, because the proofs are better corrected, than in German works. Of two friends of mine, one knew much Hebrew, the other little; the latter, however, gave instruction in Hebrew in a gymnasium; and when he called the other to help correct his pupils' exercises, it turned out that he could find out all sorts of little errors better than his friend, because the latter's perception of the words as totals was too swift."[3]

Testimony to personal identity is proverbially fallacious for similar reasons. A man has witnessed a rapid crime or accident, and carries away his mental image. Later he is confronted by a prisoner whom he forthwith perceives in the light of that image, and recognizes or 'identifies' as the criminal, although he may never have been near the spot. Similarly at the so-called 'materializing séances' which fraudulent mediums give: in a dark room a man sees a gauze-robed figure who in a whisper tells him she is the spirit of his sister, mother, wife, or child, and falls upon his neck. The darkness, the previous forms, and the expectancy have so filled his mind with premonitory images that it is no wonder he perceives what is suggested. These fraudulent 'séances' would furnish most precious documents to the psychology of perception, if they could only be satisfactorily inquired into. In the hypnotic trance any suggested object is sensibly perceived. In certain subjects this happens more or less completely after waking from the trance. It would seem that under favorable conditions a some-

---

[3] M. Lazarus: *Das Leben der Seele* (1857), II, p. 32. In the ordinary hearing of speech half the words we seem to hear are supplied out of our own head. A language with which we are familiar is understood even when spoken in low tones and far off. An unfamiliar language is unintelligible under these conditions. The 'ideas' for interpreting the sounds by not being ready-made in our minds, as they are in our familiar mother-tongue, do not start up at so faint a cue.

what similar susceptibility to suggestion may exist in certain persons who are not otherwise entranced at all.

This suggestibility obtains in all the senses, although high authorities have doubted this power of imagination to falsify present impressions of sense. Everyone must be able to give instances from the smell-sense. When we have paid the faithless plumber for pretending to mend our drains, the intellect inhibits the nose from perceiving the same unaltered odor, until perhaps several days go by. As regards the ventilation or heating of rooms, we are apt to feel for some time as we think we ought to feel. If we believe the ventilator is shut, we feel the room close. On discovering it open, the oppression disappears.

It is the same with touch. Everyone must have felt the sensible quality change under his hand, as sudden contact with something moist or hairy, in the dark, awoke a shock of disgust or fear which faded into calm recognition of some familiar object. Even so small a thing as a crumb of potato on the table-cloth, which we pick up, thinking it a crumb of bread, feels horrible for a few moments to our fancy, and different from what it is.

In the sense of hearing, similar mistakes abound. Everyone must recall some experience in which sounds have altered their character as soon as the intellect referred them to a different source. The other day a friend was sitting in my room, when the clock, which has a rich low chime, began to strike. "Hollo!" said he, "hear that hand-organ in the garden," and was surprised at finding the real source of the sound. I have had myself a striking illusion of the sort. Sitting reading, late one night, I suddenly heard a most formidable noise proceeding from the upper part of the house, which it seemed to fill. It ceased, and in a moment renewed itself. I went into the hall to listen, but it came no more. Resuming my seat in the room, however, there it was again, low, mighty, alarming, like a rising flood or the *avant-courier* of an awful gale. It came from all space. Quite startled, I again went into the hall, but it had already ceased once more. On returning a second time to the room, I discovered that it was nothing but the breathing of a little Scotch terrier which lay asleep on the floor. The noteworthy thing is that as soon as I recognized what it was, I was compelled to think it a different sound, and could not then hear it as I had heard it a moment before.

The sense of sight is pregnant with illusions of both the types considered. No sense gives such fluctuating impressions of the same object as sight does. With no sense are we so apt to treat the sensations immediately given as mere signs; with none is the invocation from memory of a *thing*, and the consequent perception of the latter, so immediate. The 'thing' which we perceive always resembles, as we shall hereafter see, the object of some absent sensation, usually another optical figure which in our mind has come to be a standard bit of reality; and it is this incessant reduction of our immediately given optical objects to more standard and 'real' forms which has led some authors into the mistake of thinking that our optical sensations are originally and natively of no particular form at all.

Of accidental and occasional illusions of sight many amusing examples might be given. One will suffice. It is a reminiscence of my own. I was lying in my berth in a steamer listening to the sailors 'at their devotions with the holystones' outside; when, on turning my eyes to the window, I perceived with perfect distinctness that the chief-engineer of the vessel had entered my state-room, and was standing looking through the window at the men at work upon the guards. Surprised at his intrusion, and also at his intentness and immobility, I remained watching him and wondering how long he would stand thus. At last I spoke; but getting no reply, sat up in my berth, and then saw that what I had taken for the engineer was my own cap and coat hanging on a peg beside the window. The illusion was complete; the engineer was a peculiar-looking man; and I saw him unmistakably; but after the illusion had vanished I found it hard voluntarily to make the cap and coat look like him at all.

'Apperception.'—In Germany since Herbart's time psychology has always had a great deal to say about a process called *Apperception*. The incoming ideas or sensations are said to be 'apperceived' by 'masses' of ideas already in the mind. It is plain that the process we have been describing as perception is, at this rate, an apperceptive process. So are all recognition, classing, and naming; and passing beyond these simplest suggestions, all farther thoughts about our percepts are apperceptive processes as well. I have myself not used the word apperception, because it has carried very different meanings in the history of philosophy, and 'psychic reaction,' 'interpretation,' 'conception,' 'assimilation,' 'elaboration,' or simply 'thought,' are perfect synonyms for its Herbartian meaning, widely taken. It is, moreover, hardly worth

while to pretend to analyze the so-called apperceptive performances beyond the first or perceptive stage, because their variations
and degrees are literally innumerable. 'Apperception' is a name
for the sum-total of the effects of what we have studied as association; and it is obvious that the things which a given experience
will suggest to a man depend on what Mr. Lewes calls his entire
psychostatical conditions, his nature and stock of ideas, or, in
other words, his character, habits, memory, education, previous
experience, and momentary mood. We gain no insight into
what really occurs either in the mind or in the brain by calling
all these things the 'apperceiving mass,' though of course this
may upon occasion be convenient. On the whole I am inclined
to think Mr. Lewes's term of 'assimilation' the most fruitful one
yet used.

The 'apperceiving mass' is treated by the Germans as the active
factor, the apperceived sensation as the passive one; the sensation
being usually modified by the ideas in the mind. Out of the inter-
action of the two, cognition is produced. But as Steinthal remarks,
the apperceiving mass is itself often modified by the sensation. To
quote him: "Although the *a priori* moment commonly shows itself
to be the more powerful, apperception-processes can perfectly
well occur in which the new observation transforms or enriches
the apperceiving group of ideas. A child who hitherto has seen
none but four-cornered tables apperceives a round one as a table;
but by this the apperceiving mass ('table') is enriched. To his previous knowledge of tables comes this new feature that they need
not be four-cornered, but may be round. In the history of science
it has happened often enough that some discovery, at the same
time that it was apperceived, i.e., brought into connection with
the system of our knowledge, transformed the whole system. In
principle, however, we must maintain that, although either factor
is both active and passive, the *a priori* factor is almost always the
more active of the two."[4]

Genius and Old-fogyism.—This account of Steinthal's brings
out very clearly the *difference between our psychological conceptions and
what are called concepts in logic.* In logic a concept is unalterable; but
what are popularly called our 'conceptions of things' alter by
being used. The aim of 'Science' is to attain conceptions so adequate and exact that we shall never need to change them. There is

[4] *Einleitung in die Psychologie und Sprachwissenschaft* (1881), p. 173.

an everlasting struggle in every mind between the tendency to keep unchanged, and the tendency to renovate, its ideas. Our education is a ceaseless compromise between the conservative and the progressive factors. Every new experience must be disposed of under *some* old head. The great point is to find the head which has to be least altered to take it in. Certain Polynesian natives, seeing horses for the first time, called them pigs, that being the nearest head. My child of two played for a week with the first orange that was given him, calling it a 'ball.' He called the first whole eggs he saw 'potatoes,' having been accustomed to see 'eggs' already broken in a glass, and potatoes without the skin. A folding pocket-corkscrew he unhesitatingly called 'bad-scissors.' Hardly any one of us can make new heads easily when fresh experiences come. Most of us grow more and more enslaved to the stock conceptions with which we have once become familiar, and less and less capable of assimilating impressions in any but the old ways. Old-fogyism, in short, is the inevitable terminus to which life sweeps us on. Objects which violate our established habits of 'apperception' are simply not taken account of at all; or, if on some occasion we are forced by dint of argument to admit their existence, twenty-four hours later the admission is as if it were not, and every trace of the unassimilable truth has vanished from our thought. Genius, in truth, means little more than the faculty of perceiving in an unhabitual way.

On the other hand, nothing is more congenial, from babyhood to the end of life, than to be able to assimilate the new to the old, to meet each threatening violator or burster of our well-known series of concepts, as it comes in, see through its unwontedness, and ticket it off as an old friend in disguise. This victorious assimilation of the new is in fact the type of all intellectual pleasure. The lust for it is scientific curiosity. The relation of the new to the old, before the assimilation is performed, is wonder. We feel neither curiosity nor wonder concerning things so far beyond us that we have no concepts to refer them to or standards by which to measure them.[5] The Fuegians, in Darwin's voyage, wondered at the

[5] The great maxim in pedagogy is to knit every new piece of knowledge on to a preëxisting curiosity—i.e., to assimilate its matter in some way to what is already known. Hence the advantage of "comparing all that is far off and foreign to something that is near home, of making the unknown plain by the example of the known, and of connecting all the instruction with the personal experience of the pupil. . . . If

small boats, but took the big ship as a 'matter of course.' Only what we partly know already inspires us with a desire to know more. The more elaborate textile fabrics, the vaster works in metal, to most of us are like the air, the water, and the ground, absolute existences which awaken no ideas. It is a matter of course that an engraving or a copper-plate inscription should possess that degree of beauty. But if we are shown a *pen*-drawing of equal perfection, our personal sympathy with the difficulty of the task makes us immediately wonder at the skill. The old lady admiring the Academician's picture says to him: "And is it really all done *by hand*?"

The Physiological Process in Perception.—Enough has now been said to prove the general law of perception, which is this: that *whilst part of what we perceive comes through our senses from the object before us, another part* (and it may be the larger part) *always comes out of our own mind.*

At bottom this is but a case of the general fact that our nerve-centres are organs for reacting on sense-impressions, and that our hemispheres, in particular, are given us that records of our past private experience may coöperate in the reaction. Of course such a general statement is vague. If we try to put an exact meaning into it, what we find most natural to believe is that the *brain reacts* by paths which the previous experiences have worn, *and which make us perceive the probable thing*, i.e., the thing by which on the previous occasions the reaction was most frequently aroused. The reaction of the hemispheres consists in the lighting up of a certain system of paths by the current entering from the outer world. What corresponds to this mentally is a certain special pulse of thought, the thought, namely, of that most probable object. Farther than this in the analysis we can hardly go.

Hallucinations.—Between normal perception and illusion we have seen that there is no break, the *process* being identically the same in both. The last illusions we considered might fairly be called hallucinations. We must now consider the false perceptions

---

the teacher is to explain the distance of the sun from the earth, let him ask . . . 'If anyone there in the sun fired off a cannon straight at you, what should you do?' 'Get out of the way,' would be the answer. 'No need of that,' the teacher might reply. 'You may quietly go to sleep in your room, and get up again, you may wait till your confirmation-day, you may learn a trade, and grow as old as I am,—*then* only will the cannon-ball be getting near, *then* you may jump to one side! See, so great as that is the sun's distance!' " (K. Lange: *Über Apperception*, 1879, p. 74.)

more commonly called by that name. In ordinary parlance hallucination is held to differ from illusion in that, whilst there is an object really there in illusion, *in hallucination there is no objective stimulus at all.* We shall presently see that this supposed absence of objective stimulus in hallucination is a mistake, and that hallucinations are often only *extremes* of the perceptive process, in which the secondary cerebral reaction is out of all normal proportion to the peripheral stimulus which occasions the activity. Hallucinations usually appear abruptly and have the character of being forced upon the subject. But they possess various degrees of apparent *objectivity*. One mistake *in limine* must be guarded against. They are often talked of as *images* projected outwards by mistake. But where an hallucination is complete, it is much more than a mental image. *An hallucination, subjectively considered, is a sensation, as good and true a sensation as if there were a real object there.* The object happens not to be there, that is all.

The milder degrees of hallucination have been designated as *pseudo-hallucinations.* Pseudo-hallucinations and hallucinations have been sharply distinguished from each other only within a few years. From ordinary images of memory and fancy, pseudo-hallucinations differ in being much more vivid, minute, detailed, steady, abrupt, and spontaneous, in the sense that all feeling of our own activity in producing them is lacking. Dr. Kandinsky had a patient who, after taking opium or haschisch, had abundant pseudo-hallucinations and hallucinations. As he also had strong visualizing power and was an educated physician, the three sorts of phenomena could be easily compared. Although projected outwards (usually not farther than the limit of distinctest vision, a foot or so), the pseudo-hallucinations *lacked the character of objective reality* which the hallucinations possessed, but, unlike the pictures of imagination, it was almost impossible to produce them at will. Most of the 'voices' which people hear (whether they give rise to delusions or not) are pseudo-hallucinations. They are described as '*inner*' voices, although their character is entirely unlike the inner speech of the subject with himself. I know several persons who hear such inner voices making unforeseen remarks whenever they grow quiet and listen for them. They are a very common incident of delusional insanity, and may at last grow into vivid or completely exteriorized hallucinations. The latter are comparatively frequent occurrences in sporadic form; and certain individuals are liable to have them often. From the results of the 'Census of Hallucinations,' which was begun by Edmund Gurney, it would appear that, roughly speaking, one person at least in every ten is likely to have had a vivid hallucination at some time in his life. The following case from a healthy person will give an idea of what these hallucinations are:

"When a girl of eighteen, I was one evening engaged in a very painful discussion with an elderly person. My distress was so great that I took up a thick ivory knitting-needle that was lying on the mantlepiece of the parlor and broke it into small pieces as I talked. In the midst of the discussion I was very wishful to know the opinion of a brother with whom I had an unusually close relationship. I turned round and saw him sitting at the farther side of a centre-table, with his arms folded (an unusual position with him), but, to my dismay, I perceived from the sarcastic expression of his mouth that he was not in sympathy with me, was not 'taking my side,' as I should then have expressed it. The surprise cooled me, and the discussion was dropped.

"Some minutes after, having occasion to speak to my brother, I turned towards him, but he was gone. I inquired when he left the room, and was told that he had not been in it, which I did not believe, thinking that he had come in for a minute and had gone out without being noticed. About an hour and a half afterwards he appeared, and convinced me, with some trouble, that he had never been near the house that evening. He is still alive and well."

The hallucinations of fever-delirium are a mixture of pseudo-hallucination, true hallucination, and illusion. Those of opium, haschisch, and belladonna resemble them in this respect. The commonest hallucination of all is that of hearing one's own name called aloud. Nearly one half of the sporadic cases which I have collected are of this sort.

Hallucination and Illusion.—Hallucinations are easily produced by verbal suggestion in hypnotic subjects. Thus, point to a dot on a sheet of paper, and call it 'General Grant's photograph,' and your subject will see a photograph of the General there instead of the dot. The dot gives objectivity to the appearance, and the suggested notion of the General gives it form. Then magnify the dot by a lens; double it by a prism or by nudging the eyeball; reflect it in a mirror; turn it upside-down; or wipe it out; and the subject will tell you that the 'photograph' has been enlarged, doubled, reflected, turned about, or made to disappear. In M. Binet's language, the dot is the outward *point de repère* which is needed to give objectivity to your suggestion, and without which the latter will only produce an inner image in the subject's mind. M. Binet has shown that such a peripheral *point de repère* is used in an enormous number, not only of hypnotic hallucinations, but of hallucinations of the insane. These latter are often *unilateral*; that is, the patient hears the voices always on one side of him, or sees the figure only when a certain one of his eyes is open. In many of these cases it has been distinctly proved that a morbid irritation in the internal ear, or an opacity in the humors of the eye, was the starting point of the current which the patient's diseased acoustic or optical centres clothed with their peculiar products in the way of ideas. *Hallucinations produced in this way are 'illusions'; and M. Binet's theory, that all hallucinations must start in the periphery, may be called an attempt to reduce hallucination and illusion to one physiological type,* the type, namely, to which normal perception belongs. In every case, according to M. Binet, whether of perception, of hallucination, or of illusion, we get the sensational vividness by means of a current from the peripheral nerves. It may be a mere trace of a current. But that trace is enough to kindle the maximal process of disintegration in the cells (cf. p. 271), and to give to the object perceived the character of *externality*. What the *nature* of the object shall be will depend wholly on the particular system of paths in which the process is kindled. Part of the thing in all cases comes from the sense-organ, the rest is furnished by the mind. But we cannot by introspection distinguish between these parts; and our only formula for the result is that the brain has *reacted on* the impression in the resulting way.

M. Binet's theory accounts indeed for a multitude of cases, but certainly not for all. The prism does not always double the false appearance, nor does the latter always disappear when the eyes are closed. For Binet, an abnormally or exclusively active part of the cortex gives the *nature* of what shall appear, whilst a peripheral sense-organ alone can give the *intensity* sufficient to make it appear projected into real space. But since this intensity is after all but a matter of degree, one does not see why, under rare conditions, the degree in question *might* not be attained by inner causes exclusively. In that case we should have certain hallucinations centrally initiated, as well as the peripherally initiated hallucinations which are the only sort that M. Binet's theory allows. *It seems probable on the whole, therefore, that centrally initiated hallucinations can exist.* How often they do exist is another question. The existence of hallucinations which affect more than one sense is an argument for central initiation. For, grant that the thing seen may have its starting point in the outer world, the voice which it is heard to utter must be due to an influence from the visual region, i.e., must be of central origin.

Sporadic cases of hallucination, visiting people only once in a lifetime (which seem to be a quite frequent type), are on any theory hard to understand in detail. They are often extraordinarily complete; and the fact that many of them are reported as *veridical*, that is, as coinciding with real events, such as accidents, deaths, etc., of the persons seen, is an additional complication of the phenomenon. The first really scientific study of hallucination in all its possible bearings, on the basis of a large mass of empirical material, was begun by Mr. Edmund Gurney and is continued by other members of the Society for Psychical Research; and the Census is now being applied to several countries under the auspices of the International Congress of Experimental Psychology. It is to be hoped that out of these combined labors something solid will eventually grow. The facts shade off into the phenomena of motor automatism, trance, etc.; and nothing but a wide comparative study can give really instructive results.[6]

[6] The writer of the present work is Agent of the Census for America, and will thankfully receive accounts of cases of hallucination of vision, hearing, etc., of which the reader may have knowledge.

Chapter XXI

The Perception of Space

As adult thinkers we have a definite and apparently instantaneous knowledge of the sizes, shapes, and distances of the things
amongst which we live and move; and we have moreover a practically definite notion of the whole great infinite continuum of
real space in which the world swings and in which all these things
are located. Nevertheless it seems obvious that the baby's world is
vague and confused in all these respects. How does our definite
knowledge of space grow up? This is one of the quarrelsome
problems in psychology. This chapter must be so brief that there
will be no room for the polemic and historic aspects of the subject,
and I will state simply and dogmatically the conclusions which
seem most plausible to me.

The quality of voluminousness exists in all sensations, just as
intensity does. We call the reverberations of a thunder-storm
more voluminous than the squeaking of a slate-pencil; the entrance into a warm bath gives our skin a more massive feeling
than the prick of a pin; a little neuralgic pain, fine as a cobweb, in
the face, seems less extensive than the heavy soreness of a boil or
the vast discomfort of a colic or a lumbago; and a solitary star
looks smaller than the noonday sky. Muscular sensations and
semicircular-canal sensations have volume. Smells and tastes are
not without it; and sensations from our inward organs have it in a
marked degree.

Repletion and emptiness, suffocation, palpitation, headache,
are examples of this, and certainly not less spatial is the consciousness we have of our general bodily condition in nausea,

fever, heavy drowsiness, and fatigue. Our entire cubic content seems then sensibly manifest to us as such, and feels much larger than any local pulsation, pressure, or discomfort. Skin and retina are, however, the organs in which the space-element plays the most active part. Not only does the maximal vastness yielded by the retina surpass that yielded by any other organ, but the intricacy with which our attention can subdivide this vastness and perceive it to be composed of lesser portions simultaneously coexisting alongside of each other is without a parallel elsewhere. The ear gives a greater vastness than the skin, but is considerably less able to subdivide it. The *vastness, moreover, is as great in one direction as in another.* Its dimensions are so vague that in it there is no question as yet of surface as opposed to depth; 'volume' being the best short name for the sensation in question.

Sensations of different orders are roughly comparable with each other as to their volumes. Persons born blind are said to be surprised at the largeness with which objects appear to them when their sight is restored. Franz says of his patient cured of cataract: "He saw everything much larger than he had supposed from the idea obtained by his sense of touch. Moving, and especially living, objects appeared very large." Loud sounds have a certain enormousness of feeling. 'Glowing' bodies, as Hering says, give us a perception "which seems *roomy (raumhaft)* in comparison with that of strictly surface-color. A glowing iron looks luminous through and through, and so does a flame." The interior of one's mouth-cavity feels larger when explored by the tongue than when looked at. The crater of a newly-extracted tooth, and the movements of a loose tooth in its socket, feel quite monstrous. A midge buzzing against the drum of the ear will often seem as big as a butterfly. The pressure of the air in the tympanic cavity upon the membrane gives an astonishingly large sensation.

The voluminousness of the feeling seems to bear very little relation to the size of the organ that yields it. The ear and eye are comparatively minute organs, yet they give us feelings of great volume. The same lack of exact proportion between size of feeling and size of organ affected obtains within the limits of particular sensory organs. An object appears smaller on the lateral portions of the retina than it does on the fovea, as may be easily verified by holding the two forefingers parallel and a couple of inches apart, and transferring the gaze of one eye from one to the other. Then the

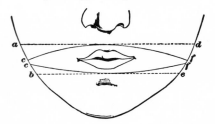

FIG. 65 (after Weber).
The dotted lines give the real course of the points, the continuous lines the course as felt.

finger not directly looked at will appear to shrink. On the skin, if two points kept equidistant (blunted compass- or scissors-points, for example) be drawn along so as really to describe a pair of parallel lines, the lines will appear farther apart in some spots than in others. If, for example, we draw them across the face, the person experimented upon will feel as if they began to diverge near the mouth and to include it in a well-marked ellipse.

Now MY FIRST THESIS IS THAT THIS EXTENSITY, *discernible in each and every sensation, though more developed in some than in others,* IS THE ORIGINAL SENSATION OF SPACE, out of which all the exact knowledge about space that we afterwards come to have is woven by processes of discrimination, association, and selection.

The Construction of Real Space.—To the babe who first opens his senses upon the world, though the experience is one of vastness or extensity, it is of an extensity within which no definite divisions, directions, sizes, or distances are yet marked out. Potentially, the room in which the child is born is subdivisible into a multitude of parts, fixed or movable, which at any given moment of time have definite relations to each other and to his person. Potentially, too, this room taken as a whole can be prolonged in various directions by the addition to it of those farther-lying spaces which constitute the outer world. But actually the further spaces are unfelt, and the subdivisions are undiscriminated, by the babe; the chief part of whose education during his first year of life consists in his becoming acquainted with them and recognizing and identifying them in detail. This process may be called that of the *construction of real space*, as a newly apprehended object, out of the original chaotic experiences of vastness. It consists of several subordinate processes:

First, the total object of vision or of feeling at any time *must have smaller objects definitely discriminated within it*;

Secondly, *objects seen or tasted must be identified with objects felt, heard*, etc., and *vice versa*, so that *the same 'thing'* may come to be recognized, although apprehended in such widely differing ways;

Third, the total extent felt at any time must be conceived as *definitely located in the midst of the surrounding extents of which the world consists*;

Fourth, these objects *must appear arranged in definite order* in the so-called three dimensions; and

Fifth, their relative sizes must be perceived—in other words, *they must be measured.*

Let us take these processes in regular order.

1) **Subdivision or Discrimination.**—Concerning this there is not much to be added to what was set forth in Chapter XV. Moving parts, sharp parts, brightly colored parts of the total field of perception 'catch the attention' and are then discerned as special objects surrounded by the remainder of the field of view or touch. That when such objects are discerned apart they should appear as thus surrounded, must be set down as an ultimate fact of our sensibility of which no farther account can be given. Later, as one partial object of this sort after another has become familiar and identifiable, the attention can be caught by more than one at once. We then see or feel a number of distinct objects alongside of each other in the general extended field. The 'alongsideness' is in the first instance vague—it may not carry with it the sense of definite directions or distances—and it too must be regarded as an ultimate fact of our sensibility.

2) **Coalescence of Different Sensations into the Same 'Thing.'**—When two senses are impressed simultaneously we tend to identify their objects as *one thing*. When a conductor is brought near the skin, the snap heard, the spark seen, and the sting felt, are all located together and believed to be different aspects of one entity, the 'electric discharge.' The space of the seen object fuses with the space of the heard object and with that of the felt object by an ultimate law of our consciousness, which is that we simplify, unify, and identify as much as we possibly can. *Whatever sensible data can be attended to together we locate together. Their several extents seem one extent. The place at which each appears is held to be the same with the place at which the others appear.* This is the first and great 'act' by which our world gets spatially arranged.

In this *coalescence in a 'thing,'* one of the coalescing sensations is held to *be* the thing, the other sensations are taken for its more or less accidental *properties*, or modes of appearance. The sensation chosen to be essentially the thing is the most constant and practically important of the lot; most often it is hardness or weight. But the hardness or weight is never without tactile bulk; and as we can always see something in our hand when we feel something there, we equate the bulk felt with the bulk seen, and thenceforward this common bulk is also apt to figure as of the essence of the 'thing.' Frequently a shape so figures, sometimes a temperature, a taste, etc.; but for the most part temperature, smell, sound, color, or whatever other phenomena may vividly impress us simultaneously with the bulk felt or seen, figure among the accidents. Smell and sound impress us, it is true, when we neither see nor touch the thing; but they are strongest when we see or touch, so we locate the *source* of these properties within the touched or seen space, whilst the properties themselves we regard as overflowing in a weakened form into the spaces filled by other things. *In all this, it will be observed, the sense-data whose spaces coalesce into one are yielded by different sense-organs.* Such data have no tendency to displace each other from consciousness, but can be attended to together all at once. Often indeed they vary concomitantly and reach a maximum together. We may be sure, therefore, that the general rule of our mind is to locate IN *each other* all sensations which are associated in simultaneous experience and do not interfere with each other's perception.

3) **The Sense of the Surrounding World.**—*Different impressions on the same sense-organ* do interfere with each other's perception and cannot well be attended to at once. Hence *we do not locate them in each other's spaces, but arrange them in a serial order of exteriority, each alongside of the rest, in a space larger than that which any one sensation brings.* We can usually recover anything lost from our sight by moving our eyes back in its direction; and it is through these constant changes that every field of seen things comes at last to be thought of as always having a fringe of *other things possible to be seen* spreading in all directions round about it. Meanwhile the movements concomitantly with which the various fields alternate are also felt and remembered; and gradually (through association) this and that movement come in our thought to suggest this or that extent of fresh objects introduced. Gradually, too, since the objects vary indefinitely in kind, we abstract from their several

natures and think separately of their mere extents, of which extents the various movements remain as the only constant introducers and associates. More and more, therefore, do we think of movement and seen extent as mutually involving each other, until at last we may get to regard them as synonymous; and, empty space then meaning for us mere *room for movement*, we may, if we are psychologists, readily but erroneously assign to the 'muscular sense' the chief rôle in perceiving extensiveness at all.

4) **The Serial Order of Locations.**—The muscular sense *has* much to do with defining the *order of position* of things seen, felt, or heard. We look at a point; another point upon the retina's margin catches our attention, and in an instant we turn the fovea upon it, letting its image successively fall upon all the points of the intervening retinal line. The line thus traced so rapidly by the second point is itself a visual object, with the first and second point at its respective ends. It *separates* the points, which become *located by its length* with reference to each other. If a third point catch the attention, more peripheral still than the second point, then a still greater movement of the eyeball and a continuation of the line will result, the second point now appearing *between* the first and third. Every moment of our life, peripherally-lying objects are drawing lines like this between themselves and other objects which they displace from our attention as we bring them to the centre of our field of view. Each peripheral retinal point comes in this way to *suggest* a line at the end of which it lies, a line which a possible movement will trace; and even the motionless field of vision ends at last by signifying a system of positions brought out by possible movements between its centre and all peripheral parts.

It is the same with our skin and joints. By moving our hand over objects we trace lines of direction, and new impressions arise at their ends. The 'lines' are sometimes on the articular surfaces, sometimes on the skin as well; in either case they give a definite order of arrangement to the successive objects between which they intervene. Similarly with sounds and smells. With our heads in a certain position, a certain sound or a certain smell is most distinct. Turning our head makes this experience fainter and brings another sound, or another smell, to its maximum. The two sounds or smells are thus separated by the movement located at its ends, the movement itself being realized as a sweep through space whose value is given partly by the semicircular-canal feeling, partly by the articular cartilages of the neck, and partly by the impressions produced upon the eye.

By such general principles of action as these everything looked at, felt, smelt, or heard comes to be located in a more or less definite position relatively to other collateral things either actually presented or only imagined as possibly there. I say 'collateral' things, for I prefer not to complicate the account just yet with any special consideration of the 'third dimension,' distance, or depth, as it has been called.

5) **The Measurement of Things in Terms of Each Other.**— Here the first thing that seems evident is that we have no *immediate* power of comparing together with any accuracy the extents revealed by different sensations. Our mouth-cavity feels indeed to the tongue larger than it feels to the finger or eye, our lips feel larger than a surface equal to them on our thigh. So much comparison is immediate; but it is vague; and for anything exact we must resort to other help.

The great agent in comparing the extent felt by one sensory surface with that felt by another is superposition—superposition of one surface upon another, and superposition of one outer thing upon many surfaces.

Two surfaces of skin superposed on each other are felt simultaneously, and by the law laid down on p. 295 are judged to occupy an identical place. Similarly of our hand, when seen and felt at the same time by its resident sensibility.

In these identifications and reductions of the many to the one it must be noticed that *when the resident sensations of largeness of two opposed surfaces conflict, one of the sensations is chosen as the true standard and the other treated as illusory.* Thus an empty tooth-socket is believed to be *really smaller* than the finger-tip which it will not admit, although it may *feel* larger; and in general it may be said that the hand, as the almost exclusive organ of palpation, gives its own magnitude to the other parts, instead of having its size determined by them.

But even though exploration of one surface by another were impossible, *we could always measure our various surfaces against each other by applying the same extended object first to one and then to another.* We might of course at first suppose that the object itself waxed and waned as it glided from one place to another (cf. above, Fig. 65); but the principle of simplifying as much as possible our world would soon drive us out of that assumption into the easier one that objects as a rule keep their sizes, and that most of our sensations are affected by errors for which a constant allowance must be made.

In the retina there is no reason to suppose that the bignesses of two impressions (lines or blotches) falling on different regions are at first felt to stand in any exact mutual ratio. But if the impressions come from the *same object*, then we might judge their sizes to be just the same. This, however, only when the relation of the object to the eye is believed to be on the whole unchanged. When the object, by moving, changes its relations to the eye, the sensation excited by its image even on the same retinal region becomes so fluctuating that we end by ascribing no absolute import whatever to the retinal space-feeling which at any moment we may receive. So complete does this overlooking of retinal magnitude become that it is next to impossible to compare the visual magnitudes of objects at different distances without making the experiment of superposition. We cannot say beforehand how much of a distant house or tree our finger will cover. The various answers to the familiar question, How large is the moon?—answers which vary from a cartwheel to a wafer—illustrate this most strikingly. The hardest part of the training of a young draughtsman is his learning to feel directly the retinal (i.e., primitively sensible) magnitudes which the different objects in the field of view subtend. To do this he must recover what Ruskin calls the 'innocence of the eye'—that is, a sort of childish perception of stains of color merely as such, without consciousness of what they mean.

With the rest of us this innocence is lost. *Out of all the visual magnitudes of each known object we have selected one as the 'real' one to think of, and degraded all the others to serve as its signs.* This real magnitude is determined by æsthetic and practical interests. It is that which we get when the object is at the distance most propitious for exact visual discrimination of its details. This is the distance at which we hold anything we are examining. Farther than this we see it too small, nearer too large. And the larger and the smaller feeling vanish in the act of suggesting this one, their more important *meaning.* As I look along the dining-table I overlook the fact that the farther plates and glasses *feel* so much smaller than my own, for I *know* that they are all equal in size; and the feeling of them, which is a present sensation, is eclipsed in the glare of the knowledge, which is a merely imagined one.

It is the same with shape as with size. Almost all the visible shapes of things are what we call perspective 'distortions.' Square table-tops constantly present two acute and two obtuse angles; circles drawn on our wall-papers, our carpets, or on sheets of paper, usually show like ellipses; parallels approach as they recede; human bodies are foreshortened; and the transitions from one to another of these altering forms are infinite and continual. Out of the flux, however, one phase always stands prominent. It is the form the object has when we see it easiest and best: and that is when our eyes and the object both are in what may be called *the normal position.* In this position our head is upright and our optic axes either parallel or symmetrically convergent; the plane of the object is perpendicular to the visual plane; and if the object is one containing many lines, it is turned so as to make them, as far as possible, either parallel or perpendicular to the visual plane. In this situation it is that we compare all shapes with each other; here every exact measurement and every decision is made.

Most sensations are signs to us of other sensations whose space-value is held to be more real. *The thing as it would appear to the eye if it were in the normal position* is what we *think of* whenever we get one of the other optical views. Only as represented in the normal position do we believe we see the object as it *is*; elsewhere, only as it seems. Experience and custom soon teach us, however, that the seeming appearance passes into the real one by continuous gradations. They teach us, moreover, that seeming and being may be strangely interchanged. Now a real circle may slide into a seeming ellipse; now an ellipse may, by sliding in the same direction, become a seeming circle; now a rectangular cross grows slant-legged; now a slant-legged one grows rectangular.

Almost any form in oblique vision may be thus a derivative of almost any other in 'primary' vision; and we must learn, when we get one of the former appearances, to translate it into the appropriate one of the latter class; we must learn of what optical 'reality' it is one of the optical signs. Having learned this, we do but obey that law of economy or simplification which dominates our whole psychic life, when we think exclusively of the 'reality' and ignore as much as our consciousness will let us the 'sign' by which we came to apprehend it. The signs of each probable real thing being multiple and the thing itself one and fixed, we gain the same mental relief by abandoning the former for the latter that we do when we abandon mental images, with all their fluctuating characters, for the definite and unchangeable *names* which they suggest. The selection of the several 'normal' appearances from out of the jungle of our optical experiences, to serve as the real sights of which we shall think, has thus some analogy to the habit of thinking in words, in that by both we substitute terms few and fixed for terms manifold and vague.

If an optical sensation can thus be a mere sign to recall another sensation of the same sense, judged more real, *a fortiori* can sensations of one sense be signs of realities which are objects of another. Smells and tastes make us believe the *visible* cologne-bottle, strawberry, or cheese to be there. Sights suggest objects of touch, touches suggest objects of sight, etc. In all this substitution and suggestive recall the only law that holds good is that in general the most *interesting* of the sensations which the 'thing' can give us is held to represent its real nature most truly. It is a case of the selective activity mentioned on p. 154 ff.

The Third Dimension or Distance.—This service of sensations as mere signs, to be ignored when they have evoked the other sensations which are their significates, was noticed first by Berkeley in his new theory of vision. He dwelt particularly on the fact that the signs were not *natural* signs, but properties of the object merely *associated by experience* with the more real aspects of it which they recall. The tangible 'feel' of a thing, and the 'look' of it to the eye, have absolutely no point in common, said Berkeley; and if I think of the look of it when I get the feel, or think of the feel when I get the look, that is merely due to the fact that I have on so many previous occasions had the two sensations at once. When we open our eyes, for example, we think we see how far off the object is. But this feeling of distance, according to Berkeley, cannot possibly be a retinal sensation, for a point in outer space can only impress our retina by the single dot which it projects 'in the fund of the eye,' and this dot is the same for *all* distances. Distance from the eye, Berkeley considered not to be an optical object at all, but an object of *touch*, of which we have optical signs of various sorts, such as the image's apparent magnitude, its 'faintness' or 'confusion,' and the 'strain' of accommodation and convergence. By distance being an object of 'touch,' Berkeley meant that our notion of it consists in ideas of the amount of muscular movement of arm or legs which would be required to place our hand upon the object. Most authors have agreed with Berkeley that creatures unable to move either their eyes or limbs would have no notion whatever of distance or the third dimension.

This opinion seems to me unjustifiable. I cannot get over the fact that all our sensations are of *volume*, and that the primitive field of view (however imperfectly distance may be discriminated or measured in it) cannot be of something *flat*, as these authors unanimously maintain. Nor can I get over the fact that distance, when I see it, is a genuinely *optical feeling*, even though I be at a loss to assign any one physiological process in the organ of vision to the varying degrees of which the variations of the feeling uniformly correspond. It is awakened by all the optical signs which Berkeley mentioned, and by more besides, such as Wheatstone's binocular disparity, and by the parallax which follows on slightly moving the head. When awakened, however, it seems optical, and not heterogeneous with the other two dimensions of the visual field.

The mutual equivalencies of the distance-dimension with the up-and-down and right-to-left dimensions of the field of view can easily be settled without resorting to experiences of touch. A being reduced to a single eyeball would perceive the same tridimensional world which we do, if he had our intellectual powers. For the *same moving things*, by alternately covering different parts of his retina, would determine the mutual equivalencies of the first two dimensions of the field of view; and by exciting the physiological cause of his perception of depth in various degrees, they would establish a scale of equivalency between the first two and the third.

First of all, one of the sensations given by the object would be chosen to represent its 'real' size and shape, in accordance with the principles so lately laid down. One sensation would measure the 'thing' present, and the 'thing' would measure the other sensations—the peripheral parts of the retina would be equated with the central by receiving the image of the same object. This needs no elucidation in case the object does not change its distance or its front. But suppose, to take a more complicated case, that the object is a stick, seen first in its whole length, and then rotated round one of its ends; let this fixed end be the one near the eye. In this movement the stick's image will grow progressively shorter; its farther end will appear less and less separated laterally from its fixed near end; soon it will be screened by the latter, and then reappear on the opposite side, the image there finally resuming its original length. Suppose this movement to become a familiar experience; the mind will presumably react upon it after its usual fashion (which is that of unifying all data which it is in any way possible to unify), and consider it the movement of a constant object rather than the transformation of a fluctuating one. Now, the *sensation of depth* which it receives during the experience is awakened more by the far than by the near end of the object. But how much depth? What shall measure its amount? Why, at the moment the far end is about to be eclipsed, the difference of its distance from the near end's distance must be judged equal to the stick's whole length; but that length has already been seen and measured by a certain visual sensation of breadth. *So we find that given amounts of the visual depth-feeling become signs of given amounts of the visual breadth-feeling, depth becoming equated with breadth. The measurement of distance is, as Berkeley truly said, a result of suggestion and experience. But visual experience alone is adequate to produce it, and this he erroneously denied.*

The Part played by the Intellect in Space-perception.—But although Berkeley was wrong in his assertion that out of optical experience alone no perception of distance can be evolved, he gave a great impetus to psychology by showing how originally incoherent and incommensurable in respect of their extensiveness our different sensations are, and how our actually so rapid space-perceptions are almost altogether acquired by education. Touch-space is one world; sight-space is another world. The two worlds have no essential or intrinsic congruence, and only through the 'association of ideas' do we know what a seen object signifies in terms of touch. Persons with congenital cataracts relieved by surgical aid, whose world until the operation has been a world of tangibles exclusively, are ludicrously unable at first to name any of the objects which newly fall upon their eye. "It might very well be *a horse*," said the latest patient of this sort of whom we have an account, when a 10-litre bottle was held up a foot from his face.[1] Neither do such patients have any accurate notion in motor terms of the relative distances of things from their eyes. All such confusions

[1] Cf. Raehlmann in *Zeitschrift für Psychologie und Physiologie der Sinnesorgane*, II, 79.

very quickly disappear with practice, and the novel optical sensations translate themselves into the familiar language of touch. The facts do not prove in the least that the optical sensations are not *spatial*, but only that it needs a subtler sense for analogy than most people have, to discern the *same* spatial aspects and relations in them which previously-known tactile and motor experiences have yielded.

Conclusion.—To sum up, the whole history of space-perception is explicable if we admit on the one hand sensations with certain amounts of extensity native to them, and on the other the ordinary powers of discrimination, selection, and association in the mind's dealings with them. The fluctuating import of many of our optical sensations, the same sensation being so ambiguous as regards size, shape, locality, and the like, has led many to believe that such attributes as these could not possibly be the result of sensation at all, but must come from some higher power of intuition, synthesis, or whatever it might be called. But the fact that a present sensation can at any time become the sign of a represented one judged to be more real, sufficiently accounts for all the phenomena without the need of supposing that the quality of extensity is created out of non-extensive experiences by a super-sensational faculty of the mind.

Chapter XXII

Reasoning

What Reasoning is.—We talk of man being the rational animal; and the traditional intellectualist philosophy has always made a great point of treating the brutes as wholly irrational creatures. Nevertheless, it is by no means easy to decide just what is meant by reason, or how the peculiar thinking process called reasoning differs from other thought-sequences which may lead to similar results.

Much of our thinking consists of trains of images suggested one by another, of a sort of spontaneous revery of which it seems likely enough that the higher brutes should be capable. This sort of thinking leads nevertheless to rational conclusions, both practical and theoretical. The links between the terms are either 'contiguity' or 'similarity,' and with a mixture of both these things we can hardly be very incoherent. As a rule, in this sort of irresponsible thinking, the terms which fall to be coupled together are empirical concretes, not abstractions. A sunset may call up the vessel's deck from which I saw one last summer, the companions of my voyage, my arrival into port, etc.; or it may make me think of solar myths, of Hercules' and Hector's funeral pyres, of Homer and whether he could write, of the Greek alphabet, etc. If habitual contiguities predominate, we have a prosaic mind; if rare contiguities or similarities have free play, we call the person fanciful, poetic, or witty. But the thought as a rule is of matters taken in their entirety. Having been thinking of one, we find later that we are thinking of another, to which we have been lifted along, we hardly know how. If an abstract quality figures in the procession, it arrests our attention but for a moment, and fades into something else; and is never very abstract. Thus, in thinking of the sun-myths, we may have a gleam of admiration at the gracefulness of the primitive human mind, or a moment of disgust at the narrowness of modern interpreters. But, in the main, we think less of qualities than of concrete things, real or possible, just as we may experience them.

Our thought here may be rational, but it is not *reasoned*, is not reasoning in the strict sense of the term. In reasoning, although our results may be thought of as concrete things, they are *not suggested immediately by other concrete things*, as in the trains of simply associative thought. They are linked to the concretes which precede them by intermediate steps, and these steps are formed by *abstract general characters* articulately denoted and expressly analyzed out. A thing inferred by reasoning need neither have been an habitual associate of the datum from which we infer it, nor need it be similar to it. It may be a thing entirely unknown to our previous experience, something which no simple association of concretes could ever have evoked. The great difference, in fact, between that simpler kind of rational thinking which consists in the concrete objects of past experience merely suggesting each other, and reasoning distinctively so called, is this: that whilst the empirical thinking is only reproductive, reasoning is productive. An empirical, or 'rule-of-thumb,' thinker can deduce nothing from data with whose behavior and associates in the concrete he is unfamiliar. But put a reasoner amongst a set of concrete objects which he has neither seen nor heard of before, and with a little time, if he is a good reasoner, he will make such inferences from them as will quite atone for his ignorance. Reasoning helps us out of unprecedented situations—situations for which all our common associative wisdom, all the 'education' which we share in common with the beasts, leaves us without resource.

Exact Definition of it.—*Let us make this ability to deal with novel data the technical differentia of reasoning.* This will sufficiently mark it out from common associative thinking, and will immediately enable us to say just what peculiarity it contains.

It contains analysis and abstraction. Whereas the merely empirical thinker stares at a fact in its entirety, and remains helpless, or gets 'stuck,' if it suggests no concomitant or similar, the reasoner breaks it up and notices some one of its separate attributes. This attribute he takes to be the essential part of the whole fact before him. This attribute has properties or consequences which the fact until then was not known to have, but which, now that it is noticed to contain the attribute, it must have.

Call the fact or concrete datum S;
the essential attribute M;
the attribute's property P.

Then the reasoned inference of P from S cannot be made without M's intermediation. The 'essence' M is thus that third or middle term in the reasoning which a moment ago was pronounced essential. *For his original concrete S the reasoner substitutes its abstract property M.* What is true of M, what is coupled with M, thereupon holds true of S, is coupled with S. As M is properly one of the *parts* of the entire S, *reasoning may then be very well defined as the substitution of parts and their implications or consequences for wholes.* And the art of the reasoner will consist of two stages:

First, *sagacity*, or the ability to discover what part, M, lies embedded in the whole S which is before him;

Second, *learning*, or the ability to recall promptly M's consequences, concomitants, or implications.

If we glance at the ordinary syllogism—

$$M \text{ is } P;$$
$$S \text{ is } M;$$
$$\therefore S \text{ is } P$$

—we see that the second or minor premise, the 'subsumption' as it is sometimes called, is the one requiring the sagacity; the first or major the one requiring the fertility, or fulness of learning. Usually the learning is more apt to be ready than the sagacity, the ability to seize fresh aspects in concrete things being rarer than the ability to learn old rules; so that, in most actual cases of reasoning, the minor premise, or the way of conceiving the subject, is the one that makes the novel step in thought. This is, to be sure, not always the case; for the fact that M carries P with it may also be unfamiliar and now formulated for the first time.

The perception that S is M is a *mode of conceiving S*. The statement that M is P is an *abstract or general proposition*. A word about both is necessary.

What is meant by a Mode of Conceiving.—When we conceive of S merely as M (of vermilion merely as a mercury-compound, for example), we neglect all the other attributes which it may have, and attend exclusively to this one. We mutilate the fulness of S's reality. Every reality has an infinity of aspects or properties. Even so simple a fact as a line which you trace in the air may be considered in respect to its form, its length, its direction, and its location. When we reach more complex facts, the number of ways in which we may regard them is literally endless. Vermilion is not only a mercury-compound, it is vividly red, heavy, and expensive, it comes from China, and so on, *ad infinitum*. All objects are well-springs of properties, which are only little by little developed to our knowledge, and it is truly said that to know one thing thoroughly would be to know the whole universe. Mediately or immediately, that one thing is related to everything else; and to know *all* about it, all its relations need be known. But each relation forms one of its attributes, one angle by which someone may conceive it, and while so conceiving it may ignore the rest of it. A man is such a complex fact. But out of the complexity all that an army commissary picks out as important for his purposes is his property of eating so many pounds a day; the general, of marching so many miles; the chair-maker, of having such a shape; the orator, of responding to such and such feelings; the theatre-manager, of being willing to pay just such a price, and no more, for an evening's amusement. Each of these persons singles out the particular side of the entire man which has a bearing on *his* concerns, and not till this side is distinctly and separately conceived can the proper practical conclusions *for that reasoner* be drawn; and when they are drawn the man's other attributes may be ignored.

All ways of conceiving a concrete fact, if they are true ways at all, are equally true ways. *There is no property* ABSOLUTELY *essential to any one thing*. The same property which figures as the essence of a thing on one occasion becomes a very inessential feature upon another. Now that I am writing, it is essential that I conceive my paper as a surface for inscription. If I failed to do that, I should have to stop my work. But if I wished to light a fire, and no other materials were by, the essential way of conceiving the paper would be as combustible material; and I need then have no thought of any of its other destinations. It is really *all* that it is: a combustible, a writing surface, a thin thing, a hydrocarbonaceous thing, a thing eight inches one way and ten another, a thing just one furlong east of a certain stone in my neighbor's field, an American thing, etc., etc., *ad infinitum*. Whichever one of these aspects of its being I temporarily class it under makes me unjust to the other aspects. But as I always am classing it under one aspect or another, I am always unjust, always partial, always exclusive. My excuse is necessity—the necessity which my finite and practical nature lays upon me. My thinking is first and last and always for the sake of my doing, and I can only do one thing at a time. A God who is supposed to drive the whole universe abreast may also be supposed, without detriment to his activity, to see all parts of it at once and without emphasis. But were our human attention so to disperse itself, we should simply stare vacantly at things at large and forfeit our opportunity of doing any particular act. Mr. Warner, in his Adirondack story, shot a bear by aiming, not at his eye or heart, but 'at him generally.' But we cannot aim 'generally' at the universe; or if we do, we miss our game. Our scope is narrow, and we must attack things piecemeal, ignoring the solid fulness in which the elements of Nature exist, and stringing one after another of them together in a serial way, to suit our little interests as they change from hour to hour. In this, the partiality of one moment is partly atoned for by the different sort of partiality of the next. To me now, writing these words, emphasis and selection seem to be the essence of the human mind. In other chapters other qualities have seemed, and will again seem, more important parts of psychology.

Men are so ingrainedly partial that, for common-sense and scholasticism (which is only common-sense grown articulate), the notion that there is no one quality genuinely, absolutely, and exclusively essential to anything is almost unthinkable. "A thing's essence makes it *what* it is. Without an exclusive essence it would be nothing in particular, would be quite nameless, we could not say it was this rather than that. What you write on, for example,—why talk of its being combustible, rectangular, and the like, when you know that these are mere accidents, and that what it really is, and was made to be, is just *paper* and nothing else?" The reader is pretty sure to make some such comment as this. But he is himself merely insisting on an aspect of the thing which suits his own petty purpose, that of *naming* the thing; or else on an aspect which suits the manufacturer's purpose, that of *producing an article for which there is a vulgar demand.* Meanwhile the reality overflows these purposes at every pore. Our usual purpose with it, our commonest title for it, and the properties which this title suggests, have in reality nothing sacramental. They characterize *us* more than they characterize the thing. But we are so stuck in our prejudices, so petrified intellectually, that to our vulgarest names, with their suggestions, we ascribe an eternal and exclusive worth. The thing must be, essentially, what the vulgarest name connotes; what less usual names connote, it can be only in an 'accidental' and relatively unreal sense.[1]

Locke undermined the fallacy. But none of his successors, so far as I know, have radically escaped it, or seen that *the only meaning of essence is teleological, and that classification and conception are purely teleological weapons of the mind.* The essence of a thing is that one of its properties which is so *important for my interests* that in comparison with it I may neglect the rest. Amongst those other things which have this important property I class it, after this property I name it, as a thing endowed with this property I conceive it; and whilst so classing, naming, and conceiving it, all other truths about it become to me as naught. The properties which are important vary from man to man and from hour to hour. Hence divers appellations and conceptions for the same thing. But many objects of daily use—as paper, ink, butter, overcoat—have properties of such constant unwavering importance, and have such stereotyped names, that we end by believing that to conceive them in those ways is to conceive them in the only true way. Those are no truer ways of conceiving them than any others; they are only more frequently serviceable ways to us.

Reasoning is always for a subjective interest. To revert now to our symbolic representation of the reasoning process:

$$\begin{array}{l} \text{M is P} \\ \underline{\text{S is M}} \\ \text{S is P} \end{array}$$

M is discerned and picked out for the time being to be the essence of the concrete fact, phenomenon, or reality, S. But M in

---

[1] Readers brought up on Popular Science may think that the molecular structure of things is their real essence in an absolute sense, and that water is H–O–H more deeply and truly than it is a solvent of sugar or a slaker of thirst. Not a whit! It is *all* of these things with equal reality, and the only reason why *for the chemist* it is H–O–H primarily, and only secondarily the other things, is that *for his purpose* of laboratory analysis and synthesis, and inclusion in the science which treats of compositions and decompositions, the H–O–H aspect of it is the more important one to bear in mind.

this world of ours is inevitably conjoined with P; so that P is the next thing that we may expect to find conjoined with the fact S. We may conclude or infer P, through the intermediation of the M which our sagacity began by discerning, when S came before it, to be the essence of the case.

Now note that if P have any value or importance for us, M was a very good character for our sagacity to pounce upon and abstract. If, on the contrary, P were of no importance, some other character than M would have been a better essence for us to conceive of S by. Psychologically, as a rule, P overshadows the process from the start. We are *seeking* P, or something like P. But the bare totality of S does not yield it to our gaze; and casting about for some point in S to take hold of which will lead us to P, we hit, if we are sagacious, upon M, because M happens to be just the character which is knit up with P. Had we wished Q instead of P, and were N a property of S conjoined with Q, we ought to have ignored M, noticed N, and conceived of S as a sort of N exclusively.

Reasoning is always to attain some particular conclusion, or to gratify some special curiosity. It not only breaks up the datum placed before it and conceives it abstractly; it must conceive it *rightly* too; and conceiving it rightly means conceiving it by that one particular abstract character which leads to the one sort of conclusion which it is the reasoner's temporary interest to attain.

The *results* of reasoning may be hit upon by accident. The stereoscope was actually a result of reasoning; it is conceivable, however, that a man playing with pictures and mirrors might accidentally have hit upon it. Cats have been known to open doors by pulling latches, etc. But no cat, if the latch got out of order, could open the door again, unless some new accident of random fumbling taught her to associate some new total movement with the total phenomenon of the closed door. A reasoning man, however, would open the door by first analyzing the hindrance. He would ascertain what particular feature of the door was wrong. The lever, e.g., does not raise the latch sufficiently from its slot—case of insufficient elevation: raise door bodily on hinges! Or door sticks at bottom by friction against sill: raise it bodily up! Now it is obvious that a child or an idiot might without this reasoning learn the *rule* for opening that particular door. I remember a clock which the maid-servant had discovered would not go unless it were supported so as to tilt slightly forwards. She had stumbled on this method after many weeks of groping. The reason of the stoppage was the friction of the pendulum-bob against the back of the clock-case, a reason which an educated man would have analyzed out in five minutes. I have a student's lamp of which the flame vibrates most unpleasantly unless the chimney be raised about a sixteenth of an inch. I learned the remedy after much torment by accident, and now always keep the chimney up with a small wedge. But my procedure is a mere association of two totals, diseased object and remedy. One learned in pneumatics could have abstracted the *cause* of the disease, and thence inferred the remedy immediately. By many measurements of triangles one might find their area always equal to their height multiplied by half their base, and one might formulate an empirical law to that effect. But a reasoner saves himself all this trouble by seeing that it is the essence (*pro hac vice*) of a triangle to be the half of a parallelogram whose area is the height into the entire base. To see this he must invent additional lines; and the geometer must often draw such to get at the essential property he may require in a figure. The essence consists in some *relation of the figure to the new lines*, a relation not obvious at all until they are put in. The geometer's genius lies in the imagining of the new lines, and his sagacity in the perceiving of the relation.

Thus, there are two great points in reasoning. *First, an extracted character is taken as equivalent to the entire datum from which it comes; and,*

Second, the character thus taken suggests a certain consequence more obviously than it was suggested by the total datum as it originally came. Take these points again, successively.

1) Suppose I say, when offered a piece of cloth, "I won't buy that; it looks as if it would fade," meaning merely that something about it suggests the idea of fading to my mind,—my judgment, though possibly correct, is not reasoned, but purely empirical; but if I can say that into the color there enters a certain dye which I know to be chemically unstable, and that *therefore* the color will fade, my judgment is reasoned. The notion of the dye, which is one of the parts of the cloth, is the connecting link between the latter and the notion of fading. So, again, an uneducated man will expect from past experience to see a piece of ice melt if placed near the fire, and the tip of his finger look coarse if he view it through a convex glass. In neither of these cases could the result be anticipated without full previous acquaintance with the entire phenomenon. It is not a result of reasoning.

But a man who should conceive heat as a mode of motion, and

liquefaction as identical with increased motion of molecules; who should know that curved surfaces bend light-rays in special ways, and that the apparent size of anything is connected with the amount of the 'bend' of its light-rays as they enter the eye,—such a man would make the right inferences for all these objects, even though he had never in his life had any concrete experience of them: and he would do this because the ideas which we have above supposed him to possess would mediate in his mind between the phenomena he starts with and the conclusions he draws. But these ideas are all mere extracted portions or circumstances. The motions which form heat, the bending of the light-waves, are, it is true, excessively recondite ingredients; the hidden pendulum I spoke of above is less so; and the sticking of a door on its sill in the earlier example would hardly be so at all. But each and all agree in this, that they bear a *more evident relation* to the conclusion than did the facts in their immediate totality.

2) And now to prove the second point: Why are the couplings, consequences, and implications of extracts more evident and obvious than those of entire phenomena? For two reasons.

First, the extracted characters are more general than the concretes, and the connections they may have are, therefore, more familiar to us, having been more often met in our experience. Think of heat as motion, and whatever is true of motion will be true of heat; but we have had a hundred experiences of motion for every one of heat. Think of the rays passing through this lens as bending towards the perpendicular, and you substitute for the comparatively unfamiliar lens the very familiar notion of a particular change in direction of a line, of which notion every day brings us countless examples.

The other reason why the relations of the extracted characters are so evident is that their properties are so *few*, compared with the properties of the whole, from which we derived them. In every concrete fact the characters and their consequences are so inexhaustibly numerous that we may lose our way among them before noticing the particular consequence it behooves us to draw. But, if we are lucky enough to single out the proper character, we take in, as it were, by a single glance all its possible consequences. Thus the character of scraping the sill has very few suggestions, prominent among which is the suggestion that the scraping will cease if we raise the door; whilst the entire refractory door suggests an enormous number of notions to the mind. Such an example may seem trivial, but it contains the essence of the most refined and transcendental theorizing. The reason why physics grows more deductive the more the fundamental properties it assumes are of a mathematical sort, such as molecular mass or wave-length, is that the immediate consequences of these notions are so few that we can survey them all at once, and promptly pick out those which concern us.

Sagacity.—To reason, then, we must be able to extract characters,—not *any* characters, but the right characters for our conclusion. If we extract the wrong character, it will not lead to that conclusion. Here, then, is the difficulty: *How are characters extracted, and why does it require the advent of a genius in many cases before the fitting character is brought to light?* Why cannot anybody reason as well as anybody else? Why does it need a Newton to notice the law of the squares, a Darwin to notice the survival of the fittest? To answer these questions we must begin a new research, and see how our insight into facts naturally grows.

All our knowledge at first is vague. When we say that a thing is vague, we mean that it has no subdivisions *ab intra*, nor precise limitations *ab extra*; but still all the forms of thought may apply to it. It may have unity, reality, externality, extent, and what not— *thinghood*, in a word, but thinghood only as a whole. In this vague way, probably, does the room appear to the babe who first begins to be conscious of it as something other than his moving nurse. It has no subdivisions in his mind, unless, perhaps, the window is able to attract his separate notice. In this vague way, certainly, does every entirely new experience appear to the adult. A library, a museum, a machine-shop, are mere confused wholes to the uninstructed, but the machinist, the antiquary, and the bookworm perhaps hardly notice the whole at all, so eager are they to pounce upon the details. Familiarity has in them bred discrimination. Such vague terms as 'grass,' 'mould,' and 'meat' do not exist for the botanist or the anatomist. They know too much about grasses, moulds, and muscles. A certain person said to Charles Kingsley, who was showing him the dissection of a caterpillar, with its exquisite viscera, "Why, I thought it was nothing but skin and squash!" A layman present at a shipwreck, a battle, or a fire is helpless. Discrimination has been so little awakened in him by experience that his consciousness leaves no single point of the complex situation accented and standing out for him to begin to act upon. But the sailor, the fireman, and the general know directly at what corner to take up the business. They 'see into the situation'—that is, they analyze it—with their first glance. It is full of delicately differenced ingredients which their education has little by little brought to their consciousness, but of which the novice gains no clear idea.

How this power of analysis was brought about we saw in our chapters on Discrimination and Attention. We dissociate the elements of originally vague totals by attending to them or noticing them alternately, of course. But what determines which element we shall attend to first? There are two immediate and obvious answers: first, our practical or instinctive interests; and second, our æsthetic interests. The dog singles out of any situation its smells, and the horse its sounds, because they may reveal facts of practical moment, and are instinctively exciting to these several creatures. The infant notices the candle-flame or the window, and ignores the rest of the room, because those objects give him a vivid pleasure. So, the country boy dissociates the blackberry, the chestnut, and the wintergreen, from the vague mass of other shrubs and trees, for their practical uses, and the savage is delighted with the beads, the bits of looking-glass, brought by an exploring vessel, and gives no heed to the features of the vessel itself, which is too much beyond his sphere. These æsthetic and practical interests, then, are the weightiest factors in making particular ingredients stand out in high relief. What they lay their accent on, that we notice; but what they are in themselves we cannot say. We must content ourselves here with simply accepting them as irreducible ultimate factors in determining the way our knowledge grows.

Now, a creature which has few instinctive impulses, or interests practical or æsthetic, will dissociate few characters, and will, at best, have limited reasoning powers; whilst one whose interests are very varied will reason much better. Man, by his immensely varied instincts, practical wants, and æsthetic feelings, to which every sense contributes, would, by dint of these alone, be sure to dissociate vastly more characters than any other animal; and accordingly we find that the lowest savages reason incomparably better than the highest brutes. The diverse interests lead, too, to a diversification of experiences, whose accumulation becomes a condition for the play of that *law of dissociation by varying concomitants* of which I treated on p. 221.

The Help given by Association by Similarity.—It is probable, also, that man's *superior association by similarity* has much to do with those discriminations of character on which his higher flights of reasoning are based. As this latter is an important matter, and as little or nothing was said of it in the chapter on Discrimination, it behooves me to dwell a little upon it here.

What does the reader do when he wishes to see in what the precise likeness or difference of two objects lies? He transfers his attention as rapidly as possible, backwards and forwards, from one to the other. The rapid alteration in consciousness shakes out, as it were, the points of difference or agreement, which would have slumbered forever unnoticed if the consciousness of the objects compared had occurred at widely distant periods of time. What does the scientific man do who searches for the reason or law embedded in a phenomenon? He deliberately acccumulates all the instances he can find which have any analogy to that phenomenon; and, by simultaneously filling his mind with them all, he frequently succeeds in detaching from the collection the peculiarity which he was unable to formulate in one alone; even though that one had been preceded in his former experience by all of those with which he now at once confronts it. These examples show that the mere general fact of having occurred at some time in one's experience, with varying concomitants, is not by itself a sufficient reason for a character to be dissociated now. We need something more; we need that the varying concomitants should in all their variety be brought into consciousness *at once*. Not till then will the character in question escape from its adhesion to each and all of them and stand alone. This will immediately be recognized by those who have read Mill's *Logic* as the ground of Utility in his famous 'four methods of experimental inquiry,' the methods of agreement, of difference, of residues, and of concomitant variations. Each of these gives a list of analogous instances out of the midst of which a sought-for character may roll and strike the mind.

Now it is obvious that any mind in which association by similarity is highly developed is a mind which will spontaneously form lists of instances like this. Take a present fact A, with a character m in it. The mind may fail at first to notice this character m at all. But if A calls up C, D, E, and F,—these being phenomena which resemble A in possessing m, but which may not have entered for months into the experience of the animal who now experiences *A*, why, plainly, such association performs the part of the reader's deliberately rapid comparison referred to above, and of the systematic consideration of like cases by the scientific investigator, and may lead to the noticing of *m* in an abstract way. Certainly this is obvious; and no conclusion is left to us but to assert that, after the few most powerful practical and æsthetic interests, our chief help towards noticing those special characters of phenomena which, when once possessed and named, are used as reasons, class names, essences, or middle terms, *is this association by similarity*. Without it, indeed, the deliberate procedure of the scientific man would be impossible: he could never collect his analogous instances. But it operates of itself in highly-gifted minds without any deliberation, spontaneously collecting analogous instances, uniting in a moment what in nature the whole breadth of space and time keeps separate, and so permitting a perception of identical points in the midst of different circumstances, which minds governed wholly by the law of contiguity could never begin to attain.

Figure 66 shows this. If *m*, in the present representation *A*, calls up *B*, *C*, *D*, and *E*, which are similar to *A* in possessing it, and calls them up in rapid succession, then *m*, being associated almost simultaneously with such varying concomitants, will 'roll out' and attract our separate notice.

If so much is clear to the reader, he will be willing to admit that

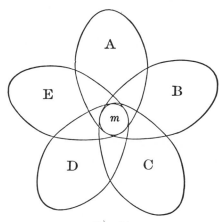

FIG. 66.

the mind *in which this mode of association most prevails* will, from its better opportunity of extricating characters, be the one most prone to reasoned thinking; whilst, on the other hand, a mind in which we do not detect reasoned thinking will probably be one in which association by contiguity holds almost exclusive sway.

Geniuses are, by common consent, considered to differ from ordinary minds by an unusual development of association by similarity. One of Professor Bain's best strokes of work is the exhibition of this truth. It applies to geniuses in the line of reasoning as well as in other lines.

The Reasoning Powers of Brutes.—As the genius is to the vulgarian, so the vulgar human mind is to the intelligence of a brute. Compared with men, it is probable that brutes neither attend to abstract characters, nor have associations by similarity. Their thoughts probably pass from one concrete object to its habitual concrete successor far more uniformly than is the case with us. In other words, their associations of ideas are almost exclusively by contiguity. So far, however, as any brute might think by abstract characters instead of by the association of concretes, he would have to be admitted to be a reasoner in the true human sense. How far this may take place is quite uncertain. Certain it is that the more intelligent brutes *obey* abstract characters, whether they mentally single them out as such or not. They act upon things according to their *class*. This involves some sort of emphasizing, if not abstracting, of the class-essence by the animal's mind. A concrete individual with none of his characters emphasized is one thing; a sharply conceived attribute marked off from everything else by a name is another. But between no analysis of a concrete, and complete analysis; no abstraction of an embedded character, and complete abstraction, every possible intermediary grade must lie. And some of these grades ought to have names, for they are certainly represented in the mind. Dr. Romanes has proposed the name *recept*, and Prof. Lloyd Morgan the name *construct*, for the idea of a vaguely abstracted and generalized object-class. A definite abstraction is called an *isolate* by the latter author. Neither *construct* nor *recept* seems to me a felicitous word; but poor as both are, they form a distinct addition to psychology, so I give them here. Would such a word as *influent* sound better than *recept* in the following passage from Romanes?

"Water-fowl adopt a somewhat different mode of alighting

upon land, or even upon ice, from that which they adopt when
alighting upon water; and those kinds which dive from a height
(such as terns and gannets) never do so upon land or upon ice.
These facts prove that the animals have one recept answering to a
solid substance, and another answering to a fluid. Similarly, a
man will not dive from a height over hard ground or over ice, nor
will he jump into water in the same way as he jumps upon dry
land. In other words, like the water-fowl, he has two distinct recepts, one of which answers to solid ground, and the other to an
unresisting fluid. But, unlike the water-fowl, he is able to bestow
upon each of these recepts a name, and thus to raise them both to
the level of concepts. So far as the practical purposes of locomotion are concerned, it is of course immaterial whether or not he
thus raises his recepts into concepts; but . . . for many other purposes it is of the highest importance that he is able to do this."[2]

A certain well-bred retriever of whom I know never bit his
birds. But one day having to bring two birds at once, which,
though unable to fly, were 'alive and kicking,' he deliberately
gave one a bite which killed it, took the other one still alive to his
master, and then returned for the first. It is impossible not to believe that some such abstract thoughts as 'alive—get away—must
kill,' . . . etc., passed in rapid succession through this dog's mind,
whatever the sensible imagery may have been with which they
were blended. Such practical obedience to the special aspects of
things which may be important involves the essence of reasoning.
But the characters whose presence impress brutes are very few,
being only those which are directly connected with their most instinctive interests. They never extract characters for the mere fun
of the thing, as men do. One is tempted to explain this as the result in them of an almost entire absence of such association by
similarity as characterizes the human mind. A thing may remind
a brute of its full similars, but not of things to which it is but
slightly similar; and all that dissociation by varying concomitants,
which in man is based so largely on association by similarity,
hardly seems to take place at all in the infra-human mind. One
total object suggests another total object, and the lower mammals
find themselves acting with propriety, they know not why. The
great, the fundamental, defect of their minds seems to be the in-

---

[2] *Mental Evolution in Man*, p. 74.

ability of their groups of ideas to break across in unaccustomed places. They are enslaved to routine, to cut-and-dried thinking; and if the most prosaic of human beings could be transported into his dog's soul, he would be appalled at the utter absence of fancy which there reigns. Thoughts would not be found to call up their similars, but only their habitual successors. Sunsets would not suggest heroes' deaths, but supper-time. This is why man is the only metaphysical animal. To wonder why the universe should be as it is presupposes the notion of its being different, and a brute, who never reduces the actual to fluidity by breaking up its literal sequences in his imagination, can never form such a notion. He takes the world simply for granted, and never wonders at it at all.

Chapter XXIII

Consciousness and Movement

All consciousness is motor. The reader will not have forgotten, in the jungle of purely inward processes and products through which the last chapters have borne him, that the final result of them all must be some form of bodily activity due to the escape of the central excitement through outgoing nerves. The whole neural organism, it will be remembered, is, physiologically considered, but a machine for converting stimuli into reactions; and the intellectual part of our life is knit up with but the middle or 'central' part of the machine's operations. We now go on to consider the final or emergent operations, the bodily activities, and the forms of consciousness consequent thereupon.

Every impression which impinges on the incoming nerves produces some discharge down the outgoing ones, whether we be aware of it or not. Using sweeping terms and ignoring exceptions, *we might say that every possible feeling produces a movement, and that the movement is a movement of the entire organism, and of each and all its parts.* What happens patently when an explosion or a flash of lightning startles us, or when we are tickled, happens latently with every sensation which we receive. The only reason why we do not feel the startle or tickle in the case of insignificant sensations is partly its very small amount, partly our obtuseness. Professor Bain many years ago gave the name of the Law of Diffusion to this phenomenon of general discharge, and expressed it thus: "According as an impression is accompanied with Feeling, the aroused currents diffuse themselves freely over the brain, leading to a general agitation of the moving organs, as well as affecting the viscera."

There are probably no exceptions to the diffusion of every impression through the *nerve-centres*. The *effect* of a new wave through the centres may, however, often be to interfere with processes already going on there; and the outward consequence of such interference may be the checking of bodily activities in process of occurrence. When this happens it probably is like the siphoning of certain channels by currents flowing through others; as when, in walking, we suddenly stand still because a sound, sight, smell, or thought catches our attention. But there are cases of arrest of peripheral activity which depend, not on inhibition of centres, but on stimulation of centres which discharge outgoing currents of an inhibitory sort. Whenever we are startled, for example, our heart momentarily stops or slows its beating, and then palpitates with accelerated speed. The brief arrest is due to an outgoing current down the pneumogastric nerve. This nerve, when stimulated, stops or slows the heart-beats, and this particular effect of startling fails to occur if the nerve be cut.

In general, however, the stimulating effects of a sense-impression preponderate over the inhibiting effects, so that we may roughly say, as we began by saying, that the wave of discharge produces an activity in all parts of the body. The task of tracing out *all* the effects of any one incoming sensation has not yet been performed by physiologists. Recent years have, however, begun to enlarge our information; and we have now experimental proof that the heart-beats, the arterial pressure, the respiration, the sweat-glands, the pupil, the bladder, bowels, and uterus, as well as the voluntary muscles, may have their tone and degree of contraction altered even by the most insignificant sensorial stimuli. In short, a *process set up anywhere in the centres reverberates everywhere, and in some way or other affects the organism throughout, making its activities either greater or less.* It is as if the nerve-central mass were like a good conductor charged with electricity, of which the tension cannot be changed at all without changing it everywhere at once.

Herr Schneider has tried to show, by an ingenious zoölogical review, that all the *special* movements which highly evolved animals make are differentiated from the two originally simple movements of contraction and expansion in which the entire body of simple organisms takes part. The tendency to contract is the source of all the self-protective impulses and reactions which are later developed, including that of flight. The tendency to expand splits up, on the contrary, into the impulses and instincts of an aggressive kind, feeding, fighting, sexual intercourse, etc. I cite this as a sort of evolutionary reason to add to the mechanical *a priori* reason why there *ought* to be the diffusive wave which *a posteriori* instances show to exist.

I shall now proceed to a detailed study of the more important classes of movement consequent upon cerebro-mental change. They may be enumerated as—

  1) Expressions of Emotion;
  2) Instinctive or Impulsive Performances; and
  3) Voluntary Deeds;

and each shall have a chapter to itself.

Chapter XXIV

Emotion

Emotions compared with Instincts.—An emotion is a tendency to feel, and an instinct is a tendency to act, characteristically, when in presence of a certain object in the environment. But the emotions also have their bodily 'expression,' which may involve strong muscular activity (as in fear or anger, for example); and it becomes a little hard in many cases to separate the description of the 'emotional' condition from that of the 'instinctive' reaction which one and the same object may provoke. Shall *fear* be described in the chapter on Instincts or in that on Emotions? Where shall one describe *curiosity*, *emulation*, and the like? The answer is quite arbitrary from the scientific point of view, and practical convenience may decide. As inner mental conditions, emotions are quite indescribable. Description, moreover, would be superfluous, for the reader knows already how they feel. Their relations to the objects which prompt them and to the reactions which they provoke are all that one can put down in a book.

Every object that excites an instinct excites an emotion as well. The only distinction one may draw is that the reaction called emotional terminates in the subject's own body, whilst the reaction called instinctive is apt to go farther and enter into practical relations with the exciting object. In both instinct and emotion the mere memory or imagination of the object may suffice to liberate the excitement. One may even get angrier in thinking over one's insult than one was in receiving it; and melt more over a mother who is dead than one ever did when she was living. In the rest of the chapter I shall use the word *object* of emotion indifferently to mean one which is physically present or one which is merely thought of.

The varieties of emotion are innumerable. *Anger, fear, love, hate, joy, grief, shame, pride,* and their varieties, may be called the *coarser* emotions, being coupled as they are with relatively strong bodily reverberations. The *subtler* emotions are the moral, intellectual, and æsthetic feelings, and their bodily reaction is usually much less strong. The mere description of the objects, circumstances, and varieties of the different species of emotion may go to any length. Their internal shadings merge endlessly into each other, and have been partly commemorated in language, as, for example, by such synonyms as hatred, antipathy, animosity, resentment, dislike, aversion, malice, spite, revenge, abhorrence, etc., etc. Dictionaries of synonyms have discriminated them, as well as text-books of psychology—in fact, many German psychological text-books *are* nothing but dictionaries of synonyms when it comes to the chapter on Emotion. But there are limits to the profitable elaboration of the obvious, and the result of all this flux is that the merely descriptive literature of the subject, from Descartes downwards, is one of the most tedious parts of psychology. And not only is it tedious, but you feel that its subdivisions are to a great extent either fictitious or unimportant, and that its pretences to accuracy are a sham. But unfortunately there is little psychological writing about the emotions which is not merely descriptive. As emotions are described in novels, they interest us, for we are made to share them. We have grown acquainted with the concrete objects and emergencies which call them forth, and any knowing touch of introspection which may grace the page meets with a quick and feeling response. Confessedly literary works of aphoristic philosophy also flash lights into our emotional life, and give us a fitful delight. But as far as the 'scientific psychology' of the emotions goes, I may have been surfeited by too much reading of classic works on the subject, but I should as lief read verbal descriptions of the shapes of the rocks on a New Hampshire farm as toil through them again. They give one nowhere a central point of view, or a deductive or generative principle. They distinguish and refine and specify *in infinitum* without ever getting on to another logical level. Whereas the beauty of all truly scientific work is to get to ever deeper levels. Is there no way out from this level of individual description in the case of the emotions? I believe there is a way out, if one will only take it.

The Cause of their Varieties.—The trouble with the emotions in psychology is that they are regarded too much as absolutely individual things. So long as they are set down as so many eternal and sacred psychic entities, like the old immutable species in natural history, so long all that *can* be done with them is reverently to catalogue their separate characters, points, and effects. But if we regard them as products of more general causes (as 'species' are now regarded as products of heredity and variation), the mere distinguishing and cataloguing becomes of subsidiary importance. Having the goose which lays the golden eggs, the description of each egg already laid is a minor matter. I will devote the next few pages to setting forth one very general cause of our emotional feeling, limiting myself in the first instance to what may be called the *coarser* emotions.

The feeling, in the coarser emotions, results from the bodily expression. Our natural way of thinking about these coarser emotions is that the mental perception of some fact excites the mental affection called the emotion, and that this latter state of mind gives rise to the bodily expression. My theory, on the contrary, is that *the bodily changes follow directly the perception of the exciting fact, and that our feeling of the same changes as they occur* IS *the emotion.* Common-sense says, we lose our fortune, are sorry and weep; we meet a bear, are frightened and run; we are insulted by a rival, are angry and strike. The hypothesis here to be defended says that this order of sequence is incorrect, that the one mental state is not immediately induced by the other, that the bodily manifestations must first be interposed between, and that the more rational statement is that we feel sorry because we cry, angry because we strike, afraid because we tremble, and not that we cry, strike, or tremble because we are sorry, angry, or fearful, as the case may be. Without the bodily states following on the perception, the latter would be purely cognitive in form, pale, colorless, destitute of emotional warmth. We might then see the bear and judge it best to run, receive the insult and deem it right to strike, but we should not actually *feel* afraid or angry.

Stated in this crude way, the hypothesis is pretty sure to meet with immediate disbelief. And yet neither many nor far-fetched considerations are required to mitigate its paradoxical character, and possibly to produce conviction of its truth.

To begin with, *particular perceptions certainly do produce wide-spread bodily effects by a sort of immediate physical influence, antecedent to the arousal of an emotion or emotional idea.* In listening to poetry, drama, or heroic narrative we are often surprised at the cutaneous shiver which like a sudden wave flows over us, and at the heart-swelling and the lachrymal effusion that unexpectedly catch us at intervals. In hearing music the same is even more strikingly true. If we abruptly see a dark moving form in the woods, our heart stops beating, and we catch our breath instantly and before any articulate idea of danger can arise. If our friend goes near to the edge of a precipice, we get the well-known feeling of 'all-overishness,' and we shrink back, although we positively *know* him to be safe, and have no distinct imagination of his fall. The writer well remembers his astonishment, when a boy of seven or eight, at fainting when he saw a horse bled. The blood was in a bucket, with a stick in it, and, if memory does not deceive him, he stirred it round and saw it drip from the stick with no feeling save that of childish curiosity. Suddenly the world grew black before his eyes, his ears began to buzz, and he knew no more. He had never heard of the sight of blood producing faintness or sickness, and he had so little repugnance to it, and so little apprehension of any other sort of danger from it, that even at that tender age, as he well remembers, he could not help wondering how the mere physical presence of a pailful of crimson fluid could occasion in him such formidable bodily effects.

The best proof that the immediate cause of emotion is a physical effect on the nerves is furnished by *those pathological cases in which the emotion is objectless.* One of the chief merits, in fact, of the view which I propose seems to be that we can so easily formulate by its means pathological cases and normal cases under a common scheme. In every asylum we find examples of absolutely unmotived fear, anger, melancholy, or conceit; and others of an equally unmotived apathy which persists in spite of the best of outward reasons why it should give way. In the former cases we must suppose the nervous machinery to be so 'labile' in some one emotional direction that almost every stimulus (however inappropriate) causes it to upset in that way, and to engender the particular complex of feelings of which the psychic body of the emotion consists. Thus, to take one special instance, if inability to draw deep breath, fluttering of the heart, and that peculiar epigastric change felt as 'precordial anxiety,' with an irresistible ten-

dency to take a somewhat crouching attitude and to sit still, and
with perhaps other visceral processes not now known, all spontaneously occur together in a certain person, his feeling of their
combination *is* the emotion of dread, and he is the victim of what
is known as morbid fear. A friend who has had occasional attacks
of this most evil of all maladies tells me that in his case the whole
drama seems to centre about the region of the heart and respiratory apparatus, that his main effort during the attacks is to get
control of his inspirations and to slow his heart, and that the moment he attains to breathing deeply and to holding himself erect,
the dread, *ipso facto*, seems to depart.

The emotion here is nothing but the feeling of a bodily state,
and it has a purely bodily cause.

The next thing to be noticed is this, that *every one of the bodily
changes, whatsoever it be, is* FELT, *acutely or obscurely, the moment it
occurs.* If the reader has never paid attention to this matter, he will
be both interested and astonished to learn how many different
local bodily feelings he can detect in himself as characteristic of
his various emotional moods. It would be perhaps too much to
expect him to arrest the tide of any strong gust of passion for the
sake of any such curious analysis as this; but he can observe more
tranquil states, and that may be assumed here to be true of the
greater which is shown to be true of the less. Our whole cubic capacity is sensibly alive; and each morsel of it contributes its pulsations of feeling, dim or sharp, pleasant, painful, or dubious, to
that sense of personality that every one of us unfailingly carries
with him. It is surprising what little items give accent to these
complexes of sensibility. When worried by any slight trouble, one
may find that the focus of one's bodily consciousness is the contraction, often quite inconsiderable, of the eyes and brows. When
momentarily embarrassed, it is something in the pharynx that
compels either a swallow, a clearing of the throat, or a slight
cough; and so on for as many more instances as might be named.
The various permutations of which these organic changes are susceptible make it abstractly possible that no shade of emotion
should be without a bodily reverberation as unique, when taken
in its totality, as is the mental mood itself. The immense number
of parts modified is what makes it so difficult for us to reproduce
in cold blood the total and integral expression of any one emotion. We may catch the trick with the voluntary muscles, but fail

with the skin, glands, heart, and other viscera. Just as an artificially imitated sneeze lacks something of the reality, so the attempt to imitate grief or enthusiasm in the absence of its normal instigating cause is apt to be rather 'hollow.'

I now proceed to urge the vital point of my whole theory, which is this: *If we fancy some strong emotion, and then try to abstract from our consciousness of it all the feelings of its bodily symptoms, we find we have nothing left behind*, no 'mind-stuff' out of which the emotion can be constituted, and that a cold and neutral state of intellectual perception is all that remains. It is true that, although most people, when asked, say that their introspection verifies this statement, some persist in saying theirs does not. Many cannot be made to understand the question. When you beg them to imagine away every feeling of laughter and of tendency to laugh from their consciousness of the ludicrousness of an object, and then to tell you what the feeling of its ludicrousness would be like, whether it be anything more than the perception that the object belongs to the class 'funny,' they persist in replying that the thing proposed is a physical impossibility, and that they always *must* laugh if they see a funny object. Of course the task proposed is not the practical one of seeing a ludicrous object and annihilating one's tendency to laugh. It is the purely speculative one of subtracting certain elements of feeling from an emotional state supposed to exist in its fulness, and saying what the residual elements are. I cannot help thinking that all who rightly apprehend this problem will agree with the proposition above laid down. What kind of an emotion of fear would be left if the feeling neither of quickened heart-beats nor of shallow breathing, neither of trembling lips nor of weakened limbs, neither of goose-flesh nor of visceral stirrings, were present, it is quite impossible for me to think. Can one fancy the state of rage and picture no ebullition in the chest, no flushing of the face, no dilatation of the nostrils, no clenching of the teeth, no impulse to vigorous action, but in their stead limp muscles, calm breathing, and a placid face? The present writer, for one, certainly cannot. The rage is as completely evaporated as the sensation of its so-called manifestations, and the only thing that can possibly be supposed to take its place is some cold-blooded and dispassionate judicial sentence, confined entirely to the intellectual realm, to the effect that a certain person or persons merit chastisement for their sins. In like manner of grief: what would it be without its tears, its sobs, its suffocation of the heart, its pang in the breast-bone? A feelingless cognition that certain circumstances are deplorable, and nothing more. Every passion in turn tells the same story. A disembodied human emotion is a sheer nonentity. I do not say that it is a contradiction in the nature of things, or that pure spirits are necessarily condemned to cold intellectual lives; but I say that for *us* emotion dissociated from all bodily feeling is inconceivable. The more closely I scrutinize my states, the more persuaded I become that whatever 'coarse' affections and passions I have are in very truth constituted by, and made up of, those bodily changes which we ordinarily call their expression or consequence; and the more it seems to me that if I were to become corporeally anæsthetic, I should be excluded from the life of the affections, harsh and tender alike, and drag out an existence of merely cognitive or intellectual form. Such an existence, although it seems to have been the ideal of ancient sages, is too apathetic to be keenly sought after by those born after the revival of the worship of sensibility, a few generations ago.

Let not this view be called materialistic. It is neither more nor less materialistic than any other view which says that our emotions are conditioned by nervous processes. No reader of this book is likely to rebel against such a saying so long as it is expressed in general terms; and if anyone still finds materialism in the thesis now defended, that must be because of the special processes invoked. They are *sensational* processes, processes due to inward currents set up by physical happenings. Such processes have, it is true, always been regarded by the platonizers in psychology as having something peculiarly base about them. But our emotions must always be *inwardly* what they are, whatever be the physiological ground of their apparition. If they are deep pure worthy spiritual facts on any conceivable theory of their physiological source, they remain no less deep pure spiritual and worthy of regard on this present sensational theory. They carry their own inner measure of worth with them; and it is just as logical to use the present theory of the emotions for proving that sensational processes need not be vile and material, as to use their vileness and materiality as a proof that such a theory cannot be true.

This view explains the great variability of emotion. If such a theory is true, then each emotion is the resultant of a sum of elements, and each element is caused by a physiological process of a sort already well known. The elements are all organic changes, and each of them is the reflex effect of the exciting object. Definite questions now immediately arise—questions very different from those which were the only possible ones without this view. Those were questions of classification: "Which are the proper genera of emotion, and which the species under each?"—or of description: "By what expression is each emotion characterized?" The questions now are *causal*: "Just what changes does this object and what changes does that object excite?" and "How come they to excite these particular changes and not others?" We step from a superficial to a deep order of inquiry. Classification and description are the lowest stage of science. They sink into the background the moment questions of causation are formulated, and remain important only so far as they facilitate our answering these. Now the moment an emotion is causally accounted for, as the arousal by an object of a lot of reflex acts which are forthwith felt, *we immediately see why there is no limit to the number of possible different emotions which may exist, and why the emotions of different individuals may vary indefinitely*, both as to their constitution and as to the objects which call them forth. For there is nothing sacramental or eternally fixed in reflex action. Any sort of reflex effect is possible, and reflexes actually vary indefinitely, as we know.

In short, *any classification of the emotions is seen to be as true and as 'natural' as any other*, if it only serves some purpose; and such a question as "What is the 'real' or 'typical' expression of anger, or fear?" is seen to have no objective meaning at all. Instead of it we now have the question as to how any given 'expression' of anger or fear may have come to exist; and that is a real question of physiological mechanics on the one hand, and of history on the other, which (like all real questions) is in essence answerable, although the answer may be hard to find. On a later page I shall mention the attempts to answer it which have been made.

A Corollary verified.—If our theory be true, a necessary corollary of it ought to be this: that any voluntary and cold-blooded arousal of the so-called manifestations of a special emotion should give us the emotion itself. Now within the limits in which it can be verified, experience corroborates rather than disproves this inference. Everyone knows how panic is increased by flight, and how the giving way to the symptoms of grief or anger increases those passions themselves. Each fit of sobbing makes the sorrow more acute, and calls forth another fit stronger still, until at last repose only ensues with lassitude and with the apparent exhaustion of the machinery. In rage, it is notorious how we 'work our-selves up' to a climax by repeated outbreaks of expression. Refuse to express a passion, and it dies. Count ten before venting your anger, and its occasion seems ridiculous. Whistling to keep up courage is no mere figure of speech. On the other hand, sit all day in a moping posture, sigh, and reply to everything with a dismal voice, and your melancholy lingers. There is no more valuable precept in moral education than this, as all who have experience know: if we wish to conquer undesirable emotional tendencies in ourselves, we must assiduously, and in the first instance cold-bloodedly, go through the *outward movements* of those contrary dis-positions which we prefer to cultivate. The reward of persistency will infallibly come, in the fading out of the sullenness or de-pression, and the advent of real cheerfulness and kindliness in their stead. Smooth the brow, brighten the eye, contract the dor-sal rather than the ventral aspect of the frame, and speak in a major key, pass the genial compliment, and your heart must be frigid indeed if it do not gradually thaw!

Against this it is to be said that many actors who perfectly mimic the outward appearances of emotion in face, gait, and voice declare that they feel no emotion at all. Others, however, according to Mr. William Archer, who has made a very instruc-tive statistical inquiry among them, say that the emotion of the part masters them whenever they play it well. The explanation for the discrepancy amongst actors is probably simple. The *visceral and organic* part of the expression can be suppressed in some men, but not in others, and on this it must be that the chief part of the felt emotion depends. Those actors who feel the emotion are prob-ably unable, those who are inwardly cold are probably able, to af-fect the dissociation in a complete way.

An Objection replied to.—It may be objected to the general theory which I maintain that stopping the expression of an emo-tion often makes it worse. The funniness becomes quite excruciat-ing when we are forbidden by the situation to laugh, and anger pent in by fear turns into tenfold hate. Expressing either emotion freely, however, gives relief.

This objection is more specious than real. *During* the expression the emotion is always felt. *After* it, the centres having normally discharged themselves, we feel it no more. But where the facial part of the discharge is suppressed the thoracic and visceral may be all the more violent and persistent, as in suppressed laughter; or the original emotion may be changed, by the combination of the provoking object with the restraining pressure, into *another emotion altogether*, in which different and possibly profounder organic disturbance occurs. If I would kill my enemy but dare not, my emotion is surely altogether other than that which would possess me if I let my anger explode.—On the whole, therefore this objection has no weight.

The Subtler Emotions.—In the æsthetic emotions the bodily reverberation and the feeling may both be faint. A connoisseur is apt to judge a work of art dryly and intellectually, and with no bodily thrill. On the other hand, works of art may arouse intense emotion; and whenever they do so, the experience is completely covered by the terms of our theory. Our theory requires that *incoming currents* be the basis of emotion. But, whether secondary organic reverberations be or be not aroused by it, the perception of a work of art (music, decoration, etc.) is always in the first instance at any rate an affair of incoming currents. The work itself is an object of sensation; and, the perception of an object of sensation being a 'coarse' or vivid experience, what pleasure goes with it will partake of the 'coarse' or vivid form.

That there may be subtle pleasure too, I do not deny. In other words, there may be purely cerebral emotion, independent of all currents from outside. Such feelings as moral satisfaction, thankfulness, curiosity, relief at getting a problem solved, may be of this sort. But the thinness and paleness of these feelings, when unmixed with bodily effects, is in very striking contrast to the coarser emotions. In all sentimental and impressionable people the bodily effects mix in: the voice breaks and the eyes moisten when the moral truth is felt, etc. Wherever there is anything like *rapture*, however intellectual its ground, we find these secondary processes ensue. Unless we actually laugh at the neatness of the demonstration or witticism; unless we thrill at the case of justice, or tingle at the act of magnanimity, our state of mind can hardly be called emotional at all. It is in fact a mere intellectual perception of how certain things are to be called—neat, right, witty, generous, and the like. Such a judicial state of mind as this is to be classed among cognitive rather than among emotional acts.

Description of Fear.—For the reasons given on p. 325, I will append no inventory or classification of emotions or description of their symptoms. The reader has practically almost all the facts in his own hand. As an example, however, of the best sort of descriptive work on the symptoms, I will quote Darwin's account of them in fear.

"Fear is often preceded by astonishment, and is so far akin to it, that both lead to the senses of sight and hearing being instantly aroused. In both cases the eyes and mouth are widely opened, and the eyebrows raised. The frightened man at first stands like a statue motionless and breathless, or crouches down as if instinctively to escape observation. The heart beats quickly and violently, so that it palpitates or knocks against the ribs; but it is very doubtful whether it then works more efficiently than usual, so as to send a greater supply of blood to all parts of the body; for the skin instantly becomes pale, as during incipient faintness. This paleness of the surface, however, is probably in large part, or exclusively, due to the vaso-motor centre being affected in such a manner as to cause the contraction of the small arteries of the skin. That the skin is much affected under the sense of great fear, we see in the marvellous manner in which perspiration immediately exudes from it. This exudation is all the more remarkable, as the surface is then cold, and hence the term a cold sweat; whereas, the sudorific glands are properly excited into action when the surface is heated. The hairs also on the skin stand erect; and the superficial muscles shiver. In connection with the disturbed action of the heart, the breathing is hurried. The salivary glands act imperfectly; the mouth becomes dry, and is often opened and shut. I have also noticed that under slight fear there is a strong tendency to yawn. One of the best-marked symptoms is the trembling of all the muscles of the body; and this is often first seen in the lips. From this cause, and from the dryness of the mouth, the voice becomes husky or indistinct, or may altogether fail. 'Obstupui, steteruntque comæ, et vox faucibus hæsit.' . . . As fear increases into an agony of terror, we behold, as under all violent emotions, diversified results. The heart beats wildly, or may fail to act and faintness ensue; there is a death-like pallor; the breathing is laboured; the wings of the nostrils are widely dilated; 'there is a gasping and convulsive motion of the lips, a tremor on the hollow cheek, a gulping and catching of the throat'; the uncovered and protruding eyeballs are fixed on the object of terror; or they may roll restlessly from side to side, *huc illuc volvens oculos totumque perer-*

rat. The pupils are said to be enormously dilated. All the muscles of the body may become rigid, or may be thrown into convulsive movements. The hands are alternately clenched and opened, often with a twitching movement. The arms may be protruded, as if to avert some dreadful danger, or may be thrown wildly over the head. The Rev. Mr. Hagenauer has seen this latter action in a terrified Australian. In other cases there is a sudden and uncontrollable tendency to headlong flight; and so strong is this, that the boldest soldiers may be seized with a sudden panic."[1]

Genesis of the Emotional Reactions.—How come the various objects which excite emotion to produce such special and different bodily effects? This question was not asked till quite recently, but already some interesting suggestions towards answering it have been made.

Some movements of expression can be accounted for as *weakened repetitions of movements which formerly* (when they were stronger) *were of utility to the subject.* Others are similarly weakened repetitions of movements which under other conditions were *physiologically necessary concomitants of the useful movements.* Of the latter reactions the respiratory disturbances in anger and fear might be taken as examples—organic reminiscences, as it were, reverberations in imagination of the blowings of the man making a series of combative efforts, of the pantings of one in precipitate flight. Such at least is a suggestion made by Mr. Spencer which has found approval. And he also was the first, so far as I know, to suggest that other movements in anger and fear could be explained by the nascent excitation of formerly useful acts.

"To have in a slight degree," he says, "such psychical states as accompany the reception of wounds, and are experienced during flight, is to be in a state of what we call fear. And to have in a slight degree such psychical states as the processes of catching, killing, and eating imply, is to have the desires to catch, kill, and eat. That the propensities to the acts are nothing else than nascent excitations of the psychical state involved in the acts, is proved by the natural language of the propensities. Fear, when strong, expresses itself in cries, in efforts to escape, in palpitations, in tremblings; and these are just the manifestations that go along with an actual suffering of the evil feared. The destructive passion is

[1] *The Expression of the Emotions in Man and Animals* (N.Y. ed.), p. 290.

335

shown in a general tension of the muscular system, in gnashing of teeth and protrusion of the claws, in dilated eyes and nostrils, in growls; and these are weaker forms of the actions that accompany the killing of prey. To such objective evidences, every one can add subjective evidences. Every one can testify that the psychical state called fear, consists of mental representations of certain painful results; and that the one called anger, consists of mental representations of the actions and impressions which would occur while inflicting some kind of pain."

The principle of *revival, in weakened form, of reactions useful in more violent dealings with the object inspiring the emotion*, has found many applications. So slight a symptom as the snarl or sneer, the one-sided uncovering of the upper teeth, is accounted for by Darwin as a survival from the time when our ancestors had large canines, and unfleshed them (as dogs now do) for attack. Similarly the raising of the eyebrows in outward attention, the opening of the mouth in astonishment, come, according to the same author, from the utility of these movements in extreme cases. The raising of the eyebrows goes with the opening of the eye for better vision; the opening of the mouth with the intensest listening, and with the rapid catching of the breath which precedes muscular effort. The distention of the nostrils in anger is interpreted by Spencer as an echo of the way in which our ancestors had to breathe when, during combat, their "mouth was filled up by a part of an antagonist's body that had been seized" (!). The trembling of fear is supposed by Mantegazza to be for the sake of warming the blood (!). The reddening of the face and neck is called by Wundt a compensatory arrangement for relieving the brain of the blood-pressure which the simultaneous excitement of the heart brings with it. The effusion of tears is explained both by this author and by Darwin to be a blood-withdrawing agency of a similar sort. The contraction of the muscles around the eyes, of which the primitive use is to protect those organs from being too much gorged with blood during the screaming fits of infancy, survives in adult life in the shape of the frown, which instantly comes over the brow when anything difficult or displeasing presents itself either to thought or action.

"As the habit of contracting the brows has been followed by infants during innumerable generations, at the commencement of every crying or screaming fit," says Darwin, "it has become firmly associated with the incipient sense of something distressing or disagreeable. Hence under similar circumstances it would be apt to be continued during maturity, although never then developed into a crying-fit. Screaming or weeping begins to be voluntarily restrained at an early period of life, whereas frowning is hardly ever restrained at any age."

Another principle, to which Darwin perhaps hardly does sufficient justice, may be called the principle of *reacting similarly to analogous-feeling stimuli*. There is a whole vocabulary of descriptive adjectives common to impressions belonging to different sensible spheres—experiences of all classes are *sweet*, impressions of all classes *rich* or *solid*, sensations of all classes *sharp*. Wundt and Piderit accordingly explain many of our most expressive reactions upon moral causes as symbolic gustatory movements. As soon as any experience arises which has an affinity with the feeling of sweet, or bitter, or sour, the same movements are executed which would result from the taste in point. "All the states of mind which language designates by the metaphors bitter, harsh, sweet, combine themselves, therefore, with the corresponding mimetic movements of the mouth." Certainly the emotions of disgust and satisfaction do express themselves in this mimetic way. Disgust is an incipient regurgitation or retching, limiting its expression often to the grimace of the lips and nose; satisfaction goes with a sucking smile, or tasting motion of the lips. The ordinary gesture of negation—among us, moving the head about its axis from side to side—is a reaction originally used by babies to keep disagreeables from getting into their mouth, and may be observed in perfection in any nursery. It is now evoked where the stimulus is only an unwelcome idea. Similarly the nod forwards in affirmation is after the analogy of taking food into the mouth. The connection of the expression of moral or social disdain or dislike, especially in women, with movements having a perfectly definite original olfactory function, is too obvious for comment. Winking is the effect of any threatening surprise, not only of what puts the eyes in danger; and a momentary aversion of the eyes is very apt to be one's first symptom of response to an unexpectedly unwelcome proposition.—These may suffice as examples of movements expressive from analogy.

But if certain of our emotional reactions can be explained by the two principles invoked—and the reader will himself have felt how conjectural and fallible in some of the instances the explanation is—there remain many reactions which cannot so be explained at all, and these we must write down for the present as purely idiopathic effects of the stimulus. Amongst them are the effects on the viscera and internal glands, the dryness of the mouth and diarrhœa and nausea of fear, the liver-disturbances which sometimes produce jaundice after excessive rage, the urinary secretion of sanguine excitement, and the bladder-contraction of apprehension, the gaping of expectancy, the 'lump in the throat' of grief, the tickling there and the swallowing of embarrassment, the 'precordial anxiety' of dread, the changes in the pupil, the various sweatings of the skin, cold or hot, local or general, and its flushings, together with other symptoms which probably exist but are too hidden to have been noticed or named. Trembling, which is found in many excitements besides that of terror, is, *pace* Mr. Spencer and Sig. Mantegazza, quite pathological. So are terror's other strong symptoms: they are harmful to the creature who presents them. In an organism as complex as the nervous system there must be many *incidental* reactions which would never themselves have been evolved independently, for any utility they might possess. Sea-sickness, ticklishness, shyness, the love of music, of the various intoxicants, nay, the entire æsthetic life of man, must be traced to this accidental origin. It would be foolish to suppose that none of the reactions called emotional could have arisen in this *quasi*-accidental way.

Chapter XXV

Instinct

Its Definition.—*Instinct is usually defined as the faculty of acting in such a way as to produce certain ends, without foresight of the ends, and without previous education in the performance.* Instincts are the functional correlatives of structure. With the presence of a certain organ goes, one may say, almost always a native aptitude for its use.

The actions we call instinctive all conform to the general reflex type; they are called forth by determinate sensory stimuli in contact with the animal's body, or at a distance in his environment. The cat runs after the mouse, runs or shows fight before the dog, avoids falling from walls and trees, shuns fire and water, etc., not because he has any notion either of life or of death, or of self, or of preservation. He has probably attained to no one of these conceptions in such a way as to react definitely upon it. He acts in each case separately, and simply because he cannot help it; being so framed that when that particular running thing called a mouse appears in his field of vision he *must* pursue; that when that particular barking and obstreperous thing called a dog appears there he *must* retire, if at a distance, and scratch if close by; that he *must* withdraw his feet from water and his face from flame, etc. His nervous system is to a great extent a preorganized bundle of such reactions—they are as fatal as sneezing, and as exactly correlated to their special excitants as it is to its own. Although the naturalist may, for his own convenience, class these reactions under general heads, he must not forget that in the animal it is a particular sensation or perception or image which calls them forth.

At first this view astounds us by the enormous number of special adjustments it supposes animals to possess ready-made in an-

ticipation of the outer things among which they are to dwell. *Can
mutual dependence be so intricate and go so far?* Is each thing
born fitted to particular other things, and to them exclusively, as
locks are fitted to their keys? Undoubtedly this must be believed
to be so. Each nook and cranny of creation, down to our very skin
and entrails, has its living inhabitants, with organs suited to the
place, to devour and digest the food it harbors and to meet the
dangers it conceals; and the minuteness of adaptation thus shown
in the way of *structure* knows no bounds. Even so are there no
bounds to the minuteness of adaptation in the way of *conduct*
which the several inhabitants display.

The older writings on instinct are ineffectual wastes of words,
because their authors never came down to this definite and simple
point of view, but smothered everything in vague wonder at the
clairvoyant and prophetic power of the animals—so superior to
anything in man—and at the beneficence of God in endowing
them with such a gift. But God's beneficence endows them, first of
all, with a nervous system; and, turning our attention to this,
makes instinct immediately appear neither more nor less wonderful than all the other facts of life.

Every instinct is an impulse. Whether we shall call such impulses as blushing, sneezing, coughing, smiling, or dodging, or
keeping time to music, instincts or not, is a mere matter of terminology. The process is the same throughout. In his delightfully
fresh and interesting work, *Der thierische Wille*, Herr G. H.
Schneider subdivides impulses (*Triebe*) into sensation-impulses,
perception-impulses, and idea-impulses. To crouch from cold is a
sensation-impulse; to turn and follow, if we see people running
one way, is a perception-impulse; to cast about for cover, if it
begins to blow and rain, is an imagination-impulse. A single complex instinctive action may involve successively the awakening of
impulses of all three classes. Thus a hungry lion starts to *seek* prey
by the awakening in him of imagination coupled with desire; he
begins to *stalk* it when, on eye, ear, or nostril, he gets an impression of its presence at a certain distance; he *springs* upon it, either
when the booty takes alarm and flees, or when the distance is sufficiently reduced; he proceeds to *tear* and *devour* it the moment he
gets a sensation of its contact with his claws and fangs. Seeking,
stalking, springing, and devouring are just so many different
kinds of muscular contraction, and neither kind is called forth by
the stimulus appropriate to the other.

Now, why do the various animals do what seem to us such strange things, in the presence of such outlandish stimuli? Why does the hen, for example, submit herself to the tedium of incubating such a fearfully uninteresting set of objects as a nestful of eggs, unless she have some sort of a prophetic inkling of the result? The only answer is *ad hominem*. We can only interpret the instincts of brutes by what we know of instincts in ourselves. Why do men always lie down, when they can, on soft beds rather than on hard floors? Why do they sit round the stove on a cold day? Why, in a room, do they place themselves, ninety-nine times out of a hundred, with their faces towards its middle rather than to the wall? Why do they prefer saddle of mutton and champagne to hard-tack and pond-water? Why does the maiden interest the youth so that everything about her seems more important and significant than anything else in the world? Nothing more can be said than that these are human ways, and that every creature *likes* its own ways, and takes to the following them as a matter of course. Science may come and consider these ways, and find that most of them are useful. But it is not for the sake of their utility that they are followed, but because at the moment of following them we feel that that is the only appropriate and natural thing to do. Not one man in a billion, when taking his dinner, ever thinks of utility. He eats because the food tastes good and makes him want more. If you ask him *why* he should want to eat more of what tastes like that, instead of revering you as a philosopher he will probably laugh at you for a fool. The connection between the savory sensation and the act it awakens is for him absolute and *selbstverständlich*, an '*a priori* synthesis' of the most perfect sort, needing no proof but its own evidence. It takes, in short, what Berkeley calls a mind debauched by learning to carry the process of making the natural seem strange, so far as to ask for the *why* of any instinctive human act. To the metaphysician alone can such questions occur as: Why do we smile, when pleased, and not scowl? Why are we unable to talk to a crowd as we talk to a single friend? Why does a particular maiden turn our wits so upside-down? The common man can only say, "*Of course* we smile, *of course* our heart palpitates at the sight of the crowd, *of course* we love the maiden, that beautiful soul clad in that perfect form, so palpably and flagrantly made from all eternity to be loved!"

And so, probably, does each animal feel about the particular things it tends to do in presence of particular objects. They, too, are *a priori* syntheses. To the lion it is the lioness which is made to be loved; to the bear, the she-bear. To the broody hen the notion would probably seem monstrous that there should be a creature in the world to whom a nestful of eggs was not the utterly fascinating and precious and never-to-be-too-much-sat-upon object which it is to her.

Thus we may be sure that, however mysterious some animals' instincts may appear to us, our instincts will appear no less mysterious to them. And we may conclude that, to the animal which obeys it, every impulse and every step of every instinct shines with its own sufficient light, and seems at the moment the only eternally right and proper thing to do. It is done for its own sake exclusively. What voluptuous thrill may not shake a fly, when she at last discovers the one particular leaf, or carrion, or bit of dung, that out of all the world can stimulate her ovipositor to its discharge? Does not the discharge then seem to her the only fitting thing? And need she care or know anything about the future maggot and its food?

Instincts are not always blind or invariable. Nothing is commoner than the remark that man differs from lower creatures by the almost total absence of instincts, and the assumption of their work in him by 'reason.' A fruitless discussion might be waged on this point by two theorizers who were careful not to define their terms. We must of course avoid a quarrel about words, and the facts of the case are really tolerably plain. Man has a far greater variety of *impulses* than any lower animal; and any one of these impulses, taken in itself, is as 'blind' as the lowest instinct can be; but, owing to man's memory, power of reflection, and power of inference, they come each one to be felt by him, after he has once yielded to them and experienced their results, in connection with a *foresight* of those results. In this condition an impulse acted out may be said to be acted out, in part at least, *for the sake* of its results. It is obvious that *every instinctive act, in an animal with memory, must cease to be 'blind' after being once repeated*, and must be accompanied with foresight of its 'end' just so far as that end may have fallen under the animal's cognizance. An insect that lays her eggs in a place where she never sees them hatch must always do so 'blindly'; but a hen who has already hatched a brood can hardly be assumed to sit with perfect 'blindness' on her second nest. Some expectation of consequences must in every case like this be aroused; and this expectation, according as it is that of something desired or of something disliked, must necessarily either re-enforce or inhibit the mere impulse. The hen's idea of the chickens would probably encourage her to sit; a rat's memory, on the other hand, of a former escape from a trap would neutralize his impulse to take bait from anything that reminded him of that trap. If a boy sees a fat hopping-toad, he probably has incontinently an impulse (especially if with other boys) to smash the creature with a stone, which impulse we may suppose him blindly to obey. But something in the expression of the dying toad's clasped hands suggests the meanness of the act, or reminds him of sayings he has heard about the sufferings of animals being like his own; so that, when next he is tempted by a toad, an idea arises which, far from spurring him again to the torment, prompts kindly actions, and may even make him the toad's champion against less reflecting boys.

It is plain, then, that, *no matter how well endowed an animal may originally be in the way of instincts, his resultant actions will be much modified if the instincts combine with experience,* if in addition to impulses he have memories, associations, inferences, and expectations, on any considerable scale. An object O, on which he has an instinctive impulse to react in the manner A, would *directly* provoke him to that reaction. But O has meantime become for him a *sign* of the nearness of P, on which he has an equally strong impulse to react in the manner B, quite unlike A. So that when he meets O, the immediate impulse A and the remote impulse B struggle in his breast for the mastery. The fatality and uniformity said to be characteristic of instinctive actions will be so little manifest that one might be tempted to deny to him altogether the possession of any instinct about the object O. Yet how false this judgment would be! The instinct about O is there; only by the complication of the associative machinery it has come into conflict with another instinct about P.

Here we immediately reap the good fruits of our simple physiological conception of what an instinct is. If it be a mere excitomotor impulse, due to the preëxistence of a certain 'reflex arc' in the nerve-centres of the creature, of course it must follow the law of all such reflex arcs. One liability of such arcs is to have their activity 'inhibited' by other processes going on at the same time. It makes no difference whether the arc be organized at birth, or ripen spontaneously later, or be due to acquired habit; it must take its chances with all the other arcs, and sometimes succeed, and sometimes fail, in drafting off the currents through itself. The mystical view of an instinct would make it invariable. The physiological view would require it to show occasional irregularities in any animal in whom the number of separate instincts, and the possible entrance of the same stimulus into several of them, were great. And such irregularities are what every superior animal's instincts do show in abundance.

Wherever the mind is elevated enough to discriminate; wherever several distinct sensory elements must combine to discharge the reflex arc; wherever, instead of plumping into action instantly at the first rough intimation of what *sort* of a thing is there, the agent waits to see which *one* of its kind it is and what the *circumstances* are of its appearance; wherever different individuals and different circumstances can impel him in different ways; wherever these are the conditions—we have a masking of the elementary constitution of the instinctive life. The whole story of our dealings with the lower wild animals is the history of our taking advantage of the way in which they judge of everything by its mere label, as it were, so as to ensnare or kill them. Nature, in them, has left matters in this rough way, and made them act *always* in the manner which would be *oftenest* right. There are more worms unattached to hooks than impaled upon them; therefore, on the whole, says Nature to her fishy children, bite at *every* worm and take your chances. But as her children get higher, and their lives more precious, she reduces the risks. Since what seems to be the same object may be now a genuine food and now a bait; since in gregarious species each individual may prove to be either the friend or the rival, according to the circumstances, of another; since any entirely unknown object may be fraught with weal or woe, *Nature implants contrary impulses to act on many classes of things*, and leaves it to slight alterations in the conditions of the individual case to decide which impulse shall carry the day. Thus, greediness and suspicion, curiosity and timidity, coyness and desire, bashfulness and vanity, sociability and pugnacity, seem to shoot over into each other as quickly, and to remain in as unstable an equilibrium, in the higher birds and mammals as in man. All are impulses, congenital, blind at first, and productive of motor reactions of a rigorously determinate sort. *Each one of them then is an instinct*, as instincts are commonly defined. *But they contradict each other*—'experience' in each particular opportunity of application usually deciding the issue. *The animal that exhibits them loses the 'instinctive' demeanor* and appears to lead a life of hesitation and choice, an intellectual life; *not, however, because he has no instincts— rather because he has so many that they block each other's path.*

Thus we may confidently say that however uncertain man's reactions upon his environment may sometimes seem in comparison with those of lower mammals, the uncertainty is probably not due to their possession of any principles of action which he lacks. *On the contrary, man possesses all the impulses that they have, and a great many more besides.* In other words, there is no material antagonism between instinct and reason. Reason, *per se*, can inhibit no impulses; the only thing that can neutralize an impulse is an impulse the other way. Reason may, however, make an *inference which will excite the imagination so as to let loose* the impulse the other way; and thus, though the animal richest in reason is also the animal richest in instinctive impulses too, he never seems the fatal automaton which a *merely* instinctive animal must be.

Two Principles of Non-uniformity.—Instincts may be masked in the mature animal's life by two other causes. These are:

a. The *inhibition of instincts by habits*; and

b. The *transitoriness of instincts.*

a. The law of **inhibition of instincts by habits** is this: *When objects of a certain class elicit from an animal a certain sort of reaction, it often happens that the animal becomes partial to the first specimen of the class on which it has reacted, and will not afterwards react on any other specimen.*

The selection of a particular hole to live in, of a particular mate, of a particular feeding-ground, a particular variety of diet, a particular anything, in short, out of a possible multitude, is a very wide-spread tendency among animals, even those low down in the scale. The limpet will return to the same sticking-place in its rock, and the lobster to its favorite nook on the sea-bottom. The rabbit will deposit its dung in the same corner; the bird makes its nest on the same bough. But each of these preferences carries with it an insensibility to *other* opportunities and occasions—an insensibility which can only be described physiologically as an inhibition of new impulses by the habit of old ones already formed. The possession of homes and wives of our own makes us strangely insensible to the charms of those of other people. Few of us are adventurous in the matter of food; in fact, most of us think there is something disgusting in a bill of fare to which we are unused. Strangers, we are apt to think, cannot be worth knowing, especially if they come from distant cities, etc. The original impulse which got us homes, wives, dietaries, and friends at all, seems to exhaust itself in its first achievements and to leave no surplus energy for reacting on new cases. And so it comes about that, witnessing this torpor, an observer of mankind might say that no *instinctive* propensity towards certain objects existed at all. It existed, but it existed *miscellaneously*, or as an instinct pure and simple, only before habit was formed. A habit, once grafted on an instinctive tendency, restricts the range of the tendency itself, and keeps us from reacting on any but the habitual object, although other objects might just as well have been chosen had they been the first-comers.

Another sort of arrest of instinct by habit is where the same class of objects awakens contrary instinctive impulses. Here the impulse first followed towards a given individual of the class is apt to keep him from ever awakening the opposite impulse in us. In fact, the whole class may be protected by this individual specimen from the application to it of the other impulse. Animals, for example, awaken in a child the opposite impulses of fearing and fondling. But if a child, in his first attempts to pat a dog, gets snapped at or bitten, so that the impulse of fear is strongly aroused, it may be that for years to come no dog will excite in him the impulse to fondle again. On the other hand, the greatest natural enemies, if carefully introduced to each other when young and guided at the outset by superior authority, settle down into those 'happy families' of friends which we see in our menageries. Young animals, immediately after birth, have no instinct of fear, but show their dependence by allowing themselves to be freely handled. Later, however, they grow 'wild,' and, if left to themselves, will not let man approach them. I am told by farmers in the Adirondack wilderness that it is a very serious matter if a cow wanders off and calves in the woods and is not found for a week or more. The calf, by that time, is as wild and almost as fleet as a deer, and hard to capture without violence. But calves rarely show any wildness to the men who have been in contact with them during the first days of their life, when the instinct to attach themselves is uppermost, nor do they dread strangers as they would if brought up wild.

Instinct

Chickens give a curious illustration of the same law. Mr. Spalding's wonderful article on instinct shall supply us with the facts. These little creatures show opposite instincts of attachment and fear, either of which may be aroused by the same object, man. If a chick is born in the absence of the hen, it "will follow any moving object. And, when guided by sight alone, they seem to have no more disposition to follow a hen than to follow a duck, or a human being. Unreflecting on-lookers, when they saw chickens a day old running after me," says Mr. Spalding, "and older ones following me miles and answering to my whistle, imagined that I must have some occult power over the creatures, whereas I simply allowed them to follow me from the first. There is the instinct to follow; and ... their ear prior to experience attaches them to the right object."[1]

But if a man presents himself for the first time when the instinct of *fear* is strong, the phenomena are altogether reversed. Mr. Spalding kept three chickens hooded until they were nearly four days old, and thus describes their behavior:

"Each of these on being unhooded evinced the greatest terror of me, dashing off in the opposite direction whenever I sought to approach it. The table on which they were unhooded stood before a window, and each in its turn beat against the glass like a wild bird. One of them darted behind some books, and squeezing itself into a corner, remained cowering for a length of time. We might guess at the meaning of this strange and exceptional wildness; but the odd fact is enough for my present purpose. Whatever might have been the meaning of this marked change in their mental constitution—had they been unhooded on the previous day they would have run to me instead of from me—it could not have been the effect of experience; it must have resulted wholly from changes in their own organization."[2]

Their case was precisely analogous to that of the Adirondack calves. The two opposite instincts relative to the same object ripen in succession. If the first one engenders a habit, that habit will inhibit the application of the second instinct to that object. All animals are tame during the earliest phase of their infancy. Habits formed then limit the effects of whatever instincts of wildness may later be evolved.

[1] Spalding: *Macmillan's Magazine*, Feb. 1873, p. 287.
[2] *Ibid.*, p. 289.

b. This leads us to the **law of transitoriness**, which is this: *Many instincts ripen at a certain age and then fade away.* A consequence of this law is that if, during the time of such an instinct's vivacity, objects adequate to arouse it are met with, a *habit* of acting on them is formed, which remains when the original instinct has passed away; but that if no such objects are met with, then no habit will be formed; and, later on in life, when the animal meets the objects, he will altogether fail to react, as at the earlier epoch he would instinctively have done.

No doubt such a law is restricted. Some instincts are far less transient than others—those connected with feeding and 'self-preservation' may hardly be transient at all—and some, after fading out for a time, recur as strong as ever; e.g., the instincts of pairing and rearing young. The law, however, though not absolute, is certainly very widespread, and a few examples will illustrate just what it means.

In the chickens and calves above mentioned it is obvious that the instinct to follow and become attached fades out after a few days, and that the instinct of flight then takes its place, the conduct of the creature towards man being decided by the formation or non-formation of a certain habit during those days. The transiency of the chicken's instinct to follow is also proved by its conduct towards the hen. Mr. Spalding kept some chickens shut up till they were comparatively old, and, speaking of these, he says:

"A chicken that has not heard the call of the mother until eight or ten days old then hears it as if it heard it not. I regret to find that on this point my notes are not so full as I could wish, or as they might have been. There is, however, an account of one chicken that could not be returned to the mother when ten days old. The hen followed it, and tried to entice it in every way; still it continually left her and ran to the house or to any person of whom it caught sight. This it persisted in doing, though beaten back with a small branch dozens of times, and indeed cruelly maltreated. It was also placed under the mother at night, but it again left her in the morning."

The instinct of sucking is ripe in all mammals at birth, and leads to that habit of taking the breast which, in the human infant, may be prolonged by daily exercise long beyond its usual term of a year or a year and a half. But the instinct itself is transient, in the sense that if, for any reason, the child be fed by spoon during the first few days of its life and not put to the breast, it may be no easy matter after that to make it suck at all. So of calves. If their mother die, or be dry, or refuse to let them suck for a day or two, so that they are fed by hand, it becomes hard to get them to suck at all when a new nurse is provided. The ease with which sucking creatures are weaned, by simply breaking the habit and giving them food in a new way, shows that the instinct, purely as such, must be entirely extinct.

Assuredly the simple fact that instincts are transient, and that the effect of later ones may be altered by the habits which earlier ones have left behind, is a far more philosophical explanation than the notion of an instinctive constitution vaguely 'deranged' or 'thrown out of gear.'

I have observed a Scotch terrier, born on the floor of a stable in December, and transferred six weeks later to a carpeted house, make, when he was less than four months old, a very elaborate pretence of burying things, such as gloves, etc., with which he had played till he was tired. He scratched the carpet with his fore-feet, dropped the object from his mouth upon the spot, then scratched all about it, and finally went away and let it lie. Of course, the act was entirely useless. I saw him perform it at that age some four or five times, and never again in his life. The conditions were not present to fix a habit which should last when the prompting instinct died away. But suppose meat instead of a glove, earth instead of a carpet, hunger-pangs instead of a fresh supper a few hours later, and it is easy to see how this dog might have got into a habit of burying superfluous food, which might have lasted all his life. Who can swear that the strictly instinctive part of the food-burying propensity in the wild *Canidæ* may not be as short-lived as it was in this terrier?

Leaving lower animals aside, and turning to human instincts, we see the law of transiency corroborated on the widest scale by the alternation of different interests and passions as human life goes on. With the child, life is all play and fairy-tales and learning the external properties of 'things'; with the youth, it is bodily exercises of a more systematic sort, novels of the real world, boon-fellowship and song, friendship and love, nature, travel and adventure, science and philosophy; with the man, ambition and policy, acquisitiveness, responsibility to others, and the selfish zest of the battle of life. If a boy grows up alone at the age of games and sports, and learns neither to play ball, nor row, nor sail, nor ride, nor skate, nor fish, nor shoot, probably he will be sedentary to the end of his days; and, though the best of opportunities be afforded him for learning these things later, it is a hundred to one but he will pass them by and shrink back from the effort of taking those necessary first steps the prospect of which, at an earlier age, would have filled him with eager delight. The sexual passion expires after a protracted reign; but it is well known that its peculiar manifestations in a given individual depend almost entirely on the habits he may form during the early period of its activity. Exposure to bad company then makes him a loose liver all his days; chastity kept at first makes the same easy later on. In all pedagogy the great thing is to strike the iron while hot, and to seize the wave of the pupil's interest in each successive subject before its ebb has come, so that knowledge may be got and a habit of skill acquired—a headway of interest, in short, secured, on which afterwards the individual may float. There is a happy moment for fixing skill in drawing, for making boys collectors in natural history, and presently dissectors and botanists; then for initiating them into the harmonies of mechanics and the wonders of physical and chemical law. Later, introspective psychology and the metaphysical and religious mysteries take their turn; and, last of all, the drama of human affairs and worldly wisdom in the widest sense of the term. In each of us a saturation-point is soon reached in all these things; the impetus of our purely intellectual zeal expires, and unless the topic be one associated with some urgent personal need that keeps our wits constantly whetted about it, we settle into an equilibrium, and live on what we learned when our interest was fresh and instinctive, without adding to the store. Outside of their own business, the ideas gained by men before they are twenty-five are practically the only ideas they shall have in their lives. They *cannot* get anything new. Disinterested curiosity is past, the mental grooves and channels set, the power of assimilation gone. If by chance we ever do learn anything about some entirely new topic, we are afflicted with a strange sense of insecurity, and we fear to advance a resolute opinion. But with things learned in the plastic days of instinctive curiosity we never lose entirely our sense of being at home. There remains a kinship, a sentiment of intimate acquaintance, which, even when we know we have failed to keep abreast of the subject, flatters us with a sense of power over it, and makes us feel not altogether out of the pale.

Whatever individual exceptions to this might be cited are of the sort that 'prove the rule.'

To detect the moment of the instinctive readiness for the subject is, then, the first duty of every educator. As for the pupils, it would probably lead to a more earnest temper on the part of college students if they had less belief in their unlimited future intellectual potentialities, and could be brought to realize that whatever physics and political economy and philosophy they are now acquiring are, for better or worse, the physics and political economy and philosophy that will have to serve them to the end.

Enumeration of Instincts in Man.—Professor Preyer, in his careful little work, *Die Seele des Kindes*, says "instinctive acts are in man few in number, and, apart from those connected with the sexual passion, difficult to recognize after early youth is past." And he adds, "so much the more attention should we pay to the instinctive movements of new-born babies, sucklings, and small children." That instinctive acts should be easiest *recognized* in childhood would be a very natural effect of our principles of transitoriness, and of the restrictive influence of habits once acquired; but they are far indeed from being 'few in number' in man. Professor Preyer divides the movements of infants into *impulsive, reflex,* and *instinctive*. By impulsive movements he means *random* movements of limbs, body, and voice, with no aim, and before perception is aroused. Among the first reflex movements are crying on contact with the air, *sneezing, snuffling, snoring, coughing, sighing, sobbing, gagging, vomiting, hiccuping, starting, moving the limbs when touched,* and *sucking.* To these may now be added *hanging by the hands* (see *Nineteenth Century,* Nov. 1891). Later on come *biting, clasping objects,* and *carrying them to the mouth, sitting up, standing, creeping,* and *walking.* It is probable that the centres for executing these three latter acts ripen spontaneously, just as those for flight have been proved to do in birds, and that the appearance of *learning* to stand and walk, by trial and failure, is due to the exercise beginning in most children before the centres are ripe. Children vary enormously in the rate and manner in which they learn to walk. With the first impulses to *imitation,* those to significant *vocalization* are born. *Emulation* rapidly ensues, with *pugnacity* in its train. *Fear* of definite objects comes in early, *sympathy* much later, though on the instinct (or emotion?—see p. 324) of sympathy so much in human life depends. *Shyness* and *sociability, play, curiosity, acquisitiveness,* all begin very early in life. The *hunting instinct, mod-*

esty, *love*, the *parental instinct*, etc., come later. By the age of 15 or 16 the whole array of human instincts is complete. It will be observed that *no other mammal, not even the monkey, shows so large a list*. In a perfectly-rounded development every one of these instincts would start a habit towards certain objects and inhibit a habit towards certain others. Usually this is the case; but, in the one-sided development of civilized life, it happens that the timely age goes by in a sort of starvation of objects, and the individual then grows up with gaps in his psychic constitution which future experiences can never fill. Compare the accomplished gentleman with the poor artisan or tradesman of a city: during the adolescence of the former, objects appropriate to his growing interests, bodily and mental, were offered as fast as the interests awoke, and, as a consequence, he is armed and equipped at every angle to meet the world. Sport came to the rescue and completed his education where real things were lacking. He has tasted of the essence of every side of human life, being sailor, hunter, athlete, scholar, fighter, talker, dandy, man of affairs, etc., all in one. Over the city poor boy's youth no such golden opportunities were hung, and in his manhood no desires for most of them exist. Fortunate it is for him if gaps are the only anomalies his instinctive life presents; perversions are too often the fruit of his unnatural bringing-up.

Description of Fear.—In order to treat at least one instinct at greater length, I will take the instance of *fear*.

Fear is a reaction aroused by the same objects that arouse ferocity. The antagonism of the two is an interesting study in instinctive dynamics. We both fear, and wish to kill, anything that may kill us; and the question which of the two impulses we shall follow is usually decided by some one of those collateral circumstances of the particular case, to be moved by which is the mark of superior mental natures. Of course this introduces uncertainty into the reaction; but it is an uncertainty found in the higher brutes as well as in men, and ought not to be taken as proof that we are less instinctive than they. Fear has bodily expressions of an extremely energetic kind, and stands, beside lust and anger, as one of the three most exciting emotions of which our nature is susceptible. The progress from brute to man is characterized by nothing so much as by the decrease in frequency of proper occasions for fear. In civilized life, in particular, it has at last become possible for large numbers of people to pass from the cradle to the grave without ever having had a pang of genuine fear. Many of us need an attack of mental disease to teach us the meaning of the word. Hence the possibility of so much blindly optimistic philosophy and religion. The atrocities of life become 'like a tale of little meaning tho' the words are strong'; we doubt if anything like *us* ever really was within the tiger's jaws, and conclude that the horrors we hear of are but a sort of painted tapestry for the chambers in which we lie so comfortably at peace with ourselves and with the world.

Be this as it may, fear is a genuine instinct, and one of the earliest shown by the human child. *Noises* seem especially to call it forth. Most noises from the outer world, to a child bred in the house, have no exact significance. They are simply startling. To quote a good observer, M. Perez:

"Children between three and ten months are less often alarmed by visual than by auditory impressions. In cats, from the fifteenth day, the contrary is the case. A child, three and a half months old, in the midst of the turmoil of a conflagration, in presence of the devouring flames and ruined walls, showed neither astonishment nor fear, but smiled at the woman who was taking care of him, while his parents were busy. The noise, however, of the trumpet of the firemen, who were approaching, and that of the wheels of the engine, made him start and cry. At this age I have never yet seen an infant startled at a flash of lightning, even when intense; but I have seen many of them alarmed at the voice of the thunder. . . . Thus fear comes rather by the ears than by the eyes, to the child without experience."[3]

The effect of noise in heightening any terror we may feel in adult years is very marked. The *howling* of the storm, whether on sea or land, is a principal cause of our anxiety when exposed to it. The writer has been interested in noticing in his own person, while lying in bed, and kept awake by the wind outside, how invariably each loud gust of it arrested momentarily his heart. A dog attacking us is much more dreadful by reason of the noises he makes.

Strange men, and *strange animals*, either large or small, excite fear, but especially men or animals advancing towards us in a threatening way. This is entirely instinctive and antecedent to experi-

---

[3] *Psychologie de l'enfant*, p. 72.

ence. Some children will cry with terror at their very first sight of a cat or dog, and it will often be impossible for weeks to make them touch it. Others will wish to fondle it almost immediately. Certain kinds of 'vermin,' especially spiders and snakes, seem to excite a fear unusually difficult to overcome. It is impossible to say how much of this difference is instinctive and how much the result of stories heard about these creatures. That the fear of 'vermin' ripens gradually seemed to me to be proved in a child of my own to whom I gave a live frog once, at the age of six to eight months, and again when he was a year and a half old. The first time, he seized it promptly, and holding it in spite of its struggling, at last got its head into his mouth. He then let it crawl up his breast, and get upon his face, without showing alarm. But the second time, although he had seen no frog and heard no story about a frog between-whiles, it was almost impossible to induce him to touch it. Another child, a year old, eagerly took some very large spiders into his hand. At present he is afraid, but has been exposed meanwhile to the teachings of the nursery. One of my children from her birth upwards saw daily the pet pug-dog of the house, and never betrayed the slightest fear until she was (if I recollect rightly) about eight months old. Then the instinct suddenly seemed to develop, and with such intensity that familiarity had no mitigating effect. She screamed whenever the dog entered the room, and for many months remained afraid to touch him. It is needless to say that no change in the pug's unfailingly friendly conduct had anything to do with this change of feeling in the child. Two of my children were afraid, when babies, of *fur*: Richet reports a similar observation.

Preyer tells of a young child screaming with fear on being carried near to the *sea*. The great source of terror to infancy is solitude. The teleology of this is obvious, as is also that of the infant's expression of dismay—the never-failing cry—on waking up and finding himself alone.

Black things, and especially *dark places*, holes, caverns, etc., arouse a peculiarly gruesome fear. This fear, as well as that of solitude, of being 'lost,' are explained after a fashion by ancestral experience. Says Schneider:

"It is a fact that men, especially in childhood, fear to go into a dark cavern or a gloomy wood. This feeling of fear arises, to be sure, partly from the fact that we easily suspect that dangerous beasts may lurk in these localities—a suspicion due to stories we have heard and read. But, on the other hand, it is quite sure that this fear at a certain perception is also directly inherited. Children who have been carefully guarded from all ghost-stories are nevertheless terrified and cry if led into a dark place, especially if sounds are made there. Even an adult can easily observe that an uncomfortable timidity steals over him in a lonely wood at night, although he may have the fixed conviction that not the slightest danger is near.

"This feeling of fear occurs in many men even in their own house after dark, although it is much stronger in a dark cavern or forest. The fact of such instinctive fear is easily explicable when we consider that our savage ancestors through innumerable generations were accustomed to meet with dangerous beasts in caverns, especially bears, and were for the most part attacked by such beasts during the night and in the woods, and that thus an inseparable association between the perceptions of darkness, caverns, woods, and fear took place, and was inherited."[4]

High places cause fear of a peculiarly sickening sort, though here, again, individuals differ enormously. The utterly blind instinctive character of the motor impulses here is shown by the fact that they are almost always entirely unreasonable, but that reason is powerless to suppress them. That they are a mere incidental peculiarity of the nervous system, like liability to sea-sickness, or love of music, with no teleological significance, seems more than probable. The fear in question varies so much from one person to another, and its detrimental effects are so much more obvious than its uses, that it is hard to see how it could be a selected instinct. Man is anatomically one of the best fitted of animals for climbing about high places. The best psychical complement to this equipment would seem to be a 'level head' when there, not a dread of going there at all. In fact, the teleology of fear, beyond a certain point, is more than dubious. A certain amount of timidity obviously adapts us to the world we live in, but the *fear-paroxysm* is surely altogether harmful to him who is its prey.

Fear of the supernatural is one variety of fear. It is difficult to assign any normal object for this fear, unless it were a genuine ghost. But, in spite of psychical-research societies, science has not

---

[4] *Der menschliche Wille*, p. 224.

yet adopted ghosts; so we can only say that certain *ideas* of super-natural agency, associated with real circumstances, produce a peculiar kind of horror. This horror is probably explicable as the result of a combination of simpler horrors. To bring the ghostly terror to its maximum, many usual elements of the dreadful must combine, such as loneliness, darkness, inexplicable sounds, especially of a dismal character, moving figures half discerned (or, if discerned, of dreadful aspect), and a vertiginous baffling of the expectation. This last element, which is *intellectual*, is very important. It produces a strange emotional 'curdle' in our blood to see a process with which we are familiar deliberately taking an unwonted course. Anyone's heart would stop beating if he perceived his chair sliding unassisted across the floor. The lower animals appear to be sensitive to the mysteriously exceptional as well as ourselves. My friend Professor W. K. Brooks told me of his large and noble dog being frightened into a sort of epileptic fit by a bone being drawn across the floor by a thread which the dog did not see. Darwin and Romanes have given similar experiences. The idea of the supernatural involves that the usual should be set at naught. In the witch and hobgoblin supernatural, other elements still of fear are brought in—caverns, slime and ooze, vermin, corpses, and the like. A human corpse seems normally to produce an instinctive dread, which is no doubt somewhat due to its mysteriousness, and which familiarity rapidly dispels. But, in view of the fact that cadaveric, reptilian, and underground horrors play so specific and constant a part in many nightmares and forms of delirium, it seems not altogether unwise to ask whether these forms of dreadful circumstance may not at a former period have been more normal objects of the environment than now. The ordinary cock-sure evolutionist ought to have no difficulty in explaining these terrors, and the scenery that provokes them, as relapses into the consciousness of the cave-men, a consciousness usually overlaid in us by experiences of more recent date.

There are certain other pathological fears, and certain peculiarities in the expression of ordinary fear, which might receive an explanatory light from ancestral conditions, even infra-human ones. In ordinary fear, one may either run, or remain semi-paralyzed. The latter condition reminds us of the so-called death-shamming instinct shown by many animals. Dr. Lindsay, in his work *Mind in Animals*, says this must require great self-command in those that practise it. But it is really no feigning of death at all, and requires no self-command. It is simply a terror-paralysis which has been so useful as to become hereditary. The beast of prey does not think the motionless bird, insect, or crustacean dead. He simply fails to notice them at all; because his senses, like ours, are much more strongly excited by a moving object than by a still one. It is the same instinct which leads a boy playing 'I spy' to hold his very breath when the seeker is near, and which makes the beast of prey himself in many cases motionlessly lie in wait for his victim or silently 'stalk' it, by stealthy advances alternated with periods of immobility. It is the opposite of the instinct which makes us jump up and down and move our arms when we wish to attract the notice of someone passing far away, and makes the shipwrecked sailor upon the raft where he is floating frantically wave a cloth when a distant sail appears. Now, may not the statue-like, crouching immobility of some melancholiacs, insane with general anxiety and fear of everything, be in some way connected with this old instinct? They can give no *reason* for their fear to move; but immobility makes them feel safer and more comfortable. Is not this the mental state of the 'feigning' animal?

Again, take the strange symptom which has been described of late years by the rather absurd name of *agoraphobia*. The patient is seized with palpitation and terror at the sight of any open place or broad street which he has to cross alone. He trembles, his knees bend, he may even faint at the idea. Where he has sufficient self-command he sometimes accomplishes the object by keeping safe under the lee of a vehicle going across, or joining himself to a knot of other people. But usually he slinks round the sides of the square, hugging the houses as closely as he can. This emotion has no utility in a civilized man, but when we notice the chronic agoraphobia of our domestic cats, and see the tenacious way in which many wild animals, especially rodents, cling to cover, and only venture on a dash across the open as a desperate measure—even then making for every stone or bunch of weeds which may give a momentary shelter—when we see this we are strongly tempted to ask whether such an odd kind of fear in us be not due to the accidental resurrection, through disease, of a sort of instinct which may in some of our remote ancestors have had a permanent and on the whole a useful part to play?

Chapter XXVI

Will

Voluntary Acts.—Desire, wish, will, are states of mind which everyone knows, and which no definition can make plainer. We desire to feel, to have, to do, all sorts of things which at the moment are not felt, had, or done. If with the desire there goes a sense that attainment is not possible, we simply *wish*; but if we believe that the end is in our power, we *will* that the desired feeling, having, or doing shall be real; and real it presently becomes, either immediately upon the willing or after certain preliminaries have been fulfilled.

The only ends which follow *immediately* upon our willing seem to be movements of our own bodies. Whatever *feelings* and *havings* we may will to get come in as results of preliminary movements which we make for the purpose. This fact is too familiar to need illustration; so that we may start with the proposition that the only *direct* outward effects of our will are bodily movements. The mechanism of production of these voluntary movements is what befalls us to study now.

They are secondary performances. The movements we have studied hitherto have been automatic and reflex, and (on the first occasion of their performance, at any rate) unforeseen by the agent. The movements to the study of which we now address ourselves, being desired and intended beforehand, are of course done with full prevision of what they are to be. It follows from this that *voluntary movements must be secondary, not primary, functions of our organism.* This is the first point to understand in the psychology of Volition. Reflex, instinctive, and emotional movements are all primary performances. The nerve-centres are so organized that certain stimuli pull the trigger of certain explosive parts; and a creature going through one of these explosions for the first time undergoes an entirely novel experience. The other day I was standing at a railroad station with a little child, when an express-train went thundering by. The child, who was near the edge of the platform, started, winked, had his breathing convulsed, turned pale, burst out crying, and ran frantically towards me and hid his face. I have no doubt that this youngster was almost as much astonished by his own behavior as he was by the train, and more than I was, who stood by. Of course if such a reaction has many times occurred we learn what to expect of ourselves, and can then foresee our conduct, even though it remain as involuntary and uncontrollable as it was before. But if, in voluntary action properly so called, the act must be foreseen, it follows that no creature not endowed with prophetic power can perform an act voluntarily for the first time. Well, we are no more endowed with prophetic vision of what movements lie in our power than we are endowed with prophetic vision of what sensations we are capable of receiving. As we must wait for the sensations to be given us, so we must wait for the movements to be performed involuntarily, before we can frame ideas of what either of these things are. We learn all our possibilities by the way of experience. When a particular movement, having once occurred in a random, reflex, or involuntary way, has left an image of itself in the memory, then the movement can be desired again, and deliberately willed. But it is impossible to see how it could be willed before.

A supply of ideas of the various movements that are possible, left in the memory by experiences of their involuntary performance, is thus the first prerequisite of the voluntary life.

Two Kinds of Ideas of Movement.—Now these ideas may be either *resident* or *remote*. That is, they may be of the movement as it feels, when taking place, in the moving parts; or they may be of the movement as it feels in some other part of the body which it affects (strokes, presses, scratches, etc.), or as it sounds, or as it looks. The resident sensations in the parts that move have been called *kinæsthetic* feelings, the memories of them are kinæsthetic ideas. It is by these kinæsthetic sensations that we are made conscious of *passive movements*—movements communicated to our limbs by others. If you lie with closed eyes, and another person noiselessly places your arm or leg in any arbitrarily chosen attitude, you receive a feeling of what attitude it is, and can reproduce it yourself in the arm or leg of the opposite side. Similarly a man waked suddenly from sleep in the dark is aware of how he finds himself lying. At least this is what happens in normal cases. But when the feelings of passive movement as well as all the other feelings of a limb are lost, we get such results as are given in the following account by Prof. A. Strümpell of his wonderful anæsthetic boy, whose only sources of feeling were the right eye and the left ear:[1]

"Passive movements could be imprinted on all the extremities to the greatest extent, without attracting the patient's notice. Only in violent forced hyperextension of the joints, especially of the knees, there arose a dull vague feeling of strain, but this was seldom precisely localized. We have often, after bandaging the eyes of the patient, carried him about the room, laid him on a table, given to his arms and legs the most fantastic and apparently the most inconvenient attitudes, without his having a suspicion of it. The expression of astonishment in his face, when all at once the removal of the handkerchief revealed his situation, is indescribable in words. Only when his head was made to hang away down he immediately spoke of dizziness, but could not assign its ground. Later he sometimes inferred from the sounds connected with the manipulation that something special was being done with him. . . . He had no feelings of muscular fatigue. If, with his eyes shut, we told him to raise his arm and to keep it up, he did so without trouble. After one or two minutes, however, the arm began to tremble and sink without his being aware of it. He asserted still his ability to keep it up. . . . Passively holding still his fingers did not affect him. He thought constantly that he opened and shut his hand, whereas it was really fixed."

No third kind of idea is called for. We need, then, when we perform a movement, either a kinæsthetic or a remote idea of which special movement it is to be. In addition to this it has often been supposed that we need an *idea of the amount of innervation* required for the muscular contraction. The discharge from the motor centre into the motor nerve is supposed to give a sensation *sui generis*, opposed to all our other sensations. These accompany incoming currents, whilst that, it is said, accompanies an outgoing current, and no movement is supposed to be totally defined in our

[1] *Deutsches Archiv für klinische Medicin*, xxii, 321.

mind, unless an anticipation of this feeling enter into our idea. The movement's degree of strength, and the effort required to perform it, are supposed to be specially revealed by the feeling of innervation. Many authors deny that this feeling exists, and the proofs given of its existence are certainly insufficient.

The various degrees of 'effort' actually felt in making the same movement against different resistances are all accounted for by the incoming feelings from our chest, jaws, abdomen, and other parts sympathetically contracted whenever the effort is great. There is no need of a consciousness of the amount of outgoing current required. If anything be obvious to introspection, it is that the degree of strength put forth is completely revealed to us by incoming feelings from the muscles themselves and their insertions, from the vicinity of the joints, and from the general fixation of the larynx, chest, face, and body. When a certain degree of energy of contraction rather than another is thought of by us, this complex aggregate of afferent feelings, forming the material of our thought, renders absolutely precise and distinctive our mental image of the exact strength of movement to be made, and the exact amount of resistance to be overcome.

Let the reader try to direct his will towards a particular movement, and then notice what *constituted* the direction of the will. Was it anything over and above the notion of the different feelings to which the movement when effected would give rise? If we abstract from these feelings, will any sign, principle, or means of orientation be left by which the will may innervate the proper muscles with the right intensity, and not go astray into the wrong ones? Strip off these images anticipative of the results of the motion, and so far from leaving us with a complete assortment of directions into which our will may launch itself, you leave our consciousness in an absolute and total vacuum. If I will to write *Peter* rather than *Paul*, it is the thought of certain digital sensations, of certain alphabetic sounds, of certain appearances on the paper, and of no others, which immediately precedes the motion of my pen. If I will to utter the word *Paul* rather than *Peter*, it is the thought of my voice falling on my ear, and of certain muscular feelings in my tongue, lips, and larynx, which guide the utterance. All these are incoming feelings, and between the thought of them, by which the act is mentally specified with all possible completeness, and the act itself, there is no room for any third order of mental phenomenon.

There is indeed the *fiat*, the element of consent, or resolve that the act shall ensue. This, doubtless, to the reader's mind, as to my own, constitutes the essence of the voluntariness of the act. This *fiat* will be treated of in detail farther on. It may be entirely neglected here, for it is a constant coefficient, affecting all voluntary actions alike, and incapable of serving to distinguish them. No one will pretend that its quality varies according as the right arm, for example, or the left is used.

An anticipatory image, then, of the sensorial consequences of a movement, plus (on certain occasions) the fiat that these consequences shall become actual, is the only psychic state which introspection lets us discern as the forerunner of our voluntary acts. There is no coercive evidence of any feeling attached to the efferent discharge.

The entire content and material of our consciousness—consciousness of movement, as of all things else—seems thus to be of peripheral origin, and to come to us in the first instance through the peripheral nerves.

The Motor-cue.—Let us call the last idea which in the mind precedes the motor discharge the 'motor-cue.' Now do 'resident' images form the only motor-cue, or will 'remote' ones equally suffice?

There can be no doubt whatever that the cue may be an image either of the resident or of the remote kind. Although, at the outset of our learning a movement, it would seem that the resident feelings must come strongly before consciousness, later this need not be the case. The rule, in fact, would seem to be that they tend to lapse more and more from consciousness, and that the more practised we become in a movement, the more 'remote' do the ideas become which form its mental cue. What we are *interested* in is what sticks in our consciousness; everything else we get rid of as quickly as we can. Our resident feelings of movement have no substantive interest for us at all, as a rule. What interest us are the ends which the movement is to attain. Such an end is generally a remote sensation, an impression which the movement produces on the eye or ear, or sometimes on the skin, nose, or palate. Now let the idea of such an end associate itself definitely with the right discharge, and the thought of the innervation's *resident* effects will become as great an encumbrance as we have already concluded that the feeling of the innervation itself is. The mind does not need it; the end alone is enough.

The idea of the end, then, tends more and more to make itself all-sufficient. Or, at any rate, if the kinæsthetic ideas are called up at all, they are so swamped in the vivid kinæsthetic feelings by which they are immediately overtaken that we have no time to be aware of their separate existence. As I write, I have no anticipation, as a thing distinct from my sensation, of either the look or the digital feel of the letters which flow from my pen. The words chime on my mental *ear*, as it were, before I write them, but not on my mental eye or hand. This comes from the rapidity with which the movements follow on their mental cue. An end consented to as soon as conceived innervates directly the centre of the first movement of the chain which leads to its accomplishment, and then the whole chain rattles off *quasi*-reflexly, as was described on pp. 130–131.

The reader will certainly recognize this to be true in all fluent and unhesitating voluntary acts. The only special fiat there is at the outset of the performance. A man says to himself, "I must change my clothes," and involuntarily he has taken off his coat, and his fingers are at work in their accustomed manner on his waistcoat-buttons, etc.; or we say, "I must go downstairs," and ere we know it we have risen, walked, and turned the handle of the door;—all through the idea of an end coupled with a series of guiding sensations which successively arise. It would seem indeed that we fail of accuracy and certainty in our attainment of the end whenever we are preoccupied with the way in which the movement will feel. We walk a beam the better the less we think of the position of our feet upon it. We pitch or catch, we shoot or chop the better the less tactile and muscular (the less resident), and the more exclusively optical (the more remote), our consciousness is. Keep your *eye* on the place aimed at, and your hand will fetch it; think of your hand, and you will very likely miss your aim. Dr. Southard found that he could touch a spot with a pencil-point more accurately with a visual than with a tactile mental cue. In the former case he looked at a small object and closed his eyes before trying to touch it. In the latter case he *placed* it with closed eyes, and then after removing his hand tried to touch it again. The average error with touch (when the results were most favorable) was 17.13 mm. With sight it was only 12.37 mm. —All these are plain results of introspection and observation. By what neural machinery they are made possible we do not know.

In Chapter XIX we saw how enormously individuals differ in

respect to their mental imagery. In the type of imagination called *tactile* by the French authors, it is probable that the kinæsthetic ideas are more prominent than in my account. We must not expect too great a uniformity in individual accounts, nor wrangle overmuch as to which one 'truly' represents the process.

I trust that I have now made clear what that 'idea of a movement' is which must precede it in order that it be voluntary. It is not the thought of the innervation which the movement requires. It is the anticipation of the movement's sensible effects, resident or remote, and sometimes very remote indeed. Such anticipations, to say the least, determine *what* our movements shall be. I have spoken all along as if they also might determine *that* they shall be. This, no doubt, has disconcerted many readers, for it certainly seems as if a special fiat, or consent to the movement, were required in addition to the mere conception of it, in many cases of volition; and this fiat I have altogether left out of my account. This leads us to the next point in our discussion.

Ideo-motor Action.—The question is this: *Is the bare idea of a movement's sensible effects its sufficient motor-cue, or must there be an additional mental antecedent, in the shape of a fiat, decision, consent, volitional mandate, or other synonymous phenomenon of consciousness, before the movement can follow?*

I answer: Sometimes the bare idea is sufficient, but sometimes an additional conscious element, in the shape of a fiat, mandate, or express consent, has to intervene and precede the movement. The cases without a fiat constitute the more fundamental, because the more simple, variety. The others involve a special complication, which must be fully discussed at the proper time. For the present let us turn to *ideo-motor action*, as it has been termed, or the sequence of movement upon the mere thought of it, without a special fiat, as the type of the process of volition.

Wherever a movement *unhesitatingly and immediately* follows upon the idea of it, we have ideo-motor action. We are then aware of nothing between the conception and the execution. All sorts of neuro-muscular processes come between, of course, but we know absolutely nothing of them. We think the act, and it is done; and that is all that introspection tells us of the matter. Dr. Carpenter, who first used, I believe, the name of ideo-motor action, placed it, if I mistake not, among the curiosities of our mental life. The truth is that it is no curiosity, but simply the normal process stripped of disguise. Whilst talking I become conscious of a pin on the floor, or of some dust on my sleeve. Without interrupting the conversation I brush away the dust or pick up the pin. I make no express resolve, but the mere perception of the object and the fleeting notion of the act seem of themselves to bring the latter about. Similarly, I sit at table after dinner and find myself from time to time taking nuts or raisins out of the dish and eating them. My dinner properly is over, and in the heat of the conversation I am hardly aware of what I do; but the perception of the fruit, and the fleeting notion that I may eat it, seem fatally to bring the act about. There is certainly no express fiat here; any more than there is in all those habitual goings and comings and rearrangements of ourselves which fill every hour of the day, and which incoming sensations instigate so immediately that it is often difficult to decide whether not to call them reflex rather than voluntary acts. As Lotze says:

"We see in writing or piano-playing a great number of very complicated movements following quickly one upon the other, the instigative representations of which remained scarcely a second in consciousness, certainly not long enough to awaken any other volition than the general one of resigning one's self without reserve to the passing over of representation into action. All the acts of our daily life happen in this wise: Our standing up, walking, talking, all this never demands a distinct impulse of the will, but is adequately brought about by the pure flux of thought."[2]

In all this the determining condition of the unhesitating and resistless sequence of the act seems to be *the absence of any conflicting notion in the mind.* Either there is nothing else at all in the mind, or what is there does not conflict. We know what it is to get out of bed on a freezing morning in a room without a fire, and how the very vital principle within us protests against the ordeal. Probably most persons have lain on certain mornings for an hour at a time unable to brace themselves to the resolve. We think how late we shall be, how the duties of the day will suffer; we say, "I *must* get up, this is ignominious," etc.; but still the warm couch feels too delicious, the cold outside too cruel, and resolution faints away and postpones itself again and again just as it seemed on the verge of bursting the resistance and passing over into the decisive act.

[2] *Medicinische Psychologie*, p. 293.

Now how do we *ever* get up under such circumstances? If I may generalize from my own experience, we more often than not get up without any struggle or decision at all. We suddenly find that we *have* got up. A fortunate lapse of consciousness occurs; we forget both the warmth and the cold; we fall into some revery connected with the day's life, in the course of which the idea flashes across us, "Hollo! I must lie here no longer"—an idea which at that lucky instant awakens no contradictory or paralyzing suggestions, and consequently produces immediately its appropriate motor effects. It was our acute consciousness of both the warmth and the cold during the period of struggle, which paralyzed our activity then and kept our idea of rising in the condition of *wish* and not of *will*. The moment these inhibitory ideas ceased, the original idea exerted its effects.

This case seems to me to contain in miniature form the data for an entire psychology of volition. It was in fact through meditating on the phenomenon in my own person that I first became convinced of the truth of the doctrine which these pages present, and which I need here illustrate by no farther examples. The reason why that doctrine is not a self-evident truth is that we have so many ideas which *do not* result in action. But it will be seen that in every such case, without exception, that is because other ideas simultaneously present rob them of their impulsive power. But even here, and when a movement is inhibited from *completely* taking place by contrary ideas, it will *incipiently* take place. To quote Lotze once more:

"The spectator accompanies the throwing of a billiard-ball, or the thrust of the swordsman, with slight movements of his arm; the untaught narrator tells his story with many gesticulations; the reader while absorbed in the perusal of a battle-scene feels a slight tension run through his muscular system, keeping time as it were with the actions he is reading of. These results become the more marked the more we are absorbed in thinking of the movements which suggest them; they grow fainter exactly in proportion as a complex consciousness, under the dominion of a crowd of other representations, withstands the passing over of mental contemplation into outward action."

The 'willing-game,' the exhibitions of so-called 'mind-reading,' or more properly muscle-reading, which have lately grown so fashionable, are based on this incipient obedience of muscular contraction to idea, even when the deliberate intention is that no contraction shall occur.

We may then lay it down for certain that *every representation of a movement awakens in some degree the actual movement which is its object; and awakens it in a maximum degree whenever it is not kept from so doing by an antagonistic representation present simultaneously to the mind.*

The express fiat, or act of mental consent to the movement, comes in when the neutralization of the antagonistic and inhibitory idea is required. But that there is no express fiat needed when the conditions are simple, the reader ought now to be convinced. Lest, however, he should still share the common prejudice that voluntary action without 'exertion of will-power' is *Hamlet* with the prince's part left out, I will make a few farther remarks. The first point to start from, in understanding voluntary action and the possible occurrence of it with no fiat or express resolve, is the fact that consciousness is *in its very nature impulsive.* We do not first have a sensation or thought, and then have to *add* something dynamic to it to get a movement. Every pulse of feeling which we have is the correlate of some neural activity that is already on its way to instigate a movement. Our sensations and thoughts are but cross-sections, as it were, of currents whose essential consequence is motion, and which have no sooner run in at one nerve than they are ready to run out by another. The popular notion that consciousness is not essentially a forerunner of activity, but that the latter must result from some superadded 'will-force,' is a very natural inference from those special cases in which we think of an act for an indefinite length of time without the action taking place. These cases, however, are not the norm; they are cases of inhibition by antagonistic thoughts. When the blocking is released we feel as if an inward spring were let loose, and this is the additional impulse or *fiat* upon which the act effectively succeeds. We shall study anon the blocking and its release. Our higher thought is full of it. But where there is no blocking, there is naturally no hiatus between the thought-process and the motor discharge. *Movement is the natural immediate effect of the process of feeling, irrespective of what the quality of the feeling may be. It is so in reflex action, it is so in emotional expression, it is so in the voluntary life.* Ideomotor action is thus no paradox, to be softened or explained away. It obeys the type of all conscious action, and from it one must start to explain the sort of action in which a special fiat is involved.

It may be remarked in passing, that the inhibition of a movement no more involves an express effort or command than its execution does. Either of them *may* require it. But in all simple and ordinary cases, just as the bare presence of one idea prompts a movement, so the bare presence of another idea will prevent its taking place. Try to feel as if you were crooking your finger, whilst keeping it straight. In a minute it will fairly tingle with the imaginary change of position; yet it will not sensibly move, because *its not really moving* is also a part of what you have in mind. Drop *this* idea, think purely and simply of the movement, and nothing else, and, presto! it takes place with no effort at all.

A waking man's behavior is thus at all times the resultant of two opposing neural forces. With unimaginable fineness some currents among the cells and fibres of his brain are playing on his motor nerves, whilst other currents, as unimaginably fine, are playing on the first currents, damming or helping them, altering their direction or their speed. The upshot of it all is, that whilst the currents must always end by being drained off through *some* motor nerves, they are drained off sometimes through one set and sometimes through another; and sometimes they keep each other in equilibrium so long that a superficial observer may think they are not drained off at all. Such an observer must remember, however, that from the physiological point of view a gesture, an expression of the brow, or an expulsion of the breath are movements as much as an act of locomotion is. A king's breath slays as well as an assassin's blow; and the outpouring of those currents which the magic imponderable streaming of our ideas accompanies need not always be of an explosive or otherwise physically conspicuous kind.

Action after Deliberation.—We are now in a position to describe *what happens in deliberate action*, or when the mind has many objects before it, related to each other in antagonistic or in favorable ways. One of these objects of its thought may be an act. By itself this would prompt a movement; some of the additional objects or considerations, however, block the motor discharge, whilst others, on the contrary, solicit it to take place. The result is that peculiar feeling of inward unrest known as *indecision*. Fortunately it is too familiar to need description, for to describe it would be impossible. As long as it lasts, with the various objects before the attention, we are said to *deliberate*; and when finally the original suggestion either prevails and makes the movement take place, or gets definitively quenched by its antagonists, we are said to *decide*, or to *utter our voluntary fiat*, in favor of one or the other course. The reinforcing and inhibiting objects meanwhile are termed the *reasons* or *motives* by which the decision is brought about.

The process of deliberation contains endless degrees of complication. At every moment of it our consciousness is of an extremely complex thing, namely, the whole set of motives and their conflict. Of this complicated object, the totality of which is realized more or less dimly all the while by consciousness, certain parts stand out more or less sharply at one moment in the foreground, and at another moment other parts, in consequence of the oscillations of our attention, and of the 'associative' flow of our ideas. But no matter how sharp the foreground-reasons may be, or how imminently close to bursting through the dam and carrying the motor consequences their own way, the background, however dimly felt, is always there as a fringe (p. 149); and its presence (so long as the indecision actually lasts) serves as an effective check upon the irrevocable discharge. The deliberation may last for weeks or months, occupying at intervals the mind. The motives which yesterday seemed full of urgency and blood and life to-day feel strangely weak and pale and dead. But as little to-day as to-morrow is the question finally resolved. Something tells us that all this is provisional; that the weakened reasons will wax strong again, and the stronger weaken; that equilibrium is unreached; that testing our reasons, not obeying them, is still the order of the day, and that we must wait awhile, patiently or impatiently, until our mind is made up 'for good and all.' This inclining, first to one, then to another future, both of which we represent as possible, resembles the oscillations to and fro of a material body within the limits of its elasticity. There is inward strain, but no outward rupture. And this condition, plainly enough, is susceptible of indefinite continuance, as well in the physical mass as in the mind. If the elasticity give way, however, if the dam ever do break, and the currents burst the crust, vacillation is over and decision is irrevocably there.

The decision may come in any one of many modes. I will try briefly to sketch the most characteristic types of it, merely warning the reader that this is only an introspective account of symptoms and phenomena, and that all questions of causal agency, whether neural or spiritual, are relegated to a later page.

Five Chief Types of Decision.—Turning now to the form of the decision itself, we may distinguish five chief types. *The first may be called the reasonable type.* It is that of those cases in which the arguments for and against a given course seem gradually and almost insensibly to settle themselves in the mind and to end by leaving a clear balance in favor of one alternative, which alternative we then adopt without effort or constraint. Until this rational balancing of the books is consummated we have a calm feeling that the evidence is not yet all in, and this keeps action in suspense. But some day we wake with the sense that we see the matter rightly, that no new light will be thrown on it by farther delay, and that it had better be settled *now*. In this easy transition from doubt to assurance we seem to ourselves almost passive; the 'reasons' which decide us appearing to flow in from the nature of things, and to owe nothing to our will. We have, however, a perfect sense of being *free*, in that we are devoid of any feeling of coercion. The conclusive reason for the decision in these cases usually is the discovery that we can refer the case to a *class* upon which we are accustomed to act unhesitatingly in a certain stereotyped way. It may be said in general that a great part of every deliberation consists in the turning over of all the possible modes of *conceiving* the doing or not doing of the act in point. The moment we hit upon a conception which lets us apply some principle of action which is a fixed and stable part of our Ego, our state of doubt is at an end. Persons of authority, who have to make many decisions in the day, carry with them a set of heads of classification, each bearing its volitional consequence, and under these they seek as far as possible to range each new emergency as it occurs. It is where the emergency belongs to a species without precedent, to which consequently no cut-and-dried maxim will apply, that we feel most at a loss, and are distressed at the indeterminateness of our task. As soon, however, as we see our way to a familiar classification, we are at ease again. *In action as in reasoning, then, the great thing is the quest of the right conception.* The concrete dilemmas do not come to us with labels gummed upon their backs. We may name them by many names. The wise man is he who succeeds in finding the name which suits the needs of the particular occasion best (p. 310 ff.). A 'reasonable' character is one who

370

has a store of stable and worthy ends, and who does not decide about an action till he has calmly ascertained whether it be ministerial or detrimental to any one of these.

In the next two types of decision, the final fiat occurs before the evidence is all 'in.' It often happens that no paramount and authoritative reason for either course will come. Either seems a good, and there is no umpire to decide which should yield its place to the other. We grow tired of long hesitation and inconclusiveness, and the hour may come when we feel that even a bad decision is better than no decision at all. Under these conditions it will often happen that some accidental circumstance, supervening at a particular moment upon our mental weariness, will upset the balance in the direction of one of the alternatives, to which then we feel ourselves committed, although an opposite accident at the same time might have produced the opposite result.

In the *second type* our feeling is to a great extent that of letting ourselves drift with a certain indifferent acquiescence in a direction accidentally determined *from without*, with the conviction that, after all, we might as well stand by this course as by the other, and that things are in any event sure to turn out sufficiently right.

In the *third type* the determination seems equally accidental, but it comes from within, and not from without. It often happens, when the absence of imperative principle is perplexing and suspense distracting, that we find ourselves acting, as it were, automatically, and as if by a spontaneous discharge of our nerves, in the direction of one of the horns of the dilemma. But so exciting is this sense of motion after our intolerable pent-up state that we eagerly throw ourselves into it. 'Forward now!' we inwardly cry, 'though the heavens fall.' This reckless and exultant espousal of an energy so little premeditated by us that we feel rather like passive spectators cheering on the display of some extraneous force than like voluntary agents is a type of decision too abrupt and tumultuous to occur often in humdrum and cool-blooded natures. But it is probably frequent in persons of strong emotional endowment and unstable or vacillating character. And in men of the world-shaking type, the Napoleons, Luthers, etc., in whom tenacious passion combines with ebullient activity, when by any chance the passion's outlet has been dammed by scruples or apprehensions, the resolution is probably often of this catastrophic kind. The flood breaks quite unexpectedly through the dam. That it should so often do so is quite sufficient to account for the tendency of these characters to a fatalistic mood of mind. And the fatalistic mood itself is sure to reinforce the strength of the energy just started on its exciting path of discharge.

There is a *fourth form* of decision, which often ends deliberation as suddenly as the third form does. It comes when, in consequence of some outer experience or some inexplicable inward change, *we suddenly pass from the easy and careless to the sober and strenuous mood,* or possibly the other way. The whole scale of values of our motives and impulses then undergoes a change like that which a change of the observer's level produces on a view. The most sobering possible agents are objects of grief and fear. When one of these affects us, all 'light fantastic' notions lose their motive power, all solemn ones find theirs multiplied many-fold. The consequence is an instant abandonment of the more trivial projects with which we had been dallying, and an instant practical acceptance of the more grim and earnest alternative which till then could not extort our mind's consent. All those 'changes of heart,' 'awakenings of conscience,' etc., which make new men of so many of us may be classed under this head. The character abruptly rises to another 'level,' and deliberation comes to an immediate end.

In the *fifth and final type* of decision, the feeling that the evidence is all in, and that reason has balanced the books, may be either present or absent. But in either case we feel, in deciding, as if we ourselves by our own wilful act inclined the beam: in the former case by adding our living effort to the weight of the logical reason which, taken alone, seems powerless to make the act discharge; in the latter by a kind of creative contribution of something instead of a reason which does a reason's work. The slow dead heave of the will that is felt in these instances makes of them a class altogether different subjectively from all the four preceding classes. What the heave of the will betokens metaphysically, what the effort might lead us to infer about a will-power distinct from motives, are not matters that concern us yet. Subjectively and phenomenally, the *feeling of effort*, absent from the former decisions, accompanies these. Whether it be the dreary resignation for the sake of austere and naked duty of all sorts of rich mundane delights; or whether it be the heavy resolve that of two mutually exclusive trains of future fact, both sweet and good and with no strictly objective or imperative principle of choice between them, one shall forevermore become impossible, while the other shall become reality; it is a desolate and acrid sort of act, an entrance into a lonesome moral wilderness. If examined closely, its chief difference from the former cases appears to be that in those cases the mind at the moment of deciding on the triumphant alternative dropped the other one wholly or nearly out of sight, whereas here both alternatives are steadily held in view, and in the very act of murdering the vanquished possibility the chooser realizes how much in that instant he is making himself lose. It is deliberately driving a thorn into one's flesh; and the sense of *inward effort* with which the act is accompanied is an element which sets this fifth type of decision in strong contrast with the previous four varieties, and makes of it an altogether peculiar sort of mental phenomenon. The immense majority of human decisions are decisions without effort. In comparatively few of them, in most people, does effort accompany the final act. We are, I think, misled into supposing that effort is more frequent than it is by the fact that *during deliberation* we so often have a feeling of how great an effort it would take to make a decision *now*. Later, after the decision has made itself with ease, we recollect this and erroneously suppose the effort also to have been made then.

The existence of the effort as a phenomenal fact in our consciousness cannot of course be doubted or denied. Its significance, on the other hand, is a matter about which the gravest difference of opinion prevails. Questions as momentous as that of the very existence of spiritual causality, as vast as that of universal predestination or free-will, depend on its interpretation. It therefore becomes essential that we study with some care the conditions under which the feeling of volitional effort is found.

The Feeling of Effort.—When I said, awhile back, that *consciousness* (or the neural process which goes with it) *is in its very nature impulsive*, I should have added the proviso that *it must be sufficiently intense*. Now there are remarkable differences in the power of different sorts of consciousness to excite movement. The intensity of some feelings is practically apt to be below the discharging point, whilst that of others is apt to be above it. By practically apt, I mean apt under ordinary circumstances. These circumstances may be habitual inhibitions, like that comfortable feeling of the *dolce far niente* which gives to each and all of us a certain dose of laziness only to be overcome by the acuteness of the impulsive spur; or they may consist in the native inertia, or internal resistance, of the motor centres themselves, making explosion impossible until a certain inward tension has been reached and overpassed. These conditions may vary from one person to another, and in the same person from time to time. The neural inertia may wax or wane, and the habitual inhibitions dwindle or augment. The intensity of particular thought-processes and stimulations may also change independently, and particular paths of association grow more pervious or less so. There thus result great possibilities of alteration in the actual impulsive efficacy of particular motives compared with others. It is where the normally less efficacious motive becomes more efficacious, and the normally more efficacious one less so, that actions ordinarily effortless, or abstinences ordinarily easy, either become impossible, or are effected (if at all) by the expenditure of effort. A little more description will make it plainer what these cases are.

Healthiness of Will.—*There is a certain normal ratio in the impulsive power of different mental objects, which characterizes what may be called ordinary healthiness of will,* and which is departed from only at exceptional times or by exceptional individuals. The states of mind which normally possess the most impulsive quality are either those which represent objects of passion, appetite, or emotion— objects of instinctive reaction, in short; or they are feelings or ideas of pleasure or of pain; or ideas which for any reason we have grown accustomed to obey, so that the habit of reacting on them is ingrained; or finally, in comparison with ideas of remoter objects, they are ideas of objects present or near in space and time. Compared with these various objects, all far-off considerations, all highly abstract conceptions, unaccustomed reasons, and motives foreign to the instinctive history of the race, have little or no impulsive power. They prevail, when they ever do prevail, *with effort; and the normal,* as distinguished from the pathological, *sphere of effort is thus found wherever non-instinctive motives to behavior must be reinforced so as to rule the day.*

Healthiness of will moreover requires a certain amount of complication in the process which precedes the fiat or the act. Each stimulus or idea, at the same time that it wakens its own impulse, must also arouse other ideas along with *their* characteristic impulses, and action must finally follow, neither too slowly nor too rapidly, as the resultant of all the forces thus engaged. Even when the decision is pretty prompt, the normal thing is thus a sort of preliminary survey of the field and a vision of which course is best before the fiat comes. And where the will is healthy, *the vision must be right* (i.e., the motives must be on the whole in a normal or not too unusual ratio to each other), *and the action must obey the vision's lead.*

Unhealthiness of will may thus come about in many ways. The action may follow the stimulus or idea too rapidly, leaving no time for the arousal of restraining associates—*we then have a precipitate will.* Or, although the associates may come, the ratio which the impulsive and inhibitive forces normally bear to each other may be distorted, and we then have *a will which is perverse.* The perversity, in turn, may be due to either of many causes—too much intensity, or too little, here; too much or too little inertia there; or elsewhere too much or too little inhibitory power. *If we compare the outward symptoms of perversity together, they fall into two groups,* in one of which normal actions are impossible, and in the other abnormal ones are irrepressible. Briefly, *we may call them respectively the obstructed and the explosive will.*

It must be kept in mind, however, that since the resultant action is always due to the *ratio* between the obstructive and the explosive forces which are present, we never can tell by the mere outward symptoms to what *elementary* cause the perversion of a man's will may be due, whether to an increase of one component or a diminution of the other. One may grow explosive as readily by losing the usual brakes as by getting up more of the impulsive steam; and one may find things impossible as well through the enfeeblement of the original desire as through the advent of new lions in the path. As Dr. Clouston says, "The driver may be so weak that he cannot control well-broken horses, or the horses may be so hard-mouthed that no driver can pull them up."

The Explosive Will.   i.) **From Defective Inhibition.**—There is a normal type of character, for example, in which impulses seem to discharge so promptly into movements that inhibitions get no time to arise. These are the 'dare-devil' and 'mercurial' temperaments, overflowing with animation and fizzling with talk, which are so common in the Slavic and Celtic races, and with which the cold-blooded and long-headed English character forms so marked a contrast. Simian these people seem to us, whilst we seem to them reptilian. It is quite impossible to judge, as between

an obstructed and an explosive individual, which has the greater
sum of vital energy. An explosive Italian with good perception
and intellect will cut a figure as a perfectly tremendous fellow, on
an inward capital that could be tucked away inside of an obstructed Yankee and hardly let you know that it was there. He
will be the king of his company, sing the songs and make the
speeches, lead the parties, carry out the practical jokes, kiss the
girls, fight the men, and, if need be, lead the forlorn hopes and
enterprises, so that an onlooker would think he has more life in his
little finger than can exist in the whole body of a correct judicious
fellow. But the judicious fellow all the while may have all these
possibilities and more besides, ready to break out in the same or
even a more violent way, if only the brakes were taken off. It is the
absence of scruples, of consequences, of considerations, the extraordinary simplification of each moment's mental outlook, that
gives to the explosive individual such motor energy and ease; it
need not be the greater intensity of any of his passions, motives, or
thoughts. As mental evolution goes on, the complexity of human
consciousness grows ever greater, and with it the multiplication of
the inhibitions to which every impulse is exposed. How much
freedom of discourse we English folk lose because we feel obliged
always to speak the truth! This predominance of inhibition has a
bad as well as a good side; and if a man's impulses are in the main
orderly as well as prompt, if he has courage to accept their consequences, and intellect to lead them to a successful end, he is all
the better for his hair-trigger organization, and for not being
'sicklied o'er with the pale cast of thought.' Many of the most successful military and revolutionary characters in history have belonged to this simple but quick-witted impulsive type. Problems
come much harder to reflective and inhibitive minds. They can, it
is true, solve much vaster problems; and they can avoid many a
mistake to which the men of impulse are exposed. But when the
latter do not make mistakes, or when they are always able to re-
trieve them, theirs is one of the most engaging and indispensable
of human types.

In infancy, and in certain conditions of exhaustion, as well as in
peculiar pathological states, the inhibitory power may fail to arrest the explosions of the impulsive discharge. We have then an
explosive temperament temporarily realized in an individual who
at other times may be of a relatively obstructed type. In other

persons, again, hysterics, epileptics, criminals of the neurotic class called *dégénérés* by French authors, there is such a native feebleness in the mental machinery that before the inhibitory ideas can arise the impulsive ones have already discharged into act. In persons healthy-willed by nature bad habits can bring about this condition, especially in relation to particular sorts of impulse. Ask half the common drunkards you know why it is that they fall so often a prey to temptation, and they will say that most of the time they cannot tell. It is a sort of vertigo with them. Their nervous centres have become a sluice-way pathologically unlocked by every passing conception of a bottle and a glass. They do not thirst for the beverage; the taste of it may even appear repugnant; and they perfectly foresee the morrow's remorse. But when they think of the liquor or see it, they find themselves preparing to drink, and do not stop themselves: and more than this they cannot say. Similarly a man may lead a life of incessant love-making or sexual indulgence, though what spurs him thereto seems to be trivial suggestions and notions of possibility rather than any real solid strength of passion or desire. Such characters are too flimsy even to be bad in any deep sense of the word. The paths of natural (or it may be unnatural) impulse are so pervious in them that the slightest rise in the level of innervation produces an overflow. It is the condition recognized in pathology as 'irritable weakness.' The phase known as nascency or latency is so short in the excitement of the neural tissues that there is no opportunity for strain or tension to accumulate within them; and the consequence is that with all the agitation and activity, the amount of real feeling engaged may be very small. The hysterical temperament is the playground *par excellence* of this unstable equilibrium. One of these subjects will be filled with what seems the most genuine and settled aversion to a certain line of conduct, and the very next *instant* follow the stirring of temptation and plunge in it up to the neck.

2.) **From Exaggerated Impulsion.**—Disorderly and impulsive conduct may, on the other hand, come about where the neural tissues preserve their proper inward tone, and where the inhibitory power is normal or even unusually great. In such cases *the strength of the impulsive idea is preternaturally exalted*, and what would be for most people the passing suggestion of a possibility becomes a gnawing, craving urgency to act. Works on insanity are full of examples of these morbid insistent ideas, in obstinately struggling against which the unfortunate victim's soul often sweats with agony ere at last it gets swept away.

The craving for drink in real dipsomaniacs, or for opium or chloral in those subjugated, is of a strength of which normal persons can form no conception. "Were a keg of rum in one corner of a room and were a cannon constantly discharging balls between me and it, I could not refrain from passing before that cannon in order to get at the rum"; "If a bottle of brandy stood at one hand, and the pit of hell yawned at the other, and I were convinced that I would be pushed in as sure as I took one glass, I could not refrain": such statements abound in dipsomaniacs' mouths. Dr. Mussey of Cincinnati relates this case:

"A few years ago a tippler was put into an almshouse in this State. Within a few days he had devised various expedients to procure rum, but failed. At length, however, he hit upon one which was successful. He went into the wood-yard of the establishment, placed one hand upon the block, and with an axe in the other, struck it off at a single blow. With the the stump raised and streaming, he ran into the house and cried, 'Get some rum! get some rum! My hand is off.' In the confusion and bustle of the occasion a bowl of rum was brought, into which he plunged the bleeding member of his body; then raising the bowl to his mouth, drank freely, and exultingly exclaimed, 'Now I am satisfied!' Dr. J. E. Turner tells of a man, who while under treatment for inebriety, during four weeks secretly drank the alcohol from six jars containing morbid specimens. On asking him why he had committed this loathsome act, he replied, 'Sir, it is as impossible for me to control this diseased appetite as it is for me to control the pulsations of my heart.' "

Often the insistent idea is of a trivial sort, but it may wear the patient's life out. His hands feel dirty, they must be washed. He *knows* they are not dirty; yet to get rid of the teasing idea he washes them. The idea, however, returns in a moment, and the unfortunate victim, who is not in the least deluded *intellectually*, will end by spending the whole day at the wash-stand. Or his clothes are not 'rightly' put on; and to banish the thought he takes them off and puts them on again, till his toilet consumes two or three hours of time. Most people have the potentiality of this disease. To few has it not happened to conceive, after getting into bed, that they may have forgotten to lock the front door, or to turn out the entry gas. And few of us have not on some occasion got up to repeat the performance, less because we believed in the reality of its omission than because only so could we banish the worrying doubt and get to sleep.

The Obstructed Will.—In striking contrast with the cases in which inhibition is insufficient or impulsion in excess are those in which impulsion is insufficient or inhibition in excess. We all know the condition described on p. 193, in which the mind for a few moments seems to lose its focussing power and to be unable to rally its attention to any determinate thing. At such times we sit blankly staring and do nothing. The objects of consciousness fail to touch the quick or break the skin. They are there, but do not reach the level of effectiveness. This state of non-efficacious presence is the normal condition of *some* objects, in all of us. Great fatigue or exhaustion may make it the condition of almost all objects; and an apathy resembling that then brought about is recognized in asylums under the name of *abulia* as a symptom of mental disease. The healthy state of the will requires, as aforesaid, both that vision should be right, and that action should obey its lead. But in the morbid condition in question the vision may be wholly unaffected, and the intellect clear, and yet the act either fails to follow or follows in some other way.

"*Video meliora proboque, deteriora sequor*" is the classic expression of this latter condition of mind. The moral tragedy of human life comes almost wholly from the fact that the link is ruptured which normally should hold between vision of the truth and action, and that this pungent sense of effective reality will not attach to certain ideas. Men do not differ so much in their mere feelings and conceptions. Their notions of possibility and their ideals are not as far apart as might be argued from their differing fates. No class of them have better sentiments or feel more constantly the difference between the higher and the lower path in life than the hopeless failures, the sentimentalists, the drunkards, the schemers, the 'dead-beats,' whose life is one long contradiction between knowledge and action, and who, with full command of theory, never get to holding their limp characters erect. No one eats of the fruit of the tree of knowledge as they do; so far as moral insight goes, in comparison with them the orderly and prosperous philistines whom they scandalize are sucking babes. And yet their moral knowledge, always there grumbling and rumbling in the background,—discerning, commenting, protesting, longing, half resolving,—never wholly resolves, never gets its voice out of the minor into the major key, or its speech out of the subjunctive into the imperative mood, never breaks the spell, never takes the helm into its hands. In such characters as Rousseau and Restif it would seem as if the lower motives had all the impulsive efficacy in their hands. Like trains with the right of way, they retain exclusive possession of the track. The more ideal motives exist alongside of them in profusion, but they never get switched on, and the man's conduct is no more influenced by them than an express train is influenced by a wayfarer standing by the roadside and calling to be taken aboard. They are an inert accompaniment to the end of time; and the consciousness of inward hollowness that accrues from habitually seeing the better only to do the worse, is one of the saddest feelings one can bear with him through this vale of tears.

Effort feels like an original force. We now see at one view when it is that effort complicates volition. It does so whenever a rarer and more ideal impulse is called upon to neutralize others of a more instinctive and habitual kind; it does so whenever strongly explosive tendencies are checked, or strongly obstructive conditions overcome. The *âme bien née*, the child of the sunshine, at whose birth the fairies made their gifts, does not need much of it in his life. The hero and the neurotic subject, on the other hand, do. Now our spontaneous way of conceiving the effort, under all these circumstances, is as an active force adding its strength to that of the motives which ultimately prevail. When outer forces impinge upon a body, we say that the resultant motion is in the line of least resistance, or of greatest traction. But it is a curious fact that our spontaneous language never speaks of volition with effort in this way. Of course if we proceed *a priori* and define the line of least resistance as the line that is followed, the physical law must also hold good in the mental sphere. But we *feel*, in all hard cases of volition, as if the line taken, when the rarer and more ideal motives prevail, were the line of greater resistance, and as if the line of coarser motivation were the more pervious and easy one, even at the very moment when we refuse to follow it. He who under the surgeon's knife represses cries of pain, or he who exposes himself to social obloquy for duty's sake, feels as if he were following the line of greatest temporary resistance. He speaks of conquering and overcoming his impulses and temptations.

But the sluggard, the drunkard, the coward, never talk of their conduct in that way, or say they resist their energy, overcome their sobriety, conquer their courage, and so forth. If in general we class all springs of action as propensities on the one hand and ideals on the other, the sensualist never says of his behavior that it results from a victory over his ideals, but the moralist always speaks of his as a victory over his propensities. The sensualist uses terms of inactivity, says he forgets his ideals, is deaf to duty, and so forth; which terms seem to imply that the ideal motives *per se* can be annulled without energy or effort, and that the strongest mere traction lies in the line of the propensities. The ideal impulse appears, in comparison with this, a still small voice which must be artificially reinforced to prevail. Effort is what reinforces it, making things seem as if, while the force of propensity were essentially a fixed quantity, the ideal force might be of various amount. But what determines the amount of the effort when, by its aid, an ideal motive becomes victorious over a great sensual resistance? The very greatness of the resistance itself. If the sensual propensity is small, the effort is small. The latter is *made great* by the presence of a great antagonist to overcome. And if a brief definition of ideal or moral action were required, none could be given which would better fit the appearances than this: *It is action in the line of the greatest resistance.*

The facts may be most briefly symbolized thus, P standing for the propensity, I for the ideal impulse, and E for the effort:

$$I \text{ } per \text{ } se < P.$$
$$I + E > P.$$

In other words, if E adds itself to I, P immediately offers the least resistance, and motion occurs in spite of it.

But the E does not seem to form an integral part of the I. It appears adventitious and indeterminate in advance. We can make more or less as we please, and *if* we make enough we can convert the greatest mental resistance into the least. Such, at least, is the impression which the facts spontaneously produce upon us. But we will not discuss the truth of this impression at present; let us rather continue our descriptive detail.

Pleasure and Pain as Springs of Action.—Objects and thoughts of objects start our action, but the pleasures and pains which action brings modify its course and regulate it; and later the thoughts of the pleasures and the pains acquire themselves impulsive and inhibitive power. Not that the thought of a pleasure need be itself a pleasure, usually it is the reverse—*nessun maggior dolore*—as Dante says—and not that the thought of pain need be a pain, for, as Homer says, "griefs are often afterwards an entertainment." But as present pleasures are tremendous reinforcers, and present pains tremendous inhibitors of whatever action leads to them, so the thoughts of pleasures and pains take rank amongst the thoughts which have most impulsive and inhibitive power. The precise relation which these thoughts hold to other thoughts is thus a matter demanding some attention.

If a movement feels agreeable, we repeat and repeat it as long as the pleasure lasts. If it hurts us, our muscular contractions at the instant stop. So complete is the inhibition in this latter case that it is almost impossible for a man to cut or mutilate himself slowly and deliberately—his hand invincibly refusing to bring on the pain. And there are many pleasures which, when once we have begun to taste them, make it all but obligatory to keep up the activity to which they are due. So widespread and searching is this influence of pleasures and pains upon our movements that a premature philosophy has decided that these are our only spurs to action, and that wherever they seem to be absent, it is only because they are so far on among the 'remoter' images that prompt the action that they are overlooked.

This is a great mistake, however. Important as is the influence of pleasures and pains upon our movements, they are far from being our only stimuli. With the manifestations of instinct and emotional expression, for example, they have absolutely nothing to do. Who smiles for the pleasure of the smiling, or frowns for the pleasure of the frown? Who blushes to escape the discomfort of not blushing? Or who in anger, grief, or fear is actuated to the movements which he makes by the pleasures which they yield? In all these cases the movements are discharged fatally by the *vis a tergo* which the stimulus exerts upon a nervous system framed to respond in just that way. The objects of our rage, love, or terror, the occasions of our tears and smiles, whether they be present to our senses, or whether they be merely represented in idea, have this peculiar sort of impulsive power. The *impulsive quality* of mental states is an attribute behind which we cannot go. Some states of mind have more of it than others, some have it in this direction and some in that. Feelings of pleasure and pain have it, and perceptions and imaginations of fact have it, but neither have it exclusively or peculiarly. It is of the essence of all consciousness (or of the neural process which underlies it) to instigate movement of some sort. That with one creature and object it should be of one sort, with others of another sort, is a problem for evolutionary history to explain. However the actual impulsions may have arisen, they must now be described as they exist; and those persons obey a curiously narrow teleological superstition who think themselves bound to interpret them in every instance as effects of the secret solicitancy of pleasure and repugnancy of pain. If the thought of pleasure can impel to action, surely other thoughts may. Experience only can decide which thoughts do. The chapters on Instinct and Emotion have shown us that their name is legion; and with this verdict we ought to remain contented, and not seek an illusory simplification at the cost of half the facts.

If in these our *first* acts pleasures and pains bear no part, as little do they bear in our last acts, or those artificially acquired performances which have become habitual. All the daily routine of life, our dressing and undressing, the coming and going from our work or carrying through of its various operations, is utterly without mental reference to pleasure and pain, except under rarely realized conditions. It is ideo-motor action. As I do not breathe for the pleasure of the breathing, but simply find that I *am* breathing, so I do not write for the pleasure of the writing, but simply because I have once begun, and being in a state of intellectual excitement which keeps venting itself in that way, find that I *am* writing still. Who will pretend that when he idly fingers his knife-handle at the table, it is for the sake of any pleasure which it gives him, or pain which he thereby avoids? We do all these things because at the moment we cannot help it; our nervous systems are so shaped that they overflow in just that way; and for many of our idle or purely 'nervous' and fidgety performances we can assign absolutely no *reason* at all.

Or what shall be said of a shy and unsociable man who receives point-blank an invitation to a small party? The thing is to him an abomination; but your presence exerts a compulsion on him, he can think of no excuse, and so says yes, cursing himself the while for what he does. He is unusually *sui compos* who does not every week of his life fall into some such blundering act as this. Such in-stances of *voluntas invita* show not only that our acts cannot all be conceived as effects of represented pleasure, but that they cannot even be classed as cases of represented *good*. The class 'goods' con-tains many more generally influential motives to action than the class 'pleasants.' But almost as little as under the form of pleasures do our acts invariably appear to us under the form of *goods*. All diseased impulses and pathological fixed ideas are instances to the contrary. It is the very badness of the act that gives it then its ver-tiginous fascination. Remove the prohibition, and the attraction stops. In my university days a student threw himself from an upper entry window of one of the college buildings and was nearly killed. Another student, a friend of my own, had to pass the window daily in coming and going from his room, and experi-enced a dreadful temptation to imitate the deed. Being a Catho-lic, he told his director, who said, 'All right! if you must, you must,' and added, 'Go ahead and do it,' thereby instantly quenching his desire. This director knew how to minister to a mind diseased. But we need not go to minds diseased for examples of the occasional tempting-power of simple badness and unpleas-antness as such. Everyone who has a wound or hurt anywhere, a sore tooth, e.g., will ever and anon press it just to bring out the pain. If we are near a new sort of stink, we must sniff it again just to verify once more how bad it is. This very day I have been re-peating over and over to myself a verbal jingle whose mawkish silliness was the secret of its haunting power. I loathed yet could not banish it.

What holds attention determines action. If one must have a single name for the condition upon which the impulsive and in-hibitive quality of objects depends, one had better call it their *in-terest*. 'The interesting' is a title which covers not only the pleasant and the painful, but also the morbidly fascinating, the tediously haunting, and even the simply habitual, inasmuch as the atten-tion usually travels on habitual lines, and what-we-attend-to and what-interests-us are synonymous terms. It seems as if we ought to look for the secret of an idea's impulsiveness, not in any peculiar relations which it may have with paths of motor discharge,—for *all* ideas have relations with some such paths,—but rather in a preliminary phenomenon, the *urgency, namely, with which it is able to compel attention and dominate in consciousness.* Let it once so dominate, let no other ideas succeed in displacing it, and whatever motor effects belong to it by nature will inevitably occur—its impulsion, in short, will be given to boot, and will manifest itself as a matter of course. This is what we have seen in instinct, in emotion, in common ideo-motor action, in hypnotic suggestion, in morbid impulsion, and in *voluntas invita*,—the impelling idea is simply the one which possesses the attention. It is the same where pleasure and pain are the motor spurs—they drive other thoughts from consciousness at the same time that they instigate their own characteristic 'volitional' effects. And this is also what happens at the moment of the *fiat*, in all the five types of 'decision' which we have described. In short, one does not see any case in which the steadfast occupancy of consciousness does not appear to be the prime condition of impulsive power. It is still more obviously the prime condition of inhibitive power. What checks our impulses is the mere thinking of reasons to the contrary—it is their bare presence to the mind which gives the veto, and makes acts, otherwise seductive, impossible to perform. If we could only *forget* our scruples, our doubts, our fears, what exultant energy we should for a while display!

Will is a relation between the mind and its 'ideas.' In closing in, therefore, after all these preliminaries, upon the more *intimate* nature of the volitional process, we find ourselves driven more and more exclusively to consider the conditions which make ideas prevail in the mind. With the prevalence, once there as a fact, of the motive idea, the *psychology* of volition properly stops. The movements which ensue are exclusively physiological phenomena, following according to physiological laws upon the neural events to which the idea corresponds. The *willing* terminates with the prevalence of the idea; and whether the act then follows or not is a matter quite immaterial, so far as the willing itself goes. I will to write, and the act follows. I will to sneeze, and it does not. I will that the distant table slide over the floor towards me; it also does not. My willing representation can no more instigate my sneezing-centre than it can instigate the table to activity. But in both cases it is as true and good willing as it was when I willed to write. In a word, volition is a psychic or moral fact pure and simple, and is absolutely completed when the stable state of the idea is there. The supervention of motion is a supernumerary phenomenon depending on executive ganglia whose function lies outside the mind. If the ganglia work duly, the act occurs perfectly. If they work, but work wrongly, we have St. Vitus's dance, locomotor ataxy, motor aphasia, or minor degrees of awkwardness. If they don't work at all, the act fails altogether, and we say the man is paralyzed. He may make a tremendous effort, and contract the other muscles of the body, but the paralyzed limb fails to move. In all these cases, however, the volition considered as a psychic process is intact.

Volitional effort is effort of attention. We thus find that *we reach the heart of our inquiry into volition when we ask by what process it is that the thought of any given action comes to prevail stably in the mind.* Where thoughts prevail without effort, we have sufficiently studied in the several chapters on Sensation, Association, and Attention, the laws of their advent before consciousness and of their stay. We shall not go over that ground again, for we know that interest and association are the words, let their worth be what it may, on which our explanations must perforce rely. Where, on the other hand, the prevalence of the thought is accompanied by the phenomenon of effort, the case is much less clear. Already in the chapter on Attention we postponed the final consideration of voluntary attention with effort to a later place. We have now brought things to a point at which we see that attention with effort is all that any case of volition implies. *The essential achievement of the will, in short, when it is most 'voluntary,' is to attend to a difficult object and hold it fast before the mind.* The so-doing *is* the *fiat*; and it is a mere physiological incident that when the object is thus attended to, immediate motor consequences should ensue.

Effort of attention is thus the essential phenomenon of will.[3] Every

---

[3] This *volitional* effort pure and simple must be carefully distinguished from the *muscular* effort with which it is usually confounded. The latter consists of all those peripheral feelings to which a muscular 'exertion' may give rise. These feelings, whenever they are massive and the body is not 'fresh,' are rather disagreeable, especially when accompanied by stopped breath, congested head, bruised skin of fingers, toes, or shoulders, and strained joints. And it is only *as thus disagreeable* that the mind must make its *volitional* effort in stably representing their reality and consequently bringing it about. That they happen to be made real by muscular activity is a purely accidental circumstance. There are instances where the fiat demands great volitional effort though the muscular exertion be insignificant, e.g., the getting out of bed and bathing one's self on a cold morning. Again, a soldier standing still to be fired at expects disagreeable sensations from his muscular passivity. The action of his will, in sustaining the expectation, is identical with that required for a painful muscular effort. What is hard for both is *facing an idea as real.*

reader must know by his own experience that this is so, for every reader must have felt some fiery passion's grasp. What constitutes the difficulty for a man laboring under an unwise passion of acting as if the passion were wise? Certainly there is no physical difficulty. It is as easy physically to avoid a fight as to begin one, to pocket one's money as to squander it on one's cupidities, to walk away from as towards a coquette's door. The difficulty is mental: it is that of getting the idea of the wise action to stay before our mind at all. When any strong emotional state whatever is upon us, the tendency is for no images but such as are congruous with it to come up. If others by chance offer themselves, they are instantly smothered and crowded out. If we be joyous, we cannot keep thinking of those uncertainties and risks of failure which abound upon our path; if lugubrious, we cannot think of new triumphs, travels, loves, and joys; nor if vengeful, of our oppressor's community of nature with ourselves. The cooling advice which we get from others when the fever-fit is on us is the most jarring and exasperating thing in life. Reply we cannot, so we get angry; for by a sort of self-preserving instinct which our passion has, it feels that these chill objects, if they once but gain a lodgment, will work and work until they have frozen the very vital spark from out of all our mood and brought our airy castles in ruin to the ground. Such is the inevitable effect of reasonable ideas over others—*if they can once get a quiet hearing*; and passion's cue accordingly is always and everywhere to prevent their still small voice from being heard at all. "Let me not think of that! Don't speak to me of that!" This is the sudden cry of all those who in a passion perceive some sobering considerations about to check them in mid-career. There is something so icy in this cold-water bath, something which seems so hostile to the movement of our life, so purely negative, in Reason, when she lays her corpse-like finger on our heart and says "Halt! give up! leave off! go back! sit down!" that it is no wonder that to most men the steadying influence seems, for the time being, a very minister of death.

The strong-willed man, however, is the man who hears the still small voice unflinchingly, and who, when the death-bringing consideration comes, looks at its face, consents to its presence, clings to it, affirms it, and holds it fast, in spite of the host of exciting mental images which rise in revolt against it and would expel it from the mind. Sustained in this way by a resolute effort of atten-

tion, the difficult object erelong begins to call up its own congeners and associates and ends by changing the disposition of the
man's consciousness altogether. And with his consciousness his action changes, for the new object, once stably in possession of the
field of his thoughts, infallibly produces its own motor effects.
The difficulty lies in the gaining possession of that field. Though
the spontaneous drift of thought is all the other way, the attention
must be kept strained on that one object until at last it *grows*, so as
to maintain itself before the mind with ease. This strain of the attention is the fundamental act of will. And the will's work is in
most cases practically ended when the bare presence to our
thought of the naturally unwelcome object has been secured. For
the mysterious tie between the thought and the motor centres
next comes into play, and, in a way which we cannot even guess
at, the obedience of the bodily organs follows as a matter of
course.

In all this one sees how the immediate point of application of
the volitional effort lies exclusively within the mental world. The
whole drama is a mental drama. The whole difficulty is a mental
difficulty, a difficulty with an ideal object of our thought. It is, in
one word, an *idea* to which our will applies itself, an idea which if
we let it go would slip away, but which we will not let go. *Consent
to the idea's undivided presence, this is effort's sole achievement.* Its only
function is to get this feeling of consent into the mind. And for this
there is but one way. The idea to be consented to must be kept
from flickering and going out. It must be held steadily before the
mind until it *fills* the mind. Such filling of the mind by an idea,
with its congruous associates, *is* consent to the idea and to the fact
which the idea represents. If the idea be that, or include that, of a
bodily movement of our own, then we call the consent thus la-
boriously gained a motor volition. For Nature here 'backs' us instantaneously and follows up our inward willingness by outward
changes on her own part. She does this in no other instance. Pity
she should not have been more generous, nor made a world whose
other parts were as immediately subject to our will!

On page 370, in describing the 'reasonable type' of decision, it
was said that it usually came when the right conception of the
case was found. Where, however, the right conception is an anti-
impulsive one, the whole intellectual ingenuity of the man usually
goes to work to crowd it out of sight, and to find for the emer-

gency names by the help of which the dispositions of the moment may sound sanctified, and sloth or passion may reign unchecked. How many excuses does the drunkard find when each new temptation comes! It is a new brand of liquor which the interests of intellectual culture in such matters oblige him to test; moreover it is poured out and it is sin to waste it; also others are drinking and it would be churlishness to refuse. Or it is but to enable him to sleep, or just to get through this job of work; or it isn't drinking, it is because he feels so cold; or it is Christmas-day; or it is a means of stimulating him to make a more powerful resolution in favor of abstinence than any he has hitherto made; or it is just this once, and once doesn't count, etc., etc., *ad libitum*—it is, in fact, anything you like except *being a drunkard. That* is the conception that will not stay before the poor soul's attention. But if he once gets able to pick out that way of conceiving, from all the other possible ways of conceiving the various opportunities which occur, if through thick and thin he holds to it that this is being a drunkard and is nothing else, he is not likely to remain one long. The effort by which he succeeds in keeping the right *name* unwaveringly present to his mind proves to be his saving moral act.

Everywhere, then, the function of the effort is the same: to keep affirming and adopting a thought which, if left to itself, would slip away. It may be cold and flat when the spontaneous mental drift is towards excitement, or great and arduous when the spontaneous drift is towards repose. In the one case the effort has to inhibit an explosive, in the other to arouse an obstructed will. The exhausted sailor on a wreck has a will which is obstructed. One of his ideas is that of his sore hands, of the nameless exhaustion of his whole frame which the act of farther pumping involves, and of the deliciousness of sinking into sleep. The other is that of the hungry sea ingulfing him. "Rather the aching toil!" he says; and it becomes reality then, in spite of the inhibiting influence of the relatively luxurious sensations which he gets from lying still. Often again it may be the thought of sleep and what leads to it which is the hard one to keep before the mind. If a patient afflicted with insomnia can only control the whirling chase of his ideas so far as to think of *nothing at all* (which can be done), or so far as to imagine one letter after another of a verse of scripture or poetry spelt slowly and monotonously out, it is almost certain that here, too, specific bodily effects will follow, and that sleep will come. The trouble is to keep the mind upon a train of objects naturally so insipid. *To sustain a representation, to think*, is, in short, the only moral act, for the impulsive and the obstructed, for sane and lunatics alike. Most maniacs know their thoughts to be crazy, but find them too pressing to be withstood. Compared with them the sane truths are so deadly sober, so cadaverous, that the lunatic cannot bear to look them in the face and say, "Let these alone be my reality!" But with sufficient effort, as Dr. Wigan says, "Such a man can for a time *wind himself up*, as it were, and determine that the notions of the disordered brain shall not be manifested. Many instances are on record similar to that told by Pinel, where an inmate of the Bicêtre, having stood a long cross-examination, and given every mark of restored reason, signed his name to the paper authorizing his discharge, 'Jesus Christ,' and then went off into all the vagaries connected with that delusion. In the phraseology of the gentleman whose case is related in an early part of this [Wigan's] work, he had 'held himself tight' during the examination, in order to attain his object; this once accomplished, he 'let himself down' again, and, if even *conscious* of his delusion, could not control it. I have observed with such persons that it requires a considerable time to wind themselves up to the pitch of complete self-control, and that the effort is a painful tension of the mind. When thrown off their guard by any accidental remark, or worn out by the length of the examination, they *let themselves go*, and cannot gather themselves up again without preparation."

To sum it all up in a word, *the terminus of the psychological process in volition, the point to which the will is directly applied, is always an idea.* There are at all times *some* ideas from which we shy away like frightened horses the moment we get a glimpse of their forbidding profile upon the threshold of our thought. *The only resistance which our will can possibly experience is the resistance which such an idea offers to being attended to at all.* To attend to it is the volitional act, and the only inward volitional act which we ever perform.

The Question of 'Free-will.'—As was remarked on p. 380, in the experience of effort we feel as if we might make more or less than we actually at any moment are making.

The effort appears, in other words, not as a fixed reaction on our part which the object that resists us necessarily calls forth, but as what the mathematicians call an 'independent variable' amongst the fixed data of the case, our motives, character, etc. If it be really so, if the amount of our effort is not a determinate function of those other data, then, in common parlance, *our wills are free.* If, on the contrary, the amount of effort be a fixed function, so that whatever object at any time fills our consciousness was from eternity bound to fill it then and there, and compel from us the exact effort, neither more nor less, which we bestow upon it,—then our wills are not free, and all our acts are foreordained. *The question of fact in the free-will controversy is thus extremely simple. It relates solely to the amount of effort of attention which we can at any time put forth.* Are the duration and intensity of this effort fixed functions of the object, or are they not? Now, as I just said, it *seems* as if we might exert more or less in any given case. When a man has let his thoughts go for days and weeks until at last they culminate in some particularly dirty or cowardly or cruel act, it is hard to persuade him, in the midst of his remorse, that he might not have reined them in; hard to make him believe that this whole goodly universe (which his act so jars upon) required and exacted it of him at that fatal moment, and from eternity made aught else impossible. But, on the other hand, there is the certainty that all his *effortless* volitions are resultants of interests and associations whose strength and sequence are mechanically determined by the structure of that physical mass, his brain; and the general continuity of things and the monistic conception of the world may lead one irresistibly to postulate that a little fact like effort can form no real exception to the overwhelming reign of deterministic law. Even in effortless volition we have the consciousness of the alternative being also possible. This is surely a delusion here; why is it not a delusion everywhere?

The fact is that the question of free-will is insoluble on strictly psychologic grounds. After a certain amount of effort of attention has been given to an idea, it is manifestly impossible to tell whether either more or less of it *might* have been given or not. To tell that, we should have to ascend to the antecedents of the effort, and defining them with mathematical exactitude, prove, by laws of which we have not at present even an inkling, that the only amount of sequent effort which could *possibly* comport with them was the precise amount that actually came. Such measurements, whether of psychic or of neural quantities, and such deductive reasonings as this method of proof implies, will surely be forever beyond human reach. No serious psychologist or physiologist will venture even to suggest a notion of how they might be practically made. Had one no motives drawn from elsewhere to make one partial to either solution, one might easily leave the matter undecided. But a psychologist cannot be expected to be thus impartial, having a great motive in favor of determinism. He wants to build a *Science*; and a Science is a system of fixed relations. Wherever there are independent variables, there Science stops. So far, then, as our volitions may be independent variables, a scientific psychology must ignore that fact, and treat of them only so far as they are fixed functions. In other words, she must deal with the *general laws* of volition exclusively; with the impulsive and inhibitory character of ideas; with the nature of their appeals to the attention; with the conditions under which effort may arise, etc.; but not with the precise amounts of effort, for these, if our wills be free, are impossible to compute. She thus abstracts from free-will, without necessarily denying its existence. Practically, however, such abstraction is not distinguished from rejection; and most actual psychologists have no hesitation in denying that free-will exists.

For ourselves, we can hand the free-will controversy over to metaphysics. Psychology will surely never grow refined enough to discover, in the case of any individual's decision, a discrepancy between her scientific calculations and the fact. Her prevision will never foretell, whether the effort be completely predestinate or not, the way in which each individual emergency is resolved. Psychology will be psychology, and Science science, as much as ever (as much and no more) in this world, whether free-will be true in it or not.

We can thus ignore the free-will question in psychology. As we said on p. 387, the operation of free effort, if it existed, could only be to hold some one ideal object, or part of an object, a little longer or a little more intensely before the mind. Amongst the alternatives which present themselves as *genuine possibles*, it would thus make one effective. And although such quickening of one idea might be morally and historically momentous, yet, if considered *dynamically*, it would be an operation amongst those physiological infinitesimals which an actual science must forever neglect.

Ethical Importance of the Phenomenon of Effort.—But whilst eliminating the question about the amount of our effort as one which psychology will never have a practical call to decide, I must say one word about the extraordinarily intimate and important character which the phenomenon of effort assumes in our own eyes as individual men. Of course we measure ourselves by many standards. Our strength and our intelligence, our wealth and even our good luck, are things which warm our heart and make us feel ourselves a match for life. But deeper than all such things, and able to suffice unto itself without them, is the sense of the amount of effort which we can put forth. Those are, after all, but effects, products, and reflections of the outer world within. But the effort seems to belong to an altogether different realm, as if it were the substantive thing which we *are*, and those were but externals which we *carry*. If the 'searching of our heart and reins' be the purpose of this human drama, then what is sought seems to be what effort we can make. He who can make none is but a shadow; he who can make much is a hero. The huge world that girdles us about puts all sorts of questions to us, and tests us in all sorts of ways. Some of the tests we meet by actions that are easy, and some of the questions we answer in articulately formulated words. But the deepest question that is ever asked admits of no reply but the dumb turning of the will and the tightening of our heart-strings as we say, "*Yes, I will even have it so!*" When a dreadful object is presented, or when life as a whole turns up its dark abysses to our view, then the worthless ones among us lose their hold on the situation altogether, and either escape from its difficulties by averting their attention, or if they cannot do that, collapse into yielding masses of plaintiveness and fear. The effort required for facing and consenting to such objects is beyond their power to make. But the heroic mind does differently. To it, too, the objects are sinister and dreadful, unwelcome, incompatible with wished-for things. But it can face them if necessary, without for that losing its hold upon the rest of life. The world thus finds in the heroic man its worthy match and mate; and the effort which he is able to put forth to hold himself erect and keep his heart unshaken is the direct measure of his worth and function in the game of human life. He can *stand* this Universe. He can meet it and keep up his faith in it in presence of those same features which lay his weaker brethren low. He can still find a zest in it, not by 'ostrich-like forgetfulness,' but by pure inward willingness to take it with those deterrent objects there. And hereby he makes himself one of the masters and the lords of life. He must be counted with henceforth;

he forms a part of human destiny. Neither in the theoretic nor in the practical sphere do we care for, or go for help to, those who have no head for risks, or sense for living on the perilous edge. Our religious life lies more, our practical life lies less, than it used to, on the perilous edge. But just as our courage is so often a reflex of another's courage, so our faith is apt to be a faith in someone else's faith. We draw new life from the heroic example. The prophet has drunk more deeply than anyone of the cup of bitterness, but his countenance is so unshaken and he speaks such mighty words of cheer that his will becomes our will, and our life is kindled at his own.

Thus not only our morality but our religion, so far as the latter is deliberate, depend on the effort which we can make. "*Will you or won't you have it so?*" is the most probing question we are ever asked; we are asked it every hour of the day, and about the largest as well as the smallest, the most theoretical as well as the most practical, things. We answer by *consents or non-consents* and not by words. What wonder that these dumb responses should seem our deepest organs of communication with the nature of things! What wonder if the effort demanded by them be the measure of our worth as men! What wonder if the amount which we accord of it were the one strictly underived and original contribution which we make to the world!

Epilogue

Psychology and Philosophy

What the Word Metaphysics means.—In the last chapter we handed the question of free-will over to 'metaphysics.' It would indeed have been hasty to settle the question absolutely, inside the limits of psychology. Let psychology frankly admit that *for her scientific purposes* determinism may be *claimed*, and no one can find fault. If, then, it turn out later that the claim has only a relative purpose, and may be crossed by counter-claims, the readjustment can be made. Now ethics makes a counter-claim; and the present writer, for one, has no hesitation in regarding her claim as the stronger, and in assuming that our wills are 'free.' For him, then, the deterministic assumption of psychology is merely provisional and methodological. This is no place to argue the ethical point; and I only mention the conflict to show that all these special sciences, marked off for convenience from the remaining body of truth (cf. p. 9), must hold their assumptions and results subject to revision in the light of each other's needs. The forum where they hold discussion is called metaphysics. Metaphysics means only an unusually obstinate attempt to think clearly and consistently. The special sciences all deal with data that are full of obscurity and contradiction; but from the point of view of their limited purposes these defects may be overlooked. Hence the disparaging use of the name metaphysics which is so common. To a man with a limited purpose any discussion that is over-subtle for that purpose is branded as 'metaphysical.' A geologist's purposes fall short of understanding Time itself. A mechanist need not know how action and reaction are possible at all. A psychologist has enough to do without asking how both he and the mind which he studies are able to take cognizance of the same outer world. But it is obvious that problems irrelevant from one standpoint may be essential from another. And as soon as one's purpose is the attainment of the maximum of possible insight into the world as a whole, the metaphysical puzzles become the most urgent ones of all. Psychology contributes to general philosophy her full share of these; and I propose in this last chapter to indicate briefly which of them seem the more important. And first, of the

Relation of Consciousness to the Brain.—When psychology is treated as a natural science (after the fashion in which it has been treated in this book), 'states of mind' are taken for granted, as data immediately given in experience; and the working hypothesis (see p. 13) is the mere empirical law that to the entire state of the brain at any moment one unique state of mind always 'corresponds.' This does very well till we begin to be metaphysical and ask ourselves just what we mean by such a word as 'corresponds.' This notion appears dark in the extreme, the moment we seek to translate it into something more intimate than mere parallel variation. Some think they make the notion of it clearer by calling the mental state and the brain the inner and outer 'aspects,' respectively, of 'One and the Same Reality.' Others consider the mental state as the 'reaction' of a unitary being, the Soul, upon the multiple activities which the brain presents. Others again comminute the mystery by supposing each brain-cell to be separately conscious, and the empirically given mental state to be the appearance of all the little consciousnesses fused into one, just as the 'brain' itself is the appearance of all the cells together, when looked at from one point of view.

We may call these three metaphysical attempts the *monistic*, the *spiritualistic*, and the *atomistic* theories respectively. Each has its difficulties, of which it seems to me that those of the spiritualistic theory are *logically* much the least grave. But the spiritualistic theory is quite out of touch with the facts of multiple consciousness, alternate personality, etc. (pp. 184–190). These lend themselves more naturally to the atomistic formulation, for it seems easier to think of a lot of minor consciousnesses now gathering together into one large mass, and now into several smaller ones, than of a Soul now reacting totally, now breaking into several disconnected simultaneous reactions. The localization of brain-functions also makes for the atomistic view. If in my experience, say of a bell, it is my occipital lobes which are the condition of its being seen, and my temporal lobes which are the condition of its being heard, what is more natural than to say that the former *see* it and the latter *hear* it, and then 'combine their information'? In view of the extreme naturalness of such a way of representing the well-established fact that the appearance of the several parts of an object to consciousness at any moment does depend on as many several parts of the brain being then active, all such objections as were urged, on pp. 27, 58, and elsewhere, to the notion that 'parts' of consciousness *can* 'combine' will be rejected as far-fetched, unreal, and 'metaphysical' by the atomistic philosopher. His 'purpose' is to gain a formula which shall unify things in a natural and easy manner, and for such a purpose the atomistic theory seems expressly made to his hand.

But the difficulty with the problem of 'correspondence' is not only that of solving it, it is that of even stating it in elementary terms.

"L'ombre en ce lieu s'amasse, et la nuit est la toute."

Before we can know just what sort of goings-on occur when thought corresponds to a change in the brain, we must know the *subjects* of the goings-on. We must know which sort of mental fact and which sort of cerebral fact are, so to speak, in immediate juxtaposition. We must find the minimal mental fact whose being reposes directly on a brain-fact; and we must similarly find the minimal brain-event which can have a mental counterpart at all. Between the mental and the physical minima thus found there will be an immediate relation, the expression of which, if we had it, would be the elementary psycho-physic law.

Our own formula has escaped the metempiric assumption of psychic atoms by *taking the entire thought* (even of a complex object) *as the minimum with which it deals on the mental* side, and the entire brain as the minimum on the physical side. But the 'entire brain' is not a physical fact at all! It is nothing but our name for the way in which a billion of molecules arranged in certain positions may affect our sense. On the principles of the corpuscular or mechanical philosophy, the only realities are the separate molecules, or at most the cells. Their aggregation into a 'brain' is a fiction of popular speech. Such a figment cannot serve as the objectively real counterpart to any psychic state whatever. Only a genuinely physical fact can so serve, and the molecular fact is the only genuine physical fact. Whereupon we seem, if we are to have an elementary psycho-physic law at all, thrust right back upon something like the mental-atom-theory, for the molecular fact, being an element of the 'brain,' would seem naturally to correspond, not to total thoughts, but to elements of thoughts. Thus the real in psychics seems to 'correspond' to the unreal in physics, and *vice versa*; and our perplexity is extreme.

The Relation of States of Mind to their 'Objects.'—The perplexity is not diminished when we reflect upon our assumption that states of consciousness can *know* (pp. 10–11). From the common-sense point of view (which is that of all the natural sciences) knowledge is an ultimate relation between two mutually external entities, the knower and the known. The world first exists, and then the states of mind; and these gain a cognizance of the world which gets gradually more and more complete. But it is hard to carry through this simple dualism, for idealistic reflections will intrude. Take the states of mind called pure sensations (so far as such may exist), that for example of *blue*, which we may get from looking into the zenith on a clear day. Is the blue a determination of the feeling itself, or of its 'object'? Shall we describe the experience as a quality of our feeling or as our feeling of a quality? Ordinary speech vacillates incessantly on this point. The ambiguous word 'content' has been recently invented instead of 'object,' to escape a decision; for 'content' suggests something not exactly out of the feeling, nor yet exactly identical with the feeling, since the latter remains suggested as the container or vessel. Yet of our feelings as vessels apart from their content we really have no clear notion whatever. The fact is that such an experience as *blue*, as it is immediately given, can only be called by some such neutral name as that of *phenomenon*. It does not *come* to us *immediately* as a relation between two realities, one mental and one physical. It is only when, still thinking of it as the *same* blue (cf. p. 210), we trace relations between it and other things, that it doubles itself, so to speak, and develops in two directions; and, taken in connection with some associates, figures as a physical quality, whilst with others it figures as a feeling in the mind.

Our non-sensational, or conceptual, states of mind, on the other hand, seem to obey a different law. They present themselves immediately as referring beyond themselves. Although they also possess an immediately given 'content,' they have a 'fringe' beyond it (p. 153), and claim to 'represent' something else than it. The 'blue' we have just spoken of, for instance, was, substantively considered, a *word*; but it was a word with a *meaning*. The quality blue was the *object* of the thought, the word was its *content*. The mental state, in short, was not self-sufficient as sensations are, but expressly pointed at something more in which it meant to terminate.

But the moment when, as in sensations, object and conscious state seem to be different ways of considering one and the same fact, it becomes hard to justify our denial that mental states consist of parts. The blue sky, considered physically, is a sum of mutually external parts; why is it not such a sum, when considered as a content of sensation?

The only result that is plain from all this is that the relations of the known and the knower are infinitely complicated, and that a genial, whole-hearted, popular-science way of formulating them will not suffice. The only possible path to understanding them lies through metaphysical subtlety; and Idealism and *Erkenntnisstheorie* must say their say before the natural-science assumption that thoughts 'know' things grows clear.

The changing character of consciousness presents another puzzle. We first assumed conscious 'states' as the units with which psychology deals, and we said later that they were in constant change. Yet any state must have a certain duration to be *effective* at all—a pain which lasted but a hundredth of a second would practically be no pain—and the question comes up, how long may a state last and still be treated as *one* state? In time-perception for example, if the 'present' as known (the 'specious present,' as we called it) may be a dozen seconds long (p. 246), how long need the present as knower be? That is, what is the minimum duration of the consciousness in which those twelve seconds can be apprehended as just past, the minimum which can be called a 'state,' for such a cognitive purpose? Consciousness, as a process in time, offers the paradoxes which have been found in all continuous change. There are no 'states' in such a thing, any more than there are facets in a circle, or places where an arrow 'is' when it flies. The vertical raised upon the time-line on which (p. 249) we represented the past to be 'projected' at any given instant of memory, is only an ideal construction. Yet anything broader than that vertical *is* not, for the *actual* present is only the joint between the past and future and has no breadth of its own. Where everything is change and process, how can we talk of 'state'? Yet how can we do without 'states,' in describing what the vehicles of our knowledge seem to be?

States of consciousness themselves are not verifiable facts. But 'worse remains behind.' Neither common-sense, nor psychology so far as it has yet been written, has ever doubted that the states of consciousness which that science studies are immediate data of experience. 'Things' have been doubted, but thoughts and feelings have never been doubted. The outer world, but never the inner world, has been denied. Everyone assumes that we have direct introspective acquaintance with our thinking activity as such, with our consciousness as something inward and contrasted with the outer objects which it knows. Yet I must confess that for my part I cannot feel sure of this conclusion. Whenever I try to become sensible of my thinking activity as such, what I catch is some bodily fact, an impression coming from my brow, or head, or throat, or nose. It seems as if consciousness as an inner activity were rather a *postulate* than a sensibly given fact, the postulate, namely, of a *knower* as correlative to all this known; and as if '*scious*ness' might be a better word by which to describe it. But 'sciousness postulated as an hypothesis' is practically a very different thing from 'states of consciousness apprehended with infallible certainty by an inner sense.' For one thing, it throws the question of *who the knower really is* wide open again, and makes the answer which we gave to it at the end of Chapter XII a mere provisional statement from a popular and prejudiced point of view.

Conclusion.—When, then, we talk of 'psychology as a natural science,' we must not assume that that means a sort of psychology that stands at last on solid ground. It means just the reverse; it means a psychology particularly fragile, and into which the waters of metaphysical criticism leak at every joint, a psychology all of whose elementary assumptions and data must be reconsidered in wider connections and translated into other terms. It is, in short, a phrase of diffidence, and not of arrogance; and it is indeed strange to hear people talk triumphantly of 'the New Psychology,' and write 'Histories of Psychology,' when into the real elements and forces which the word covers not the first glimpse of clear insight exists. A string of raw facts; a little gossip and wrangle about opinions; a little classification and generalization on the mere descriptive level; a strong prejudice that we *have* states of mind, and that our brain conditions them: but not a single law in the sense in which physics shows us laws, not a single proposition from which any consequence can causally be deduced. We don't even know the terms between which the elementary laws would obtain if we had them (p. 398). This is no science, it is only the hope of a science. The matter of a science is with us. Something definite happens when to a certain brain-state a certain 'sciousness' corresponds. A genuine glimpse into what it is would be *the* scientific achievement, before which all past achievements would pale. But at present psychology is in the condition of physics before Galileo and the laws of motion, of chemistry before Lavoisier and the notion that mass is preserved in all reactions. The Galileo and the Lavoisier of psychology will be famous men indeed when they come, as come they some day surely will, or past successes are no index to the future. When they do come, however, the necessities of the case will make them 'metaphysical.' Meanwhile the best way in which we can facilitate their advent is to understand how great is the darkness in which we grope, and never to forget that the natural-science assumptions with which we started are provisional and revisable things.

THE END

Index

James's Index for *Psychology: Briefer Course* has been rekeyed to the pages of the present edition. Anomalies in accidental matters, including mechanical errors of typography, punctuation, and alphabetizing, have been corrected silently, with one exception: 'thought,' with the comma changed from a semicolon, appears in the Emendations list (410.1b), as being a plate alteration.

Approximately twenty-five errors of varying kinds which could be called substantive were found and corrected silently, again with one exception: 'Schaefer' was emended to 'Schäfer' as elsewhere in the text, and this change also appears in the Emendations list (409.13a, found at 112.21). Page numbers were occasionally off by a digit or more, as with 'Experience, 218', which should have been '217' (rekeyed to 192). In three cases chapter numbers were incorrect. Sometimes a word was spelled wrong, as 'Longituditional', corrected to 'Longitudinal'.

In one instance, under the general entry 'Discrimination' the heading 'hearing' was omitted before the page number, and this was supplied. Under the entry 'Spontaneous trains of thought' the page number '271' referred to a paragraph with the heading 'Summary concerning Spontaneous Trains of Thought' that was deleted in the fourth printing (see Emendations entry 238.5 and Textual Note ad loc.), and so this reference is omitted in the present edition.

Index

object must change to hold attention, 199; objects as signs and as realities, 300; relation of states of mind to their object, 398
Occipital lobes, seat of visual centre, 105
Old-fogyism vs. genius, 285
Olfactory lobes, 80, 82
Olivary bodies, 83
Optic nerve, 80, 86
Optic tracts, 82
Original force, effort feels like one, 380
Overtones, 57

Pain, 67 ff.; pain and pleasure as springs of action, 381
PASCAL, 197
Past time, known in a present feeling, 249; the immediate past is a portion of the present duration-block, 245
PAULHAN, 194
Pedagogic remarks on habit, 132; on attention, 207
Peduncles, 82, 83
Perception, Chapter XX; compared with sensation, 273; involves reproductive processes, 273; the perceptive state of mind is not a compound, 274; perception is of definite and probable things, 276; illusory perceptions, 277; physiological process of perception, 287
Perception of Space, Chapter XXI
PEREZ, M., 353
Personal Identity, 179; mutations of, 183 ff.; alternating personality, 183 ff.
Personality, alterations of, 183 ff.
Philosophy, Psychology and, Epilogue, 395
Phosphorus and thought, 123
Pia mater, 80
Pigeons' lower centres, 94
Pitch, 55–56
Pituitary body, 80, 86
Place, a series of positions, 297
Plasticity, as basis of habit, defined, 126
PLATO, 211
Play, 351
Pleasure, and pain, as springs of action, 381
Pons Varolii, 77, 82, 104
Positions, place a series of, 297
Practice, improves discrimination, 221
Present, the present moment, 245
Pressure sense, 61

PREYER, 351
Probability determines what object shall be perceived, 276, 287
Problematic conceptions, 211
Problems, solution of, 239
Projection of sensations, eccentric, 20
Psychology and Philosophy, Epilogue, 395
Psychology, defined, 9; a natural science, 10; what data it assumes, 10; Psychology and Philosophy, Epilogue
Psycho-physic law, 21, 27, 47, 59, 67, 68
Pugnacity, 351
PURKINJE, 74
Pyramids, 82

Quality, 18, 27, 28, 57

RAEHLMANN, 303
Rationality, 157
Reaction-time, 114 ff.
Real magnitude, determined by æsthetic and practical interests, 299
Real space, 294
Reason, 224
Reasoning, Chapter XXII; what it is, 305; involves use of abstract characters, 306; what is meant by an essential character, 308; the essence is always for a subjective interest, 310; two great points in reasoning, 312; sagacity, 314; help from association by similarity, 316; reasoning power of brutes, 318
Recall, 252
Recency, determines association, 233
'Recepts,' 318
Recognition, 261
Recollection, 252 ff.
Redintegration, 232
Reflex acts, defined, 90; reaction-time measures one, 115; concatenated habits are constituted by a chain of, 130
REID, 274
Relations, between objects, 148; feelings of, 148
'*Relativity* of knowledge,' 28
Reproduction in memory, 252 ff.; voluntary, 238
Resemblance, 213
Retention in memory, 252
Retentiveness, organic, 254; it is unchangeable, 258–259
Retina, peripheral parts of, act as sentinels, 73

Notes

Appendix

A Note on the Editorial Method

The Text of
Psychology: Briefer Course

Apparatus

General Index

Key to the Pagination of Editions

Notes

The William James Collection is housed in the Houghton Library of Harvard University. It can be identified by the call number 'MS Am 1092', with sometimes either 'b' or 'f' as a prefix and a decimal following the numeral '2'. Many books from James's library are also preserved there; many of these are sufficiently identified by their call numbers which begin either with 'WJ' or 'AC'. Other books from his library are in Harvard's Widener Library and elsewhere, and in such cases their location is stated. Still others were sold and have not been located. However, Ralph Barton Perry made a list, noting markings and annotations; this unpublished list can be consulted at Houghton.

Since work on this edition began, the Houghton Library has reclassified the manuscripts and many letters in the James Collection. A new and detailed guide was prepared in the spring of 1977. The new call numbers are used in the present notes. Apparently, in time, the 'WJ' class will be eliminated, but thus far only a few books have been affected. Some books have been transferred recently from Widener into Houghton, while others, reported by Perry as sold or not listed at all, have turned up in the Widener stacks. The concluding volumes of this edition will contain a complete account of James's library and will give the then current call numbers and locations. Since the same volumes will contain James's annotations, extensively indexed, only those annotations that appear to have a direct bearing upon the text at hand are noted in the present volume.

James was a very active reader who filled his books with annotations and markings. The term 'markings' refers to underlining, vertical lines in margins, exclamation points, question marks, the notation 'N.B.', and 'Qu' for 'quote'. James's style of marking is distinctive: the N.B.'s are such that the same vertical stroke serves for both the 'N' and the 'B', while his underlining often has a peculiar waver. Furthermore, James habitually filled the flyleaves of his books with indexes, in some cases simply jotting down a page number or two, in others, noting numerous subjects and marking passages for attention or quotation. Pages singled out in this fashion usually have markings. Thus, for books protected in Houghton, the risk of error in attributing a given marking to James is slight. The risk is greater for materials in open stacks such as those in Widener, where the only claim made is that the book was owned or used by James and that there are markings. Where the books have been sold, we are totally dependent upon Perry's reports.

In abridging *The Principles of Psychology* James omitted most of the quotations and references and did not use the opportunity to incorporate later research. A reader familiar only with *Briefer Course* will get the mistaken impression that James was not familiar with the relevant literature and in the early 1890s was not keeping up with developments in psychology. Evidence that he did is provided by the annotations in his private copy of *Principles*, reprinted in WORKS, pp. 1443–1481, and the annotations in his copy of *Briefer Course*, reprinted in the present volume.

Most of the references in *Briefer Course* represent material used in *Principles*, the physiological accounts borrowed from Henry Newell Martin being the major exceptions, but with the documentation omitted. It seemed useful to add in parentheses references to *Principles* where the *Briefer Course* note is based on documentation supplied by James himself in *Principles*.

Works by James already published in the present edition are cited in this edition, identified as WORKS, while others are cited in the original editions.

1.3 class-room] The close connection between the *Briefer Course* and teaching is shown by the incomplete pre-publication copies described in Professor Bowers' textual introduction.

1.22 *Principles*] That *The Principles of Psychology* is unsystematic and poorly organized is a point made in an unsigned review in *Science*, 16 (October 10, 1890), 207–208: "Indeed, one derives the impression that this guiding principle is none other than the personal interests of the author. He has gathered together the various problems of which he has at various times made special study (and in part published the results), and added thereto certain other chapters allied to these in the way of introduction or corollary. It is not, and makes no pretence of being, a systematic work" (p. 207). James Sully, *Mind*, 16 (July 1891), 393–404, voices a similar judgment: "Prof. James frankly tells us that a good number of his chapters are reprints, with more or less considerable alterations, of papers sent to this and other journals. Now, to adapt a series of papers, some of which have appeared in popular magazines, to the exigencies of a scientific text-book does not strike one as an easy task, and our author has not altogether escaped the risks of the undertaking. In truth, an intelligent reader might have guessed that the book had formed itself in the way described. Thus the want of a rigorous sequence, of that progressive development which is essential to the exposition of a body of scientific doctrine, strikes the eye at a first glance. The order of subjects is not always clear, the experienced eye spies ominous gaps" (p. 393). Charles Sanders Peirce was the reviewer in the *Nation*, 53 (July 2, 1891), 15; (July 9), 32–33. According to Peirce, "Prof. James is continually wresting words and phrases of exact import to unauthorized and unsuitable uses. He indulges himself with idiosyncracies of diction and tricks of language such as usually spring up in households of great talent." The book on the whole is a "large assortment of somewhat heterogeneous articles loosely tied up in one bag, with tendencies towards sprawling" (p. 15). Granville Stanley Hall, *American Journal of Psychology*, 3 (February 1891), 578–591, describes James as an "*impressionist* in psychology" whose "portfolio contains sketches old and new" (p. 585). George Santayana in a friendly review, *Atlantic Monthly*, 67 (April 1891), 552–556, notes that the book is "essentially a collection of monographs, and in fact many of the chapters have already appeared in various reviews" (p. 553). James Mark Baldwin, *Educational Review*, 1 (April 1891), 357–371, draws attention to the same fact and notes that not all of the essays have been "revised and brought down to the latest publications" (p. 357).

I am aware of one major exception. Josiah Royce, *International Journal of Ethics*, 1 (January 1891), 143–169, does not voice the standard complaint.

9.2 Ladd] George Trumbull Ladd (1842–1921), American philosopher and psychologist, *Outlines of Physiological Psychology* (New York: Charles Scribner's Sons, 1891), p. 3. For the relations between James and Ladd see *Principles*, Works, note to 18.38.

9.8 **Psychology**] James's account of the limits of psychology as a natural science covers ground dealt with in *Principles* (Works, pp. 6–7, 183–184) but is completely rewritten. In *Principles* in this context it is not stated that "farther reflection leads to idealism" and there is no mention of a rational psychology distinct from empirical. In "A Plea for Psychology as a 'Natural Science'" James expresses the hope that the abridgment of his view in *Briefer Course* should have made it clearer (*Essays in Psychology*, Works, pp. 270–271).

10.15 *Thoughts*] The *Principles* list of the irreducible data of psychology contains four items (Works, p. 184).

11.3 **human**] For James's view of animal psychology see *Principles*, Works, p. 193.

12.1 Spencerian] Herbert Spencer (1820–1903), *The Principles of Psychology*, 2 vols. (New York: D. Appleton, 1871–1873) (WJ 582.24.6), I, 387 (sec. 173). For the text and a note on James's view of Spencer see *Principles*, Works, note to 19.24.

13.18 function] In *Human Immortality* (*Essays in Religion and Morality*, Works, p. 86), James distinguishes between productive and transmissive functions and argues that thought need not be a product of the brain.

17.10 Lewes] George Henry Lewes (1817–1878), English philosopher and writer, *The Physiology of Common Life*, 2 vols. (Edinburgh: Blackwood, 1859–1860), ch. 8 (II, 1–80) on "Feeling and Thinking." For works by Lewes from James's library see *Principles*, Works, note to 22.14.

17.10 Wundt] Wilhelm Wundt (1832–1920), German psychologist and philosopher. Wundt discusses the doctrine of specific energies in the *Grundzüge der physiologischen Psychologie*, 2nd ed., 2 vols. (Leipzig: W. Engelmann, 1880) (WJ 796.59.4), I, 318–321, in the section titled "Kritik der Lehre von der specifischen Energie." Also preserved is James's copy of the first edition (Leipzig: W. Engelmann, 1874) (WJ 796.59.2). Perry reports that both volumes of the fourth edition (Leipzig: W. Engelmann, 1893), with some annotations, were sold. Neither volume of the third (Leipzig: W. Engelmann, 1887) has been located. In volume I of his copy of the second edition James inserted a list of changes made in the fourth edition. This list contains the entry "Specific Energies, 329–31." For James's reading of the two later editions see *Essays in Psychology*, Works, note to 295.1.

17.10 Rosenthal] Isidor Rosenthal (1836–1915), German physiologist, "Die spezifischen Energien der Nerven," *Biologisches Centralblatt*, 4 (1884), 54–64, 78–87, 116–127, 154–160.

17.11 Goldscheider] Alfred Goldscheider (1858–1935), German physiologist.

In *Principles*, WORKS, p. 809, James cites Goldscheider's work on temperature and pressure spots of the skin.

19.5 **'Knowledge]** This distinction is developed in *Principles*, WORKS, pp. 216–218; James borrows the terms from John Grote (1813–1866), British philosopher. For the reference see *Principles*, WORKS, note to 217.39.

19.16 Condillac's] Étienne Bonnot, Abbé de Condillac (1715–1780), French philosopher. For the reference see *Principles*, WORKS, note to 653.29.

19.28–29 philosophers] For the names of some of the philosophers see *Principles*, WORKS, pp. 654n, 658n–659n.

19.35 *presence]* This appears to be a summary of *Principles*, WORKS, pp. 927–935.

20.14 'projected'] James discusses this theory and provides references in *Principles*, WORKS, pp. 678–689.

20.19 infant] For the remainder of this section James is drawing heavily upon *Principles*, WORKS, pp. 657–658.

21.4 blooming] See *Principles*, WORKS, p. 462.

21.17 Fechner] Gustav Theodor Fechner (1801–1887), German philosopher, physicist, and psychologist, *Elemente der Psychophysik*, 2 vols. (Leipzig: Breitkopf und Härtel, 1860) (WJ 727.13), II, 526–530, quoted by James in *Human Immortality*, reprinted in *Essays in Religion and Morality*, WORKS, pp. 90n–92n. Chapter 4 of *A Pluralistic Universe* is devoted to a general assessment of Fechner's thought.

21.33 **Weber's]** Ernst Heinrich Weber (1795–1878), German physiologist, "Der Tastsinn und das Gemeingefühl," in *Handwörterbuch der Physiologie*, ed. Rudolph Wagner, vol. III, pt. 2 (Braunschweig: Vieweg, 1846), pp. 481–588.

22.1 FIG. 1] The figure is from Theodor Ziehen (1862–1950), German psychiatrist, *Leitfaden der physiologischen Psychologie* (Jena: Fischer, 1891), p. 29. James's annotated copy is in Houghton (Phil 5265.1*). In Widener there is a copy of the third edition (1896) inscribed to James by the author (Phil 5265.1.2).

22.20 FIG. 2] Ziehen, p. 30.

23.1 Wundt's] Wilhelm Wundt, *Vorlesungen über die Menschen- und Thierseele*, 2 vols. (Leipzig: Voss, 1863), I, 88–90. Only vol. II is preserved (WJ 796.59.8). Also preserved is the English translation by J. E. Creighton and E. B. Titchener of the second edition (1892) (London: Swan Sonnenschein, 1894) (WJ 796.59.10), annotated primarily for teaching purposes.

24.31 "We] *Vorlesungen*, I, 91–92.

25.1 "So] *Vorlesungen*, I, 98.

26.12 Fechner's] For a more colorful formulation of the same view see *Principles*, WORKS, p. 518.

26.37 Fechner] For the method see *Principles*, WORKS, pp. 510–511.

27.6 Münsterberg] Hugo Münsterberg (1863–1916), German-born psychologist, James's colleague at Harvard, *Beiträge zur experimentellen Psychologie*, 4 pts. (Freiburg i. B.: J. C. B. Mohr, 1889–1892) (WJ 757.62), pt. 3 (1890), pp. 3–4. For the relations between James and Münsterberg see *Principles*, WORKS, note to 84.32.

27.37 **Relativity**] In *Principles* James holds that the law of relativity is "flatly disproved" by certain facts (WORKS, p. 661), although it is not clear that he has exactly the same principle in mind.

28.20 Wundt's] For references to Wundt see *Principles*, WORKS, p. 675n.

28.22 Hobbes's] For the statement by Hobbes see *Principles*, WORKS, p. 660n.

28.36 Hering's] Ewald Hering (1834–1918), German physiologist. No source is cited by Ziehen.

29.2 Weber] "Der Tastsinn und das Gemeingefühl," pp. 512–513.

29.3 Urbantschitsch] Victor Urbantschitsch (1847–1921), "Über den Einfluss einer Sinneserregung auf die übrigen Sinnesempfindungen," *Archiv für die gesammte Physiologie*, 42 (1888), 154–182.

29.22 Helmholtz] Hermann Ludwig Ferdinand von Helmholtz (1821–1894), German physiologist and physicist, *Handbuch der physiologischen Optik* (Leipzig: Voss, 1867), p. 408. For the text see *Principles*, WORKS, p. 666. For James's contacts with Helmholtz see *Principles*, WORKS, note to 92.16.

29.37 Hering] In *Principles*, WORKS, p. 668n, James cites Ewald Hering, *Zur Lehre vom Lichtsinne* (Vienna: Carl Gerold's Sohn, 1878), pp. 24–28.

31.6 Bird's] Golding Bird (1814–1854), English physician and medical writer.

32.1 FIG. 3] The figure could be based on Henry Newell Martin (1848–1896), Irish-born biologist, active in the United States, *The Human Body: An Account of Its Structure and Activities and the Conditions of Its Healthy Working* (New York: Henry Holt, 1881), p. 485, but similar illustrations appear in numerous books.

34.1 FIG. 5] Émile Küss (1815–1871), French physiologist, *A Course of Lectures on Physiology*, trans. Robert Amory (Boston: James Campbell, 1875), p. 441. The edition used by James has not been identified.

34.20 FIG. 6] Wundt, *Grundzüge*, 2nd ed., II, 67.

35.1 FIG. 7] The figure is based on Hermann Helmholtz, *Atlas von elf Tafeln* (figures to accompany the *Handbuch*) (Leipzig: Voss, 1867), table 1, figure 3. In the copy in Houghton (Phil 5643.8*) the explanatory wording is added in pencil in James's hand.

38.1 FIG. 9] This figure appears in *Principles*, WORKS, p. 856.

38.3 'Identical] The theory of identical points is discussed in *Principles*, WORKS, pp. 856–861.

39.1 FIG. 10] This figure appears in *Principles*, WORKS, p. 858. In *Principles* points R'R are on the left eye, and L L' on the right.

40.2 says] In *Principles*, WORKS, p. 883, James attributes this remark to Hering.

43.8 Wundt] Wundt, *Grundzüge*, 2nd ed., I, 429.

43.24 Helmholtz] At the beginning of section 20 of the *Handbuch* Helmholtz discusses the mixing of colors. He argues that mixtures of pigments do not produce the same results as mixtures of lights.

44.1 Ziehen] Ziehen (1891), p. 70.

44.5 Helmholtz] The theory sometimes known as the Young-Helmholtz theory of color perception is found in the *Handbuch*, sec. 20 (pp. 272–309).

44.6 Hering] Hering's views are found in *Zur Lehre vom Lichtsinne*.

45.30 Helmholtz] *Handbuch*, p. 358. James makes the same remark in *Principles*, WORKS, p. 607n.

47.10 Hering] For a discussion with references see *Principles*, WORKS, pp. 667–668.

47.25 König] Arthur König (1856–1901), German physiologist, and Eugen Brodhun (b. 1860), "Experimentelle Untersuchungen über die psychophysische Fundamentalformel in Bezug auf den Gesichtsinn," *Sitzungsberichte der kaiserlichen Akademie der Wissenschaften zu Berlin*, 1888, no. 37, pp. 917–931. For the text, James is drawing upon *Principles*, WORKS, p. 512.

47.34 "In] Concerning this saying see *Principles*, WORKS, note to 140.35.

47.39 Martin] Martin does not provide a reference for Hering.

49.23 Auzoux] The *Psychological Laboratory of Harvard University* (Cambridge, Mass.: Published by the University, 1893), p. 7, as item no. 34, lists a "large clastic model of the ear, showing the internal, middle, and external ear. By Auzoux, Paris. $50."

50.1 FIG. 17] The figure from Johann Nepomuk Czermak (1828–1873), Czechoslovakian laryngologist-phoneticist, *Über das Ohr und das Hören* (Berlin: Habel, 1873), p. 11, was added by Martin in the 3rd ed. (1884) of *The Human Body* (p. 535).

51.1 FIG. 18] Figure 144 in Martin, p. 537, from Jakob Henle (1809–1885), German anatomist, *Grundriss der Anatomie des Menschen: Atlas* (Braunschweig: Vieweg, 1880), p. 311.

52.1 FIG. 19] Figure 145 in Martin, p. 538; from Henle, p. 315.

52.23 FIG. 20] Figure 146 in Martin, p. 539.

53.1 FIG. 21] Figure 147 in Martin, p. 540.

53.2 Reissner] Ernst Reissner (1824–1878), German anatomist.

54.1 FIG. 22] Figure 148 in Martin, p. 541.

54.1 Corti] Alfonso Giacomo Gaspare Corti (1822–1876), Italian anatomist.

55.1 FIG. 23] Figure 149 in Martin, p. 542.

56.23 'timbre'] The discussion to 57.3 is heavily drawn from Martin, p. 546.

57.7 Helmholtz] In *Principles*, WORKS, p. 477, James cites Hermann Helmholtz, *On the Sensations of Tone as a Physiological Basis for the Theory of Music*, trans. Alexander J. Ellis, 2nd ed. (London: Longmans, Green, 1885), p. 65.

57.20 Helmholtz] Helmholtz develops this view in *On the Sensations of Tone*, pp. 128, 146, and elsewhere.

57.22 basilar] Some of the exposition which follows could be based on Martin, p. 553.

58.15 **Fusion**] In *A Pluralistic Universe*, WORKS, pp. 85–90, James surveys the development of his views on the compounding of consciousness. The problem is discussed in *Principles*, WORKS, pp. 157–164 and elsewhere.

59.26 Helmholtz] *On the Sensations of Tone*, p. 194, and elsewhere.

59.31 Wundt] Wundt discusses consonance and harmony in *Grundzüge*, 2nd ed., I, 405; II, 180, and elsewhere.

59.40 Merkel] Julius Merkel (b. 1858), German psychologist, "Die Abhängigkeit zwischen Reiz und Empfindung," *Philosophische Studien*, 4 (1888), 541–594; 5 (1888), 245–291, 499–557; 10 (1894), 140–159, 203–248, 369–392, 507–522; data from 5, 514–515 (see *Principles*, WORKS, p. 513).

62.1 FIG. 24] The figure is found in George Trumbull Ladd, *Elements of Physiological Psychology* (New York: Charles Scribner's Sons, 1887) (WJ 448.17), p. 170; Ladd attributes it to Albert von Koelliker (1817–1905), Swiss histologist.

65.10 Goldscheider] Alfred Goldscheider, "Neue Thatsachen über die Hautsinnesnerven," *Archiv für Anatomie und Physiologie*, physiologische Abtheilung, 1885, pp. 1–110 of the supplement (see *Principles*, WORKS, p. 809).

65.10 Blix] Magnus Blix (1849–1904), Swedish physiologist, "Experimentelle Beiträge zur Lösung der Frage über die specifische Energie der Hautnerven," *Zeitschrift für Biologie*, 20 (1884), 141–156; 21 (1885), 145–160 (see *Principles*, WORKS, p. 809).

65.11 Donaldson] Henry Herbert Donaldson (1857–1938), American neurologist, "On the Temperature-Sense," *Mind*, 10 (July 1885), 399–416 (see *Principles*, WORKS, p. 809).

66.31 Sachs] Carl Sachs (1853–1878), German physician, "Physiologische und anatomische Untersuchungen über die sensiblen Nerven der Muskeln," *Archiv für Anatomie, Physiologie und wissenschaftliche Medicin*, 1874, pp. 175–195.

67.16 Weber] James discusses this question in *Principles*, WORKS, p. 513.

67.18–19 Merkel's] The remainder of this paragraph is from *Principles*, WORKS, pp. 513–514; the reference is to Merkel, 5, 287.

68.1 FIG. 27] Wundt, *Grundzüge*, 2nd ed., I, 468.

68.20 Blix] George Trumbull Ladd, *Psychology: Descriptive and Explanatory* (New York: Charles Scribner's Sons, 1894) (WJ 448.17.4), p. 190n, states that Blix (see note to 65.10) denied the existence of specific organs of pain in the skin. According to Ladd, most observers found that the issue has not been decided.

68.20 Goldscheider] See note to 65.10.

69.4 Schiff] The references to rabbits and Schiff were added by James, Martin's words being "In animals a similar state of things may be produced by dividing" (p. 568). Moritz Schiff (1823–1896), Swiss physiologist, dealt with the subject repeatedly. A partial survey of his writings is given in his "On the Excitable Area of the Cortex, and Its Relations to the Columns of the Spinal Cord. A Reply to Professor Horsley," *Brain*, 9 (October 1886), 289–310. For a work from James's library see *Principles*, WORKS, note to 67.11.

70.18 Czermak] Johann Nepomuk Czermak, "Ideen zu einer Lehre vom Zeitsinn," *Sitzungsberichte der kaiserlichen Akademie der Wissenschaften*, mathematisch-naturwissenschaftliche Classe (Vienna), 24 (1857), 231–236.

71.17 *Vierordt*] Karl von Vierordt (1818–1884), German physician, "Die Bewegungsempfindung," *Zeitschrift für Biologie*, 12 (1876), 226–240. For works from James's library see *Principles*, WORKS, notes to 192.4, 795.38.

72.17 Schneider] Georg Heinrich Schneider (1846–1904), German educator, "Warum bemerken wir mässig bewegte Dinge leichter als ruhende?" *Vierteljahrsschrift für wissenschaftliche Philosophie*, 2 (1878), 377–414. For works from James's library see below, notes to 131.26 and 340.26, and *Principles*, WORKS, note to 118.38.

73.32 Goldscheider] Alfred Goldscheider, "Untersuchungen über den Muskelsinn," *Archiv für Anatomie und Physiologie*, physiologische Abtheilung, 1889, pp. 369–502.

74.12 stated] No such statement appears in the published text. For a note on James's investigations of the semicircular canals and vertigo see *Essays in Psychology*, WORKS, note to 127.1–2. His most extensive investigation is "The Sense of Dizziness in Deaf-Mutes," reprinted in *Essays in Psychology*.

74.18 Ménière's] Émile Antoine Ménière (1839–1905), French physician.

74.30 Purkinje] Johannes Evangelista Purkinje (1787–1869), Czechoslovakian physiologist.

74.30 Mach] Ernst Mach (1838–1916), Austrian physicist and philosopher. In later editions of *Beiträge zur Analyse der Empfindungen* (1886), Mach evaluates all of his writings on vertigo; see the English translation by C. M. Williams, *The Analysis of Sensations*, rev. ed. (Chicago: Open Court, 1914), pp. 135–170. James's contribution is discussed on pp. 148–149. For a note on the relations between Mach and James see *Principles*, WORKS, note to 91.41.

75.30 Delage] Yves Delage (1854–1920), French physician and zoologist, "Études expérimentales sur les illusions statiques et dynamiques de direction pour servir à déterminer les fonctions des canaux demi-circulaires de l'oreille interne," *Archives de Zoologie Expérimentale et Générale*, 2nd series, vol. 4 (1886), 535–624.

76.16 Silvius] Franciscus Sylvius (de le Boë) (1614–1672), German chemist and physiologist.

Notes

76.22   Talrich]   *Psychological Laboratory of Harvard University*, p. 3, lists five models manufactured by Talrich, "showing the convolutions," "horizontal section," "seen from below," "model of corpus callosum, seen from below," and "showing median section."

77.1   FIG. 28]   Gustav Huguenin (1841–1920), Swiss physician, *Allgemeine Pathologie der Krankheiten des Nervensystems. Ein Lehrbuch für Aerzte und Studirende*, I (Zurich: Zürcher & Furrer, 1873), 2 (for the three diagrams). The Widener copy (Phil 6117.11) was given by James on August 20, 1906. James crossed out Huguenin's lettering in the diagrams and introduced his own.

77.5   *Varolii*]   Constant Varoli (1543–1575), Italian physician.

77.13   *Vieussens*]   Raymond Vieussens (1641–1716), French physician.

78.11   FIG. 32]   Thomas Henry Huxley (1825–1895), English biologist and essayist, *A Manual of the Anatomy of Vertebrated Animals* (London: J. & A. Churchill, 1871) (WJ 540.97), p. 60. In James's copy there are instructions in James's hand for reproducing this and the following figures.

79.1   FIG. 33]   Huxley, p. 61.

79.17   Holden's]   Luther Holden (1815–1905), English physician and anatomist. In a similar context in *Principles*, WORKS, p. 24, James cites *A Manual of the Dissection of the Human Body* (1851), some editions of which were published by J. & A. Churchill. No *Practical Anatomy* by Holden was found.

79.18   Morrell's]   George Herbert Morrell, *The Student's Manual of Comparative Anatomy, and Guide to Dissection*, pt. 1 (London: Longman & Co., 1872).

79.19   Foster]   Michael Foster (1836–1907), British physiologist, *A Course of Elementary Practical Physiology* (London: Macmillan, 1876). In the first edition Foster is "assisted by" John Newport Langley (1852–1925), British physiologist; in the fifth, both are named as co-authors, while in later ones, Langley is additionally named as editor.

81.1   FIG. 34]   The figure is given in Martin, p. 169; Henle, p. 457.

83.1   FIG. 35]   The figure is not found in Martin; it is in Henle, p. 431.

85.1   FIG. 36]   Henle, p. 435. Henle identifies more regions than James.

86.9   FIG. 37]   Heinrich Obersteiner (1847–1922), German physiologist, *The Anatomy of the Central Nervous Organs in Health and in Disease*, trans. Alex Hill (Philadelphia: P. Blakiston, 1890), p. 72. Obersteiner lists the various regions in much greater detail.

87.6   *Monro*]   Alexander Monro (1733–1817), Scottish physician and anatomist.

87.25   FIG. 38]   The figure, showing more detail, appears in Ladd's *Elements*, p. 90. Ladd attributes it to Karl Gegenbaur (1826–1903), German comparative anatomist.

90.25   frog]   In *Principles* for experiments on frogs James relied heavily upon Friedrich Leopold Goltz (1834–1902), German physiologist, *Beiträge zur Lehre von den Functionen der Nervencentren des Frosches* (Berlin: A. Hirschwald, 1869). For the relations between them see *Principles*, WORKS, note to 22.32.

94.20 Schrader's] Max E. G. Schrader (d. 1903), German physician, "Zur Physiologie des Vogelgehirns," *Archiv für die gesammte Physiologie*, 44 (1888), 175–238; quotation from pp. 230–231.

97.14 Goltz] Goltz's experiments on dogs were published in the *Archiv für die gesammte Physiologie* in 1876–1892; for the complete reference see *Principles*, WORKS, note to 22.32. The present text restores the sexually stronger language used in *Principles* (WORKS, p. 34) and early printings of *Briefer Course*. The paragraph was toned down in later printings apparently at the insistence of the publisher. Professor Bowers' textual introduction should be consulted for details.

97.16 Darwin's] Charles Darwin, *The Descent of Man, and Selection in Relation to Sex*, 2 vols. (London: John Murray, 1871). A copy of this work was sold from James's library.

98.24 theories] This treatment of the efficacy of consciousness summarizes the much longer discussion in *Principles*, WORKS, pp. 132–147; the notes to that section should be consulted for references.

98.28 spinal] For discussions of the spinal soul see *Principles*, WORKS, pp. 22–23, 74–75, 81, 85, 137–138.

100.6 Spencer] *The Principles of Psychology*, I, 280–281 (sec. 125).

100.21 Allen] Charles Grant Blairfindie Allen (1848–1899), Canadian-born naturalist and writer, *Physiological Æsthetics* (London: Henry S. King, 1877) (WJ 503.49). For a note on James's marginal comments see *Principles*, WORKS, note to 147.1.

101.14 phrenological] The brief paragraph on phrenology summarizes *Principles*, WORKS, pp. 39–41.

101.24 Jackson] John Hughlings Jackson (1835–1911), British neurologist, "On Epilepsies and on the After Effects of Epileptic Discharges," *West Riding Lunatic Asylum Medical Reports*, 6 (1876), 266–309, quotation from pp. 267–268. For James's view of Jackson see *Principles*, WORKS, note to 41.15.

101.28 Meynert] Theodor Meynert (1833–1892), psychiatrist, active in Austria, *Psychiatry: A Clinical Treatise on Diseases of the Fore-Brain* (New York: G. P. Putnam's Sons, 1885) (*AC 85.J2376.Zz885m), p. 39; *Zur Mechanik des Gehirnbaues* (Vienna: W. Braumüller, 1874), pp. 18, 19. James's copy of the latter work is in Widener (Phil 6122.44). For additional works from James's library see *Principles*, WORKS, note to 27.8.

101.36 analytic] In *Principles*, WORKS, p. 41, James speaks of associationists at this point.

102.9 Rolando] Luigi Rolando (1773–1831), Italian physiologist.

102.18 Schäfer] Victor Alexander Haden Horsley (1857–1916), British physician and physiologist, and Edward Albert Schafer (Schäfer, Sharpey-Schafer) (1850–1935), British physiologist, "A Record of Experiments upon the Functions of the Cerebral Cortex," *Philosophical Transactions of the Royal Society,* series B, 179 (1888), 1–45; figure 41 is from p. 6, figure 42, from p. 10.

102.21 Starr] Moses Allen Starr (1854–1932), American neurologist, *Familiar Forms of Nervous Disease,* 2nd ed. (New York: William Wood, 1891), p. 94 for figure 43.

103.22 Broca] Pierre Paul Broca (1824–1880), French physician and anthropologist, *Mémoires d'anthropologie,* V (Paris: C. Reinwald, 1888), 1–161, reprints numerous papers under the title "Siège de la faculté du langage articulé," including the paper James appears to have in mind, "Perte de la parole, ramollissement chronique et destruction partielle du lobe antérieur gauche du cerveau," *Bulletins de la Société d'Anthropologie,* 1st series, vol. 2 (April 18, 1861), pp. 235–238.

105.2 'Wernicke'] See note to 108.15.

105.17 Schäfer] Edward Albert Schafer, "On Electrical Excitation of the Occipital Lobe and Adjacent Parts of the Monkey's Brain," *Proceedings of the Royal Society of London,* 43 (1888), 408–410.

105.17 Munk] Hermann Munk (1839–1912), German physiologist, "Of the Visual Area of the Cerebral Cortex, and Its Relation to Eye Movements," *Brain,* 13 (1890), 45–70. For additional writings by Munk on localization see *Principles,* WORKS, note to 42.5.

106.1 Seguin] Edward Constant Seguin (1843–1898), American neurologist, "A Contribution to the Pathology of Hemianopsia of Central Origin (Cortex-Hemianopsia)," *Journal of Nervous and Mental Disease,* 13 (January 1886), pp. 1–38; figure from p. 35. The legend is James's.

107.24 FIG. 46] Starr, *Familiar Forms of Nervous Disease,* p. 98.

108.15 Wernicke] Carl Wernicke (1848–1905), German psychiatrist, *Der aphasische Symptomencomplex: Eine psychologische Studie auf anatomischer Basis* (Breslau: Max Coen & Weigert, 1874). James's annotated copy is in Widener (Phil 6400.6). For additional works from James's library see *Principles,* WORKS, note to 49.25.

108.16 Charcot] Jean Martin Charcot (1825–1893), French neurologist. James perhaps has in mind Charcot's lectures "Des différentes formes de l'aphasie," *Progrès Médical,* 11 (June 9, 1883), 441–444; continued as "Des variétés de l'aphasie" (June 16), 469–471; (June 23), 487–488; (July 7), 521–523; and concluded with the original title (November 3), 859–861. For works from James's library see *Principles,* WORKS, note to 60.38.

108.22 Starr] Moses Allen Starr, "The Pathology of Sensory Aphasia, with an Analysis of Fifty Cases in which Broca's Centre Was not Diseased," *Brain,* 12 (July 1889), 82–99.

109.37 Naunyn] Carl Wilhelm Hermann Nothnagel (1841–1905), Austrian physician, and Bernard Naunyn (1839–1925), German physician, *Über die Localisation der Gehirnkrankheiten* (Wiesbaden: J. F. Bergmann, 1887). James's unannotated copy is in Widener (Phil 6963.5). Figure 47 is not copied from Nothnagel and Naunyn. Their tables 3 and 4 represent a single brain with three shaded regions. Two of these correspond with the Broca and Wernicke regions of James's figure 44, the third, with the angular convolution of figure 47.

110.14 Ross] James Ross (1837–1892), British physician, *On Aphasia: Being a Contribution to the Subject of the Dissolution of Speech from Cerebral Disease* (London: J. & A. Churchill, 1887), p. 124.

110.17 **Centres**] The several topics of this paragraph are treated at greater length in *Principles*, WORKS, pp. 65–70.

111.17 Marique] Joseph M. Louis Marique (b. 1856), Belgian physician, *Recherches expérimentales sur le mécanisme de fonctionnement des centres psycho-moteurs du cerveau* (Brussels: Gustave Mayolez, 1885).

111.18 Exner] Sigmund Exner (1846–1926), Austrian physiologist, and Josef Paneth (1857–1890), Austrian physiologist, "Versuche über die Folgen der Durchschneidung von Associationsfasern am Hundehirn," *Archiv für die gesammte Physiologie*, 44 (1889), 544–555. For works by Exner from James's library see *Principles*, WORKS, notes to 46.13.

112.21 Horsley] In *Principles*, WORKS, p. 71, for the same remark, James cites Horsley and Schafer, p. 3.

113.13 Matteuci] Carlo Matteuci (1811–1868), Italian physicist, noted for studies of animal electricity.

114.3 Helmholtz] Helmholtz's early experiments on frogs are reported in "Vorläufiger Bericht über die Fortpflanzungsgeschwindigkeit der Nervenreizung," *Archiv für Anatomie und Physiologie* (anatomische Abtheilung), 1850, pp. 71–73 of supplement.

114.11 Franklin] An allusion to the inscription on Jean Antoine Houdon's bust of Benjamin Franklin, "He snatched the thunderbolt from heaven, then the sceptre from tyrants," usually traced to the Roman poet Manilius.

115.2 Hipp's] Matthäus Hipp (1813–1893), German-born inventor.

115.12 Lange] Ludwig Lange (1863–1936), German psychologist, "Neue Experimente über den Vorgang der einfachen Reaction auf Sinneseindrücke," *Philosophische Studien*, vol. 4, no. 4 (1888), pp. 479–510; data from p. 493. In *Principles*, WORKS, pp. 98–100, James claims that Lange's data led Wundt to abandon his earlier view that the reactions being studied involve conscious feelings.

116.8 Wundt's] *Grundzüge*, 2nd ed., II, 219–291; for a discussion of discrimination time see *Principles*, WORKS, pp. 494–498.

116.21 Exner] Sigmund Exner, "Experimentelle Untersuchung der einfachsten psychischen Processe," *Archiv für die gesammte Physiologie*, 7 (1873), 601–660; 8 (1874), 526–537; 11 (1875), 403–432, 581–602; reference is to pp. 612–614.

116.22 Herzen] Alexandre Herzen (1839–1906), Swiss physiologist, "Il tempo fisiologico in rapporto all'età," *Archivio per l'Antropologia e la Etnologia*, 9 (1879), 351–352.

116.29 observers] The table is quoted from Wundt, *Grundzüge*, 2nd ed., II, 223 (*Principles*, WORKS, p. 101); for the references to Adolph Hirsch (1830–

1901), Swiss geodesist, and Wilhelm Gottlieb Hankel (1814–1899), German physicist, see *Principles*, WORKS, note to 101.12. The Exner figures are from his "Experimentelle Untersuchung," pp. 645, 648, 649.

116.37 Herzen] In *Principles*, WORKS, p. 102, James cites Alexandre Herzen, *Grundlinien einer allgemeinen Psychophysiologie* (Leipzig: Ernst Günthers Verlag, 1889), p. 101.

117.5 *Intoxicants*] For references see *Principles*, WORKS, pp. 102–103.

117.18 Wundt] *Grundzüge*, 2nd ed., II, 248 (*Principles*, WORKS, p. 495).

117.34 Cattell] James McKeen Cattell (1860–1944), American psychologist, "The Time Taken up by Cerebral Operations," *Mind*, 11 (1886), 220–242, 377–392, 524–538. The six pairs of figures are picked out from pp. 380, 383, 385, 386, 387. James's numerous letters to Cattell are in the Library of Congress.

118.19 Cattell] P. 387.

118.27 Galton] Francis Galton (1822–1911), British scientist, *Inquiries into Human Faculty and Its Development* (New York: Macmillan, 1883) (WJ 531.52), p. 190. Galton's rate is fifty ideas per minute. For letters from Galton to James see *Principles*, WORKS, note to 193.18.

118.29 Wundt] *Grundzüge*, 2nd ed., II, 280 (*Principles*, WORKS, p. 526).

119.3 American] In *Principles*, WORKS, p. 526, identified as Granville Stanley Hall.

119.7 Cattell] James McKeen Cattell, "The Time It Takes to See and Name Objects," *Mind*, 11 (January 1886), 63–65.

120.3 Romanes] George John Romanes (1848–1894), Canadian-born naturalist, *Mental Evolution in Animals* (London: Kegan Paul, Trench, 1883) (WJ 577.53), pp. 136–137.

121.7 Brücke] George Henry Lewes, *The Physical Basis of Mind* (London: Trübner, 1877), pp. 478–479, cites Ernst Wilhelm, Ritter von Brücke (1819–1892), German physiologist, from his *Vorlesungen über Physiologie* (*Principles*, WORKS, p. 91).

121.11 Thomson] Romanes, *Mental Evolution in Animals*, p. 163, cites a letter from Allen Thomson (1809–1884), Scottish biologist (*Principles*, WORKS, p. 91).

121.29 Mosso] Angelo Mosso (1846–1910), Italian physiologist, describes his plethysmograph, a device for recording variations in the amount of blood in an organ, in *La Paura* (Milan: Fratelli Treves, 1884), p. 116, and in *Über den Kreislauf des Blutes im menschlichen Gehirn* (Leipzig: Veit, 1881), p. 45.

121.35 Ludwig] Carl Friedrich Wilhelm Ludwig (1816–1895), German physiologist. Mosso worked in Ludwig's laboratory in Leipzig. The incident is reported in *La Paura*, p. 117.

121.37 Mosso's] *Über den Kreislauf*, pp. 39–45.

122.1 FIG. 50] *Über den Kreislauf*, p. 51.

122.25 Lombard] Josiah Stickney Lombard, American physician, *Experimental Researches on the Regional Temperature of the Head under Conditions of Rest, Intellectual Activity, and Emotion* (London: H. K. Lewis, 1879) (*Principles*, WORKS, p. 105).

122.31 Schiff] Moritz Schiff, "Recherches sur l'échauffement des nerfs et des centres nerveux à la suite des irritations sensorielles et sensitives," *Archives de Physiologie*, 2 (1869), 157–178, 330–351; 3 (1870), 5–25, 198–214, 323–333, 451–462 (*Principles*, WORKS, p. 106n).

123.9–10 Amidon] Royal Wells Amidon (b. 1853), American neurologist, *A New Study of Cerebral Cortical Localization. The Effect of Willed Muscular Movements on the Temperature of the Head* (New York: G. P. Putnam's Sons, 1880), pp. 48–53 (*Principles*, WORKS, p. 106).

123.22 'Ohne] A widely quoted saying from Jacob Moleschott (1822–1893), Dutch physiologist and philosopher.

123.32 Agassiz] Louis Agassiz (1807–1873), Swiss-born naturalist, one of James's teachers at Harvard. For a possible source see *Principles*, WORKS, note to 107.5.

124.1 observers] For references see *Principles*, WORKS, p. 107n.

124.13 "The] A widely quoted remark by Pierre Jean Georges Cabanis (1757–1808), French materialist. For the full citation see *Principles*, WORKS, note to 107.32.

125.4 habits] With the exception of the first paragraph, the chapter on habit is an abridgment of the corresponding chapter in *Principles*. While the new paragraph adds no novel doctrines, it serves to make more explicit James's theory of habit and his tendency to explain mental processes by means of it.

126.28 Dumont] Léon Dumont (1837–1877), French author, "De l'habitude," *Revue Philosophique*, 1 (April 1876), 321–366, quotation from pp. 323–324.

128.31 Maudsley] Henry Maudsley (1835–1918), British physiologist and psychologist, *The Physiology of Mind: Being the First Part of a Third Edition, Revised, Enlarged, and in Great Part Rewritten, of "The Physiology and Pathology of Mind"* (London: Macmillan, 1876), pp. 154–155. James's annotated copy is in Houghton (Phil 6122.1.15*). For additional works from James's library see *Principles*, WORKS, note to 75.36.

131.26 Schneider's] Georg Heinrich Schneider, *Der menschliche Wille vom Standpunkte der neueren Entwickelungstheorien (Des "Darwinismus")*, (Berlin: Dümmler, 1882) (WJ 779.39), pp. 447–448, 439–440.

132.21 Huxley] Thomas Henry Huxley, *Lessons in Elementary Physiology* (London: Macmillan, 1866), p. 286.

134.17 Bain's] Alexander Bain (1818–1903), Scottish philosopher and psychologist, *The Emotions and the Will*, 3rd ed. (London: Longmans, Green, 1875) (WJ 506.41), ch. 9 (pp. 440–459), "The Moral Habits."

134.36 Bain] Pp. 440–441.

135.10   Goethe]   For the source of the Goethe anecdote see *Principles*, Works, note to 127.39.

135.27   "One]   Julius August Bahnsen (1830–1881), German philosopher, *Beiträge zur Charakterologie. Mit besonderer Berücksichtigung pädagogischer Fragen*, 2 vols. (Leipzig: F. A. Brockhaus, 1867), I, 209.

136.5   "The]   I, 208.

136.16   Mill]   John Stuart Mill (1806–1873), *A System of Logic: Ratiocinative and Inductive*, 2 vols., 8th ed. (London: Longmans, Green, Reader, and Dyer, 1872) (WJ 555.51), II, 429. Mill is quoting Novalis.

138.12   Jefferson's]   Joseph Jefferson (1829–1905), American actor. For the reference see *Principles*, Works, note to 131.3.

140.15   four]   The original list in *Principles*, Works, p. 220, includes a fifth character, that thought "always appears to deal with objects independent of itself." James substitutes the term 'state' for 'thought' used in *Principles*.

141.25   universal]   Borden Parker Bowne (1847–1910), American philosopher, *Metaphysics: A Study in First Principles* (New York: Harper & Brothers, 1882), p. 362 (*Principles*, Works, p. 221).

142.37   Helmholtz]   Hermann Helmholtz, *Populäre wissenschaftliche Vorträge*, III (Braunschweig: Vieweg, 1876), 72 (*Principles*, Works, p. 226).

144.25   'pass]   Ralph Waldo Emerson, from the poem "Brahma," *Poems* (Boston: Houghton, Mifflin, 1885), p. 170.

152.9   'mix]   Alexander Pope, "Elegy to the Memory of an Unfortunate Lady" (line 19): "Dim lights of life, that burn a length of years" (*Poetical Works*, ed. Herbert Davis [London: Oxford, 1966], p. 120).

152.19   'acquaintance']   For other treatments of this distinction see *The Meaning of Truth*, Works, pp. 18–20, 30–31, 87–88, and elsewhere.

158.2   Schopenhauer]   For the reference see *Principles*, Works, note to 277.1.

158.27   Lotze]   For the reference see *Principles*, Works, note to 278.14.

160.23   *constituents*]   The list of constituents in *Principles*, Works, p. 280, includes the "pure Ego." James omits most of the material related to that subject; the remainder is treated under the new heading of "the self as knower."

164.38   "Is]   Quoted by Alexander Bain, *The Emotions and the Will*, p. 206.

166.17   Thackeray]   For the reference see *Principles*, Works, note to 294.25.

166.25   Guiteau]   Charles Guiteau (d. June 30, 1882), assassinated James Garfield in 1881; see *Principles*, Works, note to 294.33.

169.1   Carlyle]   Thomas Carlyle (1795–1881), Scottish historian and essayist, *Sartor Resartus: The Life and Opinions of Herr Teufelsdröckh*, 3rd ed. (London: Chapman and Hall, 1849) (*AC 85.J2376.Zz849c), pp. 207–208.

169.16   Epictetus]   *The Works of Epictetus*, trans. Thomas Wentworth Higginson (Boston: Little, Brown, 1866), pp. 6, 10, 105 (from the *Discourses*) (*Principles*, Works, pp. 297–298).

170.24 Aurelius] *The Thoughts of the Emperor M. Aurelius Antoninus*, trans. George Long (Boston: Ticknor and Fields, 1864) (*AC 85.J2376.Zz864a), p. 130 (bk. IV, sec. 23). In James's copy, dated February 1865, the passage is marked with cross-references to pp. 259, 144.

171.15 Horwicz] Adolf Horwicz (1831–1894), German philosopher, *Analyse der qualitativen Gefühle* (Magdeburg: A. & R. Faber, 1878), p. 262; vol. II, pt. 2 of *Psychologische Analysen auf physiologischer Grundlage* (1872–) (WJ 739.78).

173.15 Job's] Job, xiii.15.

173.16 Aurelius's] *Thoughts*, p. 193 (bk. VII, sec. 41).

176.9 Mill] James Mill (1773–1836), British philosopher and historian, *Analysis of the Phenomena of the Human Mind*, ed. John Stuart Mill, with notes by Alexander Bain, Andrew Findlater, George Grote, and J. S. Mill, 2 vols. (London: Longmans, Green, Reader, and Dyer, 1869) (WJ 550.50), I, 264 (*Principles*, Works, p. 267n).

177.11 'combinations'] For James's later views concerning mental compounds see "The Knowing of Things Together," *Essays in Philosophy*, Works, and "The Compounding of Consciousness," *A Pluralistic Universe*, Works.

184.31 Ribot] Théodule Armand Ribot (1839–1916), French psychologist, *Les Maladies de la mémoire* (Paris: Baillière, 1881), pp. 84–85 (*Principles*, Works, pp. 354–355). James's copy is in Widener (Phil 5545.22.2). He is not using the available English translation. For a note on the relations between James and Ribot see *Principles*, Works, note to 100.39.

185.26 Taine] Hippolyte Adolphe Taine (1828–1893), French critic, historian, philosopher, and psychologist, *De l'intelligence*, 3rd ed., 2 vols. (Paris: Hachette, 1878), II, 465–468, quoting from the journal of observations compiled by Maurice Krishaber (1836–1883), French physician. James's copy of *De l'intelligence* is of the first edition (Paris: Hachette, 1870) (WJ 684.41). For a related work by Krishaber see *Principles*, Works, note to 357.37.

187.13 Azam] Eugène Azam (1822–1899), French physician, "Amnésie périodique, ou doublement de la vie," *Revue Scientifique*, 2nd series, vol. 10 (May 20, 1876), pp. 481–489; *Hypnotisme, double conscience et altérations de la personnalité* (Paris: Baillière, 1887).

187.31 Janet] Pierre Janet (1859–1947), French psychologist, *L'Automatisme psychologique: Essai de psychologie expérimentale sur les formes inférieures de l'activité humaine* (Paris: Alcan, 1889) (WJ 642.59), pp. 128–129, 132–133 (*Principles*, Works, pp. 366–367).

190.21–22 medium] Leonora Piper (1859–1950), American trance medium. James's numerous writings concerning Mrs. Piper will be reprinted in *Essays in Psychical Research*, Works.

190.29 evidence] Frederic William Henry Myers, Oliver Lodge, Walter Leaf, William James, Richard Hodgson, "A Record of Observations of Certain Phenomena of Trance," *Proceedings of the Society for Psychical Research* (English), 6 (December 1890), 436–659; 8 (June 1892), 1–167.

193.36 Cattell] James McKeen Cattell, "Über die Trägheit der Netzhaut und des Sehcentrums," *Philosophische Studien*, 3 (1885), 94–127; quotation from p. 127 (*Principles*, WORKS, 385n).

194.18 Paulhan] Frédéric Paulhan (1856–1931), French psychologist, "La Simultanéité des actes psychiques," *Revue Scientifique*, 39 (May 28, 1887), 684–689; quotation from p. 687 with the order inverted (*Principles*, WORKS, pp. 385–386).

195.7 Wundt] *Grundzüge*, 2nd ed., II, 262–266 (*Principles*, WORKS, pp. 388–391).

196.27 Herbart] Johann Friedrich Herbart (1776–1841), German philosopher and educator, *Psychologie als Wissenschaft*, 2 vols. (Königsberg: Unzer, 1824–1825), II, 225–226 (sec. 128) (*Principles*, WORKS, p. 395).

197.19 *Involuntary*] In *Principles*, WORKS, p. 395, James uses '*Passive*' at this point.

197.26 Wesley] John Wesley (1703–1791), English clergyman.

197.26 Hall] Robert Hall (1764–1831), English clergyman.

197.26–27 Carpenter] William Benjamin Carpenter (1813–1885), British physiologist, *Principles of Mental Physiology* (New York: D. Appleton, 1874) (WJ 511.77), pp. 138–139 (sec. 124) (*Principles*, WORKS, pp. 396–397).

199.18 logic] In view of James's frequently stated dislike of logic, it is possible that this remark is autobiographical (see *Principles*, WORKS, note to 398.31).

199.29 FIG. 54] This figure appears to be based on Helmholtz's *Atlas*, table 11, figure X. James omits a pair of black diamonds, one just above the other, centered in each of the two halves.

200.1–2 Helmholtz] *Handbuch*, p. 770 (sec. 32) (*Principles*, WORKS, p. 399). The italics are added by James.

201.33 *blood*] The third condition is not stated in *Principles*, WORKS, p. 411.

202.17 Fechner] *Elemente der Psychophysik*, II, 475–476.

204.29 Lewes's] George Henry Lewes, *Problems of Life and Mind*, 3rd series, 2 vols. (London: Trübner, 1879), II, 107–108.

205.11 Helmholtz] Hermann Helmholtz, *Die Lehre von den Tonempfindungen, als physiologische Grundlage für die Theorie der Musik*, 3rd ed. (Braunschweig: Vieweg, 1870), pp. 85–88 (*Principles*, WORKS, p. 416). James's annotated copy was sold. He is not using the available English translation.

205.23 Wundt] *Grundzüge*, 2nd ed., II, 208, 209.

206.7 Helmholtz] *Handbuch*, p. 741 (*Principles*, WORKS, p. 417).

206.14 Helmholtz] Hermann Helmholtz, *Popular Lectures on Scientific Subjects*, trans. E. Atkinson (London: Longmans, Green, 1873), pp. 294–295. The italics are James's.

207.35   interest]   James discusses ways of arousing interest in connection with education in *Talks to Teachers on Psychology*, WORKS, pp. 61–65.

208.3   Herbartian]   Herbart, *Psychologie als Wissenschaft*, II, 209–229.

209.10   Psychology]   That every science must postulate determinism seems a stronger formulation of a view found in *Principles*, WORKS, p. 1179.

215.12   Hume]   For works by Hume from James's library see *Some Problems of Philosophy*, WORKS, note to 14.5.

218.36   Homer]   For both Homer and Dante see *Principles*, WORKS, notes to 1156.9 and 1156.10.

220.27   remember]   The reference is to the quotation from Helmholtz on p. 205 (*Principles*, WORKS, pp. 476–477).

221.12   Martineau]   James Martineau (1805–1900), English philosopher and clergyman, *Essays, Philosophical and Theological* (Boston: William V. Spencer, 1866), pp. 271–272.

222.6   Bridgman]   Laura Dewey Bridgman (1829–1889). Her unusual sensitivity was noted by Granville Stanley Hall, "Laura Bridgman," *Mind*, 4 (April 1879), 151, and other writers.

222.8   Brace]   Julia Brace (1806–1884), American teacher of blind deaf-mutes.

224.12   'categories']   *Principles*, WORKS, p. 520, at this point mentions Kant and Charles Renouvier.

225.2   Locke]   James could be referring to bk. II, ch. 33 of *An Essay Concerning Human Understanding*, 31st ed. (London: William Tegg, 1853) (WJ 551.13), pp. 283–288.

225.12   Hartley]   In *Principles*, WORKS, p. 529n, James quotes David Hartley (1705–1757), British philosopher, *Observations on Man, His Frame, His Duty, and His Expectations*, 2 vols. (London, 1749), I, 65.

226.37   "Locksley]   *The Works of Alfred Lord Tennyson* (London: Macmillan, 1905), pp. 101, 102.

228.15   Bain]   Alexander Bain, *The Senses and the Intellect*, 3rd ed. (London: Longmans, Green, 1868) (WJ 506.41.4), pp. 544–555, on "Compound Association" (*Principles*, WORKS, p. 536).

228.35   Hamilton]   William Hamilton (1788–1856), Scottish philosopher, *Lectures on Metaphysics and Logic*, ed. H. L. Mansel and John Veitch, 4 vols. (Edinburgh: William Blackwood and Sons, 1859–1860), II, 238.

230.1   Austen's]   The quoted text appears in *Emma* (Boston: Houghton, Mifflin, c1957), p. 132.

230.36   Hodgson]   Shadworth Hollway Hodgson (1832–1912), British philosopher, *Time and Space: A Metaphysical Essay* (London: Longman, Green, Longman, Roberts, and Green, 1865) (WJ 539.18.6), pp. 266–267. For a note on the relations between James and Hodgson see *Principles*, WORKS, note to 7.23.

231.28 Bayard] Thomas Francis Bayard (1828–1898), Democratic senator from Delaware.

232.5 *partial*] The expression '*partial recall*' is added in *Briefer Course* (*Principles*, WORKS, p. 540).

232.11 Hodgson] *Time and Space*, pp. 267–268.

233.7–8 author's] Carl Theodor Göring (1841–1879), German philosopher (*Principles*, WORKS, p. 541).

234.23 Dumas] Earlier translations of Alexandre Dumas (1802–1870), *Les Trois mousquetaires* appeared under the title *The Three Guardsmen*.

235.15 Hamilton] *Lectures on Metaphysics and Logic*, I, 352–353.

237.10 Calkins] Mary Whiton Calkins (1863–1930), American philosopher, "A Suggested Classification of Cases of Association," *Philosophical Review*, 1 (July 1892), 389–402; quotation from pp. 395–396, the term 'desistent', p. 396. The note about Calkins was added in later printings of *Briefer Course* and replaces a section titled "Summary concerning Spontaneous Trains of Thought." The omitted paragraph is given in the list of Emendations. For the history of this revision, "The Text of *Psychology: Briefer Course*" should be consulted. Calkins' article is in part a criticism of James's treatment of association.

237.22 Wundt's] *Grundzüge*, 2nd ed., II, 300 (*Principles*, WORKS, p. 529).

242.15 Mill] *A System of Logic*, I, 448–471 (bk. III, ch. 8).

245.5 Hodgson] Quoted by Hodgson in *Time and Space*, p. 105, without a source. In a marginal note in his copy of *Briefer Course*, James attributes the line to Nicolas Boileau-Despréaux (1636–1711), French poet (from "Épitre III," *Œuvres poétiques de Boileau Despréaux* [Paris: Charpentier, 1855], p. 208).

245.14 called] *The Alternative: A Study in Psychology* (London: Macmillan, 1882), pp. 167–169; published anonymously, but usually attributed to Edmund R. Clay (*Principles*, WORKS, pp. 573–574).

246.14 Wundt's] For references see *Principles*, WORKS, p. 577.

246.16 Exner] "Experimentelle Untersuchung," pp. 415–420 (see note to 116.21) (*Principles*, WORKS, p. 578).

246.21 "to] From Tennyson's "The Mystic," one of the suppressed poems, *The Poems of Tennyson*, ed. Christopher Ricks (London: Longmans, 1969), p. 230.

246.40 Wundt] For Wundt's text see *Principles*, WORKS, p. 599.

247.26 Hodgson's] For Hodgson's text see *Principles*, WORKS, p. 572n.

249.16 Volkmann] Wilhelm Fridolin Volkmann, Ritter von Volkmar (1822–1877), Czechoslovakian philosopher and psychologist, *Lehrbuch der Psychologie*, 2nd ed., 2 vols. (Cöthen: Schulze, 1875–1876), II, 26.

253.2 Mill] *Analysis*, I, 322–324 (*Principles*, WORKS, pp. 614–615).

259.39 Holbrook] Martin Luther Holbrook (1831–1902), American physician and author, *How to Strengthen the Memory; or, Natural and Scientific Methods of Never Forgetting* (New York: M. L. Holbrook, ᶜ1886), p. 38 (*Principles*, WORKS, pp. 625–626).

261.13 Loisette] Alphonse Loisette, pseudonym of Marcus Dwight Larrowe (b. 1832), American lecturer and writer.

261.35 common] In *Principles*, WORKS, p. 629, the figure-alphabet is part of a quotation from Edward Pick (1824–1899). For a note on James's source see *Principles*, WORKS, note to 629.37.

262.3 Wigan] Arthur Ladbroke Wigan, British physician, *The Duality of the Mind* (London: Longman, Brown, Green, and Longmans, 1844), p. 84 (*Principles*, WORKS, pp. 635–636).

262.13 Lazarus] Moritz Lazarus (1824–1903), German philosopher and psychologist, "Zur Lehre von den Sinnestäuschungen," *Zeitschrift für Völkerpsychologie und Sprachwissenschaft*, 5 (1868), 113–152 (*Principles*, WORKS, p. 636).

262.24 Ribot] Théodule Armand Ribot, *Les Maladies de la mémoire* (Paris: Baillière, 1881), pp. 45–46. James's copy is in Widener (Phil 5545.22.2) (*Principles*, WORKS, pp. 640–641). James is not using the available English translation.

264.9 Locke's] Not quoted in *Briefer Course*, but quoted in *Principles*, WORKS, p. 656, from the *Essay*, pp. 213 (bk. II, ch. 25, sec. 9), 200 (bk. II, ch. 23, sec. 29).

265.4 Locke] *Essay*, p. 458 (bk. IV, ch. 7, sec. 9).

265.7 Berkeley] George Berkeley, *A Treatise Concerning the Principles of Human Knowledge*, ed. Charles P. Krauth (Philadelphia: J. B. Lippincott, 1874) (WJ 507.76), p. 182 (Introduction, sec. 13) (*Principles*, WORKS, p. 696).

265.20 Galton] Francis Galton, "Statistics of Mental Imagery," *Mind*, 5 (July 1880), 301–318.

265.28 Galton's] Part of Galton's text is quoted in *Principles*, WORKS, pp. 696–702.

266.30 La Fontaine] For the reference see *Principles*, WORKS, note to 703.34.

267.37 Galton] *The Oxford English Dictionary* (supplement) does not attribute this term to Galton, but rather cites Joseph Jacobs, review of Binet's *Psychologie du raisonnement*, in *Mind*, 11 (July 1886), 415.

267.37 Binet] Alfred Binet (1857–1911), French psychologist, *La Psychologie du raisonnement: Recherches expérimentales par l'hypnotisme* (Paris: Alcan, 1886), pp. 25–26.

268.5 Legouvé] Ernest Wilfried Legouvé (1807–1903), French dramatist and writer, and Augustin Eugène Scribe (1791–1861), French dramatist.

268.19 Stricker] Salomon Stricker (1834–1898), Hungarian pathologist, *Studien über die Sprachvorstellungen* (Vienna: W. Braumüller, 1880); *Studien über die Bewegungsvorstellungen* (Vienna: W. Braumüller, 1882) (*Principles*, WORKS, p. 709). Copies of both works were sold from James's library.

268.34 says] *Studien über die Bewegungsvorstellungen*, p. 6.

269.5 Stricker] *Studien über die Sprachvorstellungen*, pp. 9–15, 29–33, 49–50, 69–70.

269.13 Bain] *The Senses and the Intellect*, p. 339.

269.27 Meyer] Georg Hermann Meyer (1815–1892), German psychologist, *Untersuchungen über die Physiologie der Nervenfaser* (Tübingen: Laupp, 1843), p. 233 (*Principles*, WORKS, p. 712).

269.36 Franz] J. C. August Franz, German physician, "Memoir of the Case of a Gentleman Born Blind, and Successfully Operated upon in the 18th Year of His Age, with Physiological Observations and Experiments," *Philosophical Transactions of the Royal Society* of London, 131 (1841), 59–68 (*Principles*, WORKS, p. 709).

270.9 Charcot] Cited by James from Hermann Wilbrand, *Die Seelenblindheit* (Wiesbaden: J. F. Bergmann, 1887) (WJ 794.48), pp. 43–49 (*Principles*, WORKS, pp. 704–706).

271.29 Münsterberg] Hugo Münsterberg, *Die Willenshandlung* (Freiburg i. B.: J. C. B. Mohr, 1888) (WJ 757.62.6), p. 139 (*Principles*, WORKS, p. 720).

272.9 Meyer] For Meyer's text see *Principles*, WORKS, pp. 713–714.

272.9 Féré] Charles Féré (1852–1907), French psychiatrist, "Sensation et mouvement," *Revue Philosophique*, 20 (1885), 337–368 (*Principles*, WORKS, p. 714n).

272.10 Scott] Perhaps Fred Newton Scott (1860–1930), American educator, in a letter to James (*Principles*, WORKS, p. 1464).

272.10 Smith] Perhaps Theodore Clarke Smith, a student at Harvard in 1888–1894, 1895–1897.

274.18 Reid] Thomas Reid (1710–1796), Scottish philosopher, *An Inquiry into the Human Mind on the Principles of Common Sense*, ch. 4, sec. 1 (*The Works of Thomas Reid, D. D.*, ed. William Hamilton, 5th ed. [Edinburgh: Maclachlan and Stewart, 1858], p. 117). For works by Reid from James's library see *Principles*, WORKS, note to 162.25.

278.25 Robertson] George Croom Robertson (1842–1892), British philosopher, "Sense of Doubleness with Crossed Fingers," *Mind*, 1 (January 1876), 145–146. Robertson cites Aristotle's *Metaphysics*, 1011ª. For the letters between James and Robertson see *Principles*, WORKS, note to 184.37–38.

278.37 Binet] Alfred Binet, "La Rectification des illusions par l'appel aux sens," *Mind*, 9 (April 1884), 206–222.

279.12 Wheatstone's] Charles Wheatstone (1802–1875), British physicist and inventor.

280.27 Helmholtz] *Handbuch*, p. 635 (*Principles*, WORKS, p. 736).

282.36 Lazarus] Moritz Lazarus, *Das Leben der Seele*, 2 vols. (Berlin: Schindler, 1856–1857), II, 31–32.

283.3–4 authorities] James is referring to Reid and Helmholtz, see *Principles*, WORKS, p. 852.

285.6 Lewes] George Henry Lewes, *Problems of Life and Mind*, 1st series, 2 vols. (London: Trübner, 1874–1875), I, 118–124 (*Principles*, WORKS, p. 751).

285.18 Steinthal] Heyman Steinthal (1823–1899), German philosopher, *Einleitung in die Psychologie und Sprachwissenschaft*, 2nd ed. (Berlin: Dümmler, 1881), p. 173. An annotated copy was sold from James's library.

286.6 Polynesian] For James's source see *Talks to Teachers*, WORKS, p. 97.

287.41 Lange] Karl Maximilian Lange (1849–1893), German educator, *Über Apperception* (Plauen: F. E. Neupert, 1879), pp. 74, 76.

288.23 Kandinsky] Victor Kandinsky (Viktor Khrisanfovich Kandinskii) (1849–1899), Russian psychiatrist, *Kritische und klinische Betrachtungen im Gebiete der Sinnestäuschungen* (Berlin: Friedländer & Sohn, 1885) (WJ 878.43). James could be referring to the case of Michel Dolinin described by Kandinsky on pp. 44–54.

289.2 Gurney] Edmund Gurney (1847–1888), British aesthetician and psychical researcher. For the relations between James and Gurney see *The Will to Believe*, WORKS, notes to 225.38 and 228.11; for information about the census and James's role in it see *Principles*, WORKS, notes to 760.28 and 760.40. Gurney figures prominently in James's own psychical investigations, to be collected in *Essays in Psychical Research*, WORKS.

290.2 Binet's] Alfred Binet, "L'Hallucination," *Revue Philosophique*, 17 (1884), 377-412; Binet and Charles Féré, *Animal Magnetism* (New York: D. Appleton, 1888), pp. 211–276 (*Principles*, WORKS, p. 771n).

293.18 Franz] *Philosophical Transactions*, p. 66 (*Principles*, WORKS, p. 778).

293.22 Hering] Ewald Hering, "Der Raumsinn und die Bewegungen des Auges," *Handbuch der Physiologie*, ed. Ludimar Hermann, vol. III, pt. 1 (Leipzig: Vogel, 1879), p. 575 (*Principles*, WORKS, p. 778).

294.1 FIG. 65] See *Principles*, WORKS, note to 783.1.

297.9 muscular] This treatment of the muscular sense is added in *Briefer Course*.

297.30 joints] In *Principles*, WORKS, pp. 826–833, James places much emphasis on the role of the joints in the perception of space.

299.25 Ruskin] John Ruskin (1819–1900), English critic and essayist. For the reference see *Principles*, WORKS, note to 817.26.

301.34 'in] George Berkeley, *An Essay towards a New Theory of Vision*, in *The Works of George Berkeley, D. D.*, ed. Alexander Campbell Fraser, 4 vols. (Oxford: Clarendon, 1871), I, 35. For a more complete text see *Principles*, WORKS, p. 847. Vols. I and II of Berkeley's *Works* were sold from James's library.

302.15 Wheatstone's] For references see *Principles*, WORKS, pp. 859–860.

303.31 Persons] For references see *Principles*, WORKS, p. 845.

303.39 Raehlmann] Eduard Raehlmann (b. 1848), "Physiologisch-psychologische Studien über die Entwickelung der Gesichtswahrnehmungen bei Kindern und bei operierten Blindgeborenen," *Zeitschrift für Psychologie*, 2 (1891), 53–96.

309.13   Warner]   Charles Dudley Warner (1829–1900), American author, "How I Killed a Bear," *In the Wilderness* (Boston: Houghton, Osgood, 1878), p. 14.

310.9   Locke]   For the reference see *Principles*, Works, note to 961.13.

314.35   Kingsley]   Charles Kingsley (1819–1875), English clergyman and author.

316.29   Mill's]   See note to 242.15.

318.8   Bain's]   Alexander Bain, *On the Study of Character, Including an Estimate of Phrenology* (London: Parker, Son, and Bourn, 1861), pp. 322–344 (*Principles*, Works, p. 972). James's copy was sold.

318.32   Romanes]   George John Romanes, *Mental Evolution in Man: Origin of Human Faculty* (New York: D. Appleton, 1889) (WJ 577.53.2), pp. 40–69, on the "Logic of Recepts" (*Principles*, Works, p. 954).

318.33   Morgan]   Conwy Lloyd Morgan (1852–1936), British biologist and philosopher, *Animal Life and Intelligence* (London: Edwin E. Arnold, 1890–1891), pp. 312, 339 (*Principles*, Works, p. 1470).

321.21   Bain]   *The Emotions and the Will*, p. 4.

322.34   Schneider]   Georg Heinrich Schneider, "Zur Entwicklung der Willensäusserungen im Tierreiche," *Vierteljahrsschrift für wissenschaftliche Philosophie*, 3 (1879), 176–205, 294–307.

324.1   emotion]   The chapter on emotion is a condensation of the chapter in *Principles*, with most of the quotations and references omitted. Most noteworthy is the omission of references to Carl Georg Lange, usually given credit by James for having independently developed a similar theory. For James's defense of the Lange-James theory see "The Physical Basis of Emotion," *Psychological Review*, 1 (1894), 516–529, reprinted in *Essays in Psychology*, Works.

332.22   Archer]   William Archer (1856–1924), British critic and journalist, "The Anatomy of Acting," *Longman's Magazine*, 11 (January 1888), 266–281; (February 1888), 375–395; (March 1888), 498–516 (*Principles*, Works, pp. 1079–1080).

334.3   Darwin's]   Charles Darwin, *The Expression of the Emotions in Man and Animals* (New York: D. Appleton, 1873), pp. 290–292. A marked copy was sold from James's library.

334.31   'Obstupui]   Virgil, *Aeneid*, bk. II, line 774.

334.40   *huc*]   Virgil, *Aeneid*, bk. IV, line 363.

335.6   Hagenauer]   F. A. Hagenauer of Lake Wellington, a missionary in Australia, one of several persons who observed aborigines for Darwin.

335.28   says]   *The Principles of Psychology*, I, 482–483 (sec. 213).

336.13   Darwin]   *The Expression of the Emotions*, pp. 253, 282–284.

Notes

336.22 Spencer] *The Principles of Psychology*, II, 548 (sec. 498).

336.26 Mantegazza] Paolo Mantegazza (1831–1910), Italian physician and anthropologist, *La Physionomie et l'expression des sentiments* (Paris: Alcan, 1885), p. 78.

336.27 Wundt] *Grundzüge*, 2nd ed., II, 420–421.

336.31 Darwin] *The Expression of the Emotions*, p. 176.

336.40 Darwin] *The Expression of the Emotions*, pp. 225–226.

337.12 Wundt] *Grundzüge*, 2nd ed., II, 423–424.

337.12–13 Piderit] Theodor Piderit (1826–1898), *Wissenschaftliches System der Mimik und Physiognomik* (Detmold: Klingenberg, 1867), p. 69 (cited by Wundt, *Grundzüge*, 2nd ed., II, 424).

337.17 "All] *Grundzüge*, 2nd ed., II, 424.

340.26 Schneider] Georg Heinrich Schneider, *Der thierische Wille; Systematische Darstellung und Erklärung der thierischen Triebe und deren Entstehung, Entwickelung und Verbreitung im Thierreiche als Grundlage zu einer vergleichenden Willenslehre* (Leipzig: Ambr. Abel [1880]) (WJ 779.39.2).

347.2 Spalding's] Douglas Alexander Spalding (c. 1840–1877), British naturalist, "Instinct. With Original Observations on Young Animals," *Macmillan's Magazine*, 27 (February 1873), 282–293.

348.23 Spalding] P. 289.

351.11 Preyer] Wilhelm Thierry Preyer (1842–1897), German physiologist, *Die Seele des Kindes* (Leipzig: Th. Grieben, 1882), p. 147. An annotated copy was sold.

351.28 *Nineteenth*] Louis Robinson (b. 1857), physician, "Darwinism in the Nursery," *Nineteenth Century*, 30 (November 1891), 831–842.

353.4 'like] From Tennyson's "Lotos-Eaters," *The Works of Alfred Lord Tennyson*, p. 56.

353.14 Perez] Bernard Perez (1863–1903), French educator, *La Psychologie de l'enfant (les trois premières années)*, 2nd ed. (Paris: Baillière, 1882), pp. 72, 74.

354.27 Richet] Charles Robert Richet (1850–1935), French physiologist, *L'Homme et l'intelligence* (Paris: Alcan, 1884), p. 482 (*Principles*, WORKS, p. 1472). James's copy is in Widener (Phil 5257.6).

354.29 Preyer] *Die Seele des Kindes*, p. 106.

356.15 Brooks] William Keith Brooks (1848–1908), American naturalist.

356.18 Darwin] In *Mental Evolution in Animals*, p. 156, Romanes gives several stories, including one from Darwin's *Descent of Man* (I, 67) about a dog barking at a parasol moved along a lawn by wind (*Principles*, WORKS, p. 1038).

356.39 Lindsay] William Lauder Lindsay (1829–1880), Scottish physician, *Mind in the Lower Animals in Health and Disease*, 2 vols. (New York: D. Appleton, 1880) (WJ 550.59), I, 526.

360.7 Strümpell] Adolf von Strümpell (1853–1925), German physician, "Beobachtungen über ausgebreitete Anästhesien und deren Folgen für die willkürliche Bewegung und das Bewusstsein," *Deutsches Archiv für klinische Medicin*, 22 (1878), 321–361; quotation from pp. 327–328.

360.34 *innervation*] The feeling of innervation is discussed by James in "The Feeling of Effort" (1880), reprinted in *Essays in Psychology*, WORKS, in *Principles*, and in "Professor Wundt and Feelings of Innervation" (1894), reprinted in *Essays in Psychology*, WORKS.

363.31 Southard] Henry Pickering Bowditch (1840–1911), American physiologist, and William Freeman Southard, American physician, "A Comparison of Sight and Touch," *Journal of Physiology*, 3 (January 1882), 232–245 (*Principles*, WORKS, pp. 1128–1129).

364.37 Carpenter] *Principles of Mental Physiology*, pp. 279–315.

365.16 Lotze] Rudolph Hermann Lotze (1817–1881), German philosopher, *Medicinische Psychologie oder Physiologie der Seele* (Leipzig: Weidmann, 1852) (WJ 751.88.4), pp. 293–294. For works by Lotze from James's library see *Principles*, WORKS, note to 7.22.

366.26 Lotze] P. 293.

375.29 Clouston] Thomas Smith Clouston (1840–1915), Scottish psychiatrist, *Clinical Lectures on Mental Diseases* (London: J. & A. Churchill, 1883), p. 317. For James's copy see *Principles*, WORKS, note to 758.18.

376.27 'sicklied] From Shakespeare's *Hamlet*, act 3, scene 1.

378.12 Mussey] George Burr (1813–1882), American physician, "On the Insanity of Inebriety," *Psychological and Medico-Legal Journal*, n.s. 1 (December 1874), 341–365; the quotations from Reuben Dimond Mussey (1780–1866), American physician, and J. E. Turner are from pp. 355–356. Burr does not cite any sources (*Principles*, WORKS, 1149–1150).

379.22 "*Video*] From Ovid's *Metamorphoses*, bk. VII, lines 20–21.

380.3 Restif] Nicolas Edme Restif (Restif de la Bretonne) (1734–1806), French novelist.

381.23 symbolized] For James's comments on a similar diagram see *Essays in Psychology*, WORKS, note to 120.13.

382.4 Dante] *Inferno*, canto 5, line 121.

382.5 Homer] *Odyssey*, bk. XV, lines 400–401.

390.8 Wigan] *The Duality of the Mind*, pp. 141–142 (*Principles*, WORKS, pp. 1170–1171).

390.11   Pinel]   Philippe Pinel (1745–1826), French physician, director of the insane asylum at Bicêtre.

393.12   'searching]   Psalms, vii.10.

395.17   Metaphysics]   The sentence is used in *Principles*, WORKS, p. 148.

400.24   *'scious*ness']   The term is used in *Principles*, WORKS, pp. 290–291.

400.32   'psychology]   James treats this topic at greater length in "A Plea for Psychology as a 'Natural Science' " (1892), reprinted in *Essays in Psychology*, WORKS.

Appendix

James's Annotations of His Private Copy
of Psychology: Briefer Course

This appendix contains transcripts of all the autograph markings that James made in his private signed copy of the second printing preserved in the James Collection in the Houghton Library, Harvard University (WJ 200.35). The first page-line reference is to the present edition; the second, within parentheses, is to the original 1892 volume. The lemma is that of the second printing, which in all the entries listed corresponds to that of the first printing. The exact text referred to is not always to be identified precisely, this being especially true of general notes placed at the head and at the foot of a page. Therefore, annotations made by James in the top or bottom margin of a page are keyed to the first or last words on that page, unless joined by guidelines to specific passages. Professor Skrupskelis has provided what annotations seem useful as an aid to the reader; reference is also made to other entries in the Appendix and to the Notes.

There are a number of inconsistencies in spelling as well as what might appear to be typographical errors in James's notes, which have been retained in their original form.

(verso of end paper) [*ink*] *Be sure to put in s'thing about P. Janet's "derivation." The supremely effective mind is the one that goes to action & solution of practical problems. That power arrested, vague excitement accrues. In my own case, fear or not remembering. [*ov. penc. vert.* 'W. F. Ellis']
    Perhaps Walter Fred Ellis, a student at Harvard in 1896–1900.

(πii, top) [*penc.*] Calkins's Articles | Dec. 1907+
    Mary Whiton Calkins, papers in the *Journal of Philosophy*: "Psychology: What Is It About?" 4 (December 5, 1907), 673–683; "Psychology as Science of Self," 5 (January 2, 1908), 12–20; (January 30, 1908), 64–68; (February 27, 1908), 113–122.

2.13 (iv.17)   synthetic] [*ink*] 'analytic' *in mrgn. for del.* 'synthetic'

10.17 (2.24)   things.] [*penc.*] 'facts' *in mrgn. for del.* 'things'

11.37 (4.17)   **teleological**] [*ink*] [*short rule*] Older psychology tho't mind essentially rational, cognitive

12.16 (4.37)   insanity—and] [*ink*] My mental state as lecturer, now. Account for it.

439

12.17 (5.1) 'Æsthetics.'] [*penc.*] 'apologize for this.' *in top mrgn., joined by guideline to* ' 'Æsthetics.' '

12.20 (5.5) **bodily activity**] [*penc.*] [*short rule*] no imp. § ex-pression
Cf. *Talks to Teachers*, WORKS, p. 30: '*no impression without correlative expression*'.

13.15 (6.9) *aphasias.*] [*penc.*] The hereditary nature of some mental peculiarities is best explained by the materialistic theory.

13.41 (7.1) on our brain] [*penc.*] materialism vs. spiritualism

14.28–30 (7.31–33) 1) . . . out.] [*penc.*] very crude.

14.28 (7.31) 1) The] [*penc.*] psychopetal

14.30 (7.33) 3) The] [*penc.*] psychofugal

14.39 (8.7) urged.] [*penc.*] Impression—elaboration—expression. | "No impression without expression | [*ink*] Sully, Illusions, Childhood. | Morgan's 2 books Bain Mind & Body | Ribot's 4. | Donaldson, G. of B. | *R. P. [*added*] Halleck E. of C. N. S. | Maudsley Responsibility, Body & Mind | Galton. I. into H. F. | *Lubbock [2'b' *ov.* 'o'], Bees A. & W | Bernstein; 5 senses | Binet's Psych des. Calc., Alt. d. l. P. | Binet et Féré: Animal mag. | Moll: hypnot. | Hirsch. Genius & degeneration.
James Sully (1842–1923), British philosopher and psychologist, *Illusions: A Psychological Study* (New York: D. Appleton, 1881); *Studies of Childhood* (London and New York: Longmans, Green, 1895).
Conwy Lloyd Morgan, *Psychology for Teachers* (London: Arnold, 1894); *An Introduction to Comparative Psychology* (London: Walter Scott, 1894).
Alexander Bain, *Mind and Body. The Theories of Their Relation* (1873).
For works by Ribot from James's library see *The Principles of Psychology*, WORKS, note to 100.39.
Henry Herbert Donaldson, *The Growth of the Brain: A Study of the Nervous System in Relation to Education* (1895).
Reuben Post Halleck (1859–1936), American writer, *The Education of the Central Nervous System* (1896).
Henry Maudsley, *Responsibility in Mental Disease* (1874); *Body and Mind* (London: Macmillan, 1870).
For Galton, see note to 118.27.
John Lubbock (Baron Avebury) (1834–1913), British banker and naturalist, *Ants, Bees, and Wasps* (1882).
Julius Bernstein (1839–1917), German physiologist, *The Five Senses of Man* (1876).
Alfred Binet, *Psychologie des grands calculateurs et joueurs d'échecs* (1894); *Les Altérations de la personnalité* (1892).
For Binet and Féré, see note to 290.2.
Albert Moll (1862–1939), German psychiatrist, *Der Hypnotismus* (Berlin: Fischer's medicinische Buchhandlung, 1889) (WJ 756.51).
William Hirsch, German physician, *Genius and Degeneration*, English translation (1896); see James's review, *Psychological Review*, 2 (1895), 290–294.

15.0 (9.0)   CHAPTER II.] [*ink*] Speak of environment | Give acct. of Nerve fibres [*penc.*], and cells | The neuron etc. | [*ink*] chemical & mechanical senses | (Wundt: lectures)
>   Wilhelm Wundt, *Lectures on Human and Animal Psychology*, see note to 23.1.

15.18–19 (9.20)   invisible . . . escape] [*ink*] Habits, viz.

16.12 (10.18)   perceiving.] [*penc.*] Prove current & its velocity *18 [*ov.* '33'] met a sec. in frog

16.26 (11.1)   fibres] [*ink*] "Five" senses give so many qualities | [*penc.*] Sense of *pain*

16.34–35 (11.10)   cerebral convolutions. [*underl. in ink*]] [*penc.*] If the opt. N. were exposed to blows we should feel them as flashes

17.5 (11.16)   cerebral cortex] [*ink*] *underl.*

17.19 (12.1)   can guess] [*penc.*] Sensations as ultimate products of analysis. Titchener's

E   ⊗   D

>   Edward Bradford Titchener (1867–1927), American psychologist, *An Outline of Psychology* (New York: Macmillan, 1896), p. 31, uses the diagram to depict the four aspects of every sensation: quality, intensity, extent, and duration.

17.32–33 (12.16)   If we could] [*ink*] You would see the words of my lecture demeaning themselves as all sorts of changing colours, and hear my person existing.

18.10–11 (13.1)   existent.] [*ink*] "Consciousness" is thus always cognitive of things and named after them usually.

19.11–12 (14.10–11)   *what . . . whats*] [*penc.*] *carets aft. 'what' and 'whats'; 'which* fact' *and '& whiches' in mrgn.*

19.37 (15.1)   sensa-] [*ink*] *underl.*

19.37 (15.2)   due . . . currents] [*ink*] *all underl.*

19.40 (15.5)   images] [*ink*] *underl.*

20.1 (15.6–7)   currents . . . convolutions] [*ink*] *all underl.*

20.10 (15.16)   extended and] [*ink*] Miss Rounds | Miss Stein.
>   Gertrude Stein (1874–1946), American author, was a student at Radcliffe in 1893–1897 and attended several of James's courses.

20.10 (15.17)   outside] [*ink*] *underl.*

20.11 (15.17)   body [*underl. in penc.*]] [*penc*] 'mind' *in mrgn. and underl. for del.* 'body'

21.13 (16.29)   **The Intensity**] [*ink*] *horiz. line in mrgn.*

Appendix

21.29 (17.10)   On the other hand] [*ink*] No! Cf. Horwicz
Adolf Horwicz (1831–1894), German philosopher.

22.5 (18.1) S^2—2, and so on.] [*ink*] See Wundt's lectures II, III, *IV [*ov.* 'II']
Lectures, pp. 12–63.

22.13 (18.11)   Fig. 2 represents] [*penc.*] minima: [*ink*] *wt.* *gm. [*intrl.*] 0.002
to 0.05 | *sound* 1 mg. of cork fall^g 1 mm. upon glass, 91 mm. from ear. | Musket-
shot 7 kilom.

22.20 (18.10)   FIG. 2.] [*ink*] Simpler diagram Wundt p 36

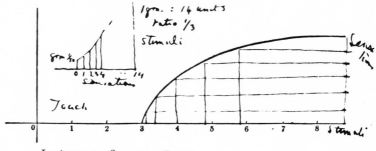

Lectures, p. 36.   FIG. 2.

25.27–30 (21.26–29)   The . . . pound.] [*penc.*] *vert. line and qst. mk. in mrgn.*

25.37,38,39(*twice*),40 (21.36,37;22.34[*twice*],36)   d] [*ink*] '∆' *in mrgn. for del. 'd'*

26.12 (22.13)   Fechner's] [*penc.*] The 3 methods eben mklh. [*short rule*] mitt-
lere fehler [*short rule*] falsch und richtige fälle [*short rule*]

26.12 (22.13)   Fechner's] [*leaf of white wove paper,* 4⁹⁄₁₀ × 8", *glued to upper
left corner of p. 22 (ed., p. 26), written in ink*] [*recto*] 4 [*ov.* '3'] Methods. | 1)
Just discernible difference or "minimal change: S + d; (S + d) − d'; $\dfrac{d + d'}{2}$ is
the *j. d. d*; and the ratio of this to S (or rather S + d − d') is the threshold. | 2)
true & false cases. *(say whether = or difft) [*insrtd. bel.* 'true . . . cases.']
$\dfrac{\text{errors}}{\text{right judgments}}$ must be the same ratio all along scale of stimulus. Fechner
made 24,500 by this method. | 3) Average error: Make 2 = 1. + and − errors
added and divided by number of trials gives A. e. which is reciprocal of sensibility. [*verso*] 4) *Equal ['E' *ov.* 'e'] seeming intervals. [*short rule*] *Where is
the law?*

26.30 (23.1)   the line] [*ink*] physico-cerebral; cerebro-mental; intra mental

27.1 (23.13–14)   The fundamental objection] [*ink*] vide *infra ['inf' *ov.* 'sup']
p. ['23' *del.*] 196

27.26 (24.5–6)   *distance*, from the starting-point,] [*penc.*] 'from . . . -point,'
del.

27.26 (24.6)   feel] [*penc.*] between the sensation we start from & the one we
compare with it, each being a unit.

442

27.38 (24.18–19)   the more . . . attend to [*all underl. in ink*]] [*ink*] "psychological"

27.39 (23.37)   *Beiträge] [*penc.*] Refer to Wundt's Lectures, Titchener, & my P. of P. vol I, p. 533+
    The Principles of Psychology, WORKS, p. 503.

28.38 (25.34)   light falling] [*ink*] 'light' *del.*

30.3 (27.3–4)   the simultaneous variety,] [*ink*] 'the' *del.*; 'contrast' *in mrgn. for del.* 'variety,'

33.1 (30.21)   *at top of* FIG. 4] rods | cone

33.1 (30.21)   FIG. 4.7] [*penc.*] "external granular"—bipolar cells

33.1 (30.21)   FIG. 4.3] [*penc.*] external plexiform zone

33.1 (30.21)   FIG. 4.2] [*penc.*] "internal granular layer" bipolar cells

33.1 (30.21)   FIG. 4] [*penc.*] 'infr arborization of bipolar cells for rods.' *written in mrgn. beside penc. drawing (see below), which is connected to left of lower half of diagram*

33.2 (30.24)   (See Fig. 5.)] [*penc.*] R. y. C. Nouvelles idées, p. 112 int. gran. layer also contains horizontal cells & spongioblasts
    Santiago Ramón y Cajal (1852–1934), Spanish anatomist, *Les Nouvelles idées sur la structure du système nerveux chez l'homme et chez les vertébrés*, trans. L. Azoulay (Paris: Reinwald, 1895). James's copy is in Widener (Phil 6127.7.10).

34.1 (30.19)   FIG. 5.] [*penc.*] The stimulation spreads to more members as we go deeper. A single cone affects several ganglion cells. p. 124

48.5 (46.34)   process.] [*penc.*] Upright vision | Stratton
    George Malcolm Stratton (1865–1957), American psychologist, "Some Preliminary Experiments on Vision without Inversion of the Retinal Image," *Psychological Review*, 3 (November 1896), 611–617; "Vision without Inversion of the Retinal Image," *Psychological Review*, 4 (July 1897), 341–360; (September 1897), 463–481.

49.10 (48.6)   "*The Tympanum*] [*ink*] Earache | Deafness

49.17 (48.14)   *tympanic membrane* [*underl. in ink*]] [*ink*] moist, soft

50.18 (49.3)   *The Auditory Ossicles.*] [*ink*] Phylogeny

Appendix

51.1 (48.34)   Fig. 18.] [*ink*] Experiment!

56.4 (54.16)   discerned.] [*ink*] 2 *vibrations ['b' *ov.* 't'] suffice?

56.23 (55.3)   **The 'timbre'**] [*ink*] Diagram of composition

56.31–32 (55.13)   effect.] [*ink*] Show beats.

58.9–10 (56.37)   Helmholtz's theory of] [*ink*] If we strike c^1 on the piano, c^2, g^2, c^3, e^3, *ut sol ut mi* sound with it.

58.10–14 (57.1–6)   One . . . for.] [*ink*] *vert. line in mrgn. and* 'denied by Külpe p. 114.' *written beside it*
        Oswald Külpe (1862–1915), Latvian-born psychologist, *Grundriss der Psychologie* (Leipzig: Engelmann, 1893) (WJ 747.51).

58.13 (57.5)   pitch] [*ink*] '11,600 as a maximum (Külpe, 111)' *insrtd. w. ink guideline aft.* 'pitch'

59.2 (58.1)   feeling] [*penc.*] Get a la_2 fork

59.26 (58.27)   ratio 8:9] [*penc.*] minor triad | la_3 ut_4 mi_4

59.35 (58.37)   place.] [*penc.*]

60.7 (59.13)   In the neighborhood of 1000] [*ink*] 'In . . . of' *del. and* 'Between 200 and' *subst. at bottom of page, joined by guideline to del. text*

60.11–12 (59.18–19)   differ equally [*underl. in ink*]] [*ink*] 'in a musical way; and yet in an absolute way c & c-sharp (on the harmonical, *c* sharp and *d*) Sanford p. 65) seem wider apart *in ['i' *ov.* 'o'] the higher than *in ['i' *ov.* 'o'] the lower octaves.' *insrtd. aft.* 'equally' *w. guideline*
        Edmund Clark Sanford (1859–1924), American psychologist, *A Course in Experimental Psychology*, part I, *Sensation and Perception* (Boston: D. C. Heath, 1894).

62.16–17 (61.15)   organs . . . touch. [*underl. in ink*]] [*ink*] Aristotle | Berkeley | Spencer

63.24–25 (62.22)   improvable by practice.] [*ink*] underl.

63.34 (62.37)   determined by the] [*ink*]
'B-Séq. | 2 things same as 3rd thing
not same as each other!——*Felt* diffs are

resultants of many smaller ones, unfelt. Stumpf treats cochlear terminations similarly.' *written across bottom of pp.* 62 *and* 63

    Charles Édouard Brown-Séquard (1817–1894), Mauritian physiologist.

63.34 (63.1) anatomical] *[ink]* Map of skin in Nerve Centres. Localization philosophy.—Motion may give order.—Autoplastic operations

64.8–9 (63.14–15) nerve-... tactile;] *[ink] underl.*

65.1 (64.1) and gullet] *[ink]* Hist. of discovery: Goldscheider & Donaldson.
    For a possible reference to Goldscheider see note to 65.10, but Goldscheider has too many papers and books on the general subject of sensitivity for definite identification.
    For Donaldson see note to 65.11. Nothing else fitting James's reference was found.

65.24 (64.30) *temperature-sensation zero* [*underl. in ink*]] *[ink]* explain

66.3 (65.4) "The change] *[ink]* adaptation

66.36 (66.6) Great importance] *[ink]* Goldscheider p. 74

67.26 (67.1) **Pain.**] *[ink]* Specific energy of pain proper— *[penc.]* disagreeableness a motor effect.

67.26–27 (67.1–2) One might suppose] *[ink]* Adaptation of pleasure. *Pleasure *[ov. illeg.]* of contrast.—of rest.

68.1 (67.15) Fig. 27] *[ink]* Horwicz on disagreeableness of too feeble stimuli.

68.6 (67.23) agreeableness the] *[penc.]* Marshall on pleasures of relief.
    Henry Rutgers Marshall (1852–1927), American architect and writer, *Pain, Pleasure, and Æsthetics* (London: Macmillan, 1894) (WJ 453.78), p. 294. James reviewed the book in the *Nation*, 59 (July 19, 1894), 49–51.

68.21 (68.17–18) special 'pain-spots'] *[ink] underl.*

68.22 (68.18–19) spots which ... feelingless.] *[ink] all underl.*

68.26 (68.23) *analgesia,* [*underl. in ink*]] *[ink]* Retardation Burkhardt | Our own results. | Wundt's scheme. | Schiff's theory

69.32–33 (69.25) concerning them.] *[penc.]* Munsterberg on Schmerz & Unlust, Unlust to me of orange peel smell.
    Hugo Münsterberg, *Beiträge*, pt. 4, pp. 216–238. See *Essays in Psychology*, Works, p. 307n.

70.0 (70.0) CHAPTER VI.] *[penc.]* Philosophy of "seizing by the middle" | Life unifies what conception can't.

71.30–31 (71.34–35) primitive ... such,] *[penc.] all underl.*

71.32–33 (71.36–37) and ... parts.] *[penc.] all underl.*

72.2 (72.11) Any relative motion] *[penc.]* Optical vertigo. | R R.—illusion

72.4–5 (72.13–14) when ... giddy,] *[penc.] all underl.*

74.4 (74.32) artificially anæsthetic [*underl. in ink*]] [*ink*] 'by induction currents' *written in bottom mrgn., joined by guideline to* 'anæsthetic'

74.12–13 (75.6) semicircular canals] [*penc.*] *underl.*

75.1 (76.3) If a man] [*penc.*] Luciani's doubts [*short rule*]

75.36 (77.6) mention.] [*penc.*] F. S. Lee (Cbl. f. Physiol. 19 Nov 92) in Aubert-Delage's book) finds dog fish make compensatory movements *of eyes and fins [*insrtd.*] (perfectly definite) when canals are irritated, & lose all power of equilibrium when all ampullae are destroyed or both auditory Nvs cut through. Removing otoliths had less effect (Woods Hole work). | Résumé of whole subject by Wlassak, 4teljsch, Bd 16 & 17. | The otolith-sensation should be likened to the fovea-sensation—or the sensation of non accommodation. The body moves as the eye moves, until the discomfort is relieved.

    Frederic Schiller Lee (1859–1939), American physiologist, "Über den Gleichgewichtssinn," *Centralblatt für Physiologie*, 6 (November 19, 1892), 508–512.

    Hermann Aubert (1826–1892), German physiologist, *Physiologische Studien über die Orientierung unter Zugrundelegung von Yves Delage: Études expérimentales sur les illusions statiques et dynamiques de direction pour servir à déterminer les fonctions des canaux demi-circulaires de l'oreille interne* (Tübingen: Laupp, 1888). The title refers to Yves Delage (1854–1920), French zoologist. James frequently filed clippings in his books. The paper by Lee, apparently, was inserted in Aubert's book.

    Marine Biological Laboratory in Woods Hole, Mass.

    Rudolf Wlassak (b. 1865), "Die statischen Functionen des Ohrlabyrinthes und ihre Beziehungen zu den Raumempfindungen," *Vierteljahrsschrift für wissenschaftliche Philosophie*, 16 (1892), 385–403; 17 (1893), 15–29.

76.0–77.11 (78.0–79.33) CHAPTER VII. . . . probe for-] *clipping laid in: brief article in* Science, n.s. 3 (January 17, 1896), 94, *titled* "Relation of the Brain and Spinal Cord in Man," *on Prof. Ranke's discoveries on the weight of the brain in proportion to the spinal cord in man and the other vertebrates*

    Johannes Ranke (1836–1916), German anthropologist.

76.0 (78.0) CHAPTER VII.] [*penc.*] Minot's paper in pamphlet case "Brain" | Schäfer's article on the Nerve-cell as basis of Neurology, in Brain, 1893, p. 134

    Charles Sedgwick Minot (1852–1914), American biologist.

    Edward Albert Schafer, "The Nerve Cell Considered as the Basis of Neurology," *Brain*, 16 (1893), 134–169.

76.1 (78.1) **Embryological Sketch.**] [*penc.*] Complication due to twisting in course of evolution, original simpler plan obscured, as in case of small bones of ear. [*short rule*] Clearing up due to patience [*short rule*] Methods of embryology & degeneration [*short rule*]

76.24–25 (78.20) I have seen.] [*ink*] Morat: Centres Nerveux fonctionnels et trophiques. Rev. Scientif. Dec 1. 94 31me Année p *679 ['7' *ov.* '8']

    Jean Pierre Morat (1846–1920), French physiologist, "Qu'est-ce qu'un centre nerveux? (Centres fonctionnels et centres trophiques)," *Revue Scientifique*, 4th series, vol. 2 (1894), pp. 642–647, 679–685.

77.11 (79.33)   probe for-] [*penc.*] Flechsig's Ideas
  Paul Emil Flechsig (1847–1929), German physiologist and psychiatrist. For works from James's library see *The Principles of Psychology*, WORKS, note to 48.2–3.

89.0 (91.0)   CHAPTER VIII.] [*penc.*] Read Ward's article, Mind, N.S. III 509
  James Ward (1843–1925), British philosopher and psychologist, "Assimilation and Association," pt. 2, *Mind*, n.s. 3 (October 1894), 509–532.

90.34–35 (93.1)   thereby . . . from [*underl. in penc.*]] [*penc.*] '& destroying the brain' *in top mrgn., joined by guideline to* 'thereby'

91.23–24 (93.35)   *centre . . . movements*] [*ink*] *all underl.*

92.13 (94.13–14)   with . . . swallows;] [*ink*] *all underl.*

92.14 (94.14)   cerebellum] [*ink*] *underl.*

92.14–15 (94.15)   jumps . . . back;] [*ink*] *all underl.*

92.15 (94.16)   optic . . . croaks] [*ink*] *all underl.*

92.17 (94.18)   *animal.*] [*ink*] Steiner.
  Isidor Steiner (1849–1914), German physiologist. For a possible reference see *The Principles of Psychology*, WORKS, note to 80.17.

94.4–5 (96.24)   It . . . colonel] [*penc.*] *all underl.*

94.7 (96.26)   *The same*] [*ink*] Meynert

94.7 (96.26–27)   *repeatedly . . . heights*] [*ink*] *all underl.*

96.16 (99.6)   First . . . post-] [*penc.*] *all underl.*

100.15 (104.1)   inhibit,] [*penc.*] *comma del.*

104.1 (108.5)   FIG. 43.] [*penc.*] Insist on Meynert's idea of association fibres

104.12 (110.3)   41] [*ink*] '1' *corr. to* '3'

112.18 (118.29)   formulational together] [*penc.*] *corr. to* 'formulation altogether'

113.15–16 (120.18)   When a frog's] [*ink*] Explain this

119.16–17 (127.15)   twice . . . read] [*ink*] *all underl.*

119.17–19 (127.15–18)   words . . . words.] [*ink*] *all underl.*

120.3 (128.8)   Dr. Romanes] [*penc.*] Bigham Elementary vs. total efficiency |
Huber on Ants | Fawcett *armless ['arm' *ov. illeg.*] & legless man [*short rule*]
  John Bigham, "Memory," *Psychological Review*, 1 (September 1894), 453–461. Bigham received his doctorate from Harvard in 1893. His contribution is part of a report from the Harvard Psychological Laboratory.
  Both Pierre Huber (1777–1840), Swiss naturalist, and Jacques Huber (1867–1914), Swiss biologist, have published works on ants. The latter's appeared in 1905.

447

125.0 (134.0)   CHAPTER X.] [*ink*] Sow an action, & you reap a habit; sow a habit & you reap a character; sow a character and you reap a destiny.

125.0 (134.0)   HABIT.] [*ink*] Waring's letter

126.1–2 (135.1)   into something] [*ink*] Make it clear that without a body we need not be in the least subject to the law of habit.

132.30 (143.11)   Most domestic beasts] [*ink*] trained dog or horse.

138.8 (150.1)   bundles] [*ink*] Commit yourself irretrievably (Foster's decision of character, p. 31. The Kreipe advertisement.
    John Foster (1770–1843), English essayist, "On Decision of Character" (1805). James could have used any one of numerous editions; for a possible case see *The Varieties of Religious Experience* (New York: Longmans, Green, 1902), pp. 178–179.
    Kreipe: see *Talks to Teachers*, WORKS, p. 49, for an advertisement that may be the one referred to here.

138.34 (150.30)   together.] [*penc.*] Skip to p. 370 | take to 375 | [*ink*] **Darwin** on poetry, Life, Vol I, p. 100 | College chapel (J. J. P.'s Hindoo) | Sudden radical conversions.
    In his autobiography Darwin complains of his growing inability to appreciate poetry, *The Life and Letters of Charles Darwin*, ed. Francis Darwin, 3 vols. (London: John Murray, 1887), I, 100–102.
    The initials seem to stand for James Jackson Putnam (1846–1918), Boston physician, a student with James in the Harvard Medical School.

139.0 (151.0)   CHAPTER XI.] [*penc.*] Refer to Maher's book, p. 232 | Lloyd Morgan's *Psych. [*ov.* 'boo'] for T. pp 1–5 & Introd. to Comp. Psych.
    Michael Maher (1860–1917), Jesuit philosopher and psychologist, *Psychology* (London: Longmans, Green, 1890).
    For Morgan, see entry 14.39.

141.19–20 (153.28)   most . . . nature [*underl. in ink*]] [*ink*] "eject"

141.31 (154.4)   **Consciousness**] [*ink*] Talk of Locke's "ideas" etc

142.20–23 (154.37–155.4)   The grass . . . effect] [*ink*] impressionistic painting

142.40 (155.23)   be.] [*ink*] *period alt. to comma and* 'yet the latter looks white.' *added*

157.2 (172.36)   halls] [*penc.*] 'h' *corr. to* 'b'

157.3 (172.37)   been so] [*penc.*] Billy & the dead cat at Lucca
    The reference is to James's son William (b. 1882). The whole family spent about six months in Florence in 1892–1893, and Lucca is near Florence.

158.35 (175.10)   led.] [*penc.*] Ladd's triune unity etc. | Higher & Lower states

160.23 (177.25)   two] [*penc.*] '3' *in mrgn. for del.* 'two'

163.25 (181.15)   This collection] [*ink*] Somatic 'content'-theory.

165.27 (183.36)   friends.] [*ink*] Read Horwicz in P. of P. I. 326 | Recall Bain's view of self love.
    In *The Principles of Psychology*, WORKS, pp. 309–311, James quotes Adolf Horwicz.

173.39–174.1 (194.4–7)   *Its . . . mind.*] [*penc.*] *vert. line in mrgn.*

174.28 (194.37)   fascinated] [*ink*] Read Jas. Mill, II. 201, 216+ | Bain. E & W. 126, –7, –32
    James Mill, *Analysis of the Phenomena of the Human Mind.*
    Alexander Bain, *The Emotions and the Will.*

175.35 (196.15)   **The Unity**] [*ink*] Vide Supra p. 23

176.28 (197.16)   [*space*] the pack] [*ink*] 'of' *added in the space*

176.29 (197.16)   spades] [*ink*] *comma added*

176.36 (197.24)   of] [*ink*] 'in' *in mrgn. for del.* 'of'

178.2 (199.5)   emerge,] [*ink*] *semicolon in mrgn. for del. comma*

178.27–28 (199.34)   *a* + idea of *b* is] [*ink*] *commas added aft.* 'a' *and* 'b'; 'plus' *in mrgn. for del.* '+'; 'are' *in bottom mrgn., joined by guideline to del.* 'is'

178.30–31 (200.1)   can never] [*ink*] Paulsen on Soul, Einleitung, Bk. I, Ch. I. § 7. | Wundt's System, p. 289 ff.
    Friedrich Paulsen (1846–1908), German philosopher, *Einleitung in die Philosophie* (Berlin: Hertz, 1892) (WJ 768.89). For the relations between James and Paulsen see *Essays in Philosophy*, WORKS, note to 90.1.
    Wilhelm Wundt, *System der Philosophie* (Leipzig: Engelmann, 1889) (WJ 796.59.6).

179.22–23 (200.37)   ultimate.] [*ink*] If you say the single state needs a supporter in which to inhere—it inheres in the stream which then supports it laterally.

179.24 (201.1)   But there] [*penc.*] Read Ladd's Phil. of M. p. 195–6
    George Trumbull Ladd, *Philosophy of Mind: An Essay in the Metaphysics of Psychology* (New York: Charles Scribner's Sons, 1895) (WJ 448.17.2).

181.6 (202.35–36)   no *substantial* identity,] [*ink*] *underl.*

181.8 (202.37)   *functional* identity] [*ink*] *underl.*

182.34 (205.1)   as its own.] [*ink*] Needlessness of Soul: Stream provides for 1) support 2) unity 3) identity 4) immortality just as well

189.39 (213.34)   common;] [*penc.*] *caret aft.* 'common' *and paren in mrgn.*

190.22–23 (214.23)   *possible*] [*penc.*] 'actual' *in mrgn. for del.* 'possible'

191.34 (216.7)   thinkers.] [*ink*] Immortality: Brain *may* be principle not so much of *production* as of *restriction* of consciousness. Schiller: R. of S. 293

Appendix

[*short rule*] | Hypnotism like Sleep.—Automatic writing | Gurney's boys | Ansel B's case | Mrs Shaler's case | Dessoir's case | Whittier case (frondate palms) | Janet's Marie. | Dissociation & synthesis.

For James's view of the functions of the brain see his *Human Immortality*, reprinted in *Essays in Religion and Morality*, WORKS.

Ferdinand Canning Scott Schiller (1864–1937), British philosopher, *Riddles of the Sphinx* (London: Swan Sonnenschein, 1891). The text is quoted by James in *Human Immortality*, in *Essays in Religion and Morality*, WORKS, pp. 94n–95n.

Edmund Gurney (1847–1888), British aesthetician and psychical researcher. For the relations between James and Gurney see *The Will to Believe*, WORKS, notes to 225.38 and 228.11.

For the case of Ansel Bourne see *Essays in Psychology*, WORKS, p. 269.

Marie is a mental patient described in Pierre Janet's *Automatisme psychologique*; for the case see *Essays in Psychology*, WORKS, pp. 266–267.

192.0 (217.0)   CHAPTER XIII.] [*ink*] Take Chapter on Reasoning here

192.0 (217.0)   ATTENTION.] [*ink*] Cf. Külpe in Monist, xiii, 38
Oswald Külpe, "The Problem of Attention," *Monist*, 13 (July 1903), 38–68.

194.39–195.7 (220.16–25)   Where . . . Wundt.] [*ink*] Baskworth | Solomons | Scripture's Camera-image, in F. Th. & D.
Leon M. Solomons and Gertrude Stein, "Normal Motor Automatism," *Psychological Review*, 3 (September 1896), 492–512, part of a report from the Harvard Psychological Laboratory.
Edward Wheeler Scripture (1864–1945), American psychologist, *Thinking, Feeling, Doing* (Meadville, Pa.: Flood and Vincent, 1895), pp. 90–91.

195.9 (220.28)   sight] [*penc.*] 'sound' *in mrgn. for del.* 'sight'

195.16 (220.36)   or to] [*ink*] Hibben's girl ['bl' *del.*] deaf when not attending.
John Grier Hibben (1861–1933), American philosopher, "Sensory Stimulation by Attention," *Psychological Review*, 2 (June 1895), 369–375.

201.29–30 (228.30–32)   1) *The . . . place.*] [*penc.*] 'Students are troubled by this which seems not to cover the case of *sensorial [1's' *ov.* 'a'] attention to an object seen for the first time.' *written at bottom of pp.* 228–229 *and linked by guideline to lemma*

207.12 (235.18)   preperception] [*ink*] *underl.*

207.37 (236.21)   less] [*ink*] 'more' *in mrgn. for del.* 'less'

208.12 (236.37)   deepen one's] [*ink*] Give child something to *be attentive with*!

209.4 (237.37)   rattling off] [*ink*] *hyphen added in mrgn.*

210.0 (239.0)   CONCEPTION.] [*penc.*] = Notion = *idea ['ea' *erased*]

211.2 (240.1)   does not] [*penc.*] Conception vs. imagination

211.10–26 (240.10–28)   Some . . . know] *clipping pasted in facing this section of p.* 240, *the beginning of a review of* C. H. Judd's *translation of* Wundt's Outlines of Psychology; *no reference given*

212.3–11 (241.10–18)   *man . . .* mean] *fragment of review (see entry* 211.10–26 [240.10–28]) *pasted in facing this section of p.* 241

212.28 (241.37)   thing] [*penc.*] Binomial theorem | undistributed middle

213.1 (242.17)   The . . . conceptualists [*underl. in penc.*]] [*penc.*] 'A student poses me by asking: "Can we then conceive the inconceivable?" as if it were like ['break up the' *del.*] resisting the irresistible etc. Explain the ambiguity.

Round square. Offer ⊖ . Suppose he says: "that is n't what I meant." This shows that he did mean s'thing distinct' *written on top and along mrgn. of page, linked to lemma by underl.*

213.19 (243.1)   that of the] [*ink*] Concepts as working instruments for reasoning etc. Their gradual acquisition, beginning with those of concrete things and their properties. The limited stock of them which most of us have.

215.0 (244.0)   CHAPTER XV.] [*penc.*] Progress of knowledge

222.11 (252.29–38)   smell. [¶] The . . . here.] [*ink*] 'The . . . here.' *del. (see Emendations entry* 222.11 *for del. text)*

223.0 (253.0)   CHAPTER XVI.] [*penc.*] Logical ass^n presupposes mechanical ass^n | Rabier | *Start ['r' *ov.* 'l'] a music box—off goes the whole tune, picked out by tooth after tooth so our memory of it by cell after cell.
      Élie Rabier (b. 1846), French philosopher.

223.1–2 (253.2)   It is obvious] [*ink*] The whole mental content is remotely associable with any one idea. | Cf. Nordau Psych. du Mysticisme.
      Max Simon Nordau (1849–1923), German-Jewish journalist, perhaps a chapter on "The Psychology of Mysticism," in his *Degeneration*, English translation (New York: D. Appleton, 1895).

223.26 (253.29)   sort of] [*penc.*] Synopsias | folding | All Scotchmen hateful—Wednesday comb & mirror

223.26–224.6 (254.1–6)   connection . . . succession,] [*penc.*] *vert. line in mrgn.,* 'See 256' *written beside it*

224.1 (254.1)   *thought-of*] [*ink*] 'between the objects of the successive thoughts' *insrtd. w. guideline aft. '-of', then del.*

224.1 (254.2)   thoughts] [*ink*] 'the' *in mrgn. w. caret bef. 'thoughts' and 'themselves' insrtd. w. guideline aft. 'thoughts', but then 'themselves' and 'thoughts' del. and instead 'the things tho't of' insrtd. w. guideline bef. del. 'thoughts'*

224.32 (255.1)   thousand] [*ink*] logical bond between ideas *vs. ['v' *ov.* 'b'] mechanical bond

451

225.23–30 (256.1–8) if we . . . thought.] [*penc.*] *vert. line in mrgn.*; 'Students find this inconsistent with p. 254' *written at top of page*

227.6 (257.36) simply by] [*penc.*] abc def ghi
constellation.
abad def ect
Cf. *Talks to Teachers*, WORKS, p. 60.

232.37 (264.37) -merchant or an] [*ink*] Munsterberg on "Constellation"
Hugo Münsterberg, *Beiträge*, pt. 4, pp. 23–32.

236.3 (269.1) also similar] [*ink*] Plenty of examples in Stratton; "the Spire"

242.5–8 (276.15–17) revival . . . call] [*penc.*] *horiz. line in mrgn.*

244.32–33 (279.21) his acts.] [*penc.*] Egoistic emotions inhibit Associations

245.6 (280.7) "Le . . . moi,"] [*penc.*] Boileau
See note to 245.5.

250.28 (286.31) things.] [*penc.*] Von Baer | Haschisch
For the reference to Karl Ernst von Baer (1792–1876), German naturalist, and hashish see *The Principles of Psychology*, WORKS, pp. 601–602.

251.0 (287.0) CHAPTER XVIII.] [*penc.*] Cf ['f' *ov.* 'p'] Memory & foreknowledge or expectancy | *Faculty ['c' *ov.* 'l'] view. Ideas not *things* but processes | No reservoir

252.2 (287.29) snug in its] [*ink*] Kay's book
David Kay, British geographer and writer, *Memory: What It Is and How to Improve It* (New York: D. Appleton, 1888).

252.8–12 (288.9–13) past together . . . instant of] [*penc.*] *vert. line in mrgn.*

256.8 (293.1) The persistence] [*penc.*] 'Show by Ebbinghaus' *linked w. guideline to* 'persistence'
Hermann Ebbinghaus (1850–1909), German psychologist; for references see *The Principles of Psychology*, WORKS, note to 625.36.

256.40 (293.37) equilibrium may] [*ink*] Memories, not memory.—Teach by as many channels as possible.

258.23 (295.37) brain-processes] [*ink*] The way to attend. Form a routine habit of naming, comparing, *expressing* yourself somehow about each impression you wish to keep:—That works it in.

261.1 (298.37) way.] [*penc.*] Romanes | Bigham

261.1 (299.1) The method] [*penc.*] Scientific texts—teach by all channels In learning don't hammer in

261.16–21 (299.17–22) **Recognition** . . . *recognize*] [*penc.*] *vert. line in mrgn.*

261.35 (299.32) *A common] [*penc.*] Chas I 649 sharp | L. M. Vibgyor
Cf. *Talks to Teachers*, WORKS, p. 80, where James uses these same examples.

263.18 (301.33)   forgotten.] [*ink*] Ebbinghaus | *The [*ov.* 'Our']
most important part of our
memory is a changed disposition
towards re-acquiring.

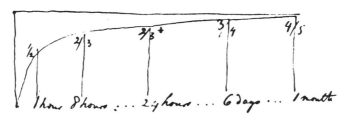

264.0 (302.0)   CHAPTER XIX.] [*ink*] Images of abstract ideas—a foot | a
pound, a minute, a difference.

267.17–19 (305.31–32)   But . . . and to] [*penc.*] *vert. line in mrgn.*

267.23–24 (305.37)   imaginative] [*penc.*] Armstrong Class

	1	II	III	IV.	V
%	13	48	29	7	3

     Andrew Campbell Armstrong (1860–1935), American educator,
"The Imagery of American Students," *Psychological Review*, 1 (September 1894), 496–505.

272.13 (311.31)   the act.] [*ink*] Scripture's (Sea*shore's) results. [*ov. penc.* 'To 329']
     Carl Emil Seashore (1866–1949), Swedish-born psychologist.

273.0 (312.0)   CHAPTER XX.] [*ink*] We can't tell with eyes closed whether
our cigar is lit or not,—can't distinguish betw. white & red wine,—can't tell
whether music good or not till we know who composer is, etc.

273.0 (312.0)   CHAPTER XX.] [*penc.*] tr

274.32 (314.1)   have aroused] [*penc.*] I said not and but is

276.15 (315.37)   mind.] [*ink*] *Vividness greatest [*ov. penc.* 'Pure sensati'] in
final processes. Whatever inhibits association-currents makes original sensation
stronger. *| [WJ *vert. stroke*] Wernicke

281.29 (322.15)   hefore] [*penc.*] 'h' *corr. to* 'b'

285.3 (326.21–22)   'Apperception'] [*ink*] Example in Dörpfeld p. 47

     Friedrich Wilhelm Dörpfeld (1824–1893), German psychologist.
James is referring to the adaptation by Herman Tyson Lukens, *The
Connection between Thought and Memory: A Contribution to Pedagogical Psychology on the Basis of F. W. Dörpfeld's Monograph "Denken und Gedächtnis"* (Boston: Heath, 1895).

285.18 (326.37)   cognition is] [*ink*] Is that (Niagara) the kind of spray I spray
my nose with.
     Cf. *Talks to Teachers*, WORKS, pp. 97–98.

285.27–30 (327.11–15)   In . . . system.] [*ink*] Porpoise | Fish.

286.9 (327.35)   'ball.' He] [*ink*] Pot of green feathers.
 Cf. *Talks to Teachers*, WORKS, p. 97.

286.10–11 (328.2–3)   his 'eggs' . . . his potatoes] [*penc.*] *each 'his' del.*

286.10–11 (328.2)   'eggs' . . . into] [*penc.*] 'already' *added w. guideline aft.*
"eggs"; 'into' *corr. to* 'in'

286.16–17 (328.9)   Old-fogyism] [*ink*] All due to fact of brain paths

288.14 (330.24–25)   *An hallucination*] [*penc.*] *Taine*

291.9 (334.10)   Sporadic] [*ink*] *wavy dash in mrgn. and* '30 coincidentals in
1300 cases = $\frac{1}{43}$ death rate and consequently chance rate = $\frac{1}{19000}$ | $\frac{1}{43}$ =
$\frac{440}{19,000}$ times the most probable no. At this rate we should expect to need
570 000 cases to yield 30 coincidentals.' *written at foot of page*

292.0 (335.0)   CHAPTER XXI.] [*penc.*] Strattons experiment.

298.29–30 (343.5)   *Thus* . . . *be*] [*penc.*] *alt. to all rom.*

298.30 (343.5–6)   really smaller] [*penc.*] *alt. to ital.*

301.4 (345.37)   definite and] [*penc.*] Selection again!

303.27–30 (349.8–11)   Touch- . . . object] [*penc.*] *vert. line in mrgn.*

305.0 (351.0)   CHAPTER XXII.] [*ink*] See Dorpfeld's Tho't & Memory. p. 15
(important)

307.22–24 (353.34–36)   M . . . P] [*penc.*]

309.7 (355.36)   A God] [*ink*] Rousseau Emile III. 21
 James's library contained the *Œuvres complètes de J. J. Rousseau*,
13 vols. (Paris: Hachette, 1865), with vols. 2 and 3 containing the
Émile.

310.1 (356.37)   title for] [*ink*] German schoolmaster and print of Sistine
Madonna

311.23 (358.37)   attain.] [*ink*] The essence of a false diamond, ruby or sap-
phire is to sink in a solution of 5 times the density of H_2O. It is usually composed of Ag & Thal. nitrate

315.30–41 (364.9–22)   Now . . . 251.] [*penc.*] *brace in mrgn. w. del. mk. and*
'(?)' *beside brace*

324.0 (373.0)   CHAPTER XXIV.] [*penc.*] We often say we are sad when no
emotion proper is there. "Religious" feelings, family feeling etc. not true

species.—Contrast betw. demonstrative and deep feeling types of character. (Rosina) Furneaux Jordan's shrew & non-shrew. 2 types of actors.

    Probably Rosina Emmet, James's distant cousin. James's letters to her are in Houghton (bMS Am 1092.9 [903a–903m]); one letter is included in *The Letters of William James*, ed. Henry James (Boston: Atlantic Monthly Press, 1920).

    John Furneaux Jordan, English anthropologist, *Character as Seen in Body and Parentage; with a Chapter on Education, Career, Morals, and Progress*, new edition (London: Kegan Paul, Trench, Trübner, 1890), pp. 7–8.

333.35–38 (385.5–9) It . . . acts.] [*penc.*] *vert. line in mrgn.*

336.5–6 (387.33) the psychical . . . represen-] [*penc.*] ? ? ?

337.33 (390.1) is the effect] [*penc.*] Bad effects of egoistic emotion on association of ideas.

338.17–18 (390.26) pathological] [*penc.*] *underl.*

338.18 (390.27) harmful] [*penc.*] *underl.*

338.21–26 (390.30–35) have . . . -accidental] [*penc.*] *vert. line in mrgn. w.* 'comment on this' *beside it*

338.26 (390.36) way.] [*penc.*] Miss Call's philosophy & American habit.
    Annie Payson Call (1853–1940), American mental health writer. James reviewed her work in the *Nation*, 52 (March 19, 1891), 246–247; 60 (February 7, 1895), 116.

339.0 (391.0) CHAPTER XXV.] [*ink*] See Perrier in Bull. de l'Ist. Psych. Internat^{le} No 7.
    Edmond Perrier (1842–1921), French naturalist, "L'Instinct," *Bulletin de L'Institut Psychologique International*, 1 (December 1901), 305–320.

340.26–27 (392.32–33) sensation- . . . idea-impulses] [*penc.*] *all underl.*

341.13 (393.27) ditch-] [*penc.*] 'pond' *in mrgn. for del.* 'ditch'

345.28 (399.9) The selection] [*penc.*] Tweedy's refusal to speak english to his parents.
    Tweedy is James's son Alexander Robertson (b. 1890), called Francis Tweedy in his early years.

346.28 (400.17) superior authority] [*penc.*] Morgan denies instinctive fear in certain birds

350.15 (405.1) may be] [*penc.*] Paedagogic remarks

350.30–31 (405.18) the . . . twenty-five are [*underl. in penc.*]] [*penc.*] Comment. Intellectual *power* fully developed at 21

353.20 (409.1) smiled] [*penc.*] Lloyd Morgan

356.38 (413.9–10) The latter condition] [*ink*] Is the pathological impotency in all fear connected with this utility?

357.38 (414.21)   to play?] [*ink*] On will, See Garman festscript, 2 last Essays.
Robert Sessions Woodworth (1869–1962), American psychologist, "The Cause of a Voluntary Movement"; Charles Theodore Burnett (b. 1873), American psychologist, "An Experimental Test of the Classical Theory of Volition" in *Studies in Philosophy and Psychology by Former Students of Charles Edward Garman* (Boston and New York: Houghton, Mifflin, 1906).

358.0 (415.0)   CHAPTER XXIII.] [*ink*] Voluntaristic psychol.—Lump feeling & conation. Refer to p. 170; 237

358.0 (415.0)   WILL.] [*penc.*] Broader & narrower sense of word will. | Scholastic faculty vs. associationism

358.25 (415.29)   emotional] [*penc.*] facultas appetendi

362.18–19 (420.16)   'resident' images] [*penc.*] Royce's exp'ts
Josiah Royce (1855–1916), American philosopher, "The Psychology of Invention," *Psychological Review*, 5 (March 1898), 113–144.

370.24–25 (430.21–22)   The moment we] [*ink*] Faculty votes.

370.36 (430.35)   *the quest . . . conception.*] [*ink*] *all underl.*

372.17 (432.30)   an . . . acceptance] [*ink*] Conversion [*short rule*]

374.27 (435.22)   or finally,] [*penc.*] Merciers cases of jealous man & defaulter
Charles Arthur Mercier (1852–1919), British psychiatrist.

376.2 (437.12–13)   An explosive Italian] [*penc.*] Germans lack inhibitions—English have too many

376.20 (437.34)   How much freedom] [*ink*] 'lying' *written in mrgn. and then del.*

378.7 (439.37)   I could not] [*ink*] Diff. betw. dipsomania and ordinary drinkhabit.

379.37 (442.8)   them,] [*ink*] *comma del.*

390.29 (455.25)   frightened horses] [*penc.*] your tomb

392.23 (457.37)   effort] [*ink*] 'Ordinary caricatures of free will. | *The ['T' *ov.* 'E'] ethical motive of belief in freedom' *written in bottom mrgn. and* 'Fullerton, in Pop. Sci. M. vols 58, 59.' *written vert. in right mrgn. beginning at foot of page*
George Stuart Fullerton (1859–1925), American philosopher, "Freedom and 'Free-Will'," *Popular Science Monthly*, 58 (November 1900), 183–192; "'Free-Will' and the Credit for Good Actions," *Popular Science Monthly*, 59 (October 1901), 526–533.

393.20 (459.6)   and] [*ink*] 'the' *in mrgn. w. caret aft.* 'and'

393.38 (459.27)   face] [*penc.*] 'take' *in mrgn. for del.* 'face'

394.23 (460.18)   world!] [*ink*] Shand, Mind. 1897, p. 289 | Bradley, Mind
Alexander F. Shand (1858–1936), British psychologist, "Types of Will," *Mind*, n.s. 6 (July 1897), 289–325.

Francis Herbert Bradley published a number of papers on the will in *Mind*. It is impossible to tell which James has in mind.

398.34 (465.17)   nam] [*penc.*] 'e' *added in mrgn.*

(verso of back flyleaf)   [*penc.*] C. K. Cummings [*diff. penc.*] 254, 288
   Perhaps Charles Kimball Cummings, a student at Harvard in 1889–1893.

(recto of end paper)   [*penc.*] Experiments to do. 21

A Note on the Editorial Method

These volumes of THE WORKS OF WILLIAM JAMES offer the critical text of a definitive edition of his published and unpublished writings (letters excepted). A text may be called 'critical' when an editor intervenes to correct the errors and aberrations of the copy-text[1] on his own responsibility or by reference to other authoritative documents, and also when he introduces authoritative revisions from such documents into the basic copy-text. An edition may be called 'definitive' (a) when the editor has exhaustively determined the authority, in whole or in part, of all preserved documents for the text; (b) when the text is based on the most authoritative documents produced during the work's formulation and execution and then during its publishing history; and (c) when the complete textual data of all authoritative documents are recorded, together with a full account of the edited text's divergences from the document chosen as copy-text, so that the user may reconstruct these sources in complete verbal detail as if they were before him. When backed by this data, a critical text in such a definitive edition may be called 'established' if from the fully recorded documentary evidence it attempts to reconstruct the author's true and fullest intention, even though in some details the restoration of intention from imperfect sources is conjectural and subject to differing opinion.

Not only every different printed version of a work, as between journal and book publication, but every printing of a book during the author's lifetime carries within itself the possibility of authoritative correction and revision which an editor must take into account. Hence, after preserved manuscripts and journal publications have been identified, the definitive form of the book text itself is established by the mechanical collation on the Lindstrand Comparator of the first printing against some posthumous printing from the same plates, followed by the identification by inspection of the precise impression in which any altera-

---

[1] The copy-text is that document, whether a manuscript or a printed edition, chosen by the editor as the most authoritative basis for his text, and therefore one which is reprinted in the present edition subject only to recorded editorial emendations, and to substitution or addition of readings from other authoritative documents, judged to be necessary or desirable for completing James's fullest intentions.

tion in the plates was made, with a view to determining its date and authority. (In the case of *Psychology: Briefer Course,* the only copy of the first printing discovered was in the Library of Congress, and of this printing only a microfilm was available. Hard copy made from the microfilm could not be collated on the comparator because of its difference in type size from that of the book. Variants were found instead by an oral proofreading of the hard copy against a posthumous printing.) Moreover, the James Collection in the Houghton Library of Harvard University contains various examples of article offprints and personal copies of his books annotated with corrections and revisions, valuable evidence of his post-publication intentions to improve the texts. The richness of the James Collection in James's working manuscripts, including various examples of the actual printer's copy, offers a valuable opportunity for an editor to secure documentary evidence not usually available to assist in the many critical and bibliographical decisions required in the formulation of a critical text.

The most important editorial decision for any work edited without modernization[2] is the choice of its copy-text, that documentary form on which the edited text will be based. Textual theorists have long distinguished two kinds of authority: first, the authority of the words themselves—the *substantives*; second, the authority of the punctuation, spelling, capitalization, word-division, paragraphing, and devices of emphasis—the *accidentals* so called—that is, the texture in which the substantives are placed but itself often a not unimportant source of meaning. In an unmodernized edition like the present, an attempt is made to print not only the substantives but also their 'accidental' texture, each in its most authoritative form. The most authoritative substantives are taken to be those that reflect most faithfully the author's

---

[2] By 'modernization' one means the silent substitution for the author's of an entirely new system of punctuation, spelling, capitalization, and word-division in order to bring these original old-fashioned 'accidentals' of the text thoroughly up to date for the benefit of a current reader. It is the theory of the present edition, however, that James's turn-of-the-century 'accidentals' offer no difficulty to a modern scholar or general reader and that to tamper with them by 'modernization' would not only destroy some of James's unique and vigorous flavor of presentation but would also risk distortion of his meaning. Since there is every evidence that, in his books at least, James was concerned to control the texture of presentation and made numerous nonverbal as well as verbal changes in preparing printer's copy, and later in proof, for an editor to interfere with James's specific, or even general, wishes by modernizing his system of 'accidentals' would upset on many occasions the designedly subtle balances of his meaning. Moreover, it would be pointless to change his various idiosyncrasies of presentation. Hence in the present edition considerable pains have been devoted to reprinting the authoritative accidentals of the copy-text and also by emendation to their purification, so far as documentary evidence extends, from the housestyling to which they were subjected in print, which was not entirely weeded out in proof. For a further discussion, see below under the question of copy-text and its treatment.

fullest intentions as he revised to perfect the form and meaning of his work. The most authoritative accidentals are those which are preferential, and even idiosyncratic, in the author's usage even though not necessarily invariable in his manuscripts. These characteristic forms convey something of an author's flavor, but their importance goes beyond aesthetic or antiquarian appreciation since they may become important adjuncts to meaning. It is precisely these adjuncts, however, that are most susceptible to compositorial and editorial styling away from authorial characteristics and toward the uniformity of whatever contemporary system the printing or publishing house fancied. Since few authors are in every respect so firm in their 'accidental' intentions as to demand an exact reproduction of their copy, or to attempt systematically to restore their own system in proof from divergent compositorial styling, their 'acceptance' of printing-house styling is meaningless as an indication of intentions. Thus, advanced editorial theory agrees that in ordinary circumstances the best authority for the accidentals is that of a holograph manuscript or, when the manuscript is not preserved, whatever typed or printed document is closest to it, so that the fewest intermediaries have had a chance to change the text and its forms. Into this copy-text—chosen on the basis of its most authoritative accidentals —are placed the latest revised substantives, with the result that each part of the resulting eclectic text is presented in its highest documentary form of authority.[3] It is recognized, however, that an author may be so scrupulous in supervising each stage of the production of a work that the accidentals of its final version join with the revised substantives in representing his latest intentions more faithfully than in earlier forms of the text. In such special cases a document removed by some stages from a preserved manuscript or from an early intermediary may in practical terms compose the best copy-text.[4]

Each work, then, must be judged on its merits. In general, experience shows that whereas James accepted some journal styling without much objection even though he read proof and had the chance to alter within reason what he wished, he was more seriously concerned with the forms of certain of his accidentals in the books, not only by his marking copy pasted up from journal articles for the printer but more par-

[3] The use of these terms, and the application to editorial principles of the divided authority between both parts of an author's text, was chiefly initiated by W. W. Greg, "The Rationale of Copy-Text," *Studies in Bibliography*, 3 (1950–51), 19–36, reprinted in *The Collected Papers of Sir Walter W. Greg*, ed. J. C. Maxwell (Oxford: Clarendon Press, 1966), pp. 374–391. For extensions of the principle, see Fredson Bowers, "Current Theories of Copy-Text," *Modern Philology*, 68 (1950), 12–20; "Multiple Authority: New Concepts of Copy-Text," *The Library*, 5th ser., 27 (1972), 81–115; "Remarks on Eclectic Texts," *Proof*, 4 (1974), 31–76, all reprinted in *Essays in Bibliography, Text, and Editing* (Charlottesville: University Press of Virginia, 1975).

[4] An extensive analysis of specific problems in the mechanical application of traditional theories of copy-text to revised modern works may be found in Bowers, "Greg's 'Rationale of Copy-Text' Revisited," *Studies in Bibliography*, 31 (1978), 90–161.

ticularly when he received the galley proofs. Indeed, it is not too much to state that James sometimes regarded the copy that he submitted for his books (especially when it was manuscript) as still somewhat in a draft state, to be shaped by proof-alterations to conform to his ultimate intentions. The choice of copy-texts in the WORKS, therefore, rests on the evidence available for each document, and the selection will vary according to the circumstances of 'accidental' authority as superior either in the early or in the late and revised forms of the text. In this connection, the earlier discussions in the textual analyses for the philosophical volumes of this edition give examples of the evidence and its application to the selection of copy-text that are pertinent to the present psychological volume. For *Psychology: Briefer Course*, the first printing of the first edition, designated as BC, has been selected as the copy-text.

On the other hand, although James demonstrably made an effort to control the forms of certain of his accidentals in the proofs, even when he had been relatively careless about their consistency in his manuscript printer's copy, he was not always equally attentive to every detail of the housestyling that printers imposed on his work. In some cases he simply did not observe anomalies even in his own idiosyncratic practices; in others he may have been relatively indifferent when no real clash of principles was involved. Thus, when an editor is aware by reason of inconsistencies within the copy-text that certain 'accidental' printing-house stylings have been substituted for James's own practices as established in manuscripts and marked copy, or have been substituted for relatively neutral journal copy that seems to approximate James's usual practice, he may feel justified in emending to recover by the methods of textual criticism as much of the purity of the Jamesian accidentals as of the substantives—both ultimately contributing to the most complete and accurate expression of James's meaning. However, although the texture of James's carefully worked-over book copy-text is ordinarily accepted in general detail over earlier documents, not every book variant may be thought of as the direct result of James's own marking whether of copy or of proof. On sufficient evidence, most are taken to have derived from this actual authority; nevertheless a decision on such grounds is impossible to make comma for comma, say, and unless contrary evidence is present the general authority of a revised book copy-text is likely to hold so long as it conforms on the whole to James's practices.

Except for the small amount of silent alteration listed below, every editorial change in the copy-text has been recorded, with the identification of its immediate source and the record of the rejected copy-text reading. An asterisk prefixed to the page-line reference (always to this edition) indicates that the alteration is discussed in a Textual Note. The formulas for notation are described in the headnote to the list of Emendations, but it may be well to mention here the use of the term *stet* to call attention in special cases to the retention of the copy-text reading. Textual Notes discuss certain emendations or refusals to emend. The Historical Collation lists all substantive readings for corresponding passages utilized in *Briefer Course* from *The Principles of Psychology* that differ from the edited text except for those recorded in the list of Emendations, which are not repeated in the Historical Collation. The principles for the recording of variants are described in the headnote to this Collation.

A special section of the apparatus treats hyphenated word-compounds. The first list shows those in the present text, with the form adopted, that were broken between lines in the copy-text and thus partake of the nature of emendations. The second lists the correct copy-text form of those broken between lines by the printer of the present edition. Consultation of the second list will enable any user to quote from the present text with the correct hyphenation of the copy-text.

Manuscript material in the Appendix that is reproduced in this edition is transcribed in genetic form,[5] without emendation, except for two features. As with many writers, James's placement of punctuation in relation to quotation marks was erratic, sometimes appearing within the marks as in the standard American system for commas and periods, sometimes outside according to the sense as in the British system, and sometimes carelessly placed immediately below the quotation mark. To attempt to determine the exact position of each mark would often be impossible; hence all such punctuation is placed as it would be by an American printer, the system that James in fact seems to have employed himself when he thought of it. Second, the spacing of ellipsis dots has been normalized. As part of this normalization the distinction is made (James's spacing usually being variable and ambiguous) between the closeup placement of the first of four dots when it represents the period directly after the last quoted word and the spaced placement (as in three dots) when the ellipsis begins in mid-sentence and the fourth dot thus represents the final period.

In this edition of THE WORKS OF WILLIAM JAMES an attempt has been made to identify the exact edition used by James for his quotations from other authors and ordinarily to emend his carelessnesses of transcription so that the quotation will reproduce exactly what the author wrote in every detail. All such changes are noted in the list of Emendations when they concern the substantives. On some occasions James altered quotations for his own purposes in such a manner that his version should be respected. Such readings are retained in the text but recorded in the list of Emendations (with the signal *stet*), and the original form is provided for the information of the consulting scholar. The general principles governing the treatment of emendation within quotations are as follows. As a rule, the author's accidentals are

---

[5] For full details of this system, see F. Bowers, "Transcription of Manuscripts: The Record of Variants," *Studies in Bibliography*, 29 (1976), 212–264.

silently inserted from the original to replace variants created in the normal course of James's copying without particular attention to such features, or of compositorial styling. For substantives, James faced the usual problem of a quoter in getting at the meat of the quotation by judicious condensation. Major omissions he was likely to mark by ellipsis dots. On the other hand, he was by no means invariably scrupulous in indicating a number of his alterations. Thus to condense a quotation he might silently omit material ranging from a phrase to several sentences. Major omissions that would require excessive space to transcribe in the list of Emendations are indicated in the text by editorially added dots, recorded as emendations. For minor condensing omissions, James's text is ordinarily allowed to stand without the distraction of ellipsis dots, and the omitted matter is recorded as part of a *stet* entry in the list of Emendations. However, James's treatment of quotations could be more cavalier. Sometimes to speed up the quotation, but occasionally to sharpen its application to his own ideas, he paraphrased a word or phrase, or a major part of a sentence. Since alteration of this nature was consciously engaged in for literary or philosophic purposes, James's text in such cases is allowed to stand but the original reading is given as part of a *stet* entry in the Emendations. More troublesome are the minor variants in wording that seem to have no purpose ideologically or as condensations. When in the opinion of the editor these represent merely careless or inadvertent slips in copying, on a par with James's sometimes casual transcription of accidentals, the originals are restored as listed emendations. Within James's quotations, paragraphing that he did not observe in the original has not been recorded and final dots have not been added editorially when he ends a quotation short of the completion of a sentence. Variation from the original in James's choice whether to begin a quotation with a capital or lower-case letter has also not been recorded. Similarly, James's syntactical capitalization or use of lower case following ellipsis has been ignored whenever by necessity it differs from the original.

Although James's own footnotes are preserved in the text substantially as he wrote them (the only footnotes allowed in the present edition), the citations have been corrected and expanded as necessary in Professor Skrupskelis' Notes to provide the full bibliographical detail required by a scholar, this ordinarily having been neglected in James's own sketchy notation. The Notes also provide full information about quotations in the text that James did not footnote.

References to McDermott (McD) are to the "Annotated Bibliography," *The Writings of William James*, ed. John J. McDermott (New York: Random House, 1967).

Silent alterations in the text of this work concern themselves chiefly with mechanical presentation. For instance, heading capitals are normalized in the first line of any chapter or section, headings may have their final periods removed, the headlines of the originals may be altered for the purposes of the present edition, anomalous typographical conventions or use of fonts may be normalized including roman or italic syntactical punctuation, which here has been made to conform to a logical system. The minutiæ of the accidentals of footnote reference have not been recorded as emendations or as rejected readings. For example, in the footnotes book titles are silently italicized from whatever other form present in the copy-text, as within quotation marks; the use of roman or italic fonts is normalized as is the general system of punctuating bibliographical references. In short, such matters involving the reference system have been silently brought into conformity with the printing practice of the time, and usually conform to that found in the styling of the period. When unusual features call for unusual treatment, special notice is always given. Abbreviations and ampersands are expanded silently.

All line numbers keyed to the text include section numbers and subheadings but do not include spaces after titles or subheadings or spaces within the text itself.

The intent of the editorial treatment both in large and in small matters, and in the recording of the textual information, has been to provide a clean reading text for the general user, with all specialized material isolated for the convenience of the scholar who wishes to consult it. The result has been to establish in the wording James's fullest intentions in their most authoritative form, divorced from verbal corruption whether in the copy-text or in subsequent printings or editions. To this crucial aim has been added the further attempt to present James's final verbal intentions within a logically contrived system of his own accidentals that in their texture are as close to their most authoritative form as controlled editorial theory can establish from the documentary evidence that has been preserved for each work.

The aid offered by this edition to serious scholars of William James's writings is not confined to the presentation of a trustworthy, purified, and established text. Of equal ultimate importance are the apparatuses and appendixes devoted to the facts about the progress of James's thought from its earliest known beginnings to final publication, and continuing to annotation in his private copy by the record of alterations there that have not previously been made public except in a few of the plate-changes of later printings. Most of the materials here made available for close study of the development and refinement of James's ideas—almost literally in the workshop—have not previously been seen by scholars except in the James Collection of the Houghton Library, and then they could not be studied in detail without tiresome collation (here fully recorded in the apparatus). In other texts the refinements of thought between journal articles and book collection are of particular interest; but in *Psychology: Briefer Course* scholars may find of especial value the corrections, revisions, and general notes from his reading that

James made in his private copy, in some part for use in the classroom, but in some part with a view to a revised edition that was never to materialize.

It is the belief of the editors of the WORKS, and the Advisory Board, that this living historical record of the development of James's psychological ideas and their expression, as found in the apparatus and the appendix, is as significant a part of the proposed 'definitive edition' for the purposes of scholarly research as is the establishment of a corrected text closer to James's own intentions than has previously been available.

F. B.

The Text of *Psychology: Briefer Course*

I. THE HISTORY

The earliest plans for *Psychology: Briefer Course* have not been preserved. Since James's publisher, Henry Holt, issued volumes of his American Science Series both in their original "Advanced Course" form and also in abridged "Briefer Course" textbooks (even a few in "Elementary Course" texts), it is natural to assume that a textbook form of the Advanced Course, *The Principles of Psychology*, had been a part of the understanding between the two men from their earliest negotiations about *Principles*. This view is strengthened by a reference in a letter to Holt of May 9, 1890, when *Principles* was in the last stages of completion: "I was in hopes that you would propose to break away from the famous 'Series' and publish the book independently, in two volumes. An abridgement could then be prepared for the Series" (*The Letters of William James*, ed. Henry James [Boston: Atlantic Monthly Press, 1920] I, 293–294). After *Principles* had been published (on September 24 or 26, 1890), in a letter dated February 12, 1891, primarily concerned with the placement of an advertisement facing the title page in volume II of *Principles*, Holt wrote: "How about that condensed edition? I see Bre'r Ladd is out with one" (Holt Business Letter Book, No. 16, p. 110, Henry Holt Archives, Princeton University Library; typed copy, Harvard bMS Am 1092 [420]). To this James responded in a February note: "As for the shorter course, don't expect it before the middle of next winter. I promise it then; but at present I have other things on hand" (bMS Am 1092.1, typed copy).

However, by late spring he was preparing for the task, as he noted in a letter of June 1, 1891, written to his brother Henry and to his sister, Alice: "I am going to work on an abridgement of my psychology in a fortnight. As it means a lot of rewriting, it will probably take me *all ['a' *ov.* 't'] summer, worse luck to it" (bMS Am 1092.9 [2666]; hereafter all quotations from letters in the bMS Am 1092.9 series will be referred to by individual number only). On June 21 he had written about his plans to Holt, as indicated in a letter of July 3, 1891, from Holt's assistant, Vogelius:

I. *The History*

We have yours of the 21st to our Mr. Henry Holt who is away on his vacation.

We think it by all means best that you should read the proofs yourself. Upon the receipt of your manuscript, we will put it in hand and send you some proofs by September 1st as you suggest.

We think the sale of the large book will be good in the fall.

We are very glad to learn that we shall have the manuscript of the "briefer course" so [incomplete] (Holt Letter Book, Henry Holt Archives, Princeton University Library; hereafter indicated as LB).

By July 6 James seems to have made some sort of start as suggested by a letter sent from Chocorua to his sister, Alice: "I'm about settling down to my tedious summer's task of abridging and partly rewriting my Psychology" (#1154). July 24 found him well advanced when he wrote to Henry Holt:

I expect to send you within ten days the Ms. of my "briefer course," boiled down to possibly 400 pp. By adding some twaddle about the senses, by leaving out all polemics and history, all bibliography and experimental details, all metaphysical subtleties and digressions, all quotations, all humor and pathos, all *interest* in short, and by blackening the tops of all the paragraphs,[1] I think I have produced a tome of pedagogic classic which will enrich both you and me, if not the student's mind.

The difficulty is about when to correct the proofs. I've practically had no vacation so far, and won't touch them during August. I can start them September first up here [in Chocorua]. I can't rush them through in Cambridge as I did last year, but must do them leisurely to suit this northern mail and its hours. I *could* have them done by another man in Cambridge, if there were desperate hurry, but on the whole I should prefer to do them myself.

Write and propose something! The larger book seems to be a decided success —especially from the literary point of view. I begin to look down upon Mark Twain (bMS Am 1092.1, typed copy).

The work was completed in mid-August although the exact date is uncertain. According to letters to his brother Henry, James was in Cambridge on August 10, 12, and 14. He then headed south and a letter of August 15 is dated from Washington, D.C., and another on August 16 from Danville, Virginia. Assuming that James did not leave Chocorua before finishing the abridgement, we may take it that it was completed before August 10, or relatively close to his July 24 estimate to Holt of ten more working days. On August 20 he addressed Henry from Asheville, North Carolina: "This date will doubtless surprise you—I came here a few days ago in search of novelty, being to that degree elaborately tired in my insides after preparing a 'briefer course' of my psychology straight on top of the year's work that I felt like

[1] By this James means the bold-face headings that begin the first paragraphs of the various sections. Obviously, this was a procedure suggested to him by other volumes of the "Briefer Course" series.

['coming s' *del.*] going where I should be reminded of nothing that I had ever seen or heard or smelt or tasted before." Toward the end he remarked, "My psychology seems to be a great success so-far, and I am quite sure that the 'briefer course' will practically be *the* book used in the colleges" (#2667). A few days later on August 23, in a letter written from Roan Mountain to his sister, Alice, he described the success of *Principles* and added, "If the shorter edition captures the market, as I have a certain degree of confidence that it will, both in England and america, I shall make several hundred dollars a year by it" (#1155).

Manuscript, combined with three short printed sections from *Principles* for the first seven chapters, and annotated pasted-up pages of *Principles*, interspersed with various leaves of manuscript for the remainder, comprised the printer's copy. This was probably sent off to Holt on James's arrival in Cambridge, or between August 10 and 14. However, publishing was held up in production by various technical difficulties detailed in a letter of October 12, 1891, from Holt's assistant, Vogelius: "We enclose specimen pages of the Briefer Psychology. [¶] After a series of delays between the type founders, proofreaders and Photo-engraving Co. we he [*stet*] hope to begin sending proofs to-morrow. [¶] Do you wish us to send proofs to A. Zimmer of Stuttgart, the German publisher? He has applied to us for price of sets.[2] [¶] To what address shall we send your books from which we made cuts?"[3] (LB). The first proofs were mailed on October 13, as noted in a letter from Vogelius of October 14: "The first lot of proofs went off yesterday. We will with pleasure forward sets of plate proofs to Germany and France as the work progresses. [¶] Kindly send us Prof. Boirac's address. [¶] The German publisher says Prof. Cossman is in Frankfort-on-the-Main. Is your Munich address later than September 11th?"[4] (LB).

[2] As it finally developed, the German translation was published in Leipzig by Quelle and Meyer.

[3] Thirty-eight new woodcuts were required in the added first seven chapters. Figures 32 and 33 were taken from Thomas Henry Huxley's *Manual of the Anatomy of Vertebrated Animals* (1871). In James's copy (WJ 540.97) are found his instructions on a scrap of paper pasted in behind Huxley's Figure 19 on p. 60 (James's Fig. 32): '*Figs 27 & 28* [i.e., actually, Figs. 32, 33] | Copy figs 19 & 20 of Huxley's Anatomy pp. *60, [intrl.] 61 omitting the lines and numerals marked out with pencil in fig. 20. (Leave the ['fig' *del.*] '4' in [*illeg. letter del.*]. | v strengthen.' On both pages the cuts are marked in pencil with the manufacturer's figures for size and, against fig. 20, the special note "leave this 4 in make more distinct." On October 24 Vogelius wrote James that the books had been shipped back to him (LB). A third cut sent to Holt, taken from Hermann Helmholtz's *Handbuch der physiologischen Optik* for Fig. 7 is illustrated on page 35 of the present volume.

[4] Émile Boirac (1851–1917), a psychologist and psychical researcher; Paul Nikolaus Cossmann (1869–1942), author of a book on philosophy in James's library. Although they seem to have been James's choice, neither in fact translated the book.

I. The History

In acknowledging the proofs on October 15, James brought up for the first time the question of royalties:

> I am glad to get at the proofs and get that job off my hands—it is hateful to have to go so often over one's own tracks. I may not be able, with my college duties so heavy, to send back the proofs quite as promptly as either the printer or I should like, but of course I'll do my aller darnedest.
>
> We have made no contract yet, and in surveying on the one hand my ruined estate, and on the other the fact that this work will surely be more lucrative than its predecessor, it seems to me fair to ask for slightly more liberal terms. What I propose is that I should pay no extra-proof correction bill and that you should pay for the index, which I can easily have made here, but have no time to execute myself. Otherwise the terms of the older contract will suffice, unless you have something better yet to propose.
>
> Mr. Vogelius asks me for the addresses of the German & French translators. Will you kindly give them to him? The German one is [incomplete] (bMS Am 1092.1, typed copy).

Holt wrote on October 17:

> It tries my faith in human nature to have one of its best exponents let an innocent and confiding publisher run on trusting in the general principle that precedent rules where action is taken without anything said to the contrary, and then bring him up with a round turn *in media res.*
>
> A publisher is never admitted to have any rights against an author, however, so I'll tell you what I'll do. If after the new book has been published two years, it has made my firm more profit than the old one did in it's [stet] first two years, I'll devote our excess pro rata with yours (if you have any) to returning the charge that will have been made against you for alterations and index. It does not follow that you will make more profit if we do, or that we will if you do. Such things can't run with absolute uniformity. "Two years" will have to mean four semi-annual settlements. We can't tell what the existing book has done at any day between them.
>
> The fact is, however, that a greater apparent profit to the publisher from the new book may not be a greater real one, as it will need more pushing against competitors than the old one. That was unique (Holt Business Letter Book, no. 17, p. 122; typed copy, Harvard bMS Am 1092.1[421]).

James responded on October 25:

> I am afraid that after the four semi-annual settlements, the amount of ciphering which will need to be done to fulfil the agreement which you propose will be more than the redistribution is worth to anyone. However since you propose it, let it stand, and see if either of us remembers it when the time comes!

He then continued:

> My impression is that the proof corrections will be comparatively slight, after we get through all this wretched twaddle about the senses which I am

469

correcting now,[5] and which had to be put in to satisfy the market. But *how* sorry I am we can't have a book of 350 pages! The fact is that the subject can't possibly be treated concisely and interestingly at the same time. And I think that as things go, the most interesting book will be the one that sells best. When I got through the job last summer I had a rather distinct impression that this work would kill most of its competitors for the reason that they are all (except Taine) so uninterestingly written. We shall see (bMS Am 1092.1, typed copy).

The recovery of the figures for the sales and royalties of *Briefer Course* is complicated by missing documents and some problems of interpretation in certain of those that have been preserved. The original contract is not known, but from various royalty statements, as for instance that of October 25, 1892, it is clear that James received a royalty of 20 cents per copy for American sales and 8 cents (raised before first payment to 11$\frac{1}{10}$ cents) for the British.[6] Whether or not Holt's proposal of forgiveness for proofreading costs and index preparation was ever instituted is not known. As it turned out, the Index was set from James's cards without further preparation and James was billed for excess proofreading charges.

Initially, production proceeded smoothly. After the first batch of proofs had been sent on October 13, Vogelius on October 24 answered some query by James: "As to the title, we have left it simply Psychology. The title page and advertisements will bear the words *Briefer Course*" (LB). On November 2 Vogelius reported that in the preceding week

[5] James was optimistic. As of September 25, 1892, he was billed for $27.42 for author's alterations in the original typesetting in excess of 10 per cent of the cost of the setting, and on October 25, 1893, for $4.20 to cover alterations in the plates of the third printing.

[6] In the October 25, 1892, royalty statement 907 copies of the *Briefer Course* were listed at 20 cents per copy for a total of $181.40, and the 500 sheets for England at 11$\frac{1}{10}$ cents for a total of $55.50. The contemporary royalty statements clash with the firm's response on October 24, 1922, to James's son Henry, that the royalty rate was originally 10 per cent but since 1907 had been voluntarily raised to 15 per cent of the list price (bMS Am 1435 [5]). An earlier letter from the firm to Henry Jr., of July 18, 1917, stated that although two raises had been made in the royalty rates for the Advanced Course (i.e., *Principles*), the *Briefer Course* rate had not been altered: "We made no offer to raise the royalty on the Briefer Course because the agents' expenses for that are so much heavier than for the other" (bMS Am 1092.1). Presumably this refers to the situation before the 1907 extension of the rate. As originally issued, the list price stated in the Holt correspondence and confirmed by the *Publishers' Weekly* was $1.60 although a preliminary Holt estimate had set it as high as $2.80. The rate for British sheets was generous. According to a Vogelius letter of May 20, 1892, explaining the financial arrangements for England, if Holt had kept to the percentages laid down in the contract James would have received only one cent per copy, whereas "we have therefore stretched a point and have given you, irrespective of the contract, 8 cents a copy on *the [*ink intrl.*] edition sold in England" (LB, typed carbon). However, Holt paid James 11$\frac{1}{10}$ cents.

the first forty-eight pages had been sent to Cossman and to Boirac (LB). We may assume that these were plate proofs, as proposed, meaning that James's corrections had been returned, incorporated, the galleys paged, and the type revised: i.e., in final form just before plating.[7] On December 2, plate proofs for pages 1–147 were sent: "Others will follow soon. If there are any changes to be made in these pages, please let us have them at once" (LB). Vogelius informed James on December 4:

From present indications the type setting of the text ought to be completed by the 12th of this month, allowing another week for revises, casting of plates, etc would bring us to Dec 19. The question then is: how soon after the 19th can you give us the copy for contents & index? We won't be able to get very much out of the printers, between Dec 25–Jan 6 as they will be celebrating. . . . Plate proofs of pp 148–209 go with this (LB).

Later, in a lost letter, James wrote about the non-receipt of proofs, to which Vogelius replied on December 21:

We have yours of the 19[th][.]
Page proofs 338–361 and galley slips 536–565 were sent to you on the 16th inst. We now mail duplicates of both.
The printer too is very anxious to get the composition completed, in fact he speculated that the missing proofs would be back on the 19th and then he would try & complete the rest so you should have the proofs to-day. But now we are entirely blocked not only in setting but in their make up ['or' *del.*] until *thes[e] gaps are [*alt. fr.* 'this gap is'] returned.
Don't let this accident prevent you from going away, [*illeg.*] let the final batch follow you. It certainly can't delay it over 3 or 4 days and this we will gladly make up in the press-work & binding. When must you have copies? How about Index & Contents? We now have sent you plate proofs of pp. 1–337. We propose to put the pages to press at once. If you have discovered any ['other' *del.*] errors please let us have them. Of course you won't have any chance to correct anything beyond *this [*alt. fr.* 'the'] unless you can give us more time[.]
We shall print new leaves for pages 86 & 89 and insert them before binding. We dislike to put in a slip of "errata" (LB).[8]

The next day, December 22, Vogelius reported receipt of "a part of the missing *page* proofs pp 342–361. We still lack pp. 338–341" (LB). On December 29 he wrote:

[7] Holt in this correspondence always refers to 'plate proofs,' which probably means proofs ready for plating, rather than what are properly called 'foundry proofs,' that is, proofs pulled from the manufactured plates. Vogelius appears sometimes to use 'plate proofs' in the latter sense, as probably in his letter of January 14, 1892.

[8] See "The Documents" for the description of the textual changes in pages 86 and 89 and elsewhere. This whole account of the production under pressure must be read in context with the account below of the special 1891 binding-up of the first six text sheets after James's sudden demand on November 18 for copies of the book by December 14 for his class.

With this we send the last page proofs of the text and also the front matter.

We hope it will be possible for you to have the copy for index in our hands on Thursday morning the 31st inst so we can put it in hand, and if we can not complete it on that day we have arranged for enough hands to come on Saturday and finish it, otherwise they will be closed from the 31st to Jan 4, and we wou'd hardly see our way clear to have bound copies in your hands by Jan 12. The page proofs can wait until you have the index copy off. Of course you'll forgo a revise on the index.

Prof Jastrow is also anxiously waiting to examine a copy of the book with a view of using it in his classes. We have promised it by ['the' *del.*] Jan 15 (LB).[9]

Vogelius apologized on December 31, responding to a lost James letter of December 30, for not having had "enough sense to send one batch of the page proofs as letter postage." He continued: "The 'à la card' index will do perfectly well without pasting on large sheets.[10] If by any chance you should have the index ready to-morrow, please express it to Robert Drummond [the printer], 444 Pearl St., N. Y. He has all directions and we have arranged with him to have a few hands come down on Saturday morning, and if possible, get it set. [¶] We don't yet give up and we still hope to have the book in your hands by the 12th. [¶] We presume you will see to it that the booksellers send on their orders" (Holt Archives, Princeton, typed carbon). James did not send off the index until January 5, 1892, on the evidence of Vogelius' letter of January 6:

Your favor of the 5th reached us at 9 am. The special delivery letter with the index came at 10 am. it had been offered at 7.35 a.m before business hours and taken back to the P. O. We are still in hopes that we can ship copies on the 11th.

As to price, we have in mind that the teachers' price should be about $2.00 but we hardly ever fix a price until we have seen the book complete. . . .

We have noted your request about the 20 copies. Several of the book sellers have already sent us their orders.

Enclosed is a duplicate bill as requested (LB).

[9] Vogelius' letter continues: "Some time ago Prof. Jastrow asked for the use of Figs. 60, 61, 62, 66, 67 & 69 from your large Psychology ['from' *del.*] for one of his papers, without thinking that you owned some of the cuts, we said 'Yes,' provided he gave credit for them to your book. He now orders them and trust you will not object, as it will be an advertisement for the book. If, however, there is some good reason why you can not loan *them [*alt. fr.* 'this'], [*illeg. del.*] will you please telegraph us to-morrow at our expense[.]" Professor Joseph Jastrow taught psychology at the University of Wisconsin from 1888–1927. The article referred to (using James's plates) was published as "A Study of Zöllner's Figures and Other Related Illusions," *American Journal of Psychology*, 4 (April 1892), 381–398. The cuts borrowed by Jastrow were from the chapter "The Perception of Space" in *Principles* and could be loaned since they were not utilized in *Briefer Course.*

[10] This sentence seems to suggest that in fact James made his own index and for economy's sake did not hire it done after Holt declined to bear the expense.

I. The History

Vogelius wrote triumphantly on January 11, 1892: "The Psychology is ready and copies have been shipped to the book sellers. Your 10 copies also go by express. We have fixed the teachers' price at $1.60" (LB).

The first post-publication discovery of error came almost immediately on January 12: "Will you kindly supply the reference page on the enclosed proof, last line. The printer left it go blank in the edition printed" (LB).[11] Another was mentioned on January 14:

> We are glad that you are pleased with the appearance of the "Briefer Psychology". We mail the copies as per your list.
>
> We shall print a cancel sheet for pp. 51 and 52 and will insert it in the next lot that we bind.
>
> We have sent Cossmann & Boirac plate proofs of the pages as fast as they were ready. The last installment was sent to them on January 8th. In view of this do you still wish us to send a copy of the book to each?
>
> As to your suggestion regarding advertising in the Philosophical Review, we think that your article will do more to call attention to the books than any advertisement that we might insert.[12]
>
> [*handwritten*] P. S. We have just succeeded in selling Macmillan & Co 500 copies of the Brief Psychology for the London market (LB, typed carbon).

On the same day, January 14, Vogelius wrote the exciting news: "We shall need to print a new edition of the Psychology, *briefer Course at once*. If you have any further corrections to make please telegraph us to-morrow, otherwise in the absence of ['them' *del.*] a telegram the new edition will go to press to-morrow" (LB).

In connection with a third printing in 1892, Vogelius wrote on March 26: "Enclosed are proofs of the pieces and pages of the Briefer Course corrections. Pages 94 & 100 need condensing" (LB). Finally, on November 29, 1892, in connection with the fourth printing that was to take place in 1893 (although dated 1892 on the title page), he wrote about corrections:

> Our attention has recently been called to the repetition of matter in the chapter on "Association", proof of which we enclose. The matter on page 271 is partly repeated on pages 277 and 278. In cutting out matter will you please see that at least three or four lines are left on page 279; in other words, if you cut out say twenty lines on page 271, please write in say two or three lines of matter anywhere between pages 271 and 279. Otherwise page 279, being a short page, would be entirely blank.
>
> We shall need to print a new edition soon and would thank you to let us have the corrections at the earliest moment possible (LB, typed carbon).

[11] The last line on p. 244 (*ed.*, 215.25) was missing the reference page number 218 (*ed.*, 193), which was supplied in the second printing.

[12] This was presumably James's "A Plea for Psychology as a 'Natural Science'," *Philosophical Review*, 1 (March 1892), 146–153.

As indicated by three printings in the year of publication 1892, and by a fourth early in 1893, *Briefer Course* was warmly received. We first hear of its sales in a letter, dated May 20, 1892, from Vogelius to James. In this, Vogelius, responding to a query from James, writes that 843 copies of *Briefer Course* had been sold and an additional 500 sheets had gone to England, bringing James's earnings to date to $208.60. The first royalties to June 30, 1892, were paid on October 25, 1892, for 907 American copies and the 500 English sheets (here paid for at the rate of $11\frac{1}{10}$ cents per set).[13] The last statement of accounts in the Holt Letter Books is of October 25, 1893, representing sales up to June 30, which listed 359 copies sold in the previous six-month interval from January to June 1893. The figures would seem to suggest that Holt printed 1,000 copies in the first impression, either 1,000 or 500 in the second, and perhaps 500 in the third. The fourth printing would have been made early in 1893.

James was characteristically generous in his gifts of copies. In his statement of June 25, 1892, Holt deducted $10.24 for copies of *Principles* and *Briefer Course* (two copies of which had been sent out in James's name on April 27 and one on May 23) from the royalties of *Principles*. Earlier, on January 19, 1892, Vogelius had billed James for $12.80 for ten copies of *Briefer Course* above the author's twenty, and these ten, together with three additional copies mailed on February 6, appear again in an invoice of September 25. On October 27, 1893, Professor Byerly was mailed a copy. The record of James's distribution of copies is incomplete, of course. As late as January 19, 1896, he asked that a copy be sent to Pierre Poisson in Alais, France.

Although James was inclined to push Holt about publicizing both books, some scheme of Henry Holt's own devising to issue a special brochure seems to have foundered on James's perversity. In the James folder in the Princeton University's Holt Archives is the typed copy of a letter, dated January 14, 1896, from James to Holt: "Thank you for your compliments, but as aforesaid, *I have no photograph*, so the thumbnail must be lacking to the world. I would send you my wife's but she has none either, and I suppose the baby's wont do. We are a non-photographic family, on the whole."[14] Holt must have returned to the attack, for on January 19 James replied:

At the risk of displeasing you, I think I won't have my *photograph [*alt. fr.* 'picture'] taken, even at no cost to myself. I abhor this hawking about of every-

[13] According to custom, royalties were paid in semi-annual installments; hence only half was paid in October, for on December 24, 1892, Vogelius sent James a cheque for $191.35 (one-half of $382.70) "for balance due on royalty account to July 1st as per our statement of Oct. 25" (LB). This amount included royalties on 60 copies of *Principles* as well.

[14] A note on the typed copy states that the original had been sold at the Author's Club Sale for Belgian Relief, April 1915.

body's phiz which is growing on every hand, and *don't [*alt. fr.* 'do not'] see why having written a book should expose one to it. I am sorry that you should have succumbed to the supposed trade neccessity. In any case, I will stand on my rights as a *freeman [*alt. fr.* 'freedman']. You may kill me, but you shan't publish my photograph. ['B' *del.*] Put ['a p' *del.*] a blank "thumbnail" in its place. Very very sorry to displease a man whom I love so much (Holt Archives, Princeton, holograph; typed copies of both letters at Harvard).

James resisted any suggestion that he should repeat his successful performance. On November 27, 1891, he had written to W. T. Harris, "I am very sorry to have to say no to you again—but it is quite impossible that I should do what you want, under any title. It would take me two years to do the work and kill me in the end. I have no facility for writing, as some people have; and I registered a solemn vow last summer, after abridging my Psychology, that I should never, never, never, write a text book again!"[15]

However, he did become interested in a revision as seen in a postcard of December 20, 1902, to Professor Eduard Claparède in Geneva: "When I come to revise my smaller psychology—next year I hope—it [Claparède's book on Association] will doubtless prove very instructive" (Bibliothèque publique et universitaire, Geneva, Switzerland). This revision, so lightly referred to here, was in fact contemplated as a financial venture but it came to nothing despite the offer to help by his ardent disciple E. L. Thorndike who, on February 29, 1902, had written a letter accompanied by five typed pages of suggestions for changes:

I hope you won't forget that you are going to let me try to help you when you get to the revision of your Briefer Course in Psychology. . . . I should be very glad to even do the routine work of indexing and proof reading for you. You ought not to be bothered with that sort of thing. I am going to take the liberty of sending you a number of suggestions about the book, because I fancy that you have been away from elementary psychology so long that the thing is a bit dead with you, and that some new ideas, even if radically wrong, may serve when you come to take the matter up, to give you a starting point in the job. There is no need to reply to this. You can just lay these things I send away in a drawer, and when you come to the task of revision you can see whether they are of any service or not.

A note attached to the pages of suggestions reads: "These suggestions are put in the most impolite and conceited way simply to save time. You will understand that they are of most service by being ignored, to have them ignored would suit me precisely." Several years later, on December 16, 1905, Thorndike tried again:

I am willing to accept a gift from you—I have been doing so long enough to have formed the habit—but on one condition, that you let me do the hack

---

[15] "Pragmatist to Publisher: Letters of William James to W. T. Harris," ed. Wallace Nethery, *The Personalist*, 49 (Autumn 1968), #37, p. 504.

work of revising your Briefer Course this spring and summer. You could get someone to do it better, but no one who would do it more promptly. You can plan what you want done to it. I will free myself for the time from crudities of style and pedagogical eccentricities and make a cast which you can chisel into shape without much waste of time.

The 'Principles of Psychology' ought never to be revised but to stay as a land mark of Psychology of its day; but *(in the Briefer Course) [*intrl.*] the renovation of the brain-physiology and the addition of the functional point of view and (if you thought wise) a diminution of the criticisms of philosophical dogmas about psychology would make the *Briefer Course [*ab. del.* 'book'] a bit more useful to classes and probably more certain to continue its sale.

Please take a day and jot down notes in a copy of the Briefer Course of what you would do to it in a new edition and send them to me to let me try my hand.

To this James replied on December 17:

Your offer is a most extraordinarily generous one to me and disinterested one from the point of view of your own book. I've no doubt that you could give to mine a new lease on life much better than I could myself for, you see it objectively, and have had experience of its way of being taken by students which I have not.

Nevertheless I must decline your offer for a reason that I am sure you sympathize with. A book is a man's own flesh and blood, as it were, and when I revise that one, and partly rewrite it, as I soon must, I want it still to be, for better or worse, my own. I have preserved those notes you sent me a couple of years ago, suggesting certain emendations, and I shall probably apply for more.[16]

Only a month later James qualified what he had said to Thorndike about the necessity for a start on revision in the near future, for a letter of January 30, 1906, to Giulio Cesare Ferrari, the Italian translator of *Principles*, is much more tentative: "You seem still to be wishing to abridge the larger Psychology rather than to translate the smaller or parts thereof. You and Papini can judge best. For my part, if I were revising the smaller book, I should omit the nerve-anatomy chapters, and bring the instinct & Will chapters near the beginning so that the reader would pass from the more concrete to the more abstract continually. Of course you are *authorized* to do whatever you like, in advance" (courtesy of C. A. Ferrari di Valbona, Rome). Later in the year he was more positive, as in his letter of October 31, 1906, to his daughter, Margaret, at Bryn Mawr when he wrote, "Give up the psychology. You

16 Thorndike's two letters and his five pages of typed notes are preserved as bMS Am 1092 (1139, 1141). James's answer, as well as others of his letters originally found in Thorndike's papers, was not included in the Thorndike collection given to the Library of Congress. Their text is reprinted from Geraldine Jonçich, *The Sane Positivist: A Biography of Edward L. Thorndike* (Middletown, Conn.: Wesleyan University Press, 1968), p. 236.

can get the gist of it by reading my book, of which the Chapters on the Senses, etc., are the hardest part, I think. At any rate, I'm going to abolish or *very* greatly reduce them in the revised edition" (#3063).

Nevertheless, there is no mention of revision again until three 1909 entries in James's diary. On Friday, April 2, 1909, he recorded, "Offered to revise psychol. for Holt for 25% royalty"; on May 12, "Letter from Holt ['abou' *del.*] with offer"; and on May 13, "Wrote to Holt offering to revise for doubled royalty on both Psychologies." It is unfortunate that the correspondence relating to this exchange seems not to have been preserved, for it is not altogether clear whether James's offer was to revise *Principles* or—as seems much more likely—*Briefer Course*. Whether he had a sudden urge for money that prompted the offer to revise or merely felt an impulse to be mischievous, or a little of both, is uncertain. The fantastic royalty terms he proposed were certain to be rejected by Holt, especially, as seems possible, if James tied a rise in the royalty rate of *Principles* to an advanced royalty for a revision of *Briefer Course.* James had always tried to push Holt into a higher royalty rate than the standard 10 per cent; and especially after the flare-up that accompanied Holt's miscalculations of royalties for *Talks to Teachers* and also Holt's refusal to take part in an auction for the right to publish *The Will to Believe*, James was not on the most cordial terms with him. James could have been serious in his proposal purely as a money-making venture, but he had moved from psychology to philosophy some years before, and his true mood was very likely better represented by two extracts from his letters. In the first, he wrote to Shadworth Hodgson on March 28, 1892, "After the stubble of psychology on which I have spent a good deal of my working force for the last 10 years I have a sort of longing for erkenntnisstheorie, and even Cosmology, and the prospect of the possibility of a little unimpeded *reading* next winter is most sweet" (#984). That this was not just the temporary reaction to the completion of *Briefer Course* may be indicated by his letter to Théodore Flournoy over two years later, in August 1894: "My intellect is somewhat stagnant. I enjoyed last year reading a good deal of stuff which might connect itself with lectures on 'Cosmology,' but no reactions of my own have yet set in, and as for psychology, it has passed away from me altogether since the publication of my book" (bMS Am 1505 [12]). After this, nothing more is heard of a revision.

II. THE DOCUMENTS

The first printing, copies of which were sent to James on January 11, 1892, may be described as follows:

title: *AMERICAN SCIENCE SERIES, BRIEFER COURSE* | [rule] | PSYCHOLOGY | BY | WILLIAM JAMES | *Professor of Psychology in Harvard University* | [publisher's device] | NEW YORK | HENRY HOLT AND COMPANY | 1892

collation: 1–31⁸, 248 leaves, pp. [2] [i–ii] iii–v [vi] vii–xiii [xiv], [1] 2–478 [479–480] + advertisements pp. [1] 2–8

contents: p. πi: blank; p. πii: boxed advertisement for 'WORKS EDITED BY WILLIAM JAMES.' (J. E. Maude and Henry James, Sr.); p. i: title; p. ii: 'COPYRIGHT, 1892, | BY | HENRY HOLT & CO. | ROBERT DRUMMOND, | *Electrotyper and Printer*, | New York.'; p. iii: 'PREF-ACE.'; p. vi: blank; p. vii: 'CONTENTS.'; p. xiv: blank; p. 1: text with HT 'PSYCHOLOGY.' | [short rule]; on p. 468: 'THE END.'; p. 469: 'INDEX.', ending on p. 478; pp. 479–480: blank; p. 1: advertise-ment leaves for 'THE AMERICAN SCIENCE SERIES.'; on p. 8: 'HENRY HOLT & CO., PUBLISHERS, N. Y.'

paper and binding: unwatermarked white wove paper 7⅜ x 5″, all edges trimmed. Blue striated cloth. Front and back covers in blind within panels: 'AMERICAN SCIENCE SERIES | BRIEFER COURSE | [within a ruled panel with decorative corners] PSYCHOLOGY | JAMES | [within a panel] HENRY HOLT & CO. PUBLISHERS'. Spine in gilt, lettering in blind panels: 'AMERICAN | SCIENCE SERIES | BRIEF-ER COURSE | PSYCHOLOGY | [short rule] | JAMES | HENRY HOLT & CO.' Figured brown endpapers on rectos, one leaf pasted down; heavy white single flyleaves front and back.

Note: In all copies of the first printing pages 86 and 89 are part of a cancellans sheet, as indicated in a letter from Vogelius of Decem-ber 21, 1891. From a pre-publication form of part of the book (for which see below) we can determine that 86.43 (*ed.*, 84.36) had the misprint '*candatus*', which was corrected to '*caudatus*' in the cancel. On p. 89 (*ed.*, p. 86) the legend for Fig. 37 read 'V^{IV}, fourth ventricle' whereas the correction in the cancel page reads 'V^{III}, third ventricle' and the cut marking was altered correspondingly. All copies of the first printing have no page number for the reference in the last line of p. 244 (*ed.*, 215.25) (Vogelius to James, January 12, 1892), whereas the necessary page number '218' is supplied only in the second printing. However, another error was important enough to warrant a cancel sheet to include p. 52 in all copies of the first printing bound after January 14, 1892 (Vogelius to James of that date). The original at 52.9–11 (*ed.*, 53.25–27) reads in error, 'runs up the scala tympani to the top, where it turns into the scala vestibuli'; but in the cancel the reading is, correctly, 'runs up the scala vestibuli to the top, where it turns into the scala tympani'.

The second printing contains these corrections and, in addition, two other material alterations. In 42.23 (*ed.*, 44.4) the blank page number within the parentheses is correctly found as '11' and in the last line of the legend for Fig. 31 on p. 79 (*ed.*, 78.11) the incorrect notation 'Fig. 33' is altered to 'Fig. 32'. In addition a few imperfections in the plates were noted and corrected. These affected the inking of 'turn,' in 64.27 (*ed.*, 65.21) and, in the line below, the end of the first 'temperature' in 64.28 (*ed.*, 65.22) and also of 'into' in 438.25 (*ed.*, 377.4). In the right column of the Index at 477.10 (*ed.*, 410.1b) the semicolon after 'thought' was changed to a comma.

In the third printing among other plate changes the most prominent are the two tonings-down of sexually explicit descriptions on pp. 94 and 100 (the pages mentioned by Vogelius on March 26, 1892, as requiring special attention in the proofreading). Full collations are provided of the passages in the list of Emendations, but recognition can readily be made by the reading 'sexual passion' in 94.23 (*ed.*, 92.22) in the first two printings but 'the sexual instinct' in the third; and in 100.11 (*ed.*, 97.13–14) 'And Goltz found' in the first two but 'It is the same, according to Goltz,' in the third.

Finally, the last major change in the text was made in the fourth printing, published early in 1893 (but dated 1892) in which a repetition of matter (referred to in a Vogelius letter of November 29, 1892) was removed, with some rewriting on pp. 271, 278–79. A footnote 2 was added on pp. 270–71 to substitute for removed matter, and rewritten text appeared in part in pp. 278–79 (see list of Emendations, 237.6, 10–27; 238.5; 243.24–31). In the revised form, p. 279 has 26 lines of text but only 21 in the original setting in the first three printings. The plates for pp. 272–277 were not touched.

A few misprints were corrected in the printings of 1892 (*i.e.*, 1893), 1904, 1908, and 1910.

In preparing this edition the following copies of *Briefer Course* were consulted:

1892 (*first printing*) The Library of Congress BF 131 .J2 1892

1892 (*second printing*) Harvard WJ 200.35; Ignas K. Skrupskelis, private copy

1892 (*third printing*) Andover-Harvard Theological Seminary Library; Northwestern University Library 150 J29p 1892.

1892 (*i.e.*, 1893) (*fourth printing*) University of Virginia *BF 131 .J2 1892

1900 (*sixth printing*) Harvard Phil 5249.2.6

1904 (*seventh printing*) University of Virginia BF 131 .J2 1904

1908 (*tenth printing*) University of Virginia BF 131 .J2 1908

1909 (*eleventh printing*) Harvard Phil 5249.2.13.5

1910 (*twelfth printing*) University of Virginia BF 131 .J2 1910.

A set of early printed sheets (the first six of the text, pp. 1–96), especially made up for James and dated 1891, was copyrighted by the Library of Congress under No. 45396 on December 14, 1891, two copies being received on the same day. Under No. 2090 on January 12, 1892, Holt then copyrighted the 1892 complete book, as published. The first notice of publication was in the *Publishers' Weekly* for February 20, 1892, No. 1047, advertised for $1.60: "Abridgement of larger work (see notice, 'Weekly Record,' P. W., Oct. 11, 1890 [976]), to make it more directly available for class-room use. All polemical and historical matter, all metaphysical discussions and speculative matter, most of the quotations and all of the book references are omitted. Brief chapters are added on the various senses. About two-fifths of the volume is new or rewritten."

The revised fourth printing was made in 1893 (dated 1892), and thereafter printings appeared in 1893, 1900, 1904, 1905, 1907, 1908, 1909, 1910 (the year of James's death), and posthumously. Various of these printings have a scattering of mechanical correction but nothing that can be identified as authorial. In the printing of 1910, however, on the evidence of the changes made in the plates, two corrections, one at 104.12 and the other at 112.18, suggest that James's annotated copy of the book may have been consulted, in which case Henry James, Jr., was probably its editor. But other corrections in this printing (BC^{12}), like that at 298.11, did not originate from James's annotations.

Two pre-publication printings of the sheets for part of the book have an interesting history. In the William James Hall offices at Harvard is preserved an 8-leaf pamphlet with the title page 'STRUCTURE OF THE BRAIN | BY | WILLIAM JAMES | PROFESSOR OF PSYCHOLOGY IN HARVARD UNIVERSITY | *Reprinted from the "Briefer Course" Psychology* | [device] | NEW YORK | HENRY HOLT AND COMPANY | 1891'. The verso of the title is blank. Leaves 2 to 8 contain Chapter VII, "The Structure of the Brain," pp. 78–90, reimposed so that p. 78 begins on a recto and the last page, the verso of the eighth leaf, is blank. A circled '61' in ink appears in the upper left corner of the title and the name 'Sanford' in the upper right. The evidence suggests that James wanted this chapter reprinted, at his own expense, for use in his class before the book would appear. Correspondence on the matter is contained in the Holt Letter Book in the Princeton University Library. The earliest reference comes in a Vogelius letter of November 2, 1891:

There are 13 pages in Chapter VII, (78–90) which will have to be printed as 16 pp, see enclosed dummy. It's a little awkward that the chapter begins on an even page as it will throw all the page numbers on the inside margin, instead of on the outside, unless we begin with page 78 on back of title page, and then leave the last two pages blank. It won't make any difference ['whi' *del.*] in the cost which of these three ways of doing it you select. To set a title, print, fold & stitch 100 copies, will cost you $8.00 (LB).

James must have selected the dummy form of reprinting. On November 4 Vogelius responded to a lost query: "The difference between printing 100 copies and 50 copies of the pamphlets will be but $1.42, in other words 50 copies will cost you $6.58; 100 copies $8.00. We will print 50 unless we hear from you to the contrary" (LB).

These fifty (or one hundred) copies were presumably printed and distributed to James's students. But James then seems to have decided that he wanted the whole book for his class at an earlier date, December 14 to be precise, than had been the plan for publication. In some perturbation Vogelius wrote on November 24:

> Yours of the 18th conveys the first intimation we have had that the Briefer Psychology was wanted on a certain day for your classes. It is rather short notice now to have it ready by Dec 14th, however, we are going to do our best, and if you will help us by doing all your cuttings and insertions in the galley proofs and not in the made up pages, we will gain considerable and think we can safely promise to have the book ready by the time you want it, although it's going to be a very close shave to do it. We have already given orders to increase the fount of type and as soon as it can be cast & delivered, the work will proceed more rapidly.
>
> Do you wish to see plate proofs? (LB).

In a typed letter of December 2 came the bad news:

> The printer just informs us that the type foundry cannot deliver the additional type for the "Briefer Psychology" under two weeks. This of course would be too late for your purpose. However we want to accommodate you and there are three ways open: I. We could use an old font of type on the last few chapters and complete the book so as to deliver copies on the 14th. This we do not want to do as it would spoil the appearance of the book. II. If you would be willing to forego page proofs, we could complete the composition with the present font of type probably this week. III. The most sensible plan although the most expensive one for us, would be to print a pamphlet of enough pages to carry your class say into the first week of January. This would give you more time on the proof reading and the making of the index and would enable us to do more justice to the press work and binding. If you agree with us, kindly let us know about how many pages you would need and on what day you must have them. We should send these directly to you *(free of charge) [*ink intrl.*] for distribution to *the members of [*typed intrl.*] your class who would buy copies of the book when completed (LB).

Two days later, on December 4, Vogelius wrote again:

> We have yours of yesterday. Before we put the plates of the Briefer Course to press for the pamphlet, we beg to inquire whether you have any further changes to make in the plates? While we have the plates on press for it [it] is our intention to print, at the same time, enough copies for our regular edition, as it will save the handling of the plates a second time.
>
> Will 200 copies see your class through? (LB).

The last we hear is a note of December 11: "Your postal card asking for 16 additional copies of the pamphlet is at hand. We will send the entire lot to-morrow morning so that you ought to have them early on Monday" (LB).

This second pamphlet, preserved in the Houghton Library (Phil 5249.2.5.3 [A]) consists of pp. 1–96, the first six sheets of the text in 8's, stabbed, within a brown-paper wrapper. On the front cover of the wrapper is printed the title page as in the 1892 edition except that the imprint reads 'NEW YORK | HENRY HOLT AND COMPANY | 1891 | (Copyright, 1891, by Henry Holt & Co.)', the verso blank. On the outside of the back cover of the wrapper is printed a Holt advertisement headed 'THE | AMERICAN SCIENCE SERIES | FOR SCHOOLS AND COLLEGES'. The pages include Chapter VII, "The Structure of the Brain," ending on p. 90, and the first six pages of Chapter VIII, "The Functions of the Brain." Pasted on the verso of the front cover is the bookplate of Ralph C. Larrabee, Boston, with the handwritten date 'Dec 16 1891'. Larrabee was a student at Harvard in 1891. From the correspondence with Holt it is evident that this is one of perhaps 216 such copies made up for the use of James's class, Philosophy 1. Because these are only the earliest printed run of sheets of the 96 pages, the pamphlet has no major textual significance. However, because copies of the book have the cancellans revised text of pages 86 and 89, as of Vogelius' letter of December 21, the 1891 pamphlet does show us what the error was on each page that led to the reprinting of the sheet, and of course it provides the faulty readings on p. 52 known otherwise only in the earliest bound copies of the first printing. The plates of the earlier 8-leaf pamphlet show the same state of the plates as in the over-run sheets found in Chapter VII of the later pamphlet, with the same errors on pages 86 and 89.

On January 14, 1892, Holt announced to James that 500 sheets had been sold to Macmillan in London. These were given a title page reading 'TEXT-BOOK | OF | PSYCHOLOGY | BY | WILLIAM JAMES | *Professor of Psychology in Harvard University* | London | MACMILLAN AND CO. | 1892'. This title, with blank verso, constitutes a conjugate fold with the preceding leaf containing the half-title 'TEXT-BOOK | OF | PSYCHOLOGY' (verso blank), which substituted for the American advertisement leaf. The British Library copy, date-stamped 5 April 1892, has been rebound, but the Bodleian Library copy (2645. e.1137=S. Psych.15), date-stamped 11 March 1892, has a binding of dark blue grained cloth, the front and back covers blind-stamped with horizontal double rules at the top and bottom. The spine is stamped in gold: '[double thin rule] | [thick rule] | TEXT | BOOK | OF | PSY-CHOLOGY | WILLIAM | JAMES | [thick rule] MACMILLAN & Cº | [rule]'. A London Library copy of the 1892 printing has a different cancellans fold, the first leaf blank and the title on the conjugate leaf reading '*BRIEFER COURSE* | [rule] | PSYCHOLOGY | BY | WILLIAM JAMES', the rest as in the British Library and Bodleian copies except that the American copyright notice appears on the title-page verso. An oddity is that although the title page differs from that in the British and Bodleian Libraries copies, the London Library copy is bound identically with the Bodleian, including the 'Text Book' title on the spine. One may venture the guess that the London Library title fold represents that printed by Holt in New York to accompany the British sheets but that Macmillan preferred another form of the title and made up their own title fold. The London Library copy perhaps represents a late bound copy when the Macmillan titles had run out.

The Holt accounts in the Letter Book do not record further sales to England; it is likely, however, that the rebound London Library copy with the title dated 1905 but otherwise the same in wording as its 1892 copy (including the American copyright notice on the verso) comes from sheets of the Holt 1905 printing sold to Macmillan.

III. THE EDITORIAL PROBLEM

No manuscripts or drafts of *Briefer Course* have been preserved; the sole substantive authority and copy-text, therefore, is the first edition of 1892, first printing, as modified by authorial plate correction in the second and third printings of the same year, and the revision in the fourth printing in 1893 (dated 1892). However, several collateral authorities may affect the copy-text, especially when *Briefer Course* relies mainly on other documents from Chapter VIII to the end, excluding the newly composed Epilogue. The first seven chapters, largely devoted to the senses, were written especially for *Briefer Course*,[17] although small parts of Chapters II and III and a larger section of Chapter VI were set from annotated pages of *The Principles of Psychology* (1890). However, beginning with Chapter VIII the text abridges and revises chapters in *Principles* on a regular basis. The following chart indicates the relationship of the two books. The exact details will be found in the Historical Collation section of the apparatus.

Briefer Course	*Principles*
I–VII (new)	
II Sensation in General	XVII Sensation (*related to*)
III Sight	XX The Perception of Space (*in part related to*)
VI Sensations of Motion	XX The Perception of Space (*in part related to*)

[17] For James's satirical account of these new chapters as 'twaddle,' see his letter to Henry Holt of July 24, 1891, already quoted.

The major collateral authority, thus, is the text of *Principles*, appropriate pages of which were pasted on sheets of typewriter paper and marginally annotated or interspersed with handwritten additions. The evidence is not clear just which printing of *Principles* James pasted up (in two copies), for the plate changes in *PP* (*The Principles of Psychology*) that would be identifiable as true revisions, not corrections, occur either in omitted or in rewritten sections of *BC* (*Briefer Course*). A fantastic story about the preparation of *BC* was promulgated by J. E. Boodin in "William James as I Knew Him," *The Personalist*, 23 (Autumn 1942), 403–404:

His *Briefer Course*, which was prepared cold-bloodedly for the market, was put together with so much impatience that it bears unmistakable evidence of its method of production—the scissors. In this connection a story is told by Dr. Dickenson [*stet*] Miller. James was in the Adirondacks for his favorite rest, when the publishers pressed him for the text book. He had no copy of the larger work with him. So he borrowed Dr. Miller's copy. He proceeded to cut the copy to pieces and to prepare his manuscript. With the naiveté of genius, he afterwards cut to pieces a new book and pasted the pieces into Dr. Miller's copy so as to make it complete. It is needless to say that this pasted copy is now a valued souvenir. A friend of James in telling the story remarked that inasmuch as James had only one copy from which to prepare his MS, it is plain to see that he was right in stating that the abbreviated work was in part rewritten. In spite of its having been an uncongenial task, the book has been the most successful, because the most human of psychological text books.

Several facts cast doubt on this anecdote, which appears to have originated with Miller, a graduate student at Harvard in the summer of 1891. First, no record exists that James was in the Adirondacks during the summer of 1891 when he prepared *BC*, but rather that he was working at Chocorua. Second, the evidence of his correspondence demonstrates that, contrary to the publisher unexpectedly pressing James for the text book while he was on vacation, James had planned to rewrite the book well ahead of his going on vacation and had arranged all details of proof and of format, as well as of the date at which he proposed to submit the finished manuscript. Third, more than one set of *PP* would have been been required to prepare printer's copy, and the anecdote about the reconstruction of Miller's copy is ridiculous: James was scarcely that naive nor would he have been inclined to waste time in reconstituting Miller's copy if he had, in fact, used it— and for this the evidence is quite contrary. Although the references to the situation are not altogether clear, it is possible, although far from certain, that the typed carbon of a Vogelius letter to James on April 8, 1891, refers to James securing copies of *Principles* in anticipation of cutting them up as printer's copy for *Briefer Course*: "We take great pleasure in sending you with our compliments, two copies of volume I of your Psychology, although we have had but one stray copy of vol I. This breaks another set of ours. Possibly some of these days we will find the man that has the odd vol. I" (LB). It is possible that the final sentence was a slip, and refers instead to a copy of vol. II that would have produced the stray copy of vol. I, the first broken set, and that the second set was broken to provide James with a second copy of the volume. But if this were for preparation of *BC*, why James did not request two copies of both volumes is obscure. He may merely have been requesting replacement of an imperfect copy.

Since James worked over the pages of *Principles* with some care, the revised wording of the *Briefer Course* variants in the reprinted parts of the text must represent his conscious intentions; hence except for a few misprints, and two cases of apparent censorship in the revised third printing of 1892, the substantives of *Briefer Course* rule through the final textual revision of the fourth printing of 1893 (dated 1892). The amount of revision dwindled as the task progressed. The early chapters, making use of *PP* from VIII on, start off with considerable stylistic as well as content revision, but by the time James had reached

Chapter XX, "Reasoning," he had relaxed, and fewer such alterations appear. The considerable recasting given Chapter XXI, "The Perception of Space," was unusual not only for the book but for the lateness of the effort; yet it was forced on James in part by the exigencies of condensing a long and sprawling chapter in *PP* and in part by the reworking of the material from a new point of view, as for instance in *BC* 300.3–304.22 condensing and revising *PP* 818.3–912.5.

Textually, therefore, and with specific reference to the substantives, the divergences of *BC* from *PP* are authoritative. In the editing of *PP* for the WORKS, careful account had to be taken of the relation of the book text to the marked up and revised pages of the antecedent articles which formed the printer's copy in whole or in part for a number of the chapters. But in *BC*, which draws directly on the revised text of *PP* in these sections, the articles are of no textual significance in the editorial process (except for the reading at 342.37), and their substantive variants from *BC* are not recorded in the Historical Collation. This information, if required, can be recovered from the apparatus of the edition of *Principles* in the WORKS.

Although the successive corrections and revisions that James made in the plates of *BC* through the fourth printing are authoritative and hence incorporated in the first-printing copy-text, one exception has been made. On March 26, 1892, Vogelius wrote to James in connection with the plans for the third printing: "Enclosed are proofs of the pieces and pages of the Briefer Course corrections. Pages 94 & 100 need condensing" (LB). Wanting James's side of the correspondence we cannot know the source of the objections or the means by which they were conveyed to James. Vogelius' letter suggests only that James's first attempts at alteration had been too lengthy to insert in the plates. At any rate, in both pages, passages of explicit description of the sexual act, in the one of frogs 94.23–28 (*ed.*, 92.22–26), and in the other of birds as well as frogs 100.11–27 (*ed.*, 97.13–28), are so modified as to interpose a veil of generality. That the originals of these passages had offended the sensibilities either of correspondents of the publisher (in view of the circulation of the book among school and college students) or of James's friends seems to be indicated, and it follows that the censorship of the passages was agreed to and performed by James and in that sense is authoritative. Nonetheless, the present textual editor has chosen to retain the original text and to provide the altered version as a rejected form in an entry in the list of Emendations on the grounds that the modern audience will prefer the first form, as presumably would James if the question of the circulation of the book had not been raised.

Among the collateral authorities, one special form of *Principles* must be considered as possessing a superior authority in a few specific readings. The James Collection preserves an interleaved and annotated copy of *Principles* (*AC85.J2376.890p) that has hundreds of James's notes referring to articles and books either overlooked or else published between 1890 and about 1897. These appear to be a combination of references possibly to be used in his classroom teaching but perhaps more especially in a revised new edition that never was actually started. Intermixed, however, are a number of outright corrections and revisions in the text that represent his second thoughts—designed textual improvements in content and in style. The problem arises whether James consulted this annotated copy when he was marking up the *PP* pages during the preparation of the *BC* printer's copy or, later, in proof. The answer is not wholly demonstrable but the evidence suggests that either (a) many of the textual revisions as distinct from simple corrections had not been written in the interleaved copy of *PP* by the summer of 1891, or (b) James did not take the special copy with him to Chocorua and did not check it later when he was reading *BC* proof in Cambridge during the autumn and winter of 1891. A typical case occurs at *BC* 388.1–2, in which *BC* corrects to 'congeners' the misprint in *PP* 1168.20 'congerers', also corrected to 'congeners' in the annotated copy of *PP*. However, the correction of a misprint is scarcely evidential, the more especially since at 388.18 the *BC* reading 'in' follows the *PP* text and ignores James's alteration to 'within' found lower down on the same *PP* page at 1168.36.[18] The best example of possible influence comes in 387.29, on the preceding *PP* page, where after 'mid-career.' *BC* omits the following *PP* sentence, ' "*Hæc tibi erit janua leti*," we feel.', which is also deleted in the *PP* annotated copy at 1168.8. Wanting confirmatory evidence, one may take it either that there was consultation here, or else that identical motives prevailed in making the cut (or even that cutting the sentence in *BC* later led to the marking of *PP*). The case is obscure. However, on the whole, the number of substantive textual revisions in the *PP* interleaved copy that are not reproduced in overlapping passages in *BC* not only is suggestive of a lack of consultation but also raises an editorial problem. If it could be shown that James was aware of these *PP* alterations when he was working on the copy for *BC* but chose to ignore them, an editor would be forced to follow the *BC* text. However, such deliberate rejection is unlikely and cannot be demonstrated. The problem then focuses on whether the text of *Briefer Course* can be legitimately revised when it repeats readings in

---

[18] A similar example occurs in 222.6–8 where in lines 7–8 'who once has shaken' in *PP* was altered in *BC* to the obvious correction 'who once had shaken', a change also made in WJ/PP; but the WJ/PP alteration in the preceding line, 'had so improved' for original 'has so improved' was ignored by *BC* in favor of dropping the 'has' to read simply 'so improved'. The evidence here is ambiguous, for the *BC* reading could normally have resulted from an independent correction of the *PP* error of the repeated perfect tense or it could have been made as a conscious improvement of the WJ/PP version. Since the *BC* reading is perfectly satisfactory and represents the specific correction of an error that James adopted for this text, the *BC* copy-text reading is here retained over that of WJ/PP although normally the editor has inserted in *BC* the WJ alterations made in the annotated copy of *PP*.

PP that James had altered in his interleaved copy. The present editor takes it that James's final intentions in the *PP* revisions should be respected when there is no indication that the specific differences in the audience aimed at between the two works would have suggested that the written-in change not be transferred to *BC*. Hence a handful of readings from the *PP* annotated copy (WJ/PP) have been incorporated in the present *BC* text: specifically 147.10–11 snowflake . . . flake] snow-flake crystal . . . crystal BC; 212.34 tell] always tell BC; 231.23, 24 (*first one*) had] om. BC; 277.6 It . . . becomes] It is only in grave lesions that he becomes BC; 277.23 *sensations*] *those* BC; 305.22 ʌ or similari-tiesʌ], ~~, BC; 328.6 evil] distressing BC; 330.30 deepʌ pureʌ worthyʌ] ~, ~, ~, BC; 330.32 deepʌ pureʌ spiritualʌ] ~, ~, ~, BC; 369.38 any one] either BC; 379.36 so] as BC; 388.18 within] in BC.

The observance of James's final textual intentions extends to another collateral document, an annotated example of the second printing of *Briefer Course*, also preserved in the James Collection (WJ 200.35). This exhibits the same double characteristics as the interleaved *PP* copy: the combination of notes and references along with textual alterations. Perhaps more clearly, this copy of *BC* was marked for James's use in the classroom although the possibility of an eventual revised edition (which we know he contemplated for some years) cannot have been absent from his mind. Here, at any rate, the adoption of the 40 textual alterations needs no defence, even to the omission in the present text of the deleted original final paragraph of Chapter XV, "Discrimi-nation."

The superiority of the *Briefer Course* substantive readings over their variant forms in the reprinted sections of *Principles* is readily enough established but that of the accidentals is in the nature of the case more difficult to deal with. One class of spellings is clearly the *BC* housestyle even though the same printer manufactured both works: invariably these are printed in such forms as 'preëxistent' or 'coöperate' whereas James's own spellings are 'pre-existent' and 'co-operate'.[19] In contrast, there is no uniformity among the Drummond compositors in the treat-ment of James's 'everyone' for 'every one', and so forth, and there is a drift to the form 'toward' instead of James's 'towards'. The evidence in

[19] Only two possible anomalies appear: at 23.34, set from manuscript, the word is broken between lines as 'pre-|existing', and at 206.3, set from *PP* text, '*co-opera-tion*' is hyphenated. Because these two examples are shaky, this edition follows standard textual theory, which forces an editor to adopt the copy-text forms when they are invariable even though they conflict with the author's known habits. The case is different for the editorial emendation of occasional printer's forms like 'every one' and 'any one' to 'everyone' and 'anyone', which represent James's own customary preferences, since in these the inconsistency of the copy-text enables an editor to emend to a uniform standard on the evidence of various printed examples of the superior forms as found in the copy-text.

the text for forms such as 'downward' or 'downwards', 'afterward' or 'afterwards', 'forward' or 'forwards', etc. is mixed, and the editor in these cases normalizes to James's preferred form. Such internal variation is readily handled: what is more important is the matter of punctuation. Admitting that departures in punctuation from unregulated and idiosyncratic copy are somewhat of a compositorial prerogative, we must also recognize on the evidence of the textual changes James made in the annotated copy of *Briefer Course* (as well as the more frequent alterations in *Principles*) that he was also on occasion concerned with matters of punctuation. There are several examples: at 209.4 he added a hyphen in printed 'rattling off'; at 379.37 he removed the comma (also in *PP*) after 'them'; at 100.15 he removed the comma after 'inhibit'; at 178.2 he corrected the comma after 'emerge' to a semicolon; and at 189.39 he added the parenthesis after 'common' (also in *PP*). Since the last case corrected an error, these five in addition to the 31 corrections and revisions of words do not indicate any great scrupulousness. It is possible to suggest, however, that just as the textual revision in the annotations of *Briefer Course* is consistently less than that in *Principles*, the same reasons entered to reduce the need to alter the punctuation. That is, since James was adapting printed copy in *BC* (in some sections already once revised in *PP* from its article form) and giving it another round of revision (in lost copy) before printing, his final intentions are the better exemplified by the *BC* text and thus the less need existed to alter the printed result by later annotation.

Moreover, some test sections indicate that the compositors of *BC* were usually careful to follow copy with a notable exactitude. For example, from 379.23 to 386.1 (The moral . . . mind.), a stretch of eight pages in the original *BC* edition, a general equation exists between the lack of any substantive alteration whatever—except for a cut or two from *PP* and the added passage in 386.1–8 ([1]If . . . intact.)—and the fact that only three punctuation variants from copy exist.[20] On the contrary, to take a typical stretch when James concerned himself with the substantives, just preceding this eight-page area, we find in only two *BC* pages from 371.4 to 372.30 (In . . . work.) five substantive revisions and no less than four independent punctuation variants.[21]

[20] The three variants are trifling and perhaps unauthoritative: the commas after 'way' at 381.1, after 'direction' at 383.1, and after 'idea' at 385.26 do not appear in *PP*. Such an extended verbatim reprinting of *PP* is evidence that (at least for the compositors in this area) copy was exactly followed. Moreover, it is interesting to notice that a number of opportunities existed for compositorial restyling, particularly in the several examples of dashes both with and without preceding commas, where the *PP* irregularity is faithfully reproduced.

[21] Three of these variants lighten the *PP* punctuation by removing commas after 'state' at 371.28, 'agents' at 371.33, and 'us' at 372.20. The fourth is perhaps slightly suspect in its substitution of a colon for a semicolon after 'beam' at 372.26, but it may be authoritative.

In general this coincidence of a rise in the level of *BC* punctuation variants from *PP* in areas where James altered the verbal readings, but a lowering of the incidence of these variants when he did not trouble to change the wording of the *PP* text, is suggestive—in combination with other evidence—of the general fidelity of the *BC* compositors to the punctuation accidentals, as indicated, for example, by the verbatim setting of punctuation (save for one comma omitted after 'defective' at 266.33) in the extended quotation in 265.36–267.11 from the *PP* copy, which James himself had no reason to touch.

Relatively consistent evidence of this nature indicates that the authority of the *Briefer Course* accidentals (barring such obvious departures as 'preëxisting' etc.), and especially of the capitalization and punctuation, is very high, even though inevitably less likely to be quite so exact as that of the substantives. It follows that the *BC* copy-text accidentals are reproduced in cases of variance from *PP* (except for positive error) on the general assumption that in the vast majority of cases the *BC* variant represents James's own marking of copy or of proof. Indeed, so strong is the presumption of authority in such variants that the *Briefer Course* punctuation has often been used as an emending agent in the text of *Principles* as representing authorial revision and correction, a procedure occasionally buttressed by the *BC* restoration of punctuation variants in the articles behind the *PP* setting.

In *Briefer Course* the treatment of quotations follows the procedures for *Principles*. That is, in general terms the accidentals of the source are silently adopted, the *BC* or *PP* variants having been taken as the result of James's inadvertence or interference when copying. However, when it seems evident that James is altering the wording for his own purposes of condensation or clarity—as in his free treatment of the extensive quotation from Martin in Chapter V—the present text reproduces his wishes but provides in the list of Emendations (under a *stet* entry) the readings of the source. On the other hand, when it seems that James has inadvertently or carelessly departed from the original in a non-significant way, then ordinarily the substantive reading of the source is restored as an emendation. In areas of *BC* where the quotations are drawn from *PP*, the exact text of the *PP* quotation, as edited, is adopted.

All editorial alterations, whether substantive or accidental, in the copy-text—the first printing, first state—are listed in the Emendations section of the apparatus save for a few simple normalizations of the bibliographical details in footnotes. A few unimportant discrepancies as between diagrams and legends are brought into conformity silently. Commas are also added silently after 'e.g.' and 'i.e.' The Historical Collation records only the substantive variants from corresponding passages in *Principles* but, for the benefit of the reader, it also lists passages in *Principles* omitted or highly condensed or paraphrased in *Briefer Course*. All page-line references to *Principles* are to the text as established in the WORKS. Since some emendations have been made in *Principles* drawn from *Briefer Course*, an indication is given in the Historical Collation when the original *PP* reading listed has been altered to agree with the *Briefer Course* lemma.

An appendix lists all the annotations, including textual alterations, that James wrote in his private copy (WJ 200.35), with a note as to the medium whether pencil or ink. The relationship between the pencil and the ink annotations is perhaps not always constant. However, there is at least a general tendency for the pencil annotations to be the earlier.

Emendations

Every editorial change from the copy-text is recorded for the substantives, and every change in the accidentals as well save for such silent typographical adjustments as are remarked in A Note on the Editorial Method. The reading to the left of the bracket, the lemma, represents the form chosen in the present edition, usually as an emendation of the copy-text. (A prefixed superior 1 or 2 indicates which of any two identical words in the same line is intended.) The sigil immediately following the bracket is the identifying symbol for the earliest source of the emendation, followed by the sigla of any later agreeing documents. Readings in parentheses after sigla indicate a difference in the accidental form of the source from that of the emended reading to the left of the bracket. A semicolon follows the last of the sigla for emending sources. To the right of this semicolon appear the rejected readings of the copy-text and of any other recorded documents, followed by their sigla. The copy-text is BC, the first-edition typesetting as represented by the first printing from the plates. If no indication of printing is given, the assumption is that the reading in BC is invariant in all impressions from the original plates. A superior number identifies the exact printing in case of need, as BC[1] for the 1892 first printing and BC[3] for the 1892 third printing. (Emendations marked as BC[1b] indicate that they are drawn from the first printing bound after January 14, 1892; BC[1a] refers to readings prior to that date. For the details of this printing, see The Text of *Psychology: Briefer Course*.)

Reference is made to PP, the first edition, first printing of *The Principles of Psychology* (New York: Henry Holt, 1890); page-line references following certain rejected PP readings in cases of collatable areas are to the edition in the WORKS. The note (*em.*) indicates emendation of the first printing of PP by the present editor to the form shown in the lemma. A superior number identifies the exact printing of *Principles* in case of need, as PP[1] for the 1890 first printing and PP[3] for the 1891 (dated 1890) third printing. Reference is also made, in one instance, to P[37], "What Is an Instinct?" *Scribner's Magazine*, 1 (March 1887), 355–365 (McD 1887:6). Emendations marked as H (Harvard) are editorial and are not drawn from any authoritative document. The word *stet* after the bracket calls special attention to the retention of a copy-text reading. It may be employed to key a Textual Note, as marked by an asterisk before the page-line number. In a quotation it may indicate that James's version (differing from the source in some respect) has been retained in the edited text. It may also be used in rare instances to indicate that a possibly questionable or unusual reading has been retained in the text.

Emendations

One special feature appearing in the Emendations is the use of *et seq.* When this phrase occurs, all subsequent readings within the text are to be taken as agreeing with the particular feature of the reading being recorded (save for singulars and plurals and inessential typographical variation, as between roman and italic), unless specifically noted to the contrary by notation within the entry itself. Readings grouped together with multiple page-line references may also be concerned with only the particular feature being recorded and not with inessential types of variation. For convenience certain shorthand symbols familiar in textual notation are employed. A wavy dash (∼) represents the same word that appears before the bracket and is used exclusively in recording punctuation or other accidental variants. An inferior caret (ʌ) indicates the absence of a punctuation mark (or of a footnote superscript) when a difference in the punctuation constitutes the variant being recorded, or is a part of the variant. A vertical stroke (|) represents a line ending, sometimes recorded as bearing on the cause of an error or fault. A hand symbol (☞) before a page-line reference draws attention to the parenthetical listing of additional lines where the forms of emendation are identical. Quotations within the text are identified in Professor Skrupskelis' Notes. The sigil WJ/ followed by the appropriate symbol (as WJ/BC and WJ/PP) indicates James's autograph revisions found in his private copies of books.

1.2 *Principles of Psychology*] H; *rom.* BC

1.22 *Principles of Psychology*] H; ' ∼∼∼' (*rom.*) BC

2.13 analytic] WJ/BC; synthetic BC

10.17 facts] WJ/BC; things BC

19.5 'Knowledge-] H; '∼ ʌ BC

*19.11 and *which*] H; *which* fact WJ/BC; *om.* BC

19.12 and *whiches*] WJ/BC; *om.* BC

20.11 mind] WJ/BC; body BC

☞22.9 forwards] H; forward BC (*also* 31.27;32.13;35.7,11;77.11,15; 82.21;83.15;84.8,9;202.23;337.29)

22.10 upwards] H; upward BC

*23.3,11;140.8 Everyone] H; Every one BC

23.34 preëxisting] H; pre-|existing BC

25.36 *die Menschen*-] H; Menschenʌ BC

25.37,38,39 (*twice*),40 Δ] WJ/BC; *d* BC

*27.26–27 which . . . unit.] WJ/BC; from the starting-point, which we feel. BC

27.39 p. 3] H; p. 4 BC

28.38 *e.g.,*] WJ/BC (∼ʌ); *e.g.*ʌ light BC

30.3 simultaneous contrastʌ] WJ/BC; the simultaneous variety, BC

31.9 aperture] H; aperature BC (*error*)

34.18 anyone] H; any one BC

35.8 backwards] H; backward BC

40.2 someone] H; some one BC

41.16 in] *stet* BC; a short way in Martin

41.18 from one side] *stet* BC; *om.* Martin

41.21 made. . . .] H; ∼.ʌ BC

41.21 cases] *stet* BC; ∼, however, Martin

41.21 the only] *stet* BC; some Martin

41.33 ²which] *stet* BC; *om.* Martin

41.42 H. Newell] H; *om.* BC

42.8 size] *stet* BC; its size Martin

42.9 and] *stet* BC; *om.* Martin

42.39 p. 531.] H; *om.* BC

44.4 p. 16] BC² (*i.e.,* p. 11); p. BC¹

45.15 retina alternate] *stet* BC; retina on which a part of its image falls, alternating Martin

45.16 (when . . . passing)] *stet* BC; , ∼ . . . ∼ʌ Martin

45.30 so called] H; ∼-∼ BC

45.38 p. 516.] H; *om.* BC

46.4 'fix'] *stet* BC; ʌ∼ʌ Martin

46.28 another. . . .] H; ∼ .ʌ BC

46.42 away] *stet* BC; aways Martin (*error*)

493

47.2   *contrast*] stet BC; *rom.*   Martin
47.5   plays] *stet* BC; has   Martin
47.9   29] H; 27 BC (*error for* 26)
47.39   524-7] H; 525-8 BC
49.7-8   , *T*] *stet* BC; *om.*   Martin
49.14   *oval*] *stet* BC; oral   Martin
  (*error*)
49.14   *o* and *r*,] *stet* BC; *om.*   Martin
49.16   by . . . -bones] *stet* BC; in another way, to be described presently
  Martin
50.18-21   "Three . . . *stirrup.*"] H;
  ∧ ~ · · · ~ ·∧ BC
50.21   one] *stet* BC; *om.*   Martin
50.26   pp. 535-36] H; *om.* BC
51.1-5   FIG. 18 . . . stapes.] *stet* BC;
  legend varies Martin (*among* BC
  figures found in Martin *the legends
  of only Figures* 18 *and* 19 *vary*)
51.22-23   for . . . nerve] *stet* BC; on its
  inner side by which blood-vessels and
  branches of the auditory nerve enter
  Martin
52, FIG. 19   vaa] Martin; *om.* BC (*error*)
52.13   *ampulla* . . . .] H; ~ ·∧ BC
52.19   anterior] *stet* BC; posterior
  Martin (*error*)
52.22   ampulla; . . .] H; ~ ;∧ BC
53.9   times] *stet* BC; times (from left to
  right in the right ear and *vice versa*)
  Martin
53.9   around] Martin; round BC
53.12   edge] *stet* BC; end   Martin
53.26   vestibuli] BC[1b]; tympani BC[1a]
53.27   tympani] BC[1b]; vestibuli BC[1a]
53.28   , *r*,] H; ∧ *r*, BC
53.30   pp. 538-40.] H; *om.* BC
54.7   *Corti.* . . .] H; ~ ·∧ BC
54.8-9   , a . . . spiralis,] *stet* BC; *om.*
  Martin
54.9   margin] *stet* BC; edge   Martin
54.10   then] *stet* BC; these   Martin
54.19   *spiralis.* . . .] H; ~ ·∧ BC
54.19   more] *stet* BC; more slender and
  more   Martin
54.20   the numbers] *stet* BC; their numbers   Martin
54.28   From . . . spiralis] *stet* BC; The
  upper lip of the sulcus spiralis is
  uncovered by epithelium, and is known

as the *limbus laminæ spiralis*; from
it   Martin
54.32   pp. 540-42.] H; *om.* BC
56.12   this . . .] H; ~∧ BC
56.12   'hum'] *stet* BC; "buzz"   Martin
56.40   pp. 543-44.] H; *om.* BC
60.7   Between 200 and] WJ/BC; In the
  neighborhood of BC
61.5   ends. . . .] H; ~·∧ BC
61.19   three] *stet* BC; these   Martin
61.23   p. 556.] H; *om.* BC
62.5-6   When . . . it,] *stet* BC; In the
  latter case, as when we move the
  hand over an object to study its
  shape,   Martin
62.10   therefore] *stet* BC; so that
  Martin
62.20   milligr.] *stet* BC; milligr. (.03
  grain)   Martin
62.20-21   millim.] *stet* BC; millim.
  (.0139 sq. inch)   Martin
62.21   felt. . . .] H; ~·∧ BC
62.23   pressed . . . .] H; ~·∧ BC
62.23   When] *stet* BC; When, however,
  Martin
62.28   meet. . . .] H; ~·∧ BC
62.32   p. 558.] H; *om.* BC
63.1   something] *stet* BC; something
  (local sign)   Martin
63.29   at one end] *stet* BC; on the one
  hand   Martin
63.38;64.21   would] Martin; should BC
64.23   together. . . .] H; ~·∧ BC
64.27   mucous] Martin; mucuos BC
  (*error*)
65.3   sensation; . . .] H; -~;∧ BC
65.4   assume] *stet* BC; must assume
  Martin
66.2   [2]of] *stet* BC; at   Martin
66.14   [2]of] Martin; *om.* BC
66.16   has] *stet* BC; had   Martin
66.21   0.1°] *stet* BC; .1°   Martin
66.39   pp. 558-63,] H; *om.* BC
67.12-15   When . . . judgments.] *taken
  from* Martin, p. 566
68.21   cold-] H; ~∧ BC
69.3-4   rabbits . . . Schiff,] *stet* BC;
  animals a similar state of things may
  be produced   Martin

69.5 If . . . were] *stet* BC; while, if the latter be   Martin

69.6 left, there was] *stet* BC; left uninjured, there is   Martin

69.7 possibly . . . was lost.] *stet* BC; probably . . . is lost, though that is impossible to say with certainty.   Martin

69.8 afferent] *stet* BC; sensory afferent   Martin

69.9 spinal] *stet* BC; *om.*   Martin

69.10 tracks] Martin; tracts BC

69.11,13 ones] *stet* BC; *om.*   Martin

69.13 first] Martin; *om.* BC

69.34 p. 568.] H; *om.* BC

74.24 causes] H; cause BC (*error*)

78.9 , in Fig. 33,] H; *om.* BC

78.11 32] BC²; 33 BC¹

79.6;104.2 *caudatus*] H; *candatus* BC (*error*)

79.17–20 *Practical . . . Physiology*] H; all rom. BC

79.18 *Anatomy,*] H; Anatomy$_\wedge$ BC

81.2 (after Henle).] H; , $\sim\sim_{\wedge\wedge}$ BC

89.11 convey] H; conveys PP,BC

90.38 fore-paws] H; fore paws PP (*em.*); forepaws BC

91.1 $C_\wedge$] PP; $\sim$, BC (*error*)

92.21;123.10 forwards] H; forward PP, BC

*92.22–26 sexual . . . even] *stet* PP, BC¹⁻²; the sexual instinct at the proper seasons, and discriminates between male and female individuals of his own species. He is, in short, so similar in every respect to a normal frog that it would take a person very familiar with these animals to suspect anything wrong or wanting about him; but even then BC³

95.29 40] PP; 4o) BC (*error*)

97.13–28 And . . . alone.] *stet* PP (mere fact); BC¹⁻²; It is the same, according to Goltz, with male dogs who have suffered large losses of cerebral tissue. Those who have read Darwin's Descent of Man will recollect what an importance this author ascribes to the agency of sexual selection in the ameliora-

tion of the breeds of birds. The females are naturally coy, and their coyness must be overcome by the exhibition of the gorgeous plumage, and various accomplishments in the way of strutting and fighting, of the males. In frogs and toads, on the other hand, where (as we saw on page 94 [*ed.*, 92]) the sexual instinct devolves upon the lower centres, we find a machine-like obedience to the present incitements of sense, and an almost total exclusion of the power of choice. The consequence is that every spring an immense waste of batrachian life, involving numbers of adult animals and innumerable eggs, takes place from no other cause than the blind character of the sexual impulse in these creatures. BC³

97.16 *Descent of Man*] H; *rom.* PP (*em.*), BC³; *sg. qts.* (*rom.*) BC¹⁻²

99.6 *Hamlet*] H; *rom.* BC

99.29 improbable] H; improbab e BC (*error*)

100.15 inhibit$_\wedge$] WJ/BC; $\sim$, BC

101.24 J.] H; *om.* PP(*em.*), BC

101.25 lowest . . . highest] *stet* PP,BC; lowest spinal centres to the very highest centres   Jackson

101.28 rest of the] Jackson; *om.* PP (*em.*),BC

101.28 *can*] *stet* PP,BC; can   Jackson

102.18;105.17 Schäfer] H; Schaefer PP (*em.*),BC

104.12 43] WJ/BC,BC¹²; 41 BC¹⁻¹¹ (*error*)

107.16 read;] BC⁷; $\sim$: PP,BC¹⁻⁶

108.22 M.] H; *om.* PP (*em.*),BC

108.28 abolished$_\wedge$] BC⁷; $\sim$, PP,BC¹⁻⁶

110.4 Fig. 47] H; Fig. 47, p. 116 BC

112.18 formulation altogether] WJ/BC, BC¹²; formulational together BC¹⁻¹¹ (*error*)

112.21;409.13a Schäfer's] H; Schaefer's BC

117.30 0.079.] H; $\sim$ $_\wedge$ BC

117.33 0.132.] PP; $\sim$ $_\wedge$ BC

118.4 similarly,] H; $\sim$: PP; $\sim_\wedge$ BC

118.21 perceive] Cattell; distinguish PP(*em*.),BC

118.23 ¹to] Cattell; in PP(*em*.),BC

119.9 drum,] *stet* PP,BC; drum (a physiological kymograph) Cattell

119.16 that] *stet* BC; *om.* Cattell,PP

119.23 them] Cattell; *om.* PP(*em*.),BC

119.40 name] Cattell,PP; the name BC

120.13 has] Romanes; have PP (*em*.), BC

120.14 whom] Romanes; *om.* PP(*em*.), BC

120.28 *alone*),] H; ∼) ∧ PP(*em*.),BC

121.7 noticed] Lewes; noted PP(*em*.),BC

121.11 Thomson . . .] H; ∼∧ PP(*em*.), BC

121.40 downwards] H; downward PP (*em*.),BC

123.1 olfactory,] PP; ∼. BC (*error*)

126.26 principle∧] PP; ∼, BC

☞126.29 Everyone] H; Every one PP (*em*.),BC (*also* 140.28;149.38;168.9; 188.1;241.21;280.9;384.21)

126.34 roughnesses] Dumont, PP; roughness BC

126.36 so] Dumont,PP; so in the nervous system BC

126.37 in . . . system] Dumont,PP; *om.* BC

128.40 154] H; 155 PP(*em*.),BC

129.5 even of an] Maudsley; of any PP (*em*.),BC

129.5 secondary] Maudsley; secondarily PP(*em*.),BC

129.8 efforts . . . produce] Maudsley; effort . . . produces PP(*em*.),BC

131.23 *f*∧] H; *f*, BC

131.28 "it] H; "we . . . . It PP (123.11–13); ∧∼ BC

134.17 "The . . . Habits"] H; *sg. qts.* PP(*em*.), BC

135.1 never] *stet* PP,BC; never, if possible, Bain

135.7 mental] *stet* PP,BC; moral Bain

135.15 'tapering-off,'] PP; "∼-∼," BC

135.16 -indulgence,] PP; -∼∧ BC

*135.28 straight] PP; strait BC

135.39 *zur*] H; zu PP (*em*.),BC

137.11 afterwards] H; afterward PP (*em*.),BC

141.20 Everyone] PP; Every one BC

142.40–41 be, . . . white.] WJ/BC; be.⁷ PP; be.∧ BC

147.10–11 snowflake . . . flake] WJ/PP; snowflake crystal . . . crystal PP(*em*.), BC

☞149.41 someone's] H; some one's PP (*em*.),BC (*also* 207.18;308.15; 394.6)

153.8 tactile∧] PP; ∼, BC

157.2 balls] PP,WJ/BC; halls BC (*error*)

160.21 acts] BC¹²; actions PP; act BC¹⁻¹¹

160.23 three] WJ/BC (3); two PP,BC

161.11 wife∧] PP; ∼ , BC

166.14;245.1;330.23 anyone] H; any one PP(*em*.),BC

166.20 salutations] PP; salutions BC (*error*)

167.37;193.3 156] H; 173 BC (*error for* 172)

169.2 thou hast] Carlyle; hast thou PP(*em*.),BC

169.4 *renunciation*] *stet* PP, BC; Renunciation (Entsagen) Carlyle

169.4 life] *stet* PP,BC; Life Carlyle

169.18 die; well, but] *stet* PP, BC; die, and Higginson

169.19 too? . . .] H; ∼ ?∧ PP(*em*.),BC

169.19–20 I will . . . reply,] *stet* PP,BC; "And I must speak what appears to me to be right."—"But if you do, I will put you to death."— Higginson

169.23 untroubled.' . . .] H; ∼.'∧ PP (*em*.),BC

169.23 We] *stet* PP,BC; What is in my power? To Higginson

169.24 the hour] *stet* PP,BC; the day, the hour Higginson

169.25–26 belongs] *stet* PP,BC; belongs to another Higginson

169.27 submit] *stet* PP,BC; I submit Higginson

169.28 of] *stet* PP,BC; *om.* Higginson

173.16 in] Job (King James); *om.* PP (*em*.),BC

174.18 things∧] BC¹¹; ∼ . BC¹⁻¹⁰

174.20 zoölogical] H; zoological PP,BC

175.6 Instincts.] H; ∼ ∧ PP,BC

176.7 *does*] *stet* BC; does Mill,PP

176.28　of the] WJ/BC; [*space*] the BC
176.36　in] WJ/BC; of BC
178.2　emerge;] WJ/BC; ~ . PP; ~ , BC
*178.27–28　*a*, . . . ¹are] WJ/BC; *a* + idea
　of *b* is PP(*em*.),BC
179.1　146] H; 161 BC (*error for* 160)
181.31　163] H; 184 BC (*error for* 181)
189.39　common);] PP,WJ/BC; ~ ₍; BC
　(*error*)
190.22–23　*actual*] WJ/BC (*rom*.); *possible* PP,BC
190.38–39　first . . . VIII] H; last . . . VII BC
194.23　easy and] Paulhan,PP; *om*. BC
194.25　one . . . another] Paulhan, PP;
　of one . . . of another BC
195.9　sound] WJ/BC, BC³; sight BC¹⁻²
197.27　he has] *stet* PP, BC; The writer
　has himself　Carpenter
198.37　incessantly] PP; incessently BC
　(*error*)
205.5　Chapter IX] H; Chap. VIII BC
205.37　qualities] PP; qualties BC
　(*error*)
206.3　coöperation] H; co-operation PP,
　BC
206.15　It] *stet* PP,BC; Hence the retinal
　rivalry　Helmholtz (Atkinson)
206.16　upon] Helmholtz (Atkinson); on
　PP(*em*.),BC
206.16　or] *stet* PP,BC; on　Helmholtz
　(Atkinson)
206.20–21　*we . . . appear*] *stet* PP,BC;
　all rom.　Helmholtz (Atkinson)
*207.37　more internal] WJ/BC; less
　external PP; less internal BC
208.18;209.12　**Free-**] H; ~ ₍ BC
209.4　rattling-] WJ/BC; ~ ₍ PP,BC
212.34　tell] WJ/PP; always tell PP
　(*em*.),BC
215.25　p. 193] BC² (*i.e.*, p. 218); p.　BC¹
216.21–23　1) . . . 2) . . . 3)] H; (1) . . .
　(2) . . . (3) BC
219.6　so;] PP; ~ : BC
220.18　assafœtida] PP; assafœdita BC
　(*error*)
221.17–19　*color . . . form*] *stet* PP,BC;
　each rom.　Martineau
221.22　and then] Martineau; then PP
　(*em*.),BC

222.11　smell.] WJ/BC; ~ . [¶] The fact
is so familiar that few, if any, psychologists have even recognized it as needing explanation. They have seemed to think that practice must, in the nature of things, improve the delicacy of discernment, and have let the matter rest. At most they have said: "Attention accounts for it; we attend more to habitual things, and what we attend to we perceive more minutely." This answer is true, but too general; it seems to me that we can be a little more precise. PP (482.8–16; PP *text continues* '[¶] *There . . . victory!' " ' *482.17–518.34 not collatable except* 'The *time . . .* bad.³² 494.4–497.16 *for details of which see* HC 117.17–118.25); ~ . [¶] The fact . . . . This [*verbatim w*. PP *except* 'said,'] answer, though true, is too general; but we can say nothing more about the matter here. BC
*224.1–2　*the . . . of*] WJ/BC (tho't of; *all rom*.); *thoughts* PP,BC
225.35　excited] PP,BC⁴; cited BC¹⁻³
225.36　some] *stet* BC¹⁻³; any BC⁴ (*resetting variant*)
☞226.35　towards] H; toward PP (*em*.),BC (*also* 364.9,18;348.20,23;352.5; 353.37)
226.37 *et seq.*　"Locksley Hall"] H; *sg. qts.* PP(*em*.),BC
226.38　*the ages*] *stet* PP,BC; *rom*. Tennyson
226.40　Yet] Tennyson; For PP(*em*.),BC
227.15　excitement;] PP; ~ , BC
227.40　position;] PP; ~ : BC
☞230.1　*Emma.*] H; 'Emma.' PP(*em*.), BC (*similar* 233.15[*thrice*];234.22–23; 259.39;265.28–29;351.12;356.40)
230.38　and] Hodgson; *om*. PP(*em*.),BC
230.38　becoming . . .] H; ~ . . . . PP (*em*.),BC
231.1　interest] *stet* PP,BC; interest, that is, those which are attended by a representation of pleasure or pain, Hodgson
231.23,24　(*first one*)　had] WJ/PP; *om*. PP(*em*.),BC

232.12 the decaying] *stet* PP,BC; that Hodgson

232.13–14 they . . . time] Hodgson; at any time they have PP(*em.*),BC

232.18–19 *habitually*] *stet* PP,BC; *rom.* Hodgson

232.28 spontaneous] Hodgson; *om.* PP (*em.*),BC

237.6,10–27 other.[2] | Miss . . . tie.] BC[4]; ~∧ (*om. fn.*) PP,BC[1-3]

*238.5 now.] BC[4]; **Summary concerning Spontaneous Trains of Thought.** —To sum up, then, we see that *the difference between the three kinds of association reduces itself to a simple difference in the amount of that portion of the nerve-tract supporting the going thought which is operative in calling up the thought which comes.* But the *modus operandi* of this active part is the same, be it large or be it small. The items constituting the coming object waken in every instance because their nerve-tracts once were excited continuously with those of the going object or its operative part. This ultimate physiological law of habit among the neural elements is what *runs* the train. The direction of its course and the form of its transitions are due to the unknown conditions by which in some brains action tends to focalize itself in small spots, while in others it fills patiently its broad bed. What these differing conditions are, it seems impossible to guess. Whatever they are, they are what separate the man of genius from the prosaic creature of habit and routine thinking. In the chapter on Reasoning we shall need to recur again to this point. BC[1-3]

239.25 149] H; 165 BC (*error for* 164)

240.9 a] H; *à* PP(*em.*),BC

242.16 "The . . . Inquiry."] H; *sg. qts.* PP(*em.*),BC

243.24–31 the unknown . . . point.] BC[4]; conditions which we have partly been able to trace, but which, so far as regards the focalization-feature, are still unknown. BC[1-3]

244.11 A] BC[4]; The PP,BC[1-3]

244.29 free-] H; ~ ∧ PP(*em.*),BC

246.21–22 to hear] *stet* PP,BC; hath heard Tennyson

246.22–23 creeping] Tennyson; moving PP(*em.*),BC

252.12;280.10 backwards] H; backward PP(*em.*),BC

253.6 try to] Mill; *om.* PP(*em.*),BC

253.7 that] Mill; *om.* PP(*em.*),BC

253.8 then is it,] Mill; is it, then, PP (*em.*),BC

253.12 one] *stet* PP,BC; *om.* Mill

253.18 him,] *stet* PP,BC; him, the place in which I knew him, Mill

253.22 in] Mill; *om.* PP(em.),BC

253.32 sensation] Mill; association PP (*em.*),BC

253.32 the idea] Mill; idea PP(*em.*), BC

253.36 on] Mill; in PP(*em.*),BC

256.19 contrary,] PP; ~ ∧BC

259.39 M. L.] H; *om.* PP; M. C. BC (*error*)

260.6 effort] Holbrook; efforts PP(*em.*), BC

260.10 his] *stet* PP,BC; the Holbrook

263.8–9 "They . . . nothing,"] H; *sg. qts.* PP(*em*),BC

265.11 he] *stet* PP,BC; he Berkeley

266.28 *fleuve*] La Fontaine; *fleur* PP (*em.*),BC

268.34 When∧] PP; ~ , BC

269.14 *is . . . recollection*] *stet* PP,BC; *all rom.* Bain

270.22 it.'∧] H; ~.' " BC

270.23–271.3 "He . . . him."] PP (*no qt. mks. but set in smaller type*); ∧~ . . . ~∧ BC

270.23 wife's] PP; wife BC

270.23 faces] PP; face BC

270.27–28 'My . . . features.'] H; "~ . . . ~." BC

270.34 *Iliad*] H; *rom.* PP(*em.*),BC

270.34 Homer] PP; H omer BC (*error*)

272.9 Charles] H; Ch. BC

275.3 thoughts)∧] PP; ~), BC

*277.6 It . . . becomes] WJ/PP; It is

only in grave lesions that he becomes
PP$^{1\text{-}2}$(*em.*),BC; Only in the gravest
lesions does he become PP^3

277.23 sensations] WJ/PP; *those* PP
(*em.*),BC

278.31–32 because . . . space] *stet* PP,
BC; *all ital.* Robertson

280.10,32 forwards] H; forward PP
(*em.*),BC

281.17 had] Romanes,PP; *om.* BC

281.29 before] PP,WJ/BC; hefore BC
(*error*)

284.14 One . . . . It] BC^{12}; Two . . . .
One PP,BC$^{1\text{-}11}$

285.4 sum-] PP; ∼ ∧ BC

285.40 173] H; 166–171 PP (*em. to*
'167–73'); 171 BC

286.10–11 'eggs' . . . and] WJ/BC; his
'eggs' broken into a glass, and his PP
(*em.*),BC

287.41 74] H; 76 PP(*em.*),BC

289.1–2 ∧Census of Hallucinations∧] H;
'∼ ∼ ∼' PP (*em. to 'Census of Halluci-*
nations'),BC

289.28 haschisch] H; hasheesh PP;
haschish BC

291.19 ∧Census∧] H; ' ∼ ' PP(*em.*),BC

293.20–21 living . . . appeared] *stet*
PP,BC; living objects, such as men,
horses, &c., appeared to him Franz

293.22 bodies,] PP; ∼ ∧ BC

295.14 XV] BC^{12}; XIV BC$^{1\text{-}11}$ (*error*)

298.11 5)] BC^{12}; 3) BC$^{1\text{-}11}$ (*error*)

298.29–30 Thus . . . be] WJ/BC; *all*
ital. PP(*em.*),BC

298.30 *really smaller*] WJ/BC; *rom.* PP
(*em.*),BC

305.22 ∧ or similarities∧] WJ/PP;
, ∼ ∼ , PP (*em.*),BC

306.24 -thumb] H; -thnmb BC (*error*)

310.17–18 truths . . . become] PP^3; truth
. . . becomes PP$^{1\text{-}2}$(*em.*),BC

*314.1–2 Such an example . . . it
contains] H; Such examples . . . they
contain PP,BC

316.29 *Logic*] H; Logic PP(*em.*),BC

319.5 substance] Romanes; surface PP
(*em.*),BC

321.24–25 diffuse] *stet* PP,BC; *ital.*
Bain

321.25 freely] Bain; *om.* PP(*em.*),BC

322.19 preponderate] PP; proponderate
BC (*error*)

328.6 evil] WJ/PP; distressing PP(*em.*),
BC

330.12 that∧] PP; ∼ , BC

330.30 deep∧ pure∧ worthy∧] WJ/PP;
∼, ∼, ∼, PP(*em.*),BC

330.32 deep∧ pure∧ spiritual∧] WJ/PP;
∼, ∼, ∼, PP(*em.*),BC

331.7 "Just] H; ∧∼ PP (*em.*), BC

332.22 William] H; Wm. PP(*em.*),BC

334.12 whether] Darwin; if PP(*em.*),BC

334.15 or] Darwin; or is PP(*em.*),BC

334.19 marvellous] *stet* PP,BC; marvellous and inexplicable Darwin

334.27 is a] Darwin; is PP(*em.*),BC

334.31–32 Obstupui . . . hæsit] Darwin,
PP; *all ital.* BC

334.34 may] Darwin; must PP(*em.*),BC

334.40 *volvens*] Darwin; *volens* PP(*em.*),
BC (*error*)

335.39 *The . . . Animals*] H; Origin of
the Emotions PP(*em.*),BC

335.39 290] H; 290–2 PP; 292 BC

336.24–25 was . . . had] *stet* PP,BC;
is . . . has Spencer

337.22 incipient] PP; incipent BC
(*error*)

340.25 *Der . . . Wille*] H; *no qts. (rom.)*
PP (*Thierische*); *sg. qts. (rom.)* BC
(*Thierische*)

341.13 pond-] WJ/BC; ditch- PP,BC

342.37 hatch] P^{37}; hatched PP(*em.*),BC

345.26;350.16–17 *afterwards*] H; *after-*
ward PP(*em.*),BC

347.8 on-lookers] Spalding; lookers-
on PP(*em.*),BC

347.10 miles] Spalding; for miles PP
(*em.*),BC

347.12 simply] Spalding; had simply
PP(*em.*),BC

347.13 and . . .] H; ∼∧ PP(*em.*),BC

347.13 their] Spalding; the PP(*em.*),BC

347.19 these] Spalding; them PP(*em.*),
BC

347.19 of] Spalding; to PP (*em.*),BC

347.22 glass] Spalding; window PP
(*em.*),BC

347.31 organization] Spalding; organizations PP(*em.*),BC

348.12 all—] H; ~,ᴧ PP(*em*); ~,— BC

348.19 takes] PP; take BC (*error*)

349.18 fore-feet] H; forefeet PP(*em.*),BC

351.27 and] H; *and* BC

358.0 XXVI] H; XXIII BC (*error*)

363.13 130–31] H; 115–6 of Vol. I PP; 115–6 BC (*error for* 140–41)

365.36 resolution] PP; resolutions BC (*error*)

367.12 *Hamlet*] H; *rom.* PP(*em.*),BC

369.23–24 tomorrow] H; to-morrow PP (*em.*),BC

369.29 inclining,] PP³; ~ ᴧ PP¹⁻² (*em.*),BC

369.38 any one] WJ/PP; either PP (*em.*),BC

371.12 moment] H; movement PP(*em.*), BC

371.22 In the] H; *ital.* PP(*em.*),BC

375.33 1.)] H; (1. BC (*error*)

377.17–21 to . . . them] BC³; rather to be suggestions and notions of possibility than any overweening strength in his affections or lusts. He may

even be physically impotent all the while. The paths of natural (or it may be unnatural) impulse are so pervious in these characters PP,BC¹⁻²

378.8 ¹at] Burr; *om.* PP(*em.*),BC

378.10 would] Burr; should PP(*em.*),**BC**

378.24 tells . . . man] *stet* PP,BC; relates a case of a gentleman Burr

379.36 so] WJ/PP; as PP(*em.*),BC

379.37 themᴧ] WJ/BC; ~ , PP(*em.*),BC

388.18 within] WJ/PP; in PP(*em.*),BC

389.38 scripture] PP; *cap.* BC

390.14 'Jesus Christ,'] *stet* PP,BC; *Jesus Christ,* Wigan

390.22 and] Wigan; *om.* PP(*em.*),BC

390.22 mind.ᴧ] H; ~ . . . . PP(*em.*),BC

393.20 and the] WJ/BC; and PP(*em.*), BC

393.38 take] WJ/BC; face PP(*em.*),BC

395.16 other's] H; others' BC

398.13 10–11] H; 2–13 BC (*error for* 2–3)

398.33 name] WJ/BC,BC¹⁰; nam BC¹⁻⁹ (*error*)

410.1b thought,] BC²; ~ ; BC¹

Textual Notes

19.11   and *which*] James inadvertently wrote in the margin of his annotated copy '*which* fact'. The next marginal change he made, 'and *whiches*', indicates that the correct annotation should have been 'and *which*' as here emended.

23.3,11;140.8   Everyone] The lack of uniformity throughout the book in the form *every one* or *everyone* may be due partly to erratic housestyling and partly to misreading a slight space that James might leave without intending to separate the two words. James's characteristic form *everyone* has therefore been imposed on the text throughout the book in order to secure consistency of style.

27.26–27   which . . . unit.] In pencil James deleted 'from the starting-point' at the beginning of the line, and added in the margin 'between the sensation we start from & the one we compare with it, each being a unit.' However, he neglected to mark with a caret the position for these added words. They cannot replace the deletion, of course; thus they must be intended (a) to replace un-deleted 'which we feel.' as well as deleted 'from the starting-point,' or (b) to conclude the sentence after 'which we feel.' The latter choice seems to offer the better reading according to the evidence.

92.22–26   sexual . . . even] For this censorship in the plates of the third printing, see the textual discourse, p. 486.

135.28   straight] Whether it was James, or rather more likely a knowl-edgeable compositor, who altered PP 'straight' to BC 'strait' to conform to the old phrase cannot be known. What can be known, however, is the correctness of the PP translation of the German *geraden festen Weg*, and thus the need to retain the original form of James's translation and to reject the BC sophis-tication.

178.27–28   a, . . . ¹are] In his annotated copy James deleted the plus sign after '*a*' and added ', plus' in the margin. After '*b*' he added a comma and inserted the word 'are' at the bottom of the page to follow the comma. By setting 'plus idea of *b*' off by commas he thereby gave emphasis to the distinctness of ideas $a+b$ from the idea of $(a+b)$, a conclusion based upon the associationist error of the nature of ideas and its mathematical correlate discussed in lines 28–34.

207.37   more internal] Perhaps James corrected the PP copy for BC from *external* to *internal* but forgot to alter the modifier from PP *less* so that BC produced a positive error, *less internal.* Curiously, this error was never corrected in the plates.

224.1–2   *the . . . of*] Initially James in ink interlined 'between the objects of the successive thoughts' after '*thought-of,*' the caret deleting the comma, and added 'the' after '*between*' and interlined '*themselves*' after '*thoughts*'; but he then deleted this revision (forgetting to delete 'the', however) and wrote in the final version, with the characteristic spelling 'tho't of'.

238.5   now.] The paragraph following in BC¹⁻³ was omitted in BC⁴ and footnote 2 at 237.6 added to take up the space. This removal followed Holt's suggestion that 243.15–24 (To . . . the unknown. [see Emendations entry 243.24–31]) duplicated the paragraph and James should make a choice. For the correspondence, see the textual discourse, p. 473.

277.6   It . . . becomes] James's correction in his own volume of PP seems the most authoritative. The BC reading was drawn from the first printing of PP, which was corrected in the third printing but with a printer's change, as well, to justify the line, thus adding a corruption to a correction. For references to this reading, see PP, WORKS, pp. 1587 and 1640.

314.1–2   Such an example . . . it contains] In the PP text, collatable in this area, two examples were given to demonstrate James's point whereas only one is given in BC. When James revised the PP text for BC he apparently forgot to change the plural to singular to agree with his deletion, and this error was never corrected in the plates. See Emendations entry 284.14 for a similar problem that was, however, eventually corrected.

Historical Collation

This list comprises the substantive variant readings that differ from the edited text as found in PP, the first edition, first printing of *The Principles of Psychology* (New York: Henry Holt, 1890). The reading to the left of the bracket is that of the present edition; the rejected variant is to the right of the bracket. The noting of variant readings is complete for the substantives; however, variants in sub-headings are not noted. In order to save space, no accidental variants except differences in the placement of single quotes are recorded save for some linguistic differences such as someone] some one, farther] further, and towards] toward, which are recorded for their intrinsic interest. Accidental variants may be recorded when they bear upon the substantive variant being shown. Variants are not repeated in the Historical Collation when the copy-text has been emended since the details may be found in the list of Emendations.

The headnote to the Emendations list may be consulted for general conventions of notation, and the Note on the Editorial Method outlines types of variants that are not recorded. One special feature appearing in the Historical Collation, as in the Emendations, is the use of *et seq*. When this phrase occurs, all subsequent readings within the chapter are to be taken as agreeing with the particular feature of the reading being recorded (save for singulars and plurals and inessential typographical variation, as between roman and italic), unless specifically noted to the contrary by notation within the entry itself. Readings grouped together with multiple page-line references may also be concerned with only the particular feature being recorded and not with inessential types of variation. The note (*em.*) indicates emendation of the first printing of PP by the present editor to the form shown in the lemma; when the emended PP reading differs from that found in the lemma, then the emended PP reading is shown within parentheses following the variant reading. The sigil WJ/PP indicates James's autograph revisions found in his private copy of *Principles*. Page-line references preceding certain rejected readings in cases of collatable areas or areas in which the content was similar, but was either highly condensed or greatly revised (or in cases of text omitted in BC) are to the edition in the WORKS.

CHAPTER II: SENSATION IN GENERAL

18.6–19　But . . . consequence.] *drawn from* 657.9–21 *Pure* . . . consequence;

18.6–7　But . . . *immediate*] *Pure*

19.13–30　Our . . . brings.ₐ] *drawn from* 653.26–654.8 Our . . . brings.4 (*out of order*)

19.14 give] merely give
19.14 *whats, or*] *om.*
19.14–15 in other words] *om.*
19.15 yet] *om.*
19.16 rather] rather | rather (*em.*)
20.18–38 The very . . . once;] *drawn from* 657.25–658.4 *The first . . . once.*
20.18 very] *om.*

20.19 outer] *om.*
20.20 comes . . . life] later comes to know
20.21 amplification] amplification and an implication
20.30 *externality,*] *om.*
20.37 many] *om.*
20.37 various] many

CHAPTER III: SIGHT

37.19–34 Any . . . other.] *drawn from* 856.4–19 *This . . . other.*
37.19 Any] This theory starts from the truth that on both retinæ an
37.19–20 of . . . retina] *om.*
37.20 see] perceive
37.21–22 of . . . see] *om.*
37.24 geometrically] *om.*
37.26 were] were consistently
37.26 in detail] *om.*
37.34–35 Similarly . . . glass.] *drawn from* 856.26–27 *Just . . . glass.* (*out of order*)
37.34 Similarly] Just so
37.36–38.5 Or . . . one.] *drawn from* 856.19–857.2 *The . . . one.* (*except* 856.26–27 *Just . . . glass. found at* 37.34–35)
37.36 Or . . . spots.] The same result may be more artificially obtained.
37.37 pictures,] pictures, smaller, or at least
37.38 look] look at them as stereoscopic slides are looked at, that is,
38.2 view] view of either eye to the picture appear
38.3 appear] appear sharp and
38.3 single.ᴧ] ∼ .⁷⁶

38.3 'Identical . . . points'] ᴧIdentical pointsᴧ
38.6–12 Here . . . itself.] 857.3–858.7 *The . . . it.*
38.13–39.11 Now . . . treatises.] *drawn from* 858.8–859.18 *It . . . treatises.*
38.13 Now] *om.*
38.14 location] *projection*
38.14 falling] *om.*
38.16 seen] *projected*
38.20–21 The . . . single.] *om.*
38.21 then] *om.*
38.24 star's] *om.*
38.25 eye] one
38.25 to . . . O] in a direction leftward of the cyclopean eye's line of sight ('leftward' *em. to* 'leftwards')
38.25 its] the
38.26 on] of
38.26 eye] one
38.26 appear] appear far
38.26 this point] the same direction
38.29 any . . . O] O
39,FIG. 10 *L' . . . R'*] *In Fig. 55 reversed to read 'R' R   L L" in* PP
39.6 positions seen] directions of projection

CHAPTER VI: SENSATIONS OF MOTION

70.6–73.23 This . . . fall.ᴧ] *drawn from* 810.7–814.33 *The feeling . . . fall.*³⁹
70.6 This] *The feeling of motion*
70.11 time.ᴧ] ∼ .³²
70.13 I] we
70.20 that it has] of its having
70.21 whilst . . . fixed] when we fix our gaze

71.8 compass-points] dividers
71.16 it.] 811.7–22 *it. A . . . results.*
71.17 time,ᴧ] ∼ , ³⁴
71.22 seem] be seen
71.28 ¹still] still | still (*em.*)
71.37 field . . . move] background moves
71.37 think] think that
71.39 seem to] *om.*

504

71.40 really] *om.*

72.1 is not] cannot be

72.4-5 field . . .¹we] object moves
we still

72.5 and . . . moving] *om.*

72.12 faster] even faster

72.31 frogs.ₐ] ∼ .³⁶

72.39-73.1 perceived.] 813.9-15 perceived. As . . . 13.3:40.7 ('13.3:40.7'
em. to '13.8:40.7')

73.2 do] shall

73.4 radiates.ₐ] ∼ .³⁷

73.5 In ourselves,] 814.1-5 Enough . . . .
Even to-day

73.5 parts of the] regions of our

73.8 -tips.] 814.8-18 -tips. Of . . .
verified.

73.16 psychologistsₐ] ∼ ³⁸

73.21 movements] contractions

73.21 how largely] that

73.22 discernment] discrimination

73.22 impressions] impressions (quite
apart from any question of measuring
the space between them) largely

73.23 surfaces] surface

73.32-74.9 Goldscheider . . . *perceived.*]
drawn from 829.20-830.4 This . . .
perceived.

73.32 Goldscheider in Berlin] This
patient observer

73.32 fingers] his fingers

73.35 rotation.] rotation. No active
muscular contraction took place.

73.36 were] were in all cases surprisingly
small, being

73.37-38 Goldscheider says] the author
says (p. 490)

73.38 eye.] 829.28-32 eye. The . . .
performed.

73.39 had] also had

74.8 *seat*] *starting point*

CHAPTER VIII: THE FUNCTIONS OF THE BRAIN

89.1-90.21 If . . . intelligence.] *drawn
from* 25.1-26.23 If . . . intelligence.

89.13 discharges] discharges itself, if at
all strong,

89.13 nerves] nerves into muscles and
glands

89.13 movements] movements of the
limbs and viscera, or acts of secretion,

89.22 station] depot

90.10 It] Whether it be instinctive or
whether it result from the pedestrian
education of childhood may be
doubtful; it

90.22-23 Let . . . on.] 26.24-27.13 An
. . . hand.

90.24-92.8 The . . . time.] *drawn from*
27.14-29.6 The . . . time.

90.28 shall] will

90.31 operation.] 27.26-28.10 operation.
We . . . overturn.

92.6 and . . . will] everything else
being cut away, will then

92.9-17 Similarly . . . *animal.*] 29.7-
30.1 The . . . animal.

92.18-94.20 Not . . . longer.] *drawn
from* 30.1-32.16 Not . . . asleep.

92.19 mentioned] described

93.10 of] at

93.24 brainless] headless

94.2 jump] jump over a stone which
he sees

94.6 done.ₐ] ∼.²

94.11-13 stimulus . . . *things.*] 31.35-
32.9 *stimulus.* Thus . . . scale.

94.15 pigeon,] pigeon, and

94.15-16 carefully . . . operation] as
they are ordinarily cut out for a
lecture-room demonstration

94.17-20 execute . . . longer.] 32.13-
16 perform . . . asleep.

94.20 In . . . words:] 84.3-6 We . . .
voice. (*out of order*)

94.21-95.2 "The . . . prey."ₐ] *drawn
from* 84.6-27 "The . . . prey."⁹² (*out
of order; verbatim*)

95.3-98.23 All . . . -physiology.] *drawn
from* 32.18-35.37 All . . . -physiology.

95.4 try . . . broadly] think about them

95.4 conception] explanatory conception

95.6 *considerations*] *perceptions and
considerations*

95.7   are] are perceptions but sensations grouped together? and what are
95.14   death] unconsciousness
95.17   main] *om.*
95.21   *chief*] *om.*
97.5   extraordinary] exaggerated
98.23–36   This . . . simple.] 35.37–40 So . . . detail.
98.37–99.24   To . . . steps.] *drawn from* 136.17–137.4 To . . . steps. (*out of order*)
98.37   this . . . should] the consequences of the dogma so confidently enunciated, one should unflinchingly
98.38   examples] the most complicated examples
98.40   physiological] material
98.40   may] must
99.1   mechanical] material
99.3   , according . . . automatism,] *om.*
99.4   given] certain
99.12   , the . . . affirms,] *om.*
99.25–39   As . . . creature.] 137.5–146.12 Another . . . efficacy. (*out of order*)
99.39–100.24   It . . . deny.] *drawn from* 146.12–147.4 *It . . . deny.* (*out of order*)
100.12   keep] immerse
100.13   under] in
100.14–15   ¹conscious . . . anything] pleasures and pains have no efficacy
100.18   with . . . impunity] *om.*
100.20   agony.] 146.31–38 agony. The . . . impunity.
100.20   attempt] attempt, in fact,
100.24   partisans . . . automatism] 'double-aspect' partisans
100.25–101.22   Probability . . . constituents.] 36.1–41.13 THE . . . way.
101.23–34   Brain . . . correspond.] *drawn from* 41.14–25 *Brain . . . correspond.*
101.24   Jackson,ₐ] ~ ,⁶
101.32–33   little more than] nothing but
101.34   ¹sensations and] *om.*
101.34–102.6   The . . . details.] 41.25–42.24 *Ideas . . . stand.*
102.7–16   The . . . by] *drawn from* 42.25–34 The . . . by (*verbatim*)
102.16–103.6   anatomical . . . be.] 42.34–49.8 the . . . forth.

103.7–105.7   One . . . eating.] *drawn from* 49.9–50.23 One . . . eating.
104.1   FIG. 43.] *different cut and legend*
104.11–13   crossing . . . exist] 50.9–11 decussation . . . measure
105.3   these very] the
105.8–107.3   The . . . imagination.] 50.24–59.1 It . . . tracts.²²
107.4–108.9   A . . . -injury,ₐ] *drawn from* 59.5–61.14 A . . . -injury.²⁹
107.11   both] *om.*
107.12   But] If
107.13   and . . . being] on the one hand, and the visual centres on the other, be
107.15   of the] the (*em.*)
107.16–18   as . . . regions] in many cases of extensive injury about the fronto-temporal regions, as a complication of *aphasic* disease
107.18   regions.] 59.19–60.27 disease. Nothnagel . . . eyes.²⁸
107.22   are . . . paths] the associative paths are
107.24   FIG. 46.] *cut om.*
108.9   -injury,ₐ] 61.13–26 - ~ .²⁹ [¶] The . . . man.
108.10–12   The . . . 44).] 61.28–63.1 Hearing . . . part.
108.12–110.16   The . . . p. 111).] *drawn from* 63.1–65.12 The . . . 18).
108.14   aphasia] this disease
108.20   lobe.ₐ] ~ .³⁵
108.22   Starr,ₐ] ~.³⁶
108.34   In] In a large majority of Dr. Starr's fifty cases, the power either to name objects or to talk coherently was impaired. This shows that in
108.35–36   our . . . probably] it must be that our ideas
109.5   centres] centres of ideation, those, namely
109.6   analysis] analysis of the facts in the light
109.9   thing] thing, act, or relation
109.10   properties] properties of each thing
109.10   the name] its name
109.15   connection] dynamic connection
109.17   whilst] as
109.18   is] is that of

109.21–22   lesion . . . Broca] limited
lesion of the left inferior frontal
convolution

109.24   is, as aforesaid,] seems to be

109.26–27   individual's mind] individual
the thought of

109.27   or] or of

109.27   name be what] printed name
be the process which

109.29   or reading] *om.*

109.30   the human voice] speech

109.32   word- . . . aphasia] *pure* word-
deafness

110.3   convolutions] gyri

110.4   brain∧] ∼ 37

110.6–7   the . . . in] a later chapter we
shall again return to these differences
in the effectiveness of

110.7   of] in

110.11   display.∧] ∼ .38

110.11   organ] centre

110.13   mind . . . less] brain, more or
less, is

110.15   vitally] critically

110.17–24   The . . . nothing.] 65.14–72.6
Everything . . . guesses.

111.3–112.7   We . . . science—] *drawn
from* 73.1–27 We . . . science;

111.3   see] see that

111.4   with . . . be] which we started
with on p. 30 [*ed.*, p. 41] is

111.5   by] by subsequent

111.8   *together.*∧] ∼.60

111.10   discharge] motor discharge

111.11–12   asking . . . well] keeping up
that old controversy about the motor
zone, as to whether it is in reality
motor or sensitive

111.17   Marique,∧] ∼,61

111.18   Paneth∧] ∼62

112.1   ¹it . . . funnel] really it is only
the mouth of the funnel, as it were,

112.2   escapes;∧] pours;63

112.8–36   so . . . states.] 73.27–87.6 and . . .
kind. (*except* 84.3–27 We . . . prey."92
found at 94.20–95.2)

CHAPTER IX: SOME GENERAL CONDITIONS OF NEURAL ACTIVITY

113.0   Some . . . Neural] ON SOME . . .
BRAIN

113.1–24   The word . . . scale?] 88.1–
92.12 The elementary . . . field.
(*except* 89.10–92.4 The . . . row.
found at 120.25–121.23)

114.1–40   The . . . second.] *drawn from*
92.14–93.25 One . . . second.

114.1–3   The . . . years.] One of the
lines of experimental investigation
most diligently followed of late years
is that of the ascertainment of the
time occupied by nervous events.

114.3   the way] off

114.4   outgoing] *om.*

114.5   The] But the

114.5–6   sensory reactions] the sensory
nerves and the centres

114.6   admiration] scientific admiration

114.13   gods.] gods. We shall take up
the various operations measured, each
in the chapter to which it more
naturally pertains.

114.16   measured.] measured. 'Velocity

of nerve-action' is liable to the same
criticsm, for in most cases we do not
know what particular nerve-processes
occur.

114.31   reaction] observation

114.35   a rod] a pendulum or a rod

114.40–116.2   The machine . . . start.]
93.25–100.3 Ludwig's . . . 0".230.

116.3–28   These . . . vary.∧] *drawn from*
100.4–35 These . . . vary.25

116.3   These . . . thus] These reaction-
time experiments are then

116.8–9   may then be] then

116.13   Even here, however,] We shall
see, however, in the appropriate chapters, that

116.13   choice] choice involved in such
a reaction

116.17   complications, . . . variations]
complications. It is the fundamental
physiological constant in all time-
measurements. As such, its own
variations have an interest, and

116.18   review.∧] ∼.24

116.19 *age.*] *age.* An individual may have it particularly long in respect of signals of one sense (Buccola, p. 147), but not of others.

116.21 Exner] Exner, Pflüger's Archiv, VII. 612–4

116.21–22 according to Herzen] Herzen in Buccola, p. 152

116.26 sec.] sec. (*loc. cit.* p. 626).

116.27 it, . . . it. The] it. [¶] *Concentration of attention* shortens it. Details will be given in the chapter on Attention. [¶] The

116.28–33 I . . . 0.213] 100.35–101.29 Wundt . . . 49 ff.).

116.34–117.5 It . . . first.] *drawn from* 101.30–102.15 It . . . first.

116.35 either.] 101.31–102.6 either. One . . . individual.

116.37 Herzen] Herzen (Grundlinien einer allgem. Psychophysiologie, p. 101)

117.5–17 *Intoxicants* . . . operations.] 102.15–103.17 Wundt . . . *activity.*

117.17–118.25 The *time* . . . bad.$_\wedge$] *drawn from* 494.4–497.16 The . . . bad.[32] (*out of order*)

117.17 thus] *om.*

117.19 -time] -time—see p. 85 ff. [*ed.,* pp. 92 ff.]—

117.22–33 The *excess* . . . 0.132.] 494.9–495.36 The exact . . . two.[29]

117.34 Prof.] Mr. J. M.

117.34 method,$_\wedge$] ~,[30]

117.40–118.1 Reacting . . . way,] 496.7–24 The nervous . . . principles,

118.1 increment of] *om.*

118.3 0.030 . . . 0.050] 0.030 sec. . . . 0.050 sec.

118.5 0.110] 10.10 PP[1-7] (*em.* PP[8])

118.16 0.118] 0.118 sec.

118.21 he says] *om.*

118.26–120.2 The . . . name."$_\wedge$] *drawn from* 525.35–527.42 The . . . name."[6] (*out of order*)

118.26–27 The . . . measured.] The time-measuring psychologists of recent days have tried their hand at this problem by more elaborate methods.

118.29 second.$_\wedge$] ~.[3]

118.36 simple] simple physiological

118.40 *association-*] the *association-*

119.2 respectively.$_\wedge$] ~.[4]

119.3 reacting] reacting (President G. S. Hall)

119.6 Wundt] Prof. Wundt

119.6 second.$_\wedge$] ~.[5]

119.7 Prof.] Finally, Mr.

119.14–16 The . . . read.] 527.1–10 "When . . . sec.

119.16 says Prof. Cattell,] *om.*

119.25 moved. . . .] 527.19–24 ~. As . . . language.

119.32 fast. . . .] 527.30–32 ~. This . . . -examinations.

120.3–20 Dr. . . . readers."$_\wedge$] *drawn from* 773.35–775.2 Dr. . . . readers."[57] (*out of order*)

120.3 Dr. . . . has] Dr. Romanes gives an interesting variation of these time-measurements. He

120.3 found$_\wedge$] 773.36–774.28 ~[56] "an . . . said,

120.15–16 Dr. R. continues,] *om.*

120.21–24 *The* . . . long.] *om.*

120.25–121.23 Throughout . . . row.] *drawn from* 89.10–92.4 The . . . row. (*out of order*)

120.25–26 Throughout . . . law] The law is this,

120.34–35 This . . . laboratory] 89.18–91.9 Where . . . extent."[4]

120.36 apply . . . summation] use the summation of stimuli

120.39–40 -quarters,] -quarters, and

121.10 sound."$_\wedge$] ~."[5]

121.14 movements."$_\wedge$] ~."[6]

121.19 defiance.$_\wedge$] ~.[7]

121.20 on] upon

121.24–124.22 All . . . secretions.] *drawn from* 103.18–108.9 All . . . itself.

121.26 somewhat] *om.*

121.28 purpose.] purpose. Elsewhere the current must be strong enough for an epileptic attack to be produced.[27]

121.29 observed] observed, and are independent of the vaso-constrictive phenomenon

121.30 his] his ingenious
121.36 arms.$_\wedge$] ~.28
121.38 legs] arms (*em.*)
122.4 head-] balance at the head-
122.9 book,$_\wedge$] ~ ,29
122.21-22 emotion.] 104.26-105.11 emotion. [¶] The . . . subject.
122.25 1867.] 1867. Dr. Lombard's latest results include the records of over 60,000 observations.32
122.29 angry] anger
122.31 Fahrenheit.] 105.21-32 Fahrenheit. The . . . addition.
122.32 by] *om.*
122.33 brain] brain, to eliminate possible errors from vascular changes in the skin when the thermometers were placed upon the scalp
123.2 an] an immediate deflection of the galvanometer, indicating
123.9 applied.$_\wedge$] ~.34
123.9 Dr.] Dr. R. W.

123.17 degree.] 106.19-22 degree. As . . . investigated.
123.17 these regions] they
123.19 skull.$_\wedge$] ~ .35
123.20-22 Considering . . . here.] 106.26-31 *Chemical* . . . phosphorus.
123.34 alleged] *om.* (*em.*)
123.39 PO$_5$] PO
123.40 urine, . . . procedure] urine, which represents other organs as well as the brain, and this procedure, as Dr. Edes says, is like measuring the rise of water at the mouth of the Mississippi to tell where there has been a thunder-storm in Minnesota.36 It
123.40 by] however, by
124.5 sleep.] 107.21-24 sleep. There . . . foundation.37
124.22 secretions.] 108.5-9 secretions. [¶] There . . . itself.

CHAPTER X: HABIT

125.1-11 There . . . discharge.] 109.1-11 When . . . are.
125.12-138.34 The . . . together.] *drawn from* 109.12-131.25 The . . . together.
125.19-20 On . . . 3the] The
125.21 change] change (on the principles of the atomistic philosophy)
126.23 *plasticity*$_\wedge$] ~ 1
126.24 The] But the
126.28 Dumont] Dumont, whose essay on habit is perhaps the most philosophical account yet published,
126.36 already; . . . and] 110.38-111.9 already. This . . . before.
126.40 time."$_\wedge$] ~ ."2
127.8-9 in . . . known] if we ascend to the nervous system, we find
127.21 career.] 111.34-112.10 career. [¶] Can . . . out.
127.27-28 for . . . that the] 112.15-19 for . . . way. The
127.29 it] them
127.30 1and] and through
128.10 chain.] 112.40-114.9 chain. The . . . matter.5

128.22 summer.] 114.21-117.14 summer. [¶] Dr. . . . life.
128.23-24 First . . . fatigue.] 117.15-118.12 The . . . keys."8
128.31 be] therefore be
129.13 Secondly,] The next result is that
129.24 Whilst] When
129.28 follow not only] not only follow
129.29 but they] they also
129.34 shower] cataract
129.39 Persons] Very absent-minded persons
130.2 hour.] 119.31-37 hour. The . . . led.
130.2 all] all of us
130.4 like.] 120.1-3 like. Our . . . way.
130.9 the shutters] my double door
130.19 In] In an
130.25 several] respective
130.27 in] of the muscles, skin, or joints of
130.30 or . . . has] the contraction has or has not
131.1 act of attention] perception
131.1 We] By it we

131.2   intellectually] *om.*
131.2   have . . . performed] be right
131.4   etc.] etc., by intellectual means
131.8   intellectual centres] centres of idea or perception
131.8   that . . . carries] the initial impulse,
131.12 example] case
131.13 this] the
131.17 result.] result. The process, in fact, resembles the passage of a wave of 'peristaltic' motion down the bowels.
131.18 sensible . . . movement] effect of
131.21 level.] 121.20–122.12 lines. That . . . p. 26.)[10]
131.23 by] the antecedents of the successive muscular attractions,
131.23 If sensations, they] 122.14–123.6 Some . . . kind. They
131.24–25 that . . . catch] which immediately call
131.28 absorbed elsewhere] off
131.35 is] be
131.40 away. . . ." Again:] 123.24–124.16

away. [¶] "So . . . well:
131.40 a pupil] one
132.13 on."ᴧ] 124.28–36 ∼ . "[14] [¶] This . . . ourselves:
132.17 probably can] can probably
132.21 says Prof. Huxley,] *om.*
132.27 structure."ᴧ] ∼ ."[15]
132.30 domestic beasts seem] trained domestic animals, dogs and oxen, and omnibus- and car-horses, seem to be
132.35 a menagerie-tiger] to a travelling menagerie in the United States some time in 1884, a tiger
133.36 -clad] -bred
135.9   damp] dampen
135.10 experiences . . . nerve] experience . . . nerves
135.14 career.] 127.39–128.4 career. Prof. . . . formed.
136.22 When] Every time
136.22–23 is . . . evaporate] evaporates
136.23 it] *om.*
137.1   of the] of a
137.11 way.ᴧ] ∼ .[18]
137.12 grandmother] aunt

CHAPTER XI: THE STREAM OF CONSCIOUSNESS

139.0   Consciousness] THOUGHT
139.1–140.10 We . . . *him.*] 219.1–220.1 We . . . indiscriminately.
140.10–141.27 If . . . selves.] *drawn from* 220.1–221.24 If . . . selves.
140.15,25 four] five
140.18 'state'] thought
140.19 states are] thought is
140.21 Each . . . continuous.] Within each personal consciousness thought is sensibly continuous. [¶] 4) It always appears to deal with objects independent of itself.
140.22 4)] 5)
140.22 its object] these objects
140.26 nomenclature] vocabulary
140.32 'state' or] *om.*
141.26 feel.'ᴧ] ∼ .[1]
141.27–30 Thoughts . . . *worth.*] 221.24–224.14 The . . . consciousness.
141.31–149.7 I . . . itself?] *drawn from* 224.16–239.25 I . . . itself?

141.31–32 by . . . say] necessarily
141.33 What . . . on] 224.17–20 The . . . stress
141.34 *before.*] 224.21–36 *before.* Let . . . states.
141.38–40 states, . . . law?] 225.3–19 states. The . . . entirely.
141.40 which] *om.*
142.8–9 an . . . sensation] *the same bodily sensation is ever got by us*
142.18 simply . . . impressions] not attending to sensations as subjective facts, but of simply using them
142.31 what is called] *om.*
142.32 sensible qualities] sensations
142.34 of an impression] or quantity of a given sensation
142.35 impressions] sensations
143.2   These] There are facts which
143.5   again.] 226.24–28 again. The . . . day.[8]
143.5   accordingly] according

143.7 all] all things
143.8 And] *om.*
143.24 we . . . there] *om.*
143.25 consciousness] feeling
143.25 subserves.] 227.10–17 subserves. [¶] All . . . stream.
143.26 sensations] ideas of sensation
144.11 goods.] 228.4–229.20 goods. [¶] But . . . brain?
144.24–25 which . . . again.'] *om.*
144.30 *'Idea'*] *'idea' or 'Vorstellung'*
144.32 *Spades.*] 230.8–39 *Spades.* [¶] What . . . show.
144.35 division.] 231.4–5 division. I . . . nature.
144.37 out] out altogether to come into existence again at a later moment
144.38 content] *quality*, or content,
144.39 ¹what] the segment that
144.39 ²what] the one that
144.40 consciousness] within each personal consciousness thought
145.6 first.] 231.19–232.12 first. And . . . me.
145.7 *a.*] *om.*
145.29 states] feelings
146.1 *b.*] *om.*
146.9–10 No . . . our] 233.17–234.6 Does . . . . Into the
146.10 thunder] thunder itself
146.13 -it.‿] -~ .¹¹
146.21 When we take] 234.17–236.15 Here . . . fact,
146.23 the] this
146.24 be] be made of
146.35 our . . . towards] the main end of our thinking is at all times the attainment of
146.36 it has] we have
147.19 transitive . . . consciousness] psychoses
147.29 Now the blunder] 237.24–27 Were . . . this
147.31 substantive] coarse
147.33 sensible things] facts
147.34 mental states] subjective modifications
147.35 any such states] feelings of relation
147.36 on] so far as

147.37 Simple . . . 'ideas,'] Substantive psychoses
147.38 copies] copies and derivatives
147.40 view.‿] ~ .¹⁴
148.3 such] the
148.5 'state,'] modification
148.7 conditions of consciousness] states
148.8 must be known] are known, these relations,
148.11 passing perishing] *om.*
148.30–31 Consider . . . of] 238.29–239.8 The . . . look at
149.8–11 There . . . mean.] 239.25–242.3 The . . . like.¹⁶
149.12–151.15 Suppose . . . understood.] *drawn from* 243.1–246.39 Suppose . . . understood.
149.15 cases.] 243.4–6 cases. Leaving . . . diverse,
149.15 here] *om.*
149.16 real] residual
149.31 Bowles.] 243.22–36 Bowles. Here . . . existence.
149.32 *want*] emptiness
149.33–34 Such . . . ¹want] The ordinary way is to assume that they are all emptinesses of consciousness, and so the same state. But the feeling of an absence
149.34 a want of] the absence of a
149.40 words.] 244.6–245.5 words. [¶] Again . . . words.
150.12 not.] 245.18–20 not. It . . . it?
150.21–22 almost . . . on] is almost altogether a matter of
150.23 presently] presently to come upon
150.23 'however,'] 'however' at the outset of a sentence
150.24 expect.] 245.33–36 expect. A . . . etc.
150.25 verbal . . . scheme] grammatical scheme combined with each successive uttered word
150.29 It . . . see,] 246.1–14 Some . . . short,
150.29–30 and inarticulate] *om.*
150.32 the chapter on Imagination] Chapter XVIII

150.35   if we overthrow] in the over-
    throw of
150.37   'states of consciousness,'] sub-
    jective feelings
151.16–17   *Let . . . fringe.'*] 246.40–
    248.10 What . . . used.
151.18–27   Nothing . . . this:] *drawn
    from* 248.11–20 Nothing . . . this:
151.19   these] all these
151.24–25   whose . . . thought] which,
    a moment hence, will be the cerebral
    correlatives of some thing which a
    moment hence will be vividly present
    to the thought
151.28–152.11   Let . . . degree.] 248.21–
    249.11 FIG. 27. | Each . . . aroused.
    [*cut and discussion differ*]
152.12–38   It . . . ideas.] *drawn from*
    249.12–250.34 It . . . ideas.
152.12   'overtones'] the 'overtones'
152.12   music:] 249.12–15 ~ . Different
    . . . another.
152.16   point.] 249.19–22 point. [¶]
    Let . . . perceived.19
152.20   *-about'*] -about' (see p. 221
    [*ed.,* pp. 216–217])
152.31   Relation to this] 250.9–24 Half
    . . . our
152.33   Any] 250.26–29 When . . . *any*
152.35   may . . . topic] is an acceptable
    member of our thinking, whatever
    kind of thought it may otherwise be
152.36   its object] it
152.37   topic] interesting topic
152.37   is] is quite
152.39–153.5   Now . . . language]
    250.35–251.32 *For* . . . words
153.5–158.35   have . . . led.] *drawn from*
    251.32–278.22 have . . . led.

153.10   thought.] 251.37–253.10 thought.
    Dr. . . . archetypes.''
153.32   thought.] 253.32–37 thought.
    [¶] So . . . all.
154.4   We see, then,] 254.8–259.27 An
    . . . time
154.5   our] his
154.15   this] the
154.26   own.] 260.19–273.6 own. [¶]
    Thought . . . correspond. (*except*
    267.14–268.35 The . . . one.36 *found
    at* 176.2–37)
154.27   peculiarity] peculiarity of
    consciousness
154.28   thought's] its
154.29   **Consciousness**] 5) *It*
155.18–19   , as . . . 15–17] *om.*
155.23   exist.] 273.34–274.3 exist. It . . .
    darkness.
155.32   We] 274.12–21 Helmholtz's . . .
    we
155.33   *things*] 274.22–23 *things* . . .
    qualities
156.17   bluer] blacker
156.27–29   Next . . . attention.]
    275.17–25 Thus . . . attention.
156.30   a man a hundred] him a
    thousand
157.3–4   be able to] *om.*
157.13   the given] our given
157.14   conclusion.] 276.9–11 conclusion.
    Another . . . out.
157.17   it.] 276.14–16 it. I . . . mind.
157.18   the æsthetic] its æsthetic
158.7   resolve . . . choose] choose . . .
    resolve
158.9–10   Taking . . . men] 277.7–35
    Looking . . . world-stuff
158.10   race] human race
158.11   name;] ~ , and what not.

CHAPTER XII: THE SELF

159.0   The] THE CONSCIOUSNESS
    OF
159.1–15   Whatever . . . authors.]
    279.1–6 Let . . . clear that
159.17–163.22   Between . . . mean]
    drawn from 279.6–283.13 between
    . . . mean

160.8 *et seq. this chap.   Me*] *Self*
    (*except* 169.38;170.6;172.23;183.20,25,
    37;184.26,37;186.24,25,30;191.3[*twice*])
160.20   *-appreciation*] -feelings
160.25,28   The] (*a*) The
160.26   The] (*b*) The
160.26   and] *om.*

160.27   The] (c) The
160.27   me] Self; and | (d) The pure Ego
160.37   reply.ᴧ] ~ .¹
161.12   house] home
161.35   A] (b) A
162.11   him.ᴧ] ~.²
163.11   life.ᴧ] ~.³
163.21   By] (c) By
163.22   self] Me
163.22–164.8   no one . . . called.] 283.13–292.14 a man's . . . on.
164.9–173.27   Language . . . all.] *drawn from* 292.14–302.15 Language . . . all.
164.9–10   kinds . . . -appreciation] primary feelings
164.39   planted?"ᴧ] ~?"⁷
165.27   friends.] friends. Of the origin of these emotions in the race, we can speak better when we have treated of—
165.28   come next.] *om.*
165.37   together] *om.*
167.16   **Mes**] SELVES
168.2   own.] 296.10–16 own. [¶] I . . . reverse.
168.21   numerator.ᴧ] ~.⁸
169.29   die."ᴧ] ~."⁹
170.5   not.ᴧ] ~.¹⁰
171.38   the advantage] advantage
172.22   be.ᴧ] ~.¹¹
173.28–30   On . . . reverse.] 302.16–307.30 All . . . them.
173.31–174.40   Unless . . . mass.] *drawn from* 307.31–309.29 Unless . . . mass.
173.31   our] his
174.13   way.] 308.13–21 way. Were . . . now.
174.18–20   All . . . and] 308.27–309.9 *My* . . . disguise.
174.21   one object] any object whatever
174.23   other] other, whether connected or not with the interests of the me
174.28   I . . . body.] *om.*
174.29   non-egoistic] altruistic
175.1–2   The . . . far.] 309.30–313.2 The . . . be.
175.2–17   The . . . Guilt.] *drawn from* 313.3–16 The . . . Guiltᴧ
175.6–7   Aspirations] Aspiration

175.19–176.1   The . . . length.] 314.2–21 Having . . . first—
176.2–11   Common- . . . idea?"] *drawn from* 267.14–18,36–39 The . . . separate.³⁴ | ³⁴"There . . . idea?" *(out of order)*
176.2–3   Common- . . . agreed] The ordinary associationist-psychology supposes, in contrast with this,
176.5   all] and all
176.9   says James Mill] *om.*
176.12–15   Similar . . . say:] 267.18–268.18 The . . . say, *(out of order)*
176.15–23   "Well . . . knows?"] *drawn from* 268.18–27 "Well . . . knows?" *(out of order)*
176.15   that] it
176.17   well?] well? The table has legs—how can you think the table without virtually thinking its legs?
176.18   my] our
176.21   thought] our thought
176.24–37   Plausible . . . ideas.] 268.28–35 Now . . . one.³⁶ *(out of order)*
176.37–177.6   "But . . . altogether.] 160.32–40 "What!" . . . identity. *(out of order)*
177.7–10   But . . . know.] 160.25–28 But . . . know. *(out of order)*
177.11–178.31   All . . . idea.] *drawn from* 160.29–161.3,18–30;162.1–163.20 All . . . sense. | In . . . known. | Just . . . idea. *(out of order)*
177.21   When . . . combine] Let it not be objected that H₂ and O combine of themselves
177.22   to] *om.*
177.22   properties,] properties. They do not.
177.26–28   Just . . . tendon.] *om.*
177.29   In] Just so, in
177.29–30   do . . . *themselves*] themselves do not combine
178.5–6   —we . . . sum—] *om.*
178.7   the new feeling] it
178.9   out of themselves] *om.*
178.13   sentence.ᴧ] ~ .¹⁶
178.14   , it is true,] *om.*
178.17   or sentiment constitutes] sentiment, etc., constitute

178.22   Psychology] Psychology,—a contention which we shall take up at greater length in Chapter X

178.31   ¹one] one and the same thing as the 'associated'

178.31–179.25   If . . . is] *om.*

179.26–180.2   In . . . same.'] *drawn from* 314.23–315.8 In . . . same.'

179.27   (see p. 141)] in as radical a way as possible

179.31   it] its own Ego

179.33–35   and . . . judgment.] 314.29–38 being . . . things.

179.36   special mystery] difficulty or mystery peculiar to itself

179.40   as I was] *om.*

180.1   it was] *om.*

180.2   of us] I nor the pen

180.2–181.31   The . . . there.] 315.9–316.35 This . . . both.

181.31–183.6   We . . . stream] *drawn from* 316.35–322.31 We . . . stream;

181.33   object of thought] fact

181.37   object] self

181.38;182.6   objects] selves

182.1   still represent] imagine

182.2   still] *om.*

182.2–3   flavor . . . activity] aroma, the echo of the thinking

182.8   round-up] time for the round-up

182.10–13   Well . . . why] 317.15–32 The . . . that

182.22–23   And . . . consciousness] 318.1–322.5 *The . . . Thought,*

182.23   yet that] The

182.27   that] which

182.34   own.] 322.11–13 own. Each . . . proprietor.

182.36   leads to] is the foundation of

183.1–2   principle . . . principle] non-phenomenal sort of an Arch-Ego, were he

183.3   known] known in time

183.4   successive part] 'section'

183.6   an] the

183.7–13   with . . . wrong.] 322.31–351.10 and which . . . facts.

183.13–191.18   The . . . any] *drawn from* 351.11–379.32 The . . . any

183.13   we . . . survey the] the *I* discovers, as it surveys this

183.14   the relative identity] a relative identity, that

183.15   retained.ᴧ] ∼.41

183.17   some common] the same

183.31–35   *a.* Of . . . survives.] 352.17–353.3 1. *Alterations . . . me's.*

183.36   also] *om.*

183.36   occurrences] occurrences in most of us

183.37   our . . . our] the . . . the

184.12   story.] 353.19–354.6 story. Dr. . . . self!44

184.14   graver] still graver

184.15   types, but] types, from the descriptive point of view. But certain cases unite features of two or more types; and

185.8   contradiction."ᴧ] 355.4–356.11 ∼."45 [¶] With . . . me.

185.12   amongst] among (*em.*)

185.13   internal] familiar

185.14–15   Another feels that] In another

185.23   enemy.ᴧ] ∼.48

186.17   live] lived (*em.*)

186.23   like] similar to

186.33   life.ᴧ] 357.36–358.12 ∼.50 [¶] A . . . her."

186.38   But] *om.*

186.40   note.] note. Kirshaber's book (La Névropathie Cérébro-cardiaque, 1873) is full of similar observations. ('La' *em. to* 'De la')

187.1   loss] lapse

187.10   possesses.ᴧ] ∼.51

187.13   Bordeaux.ᴧ] ∼.52

187.26   has no] hasn't the least

187.31–32   M. Pierre . . . B.,] 359.17–366.3 To . . . woman,

188.11   claims] pretends

189.4   her.'"] 367.11–371.22 her.'" [¶] Léonie . . . change.62

190.19–20   the . . . ¹of] *om.*

190.20   seen.] 373.4–374.37 seen. [¶] As . . . style."

190.20   , however,] myself

190.34   explore.²] 375.9–378.25 ∼·ᴧ [¶] Many . . . ways.

190.35   up] up now

191.1 remember] 1) remember
191.2 know] and know
191.2 care] 2) emphasize and care
191.3 rest.] 378.31–379.5 rest. The . . . receive.
191.6 be] be considered to be
191.7 transcendental] pure
191.12 mind.] 379.14–28 mind. The . . . formula.

191.13–14 passing thoughts . . . existents . . . them] *the passing thought . . . existent . . . it*
191.14–16 they . . . account] *that thought is itself the thinker,* and psychology need not look beyond
191.18–34 such . . . thinkers] 379.32–40 *direct . . . view*

CHAPTER XIII: ATTENTION

192.1–193.10 One . . . minimum.] 380.1–382.6 Strange . . . degree.
193.10–27 Most . . . again.] *drawn from* 382.6–23 Most . . . again.
193.10 of us] people
193.11 somewhat] of something
193.28–38 This . . . out.] 382.24–385.2, 19–44 This . . . 272.)
193.38–194.4 When . . . distinct."] *drawn from* 385.27–32 When . . . distinct."
193.41 many] many of them
194.5–15 A . . . much] 385.3–10 Each . . . becomes
194.15–195.6 harder . . . field] *drawn from* 385.10–387.6 harder . . . field
194.16 several of them] all these parts
194.17 avoided] done
194.18 on] carefully on
194.21 poetry.ₐ] ∼ .8
194.22–23 simultaneous] sinultaneous (*em.*)
194.26 difficult."] 386.3–9 difficult." [¶] The . . . momentum.
194.30 instance:] 386.13–18 instance: [¶] "I . . . again:
194.34 them."] 386.22–25 them." [¶] Of . . . difficult.
194.35 objects] ideas or things
194.37 processes] processes of conception
194.41 fifth,ₐ] ∼ ,9
195.2 time.] 386.34–387.2 time. Within . . . form.
195.3 minute] small
195.6–13 by . . . seen.] 387.6–393.7 2of . . . . Meanwhile
195.14–201.26 Attention . . . mind.]

drawn from 393.8–401.20 Attention . . . mind.
195.25 involuntary] non-voluntary
195.31–33 In . . . or it] 394.7–10 In . . . else it
195.34 our] our normal
196.4 rest.ₐ] ∼ .17
196.9 of] *om.*
196.9 chaotic] rough
196.27 hardly will it] it will hardly
197.18 place."ₐ] ∼ ."18
197.19 *Involuntary*] *Passive*
197.23–25 The . . . only] 396.2–33 Owing . . . banish
197.38 in battle] *om.*
198.23 mind.ₐ] ∼ .21
198.31 sense] sense (p. 275 [*ed.,* p. 265])
199.25 section] chapter
199.25 rivalry.ₐ] ∼ .22
200.19 away."] 399.20–400.5 away." [¶] And . . . control."
200.35 attention.ₐ] ∼ .23
201.21 interests] interest
201.27–40 These . . . object.] 401.21–411.26 At . . . adjustment.
202.1–207.37 That . . . mind.] *drawn from* 411.27–422.13 That . . . mind.
202.10–12 we . . . accommodated.] 411.36–412.1 comes . . . does.
202.13 then,] *om.*
202.14–15 which . . . clearness.] 412.2–5 and . . . sort.
202.16 attention] attention, as we have already seen, (p. 300 [*ed.,* p. 287]),
203.6 backwards."ₐ] ∼ ."38

203.12–15 This . . . show.] 412.39–413.4 I . . . it.

203.15–25 Usually . . . made.] 413.9–414.2 Usually . . . made. (*out of order*)

203.15 it . . . that] as is well known,

203.25–28 Teachers . . . men.] 413.5–9 Teachers . . . men. This would be an objection to the *invariable and universal* presence of movements of adjustment as ingredients of the attentive process.

203.37 these] the

204.15 attention."2] 414.28–415.7 attention."40 [¶] Hering . . . organs.

204.16 But] 2. But

204.21 *excitement*] *preparation*

204.25 may come] comes

204.28–31 is . . . occurs] this reinforcing imagination, this inward reproduction, this anticipatory thinking of the thing we attend to, is

205.1 mind,] mind, which shall stand ready to receive the outward impression as if in a matrix,

205.2 be] be quite

205.3–8 In . . . concerned.] 415.33–416.10 In . . . designation.

205.11 Helmholtz says:] *om.*

205.14 If] 416.16–22 The . . . c. . . . If

205.22 ear."ʌ] ~ ."42

205.23 "The] 416.32–34 "on . . . . The

205.36 itself. . . .] 417.9–17 ~ . In . . . stimulus.

205.40 intent."ʌ] ~ ."43

206.2 -cells] -cells, or perhaps spiritual forces,

206.3 within.] within. The latter influence is the 'adaptation of the attention.'

206.4–5 inwardly imagined] attended to

206.5 attended to and] *om.*

206.7 observation] observation to the passage we quoted a while ago

206.8 "In] 417.32–33 "These . . . 2in

206.8–9 he says,] *om.*

206.13 out."ʌ] 417.38–418.8 ~ ."44 [¶] In . . . again."

206.21 *appear*."ʌ] ~ ."46

206.26 obviously] ostensibly

207.4 canoe'?ʌ] ~ '?47

207.12 preperception] *preperception*, as Mr. Lewes calls it,

207.13 thing.ʌ] ~ .48

207.19 to . . . to] we may . . . we may

207.32 world.] 420.18–422.9 world. [¶] Organic . . . pedagogic.

207.37 internal] external

207.37 mind.] 422.13–423.10 mind. Prof. . . . elsewhere.56

207.37–208.6 If . . . rule.] *drawn from* 423.21–27 Second . . . rule. (*out of order*)

207.37–40 If . . . to] Second, *a teacher who wishes to engage the attention of his class must*

207.40 our] *his*

207.40 by rational links] *om.*

208.4–5 the . . . knowing] it is in every case a very delicate problem to know

208.7–17 Second . . . course.ʌ] *drawn from* 423.11–20 Second . . . course.57 ('Second' *em. to* 'Then'; *verbatim*)

208.18–28 I . . . will] 423.29–429.1 When . . . would

208.28–209.6 deepen . . . illusion.] *drawn from* 429.1–19 deepen . . . illusion.

208.31 may] might

209.6–17 Effort . . . other.] 429.19–433.27 As . . . fact.

CHAPTER XIV: CONCEPTION

210.1–5 The . . . conceptions.] 434.2–436.17 In . . . besides.

210.5–211.24 If . . . mind.] *drawn from* 436.17–438.4 If . . . mind.

210.6 a state] an act

210.13 attention's . . . singled] attention singling

210.15 from our] *om.*

210.15 confusion.ʌ] ~ .2

210.19 that. 'ʌ] ~ . '3

210.23 itself] *om.*

211.1 be] have been

211.9 Ideas.ʌ] ~ .4

211.24–29 This . . . Same.] *om.*

211.31–212.15 The sense . . . way.] *drawn from* 446.15–39 *The . . . way. (out of order)*
211.36 has . . . with] pertains to
211.36 object] subjective state
211.39 (See p. 154.)] *om.*
212.11 no such exclusion] to *include* not only Jones, but Napoleon and Smith as well
212.16–27 No . . . only.] 438.5–13 Most . . . only.
212.27–41 We . . . picture.ʌ] *drawn from* 438.13–23 We . . . perceive.⁵
212.29 when] when it is
212.29–33 —that . . . may] Thus we
212.33 Such a machine] It
212.36–37 never touches] does not touch
212.38 again, or] *om.*
212.40–41 shows . . . picture.ʌ] lets us sensibly perceive.⁵

213.1–7 The . . . unimaginable] 439.2–453.4 The . . . it, (*except* 446.15–39 *The . . . way. found at* 211.31–212.15)
213.7–214.9 is . . . view.] *drawn from* 453.4–454.18 is . . . view.
213.9 problematics,] *om.*
213.13 way.ʌ] ~.18
213.16 Socrates] Plato and Aristotle
213.31–32 It . . . p. 143.] 453.26–29 It . . . *mind.*
214.1–2 substantively, now transitively] in one context, now in another
214.2 direct] definite
214.2–3 one . . . symbol] 454.8–12 a symbol . . . to
214.3 somehow] *om.*
214.6 described] arrested
214.6 terms] means
214.9 view.] 454.18–456.6 view. [¶] The . . . suffice.

CHAPTER XV: DISCRIMINATION

215.0 Discrimination] DISCRIMINATION AND COMPARISON
215.1–4 On . . . within.] 457.1–461.20 It . . . that
215.4–216.18 Experience . . . chapter.] *drawn from* 461.20–462.20 Experience . . . chapter.
215.4 , in other words,] *om.*
215.5 *both* by] by *both*
215.5 psychology] that psychology
215.13 are] are both
215.13 Life] Experience
215.17 do both] treat them in both ways
215.19 we do most] way preponderates
216.14 *yield*] *fuse into*
216.15 to] for
216.16 that] *om.*
216.17 is what] *om.*
216.19–30 I . . . enough.] 462.20–468.13 Although . . . all.
216.30–218.16 No . . . -m.ʌ] *drawn from* 468.14–471.32 No . . . -m.¹²
216.33 may] need not so inevitably occur, and may even
216.35–36 Secondly . . . *but must*] Another condition which then favors it is that the sensations excited by *the*

differing objects should not come to us simultaneously but
217.14 quality . . . what] quality, as difference, which remains sensible, no matter of what sort
217.19 made.] 469.9–20 made. We . . . confusion.¹⁰
217.32 say anything *about*] identify
217.38 mate.ʌ] 470.3–471.13 ~ .¹¹ [¶] With . . . terms. (*except* 470.4–24 With . . . time. *found at* 218.18–39)
217.39 the . . . n] their immediate succession
217.40 ¹is] was
218.10–11 The . . . transitive.] 471.24–26 The . . . 'stream.'
218.16–17 The . . . before.] 471.32–474.19 It . . . sort.
218.18–39 With . . . time.] *drawn from* 470.4–24 With . . . time. (*out of order*)
218.28 livelier . . . did] better . . . was
218.30 constantly] constantly busy
218.40–219.2 It . . . elsewhere.] 474.21–30 And . . . *apart.*
219.2–222.11 The . . . smell.] *drawn from* 474.30–482.8 The . . . smell.

219.13–14 are . . . impossible] are almost . . . almost impossible
219.17 examples.] 475.15–20 examples.
The . . . itself.
219.21 the feelings] them
219.30 exist.] 475.32–37 exist. But . . .
unfelt.
219.35 and *d*] *d*
220.10 separate it from] heighten the
feeling thereof; whereas it dampens
and opposes the feeling of
220.14 prove . . . it] go to prove this
point
220.30 tone.] 476.40–477.24 tone.
Helmholtz . . . tones."16
221.3–5 Fluctuation . . . appears.]

477.37–478.28 Consider . . . appear.
221.8 *concomitants.*₋ₐ]~. 16a WJ/PP
221.8 this . . . a] it will be to allow the
221.9 once] thus
221.9–10 by . . . can] to
221.12 Dr. . . . law:] 478.34–479.9 The
. . . writes:
221.26–27 but . . . here.] 479.22–481.16
One . . . sheep."18
221.29 interest] interest, however,
221.30 differences.] 481.19–20 differences. The . . . sheep.
221.34 have.] 481.24–26 have. Let . . .
habit.
222.6 so] has so (*em. to* 'had so' WJ/PP)
222.8 had] has (*em.* WJ/PP)

CHAPTER XVI: ASSOCIATION

223.1–225.30 After . . . thought.] *drawn
from* 519.1–523.1 After . . . thought.
223.1 association!] 519.1–4 association!
Already . . . ones.
223.2 all . . . in] the . . . of our
223.3 in . . . education,] *om.*
223.23–24 , between . . . other,] *om.*
223.24 *connection*] *connection* between
the thoughts which thus appear to
sprout one out of the other,
224.11 small] smaller
224.12 some authors] such authors as
Kant and Renouvier
224.13 understanding.₋ₐ] ~ .1
224.14–15 from . . . others.] 520.20–23
with . . . continuum.
224.17–18 categories] infinite possibilities of transition,
224.18–23 thinkable . . . *c*?] 520.26–38
acts . . . lunacy?
224.25 our . . . unable] thought refusing
224.30 discover?] discover? If reason
can give us relief then, why did she
not do so earlier?
224.31–32 strange . . . 'reason'] 521.9–18
conditions . . . . Reason
224.36–37 opinions . . . beliefs] beliefs
. . . opinions
224.37–225.1 And . . . *presented.*] 521.23–
38 It . . . *decisions.*
225.5 prepossessions] preprocessions

(*em.*); preposessions WJ/PP
225.13 the sequence] all connections
225.14 *causal*] psychological
225.14 problem] problem of connection
225.15 associations] connections
225.16 view.] 522.13–17 view. The . . .
cognizance.
225.16–17 having the thought] thinking
225.17 have the thought] think
225.20 in] in many
225.23–26 We . . . shall] 522.23–36 But
. . . ought to
225.30 thought.] 523.1–533.25
thought. Let . . . facts. (*except* 525.35–
527.42 The . . . name."6 *found at*
118.26–120.2)
225.31–243.14 I . . . up.₋ₐ] *drawn from*
533.27–556.26 I . . . up.28 (*except* 547.7–
549.6 To . . . point. *found at* 243.15–
31)
225.31 now] *om.*
225.31 show] show, in the pages which
immediately follow,
226.6 habit] habit, so that *psychic* contiguity, similarity, etc., are derivatives
of a single profounder kind of fact
226.14–15 unavoidably] *om.*
226.16 processes] processes, and this by
unavoidable outward causes
226.18 To answer this] *om.*

226.18 based] based, however,

226.20–21 resultant (see p. 120).] resultant.[15]

228.12–13 reawakened.] 536.15–18 reawakened. [¶] Professor . . . repeated.[16]

228.15 as . . . it,] *om.*

228.32 Fig. 57] Fig. 40, p. 570 [*ed.*, p. 537]

229.12–13 , or . . . *recall*] *om.*

230.17 Hawkins—' "] 538.21–30 Hawkins—' " [¶] But . . . contemplation.

230.20 total recall] impartial redintegration

230.36 Hodgson,ʌ] ~ ,[17]

231.6 parts] parts (as in the emotional memory just referred to, where, as all *past*, they all interest us alike)

232.5 or . . . *recall*.] 540.30–39 Another . . . quick."[18]

233.2–3 a . . . book] C. Göring's 'System der kritischen Philosophie'

233.5–6 volume . . . it] volumes . . . them (*em.*)

233.7 letter] letter from Leipzig

233.7–8 the . . . death] this philosopher's recent death by drowning

234.4–5 brushed, used] brushed them, chewed his breakfast

234.6 intense.ʌ] ~ .[20]

234.11 our] our utter

234.13 perishing, and dread] and perishing

234.25 woful] dismal and woful

234.34;235.23,27 object] thought

234.35 object . . . next] coming thought

235.4–5 Any . . . admit] 544.3–11 Both . . . true

235.21–22 that . . . attention] 544.28–30 that that . . . it

235.32 *similarity.*'ʌ] *Similarity.*'[21]

235.36 *like.*ʌ] ~ .[21a] WJ/PP

235.37 summon up] remind us of

235.39–41 of . . . Now] 545.8–12 like . . . that

236.23–24 total . . . recall] impartial redintegration to similar association through what we have called ordinary mixed association

236.25–26 total . . . partial . . . focalized, recall] impartial redintegration . . . mixed . . . similar association

236.26–28 'total recall,' . . . 'partial recall,'] 'impartial,' . . . 'mixed,'

236.29–30 association . . . part] focalized part

238.4 consciousness itself] form of consciousness upon its content

238.13 interest; and the] 549.14–17 interest. As . . . . The

238.32 and Z and *c*] or *c*

238.38 achievement] achievement, be it action or acquisition,

239.2–3 a . . . forms] 550.8–15 an . . . form

239.7 (compare p. 212)] Such an end is a problem.

239.8 thing] state of things

239.25–26 (see . . . only] 550.36–551.4 What . . . great

239.33 We] If it is a thought, we

239.34 last] *om.*

239.35 pertains] relates

239.37 missing . . . them] 551.14–17 vivid . . . details

240.6–7 last . . . matter] had the thought

240.11 associates] associations

240.12 processes] process

240.19 so to speak] there

240.24–25 principally . . . lettered] underlying the thought of the object denoted by the letter contained

241.2 rousing . . . activity.] 552.10–24 helping . . . accord.[22]

241.12 and . . . case] case and the last,

241.14–17 In . . . not.] 553.12–26 When . . . not.

241.18–19 *acquaintance* . . . objects] 553.27–31 knowledge . . . ideas

241.21 Everyone] In fact, everyone

241.23–24 Just . . . is.] 554.2–14 To . . . IX.

241.26 must] *om.*

241.28–29 but . . . comes.] 554.19–29 "Our . . . attention."[26]

241.30 my] our

242.30 one . . . another] the one . . . the other

242.33–34 and . . . thought] association, and then of voluntary association

242.40 causal . . . called] 556.9–11 operative . . . of
243.1 *itself*] *om.*
243.1 objects] objects, or between the
thoughts (if similarity there be between these latter),
243.4 way.] particular and assignable
way. But
243.10 realms.$_\wedge$] $\sim$.27
243.14 up.$_\wedge$] 556.26–558.11 $\sim$.28 [¶]
There . . . memory.29
243.15–24 To . . . transitions] *drawn*

from 547.7–17 To . . . transitions
(*out of order; verbatim*)
243.24–31 are . . . point.] 547.17–549.6
whether . . . point. (*out of order*)
243.31–244.33 I . . . acts.] *drawn from*
558.12–559.17 I . . . acts.
244.21 its] it (*em.*)
244.24 (see p. 208)] *om.*
244.27 introduces] has already introduced or tends to introduce
244.28 half] *om.*
244.33 acts.] 559.17–569.23 acts. [¶]
THE HISTORY . . . used.

CHAPTER XVII: THE SENSE OF TIME

245.0 Sense] PERCEPTION
245.1 Let] 570.1–573.2 In . . . . Let
245.1–246.11 anyone . . . mind.] *drawn*
from 573.2–576.13 any one . . . mind.
('any one' *em. to* 'anyone')
245.14 has been] Mr. E. R. Clay has
245.14–15 'the specious' present]
'$\sim\sim\sim$'
245.15 a sort . . . length] 573.16–
574.17 His . . . breadth
245.19 end.$_\wedge$] $\sim$.4
246.6–8 The . . . even] 575.3–576.10
When . . . realize
246.11 clear] very clear
246.11–18 The . . . interval.] 576.14–
583.16 How . . . flow.
246.19–250.25 Let . . . by.] *drawn from*
583.16–593.34 Let . . . by.
246.35–36 *perceive . . . perceive*] *intuit*
. . . intuit
246.37 see] perceive
247.15 sort.] 584.15–585.12 $\sim$ —an . . .
wholes.
247.34 conception.$_\wedge$] $\sim$ .32

248.9 that] which
248.9 them.$_\wedge$] $\sim$ .33
248.16 yields hardly] hardly yields
248.21 up.] 587.12–588.16 up. In
. . . between."
248.25–31 An . . . memory.] 588.21–
589.8 "Whoever . . . collapse.
249.4 itself.$_\wedge$] $\sim$ .36
249.6 elapsed, and the] elapsed. The
249.16 have.$_\wedge$] $\sim$ .37
249.18–23 In . . . for] 590.3–591.26
Exactly . . . still,
249.27 *their*] *their own*
249.29–30 the feelings . . . untouched.] 591.32–592.19 outer . . .
once."41
249.36–37 at . . . raised.] 592.25–
593.6 and all . . . simultaneously."
250.1–2 *perception*] *intuition*
250.3 perception] intuition
250.8 all.$_\wedge$] $\sim$ .42
250.25–28 In . . . things.] 593.35–
604.6 Time . . . accrues.

CHAPTER XVIII: MEMORY

251.1 Memory] 605.1–610.9 In . . . .
Memory
251.1–261.13,35–40 Memory . . .
forgotten.1 | A . . . qu] *drawn*
from 610.9–629.21 Memory . . . qu.
251.9 event.$_\wedge$] $\sim$ .9
251.9 writers$_\wedge$] $\sim$ 10
251.9 such] the

252.4 along with to-day's] *om.*
252.33 object] act
252.33 memory.] 612.15–614.15
memory. [¶] It . . . *adheres.*
252.38 and] *om.*
253.4 'object.'] '$\sim$,' as explained so
often before.
253.8 it.$_\wedge$] $\sim$ .13

253.22 vain.$_\wedge$] ∼ .14

254.3 formed."$_\wedge$] ∼ ."15

254.23 memorable . . . the] experience on the proper occasion, together with its

254.24 all] *om.*

254.25 etc.] etc., etc.

254.25 as] just as

254.27 cue] occasion

254.40–41 symbolized . . . between] *om.*

254.41 *M* and] M—

254.41 *2N* and] N—

255.10–11 excitement] functional excitement

255.11 paths] tracts and paths

255.12 representation] vision

255.13 before.] 617.11–618.29 before. [¶] These . . . O.

255.19 time.$_\wedge$] ∼ .17

255.30–32 Only . . . seen.] 619.10–620.32 But . . . another."18

256.35 scale.$_\wedge$] ∼ .19

258.35–36 Did it lead . . . were] If it led . . . would be

259.18 way.$_\wedge$] ∼ .20

259.40 York.$_\wedge$] ∼ .21

260.18 memory."$_\wedge$] ∼ ."22

260.21–22 and . . . therewithal.] 626.12–627.20 the occurrences . . . improved.24

260.25 Methods have been] In the

traditional terminology methods are

261.12–13 forgotten.1] ∼·$_\wedge$ (*fn. run-on in text*)

261.13–16 The . . . too] 629.22–633.26 "To . . . 1too

261.17–262.16 often . . . experience.] *drawn from* 633.26–636.12 often . . . experience.

261.22 cloud.] 633.32–634.9 cloud. No . . . associates.

261.26–27 thus . . . consciousness] 634.13–15 effect . . . feel,

261.31 why.$_\wedge$] ∼.30

261.35 A] The most

262.5 fact.$_\wedge$] ∼.31

262.6 here] *om.*

262.14 way;$_\wedge$] ∼;32

262.17–19 In . . . association.] 636.13–640.25 EXACT . . . obvious.

262.19–263.18 If . . . forgotten.] *drawn from* 640.25–643.2 If . . . forgotten.

262.26–27 "We . . . Ribot,] 640.32–641.4 "As . . . result

262.32 life."$_\wedge$] 641.9–642.3 ∼ ."39 [¶] There . . . source."40

262.37–263.1 The . . . Pierre] 642.8–15 We . . . . M.

263.12 done] had done

263.17–18 absolutely . . . be] nothing we experience can be absolutely

263.18 forgotten.] 643.2–649.27 forgotten. In . . . 1888.

CHAPTER XIX: IMAGINATION

264.1–22 *Sensations* . . . so called.] *drawn from* 690.1–691.11 *Sensations* . . . so called.

264.7 hearing;$_\wedge$] ∼; 1

264.16 wholes.] 690.15–691.5 wholes. [¶] *After-* . . . rise.

264.19 just . . . recollection] already studied the machinery of recollection in Chapter XVI

264.22 called.] 691.11–695.30 called. [¶] For . . . interest.

264.23–267.16 Our . . . it.] *drawn from* 695.31–704.18 Our . . . it.

264.24 may] may then

265.12 no."$_\wedge$] ∼ ."6

265.13 by] by all

265.20–28 Mr. . . . find] 696.13–702.28 The . . . further

265.29 –114.$_\wedge$] – ∼ .9

267.14 *name,*$_\wedge$] ∼ ,10

267.16–37 The . . . Galton.] 704.18–20 This . . . pp. 265–6 [*ed.,* p. 256].

267.37–268.18 *This type* . . . complete-ly."] *drawn from* 707.5–24 "*The auditory type* . . . completely.$_\wedge$ (*out of order*)

267.37 Binet,$_\wedge$] A. Binet, 13

268.18 completely."] 707.24–709.19 ∼·$_\wedge$ [¶] "It . . . would."16

268.19–269.31 Professor . . . days."] *drawn from* 709.28–712.12 Professor . . . days." (*out of order*)

268.19–22 Professor . . . case.] 709.28–31 Professor . . . familiar.18

268.32 them.ᴧ] ～ .19

268.34 , he says,] *om.*

268.39 them."ᴧ] ～ . "20

269.13–14 Prof. . . . that] 710.28–31 "When . . . excited;

269.15 speech."ᴧ] 710.32–711.2 ～ ."21 [¶] The . . . darkness.

269.16–17 does indeed seem] seems

269.19–20 thinks.ᴧ [¶] These] 711.6–712.1 thinks.22 [*no* ¶] Like . . . *-images*

269.27 Herr G. H. Meyer,] a writer who must always be quoted when it is question of the powers of imagination,24 ('question' *em. to* 'a question')

269.31 days."] 712.12–714.29 days." [¶] The . . . IMAGINATION?

269.32–39 The . . . objects."ᴧ] *drawn from* 709.20–27 The . . . objects."17 (*out of order; verbatim*)

269.40–271.3 The study . . . him.] *drawn from* 704.21–706.31 *The study . . . him.*

270.1–2 individuals . . . their] *great are the differences between individuals in respect of*

270.2 imagination.] 704.23–25 *imagination. And . . . up.*

270.2 some] some individuals

270.4–5 These . . . Charcot.] *om.*

270.7 what . . . -tract] it will throw a much-used brain-tract out of gear

270.8 an . . . affected] it may affect an unimportant region

270.9 1883.ᴧ] ～ .11

270.10–13 a merchant . . . faculty.] 705.2–33 Mr. . . . sanity.

270.15 ˎway . . . described] way. He can now describe

270.19 time.] 705.40–41 time. Gradually . . . again.

270.22 it.'] 706.1–10 ～ ." He . . . tree.

270.24 A.] the port of A.

270.29 objects dating] dating objects (*em.*)

270.34 recite] read

271.4–5 Such . . . destroyed.] 706.31–707.4 He . . . profoundly.

271.6–20 Most . . . unreality.] 714.30–717.12 The . . . imagination.31

271.21–33 If . . . alive."] *drawn from* 720.1–14 Now if . . . alive. . . . (*out of order*)

271.22 parts of] centres in

271.34–272.6 Sometimes . . . pianissimo.] *drawn from* 717.13–718.9 To . . . pianissimo.

271.34–36 Sometimes . . . hearing,] To 2): The difference alleged is not absolute, and

272.6 fainter] fainter still

272.6 pianissimo] preceding pianissimo

272.6–13 *Hallucinations . . . act.*] 718.9–719.39;720.14–721.9 This . . . mind.33 | That . . . all.

CHAPTER XX: PERCEPTION

273.0 Perception] THE PERCEPTION OF 'THINGS.'

273.1–279.15 A . . . otherwise] *drawn from* 722.2–733.1 A . . . otherwise.

273.2–3 Anything] Any quality of a thing

273.4 partly] *om.*

273.5 results] result (*em.*)

273.6 are] are commonly

273.9 *perception.*ᴧ] ～ .1

273.15 of . . . *suggested*] a matter of suggestion

273.19 play.] 723.4–724.5 play. [¶] *Perception . . . act.*

274.20–21 attributes] sights and contacts

274.21 presently felt attributes] the present sensation

274.22 materials] complex objective stuff

274.25 *perception.*ᴧ] ～ .4

274.26–34 There . . . . The] 725.1–726.7 *Perception . . . . Their*

274.38–39 As . . . arise,] As we seize

the English meaning‿

275.39 show.‿] ~ .6

276.6 perceived.] 727.20–22 perceived. [¶] On . . . point.

276.7 , then,] *om.*

276.11 pure] *om.*

276.17 old] the

276.17–18 radiating] irradiating

276.18 -impression] -impression, which may have been already formed

276.18,20,22 impression] sensation

276.34 (*twice*) shot-through] irradiated

277.24 *arouse.*] 729.6–29 *arouse.* In . . . insignificant.7

278.35 things.‿] ~ .9

278.37 In] Cf. Th. Reid's Intellectual Powers, essay II, chap. XXII, and A. Binet, in

279.8 sort . . . that] identical disparity. Whence

279.15–22 Thus . . . are.] 733.1–33 A . . . used.

279.23–280.40 **Curious** . . . look.‿] *drawn from* 733.34–736.24 Curious . . . look.13

279.24–25 have . . . (p. 71)] shall learn in the following chapter

279.29 For one thing,] *om.*

279.30 whenever] 1) whenever

279.31–280.7 This . . . point.] 734.1–735.26 and 2) . . . chapters.

280.26 sensation.‿] ~ .12

280.28 from] out of

280.39–40 (with . . . must] do

281.1–4 The . . . type.] 736.25–740.11 *Other* . . . 86 [*ed.,* 731].

281.5–284.28 In . . . all.] *drawn from* 740.11–746.12 In . . . all.

282.23 the criminal] a participant

282.38 are] are perfectly

282.39–41 The . . . cue.] 741.38–42 If . . . cue.

283.3 This . . . although] 742.9–40 This . . . another."20

283.5 sense.‿] 743.2–14 ~ .21 Yet . . . out.

283.5 instances] instances like this

283.12 disappears.] 743.21–744.2 disappears. [¶] An . . . away."22

283.19 is.] 744.9–15 is. [¶] Weight . . . substance.

283.20 abound.] 744.16–19 abound. I . . . present,

283.21 sounds] they

283.22 character] acoustic character

283.26 have had myself] had myself some years ago

283.26 striking] very striking

283.39 before.] 744.38–745.21 before. [¶] In . . . chase."23

283.40 sight] sight, as we have seen in studying Space,

284.6 shall . . . see] have seen

284.6 absent] absent object of (*em.*)

284.8 a . . . bit] the standard

284.9 immediately given] *om.*

284.9 standard and] *om.*

284.11–12 our . . . all.‿] the sensations which first apprehend them are originally and natively of any form at all.24 ('any' *em. to* 'no')

284.16 'at . . . holystones'] holystone the deck

284.28 all.] 746.12–750.32 all. [¶] The . . . fact. (*except* 747.22–748.10 Enough . . . aroused. *found at* 287.12–25)

284.29–289.28 In . . . respect.] *drawn from* 750.34–764.7 In . . . respect.

284.30–31 *Apperception.*‿] ~ .29

284.38 philosophy,‿] ~ ,30

285.14 used.‿] ~ .31

285.15–20 The . . . him:] 751.25–753.12 Professor . . . true. . . .

285.40 *Einleitung* . . . 173.] *Op. cit.,* pp. 166–171.

286.31 scientific] *om.*

287.12–25 Enough . . . aroused.] 747.22–748.10 Enough . . . aroused. (*out of order*)

287.25–30 The . . . go.] 755.9–757.22 A . . . 80, 81 [*ed.,* 726, 727].39

287.41 74] 76—a charming though prolix little work ('76' *em. to* '74')

288.1 name.‿] ~.40

288.6 perceptive] perception

288.12 *images*] mental *images*

288.14 *subjectively* . . . *sensation,*] *is a strictly sensational form of con-*

sciousness,

288.20 years.] 759.12–760.6 years.
Dr. . . . convinced."41

288.35 several] two

288.38 may] *om.*

288.38–39 or . . . exteriorized] *om.*

289.4 life.ʌ] ∼.42

289.5 case] cases

289.5 a . . . person] healthy people

289.13 farther] further

289.25 well."] 761.15–764.4 well."
[¶] Here . . . minutes."

289.28–33 The . . . subjects.] 764.7–
770.29 The . . . thing.

289.33–291.24 Thus . . . results.6]
drawn from 770.29–773.12 Thus . . .
results.55

290.2 language,ʌ] ∼,50

290.4 an inner image] a *conception*

290.4 mind.ʌ] ∼.51

290.21–22 process . . . perceived] or
supra-ideational process so that
the object perceived will have

290.29 resulting way.] 772.6–8 normal
way. Just . . . way.

290.32 appearance,ʌ] ∼,52

290.33 closed.] 772.12–16 closed. Dr.
Hack . . . does.

290.40 , as well as] ʌ alongside of

291.10 a quite] by far the most

291.24 results.6] 773.12–775.2 results.55
[¶] *The* . . . readers."57 (*except*
773.35–775.2 Dr. . . . readers."57
found at 120.3–20)

291.25–27 6The . . . knowledge.] 55In
Mr. Gurney's work, just cited, a
very large number of veridical **cases**
are critically discussed.

CHAPTER XXI: THE PERCEPTION OF SPACE

292.1–14 As . . . does.] 776.2–4 *In* . . .
voluminousness.

292.14–294.10 We . . . ellipse.] *drawn
from* 776.4–782.35 We . . . ellipse.
(*plus* Fig. 51)

292.20–23 Muscular . . . degree.]
776.10–777.10 In . . . voluminous.

293.9 elsewhere.ʌ] ∼ .1

293.11 it.ʌ] ∼ .2

293.11 The . . . *moreover,*] 777.24–
778.8 *Now* . . . *of*

293.15–16 *with* . . . *volumes.*] 778.12–
15 , *inter* . . . incommensurate.

293.16 said to be] reported

293.21 large."ʌ] ∼ ."4

293.22 feeling.] 778.21–27 feeling. It
. . . order.

293.25 flame."ʌ] 778.31–781.6 ∼ ."5
A . . . hand."

293.29 butterfly.] 781.11–22 butterfly.
The . . . ear.

293.31–32 sensation. [¶] *The*] 781.24–
782.16 sensation. [*no* ¶] We . . . that

294.2–3 The . . . felt.] *om. legend*

294.4–6 On . . . along] 782.26–30
and . . . skin

294.8 across the face] horizontally
across the face, so that the mouth

falls between them,

294.11–295.35 Now . . . that]
782.35–815.6 In . . . world. (*except*
810.7–814.33 *The feeling* . . . fall.39
found at 70.6–73.23)

295.35–297.5 we . . . and] *drawn from*
821.19–823.28 1we . . . 2and (*out
of order*)

295.39 *appear.*] *appear. They become, in short, so many properties
of* ONE AND THE SAME REAL THING.

295.39 'act'] commandment, the
fundamental 'act'

296.2 appearance.ʌ] ∼ .42

296.3 essentially the thing] the thing
essentially

296.25 perception.ʌ] ∼ .43

296.31 *brings.*] 822.18–823.13 brings.
This . . . all.

296.31 our sight] sight

296.32 eyes] attention and our eyes

296.32 it is] *om.*

296.33 that] *om.*

297.5 last] last (with Bain and J. S.
Mill)

297.6–298.10 empty . . . called.] *om.*

298.12–300.2 Here . . . one.] *drawn
from* 815.7–818.2 The . . . one.

298.14   to] to itself smaller, and to

298.15   eye,] eye, our tympanic membrane feels larger than our finger-tip,

298.22–27   Two . . . must] 815.18–816.18 Thus . . . is to

298.34   them.] 816.26–27 them. In . . . reduced.40

298.38   might . . . suppose] should of course have the alternative of supposing

299.7   at first] primitively

299.7   But if] It is only when

299.8   then we might] that we

299.9   just] *om.*

299.9   This, however] And this, too

300.3–301.9   *It . . . vague.*] *drawn from* 870.30–872.10 The . . . vague. (*out of order*)

300.3   *It . . . size.*] The matter of size has been touched upon, so that no more need be said of it here. As regards shape,

300.3   visible] retinal

300.4   of . . . call] that objects throw are

300.19   2every] *om.*

300.19   made.ʌ] ~ .91

300.21–24   *The . . . do*] 871.8–21 It . . . . Here

300.38   think] attend

300.38   of] to

301.7–8   has . . . substitute] is psychologically a parallel phenomenon to the habit of thinking in words, and has a like use. Both are

substitutions of

301.10–302.22   If . . . touch.] 818.3–848.23 If . . . eyes. (*except* 821.19–823.28 1we . . . 2 and *found at* 295.35–297.5 *and* 829.20–830.4 This . . . *perceived. found at* 73.32–74.9)

302.22–303.20   A being . . . *denied.*] *drawn from* 848.24–849.37 Now . . . *denied.*

302.22–24   A . . . powers.] 848.24–849.2 Now . . . education.

302.25   *moving things*] *object*

302.25   covering] covering in its lateral movements

302.28   they] it

302.30   would be] is

302.32   so . . . down] laid down on pp. 178 and 179 [*ed.*, 816 and 817]

302.32   would measure] *measures*

302.33   would measure] *then measures*

302.34   would be] are

303.3   the image . . . resuming] and finally on that side resume

303.12   about] ready

303.13   must be] has already been

303.14–15   seen . . . visual] judged equal to a certain optical

303.15   *So*] *Thus*

303.16   2given] *fixed*

303.17   *depth . . . breadth*] *om.*

303.21–304.22   But . . . mind.] 849.38–912.5 Suppose . . . way.146 (*except* 856.4–859.18 This . . . treatises. *found at* 37.19–39.11 *and* 870.30–872.10 The . . . vague. *found at* 300.3–301.9)

Chapter XXII: Reasoning

305.1–318.18   We . . . contiguity.] *drawn from* 952.1–973.8 We . . . contiguity.

306.6   concrete] whole

306.8–10   Our . . . our] 953.12–956.22 The . . . these (*except* 955.30–956.6 "Water- . . . this."5 *found at* 318.40–319.15)

306.10   they] but they

306.14   *abstract*] *om.*

307.13   thereupon] then

307.17   *sagacity,ʌ*] ~ , 6

307.20   implications.ʌ] ~.7

308.9   *ad*] *in* (em.)

310.18   naught.ʌ] ~.9

310.19   hour.ʌ] ~.10

310.21   overcoat] horse-car

310.25–26   frequently . . . us.] 962.6–964.2 important . . . cast.12

310.38–40   laboratory . . . decompositions,] *deduction and compendious definition*ʌ

310.40 important] useful
311.18 always] always for a subjective interest,
311.23 attain.$_\wedge$] ∼ .[13]
311.36 bottom . . . up] top by friction against lintel—press it bodily down (*em.*)
312.4 chimney] collar which bears the chimney
312.6 chimney] collar
312.9 abstracted] named
312.20–21 genius . . . relation] sagacity lies in the invention of *special [WJ/PP *for del.* 'the'] new lines *which serve his purpose [WJ/PP *added*]
312.26 these points] them
312.37 view] views
313.10 ideas] ideas or reasons for his conclusions
313.10–11 circumstances] circumstances singled out from the mass of characters which make up the entire phenomena
313.16 facts . . . immediate] immediate data in their full

313.16 totality.] 967.9–20 totality. [¶] The . . . extract.
313.33 fact] total
314.1 mind.] 968.6–30 mind. [¶] Take . . . mind.
314.23 whole.$_\wedge$] ∼.[14]
315.41 on p. 221] in a former chapter (see Vol. I, p. 506 [*ed.*, p. 478])
316.37 fact] case
318.9 truth.$_\wedge$] ∼.[15]
318.11 As] And as
318.18–39 So . . . Romanes?] 973.8–11 It . . . MAN.
318.40–319.15 "Water- . . . this."[2]] *drawn from* 955.30–956.6 "Water- . . . this."[5] (*out of order*)
319.16–319.36 A . . . mammals] 973.12–977.6 I . . . they
319.37–320.12 find . . . all.] *drawn from* 977.6–20 find . . . all.
320.4 soul] mind
320.5 there reigns.$_\wedge$] reigns there.[18]
320.5,6 would] will
320.10 who] which
320.12 all.] 977.20–993.41 all. [¶] Professor . . . itself.

CHAPTER XXIII: CONSCIOUSNESS AND MOVEMENT

321.0 Consciousness and] THE PRODUCTION OF
321.1–323.12 The . . . itself.] *drawn from* 994.1–1003.13 The . . . itself.
321.8 ²part] portion
321.9 We . . . on] Let us now turn
321.11 consequent thereupon] connected therewithal
321.26 viscera."] 995.2–22 viscera." [¶] In . . . law."[1]
322.2 a new] the
322.3–5 processes . . . activities] 995.25–28 processes, and . . . already
322.6 the] the draining or
322.7 as] *om.*
322.9 attention] attention, something like this occurs
322.10 inhibition of centres] central inhibition

322.24–29 we . . . a] 996.9–1002.16 although . . . . *A*
322.31–33 It . . . once.] 1002.19–23 We . . . everywhere.
322.34 ingenious] ingenious and suggestive
322.35 review,$_\wedge$] ∼,[15]
323.2 etc.] etc. Schneider's articles are well worth reading, if only for the careful observations on animals which they embody.
323.3 this] them here
323.4–5 which . . . show] which our *a posteriori* instances have shown
323.6 shall] will
323.9–10 Expressions . . . Performances] Instinctive or Impulsive Performances; | 2) Expressions of Emotion

CHAPTER XXIV: EMOTION

324.0 Emotion] THE EMOTIONS

324.1–325.18 An . . . obvious, and] 1058.1–1064.16 In . . . tone. (*except* 1062.11–1063.16 Take . . . panic."³ *found at* 333.39–335.9)

325.18–326.39 the result . . . truth.] *drawn from* 1064.17–1066.12 The result . . . truth.

325.19–20 subject . . . downwards,] emotions

325.31 as the] as

325.41 if . . . only] but I fear that few will

326.11–14 I . . . emotions.] 1065.10–24 Now . . . strong. ('strong.' *em. to* 'strong—and . . . XLVI.' WJ/PP)

326.39 truth.] 1066.12–18 truth. [¶] To . . . reverberate.

326.40–328.13 To . . . cause.] *drawn from* 1072.4–1074.24 First . . . cause. (*out of order*)

326.40 To begin with,] *First Objection.* There is no real evidence, it may be said, for the assumption that

326.40 *certainly*] om.

327.2 idea.] idea? [¶] *Reply.* There is most assuredly such evidence.

327.6 hearing] listening to

327.24 effects.] 1072.30–1073.32 effects. [¶] Professor . . . suppose.

328.11 depart.₍ₐ₎] ~ .¹¹

328.14–33 The . . . named.] *drawn from* 1066.30–1067.9 The . . . named. (*out of order; verbatim*)

328.33 named.] 1067.9–12 named. Our . . . on.

328.34–329.4 The . . . 'hollow.'] *drawn from* 1066.18–29 The . . . 'hollow.'

328.34 permutations] permutations and combinations

328.34 changes] activities

328.35 emotion] emotion, however slight,

328.38 modified] modified in each emotion

328.39–40 emotion] of them

329.3 grief or enthusiasm] an emotion

329.5–331.31 I . . . made.] *drawn from* 1067.13–1070.10 I . . . made.

330.4 disembodied] purely disembodied

330.4 sheer] om.

330.9 'coarse'] moods,

331.12 causation] genesis

331.14 moment] moment the genesis of

331.14 causally] *om.*

331.18 the] *om.*

331.21 know.] 1069.29–38 know. [¶] "We . . . ideas."⁵

331.31 made.] 1070.10–1072.3;1074.25–1077.8 made. [¶] I . . . plausible. | "All . . . task."¹⁵

331.32–332.28 If . . . depends.] *drawn from* 1077.9–1080.7 Second . . . depends.

331.32 If] *Second Objection.* If

331.34 should] ought to

331.35–37 Now . . . inference.] 1077.12–21 Now . . . rests.

332.18 thaw!] 1078.6–1079.2 thaw! [¶] This . . . gestures."¹⁷

332.24 well.₍ₐ₎] 1079.8–1080.2 ~ .¹⁸ Thus . . . hair.' "¹⁹

332.25 simple] that which these quotations suggest

332.27 must be] is probable

332.28–333.38 Those . . . acts.] 1080.7–1090.25 Coquelin . . . defence.

333.39–334.4 For . . . fear.] 1062.11–12 Take . . . effects: (*out of order*)

334.5–335.9 "Fear . . . panic."¹] *drawn from* 1062.13–1063.16 "Fear . . . panic."³ (*out of order*)

335.10–14 How . . . made.] 1090.27–1091.14 On . . . thought.

335.15–338.26 Some . . . way.] *drawn from* 1091.15–1097.15 Some . . . way.

335.19 *concomitants . . . movements*] *effects*

335.39 (N. Y. ed.), p.] Darwin, pp.

336.9 pain."ʌ] ∼ ."27
336.10 The] About fear I shall have
more to say presently. Meanwhile
the
337.6 age."ʌ] 1093.11–25 ∼ ."28 [¶]
The . . . form.
337.17 point.ʌ] ∼ .30
337.24 lips.] 1094.18–20 lips. In . . .
reaction.
337.28 nursery.ʌ] ∼ .31
338.15 named.] 1095.19–1096.7 named.
It . . . direction.

338.18–19 they . . . them.] 1096.10–
1097.8 Professor . . . goes.
338.19 In] In fact, in
338.20 *incidental* reactions] such reactions, incidental to others evolved
for utility's sake, but
338.22 ticklishness, shyness,] *om.*
338.24 must be traced] we have already traced (*em. to* 'we shall have
to trace' WJ/PP)
338.24 origin.ʌ] ∼ .33a WJ/PP
338.26 way.] 1097.15–39 way. [¶]
This . . . defend.

CHAPTER XXV: INSTINCT

339.1–351.27 *Instinct . . . sucking.*]
drawn from 1004.1–1023.12 *Instinct*
. . . etc.
339.3 Instincts] 1004.3–5 That . . . .
They
339.5 use.] 1004.7–1005.7 use.
[¶] "Has . . . results.
339.17 appears] appeart (*em.* WJ/PP)
340.41 other.] 1006.30–1007.6 other.
[¶] Schneider . . . performance.
342.6 her.ʌ] ∼ .2
342.18 food?] 1008.26–1010.13 food?
[¶] Since . . . mankind?
342.24 terms.] 1010.18–26 terms. 'Reason' . . . end.
344.8 abundance.ʌ] ∼ .4
344.36 an] *om.*
344.37 All are] They are all
345.6 Thus] Thus, then, without
troubling ourselves about the words
instinct and reason,
345.8 mammals] creatures
345.15 *let*] set
345.16 is] might be
345.17 never seems] would never seem
345.18 must] would
345.19–22 Instincts . . . *instincts.*]
1013.35–1014.30 Let . . . flows.
346.38 any] any particular
347.38 evolved.] 1017.7–32 evolved.
[¶] Mr. . . . ludicrous.7
348.25 until] till until (*em.*)
349.19 then] and then
349.20 it,] it (with both fore- and

hind-feet, if I remember rightly),
349.28 instinctive] instructive (*em.*)
349.30 terrier?] 1019.23–1020.17 terrier? [¶] A . . . tribe.9
351.1 to . . . cited] might be cited to
this
351.10 end.] 1022.5–34 end. [¶] The
. . . fact.
351.20 they . . . indeed] we shall see
how far they are
351.27 *touched, and sucking.*] tickled,
touched, or blown upon, etc., etc.
351.27–352.2 To . . . complete.]
1023.13–1033.25 Of . . . monster.
352.2–22 It . . . -up.] *drawn from*
1056.16–1057.17 It . . . ʌup. ('up' *em.*
to '-up'; *out of order*)
352.3 *a list*] an array
352.5–6 towards] toward (*em.*)
352.23–24 In . . . fear.] *om.*
352.25–357.38 Fear . . . play?] *drawn*
from 1033.26–1039.35 *Fear . . . play?*
353.27 experience."3] 1034.27–1035.2
∼ .ʌʌ It . . . ear."17
353.39 p. 72.] 1035.33–40 pp. 72–74.
In . . . medicine." ('–74' *em. to*
'–75')
354.27–28 Two . . . observation.] *om.*
355.17–18 caverns, woods,] of caverns
and woods, (*em.*)
355.33 more than] very
355.33 dubious.] 1037.12–17 dubious.
Professor . . . take.

356.15 Brooks] Brooks, of the Johns Hopkins University,

356.18 experiences.$_\wedge$] ~ .19

356.22 like.$_\wedge$] ~ .20

357.9 stealthy advances] rapid approaches

357.12 someone] some one (*em.*)

357.13 upon ... floating] *om.*

357.14 cloth] cloth upon the raft where he is floating

357.37 remote] *om.*

357.38 play?] 1039.35–1056.16 play? [¶] *Appropriation* ... species.34

CHAPTER XXVI: WILL

358.1–360.30 Desire ... fixed."] *drawn from* 1098.1–1101.35 Desire ... fixed."

358.17 now.] 1098.16–20 now. The ... view.

359.15 prophetic] divinatory

359.20 involuntarily,$_\wedge$] ~ ,1

359.25 again,] again, proposed as an end,

359.30–37 Now ... sensations] 1100.3–28 Now ... impressions

360.1 a] an accurate

360.1 can] can immediately

360.4–5 in ... when] 1100.35–1101.12 when .... When

360.31–361.11 We .... If] 1101.36–1111.1 Or ... if

361.11–362.12 anything ... acts.] *drawn from* 1111.1–1112.3 anything ... acts.

361.12 put forth] of our muscular contractions

361.13 incoming feelings] afferent feelings coming

361.15 body] body, in the phenomenon of effort, objectively considered

361.26 proper] right

361.28–29 anticipative ... motion] of result

362.12–19 There ... motor-cue.'] 1112.4–1127.17 There ... etc.

362.19–384.27 Now ... it.] *drawn from* 1127.17–1159.40 Now ... it.

362.20 images] images, exclusively,

362.20 the only motor-] what I have called the mental$_\wedge$

362.22 cue] *mental cue*

362.22 *an image either*] *either an image*

362.25 consciousness] consciousness (cf. p. 487 [*ed.*, p. 1099])

362.33–34 a ... produces] an outer impression

362.36 such an] the

362.36 discharge] motor innervation

362.38 have already] formerly

362.39 is] would be

363.9 the] often-repeated

363.17 clothes] shirt

363.24–25 the way ... feel] much ideal consciousness of the means

363.37 1mm.$_\wedge$] ~ .32

363.39–40 do not know] need not, at this present stage, inquire

363.41 XIX] XVIII

364.5 process.$_\wedge$] ~ .33

364.17 our discussion.] the psychology of the Will. It can be the more easily treated now that we have got rid of so much tedious preliminary matter.

364.19 *motor-cue*] mental$_\wedge$cue (p. 497 [*ed.*, p. 1108])

364.30–31 without ... fiat,] *om.*

364.32–33 a ... it] movement follows *unhesitatingly and immediately* the notion of it in the mind

365.16 acts.] 1131.20–23 acts. We ... sort.

365.29 conflict.] 1132.4–22 conflict. The ... centres.35

365.39 293.] 1131.33–40 293. In ... generals!

366.19 examples.$_\wedge$] ~ .36

367.2 occur.$_\wedge$] ~ .37

367.16 *impulsive.*$_\wedge$] ~ .38

367.16 first] *om.*

367.17 or] or a

367.22 have] *om.*

367.23 are . . . by] run out again at
367.24 consciousness] mere consciousness as such
367.24 but] *om.*
367.35 *the process of*] *om.*
367.40 the sort of] *om.*
368.10 purely . . . else,] of the movement purely and simply, with all
breaks off; ('breaks' *em.* to 'brakes')
368.31–32 has . . . it,] is the seat of
many ideas
368.33 ways.ₐ] ∼ .39
368.33 these . . . be] the ideas is
that of
368.34 this] this idea
368.34–35 objects or] *om.*
368.35 block] which are present to
consciousness block
369.4 objects] ideas
369.9 thing] object
369.9 namely,] namely the existence
of
369.9–10 conflict] conflict, as explained on p. 275 of Vol. I [*ed.*,
p. 265]
369.10 complicated] *om.*
369.11 by consciousness] *om.*
369.18 as . . . (p. 149)] *om.*
369.28 patiently] patient (*em.*)
369.32–33 rupture] rapture (*em.*)
370.2 page.] 1137.19–1138.17 page.
[¶] The . . . mind.'
370.4 five] four (*em.*)
370.12–13 matter] thing
370.13–14 it . . . it] the subject . . .
the matter
370.29 volitional] motor
370.40 (p. 310 ff.)] *om.*
371.7 good] case of a Good
371.7 to decide which] as to which
good
371.16 *type*] *type* of case
371.16 great] certain
372.8 change] charge
372.22 end.ₐ] ∼ .40
372.32;373.13 four] three (*em.*)
373.3 entrance] excursion
373.5 former] three former (*em.*)
373.12 this] the
373.13 fifth] fourth (*em.*)

373.31 When . . . back,] When,
awhile back (p. 526 [*ed.*, p. 1134]),
I said
373.33 should have added] added in
a note
374.4–5 overpassed] overpast (*em.*)
374.19 *mental objects*] *sorts of
motive*
374.34–35 *must . . . as*] *are*
374.39 also . . . characteristic] arouse
other ideas (associated and con-
sequential) with their
374.40 finally] *om.*
375.1 pretty] very
375.1 the normal thing] there
375.32 up."] 1144.18–21 up." In . . .
truth.
375.38 Slavic] Latin
375.40 Simian] Monkeys
376.1 greater] greatest (*em.*)
376.6–7 sing . . . make . . . kiss] sing
all . . . make all . . . kiss all
376.20–22 How . . . truth!] But
376.35 types.ₐ] ∼ .41
376.40–377.6 In . . . impulse.] 1146.1–
1147.32 I . . . inhibition.
377.32 neck.] 1148.16–19 neck. Professor . . . Will.' ('Will' *em. to
'Will'*)
378.2 away.] 1148.28–1149.21 away.
One . . . abhor.' "44
378.29 heart.' ",] 1150.8–1152.4
∼.' "45 [¶] The . . . ridicule.''46
379.1,2 we] they
379.3 sleep.ₐ] ∼ .47
379.6 inhibition] inhibition of (*em.*)
379.23 this] the
379.23 mind.] 1153.4–24 mind. The
. . . told.
383.12 pain.ₐ] 1157.19–1158.10 ∼ .49
[¶] It . . . breasts.
384.6 'pleasants.'] 1159.17–19 'pleasants.' Pleasures . . . good.
384.27 it.] 1159.40–1163.30 it. [¶] Be-
lievers . . . power.59
384.28–390.33 If . . . perform.]
drawn from 1164.1–1172.2 If . . .
perform.
385.28 neural] neura (*em.* WJ/PP)
385.36 write.ₐ] ∼ .60

386.1–8 ¹If . . . intact.] 1165.18–1166.3
In . . . before.⁶¹
386.11 *action*] *object*
386.15 shall] will
386.27 ensue.] 1166.22–32 ensue.
A . . . 321 [*ed.*, 948].)
386.37–39 There . . . morning.]
1167.42–44 Again, there . . . morning.
(*out of order*)
386.39–42 Again, . . . *real.*] 1167.30–
33 A soldier . . . *real.*
386.42 *real.*] 1167.33–42 real. [¶]
Where . . . again.
387.4 wise] unwise (*em.*)
387.29 -career.] -career. *"Hæc tibi erit
janua leti,"* we feel. (*em.* WJ/PP)
388.1–2 congeners] congerers (*em.*
WJ/PP)
388.20 ideal] *om.*
388.20–21 It . . . word,] If I may use
the word *idea* without suggesting
associationist or Herbartian fables,
I will say that it is
388.40–389.1 for . . . names] names for
the emergency,
389.6 also] or
389.20 act.ᴧ] ∼.⁶⁴
389.33 still.] still. But exactly similar
in form would be his consent to lie
and sleep.
389.34 again . . . be] it is

389.37 ideas] thoughts
390.25 preparation."] 1171.11–17 ∼·ᴧ
Lord . . . insane."⁶⁵
390.34–391.4 As . . . so] 1172.3–1175.18
I . . . wise
391.4–392.1 that . . . made.] *drawn
from* 1175.18–1176.17 that . . . made.
391.9 *attention*] attention or consent
391.11 *seems*] *seems* as if the effort
were an independent variable,
391.12 less] less of it
391.29 *The fact*] My own belief
391.37 that] which
391.37 Such] *om.*
391.38 such . . . reasonings] deductive
reasonings such
392.2–28 Had . . . psychology.] 1176.17–
1179.27 We . . . account.
392.28–394.23 As . . . world!] *drawn
from* 1179.27–1182.20 As . . . world!
392.29 on p. 387] in Chapter VI (p.
453 [*ed.*, p. 429])
392.33 effective.ᴧ] ∼ .⁷¹
392.36 an actual science] calculation
393.38 it] the world
393.39 makes himself] becomes
394.6 be] be, as Max Müller somewhere says,
394.22 were] be
394.23 world!] 1182.20–1193.30 world!
[¶] The . . . degree.

Word-Division

The following is a list of compound words divided at the ends of lines in the copy-text, which could be read either as one word or as a hyphenated compound. These compounds were not confirmed in their forms as printed in the present edition because the copy-text did not derive from *The Principles of Psychology* at these points or from an English quotation. In a sense, then, the hyphenation or non-hyphenation of possible compounds in the present list is in the nature of editorial emendation.

16.1	light-waves		322.25	heart-beats
279.21	pasteboard		396.25	brain-cell
298.1	semicircular-			

The following is a list of words divided at the ends of lines in the present edition but which represent authentic hyphenated compounds as found within the lines of the copy-text. Except for this list, all other hyphenations at the ends of lines in the present edition are the modern printer's and are not hyphenated forms in the copy-text.

14.22	to-|day		106.4	intra-|hemispheric
15.25	air-|waves		109.35	word-|blind
17.28;32.12;57.38;75.22	end-|organs		115.5	dial-|plates
22.13	zero-|point		120.36	car-|horse
43.13	green-|blue		120.39	hind-|quarters
45.3	'color-|theories'		121.30	blood-|supply
46.19	blue-|green		122.4	head-|end
46.35	after-|image		122.32	thermo-|electric
55.9	nerve-|filaments		126.7	india-|rubber
56.39	air-|particles		138.1	fellow-|mortals
57.8	vowel-|sounds		142.1	piano-|key
65.34	heat-|spots		146.12	-silence-|and-
69.30	**so-|called**		146.26	resting-|places
90.38	hind-|legs		155.36	dust-|wreath
93.38	wiping-|movement		165.33;348.11	self-|preservation
102.9	calloso-|marginal		167.4;173.29	self-|seeking
103.23	right-|handed		175.40	wide-|spread
103.25;108.26	left-|brained		207.12	looked-|for

Word-Division

218.9   -different-|from-
221.37   -rope-|dancing
242.38   brain-|process
251.23   clock-|strokes
254.38;287.17   nerve-|centres
271.15   sense-|organs
274.35   already-|quoted
276.34   shot-|through
278.29   -finger-|touch
284.18   state-|room
286.11   pocket-|corkscrew
286.20   twenty-|four
288.20;289.26   pseudo-|hallucinations
300.4   table-|tops
308.9   well-|springs

313.11   light-|waves
332.10   cold-|bloodedly
336.12   one-|sided
343.34   excito-|motor
349.28   food-|burying
349.36   boon-|fellowship
356.38   death-|shamming
357.24   self-|command
359.4   express-|train
367.37   Ideo-|motor
383.30   knife-|handle
388.38   anti-|impulsive
393.20   heart-|strings
393.29   wished-|for

The following are actual or possible hyphenated compounds broken at the end of the line in both the copy-text and the present edition.

14.7   zig-|zagging (*i.e.*, zigzagging)
186.13   new-|comer (*i.e.*, new-comer)

238.30   brain-|tract (*i.e.*, brain-tract)

533

Index

This index is a name and subject index for the text of *Psychology: Briefer Course* and the Appendix, James's annotations in his private copy. It is an index of names only for the "Notes," "A Note on the Editorial Method," and "The Text of *Psychology: Briefer Course.*"

Names of persons, localities, and institutions, and titles of books are indexed. However, such items are not indexed if no information about them is provided —if they are only a part of the identification of a discussed item or are merely used to indicate its location. This excludes, most of the time, names of editors, translators, and libraries, and titles of reference works consulted by editors of the present text. In contrast with the practice of some earlier volumes, titles of articles in periodicals, except those by James, are not indexed.

Generally, references to books are not indexed when the title of the book does not appear in the citation. The index therefore provides an extensive but incomplete list of James's references to individual works.

The index in most cases does not include the technical names for the various parts of the brain and nervous system.

Throughout his text James frequently offers introspective evidence, makes observations about the behavior of his own children, or refers to informal studies conducted on students and friends. Since such observations bear on the question of James as an experimental psychologist, they are listed in the index under James's name. Otherwise, references to James are not indexed.

The introduction to the present edition is also not indexed.

454; and illusions, 290–291; study of, 291

Hamilton, William, 228, 235, 430, 431

Hamlet (W. Shakespeare), 99, 233, 367, 437

Handbuch der physiologischen Optik (H. Helmholtz), 204n, 417, 418, 429, 433, 468n

Handwörterbuch der Physiologie (R. Wagner), 416

Hankel, Wilhelm Gottlieb, 116, 425

Harmony, 59, 152–153

Harris, William Torrey, 475

Hartford, Conn., 222

Hartley, David, 225, 430

Harvard Medical School, 448

Harvard Psychological Laboratory, 447, 450

Harvard University, 413, 426

Hearing: and Weber's law, 24; organs of, 49–55; and accommodation, 50–51; and pitch, 55–56; and timbre, 56–57; and analysis of sound, 57–58; and compounding, 58–59; and sensibility, 59–60; and touch, 62; and brain, 108–109; and reaction time, 116; and imagination, 267–268, 269; and illusion, 283; and voluminousness, 292, 293

Hector, 305

Helmholtz, Hermann Ludwig Ferdinand von: on contrast, 29; on color, 43n, 44; on after-images, 45; on analysis of sounds, 57–58; on discord, 59; and reaction time, 114; on sensation, 142; on retinal rivalry, 199–200, 206; on attention, 203–204, 205; on illusions, 280; notes on, 417, 418, 419, 424, 427, 429; mentioned, 430, 433, 444, 468n

Hemispheres, cerebral: functions, 12–13, 92, 93, 94–98, 103–105; development, 78–79; structure, 81–87; and sexual function, 97; and reflexes, 98; and localization, 100–112; and habits, 125; influences on, 127; and attention, 192–193

Henle, Jakob, 81, 83, 85, 418, 421

Herbart, Johann Friedrich, 196–197, 284, 429, 430

Herbartians, 144, 208

Hercules, 305

Heredity, 440

Hering, Ewald: on contrast, 29–30, 47; on color, 44; on space, 293; notes on, 417, 418, 434; mentioned, 28n

Heroism, 393–394

Herzen, Alexandre, 116, 424, 425

Hibben, John Grier, 450

Hipp, Matthäus, 115, 424

Hirsch, Adolph, 116, 424–425

Hirsch, William, 440

Hobbes, Thomas, 28, 417

Hodgson, Shadworth Hollway: on red-integration, 230–231; on association, 232; on duration, 247; letter to, 477; notes on, 430, 431; mentioned, 245, 428

Hohenzollern family, 170

Holbrook, Martin Luther, 260, 431–432

Holden, Luther, 79, 421

Holt, Henry: his American Science Series, 466; James's correspondence with, 467, 469–470, 474–475; mentioned, 468, 471n, 477, 482, 483

Homer, 218, 270, 305, 382, 430, 437

Homme et l'intelligence, Le (C. R. Richet), 436

Honor, 162–163

Horace, 270

Horsley, Victor Alexander Haden, 102, 112, 422–423, 424

Horwicz, Adolf, 171, 428, 442, 445, 449

Houdon, Jean Antoine, 424

Houghton Library, 413, 416, 426, 439, 455, 459, 464

How to Strengthen the Memory (M. L. Holbrook), 260, 431–432

Huber, Jacques, 447

Huber, Pierre, 447

Huguenin, Gustav, 77, 421

Human Body, The (H. N. Martin), 41n, 42n, 45n, 47n, 50n, 53n, 54n, 56n, 61n, 62n, 66n, 69n, 417, 418, 419, 420, 421

Human Immortality (W. James), 415, 416, 450

Hume, David, 147, 150, 215, 430

Hunger, 69

Huxley, Thomas Henry: on habit, 132; on images, 150; notes on, 421, 426; mentioned, 78, 79, 468n

Hypnotism: and sensibility, 69; and multiple personality, 187, 188; and mediumship, 190; and memory, 262; and illusion, 282–283; and hallucinations, 289–290; and attention, 385

Hypnotisme (E. Azam), 428

Hypnotismus, Der (A. Moll), 440

Hypotheses, 13

Idealism, 9–10, 17, 398, 399

Ideals, 172–173, 375

Ideas: and knowledge, 18; associationist

Key to the Pagination of Editions

The plates of the Henry Holt first edition of *Psychology: Briefer Course* have been reprinted a number of times, but always with the same numbering regardless of the date. Since the original edition has been widely used in scholarly reference, a key is here provided by which the pagination of the original Henry Holt printing can be readily equated with the text in the present ACLS edition. In the list that follows, the first number refers to the page of the January 1892 original edition and its printings of different date. The number to the right after the colon represents the page(s) of the present edition on which the corresponding text will be found.

iii:1	21:25	51:52–53	81:78–79
iv:1–2	22:25–26	52:53–54	82:79–80
v:2	23:26–27	53:54–55	83:80–81
vii:3	24:27–28	54:55–56	84:81–82
viii:3–4	25:28–29	55:56–57	85:82–83
ix:4–5	26:29–30	56:57–58	86:83–84
x:5–6	27:30	57:58–59	87:84–85
xi:6–7	28:31	58:59	88:85–88
xii:7	29:31–32	59:59–60	89:86
xiii:7–8	30:32–34	60:61–62	90:87–88
[1]:9	31:33–35	61:62–63	91:89–90
2:9–10	32:35	62:63–64	92:90
3:10–11	33:35–36	63:63–65	93:90–92
4:11–12	34:36–37	64:65	94:92
5:12–13	35:37–38	65:65–66	95:92–93
6:13	36:38–39	66:66–67	96:93–94
7:13–14	37:38–39	67:67–68	97:94–95
8:14	38:39–40	68:68–69	98:95–96
9:15	39:40–41	69:69	99:96–97
10:15–16	40:41–42	70:70–71	100:97
11:16–17	41:42–43	71:71	101:97–98
12:17–18	42:43–44	72:71–72	102:98–99
13:18–19	43:43–45	73:72–73	103:99–100
14:19	44:45–46	74:73–74	104:100–101
15:19–20	45:46–47	75:74	105:101
16:20–21	46:47–48	76:74–75	106:101–102
17:21–22	47:49–50	77:75	107:102–103
18:22–23	48:49–51	78:76–77	108:103–104
19:23–24	49:50–51	79:76–78	109:103–105
20:24–25	50:51–52	80:77–79	110:104–106

335:292
336:292–293
337:293–294
338:294–295
339:295–296
340:296–297
341:297
342:297–298
343:298–299
344:299–300
345:300–301
346:301
347:301–302
348:302–303
349:303–304
350:304
351:305
352:305–306
353:306–307
354:307–308
355:308–309
356:309–310
357:310
358:310–311
359:311–312
360:312–313
361:313
362:313–314
363:314–315
364:315–316
365:316–317
366:317
367:317–318
368:318–319

369:319–320
370:321
371:321–322
372:322–323
373:324
374:324–325
375:325–326
376:326–327
377:327–328
378:328
379:329
380:329–330
381:330–331
382:331–332
383:332
384:332–333
385:333–334
386:334–335
387:335–336
388:336–337
389:337
390:337–338
391:339
392:339–340
393:340–341
394:341–342
395:342–343
396:343
397:343–344
398:344–345
399:345–346
400:346–347
401:347
402:347–348

403:348–349
404:349–350
405:350–351
406:351
407:351–352
408:352–353
409:353–354
410:354–355
411:355
412:355–356
413:356–357
414:357
415:358
416:358–359
417:359–360
418:360–361
419:361–362
420:362
421:362–363
422:363–364
423:364–365
424:365–366
425:366
426:366–367
427:367–368
428:368–369
429:369–370
430:370
431:370–371
432:371–372
433:372–373
434:373–374
435:374
436:374–375

437:375–376
438:376–377
439:377–378
440:378
441:378–379
442:379–380
443:380–381
444:381–382
445:382
446:382–383
447:383–384
448:384–385
449:385–386
450:386–387
451:386–387
452:387–388
453:388–389
454:389–390
455:390
456:390–391
457:391–392
458:392–393
459:393–394
460:394
461:395
462:395–396
463:396–397
464:397–398
465:398–399
466:399–400
467:400
468:400–401